Business Studies

David Symons
Andrew Adams

Business Education Publishers Limited 1992

© DAVID SYMONS AND ANDREW ADAMS 1992

ISBN 0 907679 43 9

First published in 1992
Revised 1993

Graphics and illustrations by Gerard Callaghan and Flora Pearson

Cover design by Caroline White

Published in Great Britain by Business Education Publishers Limited, Leighton House,
10 Grange Crescent, Stockton Road, Sunderland,
Tyne and Wear SR2 7BN
Telephone 091 567 4963 Fax 091 514 3277

Printed in Great Britain by M and A Thomson Litho Ltd, East Kilbride, Glasgow

Acknowledgements

The author and publishers would like to thank the following for permission to reproduce material and extracts from publications in which they have copyright:

The Associated Examining Board

The University of London Examinations and Assessment Council

The Virgin Group plc

Scottish and Newcastle Group plc

Courtaulds plc

The Co-operative Bank plc

The authors would also like to thank Nigel Hill, Paul Callaghan, Tom Harrison, John Ellison, Tony Gough, Jeff Hindmarch, Albert Toal and Bernie Callaghan for permission to adapt material previously published by Business Education Publishers Ltd.

Thanks must also go to Doris Richardson for her secretarial assistance, Bob Summers for 'doing our sums for us', Delia Wilson and Hilary Knox.

This book is dedicated to our long suffering families:

Gillian, Victoria and Tom; and

Mary, Rebecca, Joe, Rachel (and Mr Bannerjee).

DS

AA

Northumberland, August 1992

Preface

This book is a thorough and detailed source for students of 'A' level and 'A/S' level Business Studies. It covers the main syllabus requirements of the AEB, Cambridge, JMB and London examination boards. It is also an extremely useful source of information for students on BTEC National courses in Business and Finance and will provide a sound introduction to the world of business for those undertaking business courses in higher education.

The authors have used their experience as teachers of Business Studies to produce a book which is written in language that is appropriate to the level of language development of post-16 students. The book clearly explains the theory that underpins the way that businesses operate. It treats a business enterprise as dynamic and organic and examines the effect of the changing business environment on the individual organisation. It provides many up-to-date examples of actual practice of business theory.

The Authors

David Symons is an experienced business studies teacher who has had wide experience of the subject at advanced level. Since 1988 he has been based at the Education Development Centre in Northumberland where he has been involved in the development of approaches to flexible learning and the testing and evaluation of related materials and resources.

Andrew Adams has taught advanced level and BTEC at schools and colleges. He is currently co-ordinator at the Post-16 Education Support Unit in Northumberland. His interests lie in language development and the ways in which students learn.

Table of Contents

Part Three – Business Communication and Organisation

Part Four – Business Functions

Part Five –
Business and Society

The Beginnings of Businesses and Organisations

The Reasons Why Businesses are Formed

The society in which you live is both complex and refined. As a consumer, you demand a variety of goods and services which allow you to maintain the quality of your life. In order to satisfy your demands, suppliers must produce the goods and services which you want. Producers achieve this by combining factors of production (land, labour and capital) in the most efficient manner.

Producers hire workers, rent or buy premises, invest in plant and machinery and purchase raw materials, and then organise the manufacture of the final product in such a way that they will make a profit. Society also gains: its scarce resources are being used in the way consumers wish, rather than being wasted in producing things people do not need. Suppliers (or producers) who work this way, under a system such as that described, are known as commercial organisations or *businesses*.

There are many public sector organisations that also provide goods and services to society. Like commercial organisations they, too, must employ staff, occupy premises and raise capital. The fundamental difference between these two types of organisation is that each tries to meet a different objective: the commercial organisation, part of the private sector, will seek to make a profit; the public sector organisation will wish to provide for the public good and improve the state of society.

As an individual you lack the knowledge, skills and physical resources to manufacture products that fulfil all your needs, whether they are simple or sophisticated. It would be as difficult for you to make a biro or a floppy disk on your own as it would be for you to make a television set or a computer.

Of course, with even very limited skills, and working alone, you might be able to supply yourself with some of the goods and services that you need. You might farm and be sufficiently capable of growing food to satisfy yourself without any help from other people. But what if you require other goods and services? It is unlikely that you will also have the ability and resources to produce your own combine-harvester or tractor. Without such products, which are manufactured by others, your life would be not only unsophisticated but also much more difficult.

A similar situation exists in the supply of services. If you feel you are strong and resourceful, you may try to protect yourself and your property from the dangers threatened by thieves or vandals. If you are not sufficiently strong, however, then you may turn to the state and demand its protection.

How, then, are these goods and services produced? It is clear that individuals, working independently, are unable to meet the complex physical and social needs that they have. To meet that complexity of need, society has developed for itself a system whereby people join together to form *organisations* – and they are extraordinarily diverse. They manufacture products, which they distribute and sell. They also provide all the services that are needed. Such organisations include both the BBC and Vickers Armstrong: both make 'products'; the BBC's product is a 'service', Vickers Armstrong's is a 'good'.

Clearly, then, if the individuals within society are to have all of their various needs satisfied, there must be co-operation between them. Each worker must specialise in a certain aspect of the supply process. Workers must be organised and be allocated a specific role in which to perform co-ordinated tasks. These tasks are normally organised with the aim of producing a given product or service, although there are some organisations that do not specialise and that make an extremely diverse range of products. In the private sector of the economy, such businesses will usually have the objective of making a *profit* for their owners.

What is a Business?

The purpose of business is to provide people with the things they need. What people need varies from person to person, country to country and economy to economy. In an undeveloped or subsistence economy, needs are likely to be for the necessities of existence: for food, water and shelter. In a more sophisticated economy, needs are likely to be more sophisticated. It is possible that a middle-class European might include a set of golf clubs amongst his or her needs in an attempt to satisfy part of the need for a particular form of recreation. Such a need is relatively expensive to meet and will require expenditure on other equipment, subscriptions, travel, socialising etc. In undeveloped economies, such as Albania or Ethiopia, a person's needs will reflect their subsistence or primitive economies: food, water and shelter are the main priorities and would, unsurprisingly, take precedence over a set of Ping golf clubs.

Faster growing economies are characterised by their increasing material wealth and needs; such growth feeds off itself as it describes a virtuous circle wherein needs create wealth which, in turn, creates more sophisticated needs that in their turn create even greater wealth. And to satisfy such burgeoning needs for greater numbers of people, larger and more varied forms of organisation have to be established.

So, a business is simply an organisation that is formed to produce and supply goods or services to satisfy the needs of people (or *consumers* as they are more specifically known). Sometimes a need is *latent*: that is, it exists but the consumer is unaware of it. The latent need can be awakened and turned into a *sale* by using effective *marketing*. A business sets out to achieve the satisfaction of needs *at a profit* which is ultimately returned to the owners of the business.

The analogy of a tree can be used effectively to show the structure, functions, inter-relationships and environment of a business. There are sufficient parallels between the growth of a tree and the growth of a business to make the analogy worth pursuing. Both tree and business are organic; both cannot be easily uprooted from the soil in which they've had their births; both need sustenance from the soil and from the environment, but that environment can also be hostile and damaging at times.

The Beginnings of a Business

A tree starts as a seed. In a protected environment – a greenhouse or nursery – the seed can be nurtured in its growth into a sapling. Like the sapling, a business might also benefit from help in its formative stage; it would certainly grow more quickly if it was protected from the elements. (The terms 'incubator units' and 'business nurseries' describe just such conditions, under which tender enterprises are nurtured and encouraged to grow.) The young, small business can be given protection from rates and rent in these early years, as well as free financial, marketing and general business advice. A small business that is left, without any form of help, to cope with an ever-changing environment would do well to survive, let alone thrive.

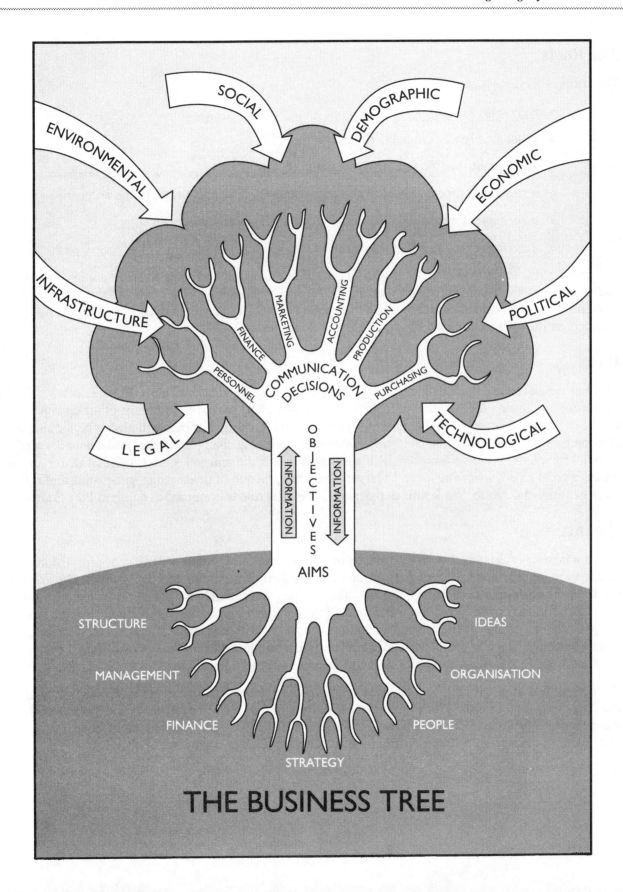

THE BUSINESS TREE

The Roots

The roots of a business are:

- a good idea (or ideas)

- sound and readily available finance

- good quality people or employees with the right skills

- a structure or form of business organisation which is appropriate to the enterprise

- management who are skilled decision-makers and effective motivators

- a strategy or overall plan for its future.

As a business increases in size, so it requires larger and better developed roots to give it a stable foundation and the means of nourishing its growth. Ideas, for example, need to be continually generated by its workforce for few businesses survive on, and remain faithful to, the original idea upon which they were founded, as the later example of Virgin Group plc clearly shows.

Ideas

As a business expands, it needs to refine and develop its original ideas and aims. If its ideas have proved successful in allowing the business to make profits, survive and grow, then perhaps other entrepreneurs will be drawn in to compete in the market. The successful, growing business will always be looking to its customers and potential customers: it will constantly be assessing changes in tastes and demand – ready to respond by refining its ideas accordingly. If a business stands still and relies on its original customer base, it runs a great risk of withering away. In larger businesses, the job of researching, generating and refining ideas generally falls to the marketing department. This vital role is examined in depth in Part Four.

Finance

When a business starts up, it requires finance or start up capital. Usually, a significant proportion of this finance will be provided by the owners of the business. People intending to start their own business will use their life savings or re-mortgage their house; they may use redundancy payments from a previous job or a legacy from a relative. Whatever the source, these amounts form the basis of the finance of the business, but are seldom enough on their own. In addition, the owner will seek more finance in the form of a loan from a bank or finance house. Most lenders will require a business plan and cash-flow forecast before they put their loan at risk; these preparations are looked at in detail in Part One.

As the business grows, then so will its need for cash if its owners wish to expand it. Money (or capital) is the 'tap root' of a business. This capital can come from only two sources: from profits generated by the business (internal finance); from additional loans (external finance). Each source brings its respective costs and risks and balancing these can result in a very skillful and tricky management decision.

People

In the early weeks and months of its existence, a business will usually employ few people: the owner will usually be one of them, perhaps along with some relatives or trusted friends. As the business expands, so the need to look further afield for the human resource becomes necessary. Both the quality and quantity of employees needed may increase and finding people who will share the values and objectives of the original business is critical. As the business first begins to expand, recruitment may still be carried out by word of mouth and be based on first-hand knowledge of potential employees. However, as growth continues, so specialists in recruitment may be consulted. In larger businesses the responsibility for recruitment is handled by the Personnel Function and its important role is explored in Part Four.

Structure

The structure of a business is primarily determined by the way it is legally formed. All business start-ups in the UK occur in the *private sector* of the economy. The private sector is that sector of the economy which is self-financing and receives no direct support from government. The three main forms of structure to consider are:

- sole trader
- partnership
- limited company.

Often a business will set up as a sole trader and, as it expands, it will change its structure to that of a limited company. The legal procedures for such structures are examined in Part One.

When a business reaches a certain size it may decide to 'go public'; that is, it will open up its share ownership to any individual or institution which has the necessary money to buy. 'Going public' happens through the mechanism of the Stock Exchange and this process is explored in Part One.

As a business grows, so does its need for people, finance etc, and in order to accommodate this change the business structure must evolve to provide safeguards for owners and employees alike.

Strategy

Business ideas need to be converted into a strategy – a long-term plan for the business. As the tree grows, so its strategy will change direction in an attempt to tap into further nourishment that will promote future growth. A business strategy which is: properly thought through; is making the best use of its present resources; is planning the development of its future resources, will go a long way to achieving success. It is important that as many employees as possible share in the objectives of the business and work towards the achievement of a common goal. If this is not attained, then conflict will ensue. Business strategy and measurement of its success is considered in Part One.

Organisation

In any small business, it is usually possible for decisions, discussions and instructions to be conducted directly between the owner(s) and the workforce. As the business becomes more complex, so the need to provide an organisational framework for efficient and effective operation and communication increases. For example, in a a small catering business, the same person that takes orders from customers over the 'phone may do the planning of the making, the making itself and the delivery. As the business grows, it may be that different people or departments have separate responsibility for such areas as:

- order processing
- buying raw foodstuffs to fulfil the order
- invoicing customers
- producing the goods
- delivering the goods
- paying bills and wages.

As you can imagine, the organisation required to co-ordinate this and satisfy the customer is considerable. If you've ever been let down by a shop, garage, or builder, then usually that will be because of poor organisation and communication in the business. Sometimes a business will choose to remain small to avoid getting involved in these challenges: for example, the self-employed electrician who doesn't even have an apprentice, trainee or helper so that the organisation and administration associated with payment of employees (PAYE, National Insurance contributions etc) can be avoided. Business organisation and communication is dealt with in Part One.

Management

Generally, the larger the business, the more managers it will have. Managers are responsible for making decisions. They should manage the resources of the business efficiently and effectively. The resources they are expected to manage include:

- people
- time
- money
- property and equipment.

People are probably the single most important resource of the business and the leadership and motivation of people is an important management issue which you will meet in Part Three.

The Branches

The larger the tree, the more branches it has: the larger the business, the more departments or specialist functions it develops. A sole trader running a small printing business is likely to have few employees. Each employee will, however, have several roles. The production assistant may take delivery of the inks and paper, set up the printing press, check the quality of the output, quote for new jobs, telephone customers and much more. The clerical assistant may receive and process orders, handle correspondence, invoice customers, pay bills, bank cheques, check bank statements, advertise in newspapers, calculate wages, and so on. The small size of the business doesn't justify one person being allocated to each separate task; jobs within the business are, as a result, varied, flexible, relatively unspecialised (and probably interesting!).

Contrast this scene with that which you might find in a large manufacturing business, such as ICL, which makes computers. Not only is the ICL business tree extremely large, but its branches are many, and each branch will have tens or hundreds of twigs. ICL will have separate departments or functions for:

- marketing
- accounting
- production
- personnel
- purchasing.

Within each of these functions there will be sub-functions or branches. For example, the production function may be subdivided into:

- manufacture
- assembly
- engineering
- inspection
- maintenance
- research and development
- production planning

Even within these sub-branches, further division of responsibility will occur. Engineering may be split into:

- plant and equipment engineering
- software engineering
- hardware engineering
- process engineering

This book will concentrate on four of the main functions of a business. You will find these in Part Four:

- marketing
- production
- personnel
- accounting.

The Trunk

The trunk of a tree provides the platform from which the branches can expand and flourish. The xylem and phloem of the tree transport the energy and nourishment from its roots to all other parts of the tree; the bark offers protection against climactic extremes and potential predators.

Most businesses start off as sole traders, partnerships or private limited companies. In such organisations the aims and direction are usually clear-cut; conflict is rare since those responsible for decision-making and strategic planning are also the owners of the business. As it continues to grow, it might widen its ownership base by selling shares to 'incomers'. Now it will have to take account of a wider spectrum of views: it is here that conflict can arise. Shareholders who are 'incomers' may want dividends and short-term returns: conversely, the original founders want long-term, steady growth which will provide security and ensure better returns in the future.

In 1986 Richard Branson's Virgin Group faced just such a situation. In order to raise additional finance to enable his planned growth, Branson 'went public' and floated shares on the London Stock Exchange; 35% of its equity was bought by 87,000 new shareholders – Branson had opened Virgin Group to 'outsiders'. It was not long before Branson realised his mistake. The new shareholders (in the main, insurance companies, pension funds and large institutional investors) sought to exert considerable influence, if not direct pressure, on the direction in which Virgin was going. Not liking what he was experiencing, in 1988 Branson bought out the new shareholders and returned the company to private status in early 1989. Though Branson's ownership of Virgin doesn't extend to owning all of its shares, those who have a stake in it tend to be those whose attitudes and values coincide with his and who have confidence in Branson's strategy and leadership.

In business, success can only be achieved by the setting, and communicating, of clear objectives. The overall strategy for the business will be set by the owner or Board of Directors (who represent the owners or shareholders in the company). It is vital that when objectives and targets are set that they are communicated to the entire workforce and thereby pervade the whole business. Failure to achieve this results in, at best, uncertainty and lack of direction and, at worst, conflict – leading to underperformance and failure to thrive. A business is held together by efficient and effective communication. The setting of objectives is covered in Part Three, as is communication in the business.

Most people in business make decisions every day. Some decisions are minor and relatively routine. A supervisor in a garage may have to make daily decisions about the sequence of work to be done there: should customer A's car be serviced before customer B's car? In this instance, the decision taken will be based on the supervisor's own experience, intuition and information. The supervisor will know how long each job is likely to take, and when customers are calling back for their vehicles, and will often subconsciously process this information before communicating the decision to the mechanics.

Generally, the more complex and important the decision, the longer the time span it takes to make: the decision-making process that considered which route would be followed by the rail link between Central London and the Channel Tunnel spanned years. The decision was based on masses of financial and statistical information, as well as other factors, such as environmental and social costs and was shaped by the influence of pressure groups. Decision-making, and the provision of information to assist in that process, is looked at in Part Three. Issues such as conflict and social costs and benefits are considered in Part Five.

The Wider Environment

The main factor which directly affects the growth of a tree is its roots and how they are nourished. Trees that grow in fertile soil, irrigated with a plentiful supply of water, are likely to grow strong. Just so with business.

However, trees are also affected by the climate and the wider environmental conditions in which they grow; acid rain; soil erosion; climactic conditions; competition with other species for light and space; felling and changes in patterns of cultivation are all factors that might affect the size and numbers of trees in a particular location. In the short-term, none of these factors may affect the tree and its growth, but in the long-term the effects may be significant and even detrimental.

Once again, in business, the tree analogy holds true. There are factors in the wider business environment which must be monitored, observed and considered. These factors include:

Economic Factors	*Other Factors*
• the market mechanism	• the social system
• the economic system	• trade unions
• the political system	• ethics
• international trade	• pressure groups
• government policies	• the condition of the world and national economy

A sensible business student will show a keen interest in such issues, many of which are studied in depth by economists.

The economic factors and issues are considered in Part Two where, as well as the theory that underpins them, your study of the wider environment will be given some relevance by looking at the wider trends that have been developing in the British and international economies in the last fifty years or so.

The other factors are considered in Part Five.

The Winds of Change

If you place your sapling in a protected place, you can be sure it will grow straight and true, but only for so long as it remains sheltered. Once unprotected, it must have the strength to stand up to all of the different weathers and winds that our 'temperate' climate can produce. So, too, with our business tree. Once out of the protection of its nursery, it will be buffeted by winds from each and every point of the compass.

L – LEGAL - this can arise out of laws added to the statute book by the British Parliament or increasingly, by the European Parliament. Examples of changes in the law which have directly affect British business are:

- the restrictions on cigarette advertising
- tougher drink driving laws

- compulsory fitting of plugs on electrical appliances.

Change never stops. The source of change may come from:

- business: the pressure for change in the Sunday trading laws is an example of this

- pressure groups: the 'Green lobby' has greatly influenced laws on emissions from power stations

- government: the creation of green belts to restrict commercial, industrial and residential development.

I – INFRASTRUCTURE - this is mainly concerned with changes to the transport and communications network. Examples of such change are:

- the construction of the Channel Tunnel

- the electrification of the east coast rail link between London and Scotland

- the restructuring of local government.

E – ENVIRONMENTAL - an increasingly important source of change as consumers become more aware of the impact of their buying habits. This has a direct 'knock-on' effect on suppliers and producers. Examples of such change are:

- consumer awareness of the importance of 're-cycling'

- the substitution of synthetic materials in place of natural furs and skins

- attitudes towards the use herbicides and pesticides

S – SOCIAL - an aspect of change which you influence and which in turn has a direct impact on your own life. Examples of social change include:

- the desire or need for more women with children to return to work

- the increased demand for convenience foods as lifestyles change

- the advent of 'consumerism'

- the move towards 'healthy eating'

- attitudes towards 'drink driving'.

D – DEMOGRAPHIC - the changing nature of the population both in terms of age and geographical location. Some examples of such change are:

- the impending shortage of qualified school leavers to fill employment openings

- the increasing proportion of the population which is of pensionable age

- the depopulation of certain rural areas of the UK.

E – ECONOMIC - the world economy, as well as that of the UK economy, runs in cycles of booms and recessions. Business must prepare a strategy for coping with, and making an opportunity of, such change. Specific economic changes which seem to be constant news are:

- the rate of inflation (Retail Price Index)

- interest rates

- unemployment

- the balance of trade.

P – POLITICAL - political change has never figured as prominently in the news as it has in the 1990s. Elections in the UK, the US and several important European countries, give rise to uncertainty about possible changes of government. But dwarfing these uncertainties are the changes brought about by:

- the demise of European Communism and the break up of the Soviet Union

- the 'opening up' of Eastern Europe

- the civil war in Yugoslavia

- the Gulf War over the invasion of Kuwait by Iraq.

The repercussions of these changes will be felt for many years to come.

T – TECHNOLOGICAL - the pace of this change is accelerating and seems inexorable. Whether technological change is considered good or bad, it is impossible to avoid being pulled along with it. Most businesses have to 'go with the flow' – or take the consequences. Current examples of technological change are innumerable, but some that have had a major impact on business and will continue to do so are:

- the increased sophistication and power of computers

- development of computer peripherals (CD-ROM, CD-TV, laser printers, optical discs, scanners, colour reprographic equipment etc)

- improved communications equipment (fibre optics, car 'phones, fax machines, electronic mail, satellites, cellular 'phone networks)

- new materials (eg Kevlar; Gore-tex etc)

- microsurgery in medicine

- increased efficiency of power generation

- CAD/CAM (Computer Aided Design/Computer Aided Manufacture).

These eight aspects of change can be remembered by means of the acronym:

LIES DEPT

Interested and perceptive business students will be ever alert for these factors or 'winds': we will not return to them specifically in this book but you will notice numerous examples of their presence.

Virgin Group: A Case Study of a Business Fable

The analogy of a tree and a business is based on the fact that both things are organic and are capable of growth by adapting themselves to changes in their respective environments. By examining a single business you can begin to determine whether these assumptions are correct. Let's look at the growth stages of the business referred to earlier, the Virgin Group of companies.

The Seed

The seed of this business was sown by Richard Branson in his schooldays, when he perceived a need that no one else noticed. On a very small amount of capital, Branson, at the age of seventeen, launched a national magazine called *Student*. Soon, Branson took on his second cousin, Simon Draper, to help him to run the business.

The Sapling

From the proceeds of this magazine Branson acquired enough capital to start up as a discount mail-order record retailer. This venture proved profitable and successful until a postal strike badly affected business, forcing him to open his first retail outlet, a record shop in Oxford Street, London. With the proceeds from these enterprises, he built a recording studio in Oxfordshire and the following year he launched the Virgin record label.

Up to this point, Virgin had been growing nicely, extending its roots and providing itself with stability and a platform for growth. Keen business acumen and an element of luck led to Virgin signing up its first star: Mike Oldfield, whose album *Tubular Bells* became the soundtrack for the film, *The Exorcist*; it sold a huge amount of copies, thus providing the business with additional finance that gave Branson the option to expand, should he so wish.

He did: he expanded into nightclubs, signed more artists on the Virgin label and set up Virgin Vision to distribute videos and films. In addition, Vanson Developments was formed with the intention of exploiting opportunities in the property development market. The following year, 1984, Branson diversified his interests again, by setting up Virgin Atlantic Airways with its North American and Japanese routes, and buying the first of several acquisitions in hotel chains. Draper was underwhelmed by his decision, telling Branson that, "This is the beginning of the end of our relationship". But Branson, as holder of a majority of Virgin shares, could afford to push through his plans in the face of his colleague's opposition, He did, and Simon Draper was given an attractive consolation prize: the right to run Virgin Music unimpeded.

At this point in their growth, many businesses act with an uncertain purpose: some nervously consolidate their financial and market positions and set out to accumulate cash in preparation for the next stage of expansion. Some, who have already accumulated spare cash, look around for attractive businesses to acquire through takeover or friendly merger, whilst a minority – usually the most ambitious – decide that they will have to find funds to feed their appetite for expansion. It was this last course of action upon which Branson and Virgin decided.

The Tree

Virgin, now a sizable and successful company, considered two possible sources for finance. For any company, large or small, there are really only two places the business tree can put out its tap root and look for extra cash: inside or outside. 'Inside' means tapping into the profits that the business has retained from previous profitable years. 'Outside' means debt: borrowing money from commercial or merchant banks or finance houses; raising equity by selling shares in one's own company or, as it is usually known, 'going public'. And going public is what Branson chose to do. The main advantage Branson gained in doing that was time: in the short-term it is quicker to raise finance from the market. The second advantage Virgin gained was a heightened public image: a public flotation normally improves a company's profile, especially if public relations are as adeptly exploited in the way that Branson manages.

There are also disadvantages. The major drawback is that there is a loss of control, since ownership of the company is now much more widely spread. Then there is the increased potential for conflict, especially between the original founders of a business, its management and, perhaps, the new members of the board of directors who may want to see a different business strategy and management policies pursued. Some directors will have 'earned' their places by being representatives of pension funds and insurance companies, investment trusts and banks – the so-called *institutional shareholders*.

As well as the dilution of power that arises because of the number of shares available on the open market, a public company is, of course, now fair game for predators. It is vulnerable to takeover since its shares can be purchased by anyone and even the largest majority shareholder, Branson himself, might be voted off the board: going public really does expose the tree to the cold winds that can blow in the financial world and make it vulnerable to external factors.

These thoughts were not the ones most in evidence when Virgin shares first went on sale, in 1986, at an offer price of 140p. The shares failed to maintain their original valuation and declined to a low point of 85p before Branson reversed his decision to go public. A major reason why Virgin shares 'failed' was because they did not prove attractive enough to the big investors, and to would-be institutional shareholders. And the reason why they were reluctant to buy in to Virgin was that they did not share Branson's faith in the long-term plans and prospects of the company.

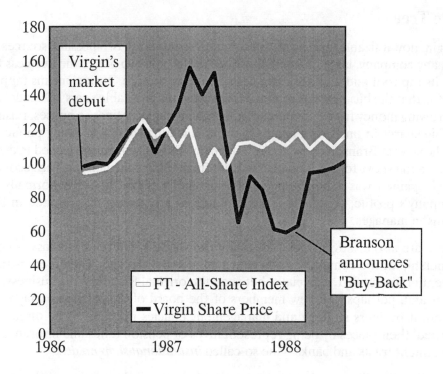

Virgin Share Price compared with FT All-Share Index 1986-1988

In 1988 Branson and his top managers, including his 'lieutenants', Ken Berry and Simon Draper, bought back Virgin shares back at their original price of 140p. In doing so, Branson effectively stifled the potential environmental threat to which he had, for the best of motives, exposed his company through that original decision to go public.

Was Virgin, then, capable of providing enough income on its own to sustain growth and fulfil Branson's desire to make it 'the greatest entertainment business in the world'? A good question. And one worth asking at this point in an unfinished story, when Virgin Music – once the core business – has just been sold to EMI for £560 million through a one-for-four rights issue. What might Branson's decision to sell mean? Has he chosen this option as a long-term tactic to raise finance to expand in a different direction? Has Branson done it deliberately to avoid having to return to the 'City' a second time in order to raise capital to finance expansion in some undisclosed direction – possibly an expansion of his airline business, which is cash-hungry and has heavy start-up costs?

The answer is, 'Probably, yes'. What has emerged is that Branson *has* changed his business strategy; his ambition to make Virgin 'the greatest entertainment business in the world' will not become reality. His new ambition – which is also the new business strategy – is summarised in the phrase, 'To create a real quality airline that manages to survive on a worldwide basis'. Eight years after he launched Virgin Atlantic, Branson has gone halfway to his target of running eighteen planes to thirteen major cities over five continents.

Where Virgin is now

At present Virgin has four major divisions: communications; travel; music and retail. (See the organisation map on page 39.) Parts of these businesses have been sold off. Fujisankei, for example, holds 25% of the music business for which it paid $150 million and WH Smith owns half of Virgin's megastores. Virgin Music has been built into the seventh largest record company in the world and it has been sold for a substantial sum to Thorn EMI, with Draper and Berry going with it as part of its sale price. Branson's energies are clearly turning to a new challenge: building an airline that can compete with the 'giants' of world aviation, like British Airways, with whom Branson is already locked in an unpleasant and litigious dispute. The resources required for starting up and running an airline are enormous: a single factor, such as the Gulf crisis of 1990-91, can plunge a successful business into illiquidity very quickly. (Branson has already witnessed this: pre-tax profits of less than £800,000 were declared for Voyager Travel in 1991, compared to £8.5 million for the previous year). But Branson's strategy is unambiguous: 'The airline is more than a business, it is a crusade.'

Where Virgin might be ...

Will Virgin's growth be organic, as it has been traditionally, or will Virgin Group become more predatory than it has been, building through acquisition? Having sold off Virgin Music, Branson currently sits on a formidable mini-mountain of cash. He seems to be turning his back on the business that metamorphosed the 'hippy entrepreneur' in to one of the country's best-known business people. At the same time, he is clearly intent upon elbowing himself in to a prominent place in the notoriously competitive airline business. Whether he succeeds or fails, there is no way presently of knowing. But what we can be certain of is that we cannot predict what the size and shape of Branson's business tree will be; at present we can only be sure that it will continue to wave in the wind for some time yet.

Adapt or Die: A Business in its Environment

The time is the late 1970s; the place is Ireland. Around a table sits a group of people obliged to find a solution to a very pressing problem. The background to their problem is simple: they have thousands of gallons of cream that no one wants. Increasingly health-conscious Irish consumers are reluctant to buy a product that they associate with fat, cholesterol and coronary heart disease. With the supply of cream steadily outstripping demand, the Irish Milk Marketing Board has a huge surplus of an unneeded product. From somewhere around that table, an idea slowly emerges ... what about blending the surplus cream with surplus Irish whiskey to make a new and distinctive liqueur? Attractively packaging the bottle whilst retaining the Irish character of the product? Giving the product a name that suggests that behind it there is a pedigree of quality and tradition? A name? Perhaps a family name? Ideas begin to emerge thick and fast as the marketing brainstorm takes on its own momentum.

A fictitious scene? Yes and no. The brainstormers that day certainly got up from that table with a new idea and a new product. They had found the answers they were looking for. What they had done was to come up with the five answers that any good marketer would want:

- whatever it is that we make, will consumers buy it?

- whatever it is that we make, can we provide it in sufficient quantity?

- whatever it is that we make, can we make it at the right price?

- whatever it is that we make, can we make it cost effectively?

- whatever it is that we make, can we make it at the right quality?

There were three further questions to which they had to get answers. Once they had designed their product, could they raise the money that would support its production and promotion? Could they get people of the right quality to develop, market and produce their product effectively? Could their organisation adapt so that the new product could be integrated into its product range? The answer to all three questions turned out to be 'Yes'; the product that they 'invented' found its way on to supermarket shelves as Bailey's Irish Cream. It was followed in a short space of time by other competing products, such as Bewley's Irish Coffee.

The moral of the above tale is that an astute business person will always, given the slightest chance in the most adverse circumstances, convert a threat in to an opportunity.

Part One – The Business Organisation

At that point in time when a business is formed, it is accepted that certain things are in place: there is a legal structure; there are people employed; there is a business idea and a business plan (or strategy, if you prefer the more widely used term); there is a management and the business has access to finance that has allowed it to get started and to continue. You might say that these things are the prerequisites that a business must have to begin trading. Each of these prerequisites is within its control and it is the responsibility of the business to ensure that they are properly in place.

This Part will lead you through: the structure of a business, its responsibilities under the law and the legal framework under which it has constituted itself; how a business is 'placed' in terms of its relationships with other businesses and within the national economy; how a business may be classified according to a number of criteria relating to its level of activity, its size, who owns it and the sector of the economy in which it is active.

As a business begins to mature the need for longer term planning and clearer objectives begin to emerge. The business looks critically at what it is hoping to achieve, how it intends to achieve it and by when it hopes to achieve it. Its managers concentrate on developing and implementing a strategy for their business and have to agree means and measures by which they can judge how successful they have been in meeting their objectives. The business will be increasingly aware of its financial requirements and a constant theme in the management of the business will be finding answers to the questions, 'How much money do we need?'; 'From where is that money going to come?'; 'What will we spend it on?'; 'How much are we prepared to pay for it?'

The organic growth of a business invariably means that more people are employed by it. As their number increases, so the challenge of motivating people to work as a team and share common, corporate objectives becomes more important. The effectiveness of teamwork, or groupwork, needs to be measured. Communication also becomes more problematic as the 'lines of communication' become more elongated and this is touched upon both here and in Part Three.

The increasing importance of management in businesses in the 1980s and 1990s forms the final section of this Part One.

Classifying Business Activity

> *"The massive Peterson Group plc is further extending its quarrying and mineral extraction operations. This is further evidence of the encroachment of the private sector into areas once seen as the public sector domain."*

That is the sort of item that you might read on the business page of any newspaper or hear as part of a radio or television bulletin. Brief as the statement is, it tells you several things about the structure of the company and that part of the economy in which the business operates.

To fully understand the statement, you must break it down into its constituent parts. The four main pieces of information it provides about the business are:

- it operates in the private sector
- it is engaged in quarrying and mineral extraction
- it is large
- it is a public limited company (plc).

The four pieces of information demonstrate the four criteria by which a business can be classified. They are:

1. by sector
2. by level of activity
3. by ownership
4. by size.

Each of these criteria will be briefly considered here; they will be referred to in different contexts, and in greater detail, later on.

1. By Sector

One distinction between the 'private' and 'public' sectors has already been made: their *objective* will be different. A second major distinction lies in their accountability: public sector organisations are accountable, in widest terms, to the public whom they serve. They are financed by the taxpayer and produce goods and/or perform services for the benefit of the public; profit is not recognised by them or the public as their main objective. On the other hand, a private sector organisation is owned by individuals, or groups of individuals, who have invested their money in it and, in return, expect to share any profits that the business makes; profit is, therefore, the main objective of a private sector organisation.

In recent years, classifying by sector has become increasingly redundant. In the late 1970s and early 1980s, the public sector was much larger than it is today. From 1979 the policies of successive Conservative governments has been to turn over many of the organisations in the public sector into private hands. This process of 'privatisation' is examined in more detail in Part Two.

2. By Level of Activity

The three broad levels of activity on which a business can operate are:

1.   the primary level (e.g. farming, fishing, mining, quarrying etc.)

2.   the secondary level (e.g. manufacturing and construction)

3.   the tertiary level (the service industries, such as banking, insurance and leisure providers).

At one time in the past, it might have been reasonably easy to use the level of activity as a criterion by which to classify a business: each business tended to stick to what it knew how to do: the brewer brewed beer; the car manufacturer made cars; the furniture store sold furniture.

Some businesses can still be categorised in this way: a farmer with no other business interests is clearly operating in the primary sector. However, in recent years, the size of businesses has tended to become bigger as they have diversified and spread their interests beyond their original level of activity.

Example 1

Scottish and Newcastle plc operates at all three levels of activity. As the diagram of the company structure shows, it has subsidiaries which produce malt (one of the raw materials of beer); retail outlets (i.e. Waverley Vintners Ltd.) and leisure companies (Center Parcs and Pontins), as well as continuing to brew beers, its original business base. Scottish and Newcastle has diversified its interests because it wishes to be less vulnerable to certain aspects of the business environment that might threaten its growth. If beer and lager sales are declining, leisure interests might be enjoying a boom time; what Scottish and Newcastle has lost on the alcoholic swings, it has made up for on the leisure roundabout.
The Group Structure for Scottish and Newcastle plc is shown on the next page.

Example 2

Nissan Manufacturing (UK) Ltd. used to sell their cars on to an independent dealer network over which they could exert little control. In January 1992, they set up their own dealer network; the new dealerships were still independent garages, but now they had to conform to a quality of service standards specified by Nissan Manufacturing (UK) Ltd.

Example 3

MFI is a well-known retailer of furniture and kitchen units. Much of what they sell is manufactured by a company called Hygena, a subsidiary of MFI group. So, unless a business is small, it is unlikely that it will be restricted to one level of activity, although a broad reference to its level of activity will usually relate back to the origins of the business.

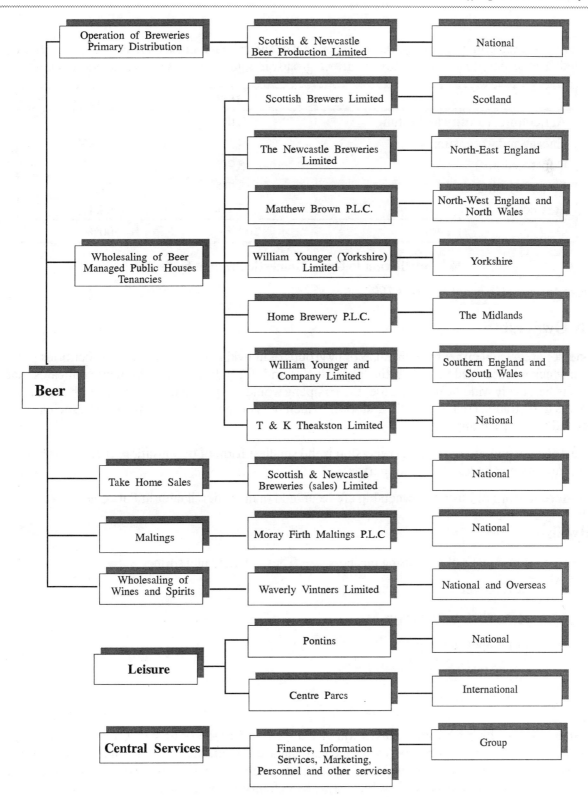

The Group Structure for Scottish and Newcastle plc

In recent years the contributions to the UK economy of the primary and secondary levels of activity have declined. The tertiary or service sector has grown greatly in significance as the Table below shows.

	1980	1990
Agriculture, forestry and fishing	2.0%	1.4%
Energy and water supply	9.3%	4.8%
Construction	5.9%	7.2%
Manufacturing	25.7%	21.2%
Services	57.1%	63.4%
Total	100%	100%

% Contribution to Gross Domestic Product by Sector

Source: Annual Abstract of Statistics 1992

3. By Ownership

Businesses are owned either by individuals or by groups of individuals. In the case of the fictitious Peterson Group which was referred to earlier, the 'plc' (which stands for public limited company) indicates that the company has a very wide ownership base; the company would be quoted on the Stock Exchange, allowing its shares to be traded (that is, bought and sold) to members of the public and institutions, such as pension funds and insurance companies.

At the opposite end of the scale of ownership is the smallest form of organisation: the sole trader, which is a business owned by a single (sole) person.

The different forms of business ownership are examined in more detail later in Part One.

4. By Size

There are various means of measuring business size. These include measuring:

- by turnover
- by number of employees
- by number of outlets
- by capital employed.

Turnover

The annual sales which a business makes will give a good indication of its size. Clearly, a company with sales of £4 million a year is likely to be, by any means of measurement, larger than a company whose turnover is £1 million a year. Measuring business size by turnover might be an accurate and valid way of comparing the size of supermarket chains, such as Safeway, Tesco, Sainsbury and Asda.

Number of employees

In a local community you will often hear people refer to firms as 'big' or 'small'. In this instance, as employment prospects are often uppermost in people's minds, 'big' and 'small' are likeliest to refer to the number of people employed by a business.

With the increasing influence of technology, the number of employees is currently much less helpful in indicating the size of a business than it was in the past. For example, shops and supermarkets, at one time labour-intensive now need fewer staff. Electronic point of sale devices, self-service, credit card payment methods and more efficient ways of restocking shelves all contribute to a reduced need for people. This trend does not mean the business is any smaller; indeed it may be growing faster as a result of the new technology.

Number of outlets

In the retail trade, the number of towns in which a business operates its branches is often a good guide to size. Consumers will perceive firms that have many branches or shops, as larger businesses than those that have few outlets. You might use this basis to produce a valid comparison of the sizes of Littlewoods and British Home Stores.

Capital employed

'Capital employed' is the total amount of money invested in a business. It is a criterion used by accountants and financiers to measure the size of a business. Generally, the more money that is invested in a business, the greater is its scale of operations.

Sometimes a business will have relatively few employees for its capital employed: it is then described as a *capital intensive* business. A business which is the converse, having many employees and relatively low levels of capital employed, is described as *labour intensive*.

	Capital	Labour
Labour intensive	Low	High
Capital intensive	High	Low

The Companies Act 1981, for accounting purposes, uses a particular method of referring to size which is broadly:

A company must satisfy two of the following three criteria over the previous two years:

Criteria	Small Company	Medium Size Company
	Must not exceed	*Must not exceed*
Turnover	£2 million	£8 million
Net assets	£0.975 million	£3.9 million
Number of employees	no more than 50	no more than 250

Types of Business Organisation

When a business starts to operate it will have already formalised its business idea into a business plan. The plan will contain a statement on what the legal structure of the business will be. Since businesses are dynamic (that is, they change in response to internal factors, over which they have some control, as well as external factors, over which they have less or no control), you would not expect that legal structure to be 'set in stone'; the legal structure, too, has to change as the business grows.

Businesses can be classified under two legal forms:

- those which are *unincorporated*. These businesses usually fall in to two types: *sole traders* or *partnerships*. In these businesses, the individuals who own them are legally responsible for their affairs. Should debts arise which cannot be paid by funds in the business, then those individuals will be legally responsible to pay off the debts from their own private resources. In the same way, if a customer is summoned to court the business for breach of contract, then *those individuals who own the business* – and not the business itself – are liable for any damages which might be awarded.

- those which are *incorporated*. Known to us as *companies*, they come in two main forms, the *private limited company* and the *public limited company*. Their owners are referred to as *shareholders*. Once a business is incorporated, its owners (shareholders) cease to have individual liability for the debts of the business. The company itself is a legal body and, in the eyes of the law, is regarded as a single entity and is treated in the same way as is an individual.

Now consider each type of business in turn.

Sole Traders (or Sole Proprietors)

The term 'sole trader' is used to describe an individual who is self-employed and operates a business alone, accepting sole responsibility for its management and finances. In practice, a sole trader rarely works alone, and will usually employ staff to assist in operating the business. There are no legal formalities governing the creation of such a business.

A sole trader's business will normally be financed solely by its owner, which means that any opportunities for raising further capital are limited. This can severely restrict the growth of the business. Also, while the sole owner is entitled to all of the profits of the business, he or she also accepts unlimited liability for any losses which the business incurs. All losses will be borne by the sole trader. The sole trader form of business is most suitable for an individual who wishes to retain absolute control of a business enterprise that only requires a modest amount of financial investment. Examples of such enterprises include: a retail shop; the service trade, such as plumbing or hairdressing; farms. Sole traders provide a valuable service to the community by offering a wide range of goods and services and making them available in a convenient way.

Responsibility for decision-making in a sole trader business rests directly with its owner; there is no individual or group to whom the owner is directly accountable, except him or herself. Such a position is attractive to someone who wants to 'be their own boss'.

Over recent years there has been an increase in the number of one-person businesses. There are often grants and tax incentives available that encourage people to set up business of this type. When the climate of business is one where unemployment and redundancies are commonplace, or rising, the result can be a flood of new small businesses into the market. In the period 1981 to 1988, the number of self-employed in the UK grew steadily from two to three million; a significant proportion of this growth was due to the number of one-person businesses being set up. In one year alone – 1988 – over 10,000 new businesses were started. (This rise is illustrated in the Figure below).

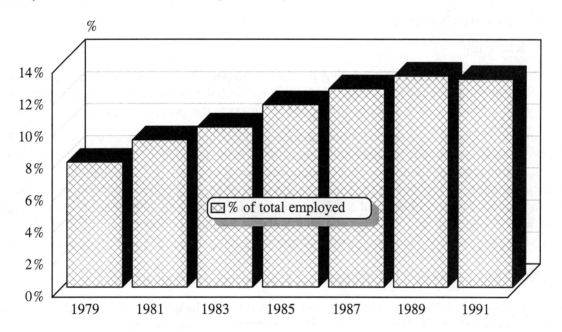

Self-employment as a proportion of the working population

Lump-sum redundancy payments, which workers in larger organisations can receive, sometimes provide the initial funding of such enterprises; with little alternative employment available, such people are often tempted to 'go it alone'. On the other hand, a large number of people make a conscious decision to become self-employed and over 200,000 employees each year take the step towards self-employment. Interestingly, the incentive that leads to this is their perception that they will gain greater independence and freedom to make their own decisions; financial rewards are found to be of only secondary importance.

As well as needing a sensible idea for a business, any aspiring business person needs to prepare a sound business plan, in order to raise any additional funding that will be required from the bank. Even with a sound business plan, it is still essential that a person undertakes training and learns the ground rules of running and organising a business if he or she is to have any chance of becoming a success.

Other factors can be critical if a business wishes to continue, the most important of which is the character of the person concerned. A profile of a successful self employed business person would include most, if not all, of the following characteristics:

- high motivation to succeed
- self-discipline
- organisational ability
- self-belief
- the ability to relate to other people
- 'self-starting' and initiative
- leadership.

Nationally, new business start-ups were running at about 1,700 per week in 1989 compared with 1,250 per week in 1988. Although the recession of the early 1990s has affected business confidence, many individuals are still prepared to take the risk of creating their own business as the previous Figure indicates.

The Department of Employment recently published a report that showed that there was a 29% growth in the number of small businesses between 1979 and 1989, from 1.3 million to 1.6 million. Whilst the Department of Employment claims that small businesses create jobs more quickly than large companies, whether national wealth is created on the same scale is debatable. Businesses employing fewer than ten people were responsible for creating half a million jobs between 1987 and 1989, a figure that represents half of the total net growth of jobs – despite the fact that they employ less than 20% of all people. Interestingly, the very smallest businesses – those employing fewer than four people – created most jobs.

The relationship between size and success: a tale of two countries

When you read Part Two of this textbook you will appreciate more fully that the 1980s saw the dismantling or collapse of a large part of UK manufacturing. The government argued that these large industries might be replaced successfully by the small businesses that would grow up to take their place, especially in the service sector.

The different experiences of the UK and Germany, regarding the encouragement of small and large businesses respectively, are worth looking at.

The Department of Employment figures make an implicit assumption that there is a link between size and success and that success favours smaller businesses. However, it is worth asking whether this assumption is true. If you look at the 1992 Annual Report of the German Daimler-Benz Company, you will find that the company is the biggest non-oil, non-utility business in Europe with annual sales of £33 billion, making it bigger than British Aerospace and ICI added together. In *International Management's* list of the top thirty EC companies, fifteen are German, six French and four British; BMW, manufacturer of luxury cars figures in that list, ahead of UK 'mega-businesses' like British Aerospace, British American Tobacco and Grand Metropolitan. In 1970 BMW had 20,000 employees; now it has 70,000. Such a fact seems to support those who assert that British business is too eager to limit the size of organic company growth; BMW has grown *organically*, as opposed to growing through acquisition, so that every job created means real additional wealth. The link between size and success is clearly seen in German businesses, such as Daimler-Benz, BASF, Hoechst and Bayer, all of whom built themselves up by developing and marketing new products and investing in the people who would make and sell them. In 1991 Daimler-Benz spent £2.9 million on research and development and £2.9 billion on capital investment, figures that, when added together, dwarf the total *sales* of the British 'giant', GEC.

Partnerships

There are no legal formalities required when individuals agree to run a business together and, in so doing, form a partnership. The agreement to form the partnership will be a contract, but there is no legal requirement as to the form this must take. All partners in a business (and there is a legal maximum of 20) will usually agree to put their capital into a business, work on its behalf and receive in return a share of the profits, usually in proportion to the amount of capital each has contributed.

Many professional people providing business services will operate as partnerships; for instance, partnerships of solicitors, chartered accountants and architects. The major risk in operating as a partnership is that, if the business should get into financial difficulties, then the individuals who make up the partnership are personally liable for any debts that the business may incur. The partners' personal wealth – such as house, car etc – will then be used to pay off the debts of the business.

One advantage of operating a business as a partnership is the increased amount of capital which it makes available to the business. This, in turn, means that the business is able to raise more loan finance from other institutions, such as the banks. The more capital that a business can raise from within itself, the more it is likely to be able to raise from external sources.

An additional advantage that partnership offers is the opportunity for shared management responsibilities and access to a wider range of experience and expertise. For example, in a partnership of solicitors it would be usual to have individuals who specialise in different areas of law: criminal law; civil law; company law; family law etc.

Perhaps the principal disadvantage of a partnership is the likelihood that partners will disagree, so that reaching a joint decision can sometimes be difficult. Since each partner in law is 'severally and jointly' liable for the actions and debts of all other partners, so the liability of each partner is unlimited. It follows, then, that each partner is ultimately responsible for the action of any or all of the partners. If one partner acts irresponsibly, then all other partners are jointly liable for his or her actions.

It is crucial, therefore, that each partner has trust and confidence in any co-partners and that the relationship is based on the utmost good faith – a rare commodity, indeed!

The relation of the partners in the partnership should be regulated by a *partnership agreement*. This agreement may vary the provisions of the Partnership Act which, broadly, are as follows:

- all partners are entitled to take part in the management of the business

- differences arising from the ordinary business operations of the partnership are decided by majority vote

- no change can be made to the nature of the partnership without the consent of all partners

- no person may be introduced as a new partner without the consent of all existing partners

- all partners are entitled to an equal share of the business and profits arising from its operation, irrespective of the amount of time they have given to it; each must contribute equally towards any losses.

If no partnership agreement exists, then any dispute which occurs will be regulated according to the terms of the Partnership Act.

Limited Companies

The most common form of business enterprise is the limited company. In the UK there are about one million registered limited companies and between them they employ the majority of the workforce in the UK, generating about two-thirds of the income made by the private sector.

A company may have as few as two members (shareholders), but since limited companies can grow to become huge multi-national, UK-registered enterprises, such as ICI and BP, they will have tens of thousands of shareholders each.

There are two forms of limited company:

- *private limited companies*, which have certain restrictions placed on the trading in their shares

- *public limited companies*, which trade their shares on the open market through the Stock Exchange.

About 99 per cent of all companies are private and, although this leaves only 1 per cent as public limited companies, they are usually large organisations in terms of turnover, assets employed and number of employees.

Many public limited companies began their lives as private limited companies. Sometimes they may revert back to the private form; one of the best known, recent examples of this is that of the Virgin Group.

If a business is launched as a limited company, it will need to have in place a legal framework for its operation. This process is usually handled by a solicitor, in consultation with the directors of the company.

The documents which must be submitted to the Registrar of Companies are:

- The Memorandum of Association

- The Articles of Association.

The submission of these documents results in the business being granted a *Certificate of Incorporation* which legally permits the business to begin trading as a limited company.

The Memorandum of Association

The Companies Act 1985 specifies that this document must include:

- *the name of the company* – in the case of a private company the name must have 'limited' as the last word; in the case of a public company it will be 'public limited company'

- *the location of its registered office* – identifying whether the company is situated in England or Scotland

- *the liability of the members* – the amount of capital they are responsible for providing

- *the capital of the company* – this sets a limit on the amount of capital the company is allowed to raise. It is referred to as the 'Authorised Share Capital'.

The Articles of Association

The articles are concerned with the internal administration of the company, and it is for those concerned in setting up the company to decide on the rules they wish included in their Articles. The Companies Act 1985 does, however, provide a set of model Articles which a company may fully or partly adopt.

The matters which are normally dealt with in the Articles are:

- the appointment and powers of the directors

- the rules in relation to shareholders' meetings and voting

- the types of shares and the shareholders' rights attached to each type

- the rules and procedures of transferring shares.

Once a company has been incorporated, its Articles may be altered if 75% of its members vote in favour of the alteration.

Both the Memorandum and Articles are open to public scrutiny, subject to the payment of a fee, at Companies House in Cardiff.

It is worth noting at this stage that a company has two main sources of control over its affairs. These are the shareholders in a general meeting, and the directors. The most important matters, such as changes in its Constitution and the appointment of directors, rest with its shareholders in a general meeting. Most decisions require a simple majority vote, although some matters may require a 75% majority. (It is worth noting that the majority and 75% votes relate to the numbers in attendance or voting by proxy and not to the total membership.)

Since voting power plays such an important role in company matters, the types of shares which the company issues are of considerable significance. Some shares, such as *ordinary* shares, usually carry full voting rights whilst other shares, such as *preference* shares, may carry no voting rights at all.

The Articles provide for the directors to be responsible for the daily running of the company, to make decisions and act on behalf of the company. If directors act contrary to the wishes of the members, or if the performance of the company brings into question their abilities as directors, they may be sanctioned or dismissed at a general meeting. In small companies, the directors will often be the sole shareholders, so such considerations will be irrelevant.

There are a number of advantages in operating a business as a limited company:

- shareholders have limited liability (financially they can only lose what they have put into or committed to the business)

- additional capital can be raised through share issues

- banks may be inclined to loan larger amounts when the shareholders' stake (equity) is larger

- the business is able to grow and operate on a larger scale, thus achieving a higher volume of output at a lower cost

- the company name is protected by law (another business cannot start up and trade under the same name).

These advantages must be offset against the possible drawbacks:

- formation of the company can be expensive (legal costs, registration fees etc)

- decision-making may become more complex and involve a greater number of people

- employees of the business can often feel distant from its owners (although management methods can be made to compensate for this problem)

- the records of the company, such as its annual accounts, are open to the public, including creditors and competitors

- affairs are strongly controlled by the provision of the Companies Acts.

Differences between private limited companies and public limited companies

The most significant difference between the two types of company is the way in which shares can be bought and sold. A private company's shares are not quoted on the Stock Exchange, which means that they are unavailable on the open market. If an individual wishes to 'buy a share' in a private company then, effectively, he or she must be invited by the existing shareholders to do so.

In practice, many private limited companies are family concerns where the majority of shares (and thus the ultimate power of decision-making) stays within the family. Any increase in share issues outside that 'family' will dilute those powers and, ultimately, may result in a loss of control. In contrast, shares in public limited companies are available for purchase through the Stock Exchange and this can lead to some interesting battles for control of a business.

Some advantages of 'floating' the company or 'going public' are that it:

- increases the opportunities for raising additional finance

- heightens awareness and increases the public profile of the business.

Some disadvantages of 'going public' are that:

- original shareholders may lose control of power and decision-making

- only certain parts of the business may be attractive to investors, requiring bits of the business to be sold separately before the flotation

- increases the likelihood of a takeover as share ownership becomes more widespread

- decisions need to be justified and explained to a wider and much more public audience.

The role of a shareholder

Buying shares entitles the owner to share in the profits of the company. The share in profits may be paid out in cash as a dividend, or a proportion of profits may be retained for re-investment on the shareholders' behalf. A shareholder may own ordinary shares or preference shares. Preference shares are less common nowadays; they have a guaranteed percentage dividend, but do not entitle the shareholder to have a voice in the running of the company. In contrast, ordinary shareholders have full voting rights which they can exercise at general meetings. The Annual General Meeting (AGM) is the time when decisions are made about:

1. the distribution of the profits; that is, what proportion will be retained for re-investment and what proportion will be paid out as dividends

2. the election of directors of the company who will represent the shareholders' interests.

The larger the number of shares a shareholder owns, the greater the shareholder's influence on these decisions. So, in a large public company, institutional investors, such as pension funds and insurance companies, usually have a greater influence on the policy and direction of the company than will a private investor.

The price of a share is represented by the value other investors put on owning the shares. Its price is influenced by many factors, some of which are within the control of the company and some of which lie outside its control. Some of the main factors are:

- profits in the period and the extent to which they meet the expectations of investors and potential investors

- the company policy regarding the proportion of profits paid out in dividends

- international occurrences, such as wars

- general economic trends (booms and recessions)

- takeover bids

- investors buying and selling large blocks of shares

- changes in market conditions which affect the business concerned

- positive or negative comments about the business by brokers and journalists.

In a private company the transfer of shares must be agreed by a majority of the other shareholders who have 'first option to purchase'. The purpose of this rule is to ensure that small to medium-sized companies, that are often family run, are given the opportunity to keep control of the business. Owning 51% of ordinary shares in a company guarantees control of the boardroom.

It is possible that an ordinary shareholder may be required to put more money into the business through a *rights issue*. For example, each shareholder may be required to buy one further share for every ten that the shareholder currently holds: this would have the effect of increasing the share capital by 10% and yet control would remain with the existing members.

The role of a director

Directors are appointed by the shareholders at the Annual General Meeting. Directors usually are also shareholders. Directors form a type of committee known as the *Board of Directors*, often just referred to as 'the Board'. It is the duty of the Board to serve the interests of the shareholders. Meetings are conducted by the elected Chairman of the Board. All directors will have either executive or non-executive status. *Executive* directors are also employees of the business, responsible not only for making policy decisions on the running of the company, but also for putting those decisions into practice, or executing them. *Non-executive* directors are *not* employees: they sit on the Board as 'outsiders': their main concern is ensuring that decisions made will benefit shareholders. Non-executive directors may hold directorships of several companies; they may be politicians or bankers; they usually have a wealth of experience in the commercial world. The Board of Directors has joint responsibility for:

- appointing the managing director and other senior managers of the company
- deciding the policy on dividend and retained profit
- the prosperity of business
- approving major capital expenditure
- development and change in company strategy.

The *Managing Director* has overall responsibility for the management of the company and the implementation of policy decisions.

Other Types of Business Organisation

Co-operatives

Co-operatives are few in number: in 1990 there were only around 2,000, compared to almost one million companies. The idea of a business co-operative is that people join together to:

- work
- share in the profits or losses of the business
- take joint responsibility for decisions.

The various forms of co-operatives operate mainly in the production, marketing and retailing sectors. Their common features are:

- the business is owned by its employees
- each employee owns one share which was bought for £1 and which carries an entitlement of one vote
- each employee receives an equal share in the profits of the business
- each employee shares an equal liability for any losses which occur
- there is either equal pay for all workers or limited pay differentials exist between workers.

Franchises

In recent years franchising as a form of business organisation has grown in popularity. There are now thousands of franchises in the UK, operating mainly in the retail trade.

A franchise exists when an individual or group of individuals (the *franchisees*) raise a sum of money to buy the opportunity to:

- use an established business model and name (e.g. Wimpy)
- sell or distribute an established or recognised product (e.g. the British School of Motoring)
- take advantage of marketing and advertising which is organised centrally by the *franchiser* (e.g. The Body Shop or Benetton).

A franchise is a legal contract which binds franchisee and franchiser. A franchise has a much lower risk of business failure than other types of business organisation.

There are many forms of contract possible in franchise arrangements. Some of the usual terms are:

- the franchisee pays a proportion of the set up cost of the franchise (the purchase of the shop site, its fixtures and fittings)
- the franchisee pays a proportion of the annual profits to the franchiser
- the franchisee must provide a standard of product or service which is expected by the franchiser
- the franchiser provides help and support on all aspects of business operations
- the franchiser provides advertising and promotion on a local (and sometimes national) scale
- the franchiser agrees not to open further franchises within a specified radius of an existing franchise.

Advantages to the franchisee

1.   a 'protected' environment in which to open a business

2.   access to 'free' help and advice from specialists and experts

3.   a ready-made market.

Advantages to the franchiser

1.   business expansion is achieved without increasing the number of direct employees

2.   business risk is shared with the franchisee

3.   franchisees are self-motivated

4.   access is gained to very wide markets through many outlets.

The Changing Shape of Business Organisations

Management Buy-outs: MBOs

These are not a new phenomenon but they have been more commonplace recently and have received more publicity. (There were over 500 MBOs in 1989 to a value of £7.5 billion and they accounted for almost one quarter of all mergers and acquisitions). Buy-outs happen when a large business decides that it will improve efficiency and performance if it stops making a particular product line and closes that part of the business. The managers of that particular enterprise (some of whom might be facing involuntary redundancy or early retirement as the result of that decision) feel that the product is a good one and that the business is still viable. Management borrows the capital in order to buy the business, its plant and equipment, and continues manufacturing the product. Usually, a management buy-out involves the transfer of place of production, stock, machinery, the existing order-book and any brand or trade name associated with the business. The business that is selling off part of its enterprise is said to be *divesting* itself of (an unprofitable) part of its business.

The frequency of MBOs shows there are reasons other than divestment why they occur so regularly.

In the 1970s & early 1980s:
MBOs resulted from companies divesting themselves of peripheral subsidiaries and the handing on of family businesses.

In the early 1980s:
1. MBOs were seen as an alternative to the full or part-closure of businesses during the recession in manufacturing;
2. as a way of resuscitating businesses which had fallen into receivership.

After 1982:
MBOs resulted from voluntary disposals as larger businesses strategically divested themselves of divisions or subsidiaries in order to concentrate upon their 'core' business.

75% of MBOs in the UK have been small – for less than £10 million. Management has usually emerged with a substantial equity share and the balance of deals has generally been met by debt.

Two sources of MBOs in the 1980s and 1990s have been:

1. 'Going privates': these involve acquiring a publicly quoted business

2. Privatisation: usually where, in preparation for the privatisation of a nationalised industry, subsidiary businesses are disposed of prior to the flotation of the new company.

The advantages of MBOs

1. They improve incentives and efficiency throughout the business, reducing the height of the organisational pyramid, increasing information flows and the effectiveness of monitoring.

2. Ownership is usually broadened, sometimes to include all employees, via an equity trust scheme.

The ethics of MBOs

MBOs that involve the buying out of existing shareholders have been more frequent since the mid-1980s, but such a situation has the potential for a conflict of interest. The conflict centres on the legal obligation that management owes to its shareholders, as opposed to its own self-interest in acquiring the business assets of the company at the cheapest possible price. And since management has access to privileged information which, of course, it needs in order to persuade the bank to put up the finance for the deal, there must be a question mark over the ethics of such manoeuvring.

Should management not act in the best interests of shareholders by maximising the proceeds from the sale of the company? To do so, of course, it would need to share out its 'privileged' information so as to ensure that shareholders secure the highest possible return on the assets of the business. The City Code on Takeovers and Mergers has now been amended to force potential buyers to do this; the result, however, is that the information which it supplies drives up the price of the bids, thus making it difficult for those with most expertise to mount a buy-out and agree terms that would give them some financial gain.

Mergers and Acquisitions

Mergers and *acquisitions* are the terms used to describe the process by which *two companies combine to form a single company which has a single management and is commonly owned.* In a merger, owners of the two businesses that join together become the owners of the new, single business and they own its total assets.

An acquisition can take one of two forms:

1.   the acquiring company erases the interests of the old ownership when the old ownership sells for cash

2.   the acquiring company does not take over all the interests of the other business, but is in a position to dominate it since it has acquired a majority of its equity shares or net assets.

Mergers can be of three kinds, any one of which may attract the interest of the Monopolies and Mergers Commission:

1.   *Conglomerate mergers*

These are the rarest type of merger, involving as they do two businesses in different fields of activity which have no obvious shared connection. For example, a car manufacturer merges with a furniture manufacturer.

2.   *Horizontal mergers*

When one firm merges with another firm that is in the same business, this is known as a 'horizontal merger'; this is one of the commonest types of UK merger and the motivation behind this type of merger is usually the desire to control the competition. The advantage that is often gained from this type of merger is in economies of scale, but mergers of this type often pave the route to a monopoly or cartel situation. Horizontal mergers have happened regularly in the car industry since the 1970s.

3.   *Vertical mergers*

Firm A merges with another Firm B: both are in the same industry, but each occupies a different stage in the overall production chain. For example, Firm A brews beer; it acquires Firm B, which manufactures bottles and Firm C, which runs a chain of pubs and hotels. It also acquires Firm D, which runs hop farms. This sort of vertical integration is then said to be *forward integration* (it has acquired interests ahead of its own part in the production process: hotel and pub outlets; bottlers) and *backward integration* (it has acquired suppliers of its 'raw materials': hops). An example of this can be seen in the figure on page 21. The main motivations for this type of merger are:

1.   the desire to guarantee supplies

2.   to control quality at all stages of the operation

3.   to move closer to the final market for the company's products.

'Temporary Mergers' or Joint Ventures

What are they?

A joint venture describes an occasion when two or more businesses decide that it will be to their mutual benefit if they merge their resources, temporarily or for the duration of a contract or project. An *international* joint venture describes businesses, from different countries, that temporarily subsume their competitve differences in order to form a strategic partnership.

Why businesses undertake joint ventures

Joint ventures can be especially advantageous to companies which want to enter new markets or move into areas of new business that might otherwise be inaccessible. Collaboration can lead to businesses entering a market from which, under normal trading circumstances, they would be barred. Such partnerships must offer the prospect of benefits that a business acting on its own would not otherwise gain. The sharing of risk – especially risks associated with spiralling costs – is an obvious advantage to any company.

The opportunities

Before the late 1980s, opportunities to penetrate the 'closed' markets of the socialist countries of Eastern Europe and the USSR were few, except when it was done in conjunction with the government itself or with a domestic business that had the approval of the government. Since the process of 'democratization' began, more opportunities have occurred.

What it involves

The companies involved in the venture can behave in a number of ways:

1. They might create a separate company and share its equity and its dividends between themselves proportionally (an *equity* joint venture); an example of this is Suntory-Allied Lyons, where the Japanese company Suntory owns 51% of the business and Allied Lyons owns 49%.

2. The companies involved might decide to allocate costs, tasks and profits between themselves (a *non-equity* joint venture). The Concorde passenger aircraft was developed in this way by British Aerospace and the French company, Aerospatiale; a more recent example is the proposed joint venture between British, German, Italian and Spanish companies to develop the European Fighter Aircraft (EFA).

The reasons for their growth

The number of ventures of this kind have seen significant growth through the late 1970s and 1980s, especially where businesses from the three important trade blocs of Japan, the EC and North America are concerned. Private businesses find it in their interest to form commercial coalitions of this kind for a number of reasons, especially in industries which are governed by sophisticated, technological change (computers; semi-conductors; avionics; pharmaceuticals etc). In such a rapidly changing environment, only the largest businesses can afford to run risks of accelerating research and development costs. Forming a joint venture can reduce risk or spread the costs of what would be an unmanagably large project between several partners. Such collaboration is common in the aerospace industry, or when huge civil engineering tasks are undertaken, such as the Channel Tunnel or Hong Kong Airport and its accompanying bridge.

A major factor leading to international joint ventures is when a business, that is large in *national* terms, wishes to be a player on the international stage. An example of this can be seen in the UK business, GEC. In national terms GEC is impressively important but, when compared with its principal competitors, it is disappointingly small. Its sales are less than one third of its German competitor (and collaborator) Siemens, and about one fifth of the American company, General Electric, GEC's strategy is shaped for it: there are few, if any, UK businesses that it could acquire that would make it a lead player on the world stage. If GEC pursued an aggressive, acquisitive policy in Europe through takeovers, such an offensive would lead to difficulties with the EC's Commissioner on competition: joint ventures are the only way forward for such a business.

Conglomerates

A conglomerate evolves as a result of a business acquiring other businesses, either through organic growth (merger) or through acquisition (takeover). *A conglomerate will have very diverse product lines which are unrelated to each other.*

Holding Companies

A holding company is the controlling company over several other companies. The holding company may control the other companies outright or it may simply hold a majority of their shareholdings. The holding company has the power to control the policies of its subsidiary companies and it will retain some functions centrally, probably reporting the accounts and results of its subsidiaries.

Typical of the structure of many holding companies is Courtaulds Textiles plc. Courtaulds is an international textile and clothing company, comprising five main business areas: branded clothing; own-label clothing; fabrics; home furnishings and spinning. Courtaulds retains some functions centrally: corporate communications; legal services; business development; accounts and financial control; tax; management services; trademark and patents etc. The remaining functions are the responsibility of the individual subsidiary businesses. However, a host of subsidiary businesses are run as limited companies; others are run as cost or profit centres.

Forming a holding company is one means of controlling diverse growth or conglomerate growth. It allows the 'parent' company to operate discrete, semi-autonomous companies which might be occupied in different fields of production activity, but at the same time it allows the parent company to exercise varying degrees of central control over its 'offspring'. This was the pattern that Courtaulds plc followed until 1990 when it was decided that its diverse interests and numerous lines of production activity meant that it made better financial sense to *demerge* the core textile business from its other activities, such as chemical and paint making, film and plastics manufacture and engineering. This was effected in March 1990, when two separate companies, Courtaulds Textiles plc and Courtaulds plc, were formed and became independent companies listed on the Stock Exchange.

The Virgin Group of Companies provides another good example of the domination a holding company maintains over its subsidiaries and we show its corporate structure on the following page.

Multi-nationals

This is another complex term which has come into use in comparatively recent times. A multi-national is a business that conducts a large part of its business outside the country in which its headquarters are located and has a significant percentage of employees and principal facilities in other countries. Some experts have suggested the following criteria for determining a business as a multi-national:

The Virgin Group of Companies

Virgin consists of 3 wholly owned separate holding companies involved in distinct business areas from media and publishing to retail, travel and leisure.

There are over 100 operating companies across the 3 holding companies in 12 countries worldwide

Virgin Music Group *1

Record companies around the world

Music Publishing

Recording Studios

*Note *1*
Thorn EMI has acquired 100% of Virgin Music Group

Voyager Investments

Virgin Retail Group

Operates a chain of megastores in the UK, Continental Europe, Australia and Pacific selling music, video and other entertainment products. Operates Games Stores in the UK. Wholesale record exports and imports

Note
Maroi of Japan own 50% of Virgin Megastores Japan

W H Smith own 50% of Virgin Retail UK

Virgin Communications

Publishing of Computer Entertainment Software

Management of investments in broadcasting including Music Box. Investments in related publishing and entertainment activities. TV Post production services.

Book publishing

Virgin Radio, Britain's first national commercial contemporary music station

Virgin Group

Investments; joint-ventures

Property Development

Magnetic Media Distribution

Management & Corporate Finance Services to the Virgin Organisation

Voyager Group

Clubs & Hotels

Airship and Balloon Operations

Storm Model Agency

Virgin Travel Group *2

UK's second largest long haul international airline (Virgin Atlantic Airways)

Freight Handling and Packaging

Inclusive tour operations (Virgin Holidays)

*Note *2*
Seibu Saison of Japan has a 10% equity investment in Voyager Travel Holdings.

Main Operating Companies of each Holding

Virgin Records
Virgin Music Publishing
Virgin Studios

Virgin Retail UK (50%)
Virgin Blockbuster joint venture
Virgin Retail Asia Pacific
Caroline International

Virgin Games
Virgin Radio (75%)
Virgin Publishing
525
Rushes
West One Television (50%)
Limelight (27%)

Vanson Developments
Virgin Management
Rapido TV (50%)
Super Channel (31%)

Virgin Atlantic Airways
Virgin Euromagnetics
Virgin Holidays
Virgin Aviation Services
Voyager Hotels
Virgin Airship & Balloon Co.
Storm Model Agency (50%)

- it conducts operations in six or more different countries

- a minimum of 20% of the business's assets and/or sales are located/ occur in countries outside the parent company's home country

- it demonstrates an 'integrated global managerial orientation'.

'Integrated global managerial orientation' means:

1. resources of the enterprise are allocated without regard to national boundaries

2. national boundaries are constraints that enter into the decision-making process: they are not part of the definition of the business itself

3. the organisational structure cuts across national boundaries

4. personnel are transferred throughout the world

5. management has a global perspective: the world is viewed as inter-related and interdependent.

The top six multi-nationals businesses in 1991 were:

Company	Home Country
Exxon	US
Royal Dutch Shell Group	Netherlands/UK
Mobil	US
General Motors	US
Texaco	US
British Petroleum (BP)	UK

Multi-nationals have a significant effect on the world economy and on the national economies of the countries in which they operate. This aspect is covered in more detail in Part Two. Indeed, such is their size that they enjoy a larger turnover than the Gross National Product of many third world countries. They offer careers in almost any part of the world, with the potential rewards that only multi-nationals can offer. The following extract from BP's Annual Report for 1988 includes the following statement which indicates the significance of jobs and people in BP.

People in BP Worldwide

During 1988, the average number of people employed by group companies was 126,000. Studies in many countries indicate that the numbers of high quality younger people entering employment will decrease over the next five years whilst the demand for their skills will rise. To overcome potential shortages, and the threat this could pose to BP's strategic plans, we are developing new approaches to recruitment and training, capita-

lising on the flexibility the group offers internationally. For example, in Australia and New Zealand we have joint training and staff exchange schemes, linking with the needs of other BP companies in South East Asia.

We are also introducing changes to remuneration packages to strengthen the link between the contribution of employees and the performance their company. New incentive schemes have, for example, been introduced for managers in Australia and France. As part of the process of creating longer term incentives for management, and for strengthening the identification with shareholders, the Executive Share Option Scheme was extended to include all senior managers worldwide.

Staff movements

The interchange of staff between BP America and the rest of the group has continued to grow. There are now around 100 staff from BP America working internationally. Worldwide movement within BP Oil has also increased and is being stimulated by its new organisation for Europe.

Restructuring has take place in most of our other business. BP Exploration has been reorganised as a result of the Standard Oil merger and the Britoil acquisition. The moves from London of the international headquarters of BP Coal to Cleveland and of BP Nutrition to Antwerp have taken place. Reorganisation has created uncertainty and job moves for many employees. Keeping them informed of change has been a major priority. Wherever possible, staff who are unable to move are redeployed within the group. Publications and videos have been used to complement direct communication between employees and their managers. Several of our businesses and departments have further developed their own identity by producing house magazines, special news sheets and videos. A number of opinion surveys were used to help managers address topics of particular interest and concern to employees.

Business Failure

For various reasons a business can come to an end. It may be the choice of the owners to terminate it, or the action may be taken by outsiders, such as creditors who are hostile towards the business because it cannot pay its debts. Different legal rules apply to termination, depending upon the status of the business. It may be a sole trader who is operating it; it may be a partnership. Alternatively, the business may be run as a limited company. The relevant rules are considered below.

Individual Insolvency

Under the Insolvency Act 1986, where a sole trader is facing insolvency or has become insolvent, there are two possible actions that may be taken:

1.   a voluntary arrangement

2.   a bankruptcy order.

1. A voluntary arrangement

From the owner's point of view, this is a more desirable alternative since it avoids the publicity attached to bankruptcy proceedings. To a creditor it is a quicker and cheaper alternative and, because it is cheaper, more assets will be left available for distribution to the creditors.

2. A bankruptcy order

Bankruptcy proceedings begin by a petition, usually presented to the court by a creditor. A creditor can petition when the unpaid debt or debts amount to £750 or more, and the creditor has either obtained a judgment debt from the court which cannot be enforced, or has served a statutory notice on the debtor to pay the amount, and the debtor has failed to pay it for three weeks or more.

If a bankruptcy order is made, a *trustee in bankruptcy* is appointed to collect in the owner's assets and distribute them according to rules laid down in the 1986 Act. The trustee has very wide powers.

In the case of first-time bankruptcy, the bankrupt owner is cleared after three years. This 'discharge of bankruptcy' lifts the various restrictions which are imposed upon a bankrupt; for example, a bankrupt cannot stand as a councillor, or obtain credit. These rules are important both to creditors as well as to those businesses operated on a sole trader basis; equally, they are important to partnerships, where the bankruptcy of an individual partner automatically terminates the partnership.

Termination of a Partnership

Just as the bankruptcy of one partner automatically terminates a partnership, so too, does a partner leaving the business also have the effect of ending it. Any partner in a firm may apply to the courts to dissolve the partnership on one of the following grounds:

1. a partner suffering from a mental disorder

2. a partner has been guilty of misconduct in his business or private life likely to be harmful to the carrying on of the business

3. a partner has been guilty of wilful or persistent breaches of the partnership agreement, such as by false accounting, refusing to attend meetings, or engaging in constant disputes with other partners.

When a partnership is wound up, its assets must be used to pay off its debts and liabilities, the individual loans to partners and the repayment of the partners' capital contributions. Finally, any residue is divided among the partners in the same proportion as any profits were divided.

Termination of Companies

In the same way that a partnership may be brought to an end voluntarily, through the agreement or actions of the partners, or compulsorily, where it is dissolved by an order of the court, so limited companies can be terminated in the same way.

The expression used to describe the process of termination for a limited company is *winding-up*. The grounds for winding-up, whether on a voluntary or compulsory basis, are set out in the Insolvency Act 1986.

Terminology

A number of technical expressions are used in company liquidations. It is helpful to define them.

A *'petition'*: an application to the court requesting the court to exercise its jurisdiction over a company liquidation. A petition is presented where the liquidation is *compulsory*. In such cases the court has a major role to play. This is not so in *voluntary* liquidations, where the liquidation is under the control of either the members or the creditors of the company.

A *'contributory'*: a person liable to contribute to the assets of a company if it is wound-up. Existing members whose shares have not been fully paid fall within the definition of a contributory.

A *'liquidator'*: the person appointed to take control of the company, collect its assets, pay its debts and distribute any surplus to the members according to their rights as shareholders. The liquidator holds a position of great responsibility. Only individuals of integrity are qualified to hold such a post. In recent years some disquiet has been voiced as a result of company liquidations in which the liquidator conducted the winding-up to the benefit of directors, rather than the company's creditors. The Insolvency Act 1986 deals with this by requiring that only an 'insolvency practitioner', a term covering liquidators, can act in a winding-up. The practitioner must be authorised to do so by the appropriate professional body (e.g. accountancy bodies; the Law Society), or by the Department of Trade and Industry (DTI). An applicant must be shown to be a fit and proper person, and must provide security, if he or she wishes to become an insolvency practitioner.

The *'Official Receiver'*: appointed by the DTI, receivers are concerned both with personal and corporate insolvencies. Official receivers are attached to courts with insolvency jurisdiction, and they act in the capacity of liquidators in the case of compulsory liquidations, being appointed automatically when a 'winding-up' order is made. The Official Receiver (OR) remains in this office until another liquidator is appointed.

Grounds for Winding-up

In the case of a compulsory winding-up, the most common ground is the inability of a business to pay its debts.

The order of priorities

The claims of company creditors are met in the following order of priorities:

1. *the costs of winding-up* (e.g. the liquidator's fees).

2. *preferential debts*. These include: income tax deducted from the pay of company employees under the PAYE system over the past year; VAT payments, owed by the company, that have accrued over the past six months; wages and salaries of employees outstanding for the previous four months, up to a present maximum figure of £800 per employee. If assets are sufficient, preferential debts are paid in full. If not, the available assets are distributed between the preferential creditors. Creditors who have provided secured loans are able to sell the assets bought by the loan to meet the company's liability towards them; e.g. a mortgage provided on premises.

3.   *ordinary unsecured debt*, such as sums owing to trade creditors. If these cannot be paid in full they are paid proportionately amongst the creditors.

4.   *the shareholders,* according to their rights under the Memorandum andArticles of Association. It may be that one class of shareholders is entitled to repayment of a certain amount of the surplus before the others; e.g. preference shareholders may receive repayment of their paid up capital in priority to ordinary shareholders.

There may be many reasons why the management of a business decides to terminate all or part of the enterprise. The decision to close down may be one imposed upon the business because of its insolvency. (Insolvency is the condition a business finds itself in when it is unable to meet its debts.) Alternatively, the decision may be a voluntary one, made in the interests of good business practice, possibly to shut down a less lucrative part of the business enterprise. Whatever the reason for the termination, it will most certainly have an impact on the employees, some of whom may be offered alternative employment, a different place of work, or be told that they are now surplus to requirements.

Recent Trends in Business Failure

The recession that began in 1990 saw a gradually rising tide of business insolvency. Whilst the 1990 figures show a 35% increase on the 1989 figures, 1991 figures surged again.

An average of 130 firms collapsed every day in 1991 during the worst business melt-down on record. According to the business information group, Dun & Bradstreet, a total of 47,777 firms 'went to the wall' with the South East of England being the worst hit. Although decreased demand in the economy, both at home and abroad, was significant, one of the main reasons for the increasing number of business failures was the reluctance of firms to pay bills and invoices on time. This has a 'knock-on' effect on other businesses in the supply chain and has a particularly adverse effect on small, recently formed businesses which then find themselves unable to maintain a satisfactory cash flow or extend their lines of credit.

Year	Liquidations & Bankruptcies
1980	10,651
1981	13,203
1982	16,567
1983	19,287
1984	21,682
1985	20,943
1986	20,680
1987	17,405
1988	16,652
1989	18,163
1990	28,935
1991	47,777

Business failures for the UK - 1980/1991

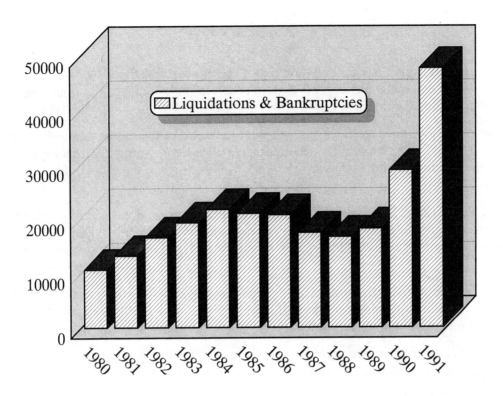

The types of business most vulnerable to the effects of recession can be seen in the Figure below.

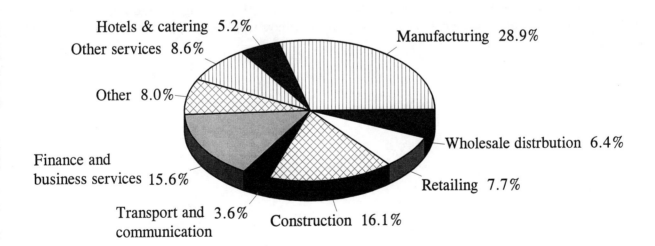

Insolvency

As already mentioned, insolvency is a general term that is used to describe the situation where a business can no longer meet its outstanding liabilities. If closure is not an option, one of the following courses of action may be taken to keep the business going. These include:

1. Calling in *administrative receivers* who will meet the debts of the business by selling off its assets. (This has proved a real growth area since 1989: there were 4,112 receiverships in 1991, 56% up on the previous year – 17% of insolvent businesses choose this course of action.)

2. Putting the business in *voluntary liquidation*. This can only be done with the consent of shareholders; the business is 'wound up', its debts are paid and any money remaining is divided amongst its shareholders. (50% of insolvent businesses choose this course of action.)

3. Asking the court to place the business into *compulsory liquidation* so that an official receiver is appointed who will 'wind up' the business. (30% of insolvent businesses choose this course of action.)

4. Asking the court to appoint an *administrator* who, in turn, will formulate a plan to rescue and restructure the business. (2% of insolvent businesses choose this course of action.)

5. The business's creditors may vote to allow management to embark on a *restructuring* of the business. (1% of insolvent businesses choose this course of action.)

Insolvency practitioners are obvious beneficiaries during periods of recession and economic downturn. They are almost always employees of accountancy firms. In 1990, the eight largest UK insolvency practitioners earned between them over £225 million from their work – an upturn of over 63% on the previous year.

1. Explain the various ways in which you can classify a business.

2. Explain how *level of activity* is becoming less useful as a means of classifying business.

3. Describe the various ways of making size comparisons between firms.

4. Analyse the significance of the contribution of small sole trader businesses to the UK economy.

5. Compile a concise list of the main features of the following forms of business organisation:

   - sole trader
   - partnership
   - private limited companies
   - public limited companies.

6. Explain the legal function of the *Memorandum* and *Articles of Association* in the formation of a company.

7. Compare and contrast the advantages of 'going public' with the decision to retain private limited company status.

8. Write a short, one hundred word article entitled '*A year in the life of a shareholder*'.

9. Explain the difference between an *executive* and *non-executive* director.

10. Describe and explain recent trends in management buy-outs (MBOs).
    Use an example, which you've researched in a newspaper or magazine, to explain the process.

11. Explain the difference between a *merger* and an *acquisition.*

12. Research and write a report on either a recent merger or acquisition: they are usually big news so you should be able to find data in the quality press.

13. Explain the function of a *holding company.*

14. Describe the process of winding up:

  - a sole trade
  - a partnership
  - a limited company.

15. Describe the recent trends in business failure and discuss the implications of the trend.

This section will take you through a concept that all successful managers regard as essential to the running of a good business: an overall strategy that will firmly fix in people's minds what the business is hoping to achieve, how it hopes to achieve it and when it hopes to achieve it. After defining what a business strategy is, you will read about how senior managers or directors develop a suitable strategy and what they need to do to carry it out. Having carried out the strategy, how do they measure whether, and to what degree, they have been successful?

What is 'Business Strategy'?

Strategy, tactics, targets, objectives are words that mainly turn up in three spheres of life: warfare, sport ... and business. They are terms that you as a student must know and use. And yet they are terms that many students find confusing.

The dictionary defines 'strategy' as:

> *'Generalship; management of an army or armies in a campaign, art of so moving or disposing troops and weapons etc in order to impose upon the enemy the place and time and conditions for fighting preferred by oneself.'*

If you change 'workforce' for 'army','employees' for 'troops', 'resources' for 'weapons' and 'competition' for 'enemy', then you will have a fair idea of what a business strategy is. It is the attempt, by a business, to create for itself the most favourable conditions it can, over a lengthy period of time ('campaign'). It involves deploying its resources, including the human resource, in the most effective ways it can. In so doing, the business will hope to achieve its objectives.

Using a sporting parallel, let's try and sort out the distinctions between 'strategy', 'tactics', 'targets' and 'objectives' before you look at how they are applied in business situations.

Put yourself in the position of a coach of a national team which has had high hopes of winning the World Cup, but which has just failed miserably to do so. As coach, you feel that your present players are not good enough but you are ambitious to succeed in achieving your *goal*: winning the next World Cup in four years' time.

To achieve that goal you might draw up a set of *strategic* plans – long-term *objective*s – which will help to bring about the result you desire. For example, you might persuade the management of the game to introduce or modify its system of leagues; you might introduce coaches into schools and focus attention on developing youth teams; you might initiate fitness programmes amongst all players. None of these plans is intended to give you immediate, short-term success: they are the preparation that is made in order to gain *eventual* success.

For your strategic plan to stand any chance of success in the long-term, you would probably wish to draw up sets of shorter term *tactical* objectives that would help you to achieve each of your strategic objectives. The objective, 'developing youth teams', might have a sub-set of tactics that not only yields short-term results but, more importantly, leads ultimately to the achievement of your strategic plan. Your tactics might include:

- raising awareness, with pupils and teachers, about the positive aspects of the game

- arranging sponsorship to provide better facilities and equipment for players

- encouraging links between senior teams and school and junior teams in particular geographical locations.

A student of business will rapidly realise that the success of a business is not just the result of luck or circumstance, but of strategic planning. A business that becomes successful in the short-term because of a stroke of luck, usually fails in the long-term. Anyone looking at the rise and fall of various companies will soon come to the conclusion that a sound business is underpinned by an equally sound corporate or business strategy that takes into account today, tomorrow and the longer term future. Planning, anticipation and foresight are qualities that a successful business looks for.

Business Strategy: Avoiding Opportunities for Conflict

Since a business is often complex – that is, it is made up of individuals and groups (shareholders, managers, directors, customers, employees etc) whose objectives might be diverse or even conflicting – it is essential that, when that business sets its own corporate objectives, the objectives of each of these group is also considered. It would be naive to think that the interests of all of these groups coincide, because they don't. And when they don't, that has the potential for conflict. ('Conflict' is discussed in greater detail in Part Five.)

Setting one objective inevitably impacts upon other, subsidiary objectives. If management sets 'growth' as an objective, this might well mean that the business will need additional finance. Or it may entail setting up new means of production. Or it may become prudent for the business to retain its profits rather than distribute them as dividends to its shareholders. Thus, taking a decision to go for growth might initially please shareholders since, once the 'growth' objective has been met, larger profits (in the form of dividends) will be paid out to them. At the same time the decision might displease managers for whom the decision may mean much re-organisation and extra work. Conversely, if dividends are suspended or reduced, shareholders might well dissent with the decision that brought this about, since they will feel deprived of their rightful share of the profit; managers, on the other hand, might now agree with the decision, since it gives them greater opportunities for promotion, bigger bonuses and individual career development.

In setting out to achieve the corporate objectives, then, it is important that the functional areas within the business (that is, departments) do not set objectives which conflict with each other or with the overall corporate strategy. To give a second example, the Engineering Department may wish to recruit only graduates to work on product development. The Personnel Department, however, knows that there are considerable financial benefits and incentives to be gained from recruiting at a lower level, and then training and 'upskilling' within the business. The objectives of the two departments conflict and it is really a question of seeing how each fits best with the corporate strategy.

Virgin Group, which is discussed in the *Business Structure: Introduction*, seems to demonstrate what is possible when a long-term strategy is properly developed and objectives are clearly communicated to all employees, resulting in everyone knowing what the strategy is and acting cohesively to implement it. If you wish to study the catastrophic results of not having and not implementing a clear and coherent business strategy, then the collapse of the ILG Group in 1990 will provide you with an excellent case study. A question about those events is included at the end of this section.

Sound strategy is developed by competent and effective management at the top of the business – strategic decisions are made at board of directors or senior management level. Decisions are made to set strategic objectives, which are specified in relation to the broader business objective.

Developing a business strategy

Developing a business strategy involves going through a four-stage process:

Stage 1 Analysing the current situation of the business

Stage 2 Setting out strategic forms of objectives, targets or goals for the business

Stage 3 Stating a policy for how the strategy is to be implemented: *strategic planning*

Stage 4 Setting tactical, short-term objectives for smaller operational areas of the business: *tactical planning.*

Stage 1. Analysing the current situation of the business

This falls into three parts

Part 1 Organisation analysis:
This critically examines the *resources* of the business, namely:

- People
- Finance
- Products
- Management
- Corporate image
- Premises and equipment.

Part 2 Competitor analysis:
This looks at *aspects of competition*, including:

- the number of competitors
- their market share
- the alternative products that competitors offer
- technological developments which may generate substitute products

- changes in strategy or direction by competition – this may reflect something the business has failed to spot.

Part 3   Environmental analysis
Looks at the changing *business environment* systematically in relation to the following factors:

- Legal
- Infrastructure
- Economic
- Social
- Demographic
- Environmental
- Political
- Technological.

Stage 2. Setting the strategic objectives for the business

These form the overall policy from which the functional parts of the business (personnel, marketing, production and finance) will formulate their own strategy.

Strategic objectives usually include statements about the following aspects of the business:

Profit	provides for growth attracts further investment satisfies shareholders/owners
Growth	keep pace with/outstrip competitors before they outstrip you growth today means increased profits tomorrow
Quality	the watchword of the 1990s becoming a prerequisite for success
Image	portray positive image in local and national environment
Employees	participation and consultation training and development loyalty and support.

Stage 3. Strategy

The formulation of strategy must always precede planning. The planners must take their guidance from the strategists. Both activities are important but they are separate.

We will now consider how the objectives get to be achieved.

Strategic Planning

A strategic plan is usually set five to seven years ahead: it will not be vague but will be quantifiable. It will involve statements on how the business intends to achieve strategic plan such as:

a.   increase exports by 10% each year for 5 years

b.   increase share of domestic market to 25% within 5 years

c.   diversify risk by acquiring business outside normal sphere of operation

d.   improve dividends to shareholders by a minimum of 8% in each of the next 5 years

e.   increase employee shareholding to 50% of the workforce etc.

Each functional area of the business, such as a department or profit centre, then develops its own strategy which is a sub-set of the whole business or corporate strategy.

Without defined objectives, specifically stated in quantitative terms, there is a possibility that individuals or departments may act in such a way that they contribute nothing to the overall performance of the business or might even act in ways which conflict with its aims.

Functional Strategies

Marketing – Part Three devotes a section to marketing strategy but a basic strategy will involve:

- identifying market segment
- achieving a positive brand and product image in the eyes of consumers
- developing a product range which meets the need of the target market segment(s).

Finance – financial strategy will involve considering the:

- debt/equity or gearing ratio
- dividend policy versus retained profits and re-investment
- return on investment performance.

Personnel – human resource or personnel strategy needs to consider things such as:

- forms and levels of recruitment needed
- availability of suitable people and demographic change
- education and training requirement
- remuneration: that is, wage and salary levels
- consultation processes.

Production – communication to ensure objectives do not conflict is especially important for production as it must produce what the marketing department requires within the financial and personnel constraints it is given. Its strategy is likely to make statements about:

- increases in productivity
- improved quality
- production technique and developments
- production volumes
- stock levels and purchasing policies.

All aspects of strategy will be compared and judged against that of competitors.

Stage 4. Making the strategy work (Tactical Planning)

Tactical plans are short-term and more sharply focused than strategy and planning. They are practically oriented and are implemented by middle management and the main body of the workforce. The success of implementation at this level will ultimately determine the overall success of the long-term strategy.

To summarise :

Managing a business strategy: the Planning Process

1. Construct the plan in consultation with those who will have direct influence on its implementation

2. Co-ordinate the planning across functional areas

3. Control the implementation of the plan by

    Reviewing the plan
    Reacting to the plan
    Revising the plan.

The whole planning process needs to be well-managed. Suitable management techniques for monitoring and measuring success in achieving objectives need to be employed.

There are three techniques which are useful to management in this respect:

1. Management by objectives
2. Overcoming barriers
3. Management by exception.

1. Management by objectives

This is an approach that percolates through the whole business. It is based on the negotiated target-setting that takes place between superior and subordinate at all levels of the business. Targets are quantified, agreed and recorded. At a later, fixed date each performance is measured in terms of the agreed target.

An obvious form of quantitative target-setting is used by sales managers who set very specific sales targets for their sales representatives; in addition, they might also set targets to recover outstanding invoices owed to them by debtors.

2. Overcoming barriers

No plan is perfect, but some are more perfect than others. Any plan is likely to run into a barrier that will make its implementation impossible. This is less likely to occur if:

realistic and attainable plans are formulated in the first instance

those concerned with implementing them have been involved in their formulation

they have been communicated clearly to the appropriate people.

Everyday barriers to success that businesses run into, and ways of circumventing (going round) them might include:

Barrier	Circumvent Barrier By
setting unattainable objectives	revising your objectives
non-co-operation of workforce	motivating your workforce
objectives not fully understood and clear	re-stating your objectives unambiguously
too high a cost	carrying out a cost/benefit analysis
workforce not sufficiently able	revising objectives
the unforeseen eventuality	drawing up contingency plans for any unexpected problems

3. Management by exception

If a business has:

- stated its strategies and tactics clearly
- drawn up plans that are well understood
- quantified targets for each member of the workforce to aim for, then senior managers need only be told of events and trends that are exceptional.

'Exceptional' events will be those which fall outside certain limits of tolerance that are already laid down by senior management. The big advantage of 'management by exception' is that it allows managers to concentrate much more fully on important and crucial decisions, rather than being occupied in making trivial decisions.

Non-profit Maximising Objectives

Most people assume that a business will usually have as its main objective the maximisation of its profits. However, this is not true in all businesses and it is certainly not true of all organisations, especially when they are part of the public sector. Even a sole trader is not always seeking the highest level of profit, but simply enough profit to satisfy his or her particular wants or needs. This is sometimes referred to as *satisfactory profit*.

An example is that of a keeper of a cornershop who chooses to close at 5.30 in the evening rather than be 'open all hours'. This is because the shopkeeper will want to do other things, such as spending time with family or enjoying a hobby. It is important to see business in perspective: it can ruin health or destroy family life as one pursues an ever-greater level of profit.

It is possible to identify objectives, in large businesses as well as small ones, other than just the 'profit objective'. Consider a large business in which different groups hold different objectives. One important factor you should remember is that, in large businesses, there is a distinction between *ownership* and *management and control*.

The most important group in the business is its *owners*: they are the shareholders who have bought a part of the company, and their degree of ownership is in proportion to the percentage of the share which they hold. In many businesses, the major shareholders are often large financial institutions, such as insurance companies, pension funds and unit trust investment companies. Their objective is to earn the maximum return on their investment, and to do this the investment managers of these institutions will buy and sell shares in companies according to their assessment of the potential profitability of each business. This means that a company must be sufficiently profitable to satisfy such *institutional shareholders*.

A second group which is involved in the business is its *managers* and *executives*. Often, in smaller businesses, they are the owners. In the larger corporate bodies, in which there is a substantial share capital, ownership and management will invariably be in different hands, with the shareholders electing a *board of directors* as salaried, professional managers of the business. While the owners have ultimate control over the managers, with the power to dismiss them, the business could not be effectively carried on without permitting managers a broad degree of commercial freedom. Having this freedom, managers may pursue policies which are more personal than organisational. Some examples may illustrate this point.

- A manager's power or salary is sometimes linked to the company's sales rather than overall performance. As a result, managers may prefer *sales maximisation* to *profit maximisation*.

- Executives may also regard the *size* of the business as a reflection of their power and so might encourage the *growth* of the business, even if this means a lower profit per share to its shareholders. Furthermore, the executive may wish to see any profit that the company does make re-invested in the business to encourage further growth and new developments. This may conflict with the aims of its shareholders, who would rather see profits distributed to them in the form of dividends on their shares, thus giving them an immediate return on their investment.

Such conflicts are rarely seen in public. Instead, the shareholders will put pressure on the managers in more discreet ways, such as by threatening to vote them out of control if they do not follow the shareholders' wishes. The success of such action depends on whether or not the directors can command the confidence of a majority of all shareholders (51%), and can therefore choose to ignore the wishes of blocks of shareholders who remain in the minority when it comes to the vote.

A final point to consider, when looking at the objectives of managers, is what are known as *behavioural* objectives. These are distinct from economic objectives and refer to a manager's desire to increase his or her power, status or workforce.

Measuring Business Performance

So far you've considered how a business develops its corporate strategy and how its managers carry it out through planning. Having set its objectives and tried to carry them out, the business must now devote its energies to finding out how well (or badly) the business has performed in its efforts to achieve its objectives.

There are three aspects of business operation which allow the assessment of its performance:

1. Economy

2. Efficiency

3. Effectiveness.

These aspects have become increasingly important in recent times, in particular as measures for assessing the quality of business management. Since they are closely related, their meanings need to be made clear.

Economy relates to the ability of a business *to obtain its inputs at optimum cost*. Optimum cost does not mean 'at the cheapest price', for it may be that buying the cheapest available materials or labour will have a detrimental effect on the quality of the finished product. The economical business will get the *balance between cost and quality* exactly right.

Efficiency is the *best use of resources to achieve production of goods or services*. Efficiency emphasises the optimum use of resources. You would say a car engine was efficient if, for a given performance, it consumed less petrol than any of its competitors. Consequently, a business which is able to use fewer resources (money, machines, material and people) than its market competitors can be properly described as an efficient business.

Effectiveness is concerned with the achievement of set organisational goals or objectives. Effectiveness is measured by *how close an organisation comes to attaining its strategic objectives*. Effectiveness is thus appropriate to the work of any business, whether it is the RSPCA, the local housing department, a travel agency or a major oil company.

A business seeks to be economical, efficient and effective, but it does not follow that because it achieves one it will also achieve the others.

For any business to operate economically, effectively and efficiently, every individual employee and every department must work together as a co-ordinated whole. Each part of the business must try to achieve a similar high standard. If there is one weak element in the system, it will tend to undermine the rest. For example, even the best planned business, using the latest technology, will prove ineffective if its workforce is poorly trained or is unmotivated.

Conversely, as one often sees with successful football clubs, when all the elements work together in harmony, the end result can be greater than just the sum of the individual parts. *Synergy* is the name given to this beneficial outcome. For example, a well-motivated worker in a good group can spark off ideas or suggestions for improvements that can then be developed and refined by fellow group members. The workers in the group are not simply carrying out their tasks, but are actually improving the business's chances of success by inspiring change through innovation.

The easiest of the '3 Es' to measure is economy or *cost minimisation*. The business can judge, through regular monitoring of material, labour and overhead costs, whether it is being economical in providing inputs to the business. Budgets to stick to – and targets for improvements – can be set and assessed periodically, providing feedback for action.

Efficiency and effectiveness are much more tricky to measure. Efficiency concerns how well a business turns its inputs into outputs (products or services). An ability to measure this depends on having something to measure it against. This means the business must have a good idea of what is possible. In other words: what is the maximum efficiency of the business, given a particular level of inputs?

Effectiveness is intangible. It is about the measurement of how well the business is meeting its objectives. Certain objectives, mainly those expressed in quantitative terms, do provide a yardstick for measuring effectiveness. For example, if the objective of a coalmine is to increase the productivity of its mining operation by 10% over a given period, then figures collected during, and at the end of, the year will permit monitoring and assessment of its success or failure. What if the objective is to achieve an improved public image for the business, or to improve employee motivation? How can such things be measured?

Ways of Measuring Performance

Three of the most common ways of measuring performance are by:

1.   *productivity*

2.   *ratios*

3.   *budget analysis.*

1. By productivity

This involves determining the actual output and production achieved and dividing it by the input of resources needed to produce. Take the example of a coalmine. Suppose coalface A produced 120 tonnes of coal in a shift, while coalface B produced 80 tonnes.

Clearly, coalface A has a higher output or production. But how efficient was coalface A in the use of its workforce? Coalface A used 60 men and, thus, its productivity was 120/60 = 2 tonnes per man shift. Coalface B used 20 men and so its productivity was 80/20 = 4 tonnes per man shift. If you compare the two, Coalface B appears to be more efficient. However, the management of the mine, in seeking a reason for this discrepancy in productivity, has found that coalface A had more difficult working conditions. Its miners worked equally hard, but more of them were needed to overcome the inherent geological problems. Coalface A is more effective in producing coal (120 tonnes), but less efficient in the use of its manpower (2 tonnes per man).

The productivity of labour

The managers of a steelworks will always want to know how its output per worker (productivity) measures against that of its competitors. They are likely to use a formula such as:

$$\frac{\text{Total output of steel in month (in tonnes)}}{\text{Total number of production employees}} = \text{tonnes per worker}$$

The output (tonnes per worker) is a measure of the productivity of the workforce. Clearly, the more tonnes per worker produced, the lower the cost of the steel is likely to be and the more competitive the business will become. Increased productivity can result from greater levels of steel production from the same number of workers, or the same level of steel production from fewer workers.

As well as being important to the business as a whole, productivity levels can be very important to individual employees. Increased productivity usually leads to rewards, either in the form of productivity bonuses or other incentives. It also provides a platform for the workforce to negotiate pay rises which recognise their productivity achievements.

In recent years productivity, linked with improved quality, has become the watchword of UK industry. If consumers are to buy UK goods and services, they will expect quality at a competitive price. If consumers can't obtain this from within the UK, then they will look to buy foreign products which meet their requirements.

There is no better example of this than the current situation facing British Coal, whose largest customers are the recently privatised electricity generating companies. Before privatisation, the Electricity Boards were contractually obliged to buy a large percentage of their coal requirements for their power stations from British Coal. This had the effect of protecting the British coal industry from low-cost imported coal.

Since privatisation the electricity generators are increasingly looking to buy coal of an appropriate quality at the most competitive price. To retain its market share, British Coal has been forced to become more productive, concentrating its production in the most profitable coalmines where seams are thick and mechanisation allows the mining of low-cost coal. As a result, smaller and less productive coalmines are closed – one of the social costs of the free market economy. (This will be explored in more detail in Part Five.)

So far you have read about the productivity of labour although, in most discussions of productivity, the distinction between the productivity of labour, land and capital is usually blurred. For example, British Coal's increases in productivity may come as much from mechanisation (capital) and economies of scale, as they do from the increased efforts of its workforce. Productivity can be easy to measure, but the reasons for increases and decreases in it are often trickier to pinpoint.

The productivity of land

There exists no better example of increased productivity than that of agricultural land over the past fifty years. In 1945 an acre of land could produce, roughly, half a tonne of wheat. By 1990, one acre was producing almost seven tonnes. This staggering increase has resulted in an over-production of wheat in the Western world and, in the EC, it has led to the creation of cereal 'mountains'. Farmers have been forced by market conditions to intensify their farming methods in order to remain in business: they either produce low-cost food of the required quality, or they fail to make a profit and are eventually forced out of business.

In the case of land, it is evident that the major reasons for its increased productivity have been the introduction of greater mechanisation and the development of improved fertilisers. Labour, too, has become more skilled and specialised. But, beyond knowing these facts, it is very difficult for the farmer to attribute percentages of the improvement to individual factors.

The productivity of capital

A crude measure of the productivity of capital is the one used by accountants; this is explained in detail in Part Four.

- Turnover
- Capital employed.

The 'turnover' and 'capital employed' figures are found in the financial statements of a business. The ratio is a measure of *the volume of sales which is produced from the level of capital which is invested* in the business. Increased sales from the same capital employed will indicate improved productivity of capital. But so will the same level of sales from a smaller level of capital: this may, on the face of it, seem a desirable outcome, but lower levels of investment may spell long-term problems for the business. This highlights one of the difficulties in measuring performance through productivity alone.

Improving productivity

In most instances, a business will seek to maintain or increase its volume of production or services while continually increasing its productivity. One major argument for improving productivity is that doing so results in less waste of resources. Clearly, the threat of competitors gaining a productivity advantage (and thus pressurising product prices and profits) is also a factor.

To illustrate these ideas, take as an example a shirt manufacturer. Suppose that, in order to produce 1,000 shirts, the company faces labour costs of £1,000, or £1 per shirt. However, with the introduction of sophisticated, computerised cutting machines, the same labour force is now able to produce 2,000 shirts at no extra cost. The labour cost per shirt is now only 50p.

If the shirts were sold at the same price, there would be 2000 × 50p or £1,000 extra profit. This could be available for distribution among the shareholders in higher dividends, or amongst the employees in the form of a pay rise. The selling price could also be reduced, which would benefit existing customers or attract new buyers for the company's product. If every business in the UK was able to increase its productivity then, in theory, the whole country would stand to benefit.

There appear to be many benefits to be gained from an increase in productivity. Improved productivity, superficially at least, appears to be the key to business success. Unfortunately, when productivity increases this does not always mean that a manufacturer can correspondingly increase sales. In our example the increase in productivity may have adverse effects for the workforce. Half the shirt workers may be made redundant if the previous sales figure of 1,000 shirts cannot be improved upon. As a result of increased productivity, the employer now feels that only half as many workers are needed in order to produce the same level of output: the rest can be let go.

The unions, therefore, may argue that it is against their own best interests to improve productivity at a time when demand for the product is not increasing. However, if all the workers were kept in jobs, the comparatively low productivity may mean that the product is no longer competitive. Consequently, the business would start making a loss and may eventually go out of business altogether, with *all* of its workforce losing its jobs.

Potentially, it is possible to improve productivity in any of a business's productive resources. The possibilities range from using better materials; implementing improved methods of work; acquiring better machinery, or adopting new technology. It may simply mean encouraging workers to work harder. Some employers use incentives, such as bonus payments, to increase productivity. Others ignore these 'carrots' and offer the 'stick' of threatened redundancy or short-time working. In the long run it may be difficult to make people continually work harder and constantly improve productivity using such methods – there is a physical limit to the amount people can produce and, eventually, no amount of incentives or threats can get them to work harder.

Generally, the biggest increases in productivity have come from new technology and new machinery. For example, automation and robotics in the motor industry have meant that fewer people are needed in car plants to produce the same output of cars. Automation means that machines can stamp out an endless stream of parts, with little human attendance; robot arms can handle spray guns or welding equipment and they can mimic human movements in a tireless fashion. This partly helps to explain why jobs in the manufacturing sector have decreased, particularly over the last twenty years or so.

The service industries, however, is one area in which jobs are increasing. The service industries offer a personal service where it has not been easy, or desirable, to replace people by machinery. Even in those industries, however, there are areas where technology can improve efficiency, for instance in health service laboratory testing, and in computerised holiday bookings.

2. By ratios

Ratios show the relationship between two quantities. They are frequently used to measure the financial performance of a business, as you will discover in Part Four. However, they can also be used to measure economy, efficiency and effectiveness. Some useful examples are:

Economy $\dfrac{\text{Total wastage in production}}{\text{Units produced}}$ = Wastage per unit

Efficiency $\dfrac{\text{Machine time per week}}{\text{Units produced per week}}$ = machine time per unit

Effectiveness $\dfrac{\text{Annual no. of customer complaints}}{\text{Number of goods sold in year}}$ = % complaints

Care must be taken when setting targets in order to improve a particular ratio. Inevitably, setting one target will have a 'knock on' effect on another part of the business: this must be recognised and action taken. For example, if wastage per unit is significantly reduced, then perhaps reduced quantities of materials need to be purchased – if this fact is not recognised, and the appropriate people informed, then increased stock levels will result, tying up cash that can be put to better use elsewhere in the business.

Failing to recognise that reducing wastage in one department may have a detrimental effect on another ratio which measures the levels of working capital in the business, is just one possibility that must be monitored. The astute manager knows that an improvement in one ratio can cause a negative affect on another and a keen eye will be kept on such a consequence.

3 By budgets

Budgets, and budgetary control, measure and monitor costs and can, therefore, be considered mainly to be a measure of economy.

Each budget constitutes the planned use of resources for the coming year, or for some specified period. Every type of resource can appear in the budget: labour, materials, machines, etc. Each item is expressed in monetary terms in order to enable comparisons to be made. If one department, therefore, requires new machinery, while another asks for new personnel, the overall effect of each decision on the business's total budget can be compared in terms of how much each will cost.

Each department is usually given an individual annual budget and, together, these individual budgets form the budget for the business as a whole. The business may seek to apply some overall measure of financial constraint and make each department justify any increase in its resources. Clearly, in time of severe financial constraints with cutbacks in spending, departments may find themselves competing for the reduced global sum, the overall budget available to the business. Such budgets are plans for the future. Middle and lower management are responsible for keeping to their budgets once they have been agreed. It is the responsibility of top management to ensure that each department's budget is reasonable and the resources which have been allocated will be used in a way which will achieve the strategic objectives of the business.

Budgets are not only plans, they are also 'tools' to allow the measurements and control of performance of a department or section. If a department is budgeted to spend £120,000 on labour costs in a year, then this can be considered to be £10,000 per month. If, in one month, the amount rose and became, for example, £15,000, this variance of 50% overspend would justify management investigation. If there was good reason for the variation, then no action need be taken. However, it may mean that the department will have to trim its labour costs in later months, or that extra finance will have to be found by cutting back elsewhere, and the added extra labour cost accounted for in the overall plans. Budgets and budgetary control systems thus provide a means of planning for those resources which will be needed in the future, and form the basis of management control over the use of resources.

Budgeting is an important control instrument, but it is of limited use in evaluating efficiency and effectiveness.

Dangers of Performance Measurement

One of the main dangers of performance measurement is the temptation of businesses to concentrate on the most easily understood and most tangible 'E': economy. Businesses can fall into the trap of believing that, if input costs are minimised and the business thereby is economical, then it follows that it is also efficient and effective. For example, reducing the training budget of the business will certainly make it more economical in the short-term, but it is likely to have a detrimental effect on both efficiency and effectiveness, particularly in the longer term.

Whether in the public or private sector, to achieve success a business must not only produce an output which the customer wants, it must also ensure that its internal operations are managed efficiently. There are many examples of businesses whose products were in great demand by customers, but which proved themselves unable to organise *effectively* their production and internal operations. For instance, the Sinclair computer company had a product which was initially a market leader, but it was plagued with production delays which deterred potential customers and eventually led to Sinclair being taken over by Amstrad, its major rival.

For these reasons no business can afford to ignore performance measurement.

1. Assess the importance of 'strategy' to a business.

2. Assess the similarities and differences of the following terms:

   - goals
   - targets
   - tactics
   - objectives
   - strategic plans.

3. Explain the meaning of *conflict of objectives*.

4. Give three examples of how objectives in a business might conflict.

5. Describe the stages in developing a business strategy.

6. Explain the process of *competitor analysis*.

7. Explain the process of *environmental analysis*.

8. Describe the process of *strategic planning*.

9. What do you understand by the term *functional strategy?*

10. Explain the techniques of managing a business strategy.

11. Are non-profit maximising objectives a good idea?

12. What are the alternative objectives to profit maximisation?

13. What are the three 'Es'?

14. What is meant by the term *productivity*?

15. Note down a formula for calculating the productivity of:

    - labour
    - land
    - capital.

16. Why is productivity seen as increasingly important in the measurement of the performance of British industry?

17. Explain the role of budgets in performance measurement.

Getting the financial structure of a business right is a critical job. Anticipating when the business will need finance, how much it will need and where is the most cost effective and beneficial source to get it from is a vital aspect of the foundation of any successful business.

Any business starting up will need finance for two main purposes:

- to buy fixed assets such as land, premises, machinery and vehicles
- to provide working capital, for the day-to-day running of the business, such as the payment of wages and suppliers.

Once a business has been operating for a period of time, it will hope to grow; more finance is usually needed for this purpose.

In broad terms, finance (or *capital*, as it is more properly called) can come from only two sources:

- from lenders (known as *borrowing* or *debt*)
- from investors (known as *equity*).

In practice, a business will usually seek to strike a balance between the funds which it acquires from each of the two sources. Each source will have a cost and a risk factor attached to it; the ability of the business to manage cost and risk can make the difference between bankruptcy, survival and growth.

Borrowing as a Means of Raising Finance

Any new business will find that it is difficult to raise finance from outside sources and anyone hoping to establish a new business may be forced to provide their own capital. A person starting in business as a sole trader, therefore, will normally provide at least part of the start-up finance and, similarly, a partnership will rely heavily on the partners to make a contribution to the initial capital required. However, many businesses will also need to borrow money from an outside source and this will depend upon a number of economic factors. Any prudent banker making a loan will want an acceptable rate of return (in the form of interest charge), some guarantee of security on the loan (collateral) and a reasonable prospect of financial success for the business. Therefore, anyone who seeks to borrow money from a bank should approach the matter in a business-like manner. If you want a loan to run a business, the first step is to approach the bank manager in the way that a business person would. This involves the preparation of a *business plan*.

Preparing a Case for a Business Loan

As we have seen, when a business seeks finance from a bank, the bank manager will want to be convinced that the business is sound and there is a high probability that the loan will be repaid. If the business has been in operation for some time, then the bank will wish to see sets of accounts for previous years. These will need to have been prepared by an accountant who will verify their accuracy. If the business is just beginning, and requires a start-up loan from the bank, there will be no accounts of previous years' trading. Thus, in order to allow the bank to judge the potential of a new business and the safety of its loan, the borrower needs to produce the following:

1.   a business plan; and

2.   a cashflow forecast and a projected profit and loss account.

A Business Plan

A *business plan* is what it appears to be, a plan of operation for a business in the short – and/or medium – term. If the business idea is viable and the plan is well prepared, it will help the case for the loan by impressing the bank that the business will be run by competent people. However, if the idea is not viable, then no amount of good presentation will help.

A business plan should include some brief background introduction to the business, setting out the product or service it is intended to supply and an indication of the scale of operation. The plan should specify those who will be directly involved in running the business, either the partners or the directors, and indicate the relevant experience that they have. Clearly, if the person starting the business has a number of years of useful experience in that particular trade or industry, it is likely that he or she will be more sure of what they are doing than someone who is completely new to the business. This does not mean that a total lack of experience will be a complete bar to a business start-up loan, but it does mean that a borrower in such a situation will have to prove that some extensive groundwork on the business project has been done.

The next part of the plan should discuss the product or service to be supplied and evaluate the need for it in the area in which the business will operate. This means that existing competition will have to be assessed and a reasonable estimate made of market potential. Other problems to be considered include the availability of skilled labour, supplies of raw materials and suitable premises. The plan should indicate the proposed level of output over the coming period and the price which it should be possible to charge for the product or service. If the borrower has some experience of the problems involved in running a business, this will help to convince the bank of the potential success of the business idea. A good business plan will also weigh up the strengths and weaknesses of the proposal. It should be honest with the bank manager: if the strengths and weaknesses have already been considered and the business idea is still considered to be viable, despite the possible drawbacks, then a bank manager should also be convinced.

A Cashflow Forecast and a Projected Profit and Loss Account

The *cashflow forecast* is an attempt to show the anticipated inflow and outflow of money from the business in the coming year. *Inflow* is the revenue from sales of the product or service. Unless the proposed business is in retailing, it is often common for a supplier to have to wait some considerable time for eventual payment after the goods have been delivered. Most business customers expect to be given some element of trade credit; others are simply slow payers. This is fine if it is you who owes the money, but it is potentially disastrous when it is your business that is waiting to be paid.

If you consider the costs of operation that make up the outflows, the business will have to pay wages and other bills on a much more prompt and regular basis than some other payments. It may be fine to leave the bill for the supply of raw materials to be paid until the end of the month, but try explaining to your workforce that they are not getting their wages for the next six weeks! Therefore, at different times throughout the trading year, the business will find that it has varying levels of cash shortage at those times when it must pay bills but is waiting to be paid itself. These circumstances need to be anticipated so that agreement can be made with the bank to provide sufficient funds at the times when they will be needed. In essence, this is all that a cashflow forecast is – a monthly statement of cash spent and cash received leaving a balance which may be in surplus, or in debit, which will need financing by the bank. It should be borne in mind that severe cashflow problems that are not resolved by appropriate borrowing can lead to a business collapsing. Creditors may soon lose patience with the business debtor who regularly pleads that the debt will be paid as soon as its outstanding accounts are settled. The unsympathetic creditor may respond by bringing bankruptcy proceedings.

Thus the cashflow forecast is not simply a means of impressing a bank manager sufficiently to be granted the loan. It is, in fact, a very useful (and often vital) management tool and should be compared carefully with what actually happens once the business is operating. If the actual cash balances regularly appear lower than those forecast, then it is time to consult the bank manager again to ensure that additional finance can be arranged.

The second financial statement required is a *projected profit and loss account*. This will simply show the total projected sales from the business in the coming year and place against it a total for the projected costs of operation. This will allow a projected net profit to be estimated by subtracting costs from revenue. We will consider the structure and interpretation of the profit and loss account in more detail in Part Four.

Short-term Borrowing

Borrowing over fewer than three years is considered to be short-term finance. Mostly, such borrowing is needed to maintain a satisfactory cashflow and act as a buffer between paying suppliers and employers and receiving money from debtors. Occasionally, short-term finance is used to buy an asset which has a relatively short life, a car or van, for example.

Bank Overdraft

This is generally the most common and cheapest way of raising short-term finance from outside the business. An overdraft occurs when a business has a negative sum in its current account with the bank. The bank will agree an overdraft limt and the business should avoid exceeding this.

Many businesses will operate permanent overdraft facilities which will give them some flexibility in their cashflow management.

The advantage of an overdraft, or overdraft facility as it is often called, is that a business will only be required to pay interest owed on a daily basis on the amount. The bank manager may have granted an overdraft facility of £5,000, but on a particular day a business is only £2,000 overdrawn. Interest is due only on the

£2,000 and not on the £5,000, which is the *potential* loan. The interest rate will vary with changes in the economy.

The business should avoid using an overdraft to finance capital spending, such as the purchase of new plant or machinery. This should be financed through other forms of loans. In fact, it is wisest to restrict the use of an overdraft to solving a business's cashflow problems in circumstances where money is owed to the business, but has not yet been received by it, though its debts now have to be paid.

Short-term loan

This is more specific than an overdraft. It is normally negotiated for a specific sum in order to purchase a particular asset. The loan is over a fixed period of time: monthly repayments will be agreed and interest charged on the full sum borrowed.

Factoring

A further means of raising short-term finance open to businesses facing cash flow problems is factoring. This involves a business, which has debts owed to it, selling the right to this money to a factor (an organisation willing to provide immediate cash in return for the right to collect and keep the monies owed by the business's debtors).

The factors are often subsidiaries of clearing banks or major financial groups. The factor will usually pay the business less than the face value of the debts (usually 3 – 10% less) and so, if the factor can collect the debts in full, this percentage is the profit on the transaction. This illustrates how *a debt is an asset owed by the business and, like any other type of asset, can be sold if a suitable buyer is available*.

This method of short-term fund raising is particularly useful to smaller firms who wish to avoid the task of debt collection and who need an efficient cashflow in order to aid expansion.

Hire purchase

In the same way as individuals can use hire purchase to buy goods when they have insufficient money immediately to hand so, too, can a business. A piece of equipment with a fairly short lifespan (usually three years or less) is bought by making a down-payment, followed by a series of regular sums (covering the cost of interest as well as the cost of the equipment). The arrangement will operate through a finance house which accepts the value of the equipment as security for the loan, since it retains the ownership of the property until the borrower has paid the final instalment. The interest rate is fixed at the time the agreement is arranged.

Bill finance

One form of factoring, bill finance, involves a business selling a specific debt to a discount house or bank. The business receives the amount (less commission) straight away and the bank collects the full sum when it falls due from the debtors.

For example, suppose Business A sells a piece of equipment to Business B for £20,000. Business A, in order to ease its cashflow, sells this debt to a bank for £18,000. Business A gets £18,000 immediately; the bank eventually collects the full £20,000 debt from Business B, thereby making a £2,000 'profit' on the deal. Bill finance is cheaper than an overdraft and has clearly identifiable costs. It is often used in conjunction with an overdraft as a source of short-term funds.

Medium-term Borrowing

Approximately 40% of all business loans are now taken for periods ranging from three to ten years. Most of these loans are secured against the assets of the business or are guaranteed by the owners of the business. Borrowing money in this way has major advantages for a business. It allows the liability to be spread over a longer period and the repayments can be made on a regular monthly or quarterly basis. The period for which the loan is given is usually sufficient to allow the business to make profits from the investment in new plant or machinery for which the loan was first negotiated.

Such medium-term loans are especially useful for the purchase of assets which have a particular lifespan. So, for instance, if a machine lasts five years before it needs replacing, it is sensible to take out a five year loan to finance it and spread its cost over its lifetime.

A medium-term loan may also be used to refinance an overdraft. In this way, the cost of finance can be spread over a longer term, avoiding financial difficulties should an overdraft facility come to an end.

Normally, then, a medium-term loan is designed for a business which has established itself and has solved the initial start-up difficulties which most companies face.

Term loan

This is the main form of medium-term finance. It can be provided by the clearing banks as well as merchant banks. The conditions for such a loan vary quite widely and are usually open to some negotiation. The stronger the financial position and prospects of the borrower, the more favourable terms the business is likely to obtain from the lender. Among the elements which can be varied are the repayment pattern and the interest rate. The rate may be fixed or floating (that is, varying according to changes in the economy).

Leasing

Leasing is available to most businesses when buying specific pieces of plant or equipment. A leasing company buys the asset and then leases it to the business at an agreed rental. Agreements are normally for periods of about between five and ten years. The business sometimes has the option of buying the equipment for a nominal sum when the lease ends. This is a much favoured method for a business which wishes to provide its employees with company cars.

Long-term Borrowing

Long-term loans are usually provided to allow a business to buy plant or machinery which will have a prolonged lifespan. Long-term is normally ten years or longer and, as well as being used to buy plant, it may also finance takeovers or other forms of expansion. However, if the business is sound, as it must be if it is to contemplate such long-term finance, it may be better advised to raise finance through a share issue, rather than take on such long-term debts. Banks may well be reluctant to make such long-term loans to a small business if they lack confidence about its long-term prospects for growth. Certainly, no long-term loan of this sort will be given by a bank without concrete guarantees and security. It is also likely that the bank will seek a higher rate of interest on such loans. You may argue that the business is wiser to seek shorter term and cheaper loans, but this ignores the advantages that the business gains from not having to repay its debts quickly. It is able to schedule its debts repayment in line with its revenue growth without having the problem of continually renegotiating its loan position.

Debentures

Companies often borrow money by means of issuing debentures. These may be secured or unsecured. The definition of a debenture is very wide and includes all forms of securities: in other words, undertakings to repay any money borrowed, which may or may not be secured by a charge on the company's assets. A *charge* simply means a legal right to take the asset. Debentures usually consist of trust deeds which will create a fixed charge over a specific piece of company property by mortgage, and/or a floating charge over the rest of the company assets. The difference between *fixed* and *floating* charges is that a company is not free to do what it wishes with assets which are subject to a fixed charge. In other words, it is not free to sell or mortgage them. However, a company is free to do what it likes with any of its assets covered by a floating charge.

The floating charge will normally be created over a class of assets, such as the company's trading stock. A floating charge is said to 'crystallise' and become a fixed charge should money become repayable under a condition in the debenture which is then not paid. This might happen, for instance, when repayment on part of the interest on the loan is due. The lender may subsequently take steps to enforce his security, because the interest due has not been paid by the borrower.

The principal rights of a debenture holder are outlined in the debenture deed and will include:

- the date of repayment of the loan and the rate of interest
- a statement of the assets of the company which are subject to fixed or floating charges
- the rights of the company to redeem the whole or any part of the monies owing
- the circumstances in which the loan becomes immediately repayable, such as if the company defaults in payment of interest
- the powers of the debenture holder to appoint a receiver and manager of the assets charged.

Mortgage

Mortgages are available to businesses which wish to buy land or buildings. Building societies do not lend to businesses, so the usual source of the mortgage is a bank. The period of the loan is usually between twenty and thirty years.

Sale and leaseback

Often seen as a 'last resort' by which to raise larger sums of money, this involves selling a fixed asset which is owned by the business (usually land or buildings) to a buyer. The asset is then leased back from the buyer by means of a rental agreement.

Legal Restrictions on Borrowing by Business

As far as a sole trader is concerned, there is no limitation on his or her borrowing powers but, of course, a sole trader remains personally liable to the full extent of his or her personal wealth for any debts entered into. In a partnership, every partner is the agent of the firm and its partners. Therefore, in a trading partnership, every partner has the power to borrow money for a purpose apparently connected with the partnership business. This rule has the effect of making every partner in a firm jointly liable, with all other partners, for all of the debts incurred by the firm while that person is a partner.

The law makes a distinction between the borrowing of non-corporate and corporate businesses. Each will be examined in turn.

Non-corporate Bodies

If you are to consider the legal rights which a business lender, such as a bank, has when it lends money to a sole trader or a partnership, you will need to determine whether the loan is secured or unsecured. An unsecured loan means that the lender has no rights over the borrower's property in the event of the borrower defaulting on the repayments. The lender's only option is to bring a court action in an attempt to recover the debt. In the present economic climate, it is more usual for a lender, such as a bank, to demand the added protection of a secured loan. One of the most common forms of secured loan is a 'commercial mortgage', which uses freehold or leasehold land, or other business assets, as security.

Corporate Bodies

Power to borrow money is usually conferred on the company directors in the Articles of Association. There is nothing to prevent a business limiting its own borrowing powers to a specific amount in its Memorandum of Association. It can do this, for instance, by including a limit on borrowing of not more than two-thirds of the value of its paid up capital. In effect, the company will be introducing a self-imposed loan gearing. Power to borrow will also carry with it an implied power to offer company property as security for a loan. As a general rule, if a business borrows beyond its powers, then the loan and any security given for it is void on the grounds of *ultra vires,* which is the legal term given to an act which is beyond the powers of the company.

The Issue of Shares as a Means of Raising Finance

If a business wishes to expand, it may be faced with the problem that the funds needed to finance its expansion cannot be met either internally, from business profits, or through borrowing from financial institutions. One of the other options open to it is to bring in new capital from outside sources. This means issuing shares and spreading the ownership of the business. Many small businesses may resent this reduction in their direct control. However, broadening ownership need not always lead to a reduction in control; it is often found that new investors are not interested in the day-to-day management of the business and only want a safe and profitable return on their investment. There are many professional investors who are looking for small businesses in which to invest funds and this can have a number of major commercial benefits.

The additional capital introduced into the business by the sale of its shares can give it a much sounder financial base and also open up other avenues for raising funds. The company's bankers will recognise that the new investors have endorsed the future potential of the business and so it may be easier to arrange overdrafts or other forms of short- and medium-term finance.

If the new share capital is sold to a professional investor, such as a merchant bank, then it is likely that the bank will want to appoint a representative to the board of the company. This may seem like an imposition on the management and policy-making functions of the business, but often such appointees have wide business experience; as they seek to protect their investment they will want the business to succeed and, to this end, will usually offer sound advice.

It is unlikely that professional investors will want to share in the capital of small businesses or those which are just starting up, but, for a medium-sized business in need of funds to expand, it may prove to be a mutually profitable move. Small businesses will not be able to get professional investors to buy their shares, but must seek individuals who are willing to buy shares.

Before moving on to consider the mechanics of share issue and the restrictions involved in raising capital in this way, you need to consider some of the distinctions between the expressions used. Unfortunately, the use of the term 'capital', when applied to companies, can have many different meanings, so in order to try and minimise confusion, we will begin this section by considering some of the more widely used expressions.

Authorised capital

This expression refers to *the value of shares that a company is authorised to issue* and is included in the capital clause of the Memorandum of Association of a company.

Issued capital

This is *the value of the company's capital which has actually been issued to the shareholders in the form of shares*.

Paid up capital

This is the amount of *capital which has actually been paid to the company on the shares issued*. It is possible to issue shares which are not paid for or which are partly paid. Under the European Communities Act, 1972, if a company makes a reference to share capital on its business stationery or order forms, it must refer to its paid up share capital – that is, the amount of capital the company has actually raised and received.

Unpaid capital

If shares which have been issued are not fully paid for, then the amount outstanding is referred to as unpaid capital. For example, if 10,000 shares are issued, each having a nominal value of £1, and only 50p has been paid up on them (in other words, paid to the company), then the issued share capital is £10,000, the paid up capital is £5,000 and the unpaid capital is £5,000. Shareholders may be required to pay up the unpaid amount on their shares by the company making a 'call' on them to do so. This may happen if the business begins to face financial difficulties and cannot meet its debts.

Classes of shares

Most companies in the UK have one class of shares which is referred to as 'ordinary shares' or as the 'equity share capital' of the company. However, there is nothing to prevent a limited company from having more than one class of shares. If different classes of shares are issued, they will confer on their purchasers certain rights, relating to such matters as voting rights, payment of dividend (in other words, the sum distributed to shareholders out of any profit made) and the return of capital to shareholders should the company go into liquidation. The two main types of shares are preference shares and ordinary shares.

Preference shares

The main characteristic of a preference share is that it will grant its holder the right to a preferred fixed dividend. This simply means that the holder of a preference share is entitled to a fixed amount of dividend, for instance 6% on the value of his share, before the ordinary shareholders are paid any dividend. A preference share is, therefore, a safe investment with a fixed reward, no matter how small or how large is the company's profit. Some preference shares are non-cumulative, while others are *cumulative*. This means that, if in any year, the company's profits are not sufficient to declare a dividend, the shortfall must be made up out of profits of subsequent years. Often preference shares carry no voting rights.

Ordinary shares

Ordinary shares are often referred to as the 'equity share capital' of a company. These are the shares which involve risk, for having declared a dividend and paid the preference shareholders, the company will now pay a dividend to the holders of ordinary shares out of the remainder of the profit. It follows, therefore, that an ordinary shareholder in a well-managed company, which is making high profits, will receive a good return on his or her investment and the nominal value of those share will rise: so, for instance, a £1 ordinary share could rise in its market value to £1.50. Unfortunately, the opposite is also true. If there is no profit, then there is no dividend and the shares may fall in value, so inevitably ordinary shares involve a certain risk. This risk is reflected in the amount of control that an ordinary shareholder has over the company's business, for while voting rights are not normally attached to preference shares, they are to ordinary shares. The ordinary shareholder can usually voice an opinion in the company's annual general meeting (AGM) and vote on major issues involving the running of the company. Ordinary shares also carry the right to a share of any surplus assets, once liabilities have been met, should the company be wound up. While preference shares normally carry no such right, their capital is usually repaid in preference to the capital of ordinary shareholders.

Raising share capital

You have already seen that the basic classification of companies is between those which are *public* and those which are *private* companies. Under the Companies Act 1985, a public limited company is one which, by its Memorandum of Association, states that it is a public limited company and has a nominal share capital of a least £50,000, of which at least one-quarter is paid up capital. All other companies are private. Also, a private company has no right to invite public subscription for shares by issuing a prospectus. (A *prospectus* is an advertisement offering shares or debentures for sale to the general public.)

Such a legal restriction effectively limits the ability of a private company to raise large amounts of capital, for it must rely totally on those individuals who are aware of its existence and who might be willing to subscribe to its shares. A public company, however, is not limited in its membership size or the rights of its shareholders to freely transfer their shares. However, only certain public companies are quoted on the Stock Exchange, so shareholders in unquoted companies have greater difficulty in buying and selling shares. To raise initial capital, or increase its issued capital, a public company will issue a prospectus to invite the public to subscribe for shares or debentures. The prospectus must, however, contain certain information including:

- Particulars of all contracts entered into by the company in the last two years which are likely to influence prospective investors

- An auditor's report showing the company's assets and liabilities, profits, losses and dividends paid over the last five years

- If the proceeds of the share issue are to be used to acquire property, or a business, a statement giving particulars of the prospective vendors and the purchase price.

The role of the merchant banks

Merchant banks have a variety of roles within the financial sector, ranging from the lending of large sums to companies, to financing mergers and takeovers, to assisting in exporting and importing. One of their major roles is to arrange the flotation of new companies on the Stock Exchange. The steps listed above will usually be handled by a merchant bank, including the preparation of the prospectus. The prospectus is often published in the 'quality' newspapers and, of course, must be truthful. An investor who can show that he or she was induced to buy shares because of false statements of fact in the prospectus, may sue to reclaim any money paid, terminate the share issue, and possibly obtain damages from the persons responsible.

It is usual practice, when a company makes an invitation to the public for a share issue, to have the issue *underwritten*. In return for a commission, an underwriter, again usually a merchant bank, will agree to subscribe for any shares which the public does not take up. This can be a very lucrative business, if all of the shares are taken up by the general public. In this instance, the merchant bank will receive its commission without actually purchasing any shares. However, should the issue be undersubscribed, the merchant bank may find itself in the position of having to purchase a large number of shares of which it may subsequently have difficulty in disposing.

Retained Profits as a Means of Raising Capital

You have looked at the need which a business might have for finance and at the main avenues which it might explore in order to obtain funds: borrowing and the issue of shares. In all of this, it is easy to overlook the fact that retained profits are still the biggest source of finance for businesses in the UK.

Whatever profitable businesses decide to do, they must first pay Corporation Tax to the Inland Revenue before they pay out dividends to their shareholders or retain what profit is left for re-investment. The trend in recent years has been towards a reduction in the rate of Corporation Tax. This has left more profits available for businesses to pay out as dividends,or to re-invest in their company.

1.   State the two main categories of the requirement for business finance.

2.   Describe the process of applying for a business loan.

3.   What should be included in a business plan?

4.   Explain the purpose of a cash-flow forecast when applying for a business loan.

5.   Describe the main features of:

      - a bank overdraft
      - factoring
      - hire purchase
      - bill finance.

6.   Why do businesses need medium-term borrowing?

7.   List the main sources of medium-term borrowing.

8.   What are *debentures*?

9.   Why is *sale and leaseback* considered as a 'last resort' form of borrowing?

10. In what ways does the law regulate borrowing by business?

11. Explain the difference between *authorised* and *issued* share capital.

12. What is meant by *unpaid* capital?

13. What is a *preference* share?

14. Explain the rights of an ordinary shareholder.

15. Describe the information which is likely to be obtained in a *prospectus*.

16. Explain the role of merchant banks in raising business finance.

17. Why are *retained profits* an important source of business finance?

18. How does Corporation Tax affect the level of retained profits in a business?

19. Complete a diagram which illustrates the main forms of finance available to:

      - a sole trader
      - a private limited company
      - a public limited company.

20.   In what ways do interest rates influence the type of finance which is chosen by a business?

21.   Produce a summary chart of the relative advantages and disadvantages of *equity* and *debt* as sources of finance.

People at Work: Individuals and Groups

Personal Relationships in the Working Environment

People at work are in an environment where they develop personal relationships with their colleagues. In a business, the staff work together as a team. They have to communicate with each other in order to maintain any sort of contact with the business to which they belong. It is impossible for an individual who works in a business to be totally outside its communication network. Whether a person's function is critical to the total business or not, if that person does not mesh into the internal communication network, then he or she will be seen as contributing nothing to it.

People communicate within businesses primarily to pursue the work of the business. But the business itself is a collection of individuals who follow a common purpose. As members of the group, those individuals may well be conscious of their group identity, especially if the business for which they work deliberately encourages such awareness. Some companies use various techniques and strategies for developing staff loyalty and even affection for their employer: company songs; social functions for all the family; sports facilities; welfare benefits, and a generally paternalistic approach towards the well-being of staff give employees a belief that they are part of a community.

The benefit to the employer is a dedicated workforce, anxious for 'their' business to prosper, whilst the benefits to the employee are both material (e.g. generous sickness payments) and psychological (e.g. the employee feeling needed and recognised by the business).

The Social Motivation to Work

Most people who work do so primarily to earn a living, rather than as a way of spending time with others. Yet the social aspects of work do meet a fundamental need. (e.g. the pools winner who carries on working for the same employer, even though the economic reason for doing so no longer exists.)

The social dimension of a person's work is part of any study of business for two reasons:

- the individual has a feeling of well-being if personal relationships at work are successful
- if staff relate to each other in a socially harmonious way, the internal pattern of communication within the business will work smoothly.

Satisfying Needs

What the needs of a particular individual are may not be clearly understood by management. One theorist, Maslow, believed that people's needs were ranked in ascending order, with the most basic needs at the bottom and an increasing order of complexity and importance being evident as one moves upward through the hierarchy.

Maslow's Hierarchy of Needs

Maslow believed that an individual is motivated by the needs of each level, but once that need has been fulfilled, motivation will come only from a higher level of need. So, for example, a man who is hungry will be motivated by money, so that he can buy food, but once he has enough money to satisfy his physical needs, he will then need other motivators (such as praise or encouragement) in order to stimulate him to greater efforts.

Maslow placed self-fulfilment at the top of his hierarchy of needs: this involves a person achieving full personal development. To enable an individual to achieve this, a business must be prepared to allow individuals to use their talents and abilities freely and to the full. Successful managers will develop more and more of the employees within their span of control to achieve the higher level of needs.

Dissatisfiers and Satisfiers

Other writers, such as Herzberg, suggest that there are two distinct sets of factors affecting motivation. Herzberg refers to these factors as:

- dissatisfiers or maintenance factors; and
- satisfiers.

Dissatisfiers

These are factors which cause employees to feel dissatisfied, though they might not be damaging to the business. Such factors will not produce improvements in motivation of the staff; for example, if working conditions are overcrowded, noisy and badly ventilated, then people will grumble and complain and this will detract from their work. If conditions are improved by a better-planned working environment, then the cause of dissatisfaction is removed. But does this provide more motivation to work? No: it simply removes the dissatisfaction.

Satisfiers

Once the source of dissatisfaction is removed, employees become more amenable and so management may then seek to improve motivation. 'Satisfiers' normally fall within a person's job. For example, it could be that an employee would prefer to have greater discretion to make decisions about work, rather than being forced to follow directions 'from above'. Thus, a salesperson may be allowed to plan his own visits to customers, rather than be expected merely to follow head office instructions. As a result of this increased latitude to decide, the job may seem now to be more satisfying and the salesperson regards him or herself as being more autonomous. The salesperson may be much keener to demonstrate an ability in choosing the most profitable customers to visit and the result can be increased sales for the business.

Some of the factors which are classified as 'satisfiers' are:

- an increase in job interest
- a higher level of achievement in the job
- a greater recognition by superiors of achievement
- increased authority and responsibility.

If 'satisfiers' are incorporated into an employee's job, motivation may increase. To achieve this, some businesses will apply a technique known as 'Job Design'.

Job Design and Redesign

Conditions and pay are important, but in themselves they cannot create interest in a boring job. People wish to be treated as 'thinking adults', not 'organic machines' who have no ideas or emotions. Better 'design' of job can lead to higher productivity, better benefits and higher pay. However, if 'efficient' methods of production lead to less variety in the job, or the employee is asked to perform fewer tasks which require less skill, or there is a restriction in the freedom to make decisions, then the job design will have failed in its objective.

Outside their work, employees make decisions and accept responsibility. Why, then, does management so often prevent this happening *at* work? Such reluctance to delegate decision-making is often counter-productive, discouraging initiative and failing to exploit the full potential of the workforce. Workers cannot be given a completely free rein, since it is management's responsibility to control a business's operations: however, a workforce should be allowed the freedom to take decisions which do not conflict with overall policy.

The consequences of poor job design

If jobs are not designed to meet people's needs, this results in:

1.   the potential of the workforce not being fully used and the business's most expensive resource being wasted

2.   the individual worker gaining little satisfaction from the job which, in turn, may adversely affect the quality of output or the service given

3.   employees' expectations not being realised, which will lead to frustration and resentment. This leads to low motivation, non-co-operation, absenteeism, poor quality work, industrial unrest and a high turnover of staff.

Principles of job design

A well-designed job will:

1.   exploit an employee's skills and abilities, both mental and physical

2.   allow the individual authority and responsibility, to use discretion and make decisions

3.   offer some opportunity for group work

4.   be reasonably demanding and present a suitable level of challenge

5.   recognise that an employee is making an identifiable contribution to the eventual product or service

6   provide variety in the range of tasks to be performed and keep people's attention by changing their patterns of work.

7.   be regarded as worthwhile and meaningful by the employee.

Methods of job design and redesign

The following represent some of the most popular and successful methods of designing and redesigning work:

1.   job rotation

2.   job enlargement

3.   group work and group technology

4.   autonomous group working

5.   job enrichment.

1. Job rotation

Workers are trained to be able to tackle a number of different jobs and are moved from task to task to give them variety. Rotation must not happen too often, as work speeds have to be built up after each change. The best results are obtained where the workforce itself decides when to change jobs.

Disadvantages:

- a worker will not be on any one job long enough to build up satisfactory skills or working speed

- swapping one boring job for another does not bring motivation. Some individuals resent changing jobs regularly and prefer certain types of work.

2. Job enlargement

A process or operation can be subdivided into a series of short, cyclical and repetitive tasks. For example, an individual checks a small part of the information on a form before passing it to someone else to complete another part. Each person does only a few seconds of work on each item before it is passed to the next worker. Each worker has a different task to do in a predetermined order. An alternative arrangement is to allow each employee to complete the whole process so that more satisfaction is gained by a worker.

Critics suggest that 'job enlargement' now consists not of one short, boring task, but many of them! Many businesses have adopted an alternative approach to the problem of repetitive tasks. Instead of treating people like programmed human machines, they have replaced them with real machines that run tirelessly under a variety of unpleasant working conditions. This has the added advantage that people are now required to set, modify, maintain and programme the machines; this places a greater demand on people's ingenuity, skills and flexibility. For this type of flexibility, human beings are ideally suited! However, for relatively short production runs, where a wide variety of products are made, automated machinery would be too expensive since it may be standing idle, other than when it is needed for that particular operation.

3. Group working and group technology

Some businesses (e.g. Volvo cars in Sweden) have moved from the production line method of manufacturing to one where groups of workers complete a whole task, such as building an engine. As a result, Volvo has experienced an increase in employee morale and motivation; as a result of group work, there has been a discernible upturn in productivity.

Businesses have changed their production methods to take advantage of group technology. Instead of many different departments, each filled with a particular variety of machine, they have grouped together machines that can produce a specific product by a group of workers. For example, instead of turning, milling, drilling, polishing and plating departments, each of which contains its own specific type of machinery, groups of workers are each given the full range of machines they need to manufacture the complete product. The advantage of this approach is that it allows workers to identify with the business's product as a completed whole, rather than viewing their own part as a separate part that has nothing to do with the whole product. Grouping can also speed up manufacture, since it removes problems, such as one department proving to be a bottleneck in an integrated production process.

4. Autonomous group working

This involves an experienced group of workers being given greater control over the order, planning and timing of its own operations. Instead of following instructions from a supervisor, employees now have discretion in decision-making and have to agree between themselves on the individual tasks. For example, a group of forklift drivers in a brewery is given customers' orders and allowed to decide how the transport is to be loaded. The role of the supervisor changes to one where he or she becomes a communication link and a problem solver for the group.

Disadvantage
The group has to be willing to accept extra responsibility and the supervisor has to be willing to relinquish authority to the group. It may be more difficult in such circumstances for management, rather than its workforce, to adjust to its new role.

5. Job enrichment

Job enrichment is the redesigning of jobs so that they will include some of the 'satisfiers', or motivating factors, that Herzberg describes and which provide opportunities for an employee's psychological development. The employee's full potential will be realised by allowing him or her to tackle more complex tasks. The new tasks are designed to 'stretch' people and give them greater challenges in their daily work. Employees will have opportunities to utilise previously neglected skills and expand their capabilities.

Disadvantages
Management must recognise that people vary in the degree to which they are attracted to take up these challenges. Employees must not be forced to accept their new role, since they will resent the new tasks, rather than feel motivated by them, if they feel that they are being imposed upon them. It is best if the changes are presented as opportunities, rather than demands; employees should be given the chance to continue to do the jobs that they have always done.

The aim of job enrichment is to improve productivity and task efficiency, while at the same time increasing workers' satisfaction. This is done by :

- building into people's jobs greater scope for personal achievement
- recognising achievement
- providing more responsible and challenging work
- creating opportunities to make decisions in people's own sphere of work.

Trials and experiments in job enrichment have been carried out by ICI. A number of different job categories were chosen and attempts were made to ensure that any changes that were noted were brought about solely by the job enrichment factors and not by some other external effect.

The sales representative experiment

One of the successful trials, carried out by ICI, involved some of its sales representatives. Initially, these individuals, working outside the company premises, had a number of restrictions placed on their work. They were expected to visit their customers according to schedules specified for them by their superiors and they had to make written reports on each call. If a customer complained of faulty material, the sales representatives were not allowed to take any action on their own initiative. They were given price lists for all products and were not permitted to vary the prices offered to the customers.

After determining the initial sales levels, (which had been falling) and deciding on a 'control' group, a number of changes were made:

- the representatives were allowed to decide when to call on customers and what to write in their reports about customers

- where customers had a complaint regarding product performance, representatives had authority and could exercise their own judgment to make a small settlement

- where customers had faulty or unwanted products, salespeople had the right to decide whether to return material or make a settlement

- representatives were given the discretion to offer up to 10% discount if they felt this was the only way to make a sale.

The result at the end of year was a sales increase of over 18%, while those who formed the 'control' group actually experienced a decrease in sales.

Difficulties in adoption of job enrichment

The above example of successful job enrichment is only one example of the many which have been achieved. However, while it may be thought that such a successful technique would have become commonplace, an analysis of 125 industrial firms in the US showed that only five had attempted to formally introduce job enrichment programmes. Three major problems exist:

- the difficulty in measuring productivity benefits

- the difficulty in redesigning existing jobs

- the difficulty that all employees may not react in the same way to the job enrichment changes.

Measuring Productivity Benefits

It is unlikely that management would be willing to introduce expensive and time-consuming changes to job design if such changes were not guaranteed to result in improved productivity. If management is to be made interested, then satisfying employees' needs must be linked to reaching business goals. It is reasonably simple to assess the effects of change to jobs which are directly related to production or sales (as in the previous example). Any alterations to the job can be related to the consequential changes in the output. Problems arise with those jobs in which the improvements cannot be easily and objectively measured over a short time.

Suppose the changes result in improved employee attitudes towards the business. These could not easily be measured in the short-term. The output of some jobs, especially those in the service sectors, is difficult to measure in a precise way. For example, suppose an office administrator has responsibility for analysing problems and producing reports for the guidance of management. If the administrator's motivation was improved, it would be difficult to monitor the expected outcome. Would there be an expectation that reports would be produced more quickly, with a greater degree of competence? The problem is that the reports may take longer to produce if the work is done in a more diligent fashion. Only a subjective appraisal of the scheme's success is possible. Thus the employee's superior may express the opinion that the reports are now an improvement over the standard previously attained. There is no doubt that this form of appraisal, because it is not based on hard fact, has less impact when it comes to persuading managers to change long-established work systems.

Difficulty in redesigning existing jobs

Many businesss, such as Volvo, find that radical changes may be readily achieved when introduced in a new factory or office with a mainly new workforce. In long-established businesses, entrenched attitudes and customs and practices built up over a number of years are not easily discarded. The resistance to change may be as much due to fear of the unknown as to worries over the potential loss of status.

Furthermore, it is difficult to change job structures whilst trying to maintain output. Most successful business are busy and are reluctant to chance any possible breakdown in the supply of goods and services that might result from major job re-structuring. Finally, available technology may restrict the manner in which jobs are performed, making it difficult – if not impossible – for them to be redesigned.

Employees' reactions

While some studies indicate that the majority of employees tend to react in a particular manner, this does not necessarily indicate that all are enthusiastic for change. Suppose a worker performed a repetitive and essentially boring task. He may become extremely skilled at this task and so be respected for being so adept. Consequently, he receives a high wage. Such a worker may regard the job merely as a means of earning a good wage and he is unlikely to welcome any change.

It may be true also that many workers do not wish, or because of factors like age no longer wish, to increase their responsibilities. They may feel inadequately equipped to deal effectively with the new challenges. The demands of their private lives may deter them from accepting greater responsibilities.

Attitudes and personality

An 'attitude' describes the way a particular person will characteristically respond to an object or situation. In the workplace, some people's attitudes are 'instrumental', that is they see work as a means of earning money and do not expect to gain any other satisfaction from the job.

Personalities can be categorised broadly as:

- extroverts – people who are outgoing and seek the company of others
- introverts – people who are more comfortable with their own small group or prefer to keep to their own company.

Again, be cautious: the vast majority of people are part introvert and part extrovert, depending upon the situation in which they find themselves.

People in Groups

An image of a successful business might be one where people work together and where their efforts are integrated in such a way that the workforce acts together as a team. When the business is small, the team is likely to include all of the staff; when larger, departments and sections emerge along specialist and functional lines. So the business may consist of a number of teams, made up of groups of staff.

But *how* do people work in groups? What types of organisational groups are there? What makes groups *effective* units? What is the relationship between the manager and the group?

Groups and their Characteristics

The operations of a business are broken down and divided between various departments. This allows staff to specialise and develop expertise in particular jobs or functions. Usually, to complete a complex task, a group of individuals is required to work together. There must be co-ordination and co-operation between the individuals who make up the group, as well as between the separate work groups that make up the business.

Most work groups have these characteristics:

1. *They share common goals*

    Each of the group's members wishes to achieve a common purpose; each believes that this goal can be most successfully accomplished by working collectively.

2. *They influence each other*

    Social interaction means that people in a group influence the values, ideas, beliefs and attitudes of other members of the group. Their influence may be as a result of discussion between the various members; e.g. at a committee meeting where people may be encouraged or persuaded to adopt the beliefs of the majority.

3. *A group structure*

    A group usually has some form of structure or set of rules, however informal, so that members can relate more easily to one another. Group names, or the values that a group shares, may be stable and consistent over a long period and may well outlast the original group members; e.g. where a number of employees form a football team which lasts for long after its founders have given up playing football – or even working for the business.

Types of Groups

In business, there are three main types of groups. These can be referred to as:

1. executive or command groups

2. committees and project (or task force) groups

3. informal groups.

The first two types of groups are *formal* in that it is for management to decide the make-up of the group and its assigned tasks. The third type of group is *informal* and grows out of the natural affinity that people have for each other in certain situations.

1. Executive or command groups are composed of managers and their staff. They plan, organise, motivate and co-ordinate the different groupings within a business. Each of these groupings or departments will have its own specialism and will co-ordinate with other groups.

For example, a production planning manager will be the head of a group providing plans to guide the production of goods manufactured on the shop floor. At the same time the production planning manager is part of a unit headed by the production director; this group will meet regularly to discuss production problems, relating to matters such as quality and quantity.

The manager of each group is a link between fellow members of the work group and the executive or command group. So, while each formal work group has a responsibility to carry out specific tasks in the business, (e.g. work study), it must co-ordinate with other groups (e.g. production) to provide a service that will benefit the business as a whole, rather than simply performing its own tasks in isolation. Thus, the work study department should aim to improve efficiency in areas of greatest priority to the business. Clearly it will not benefit the overall business if the work study department only evaluated those areas of the business which members of the work study department regard as being of greatest personal interest.

2. Committees or project groups. Formal groupings into committee or project groups may be established on a long-term basis; e.g. a safety committee that meets every week to discuss a particular area of responsibility. Alternatively, formal groupings may be short-term and set up to complete a specific, limited project; e.g. to design packaging for a product. The group would be disbanded at the end of the project, but might be reconvened for the next task. A long-term committee will have defined objectives and a structure that will endure beyond the participation of its original members.

The more formal the committee, the greater is the need for elected officers, such as a secretary and a chairman. Rules and procedures will help to reinforce the status of the committee and enable individual members to define their roles more clearly.

3. Informal groups. Informal groups will vary in their degree of informality. They can range from semi-formal groups, such as casual meetings called by managers to discuss current problems, to the informal group which congregates at the drinks machine during breaktimes and discusses a variety of subjects, including the latest rumours, the shortcomings of management and the state of the world.

The advantages of informal groups are that they:

- provide psychological security – most people feel that there is 'safety in numbers'; people feel more assured when they know that there are others in the same position as themselves

- allow people to establish their own identity or status; in a large business, individuals can often feel that they are insignificant parts of an enormous structure

- help to satisfy people's needs for friendship and support

- provide an informal communication network which supplements more formal channels, the 'grapevine', by which one group can pass messages to each other – the network is sometimes used by managers as an unofficial channel for passing on information

- may provide solutions to problems for a group; e.g. if a member is experiencing difficulties, the rest of the group may recognise this and so work harder to 'carry' the less productive member.

The disadvantages of informal groups are that they:

- can show resistance to change, despite management's concern to improve group working. (It is often easier to 'sell' changes to individuals rather than to groups.)

- inhibit individuals from expressing their attitudes if these differ radically from group attitudes; such conformity can lead to less innovation and creativity

- the 'grapevine' is often the source of rumours which are untrue but can cause disharmony in a business. The vacuum created when management fail to provide positive information may be quickly filled by rumours created by the mischievous or the ill-informed

- the group may test its strength against the rules laid down by management; this may lead to conflict with a 'them and us' situation developing with management. A striking and important psychological characteristic of the group is that people within it may behave very differently from the way they behave outside it. A manager may find that an employee, who is amenable and easy to get on with face to face, behaves obstructively when in a work group. Possibly this is as a result of the individual genuinely assuming the cultural values of the group, even when these values conflict with individual values.

Practical Studies of Group Working

One of the largest social studies ever carried out in industry was undertaken at the Hawthorne plant of Western Electric in the US during the 1920s and 1930s. Groups at work were studied and individual group members were interviewed. Over a period of two years, 20,000 employees were interviewed. The findings confirmed earlier studies which identified the human problems facing management. The results showed that, when the objectives of a group of workers and management coincided, the group could be motivated to produce a much higher output. If the objectives did not coincide, it was evident that the group could hold down output, regardless of the wishes of management.

At present, there are a number of interesting developments concerning work groups. These include the use of 'think tanks', 'brainstorming', group technology, autonomous groups, quality circles and many others. However, many of the new developments have their basis in the ideas produced by earlier work.

A brief summary of this earlier work revealed that:

1. people are mainly social animals who prefer the company of others

2. work is often conducted as a group activity

3. small, primary, informal groups are important to carry out particular tasks in a business

4 the social world of adults may centre on their work activity

5. for high morale and high productivity, the need for recognition, job satisfaction, security and a sense of belonging may be more important to employees than the physical conditions under which they work.

Group Effectiveness

Group size, needs and skills are among the most important factors that determine whether a group becomes effective and efficient.

Group Size

There have been many studies on the effectiveness of small group size, the ideal or optimum size seeming to vary from three to seven, with five appearing as favourite. Larger groups than that seem to suffer, since not every member contributes effectively. Odd numbers in a group are often preferable; this avoids the possibility of an equal split when trying to reach a decision. Of course, the size of the team is often a reflection of the scale of the task it is being asked to do.

Group Needs

For a group to be effective, three needs have to be met:

1.   the need for hard work and effort

2.   the possession of relevant skills and abilities

3.   the need to tackle the problem in the best way.

Group Skills

Groups contain individuals who bring different strengths and abilities to a task. These skills may be essentially physical (e.g. using a lathe or computer). With physical skills of this kind, weaknesses can be identified and corrected by training and experience. However, with some groups, the skills needed may not be so readily identifiable and weaknesses that exist may be more difficult to remedy. The group may lack cohesion because the person who leads it is a poor communicator; the individual members of the group, whilst recognising that a problem exists, fail to link it to their leader's failure to provide them with unambiguous instructions. Managers must work as a team and may meet together to discuss and attempt to resolve problems.

Researchers have studied management teams and the reasons for their success or failure. After analysing over many years the skills and abilities of each individual member, the researchers put together teams which were then given tasks to complete. The performance of each competing team was then compared. Sometimes they put together a team composed only of those who recorded the highest scores in tests of mental ability. You might assume that such a team would beat all others easily. However, where human relations are concerned, what appears obvious is not always confirmed by results. In reality, the most intellectually able teams performed poorly in competition, in some cases actually coming last! All too often, individual members were interested more in debating their particular point of view and pointing out the flaws in arguments of others than getting on with their job – often other important and pressing matters were neglected. The conclusion seemed to be that teams composed of a mixture of abilities give the best results.

Leadership

> *'As for the best leaders, the people do not notice their existence; the next best, the people honour and praise; the next the people fear; and the next, the people hate. But when the best leaders' work is done, the people say "We did it ourselves".'*

Leadership can be defined as: *the ability to lead groups or teams of people toward the achievement of the objectives of the business.* If you consider that management principally means 'getting things done through people', then having effective leadership qualities must be the hallmark of a good manager.

What are the key qualities of an effective leader? He or she should have:

- a clear vision of what the business is seeking to achieve and know its aims and objectives
- an understanding of what needs to be done so that the business meets its objectives
- an appreciation of the qualities needed for people in 'the team'
- the respect and authority to recruit the right people for the right jobs
- a personality that gains more satisfaction from the success of the team than from personal praise or reward
- personal qualities, such as empathy, encouragement, communication ability etc. which are respected and trusted by the team
- intelligence, expertise and knowledge, which is valued by the team and provides the confidence that the whole group can feed off
- confidence in his/her own ability
- an acceptance of the need for change
- the ability to anticipate and plan for change rather than simply react to it after it has occurred i.e. be *proactive* rather than *reactive*
- the ability to stand aside and let team members take responsibility (and recognition)
- a clear-thinking, analytical mind.

A leader must have boundless energy and great stamina. The team will have a strength of its own, but this strength will be a reflection of the confidence and commitment of its leader.

An effective leader must:

- be clear about what direction needs to be followed and lead the team towards achieving realistic goals
- have the logic to plan in the long-term
- be someone who can recognise problems and develop solutions which work – not just now or next week but in the longer term.

Long-term solutions are the product of a team that is well-led; solutions belong to the whole team. Making sure that solutions are the property of the whole team ensures that they have the greatest chance of being successfully and enthusiastically implemented.

An effective leader will give the team the right mix of freedom and direction to succeed in achieving the desired objectives.

An effective manager and a good leader are not necessarily the same – quality leadership is an honour which must be earned.

A well-led team will say, when the job is done, "We did it ourselves".

1. Explain Maslow's *hierarchy of needs*.

2. Distinguish between Herzberg's *dissatisfiers* and *satisfiers*.

3. List the principles of *job design*.

4. Explain the consequences of poor job design.

5. Explain the processes of:

   - job rotation
   - job enlargement
   - group work and group technology
   - autonomous group working
   - job enrichment.

6. List the difficulties of re-designing jobs.

7. Describe the characteristics of *work groups*.

8. Describe the characteristics of

   - executive or command groups
   - committee or project groups
   - informal groups.

9. List the factors that determine *group efficiency* and *effectiveness*.

10. Describe the qualities of an *effective* leader.

The operation of any business requires an effective form of management. It is a manager's job to see that the objectives of the business are met. However, there are many differing objectives in any business. There are the objectives of the owners of the business – the shareholders of a private company – which may differ from those of its managers who have objectives of their own. Conflicting objectives can result in tensions where different factions – management, owners, shareholders, workers – appear to be pulling the business in different directions.

The Growing Importance of Management

Management has become increasingly important during the 1980s and 1990s and it will continue to be seen as crucial in the successful operation of a business. Management or, more precisely, better management, is seen as the way to ensure the continued growth of business and the economy. ('Growth' here means an increase in the total output of a business's goods and services.)

In the 1990s management will need to cope with some significant challenges:

- the 'Single Market'; that is, the open market within the European Community (EC). The result of the open market has been a much higher level of competition and an increase in opportunities for well-managed businesses, both in the UK and other EC countries

- increased competition will mean that costs and prices will become more significant

- quality; people may not want the cheapest, but may relate price and quality when making their decision to purchase

- rapid change: this is a strengthening feature of the markets – management needs to be adaptable and skilful in changing the business, its systems and its products, to fit quickly changing market conditions

- developing technologies: an important factor that improves business performance is investment in research and development and in capital equipment, especially in developing technologies

- developing human resources – that is, people in organisations – is essential in assisting staff to acquire the skills to cope with new methods of work and for managers to manage complex organisations and organisational change.

The 1990s will see a renewed skills shortage because of the changing demography of the British population and the needs of a developing economy. Whilst management was important in the 1980s, it seems that a fresh emphasis needs to be placed upon management as a specialised function.

UK industry has often been criticised for its lack of attention to management training. In 1987 two reports, by the Training Commission and the CBI respectively, agreed that it was the failure of management training which partly helped to explain the poor performance of the economy in that decade.

Management as a Specialist Function

The rising importance of management in a growing economy has produced two effects:

1.   The use of the word 'manager' as a job title, though there are other words to describe senior managers: Director; Chief Executive; Managing Director etc. The term 'manager' as a job description indicates that management is a distinctive, separate function within a business. The term 'management' is a way of describing what managers do.

2.   The distinction between *general* managers and *functional* or specialist managers: Marketing Manager; Property Manager; Training Manager; Divisional Manager; Personnel Manager; Product Manager etc.

What is Management?

Management has become increasingly important in recent years, but what exactly is management? Some authorities on the subject suggest that there are as many definitions as there are managers. A simple and easily understood definition of management is that it is:

> *the process of deciding what is to be done and of getting it done through people.*

The definition emphasises the importance of decision-making (or policy-making). It emphasises also that a manager properly does his or her work by getting other people to do their work.

The Functions of Management

A standard list of managerial functions might include:

1.   creating
2.   planning
3.   organising
4.   motivating
5.   communicating
6.   controlling.

Consider each in turn.

1.   *Creating* means finding solutions to problems; business abounds with problems of all kinds.

2.   *Planning* the future – *how* to implement solutions to problems – and *when*. Setting the goals and objectives of the business and deciding the approach through which they can be met.

3. *Organising*: that is, blending resources together in order to make things happen. For example, changing technology can lead to a change in the balance between labour (people) and the capital used (the cost of the technology). Such a change may change the balance of skills that are needed within a workforce.

4. *Motivating people* to give a higher work performance, in terms of quantity and quality, than those with no interest in the job. The factors which influence people to work effectively are complex and are seldom purely financial.

5. *Communicating* In order to manage people, systems and procedures, and to meet objectives, there has to be an effective communications system. Managers need to be skilled communicators, orally and in writing.

6. *Controlling* involves comparing what is happening with what has been planned – and then making necessary corrections when events begin to deviate from plans.

Some Management Theorists

Frederick W Taylor

Taylor viewed the objective of management as maximising the prosperity of a business for the mutual benefit of both the owners and their employees. The method of achieving this, he stated, was 'through the efficiency of human beings'. He argued that people, in the main, were motivated by money and that if management concentrated on a particular method, then the profitability of the business would be assured. Taylor suggested that any management should:

1. Observe a task or process; collect information about it; define its purpose; and produce an analysis of the present method.

2. Following the analysis, decide on the best method of performing the task or process.

3. Select and train the most suitable people for the job.

4. Ensure an objective method of payment, relating the level of reward to the amount of effort, e.g. piece rates.

Taylor believed that, if management designed jobs which made maximum output possible and people were effectively selected and well-trained, productivity would increase and, ultimately, the business would achieve higher levels of profit.

Henri Fayol

Fayol's approach to management was 'scientific': that is, he believed principles of management could be developed from observation and experience, just like any other science. Thereby would evolve a 'theory of management' which could be employed for the benefit of any type of organisation.

Fayol defined the tasks of management, which he referred to as the elements:

1. forecasting and planning

2.   organising

3.   communicating through clear lines of command

4.   coordinating

5.   controlling.

Despite the scientific and formal nature of Fayol's research and findings, he also recognised the need for managers to take account of:

- the sensitivity of people

- the need for an adequate reward system for employees

- employees' desire for stability and security of employment.

Douglas McGregor

In 1960 McGregor published *The Human Side of Enterprise*, in which he presented his *Theory X* and *Theory Y*. Theory X suggests that people are basically lazy and uninterested in work. They lean toward job security, rather than being ambitious. If they are to work efficiently and effectively, they must be supervised.

Theory Y, McGregor's own belief, concludes that all people can be motivated to work effectively and it is up to management to provide the conditions for this to happen.

Peter Drucker

A different list of management functions has been devised by Peter Drucker, a contemporary expert on management. He lists five functions:

1.   *Setting objectives* for the business, including communicating those objectives (with targets) to other people in the business.

2.   *Organising the work.* This includes dividing the work into activities and jobs. The jobs are integrated into an organisational structure.

3.   *Motivating employees.*

4.   *Measuring performance against objectives.*

5.   *Developing people.*

Management Style

The style that management adopts is extremely important.

To decide which management style a business will use, it needs to consider:

- the personality, skill, experience and ability of the manager

- the situation

- the need for the workforce to participate in decision-making.

Personality

All managers differ in their ability to adopt a particular style successfully. Clearly, a manager should evaluate his or her own personality and talents before adopting a particular management style. For example, an inexperienced manager may find that democratic management is difficult to handle.

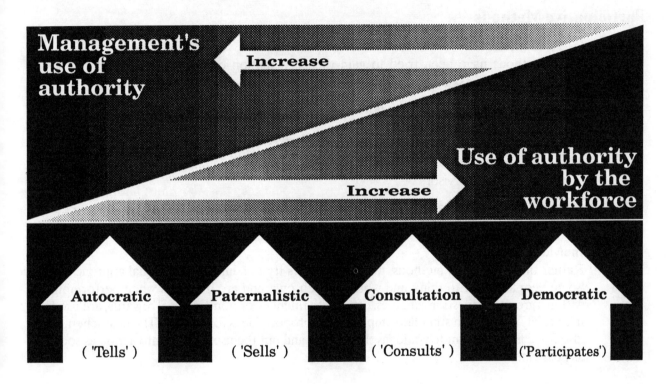

Style

Situation

Sometimes the situation itself may dictate the style to use. For example, in a crisis the workforce may look to management for a strong lead in decision-making. In fact, they may expect, and feel the need for, a largely autocratic style.

Participation

The workforce may not feel the need to participate in certain decisions. If the decision involves a problem that is not directly related to a person's task, then there may be little interest in active involvement. However, keeping people informed of decisions on changes may still be important and could be considered to be a lesser form of participation. Some businesses make an effort to keep all employees informed of top-level decisions. They do this through briefing meetings and in-house magazines and newspapers which are designed to give news, views and interests for dissemination throughout the business as a whole.

Participation in decision-making has the advantage of more fully exploiting the untapped potential of all employees. Employees become more interested in the business, want it to succeed and, consequently, work harder to achieve this. New processes are more likely to succeed where the people who have to make them work are involved in deciding the changes to be made.

Participative Methods

1. Group methods
    Many methods have been tried to gain the participation of employees as part of the management process. Group methods include:

    - *staff committees* which may be both formal and informal

    - *quality circles* where groups meet to consider particular problems

    - *autonomous work groups* in which some work decisions are made by the group, rather than by their supervisor

    - *project teams* where a group representing different departments in the business meets on a regular basis in order to tackle specific problems.

2. Individual approach
    Rather than use group methods, many businesses try to stimulate individual approaches. Some people prefer to think and work on their own and are inhibited when performing within a group. Suggestion schemes, often with financial or non-financial rewards, are used in a variety of forms to stimulate employees to propose ideas for change. The best schemes also force management to vet ideas thoroughly and put the useful ones into action as soon as possible.

Types of Problems

It would be wrong to think that all management problems can be resolved by committee or through wider consultation. Participation is a relatively slow process and, when time is short, it is better for an individual to make the decision. Generally, the problems best tackled by participative means are those which do not have 'one best answer' but offer a variety of options from which to choose. There are, of course, many problems whose nature demands a technical answer which can only be made by experts.

Interpersonal Skills

The interpersonal skills needed by a manager must include the ability to be a good listener as well as a good communicator. At meetings the manager will often act as a leader in proposing new ideas, or in counselling certain courses of action. However, the manager should 'take a back seat' and adopt a chairperson's role in encouraging debate and decision-making by others. Often a consensus decision – where all agree to the decision without a vote – is preferable.

Consultation

Consultation between management and workers requires skills of 'listening and asking'. It may also involve management taking the initiative to inform workers by using various techniques. Consultative committees are set up with representatives of management and elected representatives of staff. Consultative committees allow management to listen to the ideas and problems of staff through their representatives. Management should also be encouraged to include items on the agenda which enable them to establish employees' views. The downward communication process should be carried out by each team or group leader.

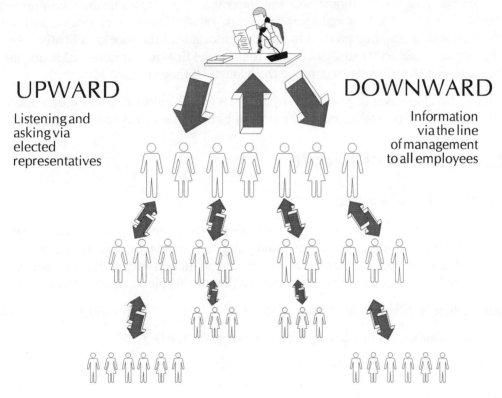

UPWARD

Listening and asking via elected representatives

DOWNWARD

Information via the line of management to all employees

Consultation

Items for Consultation

Policy and strategic objectives are decisions made by the most senior management and, being fundamental to the business, are not usually open to consultation, though how such policies are put into practice is often the matter for detailed discussion. While technical and urgent decisions are best made by the individual manager, consultation should be used where it does not slow down decision-making. Long-term decisions, or those which will affect a large number of employees, their work practices or working conditions, are better discussed in advance of planning and action. Good consultation is a practice which should help to reap long-term advantages, if it is used at the right times and is effectively operated.

Conclusion

1. A manager should be able to adopt a particular style in the light of a particular situation. It is probably accurate to say that most managers have a 'natural' or 'preferred' style which fits the individual's personality, or which the manager learned from observing other managers.

2. Subordinates have views on the managerial style they prefer. Although it varies, depending upon the problem involved, there is much evidence that the 'consultative' style is widely preferred. This style demonstrates the importance of communication systems within a business and the need for managers to be highly skilled communicators. Consultation is a difficult and demanding process to handle, especially in the face of a hostile workforce. Participative methods and styles do not remove the final responsibility of management to manage, but they do help to improve the 'climate' if they are used effectively.

The management task has never been easy; if anything it is growing more difficult as organisations become more complex, workers' expectations become more sophisticated and technological change accelerates.

The Management of People

Assessing the Value of People

One problem which faces the management of a business is the need to value the work performed by its workforce. This problem is often crucial, for usually the most expensive and important resource of any business is its human resource: its personnel. All managers need systems that assess the value of the contributions made by individuals in the workforce, so that the business can appropriately reward them.

There are two systems which are widely used:

- *job evaluation* (in which the job or position is assessed)
- *merit rating* (where the value of an individual is assessed and rewarded).

Job evaluation

A business should determine and evaluate the worth of any job and try to allocate pay in relation to its value. Many methods have been devised to achieve this, but all have their critics. The two main methods are ranking and points rating.

- *Ranking* determines which job in the business is the most important and then ranks all other jobs in descending order of importance. This is not easy to complete objectively. For example, how would you compare an office supervisor with a production supervisor?

- *Points rating.* In this evaluation, points are allocated to how the job matches up to several important factors; for example, responsibility for people or finance; skills or qualifications required. The points are totalled and the job is graded according to the total. By such means jobs in an employer's office, or in the factory, can be awarded points in the same way and so can be comparably graded and rewarded.

Once job evaluation has been carried out, it becomes possible to assess appropriate pay levels. Pay bands are established. Jobs with similar points, for example 100 - 150 points, may fall within the same 'pay band' and attract the same salary. Any change in the 'Job Specification' (that is, the detailed description of the job position the employee holds) may move the job into a different pay band.

Merit rating

This can be more controversial than job evaluation and is not always readily accepted by trade unions. Here, an individual worker is assessed and his or her performance is then graded. Grading does, however, present major difficulties in implementation. For example, two people doing a similar task, on the same pay scale, may adopt different approaches to the job. The performance of one may be considered by the manager to be only just satisfactory, while the other may be judged to be outstanding.

Unless there is a *quantitative* measure of output, such as the number of units produced in a day, such a comparison may be based on subjective judgment by the manager. To reward the person judged to be outstanding, an increase in wages called a 'merit award' can be given. The problem arises in finding an objective method of determining how good people are at their jobs. The pay award ought not to be made on the mere whim of an individual.

Some businesses lay down a set of criteria against which people are rated every year. Examples of the criteria used include: attitude to work; how well objectives are met; time-keeping. Such criteria are identified in advance and then it is left to an individual manager to decide how well a member of staff measures against them. For example, a worker may be graded as being less than satisfactory, satisfactory, good or outstanding. Often the manager discusses the rating with the individual worker before it is submitted to senior management, in order to encourage future improvement. High ratings naturally attract higher pay awards. This measure of the 'worth' of an individual can be the basis for the establishment of a plan for the improvement of the person concerned, including training where it is needed. Job evaluation and, perhaps, merit rating could be said to be an attempt to judge what is a fair day's pay.

Work study

Basically, 'work study' is an attempt to find, objectively, the best method of working and to measure the amount of work that is required in order to complete a particular task. There are two main approaches to work study: method study and work measurement.

Method study uses a variety of techniques to find the best method of doing a job. The work to be done is studied. Trials are carried out and the method which achieves the desired results in the shortest time is usually chosen. Wasted effort can thereby be eliminated. One problem of method study techniques is the possibility of oversimplifying any job, so that it becomes monotonous and boring to the workers who may then become unmotivated.

Work measurement. Work study practitioners are trained to study a job of work and determine how long it should take a trained worker to complete a specific task or sequence of tasks. The various components, or elements, of a job are determined. A simple example might be: picking up a cardboard box; packing a number of components; adding packing material; sealing the box and putting it on to a conveyor. For each box packed, a stopwatch is used to determine the time taken. The problem for the person timing the task is to decide whether the work is being carried out quickly or slowly. This is called *rating*. Taking into account the rating, by determining the time taken and the rest allowances, a standard time for any job is fixed and it is measured in 'standard hours' or 'standard minutes'. If more measured work, for example nine standard hours, is completed in an 'eight standard hour' day, then a higher bonus is paid.

Work study provides a method for estimating, in advance, how long a job will take and measuring the productivity of the work completed. Work study can provide a measure of efficiency in what is a business's most expensive resource, labour.

Approaches to Managing People

The basis of the relationship between managers and those managed is the *contract of employment*. However, there are other relationships which determine, in practice, how the business operates.

Essentially, these other relationships evolve from the attitudes of both the managers and the workforce. They will be determined by the willingness of the workforce to accept the 'right' of management to manage. They will also be influenced by management's view of the workforce. It may be that managers regard the workers as merely 'cogs' in the production process, whose hopes and aspirations, quality and standard of living, are of no concern to them.

The Consensus Approach

One approach to resolve this possible conflict of interest is based on the belief that the managers, workforce and the business itself essentially all hold the same common objective – that the business will prosper and achieve its overall aims and, in doing so, all will benefit: the owners of the business will receive what they desire, whether it is greater profit or a higher level of service; managers will benefit since they will receive promotion and higher salaries in return for their efficiency; workers will gain secure employment and higher wages in return for their labour. This approach is called the *consensus approach* because it assumes a consensus, or agreement, between all three of the parties.

The Conflict Approach

An alternative view is that each of the groups is seeking to pursue its own objectives, which are not necessarily the same. The owners may seek profit; the managers may look for power and status; workers want a greater share of the final profits. As each group is seeking to achieve its own objectives, there will be disagreements about the way the business is run and operated.

Within these two basic approaches is a number of different ways of defining the management style that a business adopts.

The Consensus Approach

The pluralistic viewpoint

While workers and management do not hold exactly the same aims and opinions on all issues, there is agreement on most major points; both workers and management wish to see the business succeed.

Management will accept the existence of trade unions as the legitimate representatives of the workforce and attempt to negotiate with them in order to ensure the most efficient implementation of its decisions.

However, trade unions are seen as a necessary evil, and the framework of the relationship is one in which the managers have the right to make major decisions independently and then agree with the workforce the means by which such decisions will be carried out.

To achieve such consensus, there is often a formal negotiating procedure established to which both sides adhere, and all contact between managers and workers, on such issues as wages and conditions, is made through this formal negotiating channel. The workforce is not consulted before the decisions are made, but it is clearly in the interests of management to bear in mind the likely reaction of the trade union to any management decision which will be put before them. This type of management style is typical of many businesses in the public sector.

The consultative style

This form of management style also relies on the consensus approach. It takes the process one stage further than the pluralistic approach, in that it involves the workforce in the decision-making process. Management seeks to ascertain the workers' views before a decision is made, but nevertheless it still retains the right to take the final decision itself. Clearly, this improves the workers' input into the decision-making process, and will allow the workforce to feel that its opinions count. However, its success as a management style really depends on how far the views of the workers are heeded. Some consultative procedures may appear to the workers to be a mere sham or facade if their opinions are continually ignored following consultations. An example where this has happened has been seen in British Coal's consultative machinery for deciding whether or not uneconomic coalmines should close. Unfortunately, because some mines have been closed despite the union's opposition during the consultation process, the unions now feel that their views count for nothing and that consultation is meaningless. Other organisations use this consultative process much more effectively by giving due weight to its employees' views in the final decision.

Worker participation

This approach involves the workforce taking a full and equal part in the decision-making process of the business. Such participation may happen on a number of levels. The most common would be in shop-floor or section committees, where workers and management regularly meet to decide on the practical operation of the business. Workers not only make suggestions about changes in working methods, or work rules, but also have a vote on whether their ideas, or management's, should be implemented. This democratic approach can be extended upwards through the business, with middle managers and representatives of the workers (e.g. shop stewards) deciding on more major decisions. Finally, a business may involve workers in policy-making by having worker directors. In this way the workforce is not only informed immediately of any policy changes which are to be made, but also can influence the decisions as they are being made.

Worker control

The most extreme form of the consensus approach involves complete worker control of the operation of the business. The workforce appoints some of its members to manage and administer the business, while others are involved in the production process. Such businesses are sometimes called 'workers' co-operatives', and are becoming increasingly common as the recession has encouraged redundant workers who have traditionally been employees of other businesses to come together and establish their own enterprises.

Sometimes problems arise in such businesses, as part of the workforce may resent some of their members appearing to hold and wield the decision-making power. However, if such problems can be overcome, the co-operative business can prove very successful, as not only do the workers feel they have a part in the decision-making, but also they normally receive a share of any profits made. A more limited form of worker control comes where employees are given, or purchase, part of the company's share capital. This encourages them to identify with the business and be more committed in their attitude, thus reducing industrial relations problems.

The Conflict Approach

The traditional management view

In more traditional businesses, there is a management view that management's job is to manage without any interference from its workforce. Management's objective will be to make the business as efficient and profitable as possible. It will use its employees only as a means of achieving this end. This does not mean that the employees will always (or even sometimes) be treated badly. Often, the converse is the case: if the business is to function smoothly, conditions and pay must be acceptable and workers must be kept happy. However, ultimately all decision-making must lie exclusively with management.

From 1979 successive governments encouraged business to take the view that saw trade unions and their supporters as being outside the organisational structure and, therefore, a presence that should be positively discouraged and, whenever possible, banished. They should be seen as an alternative focus of loyalty for the worker and, as such, a challenge to the aims of the business. Often management may allow a 'tame' company union, which will share the management's view of the business, so that if differences do occur they can be overcome by goodwill and the mutual aim of organisational success.

An example of this type of management approach, which gained considerable publicity, was the government's decision to ban trade unions from the Cheltenham GCHQ monitoring unit, because the government believed that trade union activity might be detrimental to its efficient operation. The civil service unions unsuccessfully resisted such measures, arguing that their members were equally loyal employees. A further example of this type of approach occurred in the Fleet Street newspaper-publishing business, where employers such as Rupert Murdoch and Eddie Shah sought to de-unionise their newspapers, or have only those unions which would unquestioningly accept management decisions. Such arrangements have been aided by single union agreements, where the business has refused to allow more than one union to operate within it. In doing so, it avoids inter-union disputes, and will be likely to accept a single union which it regards as the most malleable. An example of a single union agreement is that in force at the Nissan car factory in Sunderland. Honda Rover has agreed a similar deal, as has the Toyota workforce as that company establishes itself on a greenfield site in Derbyshire.

The Trade Union View of Industrial Conflict

It is sometimes argued that all trade unions are extremely militant in their views towards employers. This is simply and demonstrably untrue. A trade union will normally only react with some form of industrial action in response to management attitudes which are directly opposed to the best interests of its members. Nevertheless, most trade unions rightly see their role as one of protecting their members' interests and improving their pay and conditions. In most instances, this will mean ensuring the continued success of the employing business, as in this way the trade unionists' jobs can be made more secure and their future prosperity enhanced. However, trade unions will normally seek to gain for their members a larger share of the business's profits or budget. In this way, it will often find itself in conflict with the employer.

Of course, the majority of wage negotiations will be resolved peacefully, but when an impasse is reached the trade union may recommend to its members that they should pursue their claims through some form of collective action. It is unfortunate that it is normally these disruptive instances which receive most adverse publicity. Trade unionists are often blamed by the press for their selfishness. Yet many such claims are rightful, and industrial action is the only course of action open to workers.

Thus, the way in which a business is managed is often a consequence of the attitudes and objectives which exist on the part of both management and workforce. It has been a criticism of British industry in the post-war period that there have been too many instances of industrial strife which have seriously damaged the nation's productive capacity and international reputation, and that entrenched and intransigent attitudes on both sides have been the root cause.

Such criticisms do have some basis in truth, but industrial conflict cannot be held to be totally responsible for Britain's industrial performance. In fact, in recent years there has been, with some notable exceptions such as the miners' strike, a much lower incidence of industrial unrest in this country than in many of our competitors' economies. Therefore, what is required for the future is a positive attitude on the part of both workers and management towards the work relationship. This requires an acceptance that the worker must be given a fair reward for his labours and has the right to some greater degree of participation in the running of the business. It would be a desolate future for the British economy if the country were to regress completely to the class-ridden industrial relations picture of the pre-war years.

Enlightened managers and enlightened unions accept that conflict is, generally, bad for business. Both will hope to achieve their respective aims without inspiring industrial action which may well prove harmful to both parties. An important managerial skill is to bring about a situation in which the aims of management and workforce coincide in a desire to create and sustain a successful business. Motivating the workforce and giving individuals a sense of common purpose leads them away from adversarial situations. Thus the aims of this section are to consider:

1.   the ways in which employees can be motivated

2.   the factors, methods and processes which are important in achieving motivation.

Why Motivating People is Important

If a business is to grow, it will seek new methods to improve effectiveness and efficiency. To cope with crises and challenges in a manner which creates improvements will require an active, creative and well-motivated work force. To survive the challenge of competition, a business needs continuous innovation and improvement. All of these ideas for change must come from its staff. The process of achieving a well-motivated staff is not a simple one. People are complex and individualistic. Unlike machines, they do not always 'think' or act in the same way.

A 'Motivation Model'

Businesses hope both to achieve their goals and satisfy the needs of their employees at the same time. Good managers will try to ensure that the goals of the business are achieved. A major way of achieving this is by making sure that good work is rewarded and those who have done it are recognised as achievers. The questions below form a model which typifies this approach. This is, of course, an ideal model which may never be fully achieved in the real world. However, it can be used to analyse and test the 'needs and rewards system' of a business in order to judge how effectively it operates.

The model might be used by management to formulate questions, which must be answered in a real situation. The answers they arrive at might form the basis for correct decisions and to corrective action. An effective manager should know the answers to:

1.   Do I know all of the needs of my staff and the rewards they expect?

2.   Have I ensured that my staff are aware of the tasks I have set them and the type of effort they need to make to finish the job?

3.   Have I made sure that my staff have the knowledge, skill and experience that they need?

4.   Am I satisfied that my staff have a full understanding of what goals must be achieved?

5.   Have I ensured that my staff receive recognition for their efforts when they achieve their goals?

6.   Have I identified whether the rewards that my staff receive are those which they expect?

7.   Am I satisfied that the rewards my staff receive are high enough to continue motivating them?

Carrots are Nicer than Sticks ...

From the model, it is obvious that the needs of staff, and the rewards that the business gives, are at the heart of the motivation process. Rewards can be many and varied. Some businesses have attempted to apply what is commonly known as the 'carrot and stick' approach. Put simply, a donkey is likely to move forward if a carrot is dangled in front of its nose. A kick to its other end will achieve the same result. Similar treatment can be used with people: a manager may offer a 'carrot' by encouraging his production workers to reach higher output targets and by offering a weekly bonus once those targets are met. The manager may also use the 'stick', by dropping subtle (or unsubtle) threats to the production supervisors that, "If the quality drops, changes will have to be made around here"!

FW Taylor, author of *Scientific Management*, wrote, around the turn of the century, that all a work force wanted was a chance to earn more money, and nothing else was important. Taylor devised financial incentives schemes where the increased output of workers produced large bonuses for themselves. The problem was to find a scheme which was 'fair' to both management and workers. Today, many schemes are based upon measured work systems, devised by work study practitioners. No one suggests that money is unimportant, but many question whether it is the only important reward that people seek from work. People differ in the priority they give to the rewards they expect from their work. Nevertheless, there is evidence to suggest that for most people the following factors appear on an individual's list of priorities:

- money
- performing useful and interesting work
- using a full range of abilities and skills
- avoiding boredom

- meeting people
- working with people
- obtaining a sense of achievement
- having achievement recognised
- promotion
- security
- fringe benefits
- paid holidays.

Money as a Motivator

It is sometimes unclear exactly what value money has in motivating a particular individual – even pools winners have been known to return to work because they miss the socialising that work brings. On the other hand, there are people who take dangerous jobs which others would avoid, mainly because of the high pay such work carries. In fact, for the majority of employees, money is only one of several important factors in motivation.

Financial incentives as motivators

Financial incentive schemes which pay a money bonus for extra output have been in use for many years. The most successful schemes are based on a system that simply pays more money for more work. In other words, the striking of a bargain that balances pay with effort. Of course, the 'rate' that links money to effort should be assessed objectively, and recognised and accepted by both management and workforce. Previously, it was the practice to adopt what were referred to as 'piecework' methods. These were based on rates of pay which were arbitrarily determined. The methods used were often the source of bitter argument. It was even suggested that some businesses actually produced less because of the time wasted in industrial action caused by piece rate disputes. Nowadays work study measurements are found to be more accurate and acceptable to the workforce.

Many businesses have found that up to 30% extra output from the same workforce can be achieved after incentive schemes have been applied. A bonus which is paid immediately allows workers to see quickly the benefit of their greater efforts.

A problem exists when a bonus is linked to a more general output of the business, rather than directly to the individual worker's own efforts. For example, British Coal clerical workers may receive a bonus based upon the fluctuating output of faceworkers. The reason for this is that clerical work is a service necessary to achieve the output of coal, though it is only indirectly linked to the physical productive process. To summarise, the two major factors that management should be aware of in introducing bonus schemes are:

- the need to pay bonuses as quickly as possible once they have been earned
- the problem of attempting to tie the bonuses of those who are not involved in physical production to the output levels of the business as a whole.

Incentive schemes and output bonuses

Incentive schemes allow workers to (partially) determine their own output and so regulate their own pay. Traditionally, such decisions have been the province of management, but may now be decided, to some extent, by the individual worker. Allowing some element of discretion in work methods, or delegating decision-making powers to staff, may further increase the level of motivation. There is a possibility that bonus levels may fall if output, for a reason which is outside the control of the workforce, cannot be sustained. This is a fear that some workers guard against this, by deliberately 'hiding' extra output and so not claiming the full bonus due each week. In this way they can add 'extra' output when it is needed. Consequently, bonus levels will often show an unnaturally even level for considerable periods of time.

The workforce may also arrange amongst itself an artificial 'ceiling' above which bonus levels are not allowed to rise. They will do this because they fear that unusually high bonus levels may attract unwanted attention from senior management. The workforce may even fear that management may reduce their basic rate of pay, so they might end up working harder for smaller rewards.

An advantage of the change over to a bonus incentive system of working is that it might highlight 'hidden' problems within the business. Often the increased level of output of the workforce may reveal inadequacies in other parts of the business's production process. The purchasing, supply and storage of raw materials may have appeared to have been adequate in the past. Previously, a hold-up in supplies to the factory floor may have been welcomed by the workforce as an unofficial break from the demands of production. With the introduction of the incentive scheme, any failings in the material supply system will be emphasised by the increased demands of the workforce for extra output. The supervisor may discover that both higher management and workforce are keen to get supplies 'to the right place at the right time'.

Types of Incentive Schemes

Incentive schemes for direct workers

Production, or direct, workers are usually tied to schemes that provide an early 'feedback' on progress by paying the bonus a week after it has been earned. The main types of scheme are:

1. piecework

2. measured day work

3. high day rate scheme.

1. Piece work

The oldest type of scheme is the piecework system, so called because a bonus is paid for each 'piece' of work produced. Usually the price paid for each 'piece' of work is settled by 'negotiation', which may often result in bitter arguments between management and workforce. The modern version is referred to as the 'straight proportioning scheme'. This is determined by work study methods, based on 'standard hours' worked, and is judged to be a fairer system than the old one. The bonus is directly proportional to the output which has been objectively rated.

2. Measured day work

'Measured Day Work' has replaced earlier bonus schemes in many businesses. It has the advantage of maintaining a steady output and stable bonus, which is of benefit to both management and workforce. The bonus is paid on an agreed output of work which, with certain safeguards, the worker agrees to maintain. Such agreements are usually reached after employees have had some experience of this form of working.

3. High day rate scheme

Perhaps a greater trust in workers is shown by the 'high day rate' scheme. Here the workforce is expected to produce levels of output which are predetermined by management. Often the pace of work is dictated by the speed of machinery or a conveyor with which the worker must keep pace. An attraction of such a scheme is that the worker receives a higher than average rate of pay which does not fluctuate. Those who cannot maintain the output levels, however, are likely to be disciplined or removed.

Incentive schemes for indirect workers

Indirect workers are those whose work does not directly produce the product. In a car factory, the assembly worker is clearly *direct* production, whereas the production engineer is *indirect*. To reward indirect workers on the output of direct workers, is not considered the best approach. There are other methods which will improve motivational response. Two of the more popular methods are:

- profit sharing
- lump sums.

Profit sharing

With this method, shareholders allocate a share of the annual profits, (usually a global sum of between 3% and 10%) to the whole workforce. By agreeing to this use of profits, shareholders are taking money out of their own pockets. Before agreeing to such a scheme, shareholders need to be convinced that rewarding employees in this way will result in even higher levels of performance from the business in the future.

Results of recent research have shown that companies that engage in profit sharing are considerably more profitable than non-profit sharers. The profit share may be paid out in the form of cash or as an entitlement to shares in the company. Cash provides an immediate, tangible reward, whereas shares (unless they are sold again straight away) are medium-term and provide the employee with a 'stake' in the business.

Lump sums

If awards based on merit are to be paid, then payment as lump sums is much more effective as a motivator than smaller sums paid with the employee's monthly salary. Even more effective can be the timing of the lump sum payment – just before holidays and at Christmas are the times when most employees find that some extra cash is welcome. Employees value lump sum payments: they tend not to take them for granted as much as bonuses that are added to their monthly salary.

The main advantage to the business of lump sum payments is that they are not cumulative: if 3% of an employee's salary is paid out as an extra lump sum bonus, that 3% is only 3% of this year's salary, not of every salary after that. The same bonus will be paid the following year, but only if a certain level of performance is reached. The objectives of lump sum cash payments and share ownership schemes are:

1. to increase employee commitment to the business
2. to give employees a share in the success they've created.

A possible drawback to this system of rewards occurs when profits are squeezed by recession or market conditions. The work force may resent the reduction in the level of payouts when they feel their own effort is as good as ever and there will be a tendency for them to blame management for this.

1.   Explain why management is considered increasingly important in the 1990s.

2.   Define *management*.

3.   List the challenges facing management in the 1990s.

4.   List the main functions of management.

5.   Briefly explain the management theories of:

- Frederick Taylor
- Henri Fayol
- Douglas McGregor
- Peter Drucker.

6.   Explain the factors which influence management style.

7.   Explain the process of *job evaluation*.

8.   What do you understand by *merit rating*?

9.   Describe the *consensus approach* to management.

10. Describe the features of the *conflict approach* to management.

11. Explain the importance of motivating people.

12. List eight rewards people might expect from their work.

13. How effective is money as a motivator?

14. Describe the main features of *incentive schemes*.

15. State what you understand by

- piecework
- measured day work
- high day rate scheme.

16. What type of incentive schemes may be used for indirect workers?

1. Before 1981 management buy-outs were unknown in the UK. In 1986 there were 281 with a total value of £1.2 billion. Analyse the reasons for this growth.

   AEB P2 1989

2. In 1988 a number of firms decided to revert to private limited company status after being quoted on the Stock Exchange for some time. Discuss factors which might influence them to make such a move.

   AEB P2 1990

3. (a) Explain the following terms:

     (i) owners' equity

     (ii) rights issue

     (iii) depreciation.

   (b) A medium-size retail chain wishes to expand. To do so it needs to raise additional capital. Suggest possible internal sources of funds for this exercise and comment on the relative merits of financing the remainder by either equity or debt methods.

   UCLES P2 1991

4. (a) Why is 'job enrichment' considered an important part of motivation?

   (b) How can the concept of 'job enrichment' be effectively applied to production workers on an assembly line?

   UCLES P2 1990

5. (a) Explain the sources of finance likely to be available to a public limited company.

   (b) What factors should such a firm take into account when choosing sources of finance?

   UCLES P11991

6. (a) What is a 'small' firm and why do such firms exist?

   (b) From a human perspective, what problems and opportunities might such firms present?

   (c) What effect might an increase in the proportion of small firms have on the UK economy?

   UCLES P2 1985

7. "The job of a Manager is to make decisions rather than to motivate others."

   Discuss this statement with relation to the Production Manager of a soft drink canning factory.

   UCLES P2 1986

8. (a) What do you understand by the term 'gearing', and how might it be measured?

    (b) How might a finance house use gearing ratios when considering an application from a medium-sized manufacturing company for a loan of £5,000,000 for expansion purposes?

    (c) What alternative source of funds might the firm examine?

UCLES P2 1987

9. Discuss how economic and other constraints might influence the exploration and development policy of an oil company.

UCLES P2 1989

10. (a) Outline the leadership qualities which you think a successful manager might have.

    (b) Do motivational factors influencing production workers and the sales force differ? How might these be utilised by an organisation?

UCLES P2 1989

11. (a) British Industry has failed to react to change. What have been the consequences of this?

    (b) Discuss ways in which creativity might be encouraged and effectively harnessed in busines.

UCLES P2 1988

12. Akio Morita, Chairman of Sony, suggests in his recent book that Japanese workers are treated as "part of the family" even by large companies. Do you believe that UK industry could benefit from such an approach?

UCLES P2 1988

13. (a) Explain the benefits to a self-employed sole trader of forming a private limited company to conduct his business.

    (b) Discuss factors which would limit the size of a firm within an industry.

UCLES P2 1989

Other Questions

14. Following 'computer aided design', and 'computer aided manufacture', a new phenomenon has been identified which particularly affects small businesses, called 'computer aided bankruptcy'. How might such bankruptcy occur, and why are small firms particularly at risk?

15. Discuss the difficulties and dilemmas faced by management in the long-term as opposed to the short-term.

16. Are all attempts to motivate workers merely gimmicks or are they based on established motivational theories?

Case Study

The Driver's Bonus

John Carr is the owner and Managing Director of a small, but successful, laundry in Leeds. The company employs over 300 people in its two plants near the city centre.

He has recently appointed a new Production Manager, Tom Lawson, with the main priority of improving productivity and increasing the company's competitiveness. As the first part of his programme is to improve productivity, Tom used the services of a firm of management consultants to design a productivity bonus scheme for the transport section of the company.

This bonus scheme was the first of its kind to be introduced into the company and, if it proved successful, then a larger scheme encompassing all the laundry workers would be introduced in due course.

The transport section has had the same ten drivers for over eight years. They have always worked as a team, and any absenteeism has been covered by the others agreeing to do overtime, without any trouble. The drivers had previously been paid on a day rate basis. Their basic rate paid a weekly wage of £210 but, with overtime and the 'Christmas bonus', this averaged out at about £260 per week over the year. Once the productivity bonus scheme had been introduced, Tom Lawson announced his pleasure at its success. The company had taken on several new contracts with commercial organisations and the drivers were handling 78% more work. Their wage (including bonus) now averaged £280 per week and no overtime was necessary.

However, in spite of the newly re-arranged work routines and the work study-based times, the drivers felt that some routes were harder to complete than others in the times allocated. At first, they swapped routes in order to even out earnings; this created arguments about relative inequalities. Later, they 'modified' time sheets so that time saved on 'easy' journeys was balanced out by the extra time needed for the 'harder' journeys. This gave a constant bonus payment each week. Mr Lawson turned a blind eye to this 'creative' time sheet completion, as he knew that the journeys were still being done. Usually, drivers rushed to return to their depot, and chatted to the other drivers, drank tea and completed their time sheets.

After three months of the scheme, John Carr spoke to Tom Lawson and agreed that the bonus scheme seemed to be more productive, but there were grievances. Customers said that the drivers were not interested in listening to suggestions or complaints. Furthermore, delivery vans were dirty, even though the bonus scheme allowed for cleaning time. The drivers approached John Carr, suggesting that the time sheets were unnecessary. They preferred to return to a day rate that would give them £210 per week, plus a fixed bonus of £70. This would save completing time sheets, allow time for cleaning vans, listening to customers and still keep to present schedules. Mr Carr felt sympathetic towards the drivers. Mr Lawson had reservations, but promised to investigate the matter, discuss it with his staff and reply by the following Monday.

Task

You are employed as Tom Lawson's assistant in the production department of the company. He has asked you to prepare a report on the new bonus scheme.

You should consider the following issues:

    (a)   the reasoning behind the new bonus scheme

    (b)   the problems identified in running the scheme

    (c)   alternative suggestions for changes to the scheme, their relative merits and demerits

    (d)   your recommendations for changes to the scheme.

Case Study

The Rota Row

A group of machinists met together for a reunion after not seeing each other for some years. They talked about the 'old days' and how their factories were managed. At one time, the union had successfully fought for a reduction in the hours they had to work each week. Naturally, there still had to be continuous working on the production lines. With each machinist working fewer hours per week, there had to be changes in the shift and rota patterns. For many, changes in their start and finishing times caused social or transport problems.

One machinist, Joan, said that in her factory there had been rumours about how the problems would be solved, until one day the supervisor pinned up on the noticeboard a list of the new working arrangements. A number of machinists were upset at the new rotas and shift times, but little could be done and some of them left to work elsewhere.

Jill, another machinist, recalled that the supervisors were called to a meeting organised by the production manager. Afterwards, supervisors called their own staff together for a meeting. The supervisor explained what the new plans were for future working arrangements. The benefits of the new arrangements were stressed and questions were invited, although some machinists said afterwards that questions seemed to do little good when management's mind seemed to be made up.

June said that, in her factory, the supervisors were instructed to have discussions with their own machinists about the problem of changes. The supervisors then attended a meeting, chaired by the production manager, where the various viewpoints put forward by the employees were discussed. Minutes of the meeting were taken and much discussion took place. Within a week of the meeting the production manager sent a copy of the new arrangements to all employees; these new arrangements seemed to take account of many of the points that had been raised at the previous meeting.

Task

    1.   Identify possible social (and other) problems that machinists of different ages and circumstances may have with changes in shift times and work rotas.

    2.   Analyse the incidents described by Joan, Jill and June and describe the management styles that were exhibited.

    3.   Question family, friends and fellow students and discover whether any major changes have been made to their work patterns and how management handled those changes. Write short notes on any examples you identify and orally present the examples to small groups for discussion.

Case Study

The Mail Order Blues

The office staff of J H Mail Order Co. were having a discussion during their lunch period. Jean said that the pay was 'alright,' but what annoyed her most in the job were the rules and restrictions. One of her jobs was to write to customers when they had queries; she was only allowed to send printed 'standard' letters, even though they did not always fully answer a customer's questions.

Anne, Joan and Bill said that their jobs were boring. They all dealt with customers' orders, but worked on a 'production line', where each of them dealt with only part of the paperwork and passed the orders on for others to complete. Anne said that they felt 'out-of-touch' with their customers. Jim said that he had worked there for ten years, but was not allowed to make any decisions for himself. Often, he knew more about the job that his supervisor, but, for example, was not allowed to place orders for materials with suppliers, even though he knew that some suppliers were slower than others. His supervisor was involved in too much work, dealing with the rest of the section, to give these orders full attention. In the clerical department, Alan said that he had been trained to use the word-processor, but management did not understand its capabilities for writing good financial reports. This resulted in his being asked to input only what senior managers had hand written.

Janet said it was a shame they never really got to know people or what they did in other departments. She often wondered why another department was still completing its paperwork in a particular way, since the new computer had been brought in last month. Janet was discouraged from raising this point as she had been told it might look like 'interfering'. She felt that the organisation was a series of 'watertight' departments, where employees seldom met, inside or outside work.

Frank said that his section worked hard to complete the stock check over the weekend. None of the management seemed to be aware of this, and there were never any 'pats on the back'. Tony said that the only time his manager spoke to him was to reprimand him for being late one morning.

Task

You are employed as a member of a team of Management Consultants, engaged by J H Mail Order, to carry out a survey of organisational practices. Your specific task is to investigate staff motivation and, to this end, you are expected to produce an informal report. Use the information in the case study to help you. You should include:

(a) possible reasons for poor motivation of staff

(b) suggestions on re-designing jobs to improve motivation.

Case Study

The Bitter Pill

Health Products Ltd. is a producer of pharmaceutical pills, powders and other medicines for retailing and for prescription in chemists' shops throughout the UK and abroad. The latest technology is used in much of its manufacturing; production management works closely with research and development. Although they rarely admit it, many of the production managers enjoy the technical challenge of manufacturing the products. In fact, many can be said to manage products and processes better than people.

Every Monday the management team meets to discuss the priorities and problems of the job. This Monday, the least technological part of the process was under discussion for the first time. The problem lay in the packing section, which had just been taken over by a new manager, Mr Ray East, and it was he who raised the particular problem. The products were packed using production line techniques where operatives stood at 'stations', two metres apart. Here, each operative had quantities of a number of the products which they then placed into boxes which slowly moved by them on a conveyor. Sometimes the order attached to the box required the products of a particular individual; sometimes they did not. The problems that Mr Fox found on his appointment were recounted to the meeting. Absenteeism was the worst problem, and meant either high overtime bills or orders being unavailable to customers when they had been promised them, or both. Mr Fox's discussions with his packers revealed a lack of job interest and a high level of boredom. This situation resulted in mistakes being made, accidents happening and incidents of suspected sabotage.

One day the conveyor belt had ground to a halt to a chorus of cheers from the operatives, who promptly sat down; when the repair was finished, they groaned. The repair showed that the breakdown was caused by a bolt dropped into the conveyor cogs. Sabotage was suspected, but impossible to prove. Statistics showed that accidents and mistakes were increasing. There seemed a lack of team spirit and the operatives were unwilling to help each other when the opportunity arose. The operatives were paid an equivalent rate to other operatives in the region doing the same type of job.

Mr East proposed that the production line would be scrapped; the operatives would work in groups and sit at 'desks' which would stock all of the company's products; this would allow one packer to complete a whole order for a customer. Small groups might even deal with particular sets of customers, whom they might come to see as 'theirs'. The 'desks' would be arranged so that operatives could see, and talk to, each other as they worked. The details had not yet been fully worked out, as Mr East wanted to consult the packers first in order to seek their active participation in making the changes. Some of the managers welcomed the idea, but others were unconvinced. Their criticisms were:

> *"Asking the workforce for their ideas will only complicate the issue: explain the plan to them and tell them to get on with it."*
> *"They only work for the money, give them a bonus for better work."*
> *"We tried participation ten years ago and it did not work."*

and other disheartening statements.

Task

As Mr East's assistant you have been asked to prepare an informal report, for the next meeting of the management team, to help him sell his idea for improving the effectiveness of the packing section.

In the report you should:

(a)   prepare arguments to answer the criticism of Mr East's proposals
(b)   stress the advantages of group working for the packers
(c)   suggest the likely consequences of adopting the proposal.

Undertake a role play exercise of a meeting, between Mr East, his assistant, and some of the packers, where their active participation is sought for planning the proposed change.

Part Two – The Business Environment

You are already familiar with the analogy of a tree to illustrate the fact that a single business, and 'business' in general, are both organic; that is, they must not merely survive but they must also grow. If a sapling, planted in a rich and fertile soil, is watered regularly and allowed to grow in a completely protected place, away from the elements, the buffeting and damaging winds, you might feel confident that it will not only stay alive but will also grow straight and true.

But what if you plant your sapling and leave it exposed to the full effects of the elements? In business, the elements that affect the growth of the 'business tree' are external factors that lie outside the control of the business itself. These factors can be categorised as domestic (that is, British) and foreign; they can be governmental and non-governmental. This section introduces you to the backdrop of the major political, economic and social factors against which UK (plc) has had to work over the past fifty years. Though much of this section might appear to be 'history', rather than what is currently happening, it is important that you understand how business learns to function most effectively, even where there is a constantly evolving political situation.

This Part covers several central, 'macro' issues where economics impacts upon business:

- The Market Mechanism: A Simple Theory in a Complex World

- The Shaping of the UK Economy, 1979 to the present: this includes the policies of British governments; their economic objectives in theory and practice

- International Trade: its mechanisms, its restrictions, the 'big players' in the world economy.

The Market Mechanism: A Simple Theory in a Complex World

How Supply and Demand Meet in the Market

At its simplest level, the word 'market' describes the interaction between a seller and a buyer when a deal is struck or contract made. Although the term 'market' has existed for centuries – certainly since the Middle Ages – it began to enjoy a much wider use in the UK in the mid 1980s.

Part of the reason for this increased usage was because the three Conservative administrations, which were led by Prime Minister Margaret Thatcher, more and more came to adopt the monetarist doctrines of the American economist, Professor Milton Friedman. Friedman was increasingly supported by Thatcher in his belief that central government should, ideally, refuse to interfere with the mechanism of supply and demand so that prices and rewards would be set only by the market; such a 'hands off', non-interventionist attitude by the government was neatly summed up in Margaret Thatcher's phrase, "You can't buck the markets".

The basis of the market system is the interaction of the forces of demand and supply. *Demand* is the willingness and ability of consumers to purchase the goods and services they want: this implies that consumers not only desire the product, but also that they have the money to be able to buy it.

Supply is the willingness and ability of producers to meet these demands. Again, this implies that suppliers not only want to produce the goods and services, but also have the necessary combination of raw materials and finance, and an appropriately skilled workforce, to ensure that production is feasible. When suppliers and consumers transact they do so by entering into legally enforceable agreements, called *contracts*.

The *market mechanism* was seen by successive Conservative governments in the 1980s as a simple system of resource allocation. 'The market' was seen as neutral; a mechanism that should work within the existing distribution of income and wealth. The market mechanism accepts that there are rich people and there are poor people and it is not the market's responsibility to change that. The market is based on the belief that individuals will seek to maximise their personal satisfaction by demanding that combination of products and services which will give them the greatest level of satisfaction for the money they have.

The market system is based on the following ideas:

- it gives freedom to the individual consumer to spend money as he or she wishes

- it indicates consumers' demands and needs to producers and so ensures production of what consumers actually want

- it encourages competition between producers and so leads to a greater level of efficiency in the production of goods and services

- it adequately rewards the most efficient organisations, through high profits, and the best workers through high wages.

The market mechanism is not only relevant to the private sector of the economy: it has also become an increasingly important concept for the public sector. The market mechanism has assumed a more important role throughout the public sector as public authorities (such as hospitals and local councils) have been made to act as both suppliers and consumers.

What is Demand?

The *demand* for any product means the amount of a product that consumers are willing to buy at a range of different prices. The market demand for a product means simply *the total amount that will be bought in a specific market over a stipulated period.*

What Determines Demand?

1. *The price of the product*

    Usually, the higher the price set by the producers, the less of the product will be demanded by consumers; conversely, as price falls, more of that product will be bought, as existing buyers now demand more of it, or new consumers are attracted to it, or both. However, demand is not infinite, even for 'free' products or services. For example, a visit to your doctor would not cost you anything directly, yet you would not visit your doctor every week.

2. *Consumer needs, tastes and preferences*

    Demand is determined not only by price, but also by *need*. If cigarettes were free, the majority of people would still not smoke, because they believe that smoking is harmful. Therefore, the need and, consequently, the demand, for a product is influenced by each individual's tastes or preferences.

3. *Consumer income*

    Different individuals desire different products and services and, obviously, have varying abilities to pay for them. As income increases, more and more products are demanded.

4. *The 'pool' of consumers*

    The number of consumers in a market will influence demand. If the number of consumers rises, demand increases.

5. *The price of other goods and services*

    The level of demand for a product can be influenced by the price of other products and services. For instance, if the price of Mini Metros rose, you might choose to buy a Ford Fiesta because it is a *substitute*. The demand for Escorts would increase, even though they have remained at the same price. Alternatively, if the price of petrol rose, this might affect the demand for both Fiestas and Metros since people would travel less and would demand fewer cars and decreases in the price of them. Petrol is a *complementary* product to cars. If the price of the complement rises, demand for the first product is likely to decrease.

Finally, the price of other purchases in a consumer's budget will influence demand. If a person's rent rises, that person will have less money to spend on other things. If the price of a necessity goes up, the consumer will switch spending from less necessary purchases to pay the higher price for the necessity.

Factors which determine the level of demand for a product or service are as follows:

1. the price of the product or service

2. the tastes or preferences of consumers (is the product enjoyable; fashionable; etc?)

3. the level of income of consumers

4. the number (or 'pool') of consumers of the product

5. the price of other goods/services which are:

    substitutes

    complementary products

    also bought by the consumer.

One fact, however, is certain: a consumer will not buy a product unless it gives some level of *satisfaction* (or *utility*) when it is bought.

Expressing demand graphically

It is easier to show ideas graphically. The *demand curve* is one such idea.

If Ford found that it could sell varying amounts of its Fiestas in a certain period (say, one month), this could be tabulated:

Price £	Quantity of Fiestas Demanded
8,000	4,000
7,500	10,000
7,000	15,000
6,500	20,000
6,000	25,000
5,500	35,000

Demand Schedule for Ford Fiestas

Alternatively, this information could be presented in graphical form as seen on the next page.

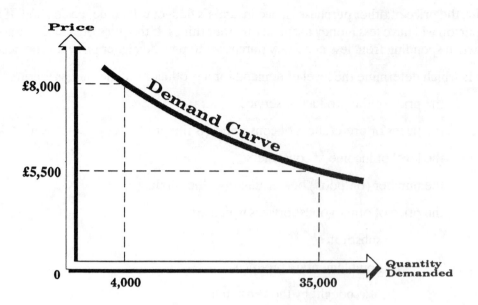

Demand Curve for Ford Fiestas

As you can see, the demand curve is typical in that it slopes from top left to bottom right. It graphically expresses the relationship between the *quantity of a product* that consumers are willing to purchase and a *range of prices*.

Changes in price

If Ford decided to set a price of £6,500, it would find that it could sell 20,000 cars. If it increased the price to £7,000, it would sell fewer – only 15,000 Fiestas. Changes in the price of the product cause movements up and down the demand curve – or more precisely *along* the demand curve. This is known as an *extension* or *contraction* in demand. A change in price does *not* move the demand curve itself, but merely changes the quantity bought because the price has changed. This is important to note.

Changes in the price of the product do not shift the demand curve but merely move quantity demanded along it. Does this mean that the demand curve cannot move? No. In fact, the other factors mentioned earlier as influencing demand (those numbering (2), (3), (4) and (5)) will shift the demand curve if they change. The following examples illustrate such changes.

The figure overleaf shows the *demand curve* for the records of a top rock group which is fashionable. People like them and buy their records. If their records were cheaper, perhaps more would be sold. If the records were more expensive, fewer might be sold. Consider, however, what would happen if people's tastes changed and the group was no longer popular. If the price had been higher, proportionately fewer records would have been bought, and so on at various possible prices. In fact, the whole demand curve has shifted to the left, from D1 to D2.

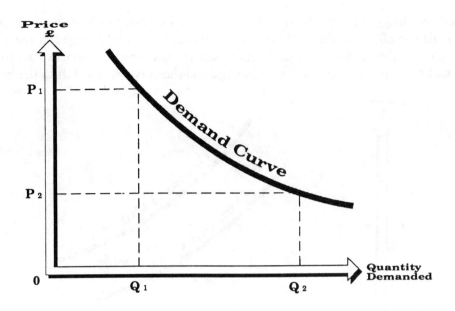

A Change in Price Moving Demand along the Existing Demand Curve

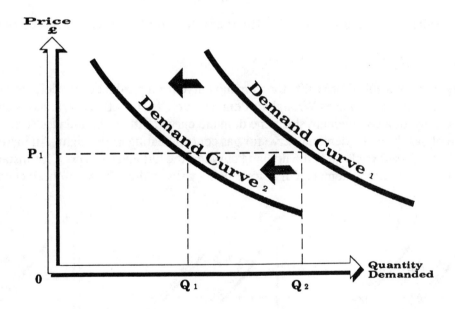

Shift in Demand Curve to the Left as a Result of a Change in Preference

Obviously, the reverse would be the case if the group became even more popular and even more people bought their records (in other words, there would be a shift to the right).

A change in the income of consumers

Now consider what result an increase in consumers' income would have on a product's demand curve. In the south east of England, during the middle 1980s, there was a general increase in the income of consumers.

This increased the demand for products generally, but had a particularly strong impact on the price of housing. How did this affect the demand for housing in the south east? As you can see, the demand curve for housing shifted to the right because of the increased incomes enjoyed by consumers. Conversely, a fall in income would mean there would be lower demand and the curve would shift to the left.

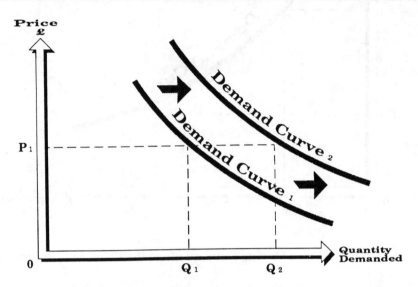

Shift in Demand Curve to the Right as a Result of an Increase in Consumer Income

A change in the price of other goods

A fall in the price of a substitute shifts the demand curve for a product to the left, and *vice versa*. So a fall in the price of Levi's jeans moves Wrangler's demand curve to the left, as Wrangler's are jeans *substitutes*. A fall in the price of a complement shifts the demand curve to the right and *vice versa*: for example, a fall in the price of gas shifts the demand curve for gas central heating to the right. An increase in the price of other goods purchased could shift the demand curve to the left and *vice versa*: for instance, an increase in the price of food moves the demand curve for cinema visits to the left. All of these changes are illustrated in diagrams below.

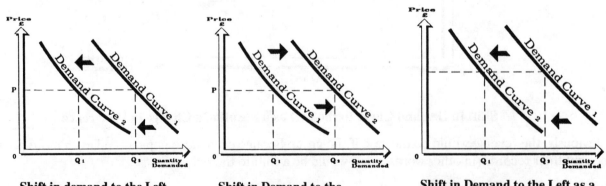

Shift in demand to the Left Resulting from a Fall in the Price of a Substitute

Shift in Demand to the Right Resulting from a Fall in the Price of a Complememt

Shift in Demand to the Left as a Result of an Increase in the Price of Other Goods Purchased by the Consumer

Elasticity of Demand

Elasticity of demand is the term that describes the responsiveness of demand to a change in price. In effect, how far will the demanded quantity stretch or shrink if its price is lowered or raised? A producer will find this information useful in two respects:

1. if s/he wishes to raise the price, s/he needs to know how many sales might be lost

2. if s/he decides to increase output, s/he will need to know by how much the price should be lowered in order to gain the extra sales that are required.

If a product has a demand which does not respond to variations in price, it is said to have an *inelastic demand*. This situation can be seen when price rises or reductions have little effect on the quantity of a product that is sold. This is a characteristic of most necessities. A substantial price increase in the price of bread means that people will still buy it, but they will make do with less of the other things. When a product does not have any close substitutes, then a rise in its price will not result in consumers switching their purchases to alternative products.

Suppliers will have as their objective the achievement of an inelastic demand curve, since this will mean that they will be able to raise their price without losing a substantial amount of custom.

The converse is true when a product has an *elastic demand*. Elastic demand occurs when even a relatively small price increase results in a substantial reduction in sales. This happens either because consumers no longer buy the product at all (this is known as the *income effect*), or because they shift their purchasing to an alternative product (this is called the *substitution effect*).

The slope of the demand curve can graphically illustrate this. (See the diagram below.)

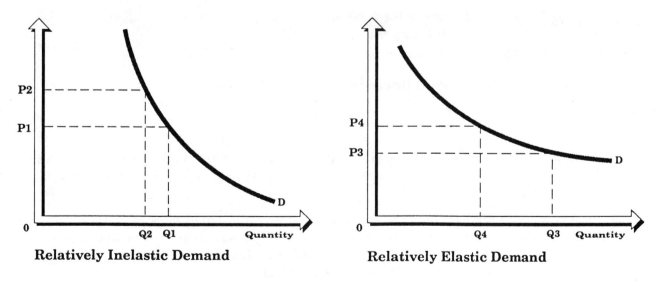

Relatively Inelastic Demand   **Relatively Elastic Demand**

Elasticity of Demand

The diagram on the left, showing a product with inelastic demand, illustrates that a relatively large price increase (from P1 to P2) will have only a limited effect on the quantity purchased (a fall in quantity from Q1 to Q2). The diagram on the right, showing a product with elastic demand, illustrates a much smaller increase in price (a rise from P3 to P4) but a much more dramatic reduction in demand (the quantity purchased falls from Q3 to Q4). Expressing this numerically, you can see that:

$$\frac{\% \text{ change in Quantity Demanded}}{\text{change in Price}} = \text{Price Elasticity of Demand}$$

A percentage change is used both for 'quantity demanded' and for 'change in price'. If you do not use a percentage, then the scale of the change in 'quantity demanded' or the price change may be deceiving. A simple example:

Price £	Quantity Demanded
5	100
6	75

In this case, an increase in price of 20% (from 5 to 6) results in a 25% fall in demand (from 100 to 75 units). This is a more than proportionate fall in demand. (Expressed simply, demand shrinks more than price stretches.) Thus demand is said to be *elastic*. The equation would show:

$$\text{Elasticity of Demand} = \frac{25\%}{20\%} = 1.25$$

If elasticity is greater than 1 (that is, demand changes in a greater proportion than price), then it is said to be elastic. A less than proportionate change would result in a figure less than 1. For example: if price rose 20% and demand fell by only 5%. This would indicate inelastic demand. The example below illustrates this.

$$\text{Elasticity of Demand} = \frac{5\% \text{ fall in quantity demanded}}{20\% \text{ price rise}} = 0.25$$

Percentages are used to avoid confusion, for example:

Price £	Quantity Demanded Units
50	10
60	7.5

The change in price may look substantially greater than the fall in demand. In fact, there is a 20% rise in price (from £50 to £60) and a 25% fall in demand (from 10 units to 7.5 units). Demand, in this case, is *elastic*, having a value of 1.25.

Products will not necessarily have the same elasticity of demand throughout a range of prices. As the price rises, the demand for a product usually becomes more elastic, because consumers tend to switch demand to cheaper substitutes. This switch in demand from one product to another can also be calculated by using what is called 'cross elasticity'. This simply illustrates how a change in the price of one product affects the demand for another product. So:

$$\text{Cross Elasticity of Demand} = \frac{\% \text{ change in quantity demanded of product A}}{\% \text{ change in price of product B}}$$

This can occur when consumers switch to cheaper substitutes, but it is also important when considering the effect of the price change of one product upon its complement. (Remember these are products which tend to be purchased together, such as cars and petrol, electricity and electric central heating.) Here a rise in the price of one product will result in the fall in demand for the other. For example, as petrol goes up in price, so demand for large petrol-hungry cars will fall.

A further variant of elasticity is that which relates to a rise or fall in income and its effect on demand for a product or service. Thus, an increase in a person's income will usually result in an increase in the demand for a product. This is more pronounced for what are referred to as 'superior goods', such as holidays and consumer durables.

Alternatively, an individual whose income rises may well demand less of an 'inferior good', such as poor quality food. This is because they are now able to purchase better quality products since they now have a higher income to spend. So, for instance, as income rises a person may buy fewer sausages but more steak.

Income elasticity can be defined as follows:

$$\text{Income Elasticity} = \frac{\% \text{ change in quantity demanded of a product}}{\% \text{ change in income}}$$

When the quantity demanded of a product *increases* positively in response to a rise in income, this is the normal, expected response and indicates that the product is acceptable or superior. If the quantity demanded of a product actually *falls* when income rises, this indicates a negative income elasticity and the product is likely to be an inferior good.

It is not only the producer who benefits from knowing how to anticipate the elasticity of demand. Clearly, the government, through its taxation policy, is extremely influential in the raising and lowering of prices. The Chancellor of the Exchequer must be aware of the likely effect, either of a change in the general level of taxation (such as increases or decreases in VAT or income tax), or of specific tax (for example, a change in the duty on petrol, alcohol or tobacco). If it is the government's objective to increase its tax yield from petrol duty, then it must be confident that the tax increase – and the consequent price increase – will not result in such a reduction in the demand for petrol that the overall tax revenue from it falls. The most appropriate goods to tax specifically, therefore, are those with inelastic demand since increasing the tax on them will not deter consumption. These products are mostly those which have no close substitutes: inevitably the Exchequer taxes products like petrol, alcohol and tobacco.

Supply

The supply of a product or service is determined by the willingness and ability of producers and suppliers to meet the demands of consumers at a variety of prices. If the price offered by consumers is relatively high, producers are willing to supply more if they can. Of course, this is not always possible: for example, the dramatic increase in house prices in the south east of England and, particularly, in Central London. Why, then, do housebuilders not respond to these higher prices by substantially increasing the number of new houses they build? In fact, many new houses have been built, but not enough to meet demand. Builders wish to build, but are restrained by the lack of suitable available land and by local authority planning restrictions.

Conversely, as the price of a product falls, the tendency is for suppliers to *reduce* production. There are three main reasons for this:

1.   efficient producers will make less profit per unit supplied

2.   inefficient suppliers will not be able to make any profit at all, and so will go out of business

3.   alternative products become more attractive to producers as they can earn a higher price for them. Consequently, suppliers transfer their productive resources to the manufacture and supply of these goods.

The pattern of the supply curve is shown in the Figure below.

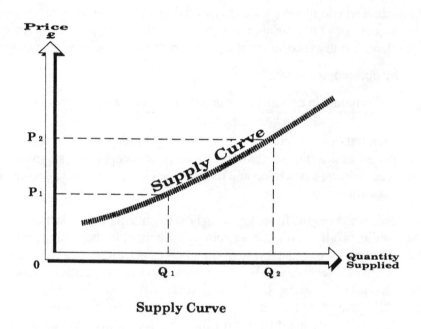

Supply Curve

There are many reasons why a producer is able to supply a certain quantity of a product at a certain price, but the main reason relates to the costs of production. Consider what will happen as a producer increases the level of output. Initially, the costs of production for each unit (referred to as the *average cost of the product*) will fall as the producer is able to take advantage of economies of scale (the more that is produced the less it costs per unit). Such *economies of scale* include bulk buying, specialisation, mechanisation and an increased ability to raise finance. Eventually, as production increases past a certain level (known as the *optimum level of production* or the most efficient level of production), these savings may decrease; it is said that the producer begins to suffer from *diseconomies of scale*. Examples of diseconomies of scale include: more problematic labour relations; the need to employ people who perhaps do not have the requisite skills for the job and an increased reliance on outside suppliers.

As in the case of demand, the supply of a product can be illustrated using either a schedule or a graph. Using the same example, Ford is willing and able to supply more Fiestas as their price increases:

Price £	Quantity Supplied per Month
8,000	45,000
7,500	35,000
7,000	28,000
6,500	20,000
6,000	13,000
5,500	5,000

Supply Schedule for Ford Fiestas

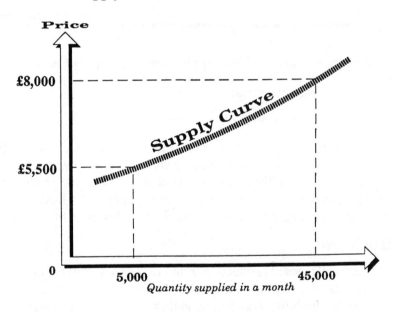

Supply Curve for Ford Fiestas

As you will notice from the figure, the supply curve usually slopes from top right to bottom left, in the opposite direction to the demand curve. The higher the price the supplier is able to achieve by selling the product, the more of it that will be produced. Now consider the factors that will influence the *supply* of goods and services.

What Determines Supply?

1. *The price of the product*

    The price that consumers are willing to pay is, obviously, the most important factor affecting the level of supply, and changes in the price that the producer can get for his products will move supply along an existing supply curve. As in the case of demand, this is technically referred to as *extensions* and *contractions of supply*. This is shown in the Figure overleaf.

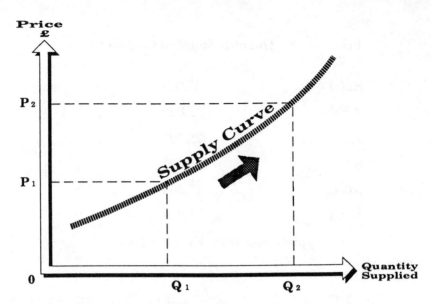

A change in price moves supply along the Supply Curve

However, there are other important determinants of supply:

2.   *The objectives of the producing business*

Many producers are not, surprisingly enough, interested in making the maximum profit. They may prefer instead to make a *satisfactory profit*. This simply may be sufficient profit to give a reasonable return on the money invested and provide the producer with a decent living, without incurring the risks associated with expanding the business. In such a case, even a price rise might not be sufficient to encourage the business to expand its production.

3.   *The cost of production*

One factor affecting all types of production is the cost of the inputs required to manufacture the product; e.g. labour, materials and power. If these inputs increase in price, then the business's level of profitability will change, and the amount of the goods or services it is willing to provide may reduce, if the price of the product does not rise proportionately.

4.   *Alternative products which the supplier might produce*

For some businesses, the choice is one of producing one product instead of another. For instance, a company producing plastic ashtrays might produce plastic dustbins. If the price of dustbins rises, and that of ashtrays does not, the business may simply transfer production from ashtrays to dustbins.

5.   *The technology which is available*

The level of available technology will influence the level of supply. If a new process is introduced, or new production machinery is developed, suppliers may be willing to increase the level of production – even though the price which can be charged remains the same. The introduction into the manufacturing process of new materials which are cheaper will have the same effect. For instance, the availability of man-made fibre has increased the willingness of shirt manufacturers to produce at a relatively low price.

6.   *The influence of government*

The government may be influential in promoting or discouraging the production of certain goods or services. An increase in the tax on cigarettes will result in a reduction in demand for the product and a consequent reduction in supply. Exporters may benefit from government help through tax concessions or subsidies.

Changes in the Supply Curve

One of the crucial factors determining the level of supply of a product is the ease with which producers can increase or decrease output in response to a rise or fall in demand and price. The supply of certain products cannot be increased quickly, even though the price has risen. If the price of apples rises in October, farmers must wait until the following harvest to raise their level of supply.

The supply of other products can be changed relatively easily. If the demand for a pop group's records increased substantially, their record company would be able to increase supply of records to the shops almost immediately. This relationship, between price and the responsiveness of supply to change, is called the *elasticity of supply*.

Movement of the Supply Curve

Just as the demand curve moves to the left or right when the factors influencing demand change, so the same is true for supply.

The following statement, then generally holds true:

* *changes in the price of a product cause a movement along an existing supply curve* (an extension or contraction of supply).

The other factors which can cause a shift in the supply curve are:

* changes in the objectives of the supplier
* changes in the cost of inputs
* changes in the price of other products that the supplier can produce
* changes in technology or the production process
* changes in government policy.

Let us consider a few possible shifts in the supply curve:

* if the supply process is revolutionised (e.g. by the introduction of robot welding machines in the production of cars), this will mean that producers are willing to produce more cars at the existing price. This would result in a shift of the *supply curve* to the right.
* conversely, an increase in the selling price of another product, which the supplier is also capable of making, may encourage manufacturers to switch production, and so result in

a shift in supply to the left. (For instance, an increase in the profit to be made from bingo encouraged many cinema owners to stop showing films and switch to bingo, which resulted in a reduction in the supply of cinemas).

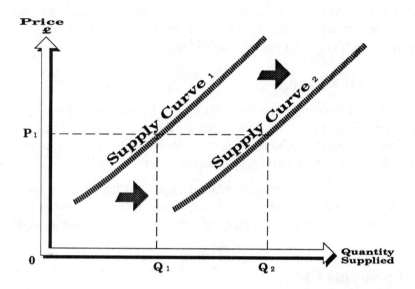

Shift in Supply to the right as a result of improved production techniques

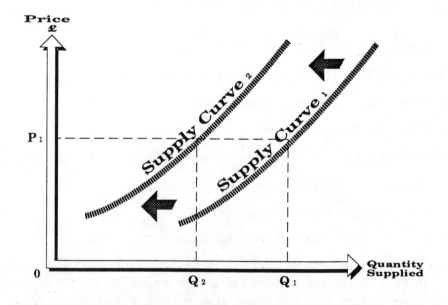

Shift in Supply to the left as a result of an increase in the price of an alternative product

The Interaction of Demand and Supply

The market is made by the combination of supply and demand for a product or service. All that the market does is that it fixes a price at which consumers are willing to buy; this price is equal to the amount that suppliers are willing to produce. As you can see in the Figure below, there is a point at which the price (£6,500) attracts 20,000 buyers, and this is also the price at which Ford is willing to supply 20,000 cars. The level of supply equals the level of demand: the market is said to be in *equilibrium*. Both consumers and suppliers are satisfied. There are no consumers willing to pay £6,500 for a Fiesta who cannot get one. In other words, there is no shortage of supply. Similarly, Ford does not have any excess stock which it cannot sell at that price, so there is no surplus production.

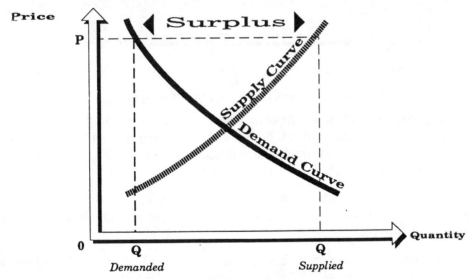

Price set too high causing a surplus of supply

This situation is fine in theory, but in practice what often happens is that there is an excess of demand over supply or vice versa. This is because the price which is set (usually by the producer) is not the equilibrium price. The following Figures illustrate this more clearly.

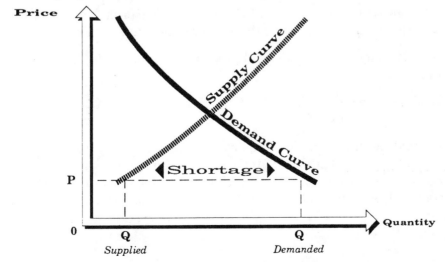

Price set too low causing a shortage of supply

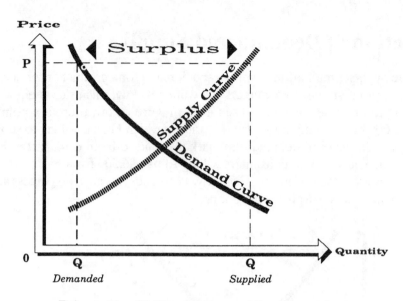

Price set too high causing a surplus of supply

In the two diagrams, the producer has misjudged demand when setting the price of the product. The first Figure illustrates a situation in which the producer has set a price which is too high: it will not, therefore, attract sufficient buyers to meet the level of supply which the manufacturer wishes to create. The result is a *surplus* of products and the producer is left with unsold goods.

In the second Figure, the producer has underestimated demand and the result is a shortage. The producer has more customers than the business is willing to supply at that price; the result is a shortage of products and a line of disappointed customers.

In situations such as this, what usually happens is that the supplier responds quickly and readjusts the price:

- *upwards* if there is an evident shortage of the product

- *downwards* if it is necessary to eliminate a *surplus*.

In either case, this moves the price closer to the equilibrium position.

An alternative course of action is to change the *level of supply*. If there is a surplus, the manufacturer reduces the level of supply and so shifts the supply curve to the left and finds a new equilibrium.

In the case of a shortage, the manufacturer responds by increasing output, if this is possible, and the new equilibrium is established.

The demand curve can also shift because of changes in the factors that are influencing demand, and the equilibrium position can change because of this.

In theory, the market should, eventually, reach an equilibrium position, where supply meets demand at a price which satisfies both consumer and producer. At the point of equilibrium, there are no sellers who do not find a buyer and no buyers who cannot find a seller. However, in the real world, most markets are not in equilibrium. You constantly see 'cut price offers' (indicating excess supply), queues (indicating excess demand), or stockpiling.

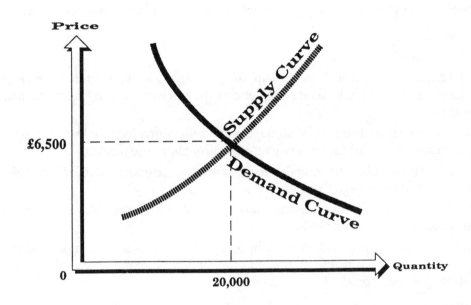

Demand and Supply Curves for Ford Fiestas showing market equilibrium

Different Forms of Market

The process of supply and demand, and the interaction between the two, determines a market price for a product. However, to say this is to assume that there is always a perfectly free market in operation, something that, in real life, exists only rarely.

To achieve this perfectly free interaction between buyers and sellers, there must be many buyers who are all in competition to buy the producer's goods. There must also be many sellers, all of whom are competing for the consumer's custom. This, again, is rarely the case. In most of the product markets in the UK today, you will normally find only a few major suppliers who dominate the market, a lack of competition that can have serious disadvantages for the consumer. This type of market is described as an *oligopoly* but, before you look at such markets, consider some of the other different market structures which exist – at least in theory.

Perfectly Competitive Markets

If a situation existed where there were many buyers and many sellers, all competing against each other for products of a similar quality, and the contractual terms offered and accepted were all relatively similar, you could say that the market was perfectly competitive.

In reality, there are few circumstances where such a situation exists and there is so-called *perfect competition*. However, this model can be useful in measuring the competitiveness of other markets. For a perfectly competitive market to exist, seven conditions would have to be fulfilled. These would be:

- many sellers
- many buyers
- no seller or buyer who is either supplying or buying a significantly large share of the market, so that no individual is influencing the price of the product or the market as a whole
- an awareness, on the part of all buyers and sellers involved, of the contractual terms (including the price) that is being offered throughout the market
- freedom for suppliers to enter the market and produce goods – if there is sufficient profit incentive to encourage them to do this
- similar freedom for existing suppliers to leave the market if they believe there is insufficient profit to be made
- relatively similar products, offered by all producers, which are comparable in terms of price, quality, delivery, etc. so that no supplier enjoys a competitive advantage through offering a better product.

If these conditions were met, in theory there would be competition between suppliers for potential customers and, as a result, the price would be kept as low as possible. The most efficient suppliers, those who can keep their production costs down, will make the most profit and so be able to pay the highest wages; high wages will, in turn, attract the best labour; higher profits mean higher rents can be afforded – so the business will secure the prime locations, produce the best products and make the most profit. Other, less efficient producers, will be less cost-effective and so will make less profit. The least efficient will make no profit and will, consequently, be driven out of business.

Perfect competition will therefore:

- encourage efficiency in production
- keep prices down for consumers.

Perfect competition rarely exists in the real world. It is, however, a useful concept for explaining the behaviour of markets. When a market does not have the characteristics of perfect competition, there will be a tendency for one side of the market to gain significant advantages – and such advantages are usually to the benefit of the producer.

Imperfectly Competitive Markets

The concept of the optimum, or most efficient, production level is important in determining how many producers will be able effectively to compete in a market and, by implication, how competitive it is. If the optimum level of production in an industry is such that one producer can meet total market demand, it is likely that only one producer will exist. In such a situation a *monopoly* will evolve. If one supplier's optimum production is such that only a proportion of market demand can be supplied, a few suppliers may end up sharing the market, and what is termed an *oligopoly* will evolve.

In the UK economy, most markets for manufactured products are oligopolies. Here a relatively few dominant suppliers are in a powerful position and can, therefore, dictate contractual terms to the buyer. The consumer has little influence on the selling price of the product, and in many cases the manufacturer determines the product range which will be offered to the consumer.

A perfect example of this practice can be seen in the market for washing powders and detergents. The market is a two-company oligopoly dominated by Procter and Gamble and Unilever. There appears to be considerable competition between these two giants, but this competition rarely involves the price of the product. Both companies see it as being in their mutual best interest to keep washing powder prices high and to compete through advertising rather than through price. Such behaviour is common in many markets and, because of this, both the government, through agencies such as the Office of Fair Trading and the Monopolies and Mergers Commission, and the courts have occasionally sought to redress the balance between the unequal bargaining position of consumers and suppliers.

In the following diagram we show the different types of market that exist, and their respective structures.

Market Form	Nature
a. Perfect Competition (Price Takers' Market)	Many producers with similar products. Many consumers, therefore high level of competition with prices determined by the market.
b. Imperfect Competition	
i. Imperfectly Competitive Market	Many producers but with different products.
ii. Oligopoly (Price Searchers' Market)	Few producers with relatively similar products. Normally many consumers but producers are in the dominant position, particularly if they work together. Price often determined by major price leader with other firms following suit.
c. Monopoly (Price Makers' Market)	One producer with individual product different from others. If product is in high level of demand then single producer is able to charge what the market will bear

Theoretically, all of these market forms can exist, and all are to some extent found in the UK. However, the most important form of market structure in this country is the oligopoly. It has been estimated that about 20 of the 22 main industrial and service sectors of the UK economy are oligopolies. Thus, in the case of most of the goods and services you purchase, choice is limited to those supplied by a few major companies. This may not always appear to be true, because oligopolists often produce a range of brands of the same type of product. They try to create *brand differentiation*. Consumers see a wide variety of brands on the supermarket shelf and believe, when they choose a 'rival' product, that they are purchasing from a different manufacturer. In fact, both brands are made by the same company. The washing powder market is a prime example of oligopoly.

This does not always not always mean that consumers do not have a choice. They are able to choose between a number of retail outlets. At this stage (that is, prior to entering into a contract for goods or services), the consumer may be able to buy from numerous shops or supermarkets. It is at the production stage, however, that the oligopoly market form is most evident. Most consumer durables, such as fridges, TVs, cookers, etc, are produced by a relatively small number of companies. Most of the processed food you eat is canned, if not actually grown, by big companies such as Heinz or Cavenham.

The Formation of Oligopoly Markets

Oligopoly markets have evolved as massive companies have grown up. These businesses dominate most markets. Their growth is the result of economies of scale gained from large-scale production. As output increases, the average cost of production falls as businesses are able to use more specialist methods of manufacture, mass production or increased mechanisation.

Essentially, such investment in new plant, machinery and methods means that a producer may be much more efficient, in terms of cost per individual item made, if it produces on a very large scale, rather than if it only makes a few units of production. The cost of the factory rent, rates, etc must be paid whatever the level of production, so if more is produced, the initial (or fixed) cost is shared out over more products. To a great extent, it is the size at which the plant or factory is most efficient – its *optimum size* – which determines how large it will become and how much of the market it can supply.

The Level of Market Concentration

The growth of oligopolies is very pronounced in the UK economy. This growth is measured by the *level of concentration* in individual markets. This indicates how many producers supply a large percentage of the total market demand. A high degree of concentration, with only a few producers supplying most of the market, indicates an oligopoly. A low level of concentration suggests production is shared among many suppliers and, therefore, competition is, presumably, greater.

Does an oligopoly market always mean that there is a lack of competition? Obviously, from the examples already given, you will realise that there is some competition between oligopolists.

Competition can be seen in the continuous advertising campaigns by which the market leaders attempt to maintain or extend their market share. Their aim is to try to tie consumers to the producer's particular brand. Often, such brand names are considerably more expensive than those products which are not extensively marketed. Branded products in supermarkets are normally about 10% more expensive than the supermarket's own label, which is usually not heavily marketed. In the washing powder market, it is estimated that 40% of the total selling price is accounted for by advertising costs. This also means that Procter and Gamble, and its main rival Unilever, are always among the top twenty largest spenders on advertising in the UK.

Manufacturers use sales gimmicks, such as competitions and free gifts, to attract and hold customers. However, does the consumer really benefit from this type of competition? The main advantage to the consumer of fierce competition is that prices will tend to be kept as low as possible. Suppliers will be forced to reduce profit margins in order to attract new custom through low prices. If this were true in oligopoly markets, there would be little cause for concern. However, as you have seen, the oligopolist's main concern is with maintaining a market share which allows the business to produce at an optimum level. If it has reached this level, an oligopolist will have no incentive to lower the price. Competition through advertising is an attempt to maintain market share (and maintain output at optimum size), rather that to increase it. It is only when a new competitor tries to enter the market and tries to become established, that a price war develops from which the consumer just might benefit.

Supplier Dominance

It is the consumer who generally loses out in an oligopoly situation and dominant suppliers who will be able to demonstrate market power. The consumer is in an unequal bargaining position for two reasons:

- lack of choice – the consumer is restricted to a limited number of suppliers
- lack of competition – there is no effective competitive drive between the dominant suppliers.

The Continued Growth of Oligopoly Markets

The UK has the highest degree of market concentration (i.e. the greatest number of oligopolistic industries) in the world. This trend is continuing and will not be reversed unless either:

- new producers enter the market, thereby reducing concentration; or
- the government takes steps to prevent the extension of oligopolies.

In 1991 the Monopolies and Mergers Commission carried out its biggest ever investigation, into the supply of cars. Its report largely absolved car manufacturers of profiteering and keeping the price of their products artificially high, a conclusion that was fiercely condemned by the Consumers' Association as a 'sell out'. The Consumers' Association agreed with those aspects of the MMC report which criticised the manufacturers' policy that restricted dealers to their own product only as well as the informal arrangement that limited the import of Japanese cars to 11% of the UK market. The Consumers' Association wishes to see the system of exclusive franchises abandoned and a completely free market develop.

New Suppliers Entering the Market

New suppliers find it difficult to enter an existing market. Eddie Shah's attempt, in 1986, to enter the capital-intensive newspaper market with *Today* , required him to make large-scale investment in the new technology which would allow him to print the paper cheaply; Shah had also to institute a major (and costly) advertising campaign on TV in order to attract readers away from their existing newspapers. Initially, *Today* was commercially unsuccessful, but Shah lacked the resources to run it at a loss for a long enough period of time that would allow the paper to properly establish itself. This forced him to sell control to Rupert Murdoch; now that the paper is making a profit, this is earned by Murdoch's International News group, which publishes the *Sun, News of the World, Times* and *Sunday Times*. One of the main forms of new competition is entry into the market by a foreign competitor. An example of this has been in the car industry, where the market dominance of Ford, Rover Group and Vauxhall has been challenged by the *market penetration* of Japanese car manufacturers. The effects upon UK oligopolies of entry into the Single Market looks likely to be interesting, as domestic oligopolists and their European competitors already jockey for position under the watchful eyes of the European Commissioner for Competition.

1. What is the *market*?

2. Define *demand* and *supply*.

3. List and explain the five factors which determine demand.

4. Sketch and label a demand curve.

5. On a graph show the effect on the demand curve of:

    - changes in price

    - change in income

    - a change in the price of other goods.

6. Explain what is meant by *elasticity of demand*.

7. Note down the formula for calculating *price elasticity of demand*.

8. What do you understand by *cross elasticity of demand*?

9. Define *income elasticity*.

10. List *three* reasons for suppliers reducing production.

11. Sketch and label a supply curve.

12. List and explain the six determinants of supply.

13. Describe factors which can cause a shift in the supply curve.

14. Describe the effect of a shifting supply curve.

15. What do you understand by the equilibrium?

16. Describe the main features of an oligopoly.

17. What conditions exist in a perfectly competitive market?

18. In a diagram, show the different types of market that can exist.

19. How are oligopolies formed?

20. Explain the role of the Monopolies and Mergers Commission.

The Shaping of the UK Economy 1979 to the Present

In the period 1945 to 1979, both the Labour and Conservative parties enjoyed some success at General Elections. For over three decades, there had been some form of consensus amongst all of the UK political parties; all believed, to a greater or lesser extent, in a corporate state and mechanisms of planning and in tripartite committees that represented industry, the unions and government (e.g. The National Economic Development Office).

Post-war governments

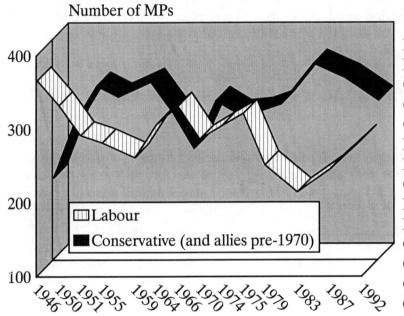

Number of MPs

Labour

Conservative (and allies pre-1970)

Winning Parties and their majorities

Labour, Attlee, majority: 147
Labour, Attlee, majority: 6
Conservative, Churchill, majority: 16
Conservative, Eden, majority: 59
Conservative, Macmillan, majority: 99
Labour, Wilson, majority: 5
Labour, Wilson, majority: 97
Conservative, Heath, majority: 31
Labour, Wilson, no overall majority
Labour, Wilson, majority: 5
Conservative, Thatcher, majority: 44
Conservative, Thatcher, majority: 144
Conservative, Thatcher, majority: 101
Conservative, Major, majority: 21

After the tenth post-war election, in 1979, over three terms in office, the Conservative governments led by Margaret Thatcher, set about dismantling many of these mechanisms. By the time she left office in October, 1990, she had abolished exchange controls, the City had been deregulated ('Big Bang'), and most of the planning system was gone.

The events that have taken place in the UK since 1979 have been, at least partially, dictated by international events that took place before that date. In common with governments in other countries, British governments have tried to reduce public spending substantially. There are three principal reasons for them wanting to do so:

1. The depression that was begun by the oil price rises in the early 1970s resulted in a depression. Government, faced with much higher unemployment figures and the need for government to give financial support to industry throughout the remainder of the decade, needed to cut back in the years after 1979.

2. Much of government expenditure, such as pension payments and unemployment benefit (usually called 'transfers'), automatically rose as the rate of inflation rose. When an economy is contracting (as the UK's was in 1979 to 1983), then such indexed payments account for a larger share of the country's gross domestic product (GDP).

3. The changing structure (or demography) of the UK's population can be seen in the large increase in the number of pension-age dependants the country has to 'pay'; the number has risen, both in absolute terms and as a proportion of the population. (Some of the implications of this 'demographic time bomb' are explored in Part Four.)

The Policies of UK Governments: their Economic Objectives in Theory and Practice

The 'Great Depression' of the 1930s plunged the UK into an unparalleled economic crisis. Mass unemployment, social deprivation, bankruptcy and economic decline faced the British people, while the government sat back and allowed market forces to take their course. There was little attempt at overall management of the economy because:

- the causes of the depression were not fully understood

- the government did not have the policy instruments capable of rectifying matters.

The Setting of Objectives

A major step forward in understanding the causes of depression came from John Maynard Keynes, an economist, who published his famous book, *The General Theory of Employment, Interest and Money* in 1936. Keynes was severely critical of the lack of government intervention to ameliorate the depression: in fact, Keynes argued, government only made matters worse by reducing public expenditure. Keynes raged:

> 'The Government's programme is as foolish as it is wrong . . . Not only is purchasing power to be curtailed, but road building, housing and the like are to be retrenched. Local authorities are to follow suit. If the theory which underlines all this is to be accepted, the end will be that no one can be employed, except those happy few who grow their own potatoes, as a result of refusing, for reasons of economy, to buy the services of anyone else . .'

(JM Keynes: *Essays in Persuasion, 1931*)

By 1944 the Government was willing to publish the economic objectives which would be pursued by post-war governments. It committed itself to the role of managing the economy and ensuring that certain basic objectives were sought. It stated:

> *'The Government believe that, once the war has been won, we can make a fresh approach, with better chances of success than ever before, to the task of maintaining a high and stable level of employment without sacrificing the essential liberties of a free society. '*

(Government White Paper on Employment Policy, 1944)

Four objectives formed the cornerstones for successive governments from the mid-1940s until 1979:

- a high and stable level of employment

- price stability

- economic growth

- a balance of payments equilibrium.

The Conflict of Objectives: the Economic Problems of the UK

The only question was whether all four objectives could be met at the same time. For example, high levels of employment can increase the level of demand in the economy. This can then lead to rising inflation which may cause a fall in business confidence as business people are deterred by increasing costs. As their confidence in the future is weakened, they become less likely to invest in new projects or re-invest in existing ones. This decline in investment results in consequent job losses. It was necessary, therefore, for governments to choose a combination of policy objectives which would be at once politically acceptable and economically viable.

In reality, the conflict between these objectives proved to be less problematic than had been anticipated, at least in the relatively stable and prosperous 1950s and 1960s. It is true that, while these decades did not produce for the UK the spectacular economic growth experienced by Germany and Japan, production gradually increased and the effects of inflation and unemployment were not felt. The balance of payments was a problem but, in a period of cheap energy and raw materials, the comparatively small trade deficits were insignificant ripples on a calm economic sea.

The full impact of the problem economy was not felt until the late 1970s, when the objectives became much more difficult to attain. What were the major problems facing the economy and what were their underlying causes?

Objective 1: A High and Stable Level of Employment

The first objective was to create high and stable levels of employment. Since 1979, however, the UK has faced rapidly increasing unemployment. By the early 1980s levels of unemployment, unknown since the depression of the 1930s, were being experienced. More disturbing was the increase in long-term unemployment.

The late 1980s saw a decline in the number of unemployed, but numbers began to rise again in 1990. The number of unemployed rose steadily throughout 1992; at the time of writing they have falling for six consecutive months but still stand at over 2 million. Let us now examine the causes of the unemployment which has hit the UK particularly hard. An examination of the unemployment figures for the last thirty years offers an opportunity to pinpoint just when the dramatic rise began; it allows us also to isolate some of its causes. The figures below show this change:

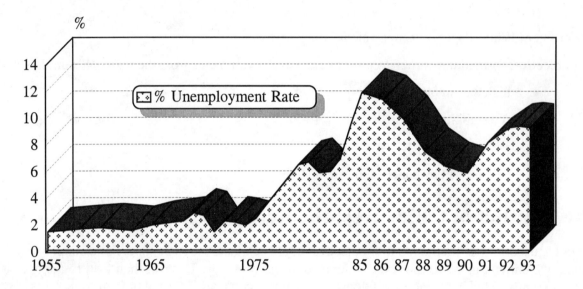

Unemployment is shown as a percentage of the workforce: between 1955 and 1970 it remained between 1% and 2%. It would be wrong, however, to assume that recent governments have attempted to place 100% of the workforce in employment: when the government states that it 'seeks to achieve full employment', it is describing a situation where there are more vacancies than there are people actively looking for work.

Of course, some of those who seek work will not always be able to find the exact job they want, at the wage they require, or in the area where they live. Thus, in the 1950s and 1960s, when this country was described as having full employment, there were areas in the country, such as Scotland, the North East of England and South Wales, where unemployment rates were above the national average. This is described as regional unemployment.

Unemployment is, in fact, often categorised according to its causes. There are four main categories:

- frictional unemployment
- seasonal unemployment
- structural unemployment
- cyclical unemployment.

Frictional unemployment

Temporary breaks from employment, lasting a comparatively short time, are known as *frictional unemployment*. It does not usually lead to the social problems associated with long-term unemployment. As long as the frictionally unemployed form only a small proportion of the workforce, the effects on overall productive output are minimal. In fact, the movement of workers to more efficient and rewarding jobs is often encouraged by government.

Seasonal unemployment

Some industries tend to operate seasonally and so those who work in such employment will find themselves temporarily unemployed in the 'off season' e.g. agriculture and building workers. It is not a major problem in the UK, although it does cause hardship for those whose jobs are seasonal.

Structural unemployment

This is a long-term version of frictional unemployment: it exists mainly because of immobility in the labour market. This results from basic changes in the demand and supply for goods and services in the economy. For example, the textile industry has suffered widespread unemployment as a result of foreign competition from South East Asia.

Much regional unemployment can be explained by the decline in demand for the products of the basic industries which predominated in those areas. In areas such as Scotland, South Wales and the North East of England the decline of coal, steel and shipbuilding has been particularly marked. Such unemployment, resulting in deep structural changes in demand patterns, is often difficult to solve in the short-term, given the existing immobility of labour.

Structural unemployment may result from supply changes; for instance, a reduction in the demand for a particular type of labour created by the introduction of robot machines. This is known as technological unemployment. Similarly, technological advances in the printing industry have meant that computer typesetting and compositing of newspapers is now perfectly feasible, a process which was bitterly resisted by the Fleet Street print and graphics unions. Technological unemployment will always occur in a dynamic economy but, often, attitudes to change are deeply influenced by the general level of unemployment in the economy.

Cyclical unemployment

The economy has always followed a cyclical pattern, alternating from boom to slump, with levels of unemployment reflecting this cyclical trend. This cyclical pattern in the post-1945 period has been less well defined.

Cyclical unemployment is the result of an overall lack of aggregate demand for goods and services in the economy. The business cycle has tended in the past to follow this fairly regular pattern. However, since the middle 1970s, the UK has been faced with continuous and growing large-scale unemployment. This is, partly, as a result of world recession but, partly, as a result of government attempts to reduce the level of inflation by lowering aggregate demand in the economy.

Objective 2: Price Stability

The general level of prices can change in either a downward (deflationary) or upward (inflationary) direction. Deflationary trends occurred in recent UK history when prices fell for much of the pre-war period, rising only after 1935. The post-war period, however, has been one of continuous inflation, as the table below shows.

UK Inflation Rates 1960-1993

Year	% Increase	Year	% Increase
1960	1.2	1977	15.8
1961	2.7	1978	8.3
1962	3.2	1979	13.4
1963	1.7	1980	18.0
1964	3.9	1981	11.9
1965	4.7	1982	8.6
1966	3.7	1983	4.6
1967	2.4	1984	5.0
1968	4.8	1985	6.1
1969	5.2	1986	3.4
19 70	6.4	1987	4.2
1971	9.4	1988	4.9
1972	7.1	1989	7.5
1973	9.2	1990	7.7
1974	16.1	1991	9.0
1975	24.2	1992	4.1
1976	16.5	1993	1.8

What is inflation?

A simple definition of inflation is 'a rise in the level of prices that is sustained over a period of time'. The definition tells us nothing about why inflation is regarded by business, government and nation as undesirable or even evil: it is because inflation makes goods and services more expensive for the business to provide, thereby making the business less competitive. Similarly, on a national scale, if the goods of 'UK plc' become more expensive in comparison to those of 'Japan Inc.' or 'Germany Ltd.', then UK exports become less attractive to consumers whatever country those consumers are in.

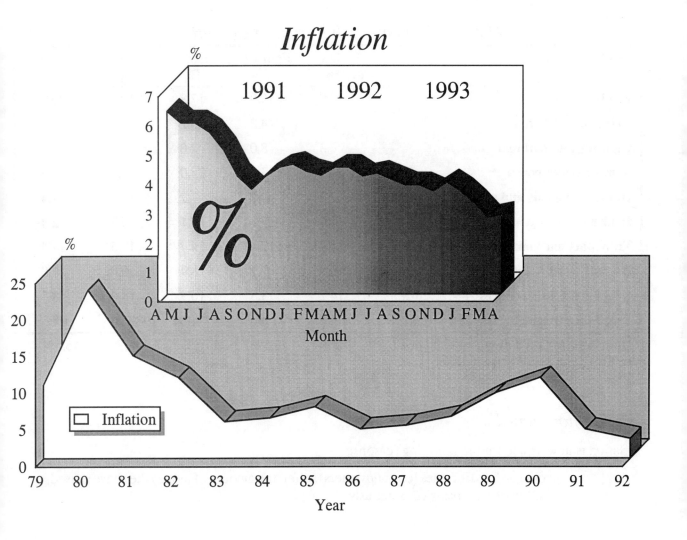

How is it measured?

The rate of inflation in the UK is measured using the Retail Price Index (RPI) which is a monthly index that shows the annual percentage change in consumer prices. The index is made up of a 'basket' of goods and services, the prices of which are monitored on a monthly basis. The individual items which make up the 'basket' do not, however, have an equal weighting in the index: in the UK food has a weighting of 13.9% whilst recreation and education has a weighting of 8.5%. This results in an increase in food prices exerting a greater effect on the RPI than the same percentage increase in the price of recreation and education. The weightings signify the importance of each of the items in the average monthly family budget.

Our partners in the EC have different lifestyles and preferences, and so use different weightings to those used in the UK Retail Price Index. This difference in practice gives rise to potential difficulties in accurately comparing the rates of inflation in different European countries.

How we Compare with European Countries

Product/Services	UK %	France %	Germany %	Italy %	Spain %
Food	13.9	19.9	17.8	19.6	29.8
Drink and Tobacco	6.7	4.8	5.2	3.2	3.2
Clothing and footwear	6.3	8.0	7.0	10.8	8.7
Rent, fuel and power	23.8	13.8	25.0	7.6	18.6
Household goods and services	7.2	7.6	7.2	10.6	7.4
Health costs	1.6	7.5	4.1	6.7	2.4
Transport and communications	17.8	17.4	14.4	13.5	14.4
Recreation and education	8.5	7.7	8.4	10.0	7.0
Other goods and services	14.2	13.3	10.9	18.0	8.5
Year index weighted	1990	1990	1985	1989/90	1983

	UK	France	Germany	Italy	Spain
Housing costs excluding fuel and power in European retail price indices	17.2%	8.5%	17.8%	4.6%	15.5%

Why it's not wanted ...

Inflation is unwelcome for the following reasons:

- people on fixed incomes (e.g. pensioners) suffer: the amount of money they have is fixed, whilst prices are rising continuously

- lenders lose; borrowers gain

- speculative investment in property and commodities becomes more attractive than investment in industry

- international trade competitiveness is reduced, since exports become relatively more expensive and imports become relatively cheaper.

How high is it?

The rate of inflation can vary enormously, from zero (which is rare), to a small part of a percentage point ('creeping inflation'), to rises in double, treble or (rarely) four figures ('hyperinflation', as in Germany in the 1930s or in Bosnia, Serbia and Russia today). An indication of inflation can be gained by looking at *The United Kingdom in Figures*, a collection of statistics published annually by the Government Statistical Office. A glance at the table, 'Internal Purchasing Power of the Pound', will show you that what you would pay £1 to buy in 1990, could have been bought for 2p in 1914, 10p in 1960, 53p in 1980 and 91p in 1989. The highest measured rate of inflation that has occurred in the UK was 26.9% in 1974-5 which, though unacceptably high, compares very favourably with the world's highest recorded rate of (hyper)inflation: in Germany in 1923 inflation reached 755%.

The 1960s were successful years in achieving relative price stability. Only from the late '60s did the pace of inflation quicken, reaching a peak of nearly 27% in August 1975. Since then, the trend has varied upwards and then downwards again to its present level of around 4.0%. Currently, the trend is downward: inflation fell from 9% in January 1991 to 1.4% by mid-1993. Inflation has been a world-wide problem in the post-war period and its causes are difficult to identify. Currently, the UK is improving its inflationary tendency relative to some of its major competitors, like Germany, though it must improve its performance even further to match low-inflation competitors like Japan.

UK Inflation compared to its trading rivals: 1991

	Year on Year Increase %
Italy	6.0
EC average	4.9
UK	4.5
Germany	4.2
US	3.1
France	3.1
Japan	2.9

What causes it?

Two basic theories have emerged on the causes of inflation:

- demand-pull inflation
- cost-push inflation.

There are other explanations, including that of the monetarists who place the cause of inflation in a much wider social and economic context.

Demand-pull inflation

One view of inflation is that changes in the price level are linked to changes in aggregate demand and supply. By *aggregate demand* is meant the total demand for goods and services. *Aggregate* supply is simply the total supply of such goods and services.

Keynes was concerned with situations where a very low level of aggregate demand resulted in massive cyclical unemployment. As aggregate demand expanded, producers responded by increasing their production of goods and services, thereby increasing aggregate supply and reducing the level of unemployment. The general level of prices remained unchanged as output increased. However, as the economy approaches its full employment level it becomes increasingly difficult for output (*aggregate supply*) to continue to expand smoothly in response to increases in aggregate demand.

Clearly, an economy is made up of many different sectors and production difficulties will be experienced in some sectors before it is felt in others. In the same way, some markets will begin to show symptoms of excess demand and, gradually, more sectors will reach this situation, until aggregate demand in the overall economy generally exceeds the aggregate supply that the economy is capable of producing with full employment. At this point, when output cannot expand further, the effect of excess demand is to put pressure on prices.

The mechanism by which excess demand results in prices being increased can be briefly illustrated as follows:

If overall aggregate demand exceeds aggregate supply in the economy, this will manifest itself in a number of ways which can be observed in the various sectors.

For example: unemployment is low; numerous job vacancies exist; overtime is offered and worked by employees; shortages of goods exist.

These conditions will affect producers in two ways:

- There will be a vigorous demand for labour which enables the trade unions to press for, and obtain, higher wages for their members. Employers concede these increases, which are then passed on to consumers in higher prices

- A response to market demand is sometimes made directly by producers raising their prices to what the market will bear.

Prices then begin to increase in the overall economy and, as the inflationary process begins, something else starts to happen: expectations reinforce price rises. This effect is created by both the worker and by the consumer. In wage negotiations, unions will, naturally, demand a higher settlement if they anticipate a rise in the level of prices in the coming year. This reinforces the increase in wages and, once again, prices rise. Workers will either spend the cash they have or borrow; in either case, it will simply add to overall aggregate demand in the economy.

Cost-push inflation

An alternative explanation for increases in inflation is that the inflationary stimulus does not come from the demand side of the economy but from the supply side. Inflation is caused by increases in the costs of the factors of production which, in turn, leads to producers passing on their cost increases to consumers as higher prices. The original increases in costs may be caused by:

- trade unions pushing up wages ahead of what is justified by productivity

- independent increases in the costs of raw materials.

Successive governments of differing political persuasions have tried to lay the blame for inflation on trade unions. Recent evidence indicates that, for most of the 1970s, the objective of trade unions was one of simply trying to maintain wage levels in line with inflation, rather than trying to outstrip inflation with excessive pay demands.

Monetary Causes of Inflation

'Monetarist' economists, such as Milton Friedman, see the cause of inflation as an excessive increase in the money supply. Put simply, any increase in the quantity of money in circulation leads, after a time lag, (during which real output may change), to increases in the level of prices, and *vice versa*.

If money supply increases by a greater proportion than the increase in the output of goods and services, then inflation will result.

Causes of Recent Inflation in the UK

Several factors can be suggested as the possible cause(s) of inflation in the UK in the 1970s and 1980s. First, examine the evidence for demand-pull inflation, using the statistical indicators of excess demand. You will see that unemployment levels have been extremely high and rising in the 1970s and 1980s, compared with earlier decades. The conclusion must be that excess demand is not the cause of inflation.

Alternatively, consider the cost-push theory. There are two possible explanations:

- wage-push inflation
- a rise in import prices.

Wage-push

The 1970s and 1980s certainly saw an increase in wage levels. These are illustrated in the table below:

Percentage changes in wage rates

Year	% change	Year	% change	Year	% change	Year	% change
1961	4.2	1971	12.9	1981	12.9	1991	8.0
1962	3.6	1972	13.8	1982	9.4	1992	4.9 (est.)
1963	4.8	1973	13.7	1983	8.4		
1964	4.8	1974	19.8	1984	6.0		
1965	4.3	1975	29.5	1985	8.5		
1966	4.6	1976	19.3	1986	7.9		
1967	3.9	1977	6.6	1987	7.8		
1968	6.6	1978	14.1	1988	8.7		
1969	5.3	1979	14.9	1989	9.1		
1970	9.9	1980	11.4	1990	9.7		

Source: 'Economic Trends', April 1991

At first sight, the statistics seem to suggest evidence of a wages explosion (from 1970 onwards) which resulted in higher prices after an appropriate time lag. Other statistics, such as those detailing industrial disputes, seem to suggest a more militant attitude on the part of the unions. There is no doubt that, superficially at least, the evidence for wage-push is inviting. But, on closer inspection, the argument is less compelling. For example, once inflation gets under way, it becomes difficult to clearly distinguish cause and effect. It may have been that wages were merely responding to anticipated inflation, rather than causing it. Furthermore, monetarist economists conclude that monetary expansion is essential to permit wage-push inflation to continue. But, even if this is true in principle, in practice governments may not react by allowing unemployment to rise to levels that are sufficient to damp down wage settlements.

Rise in import prices

An alternative, or complementary, cost-push cause, is seen in the rise in import prices which occurred after the early 1970s. One major element in inflation was the rise in oil prices, which led to increased production costs, which in turn resulted in higher prices, which led to a stimulation for wage increases – which thereby fuelled wage-push inflation.

The truth is that inflation is probably caused by many factors which interact with each other. This complexity makes identifying the cause extremely difficult and gives rise to governments looking for easy, obvious targets – whether they be irresponsible trade unions or excessive growth in the money supply. It is this difficulty in determining the underlying cause of inflation which results in conflicting approaches to solutions.

Objective 3: Economic Growth

Only by achieving growth in production can the UK economy provide people with an increase in their wealth and standard of living. UK post-war growth has been relatively low: 2 to 3% in good years and 0% (or even a negative figure) in poor years. Even in the late 1980s, when growth figures were reasonably impressive, much of its benefit was lost to foreign suppliers.

The reasons for the UK's poor performance are tied in with the reasons for economic growth itself. Long-term growth represents an increase in potential aggregate supply and so, initially, it is determined by the economic resources available to the economy, together with their efficient and full utilisation. Capital, and how it is used, is probably the most decisive factor of production in determining growth rates.

Objective 4: Balance of Payments Equilibrium

The UK has also experienced fluctuating fortunes in trying to achieve a balance of payments equilibrium. In the early 1960s, the balance of trade deteriorated into increasing deficit, resulting in the devaluation of the pound in 1967. Thereafter, a trade surplus resulted, but this did not last beyond the early 1970s. In the early 1970s the current account moved into massive deficit, reaching almost £3.55 billion in 1974. This was the result of many factors, most important of which were the price rises in primary products (especially oil) and the decline in the growth of world trade. To some extent, these deficits were alleviated by surpluses on 'invisibles', but that still left an unfavourable overall deficit. This was resolved by relying on both overseas borrowing and drawing on official reserves of foreign currency.

The years after 1977 showed a considerable improvement, reaching a current account surplus of over £2.5 billion in 1980. An important element in this improvement has been the effect of North Sea oil in reducing the petroleum trade deficit.

More recently, the balance of payments has plunged into deficit again: in 1991 the deficit had decreased to £4.4 billion on the current account, from a £15.2 billion deficit in the previous year. This substantial improvement was due, in part, to an increase in visible exports, which drove the volume of sales abroad to record levels. The deficit on manufactures fell to £3.5 billion in 1991, from a peak of £11.4 billion the previous year. However, the chief contributor to this improved situation was the UK economic recession, which resulted in a reduced demand for visible goods, especially manufacturing inputs: the deficit in these goods dropped sharply from a 1990 deficit of £18.7 billion to a 1991 figure of £10 billion.

The government claimed in the 1980s that the international market would sort itself out and that the situation was not one to cause any grievous concern. Many economists in the 1990s would strongly disagree with that assertion. The parlous situation in which the UK finds itself is exemplified when the focus is placed on a single area of the economy, such as food and drink. The graphs below illustrate all too clearly the lack of competitiveness shown in what were, until recently, traditionally strong areas of the economy.

UK's gap in food and drink

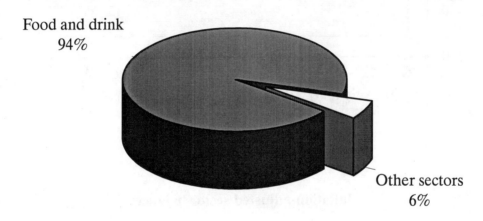

Food and drink
94%

Other sectors
6%

UK: total deficit £5.8bn 1991

Balance by country

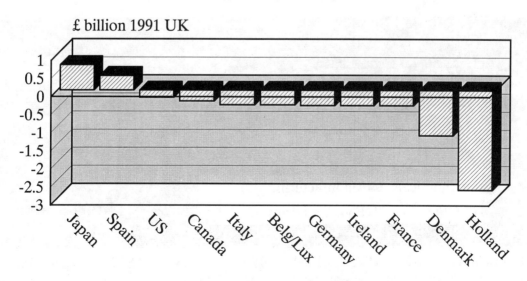

£ billion 1991 UK

Balance by product

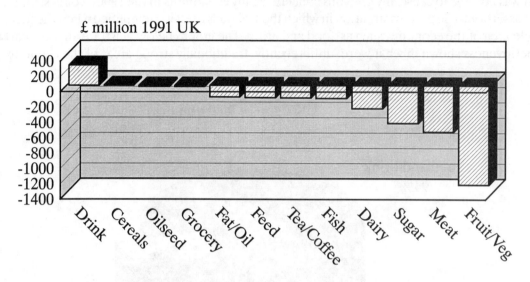

£ million 1991 UK

Inflation-adjusted sector balances

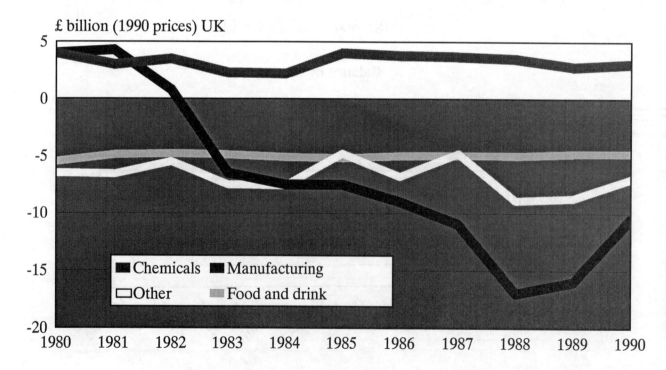

£ billion (1990 prices) UK

The Management of the Economy

The most distinctive feature of government economic management in the post-1945 period is that it can be divided into two distinct eras:

1. The Era of Keynesianism and Demand Side Economics

In the thirty five years or so, following the White Paper of 1944 on economic objectives, both Labour and Conservative governments pursued policies that owed much to the ideas of Keynes and the economists who followed in his footsteps.

2. The Era of Monetarism and Supply Side Economics

In the late 1970s there emerged a strong challenge to Keynesian thinking, described as the *monetarist revolution,* in which the four basic economic objectives stated in 1944 were reduced to a single aim: the elimination of inflation.

Achieving that, monetarists believe, would mean that all the other problems would subsequently be solved. This 'revolution' has been accompanied by the re-appraisal of the basic causes of inflation and the appropriate methods of economic control.

The Conservative Government of 1979 proclaimed that inflation was the number one economic 'evil'. Tackle price rises, they claimed, and everything else would fall into place. Mrs. Thatcher was keen to embark upon what became known as the 'Monetarist Experiment'. The basis of monetarism is that inflation is caused by too much money circulating in the economy. Any expected rise in inflation was likely to be self-fulfilling, due to several factors:

1. *Consumers*

   If consumers expect prices to rise in the future, they will be tempted to 'buy now', prior to any increase. The resultant increase in demand will inevitably lead to pressure upon prices, thus creating inflation.

2. *Trade Unions*

   Similarly, if unions foresee rising prices, then they will invariably make pay claims higher than this anticipated rate of inflation, in an attempt to achieve a rise in the actual standard of living of their members. Should these pay claims be met, then this again causes inflationary pressure.

3. *Borrowers*

   Anyone who believes inflation is rising is well advised to borrow money now, as the inflation rate will erode the real value of the repayments. Thus, increased borrowing may occur, with a knock-on effect on spending and, consequently, prices.

4.   *Lenders*

People who are lending money, and who anticipate price rises, will obviously attempt to increase their rates of interest to guarantee a decent real rate of return. The consequence of this is to put further pressure on the inflation rate.

These four factors mean that controlling inflation is much more difficult if there is an expectation that prices will rise.

The monetarist experiment – the early years

The Labour Government, which lost to Mrs. Thatcher's Conservatives in the 1979 General Election, had already begun to face one unpleasant fact of economic life: it had to curb public spending (or, as Chancellor Denis Healey preferred to phrase it, to 'cut the fiscal deficit'). The only real alternative that a government has is to raise taxes, but this, of course, is unpopular with voters at all times – and especially so when real income is already being reduced by slow growth.

The government has two options open to it:

1.   either to reduce its state benefits (child benefit, old age, sickness, unemployment benefit etc); or

2.   reduce its public investment programmes.

The first option is rarely the one taken, since reducing benefits seems to make the government politically and morally vulnerable to its opponents and to invite criticism that it is taking an inequitable approach to its electorate. Instead, a government will wield its axe over public investment programmes which, in practice, may simply mean the cancellation of a few dozen large contracts with companies in the private sector. (This is the current approach that Germany has been forced to take as a result of re-unification, rising inflation and workers who insist on maintaining their living standards.) As Sir Humphrey Appleby might justify it, by the time the crumbling sewers and potholed roads have become the focus of public attention, the government responsible for their dilapidated condition will have long gone.

The situation which Thatcher inherited consisted of an inflation rate which was 13.4%, and an unemployment rate of 5.4% or, some 1.5 million people. In order to tackle inflation, there would inevitably be a cost: higher unemployment.

The Government believed that a reduction of inflation to single figures by 1981 would result in the loss of some 700,000 jobs, or an increase in the unemployment rate to 7.5%. This, they felt, was politically acceptable as a short-term measure. The political implications of this policy are interesting. The 1979 Conservative election campaign had featured a large drive against Labour's failure to curb unemployment. Posters proclaiming 'Labour isn't working', accompanied by pictures of lengthy 'dole' queues, helped Mrs. Thatcher into power. To embark upon policies which would inevitably cause an increase in unemployment would appear to have been a politically dangerous move. However, the Thatcher strategists were convinced that, by 1982, the unemployment rate would start to fall again since, by that time, inflation would have been eliminated.

However, events did not turn out as expected. By 1981 it was clear that the actual unemployment rate in 1981 was 10%, whilst inflation was still running at 11%. The optimistic predictions of 1979 seemed to be ill-founded.

The Conservatives continued their policies of severe fiscal and monetary contraction. Public spending was drastically reduced ('The Cuts'), whilst monetary policy saw the development of the Medium-Term Financial Strategy.

The Medium-Term Financial Strategy

This policy was based upon the theory that, if people were told that inflation would be low, they would reduce spending and borrowing by acting in a rational manner. The aim of the Medium-Term Financial Strategy was to publish a variety of economic indicators to convince the nation that inflation was about to fall. The Chancellor used his Autumn Statement to signal the Government's monetary targets, such as the level of increase in the money supply and the PSBR (the Public Sector Borrowing Requirement), for the next three to five years. It was hoped that these would dampen expectations of rising prices, and thus bring about a fall in the rate of inflation itself.

Problems with the Medium-Term Financial Strategy

The Government ran into problems on two fronts:

1. *Lack of understanding*

    Much of the Government's target audience simply did not understand these figures and their implications, so they remained sceptical that inflation would fall; consequently, they did little to moderate spending and modify pay claims.

2. *Credibility*

    If anyone fails to meet a target, their whole credibility is challenged. The Government invariably overshot their monetary targets and so lost credibility. This worsened the problem. Finding themselves with little immediate success, in terms of either inflation or unemployment, the Government tightened its policies further, with the result that the country was thrown into a severe recession in 1981-82. Some Conservatives – the 'Wets' – began to call for a reversal of policies – for a return to Keynesian expansionist policies.

'TINA': 'There Is No Alternative'

The 'Wets' received scant encouragement from Mrs. Thatcher, who openly claimed that things would get worse before they got better, but that things would only improve if the government continued to pursue its policies fully. The phrases, *'There is no alternative'* and *'The lady's not for turning'* became popular amongst Government supporters.

In March 1982, Government popularity was at rock bottom. However, by June 1983, when the next election was held, the Conservatives were re-elected with a massive majority. The economy had begun to recover, at least in respect of falling inflation, although the reasons for the improvement were not universally agreed upon.

Explanations fell broadly into two categories:

Government supporters claimed that the strict monetary and fiscal policies which had been implemented had resulted in the reduction in inflation, but at a huge cost in unemployment.

Government critics argued that it was the rise in unemployment which had actually led to falling inflation. The shock to the economy had been so severe that inflation had been forced to fall. Three million unemployed was far too high a price to pay for the control of inflation.

Nevertheless, the Conservatives were elected to a second term of office, which saw them implement more strongly than ever the new 'supply-side policies'.

The Importance of Supply Side Economics

The overall aim of successive Conservative administrations since 1979 has been to reduce the role of the Government in the economy, to 'roll back the frontiers of the state'. Since 1982, Tory administrations under Margaret Thatcher were vociferous in their proclamations of belief in 'Supply Side Economics'.

A definition of supply side economics

Historically, before 1979, governments had adopted Keynesian policies which saw government intervene in the running of the economy in order to correct market failures and thereby influence the level of aggregate demand. The dual problems of high inflation and high unemployment in the mid 1970s led to the development of a new school of thought.

Monetarism was one part of the supply side 'revolution'. Believers in monetarism held that economic growth and prosperity flow from enterprise and entrepreneurial activity, which are fostered and promoted by free markets. They claim that government intervention is not necessarily the way to solve market failures. What is needed is to create a structure and culture under which markets can operate more effectively and efficiently. Therefore government policies should be designed in order to nurture the entrepreneurial spirit.

Supply side economic policies are, therefore, aimed at freeing the 'wealth makers' from the constraints of market distortions, on the basis that this will then create a 'knock on effect', whereby markets will expand, thus solving problems of unemployment.

Supply side policies

Various policies have been adopted as 'supply side economics'. Monetarist policies have already been considered.

The range of other policies includes the following:

- privatisation
- income tax reforms
- labour market policies
- deregulation of the financial sector
- deregulation of the bus services

- deregulation of the broadcasting industry
- deregulation of the legal system
- the move towards the Single European Market.

Other government policy options available

Fiscal Policy

This policy has been applied by governments since the 1940s in their attempts to control the economy. It is based on Keynesian principles, but is still implemented today. Keynesians argue that unemployment and inflation are the result of the disequilibrium in the economy's aggregate supply and demand. The assumption is that the economy tends to experience a series of booms and slumps with the fluctuations of the business cycle. Thus fiscal policy is essentially counter-cyclical; that is, when the economy is in recession the government pursues *expansionary* measures and, conversely, when the economy becomes 'over-heated' the government follows a *contractionary* policy.

Fiscal Policy to Expand the Economy

If unemployment exists, there are two ways in which a government can stimulate aggregate demand:

- by reducing the revenue it raises in taxation (tax cuts)
- by increasing its own expenditure.

Now look at how each of these policies work.

1. Tax cuts

What is taxation?

Government, both local (such as a county council) and central, raise money (revenue) to spend on public services (expenditure) by taxing individuals, households and businesses:

- through *direct* taxation e.g. income tax, corporation tax, unified business rate, 'poll tax' or council charge
- through *indirect* taxation e.g. value added tax, customs and excise duty.

Central government sometimes decides to use taxation as a *fiscal* instrument by reducing or increasing the amount of money in the economy (the circular flow of money): reducing income tax by 1p in the pound gives the population another one billion pounds a year to dispose of. It can do this in several ways (e.g. by offering greater incentives for people to save), but changing rates of taxation has proved one of the most popular with successive governments, whatever their political complexion.

Simply altering the level of taxation can be a crude fiscal instrument, one that is often criticised for being 'non-discriminatory' or 'non-selective'; that is, it affects every taxpayer in the same way. Taxation that acts in this way is said to be *regressive*. An example of this kind of taxation would be the imposition of a tax on bread, the result of which would be that everyone pays, irrespective of how small or large their income may be. The 'poll tax', introduced by the 1987 Conservative government, was such a regressive and much despised tax. It levied a charge upon a household and its members, irrespective of the income generated by its members or the size of the 'estate'. As a result, a tenant on a small yearly income, living in a tiny, dilapidated cottage would pay the same tax as the landlord who lives in a hundred-room mansion.

The converse of regressive taxation is *progressive* taxation, which aims to take a greater proportion of an individual's income. Income tax was designed to be such a tax, though nowadays chancellors of the exchequer are more subtle in its use, adjusting thresholds and allowances as well as its overall rate. In the 1992 Budget, for example, Chancellor Lamont was adjudged to have pulled off something of a coup, not by dropping the overall rate of income tax, but by dropping the tax band to 20%.

How do income tax changes affect business?

If the percentage rate of income tax increases, then some individuals will regard this as a disincentive to work harder; they will see that the more they earn, the higher the proportion of their income will be deducted in the form of income tax. This is likely to have two major effects on business:

1.   the motivation to work may diminish unless an alternative, non-financial motivator can be found

2.   individuals will have less disposable income to spend on goods and services which business produces.

If the percentage rate of income tax falls, then some politicians would argue that people are motivated to work harder and spend more. An income tax reduction will mean:

- an increase in personal disposable income, which will mean more to save or spend on goods on services

- a greater motivation to work

- a consequent increase in business output.

If, instead of a rise in income tax, there is a rise in VAT and excise duty, then prices will rise, demand will fall and the result is a tendency towards inflation (accompanied by a consequent loss of revenue to the government, perhaps). If those duties are decreased, however, prices should fall and there will be an increase in demand, but the tendency will still be inflationary.

If a government raises corporation tax, then businesses will probably wish to maintain the level of dividend they pay. So they will retain less profit, which will mean a lower level of investment in the business. In the long term, either lower dividends or lower investment will show through in a lowering of personal or organisational demand.

Decreasing corporation tax will lead to a higher level of retained profit, which leads to higher levels of investment or higher dividends. Theoretically, these will feed through the economy and show themselves in increased demand, which may be consumer demand or organisational demand.

The government may choose to undertake all or some of these policy measures. Their effectiveness depends on the willingness of individuals and businesses to raise their level of spending. It could be nullified if the extra spending is on imported goods or if savings are chosen in preference to more spending.

2. Increase in government expenditure

Additionally, the government may also increase its own spending. It can do this by:

- greater expenditure on goods and services or by employing more people in the public sector. This will create an immediate and direct increase in the level of demand
- increased expenditure on transfer payments (benefits, grants etc.) which will result in positive changes in consumer spending
- a higher level of capital investment by building more schools, hospitals, roads, etc.

While this type of spending may provide tangible benefits to society, it does take longer to bear fruit as projects must be planned, designed, and approved before implementation. There may, therefore, be a time lag in the period between electing to proceed with such expansion and the positive effect being felt in the economy.

Public Sector Current Surplus

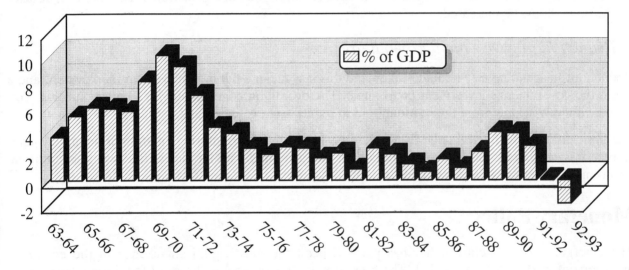

General Government Current Surplus

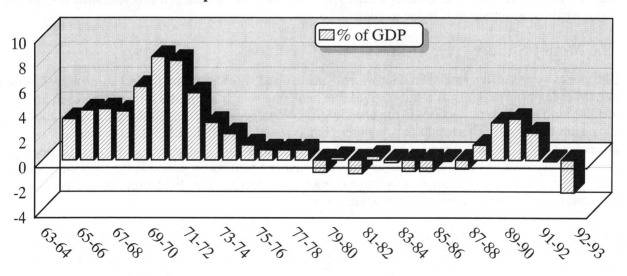

The overall impact of such changes is that the government should face a budget deficit. Revenue falls while expenditure rises. This is known as budget deficit financing and will lead to increases in borrowing by the government (the Public Spending Borrowing Requirement). The estimated PSBR for 1993-94 is £50 billion.

Fiscal Policy that Contracts the Economy

If the policy objective is reduction in inflation, the government must pursue methods which are the reverse of those already outlined.

1. Tax increases

Taxes should be raised to discourage spending. Here the most effective means of reducing expenditure is to tax more heavily those people who spend the greatest proportion of their income (for to tax those who save heavily may simply result in a reduction in savings rather than in expenditure). This means that taxes on the poor should be increased.

2. Reduction in government expenditure

Reductions in spending may be undertaken and this may mean a fall in public sector employment and a fall in the government's investment programme. The overall outcome should be a budget surplus. This would withdraw income from the economy and so reduce aggregate demand.

The basic difficulty with fiscal policy is not that it is ineffective in countering inflation or unemployment. Rather, it is its inherent inability to reduce both at the same time. This flaw led to the development of the government's alternative means of control, monetary policy.

Monetary Policy

The emergence of monetary policy has perhaps been the most significant change in the economic management in the post-war period. The crux of monetary control is the need for the government to regulate the expansion of the country's productive capacity. To understand this you must first be clear about what the government is trying to control.

The Money Supply

The money supply is that stock of money which is made up of notes and coins in circulation as well as bank and other financial deposits. It is not obvious that bank deposits, often in the form of figures in accounts, are also money. Most transactions in the economy involve large amounts of money and rely on cheques as the means of transfer. This results in commercial banks readjusting their accounts as money is drawn from an account in one bank and moved into an account in another bank. In most cases there is no need for a physical movement of notes and coins as there are similar transfers occurring in the opposite direction. Thus banks do not need to keep currency to cover all of the deposits they hold, only enough to allow them to meet their customers' demands for notes and coins.

Therefore, depending on the measure of the money supply used, bank deposits account for between two-thirds and three-quarters of the money supply. How, then, does the government attempt to control the growth in the money supply?

Means of controlling the money supply

To stop the money supply from growing, the government uses three methods:

- Control of the demand for money so that borrowers seek fewer or smaller loans from their banks
- Control of the supply of money so that the commercial banks make fewer or smaller loans
- Base control i.e. the control of the production of the original notes and coins.

Credit and Savings

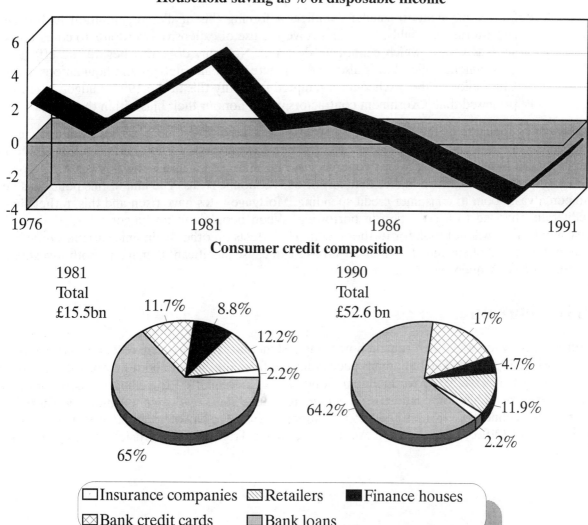

Household saving as % of disposable income

Consumer credit composition

1981
Total
£15.5bn

11.7%   8.8%
12.2%
2.2%
65%

1990
Total
£52.6 bn

17%
4.7%
11.9%
2.2%
64.2%

☐ Insurance companies   ▨ Retailers   ■ Finance houses
⊠ Bank credit cards   ▦ Bank loans

Policies for control of borrowing are aimed at two potential 'target areas'.

Domestic consumers

Early evidence suggested that the interest rate was not the sole determinant of domestic borrowing. 'Weekly payments' are often perceived as being more important, as they illustrate how much people can afford. As a result, credit companies have been guilty of extending the terms of loans as rates have gone up (i.e. extending the length of time over which the loan will be repaid), thus giving the impression that payments are staying the same or even falling. Indeed, as credit companies are faced with increased rates, they tend to launch 'hard sell' promotional campaigns, which can actually lead to an increase in borrowing.

Commercial borrowers

This section of demand for borrowing is far more 'interest rate conscious'.

Large businesses, faced with higher interest charges, often adopt the following policies:

- Reduction in investment – leading to job losses and further problems for the development of the economy

- Slower payment to smaller suppliers – forcing the smaller organisation to borrow short-term. Invariably, this will involve the use of expensive overdrafts to cover costs, such as wages, which cannot be deferred. Not only does this negate the effect of government policy, but it also leads to increased bankruptcies and liquidations. (The Chancellor of the Exchequer attempted to rectify this in the 1992 budget, when he promised that government contractors would honour their bills within thirty days.)

Interest rates appear to be the only economic weapon which the government has been willing to use: it has been called the 'one club armoury', since its opponents regard it as a blunt and primitive weapon or as inappropriate as a golfer's bag which contains just one 'stick'. As a result, the UK has seen a period of spiralling interest rates, much higher than any of our economic rivals. The aim of this policy has been to dampen a vast boom in consumer credit spending. Mortgage rates have risen and this, rather than high credit rates, has led to a reduction in borrowing. When people can no longer afford their mortgage repayments, they will not look for further credit. The effects on other economic variables remains to be seen, but a period of sustained high interest rates can cause significant damage to both investment and exports, with consequent problems for the future.

Privatisation

A further policy to reduce government borrowing and increase its short-term revenue has been privatisation. Since 1979 roughly £40 billion has been collected from the sale of about fifty privatised businesses. The present Conservative Government of John Major is committed to selling off parts or all of the remainder of the public corporations in an attempt to reduce State involvement in industry. These include: the British Technology Group; the electricity supply industry in Northern Ireland; British Coal; British Rail; the Post Office; Civil Aviation Authority; London Transport and Nuclear Electric and Scottish Nuclear.

The Arguments against Privatisation

There are three major arguments put forward against privatisation:

Financial

The industries which are currently being sold off, or have been sold off, are necessarily the more profitable areas of the public sector, for it is unlikely that private investors would wish to take over a loss-making concern. The possible result of such a policy might be that the government will be left with only the major loss-making nationalised industries (such as Nuclear Electric?) and with no possibility of cross subsidy.

Private monopoly

Government is in danger of merely transferring a State monopoly to a private monopoly, with no attempt made to introduce competition to improve efficiency.

Job losses

Trade unions claim that privatisation will be accompanied by large job losses – hardly desirable in times when unemployment is already high, but this has certainly been the case in even the most profitable privatised companies, such as British Telecom.

The Conservatives Nationalised Inheritance

In 1979 the Conservatives inherited a network of nationalised industries, yet they believed that the State provision of goods and services should be kept to a minimum. Public goods, such as defence and policing, would still be provided by the State. Merit goods, such as education and health care, would be opened up more and more to market competition. The nationalised industries themselves, it was envisaged, would be 'streamlined' and then sold off as soon as they came in to profit.

The network of nationalised industries was large. The scope of the corporations was considerable, the number of employees vast. The industries took up a significant portion of UK investment, squeezing out private sector investment. For several years the Conservative government felt that they had been a drain on the PSBR. There was also considerable criticism that many of them were 'cosy monopolies', which were not exposed to the rigours of market forces and, as such, showed a tendency to be inefficient and lacking in innovation.

The Thatcher Belief

The Conservative government believed that market failure was, in itself, insufficient grounds for government intervention. The government, it was claimed, had proved itself to be no better, and at times far worse, than the private sector in running the nationalised industries. Thatcher called for a programme of privatisation.

The Privatisation Programme

The programme itself started relatively quietly. The initial moves were not heralded as a major policy departure, but the 'sell-offs' soon gathered pace. Between 1979 and 1991 the following were privatised:

Nationalised Industry	Year privatised	Price £m
British Petroleum	1979-87	6090
British Aerospace	1981	390
Cable & Wireless	1981	1021
Amersham International	1982	64
National Freight Corporation	1982	354
Britoil	1982	1053
Associated British Ports	1983	97
Enterprise Oil	1984	384
Jaguar	1984	297
British Telecom	1984	4793
British Gas	1986	6533
British Airways	1987	854
Royal Ordnance	1987	186
Rolls Royce	1987	1032
British Airports Authority	1987	1223
Rover	1988	48
British Steel	1988	2427
The Water Authorities	1989	5240
Electricity Boards (distributors)	1990	5200
CEGB (Electricity Generators)	1991	3600
Scottish Electricity Generators	1991	2880

In addition, the following were sold: Ferranti; The Forestry Commission; Sealink; Unipart; Short Bros.; The Plant Breeding Institute; British Rail Hotels.

The Proceeds from Privatisation

The increased pace of the sale of public assets, resulting in increased revenues to the Treasury, is well illustrated in the table below (assets are in £billions):

1979 - 80	0.4
1980 - 81	0.2
1981 - 82	0.5
1982- 83	0.5
1983 - 84	1.1
1984 - 85	2.1
1985 - 86	2.7
1986 - 87	4.5
1987 - 88	5.1
1988 - 89	7.1

1989 - 90	4.2
1990 - 91	5.3

The Government has increased its expectations about the revenue receipts from the privatisation programme. Its forecasts are:

1991 - 92	8.0
1992 - 93	8.0
1993 - 94	5.5
1994 - 95	5.5.

Whilst most people equate the word 'privatisation' with the sales of public assets, such as state industries, remember that it has happened at local level, too. Local authorities have privatised services, such as refuse disposal and leisure centres, and health authorities have contracted out cleaning and laundering to private companies

British Telecom – an Example of Privatisation

British Telecom was privatised in 1984, with no major restructuring. This meant, effectively, that a public monopoly was transferred directly into private hands.

The policy dilemma

In order to guarantee a good sale price, and thereby substantial revenue for the Treasury, there was a need to keep any legislation which applied to BT fairly light. Private investors would not be attracted to an organisation which was still operating within a political straitjacket. However, the transfer of a complete monopoly could lead to inefficiency in terms of costs, prices, innovation and so on. The Thatcher strategy was to privatise first and then regulate later, if at all. Some constraints were placed upon BT in its initial phases within the private sector:

OFTEL was established to act as a regulator or 'watchdog' over the telephone industry. Consumers were to pass any complaints on service or prices to OFTEL, who would investigate and then make recommendations for action. As with most watchdog organisations, OFTEL had no power to implement its own recommendations, and had to rely on the good business sense of BT's managers who wished to avoid bad publicity. This seems to have worked to a degree, although critics would still claim OFTEL is a 'toothless watchdog'. (Similar concerns were voiced about OFWAT, the 'watchdog' responsible for the ten regional water companies which were privatised in 1989; in 1992 they returned a collective profit of £1.5 billion at a time when its inefficiency meant that 30% of mains water was lost to 'seepage', resulting from old pipes, and a quarter of the country's households were faced with rationing and restrictions on the use of water.)

Price restrictions

Until 1989, BT was limited as to the size of its price rises. The formula of Retail Price Index minus 3% was applied, meaning that BT could raise prices by no more than 3% less than the prevailing rate of inflation. Despite this restriction, BT has still managed to accrue vast profits in its early years in the private sector - upwards of £2 billion p.a. Critics suggest that this is potential revenue lost to the government. Supporters argue that the tax on these profits still boosts Treasury funds and, had, BT been left in the public sector, it would not have performed so well anyway.

The original RPI -3% formula was imposed only until 1989. From then until 1993 the current pricing formula has restricted BT from increasing prices by RPI minus 6.25%. In 1991 BT announced a half-yearly profit of £1.61 billion, a 5.1% increase on 1990. The *Financial Times* analysed BT's accounts and concluded that it could safely cut its prices by £1 billion per annum and still be earning for itself profits as high as the rest of UK industry and higher than any other European telecommunications carrier.

British Telecom's Pre-Tax Profits

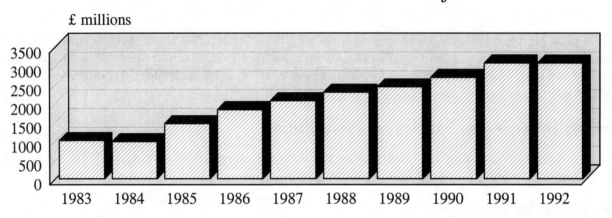

The price structure was reviewed in 1992; BT, which claims that recession and increased competition have adversely affected their profits, are prepared to accept a new formula of RPI minus 7.25 for the first part of the five year pricing regime, but will then want a reduction in the formula below that level. (BT returned a reduced profit of £3.07 billion in 1991-92).

There is no guarantee that such constraints will be reimposed by the government, nor is there any indication of what BT's policy would be, should such constraints not be enforced. Perhaps, in the longer term, competition will emerge that may curb BT's prices and profits, but as long as it remains a virtual monopoly, a tough regulatory body is needed. Perhaps OFGAS, who won a reduction in gas prices for domestic consumers by threatening to take British Gas to court, might stand as an example. The Telephone Users' Association, in their submission to OFTEL's current review of BT's prices, is that an open audit of BT's business would be good for competition. It also wants made clear where BT 'cross subsidises' one service at the expense of another (e.g. where domestic consumers subsidise business consumers).

Competition

Competition for BT's market is negligible. Mercury Telecommunications (owned by Cable & Wireless) is licensed to compete over a limited range of services, but its operations do not really affect BT's market share to any great extent. (Independent estimates put Mercury's share of the UK telecommunications market at only 5%.) The idea of constructing a second telecommunications network is inefficient (BT is a natural monopoly), and as such direct competition is difficult to foresee. A glimmer of hope that increased competition might materialise, lies in the applications made by the National Grid (owned by the twelve regional electricity operating companies) for a telephone licence to compete with BT and Mercury for customers in the business market. British Waterways, British Aerospace and British Rail have applied for similar licences.

Wider Share Ownership

One final point about privatisation. A major objective in the 1980s was to bring about a 'share owning democracy', an ideal which was inherent in much government thinking. Initially, the 'people's shares' (or 'popular capitalism', or 'shareholding democracy') certainly attracted a large number of new shareholders.

However, a large number of people also used the initial phase of privatisation to 'make a killing'. Very large profits were made because shares were heavily over-subscribed. Many realised a fast profit as they quickly sold out to large financial institutions. The 'Crash of '87' also saw many small investors frightened off share buying as their prices tumbled; many people were exposed to the harsh realities of the stock market for the first time. The long-term effects of this event have still to be assessed, but doubtless some people have adopted the philosophy of 'once bitten, twice shy'.

By March 1992 there were again fewer than ten million shareholders in the UK (*Source: National Opinion Polls, March 1992*), though a Treasury survey, conducted in 1991, showed that since 1981 individual share ownership had risen from 7% to 25% of the adult population.

54% of individual shareholders have shares in only one company, usually one that has been privatised. Only 17% of shareholders have holdings in four or more companies. (A comparison of these figures with those for 1990 – respectively 60% and 17% – suggests a slight broadening and deepening of the ownership pattern.)

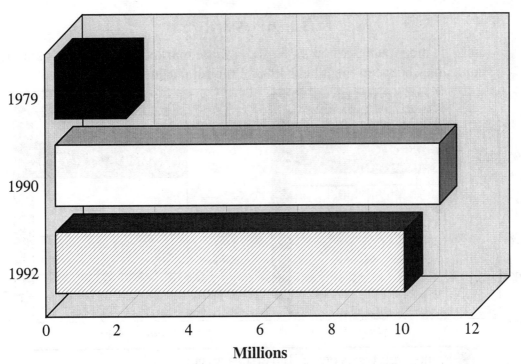

Number of Shareholders

25% of adults in the UK now own shares, up from 7% at the end of the 1970s

Evidence suggests that a majority of shareholding 'Investors' have tended to take a quick profit on those shares by selling their stake to institutional shareholders, such as pension funds and insurance companies. The proportions of individuals' shareholdings are shown in the figure below.

Value of Shares

54% of individual shareholders have shares in only one company, normally one of those that has been privatised. They tend to take a quick profit on these shares by selling their stake to institutions.

Individuals with shareholdings worth:

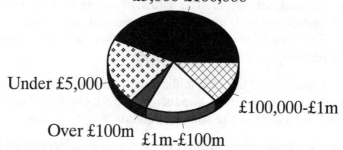

£5,000-£100,000

Under £5,000

£100,000-£1m

Over £100m   £1m-£100m

Two thirds of shares owned by individuals were in holding of less than £100,000 (1989 figures)

Whether successive governments since 1979 have been successful in widening the base of share ownership is doubtful, as the figure demonstrates.

Who owns shares

In 1989, individuals owned 21% of UK share market. Pension funds and insurance companies between them held 49% of the total value of shares.

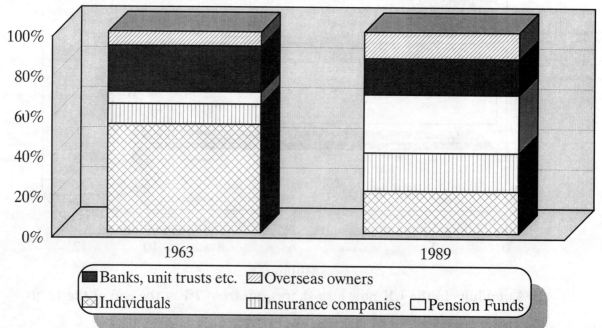

Nationalised Industries

The few remaining large businesses in this category are British Rail, British Coal, the Post Office and London Transport. They are controlled by management boards, appointed by government ministers, who give them the responsibility for day-to-day decision-making. General policy is guided by the government, which believes that national corporations should conduct themselves as commercial enterprises. Their efficiency is scrutinised by the Monopolies and Mergers Commission and they are expected to conduct themselves in accordance with the following 'guidelines'. They are expected:

- to follow clear government objectives which have been set out for them
- to achieve a required rate of return of 8% or greater
- to have financial targets and performance aims
- to have a corporate plan
- to hold performance reviews
- to have, and stick to, principles relating to investment appraisal and pricing
- to have external financing limits
- to have a systematic monitoring of their performance.

Regional Policy

The policies previously mentioned have been aimed at solving problems in the country as a whole by seeking to reduce the aggregate level of inflation or unemployment. A glance at the map on the next page, which shows each region's share of manufacturing output, reveals that the UK is not homogenous, but is diverse and uneven in what it produces and how much is produced. For example, only 14% of the output of Greater London is accounted for by manufacturing, whilst in the West Midlands manufacturing accounts for one third of that region's Gross Domestic Production. In Greater London, the banking and financial sectors account for 25% of regional GDP, a figure far higher than that for the West Midlands. However, in the UK there are some regions which have specific problems of unemployment above the national average, low growth rates and many associated social problems such as crime, poor housing and so on.

Successive governments have made various attempts to alleviate these particular problems through Regional Policy. They have attempted this by two different types of policies which:

- encourage unemployed workers to move to more prosperous regions
- induce companies and firms to move to the regions of high unemployment.

1. Encouragement of the mobility of labour

Some workers are less able to move from one area to another in search of work because they are highly immobile. The government has tried to help by giving financial incentives (travelling and re-settlement grants), encouraging re-training (through Skills Centres and Government Training Schemes) and improving workers' knowledge of opportunities in other regions (through Job Centres and Department of Employment). Such policy may well alleviate unemployment in the short-term, but it tends to have the longer term effect of moving workers away from their traditional home areas, leaving these regions to decline and to some extent reinforcing regional inequality in the UK.

Percentage share of manufacturing in regional GDP (1988)

2. *Encouraging business to re-locate in the regions*

The government has previously sought to give financial assistance to businesses willing to locate in the regions. Certain regions, such as the North East and West Cumbria, have in the past been designated Development Areas. In these areas, Regional Development Grants are available which help businesses purchase new capital assets and also provide a grant for each new job created. Additionally, other areas were designated as Intermediate Areas. These included the West Midlands, Humberside and parts of

Yorkshire, Lancashire, South Wales and the South West. In these regions, lesser grants were available for businesses which created new jobs.

At present the UK appears to lack a strong regional policy. Industrial policy is designed to encourage enterprise and economic growth in all areas of the country. In those areas where extra help is needed, this is presently provided by the Department of Trade and Industry's Enterprise Initiative. Aid is concentrated on Assisted Areas (Development Areas and Intermediate Areas), which account for over 35% of the working population. (These can be seen in the maps below.)

The two main instruments for rendering regional aid are:

1.   regional selective assistance, which is available through the Assisted Areas, for investment projects carried out by businesses that meet certain criteria

2.   Regional Enterprise Grants; these are available in Development Areas and other areas covered by EC schemes to support investment and innovation in business that employ fewer than twenty five people.

1993 Assisted Areas   **Pre-1993 Assisted Areas**

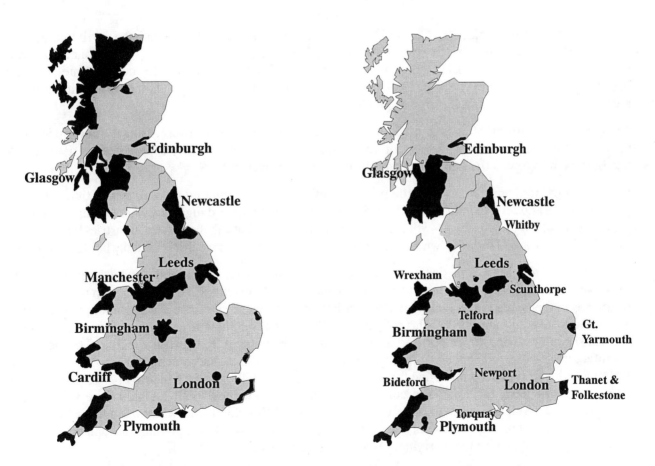

Key: ▬▬ Development and intermediate aid area

In the 1980s the government was of the view that its supply side policies would prevail, and that it should serve as a catalyst to the creation of business, rather than directly intervening to ensure its creation. Assistance which is currently provided for businesses is no longer in the form of grants or subsidies for factories, but is given or lent as money to carry out market research, financial planning or export drives. That help is available regardless of area. Part of the aversion to regional aid that could be seen in successive governments in the 1980s is suggested by a phrase that Mrs. Thatcher used before she was deposed: people in areas of high unemployment, she asserted, should stop being 'moaning minnies' and look after themselves. This complemented an earlier opinion, by one of her senior colleagues, that the unemployed should 'get on their bikes and look for work'. Such opinions together scarcely formed a coherent regional policy.

Instead, the EC has become an increasingly important source of funds, particularly in view of the reduction in the UK government direct support, through its Regional Fund. This provides money to finance specific projects in the poorer areas of Europe. Unfortunately, several of the UK's regions now fall within the category occupied by the likes of Sicily, Estremadura and Calabria.

How Successful has Government Economic Policy been since 1979?

Any answer must be subjective. Certainly, some measure of success can be claimed in the control of inflation. Having inherited a rate of over 13%, this has been reduced to 1.4% at least for a while. However, critics would argue that the cost in terms of lost jobs was socially unacceptable. At the current time, inflation has fallen from a rate of over 8% in 1989, to about 4% and for the first time in half a century it has fallen below the rate for Germany, if only marginally.

Unemployment currently stands at just over 2.3 million (or 9% of the workforce), using the current method of calculation. This is an improvement on the 3.26 million which the country experienced in 1986, but is nowhere near as low as the figure inherited by the Conservatives in 1979.

It has been pointed out that many of the new jobs which have been created are either part-time, or in the growth leisure and service industries. The UK's manufacturing base is dangerously narrow, and economic growth without manufacturing growth can only be short-lived; 'What will the service industries be servicing,' Lord Weinstock asked in 1984, 'when there is no hardware, where no wealth is actually being produced?'

There has been a long-term decline in the share of UK output accounted for by agricultural and manufacturing sectors as the economy has become more service-oriented. The contribution that manufacturing has made to the Gross Domestic Product has declined markedly since the beginning of the 1960s, when it was 35%, to today's 20%. This reduction in the level of manufacturing means that British citizens are consistently relying on imports to satisfy their needs, as no UK substitute exists. The deficit in manufacturing – ever present since the final three months of 1982 – had reached £1285 million by early 1992, with the current account deficit forecast to rise from £4.4 billion to £6.6 billion in 1992. In the single month of April 1992, the trade and current account deficit widened to £1.1 billion. The value of exports stood at £8.8 billion, whilst the level of imports stood at £10.2 billion and, whilst taking a single month's figures can be misleading because of 'exceptional items' (e.g. imports of diamonds, aeroplanes etc), this month is unexceptional as the worrying trend in the Figure overleaf illustrates.

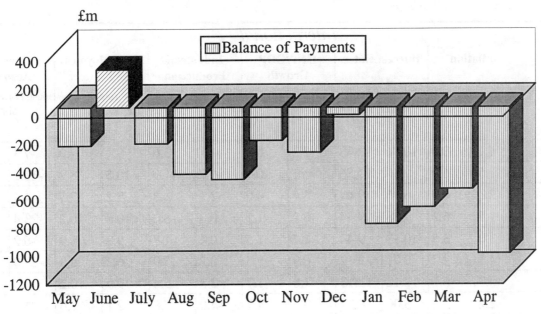

This lack of UK manufactured goods not only exists in the high-tech consumer market, but also in what could be referred to as 'low-tech' markets, or even the 'no-tech' markets. The UK construction industry is currently importing materials, such as bricks and putty, because of the limited supply from domestic producers. Thus much of the benefit of the mid-1980s boom in house construction has been lost abroad.

The balance of payments appears to be a problem which is resistant to control. The figure for 1988 was some £15 billion in deficit; in 1989 it was nearly £20 billion, and in 1990 it was £16 billion. The main explanation of this lies in the boom in consumer spending mentioned above. However, criticism also exists of the problems of British companies' export levels. These are hit by a strong pound, but many critics perceive a general lack of competitiveness. The government is attempting to alter the negative attitude of UK firms towards world trade and, in particular, trade within the Single European Market. Whether the situation improves or worsens as a result of these developments remains to be seen. The government claims that the balance of payments deficit is an irrelevancy, and that market forces will rectify the situation in the near future.

Economic growth has fluctuated a great deal during the 1980s and early 1990s. The recession of the early 1980s, when growth was negligible, gave way to a boom during the mid-1980s (Between 1983 and 1987 the *Financial Times* index of stockmarket shares multiplied by a factor of five). The UK experienced growth rates which were comparable with its rivals. However, the manufacturing base was not growing and, as such, growth has slowed down considerably. High interest rates have deterred recent investment, whilst the high value of the pound, partly as a result of these interest rates, has made it increasingly more difficult for UK firms to export. (A current comparison with the UK's major competitors can be made by looking at the following table of economic indicators.)

	International										
	Inflation		Interest Rates		GNP/GDP Growth		Industrial Production		Unemployment		Current Account	
	annual change %		3 m'th money mkt, %		annual change %		annual change %		rate %		last 12 months, $bn	
UK	4.1	8.9	10.81	12.38	-2.2	0.3	-1.1	-3.6	9.4	7.0	-7.3	-25.8
Austria	1.5	6.9	7.50	11.56	-1.1	0.1	-0.7	-1.9	10.5	8.7	-10.2	-14.1
Belgium	2.3	4.0	6.96	9.44	3.4	4.0	-2.1	3.2	8.2	7.5	4.4	3.9
Canada	1.7	6.2	7.38	9.44	-0.2	-1.1	0.8	-8.0	10.6	10.2	-23.4	-18.8
France	3.0	3.5	10.18	9.44	1.7	1.5	0.4	-1.7	9.8	8.9	-6.2	-10.0
Germany	4.3	2.7	9.71	9.12	0.9	5.5	0.2	5.9	6.2	6.3	-23.0	39.8
Italy	5.3	6.7	12.12	12.13	1.0	1.7	-2.3	-5.4	9.9	10.2	-33.6	-33.2
Japan	2.2	3.4	5.00	8.27	3.2	4.7	-4.0	7.8	2.1	2.0	81.1	36.9
Netherlands	4.4	2.5	9.60	9.24	3.9	4.2	-0.4	3.7	7.0	7.3	10.4	10.0
Spain	5.9	6.8	12.88	15.15	4.9	5.0	-0.5	-1.1	16.5	15.7	16.31	-15.8
Sweden	5.1	10.0	11.50	12.25	2.1	2.3	-11.8	-4.4	3.4	1.9	-3.6	-5.7
USA	2.6	5.7	4.44	6.56	-0.8	1.3	1.4	-2.6	7.3	6.5	-8.6	-92.1
OECD	4.2	6.1	–	–	3.5	4.5	-0.8	0.3	7.2	6.4	–	–

Economic Indicators of the UK and its major trading competitors, 1992

Similarly, imports remain attractively priced to UK residents and, as such, much of the benefit of the recent growth years is disappearing from the country. With regard to overall economic policies, the government would appear to have invented a new alternative. After Keynesianism and Monetarism, demand side and supply side economics, there is now a policy called 'suck it and see', a combination of a number of alternative approaches whose chance of long-term success is a matter for considerable and continuing debate.

The Debate Between Private and Public Sectors

Since 1979 the government has followed, with varying commitment and consistency, policies of deregulation and privatisation. *Deregulation* describes the attempts that government has made to reduce or abolish the legislative and bureaucratic burdens which local and national government place on business. Under the Deregulation Initiative, all EC and UK proposals are examined to find what impact they are likely to have on business. The costs to business are considered before the decision to adopt legislation is made and existing controls are also reviewed in order to see which are obsolete and are, therefore, candidates for the scrapyard.

The government also believes that the most effective way of improving the performance of nationalised industries is to expose them to market forces, through *privatisation* and the promotion of share ownership amongst employees and the general public.

State Intervention in the Economy: Competition

One example of the way in which the State influences the economy is shown when the government, sometimes reluctantly, attempts to prevent the growth of dominant firms (oligopolies) by restricting merger and takeover activity through competition policy. It will normally only intervene if it can see clear disadvantages arising out of the increased concentration in a market or the behaviour of market suppliers. It steps in only if such behaviour is felt to be detrimental to the public interest. However, the definition of 'public interest' varies a great deal! There are many recent examples of the government allowing companies to take over competitors and so achieve market dominance. One example was the British Airways takeover of British Caledonian which gave BA 93% of the UK domestic flight market – yet the government was still happy to allow it to go ahead.

How and Why does the Government Intervene?

The market system is, theoretically, an efficient mechanism for allowing individual consumers the freedom of choice to spend their wealth as they wish. It also acts as a means of indicating to producers which goods and services are in demand, and it benefits society in general by ensuring that scarce resources are not wasted. The problem of how products are to be allocated to competing consumers is solved through the power of the purse. Those who have sufficient income can purchase what they desire; those with less money are left wanting.

The Type of Goods and Services Provided

The market system is perfectly capable of providing private goods. We are referring here to goods which are produced by the private sector and consumed by private consumers. Others are not affected by the production and consumption of private goods, either to their advantage or detriment. Private goods alone, however, cannot meet all the demands and needs of society. Society needs to be supplied with two further types of goods or service.

These are:

- public goods
- merit goods.

Public goods

Public goods are goods or services whose benefit is indiscriminate or diffuse; that is, the benefit gained from such products is not derived by specific consumers. For example, a police service will help society as a whole. If you are protected by a police service, criminals who are likely to commit offences against you are deterred or arrested. This public service, however, not only protects you, but also the rest of society. To charge a single individual for the benefit gained ignores the fact that the rest of society is also benefiting. Therefore it is fairer to charge society as a whole for the provision of the service, rather than charge individuals.

Merit goods

The second category of products and services provided by the State are those which provide some element of benefit to society as a whole, but which might be produced by private enterprise and sold through the market mechanism. These are merit goods. Examples of such goods include education, the Health Service, parks and museums.

What differentiates merit goods (such as education) from private goods (such as clothing) is that the benefit gained does not fall solely on the individual, but on society as a whole. If you were to wear well-tailored clothing the rest of society would gain no benefit whatsoever. Yet with a trained and educated population, society can enjoy more production, research and innovation, all of which lead to a better standard of living for everyone.

The Extent of State Provision

The extent to which the State should intervene in this manner is something of a political debate involving the exercise of value judgments. It may be argued that education and health care should be the right of everyone regardless of their status or income. This is part of the rationale for the establishment of the State education system and the National Health Service. Others would argue that people with money should be allowed to spend it as they like and not have it taken from them in taxation to finance the schooling and health care of others. They should be allowed to send their children to 'public' schools or enrol on private health schemes. The Thatcher Government took this view – to what many saw as an unacceptable extreme in its policy of encouraging the development of private education and health schemes. The full scope of this debate is somewhat beyond the limits of your course and you need only note that where merit goods exist and society does benefit, there is a justification for State finance and provision.

The Scope of Public Enterprise

There is considerable debate as to which aspects of the State's activities should be included under the heading 'public enterprise'. The relevant organisations are often referred to as *public corporations* or *nationalised industries*, but using such titles can be somewhat misleading. Even the Government itself has found difficulty in defining what it regards as a nationalised industry. For instance, one official definition used in a National Economic Development Office Report (NEDO) in 1976 included under this heading only those public corporations operating in the market economy. It therefore omitted public corporations such as the BBC, which does not charge for its service but gains revenue from the government who in turn raise those revenues directly through the licence fee system. Earlier, in 1968, a House of Commons Select Committee defined nationalised industries as having three characteristics which set them apart from other aspects of the government's activities. These were:

- that such enterprises were wholly owned by the State or sufficiently owned by the State to be controlled by it

- that the industries operated in such a way that the majority of revenue came from sources other than from direct Parliamentary or Treasury subsidy

- that such enterprises are run by Boards of Directors appointed by an appropriate Minister of State.

By this definition, the major industries included in such a category would be British Coal, the Central Electricity Generating Board and the Post Office. Some of these industries, either in their entirety or in part, are regarded by a Conservative government as strong candidates for denationalisation. However, it is clear that nationalisation has tended to be concentrated in the following areas:

1. Energy and water supplies

2. Transport

3. Communications

4. Basic heavy industry.

There are also a number of other miscellaneous public corporations which do not fall under the definition of a nationalised industry previously cited. Among the most important of these is the Bank of England, which reports directly to the Treasury. The British Broadcasting Corporation, the Independent Broadcasting Authority and the Scottish and Welsh Development Agencies are also government-controlled bodies, but are financed directly from the central Exchequer, and so can be excluded from the mainstream of nationalised industries.

The Justification for Nationalisation

The arguments in support of nationalisation are many and varied but they are matched by a number of arguments against public sector involvement in industry. In considering the scope of public corporations, it is therefore useful to become familiar with some of the arguments both for and against nationalisation.

The arguments for nationalisation

1. *Natural monopolies*

   Some industries may be regarded as natural monopolies or may require vast investment. A duplication of such industries would prove to be a waste of resources. Natural monopolies occur most frequently with the provision of public utilities such as water, gas and electricity. To have two electricity grid systems running parallel throughout the country would obviously be wasteful, and so it is most economically efficient to have only one. Furthermore, it is argued that if a monopoly does exist it is better to have it under State control than to subject consumers to the possible abuse of monopoly power at the hands of a private industrialist. This reasoning obviously assumes that a government-owned organisation will not abuse its position – probably a mistaken assumption!

2. *National security*

   Some industries should be controlled by the State for reasons of defence and national security. An example of this is the United Kingdom Atomic Energy Authority.

3. *Job protection*

   The State may wish to safeguard jobs by supporting industries which would otherwise close if left in private control. Such a decision involves the government making a value judgment that it is better to finance these loss-making industries than to incur the financial and social problems involved in large-scale unemployment.

4.   *Consumer interest*

As nationalised industries are not operated purely on a profit-making basis, the possibility exists for the interest of the workers in the industry and those of consumers to be put first. For example, people living in a remote village will be able to have telephone facilities which may not be provided by private enterprise, or which otherwise would be prohibitively priced.

5.   *Economies of scale*

Certain industries can be better managed on a large scale, with the possibility of gains from economies of scale. It is, therefore, in the interests of efficiency to have them nationally co-ordinated.

6.   *State control of the economy*

If the State controls important sectors of the economy, such as transport, energy and communications, it will be able to implement its plans for the economy as a whole through its policies for these industries.

The arguments against nationalisation

1.   *Disruption of the free market economy*

Nationalisation is perhaps the first step away from the free market economy, with the balance of economic power shifting towards the State. Eventually a situation could be reached where all the means of production are in the public sector and the State is the sole employer. This increases the monopoly power of the State in the supply of goods and services and also establishes a monopoly (a sole buyer) in the labour market, where the government is the only employer.

2.   *Reduction of competition and efficiency*

It is argued that State ownership reduces competition, which in turn will adversely affect efficiency.

3.   *Misallocation of resources*

Industries which are no longer economically viable should not be supported if the market for their product is in decline. This will lead to a misallocation of resources, with growth industries being 'starved' of capital which they could possible use to create more secure employment.

4.   *Heavy subsidy*

Historically, the nationalised industries have required heavy subsidisation which increases the burden on either the taxpayer, the Public Sector Borrowing Requirements (PSBR), or both.

5. *Private ownership may still exist*

    A natural monopoly does not necessarily preclude private ownership, as can be witnessed in the US where industries such as the telecommunications and electricity generation industries are privately owned but publicly regulated.

6. *Undesirability*

    A monopoly, no matter who controls it, is undesirable. There is no guarantee that the government will not abuse its economic power by raising the price or limiting supply. The only legally protected monopolies are those in the public sector.

A Summary

Arguments such as the 'Public or Private?' debate have formed the backdrop against which managers and businesses have had to take decisions.

Since 1945, successive governments, of whatever political persuasion, relied on consensus to achieve their aims. They varied little in their economic objectives or in the ways in which they manipulated the mechanisms that they believed controlled the economy.

After 1979 such consensus largely disappeared as four successive Conservative governments developed a different approach to managing the economy. 'Keynsian' economics were replaced by a 'Friedmanite' or 'monetarist' approach and a reliance on supply side economics characterised the second and third administrations of Margaret Thatcher.

A determination to control inflation became the key emphasis in economic policy in the 1980s. This emphasis was accompanied by government's determination not to interfere in areas of economic affairs where the market mechanism should be allowed to work with no outside interference in it.

Towards the end of the 1980s, international affairs were as changeable as they had ever been. With established 'trading blocs', such as North America and the EC, becoming increasingly hostile towards each other, channels that had been created (like GATT) to speed up the free flow of trade between nations, were becoming clogged up.

The dramatic disintegration of Communism in the so-called 'Eastern bloc' led to the dismantling of the 'Soviet Empire' and the re-creation of individual nation states. For the most part, this revolution was non-violent; it has opened up previously undreamt of opportunities for business people from the rest of the World. It has also opened up a second front to the EC, which is already facing the 'challenge of the East' – the economic super power of Japan and the fast-rising 'Tiger Economies' of Taiwan, Singapore, Hong Kong and Malaysia. How these events and challenges are being dealt with forms the final section of Part Two.

1. What were the major objectives of UK governments up until 1979?

2. Describe the main categories of unemployment.

3. Define *inflation*.

4. What are the adverse effects of inflation?

5. Describe briefly the two theories of the origins of inflation.

6. What is *monetarism*?

7. What is the *supply side*?

8. Describe the main features of the privatisation policies of the Thatcher Governments.

9. Has privatisation helped or hindered competition?

10. What is meant by the phrase *mobility of labour*?

11. Define each of the following terms:

    - private sector

    - public sector

    - public goods

    - merit goods.

12. Distinguish between a *monopoly, oligopoly* and a *cartel*.

International Trade

Trading between nations is almost as old as humankind itself and few nations are, or can be, independent of others. In the same way as a business trades or carries out transactions with other businesses, so do nations. And, like businesses, nations also need to keep a record of their income and expenditure. The national 'balance sheet' is known as the balance of payments and, at the end of a trading period, it will show either a profit (*surplus*) or a loss (*deficit*). The global economy, according to the World Resources Institute, was valued in 1992 at US$20 trillion and, whilst much of this will not be traded between nations, the figure gives some indication of the extent of world trade.

The balance of payments is made up of the *balance of trade*, which records transactions which take place concerning *visibles*: that is, tangible goods. The balance of trade excludes trade in services, or *invisibles*: it includes raw materials, semi-processed or intermediate products and finished manufactured goods which can be seen and recorded as they cross national frontiers.

The possibility of trade arises where one party has a surplus of a product or service that another party needs. If it were not for surpluses there would be no trade of any sort.

The first part of this section attempts to answer the question, why is there international trade? It then examines the mechanisms by which trade takes place and how it is measured before going on to examine the performance of the UK economy and the arrangement of trading 'blocs' in which it operates.

Imports and Exports

1. *Visible trade*

    Most of us tend to visualise imports and exports as tangible products being taken in and out of the country – Japanese cars shipped into the UK or British machinery sold abroad. This is called 'visible' trade, for the obvious reason that the goods are tangible and can be seen. This trade is vital for the survival of the UK, because this country is not self-sufficient in many of the products that it needs. About half of the food eaten in the UK is produced in other countries; as we saw illustrated in the pervious section the UK has a £5 billion food trade gap. It also has a scarcity of raw materials and so must import such commodities as copper, zinc, iron ore, and rubber.

The UK spends about one third of its national income on imports, a proportion that has increased as the UK has grown richer. It can only continue to purchase goods from abroad by earning foreign currency through selling its own products and services to foreigners. Fortunately, the UK is able to sell products and services abroad and this has meant that it has been able to pay its way in the world.

To illustrate the types of visible trade, see the table below.

Visible Trade of the UK				
Exports	**%**	**Imports**		**%**
Food, beverages and tabacco	7.8	Food beverages and tabacco		10.3
Basic materials	2.0	Basic materials		4.2
Fuels	6.0	Fuels		5.0
Manufacture	82.2	Manufacturers		79.0
Others	2.0	Others		1.5
Total	**100.00**	**Total**		**100.00**

Source: Monthly Digest of Statistics April 1992 (HMSO)

The UK still accounts for 10% of world trade, but this is a declining percentage. In most years since 1945, the UK has imported more goods than it exported, which has meant a deficit in the balance of visible trade. However, since the exploitation of North Sea oil in the late 1970s, the country has not found it necessary to import as much oil and, in fact, has become a net exporter of oil. This has meant that exports have improved relative to imports, leading to a visible trade surplus in several of the last years. Unfortunately, the rest of our visible exports have not fared as well: the improvement in the oil trade has been offset by a decline in the import/export balance for other goods, especially in manufactured products.

The late 1980s saw an increase in imports but this was not accompanied by any similar increase in the level of exports. Therefore a rapid deterioration of the visible trade balance resulted.

How this situation has changed over the years can be seen from the table below.

Visible Trade Balance	£ Million					
	1980	**1981**	**1982**	**1983**	**1984**	**1985**
Visible Exports	47149	50668	55331	60700	70265	77991
Visible Imports	45792	47416	53421	62237	75601	−81336
Visible Balance	1357	3252	1910	−1537	−5336	−3345
	1986	**1987**	**1988**	**1989**	**1990**	**1991**
Visible Exports	72627	79153	80346	92389	102038	103704
Visible Imports	82186	90735	101970	116987	120713	113823
Visible Balance	−9559	−11582	−21624	−24598	−18675	−10119

Source: United Kingdom Balance of Payments (HMSO)

2.   *Invisible trade*

As the table shows the UK has had a massive *visible* trade deficit for many years. If this was the only type of trade in which countries were involved, then the UK would have gone deeper and deeper into debt. However, another important aspect of international trade is the import and export of services. As these are not physical products and cannot be seen, this is known as *invisible trade*. Examples of invisible exports are the UK's provision of banking, shipping and insurance services to the world. For these, the UK receives payments from abroad and although it may, at times, have to pay out large sums, for instance on claims for the Los Angeles riots, the Piper Alpha oil rig explosion or the Exxon Valdez spillage, its receipts for these services outweigh the costs which it might have to bear.

Another important form of invisible trade is tourism. The position of tourism in the balance of payments can produce confusion. For example, an American tourist coming on holiday to London is, in fact, part of our *invisible exports*. Although the tourist is coming into this country, he or she is bringing in money to spend in the UK, which is the equivalent of selling a British product abroad. Conversely, when a British tourist goes on holiday to Spain, that is part of our *invisible imports,* since sterling spent abroad is the equivalent of staying in the UK and importing a foreign product.

The following table shows the balance in invisible trade for the UK for recent years.

Invisible Trade Balance	£ Million					
	1980	**1981**	**1982**	**1983**	**1984**	**1985**
Invisible Balance	1487	3496	2741	5302	7146	6222
	1986	**1987**	**1988**	**1989**	**1990**	**1991**
Invisible Balance	9747	7423	6103	4195	4292	5719

Source: United Kingdom Balance of Payments (HMSO)

The sum of visible and invisible trade is called the *Current Account of the balance of payments*; it represents the country's ability to pay for goods and services without having to borrow.

Current Account of the Balance of Payments 1980/90	£ Million					
	1980	**1981**	**1982**	**1983**	**1984**	**1985**
Visible Balance	1357	3252	1910	–1537	–5336	–3345
Invisible Balance	1487	3496	2741	5302	7146	6222
Current Account Total	2844	6748	4649	3765	1810	2877
	1986	**1987**	**1988**	**1989**	**1990**	
Visible Balance	–9559	–11582	–21624	–24598	–18675	
Invisible Balance	9747	7423	6103	4195	4292	
Current Account Total	–188	–4159	–15521	–20403	–14383	

Source: United Kingdom Balance of Payments 1991 (HMSO)

A little help on interpretation: If the figures shown have a minus sign (–) in front, this means that more money has left the country than has come into it, in other words a trade deficit. If there is no sign, or a positive sign (+), then this means that more money has come into the country than has gone out and so there is a trade surplus. Thus, on its current account the UK has had a trade deficit for each year since 1986.

UK Trade

Selected areas, 1990, seasonally adjusted

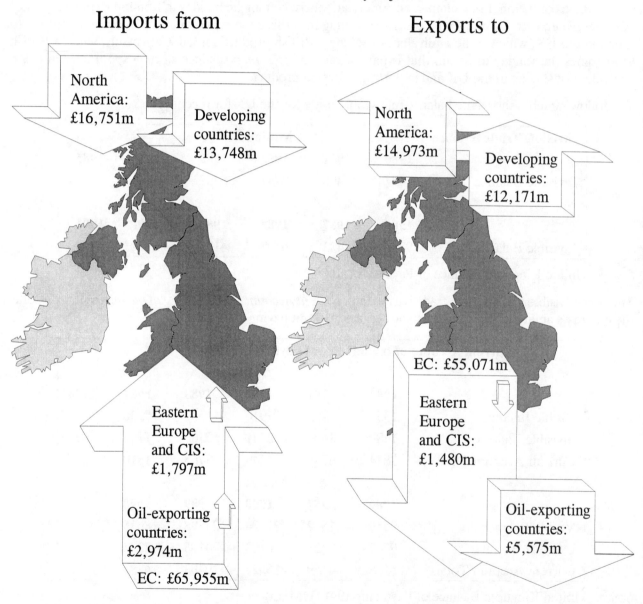

Why Should the UK Trade?

Every economy has a certain combination of resources which may be combined to produce goods and services. Each country has a different mix of resources. The UK has a workforce capable of producing highly sophisticated technological products, but has a shortage of many of the raw materials required to manufacture them. If every country in the world were to attempt to produce all its needs domestically and no international trade took place, then the world and its population would be much poorer, for each country would have to divert some of its resources from producing those products which it is most capable of making, towards less productive but necessary goods and services. The problem is: which goods and services should each country produce?

Countries tend to try and produce some of the basic necessities they need domestically so as not to be totally dependent on others. So the UK decides to produce some food in this country which could be produced more cheaply abroad. However, a country should specialise in the production of those goods or services *for which it has a comparative advantage over others.* Trade encourages specialisation and also makes it feasible.

Comparative advantage in trade

Some countries can produce many goods more cheaply and effectively than the rest of the world. Does this mean that the less efficient countries should produce nothing and buy from the cheaper country? No, it simply means that they should produce those products in which they have the *least comparative disadvantage* and the country which can produce most cheaply should specialise in those goods and services in which it has the greatest *comparative advantage.*

For example, there are two countries: one has an agricultural economy while the second has a highly trained manufacturing workforce. If both specialise in the production of those goods which they can make most efficiently, then the overall output of both agriculture and manufactures will be *maximised.* They can then trade between each other so that both end up with sufficient food and manufactures to meet their needs.

Least comparative disadvantage in trade

What if one of the countries is more efficient in the production of *both* types of output? Clearly, it would be unrealistic for the less productive one to produce nothing. If it did, it would have nothing to trade and would not survive. Therefore it is most sensible for the less efficient country to produce those things in which it has the least comparative disadvantage.

Reality of world trade

Of course, the situation outlined is a simplification of what actually happens in international trade. In many countries, industries have grown and developed prior to the establishment of an effective system of international trade and transport. The capital investment which has already been made has created an industrial structure which cannot easily be changed. A country's labour force may well have developed certain specific trades or skills. To change them would cause considerable social and economic upheaval. Overall, there is a gross imbalance in the terms of world trade, with developed nations (the 'Western' countries or 'the North') benefiting from a net inflow of US$50 billion each year.

Balance of payments

How does the UK assess the value of its trade? How important is the balance of payments to the economy as a whole?

A country's balance of payments statement is simply a comprehensive summary of all of the individual trading activities in which both the private and the public sector of the economy take part. The balance of payments statement covers a specific period and the most important time period over which it is measured is one year. At this time, the government uses the figures to determine how much the country has bought or sold in the previous twelve months and whether this trade has resulted in a surplus or a deficit.

The mechanics of the balance of payments

The system used to analyse the balance of payments is known as *double entry book-keeping*. All that this means is that every trading transaction is entered into the account twice. For instance, if ICI sells £1m worth of chemicals to France, the value of the chemicals (£1m) is entered into a trade account as a credit. The French company buying the chemicals must also pay for the goods, either in francs or by transferring the payment into £ sterling. This is entered into a second account as an increase in the country's currency holdings. This increase, whether in francs or pounds, is shown in sterling. If the payment has been made in francs, this entry is made by converting the value of the francs at the prevailing exchange rate.

The current account

The balance of payments is made up of several accounts, the first of which is the *Current Account*. This itemises the transactions in goods and services: visible exports and imports. Imports make up the largest item on the debit side of this account. Fortunately, the rest of the world buys many of our products to compensate for our visible imports and, also, the UK often acts as a middleman for the rest of the world's trade. So many of the imports seen on the debit side of the account as visible imports are then re-exported, following manufacture into some finished product or simply after being re-packaged.

Despite these exports and re-exports, the Visible Account has often been in deficit and such a deficit has come to be known as the 'Trade Gap'. The exploitation of North Sea oil has had a considerable impact in reducing the visible trade deficit and in some years this account managed to reach a surplus position. The visible trade account is sometimes called the 'balance of trade'.

The second part of the trade account is the *invisible* trade account. This covers all the non-physical services which the UK provides and buys. The UK is second only to the US with regard to invisible trade. The City of London is the major financial centre in the world; its provision of banking, insurance and shipping services is a major foreign currency earner for the UK. The invisible trade balance is normally in surplus and this helps to offset any visible trade deficit, helped by earnings from tourism.

Investment and other capital transactions

The second part of the balance of payments is sometimes called the *Capital Account,* but is more correctly called *the Investment and Capital Flows Account*. This covers all transfers of capital into and out of the country. These occur as a result of investments, government lending or borrowing and the transfer of money through bank accounts. It is sub-divided into:

- official capital flows
- private capital flows.

Official financing

If the overall balance of payments is in deficit, the country has spent more abroad than it has received and this has to be financed in some way. It can do this either by borrowing or by drawing from the foreign currency reserves which have accumulated as a result of previous trade surpluses.

The government will borrow foreign currency, either from the International Monetary Fund (IMF) or, occasionally, from foreign banks. If the overall balance is a surplus, then the government can use the surplus currency to add to its reserves or to repay debts it has already incurred.

The reserves

The government is reluctant to deplete its reserves since it must also use these foreign currency assets to maintain the value of its currency when it comes under speculative pressure.

The value of the pound

Sterling as a reserve currency

Much of the world's trade is carried on in US dollars and, to a lesser extent, in other major currencies, such as £ sterling and deutschmarks. These are *reserve currencies* because most countries in the world tend to hold these three currencies or gold. This means that the value of these currencies can be influenced, not only by the actions of their own countries' governments and by trade transactions, but also by that of other countries, organisations or individuals. This has placed a strain on the pound in recent years and the UK government has said that it no longer wishes to see the pound regarded as an international means of exchange. This problem is heightened by speculation in sterling which influences its value. However, until a more suitable system is established, then it is likely that the pound will remain as a reserve currency.

Fixed and floating exchange rates

Before 1971 the pound's value in relation to other currencies was fixed; after that date a system of floating exchange rates was introduced. In theory, this was based on the value of a currency being determined by its supply and demand. If the UK does not sell much abroad, then foreigners do not have a high demand for pounds since they do not need as many of them to pay British exporters.

As demand for exports falls, there is a corresponding fall in the demand for pounds. In the same way that a fall in demand for any commodity will reduce its price, this fall in demand for sterling will reduce its price. In this case, the price of the pound is the value that it holds against other currencies. If the exchange rate falls, UK exports become relatively cheaper on world markets as foreign buyers do not have to pay as much in their own currency to purchase British goods. So the goods become more attractive and foreigners now buy more British goods and, in order to pay for them, they must have more pounds. Demand for pounds goes up and eventually the value of the currency will stabilise at a point where the balance of payments is in equilibrium.

World Market

World trade in merchandisable goods in 1989-90, in $ billions.
Excludes services which are worth about 20% of merchandise trade
Exports From...

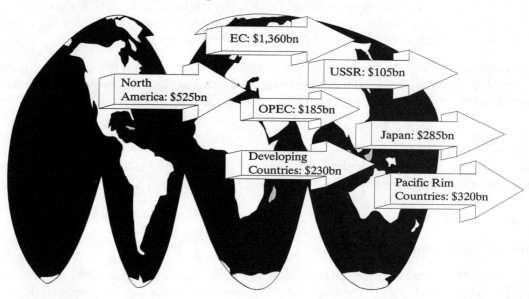

Imports to...

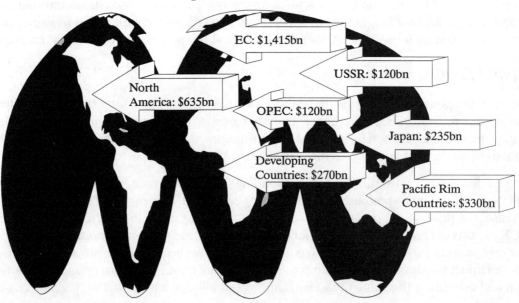

In theory, the price of the pound, (its exchange rate) will rise or fall according to the demand for it and the supply of it, until demand equals supply at the point where imports match exports and the balance of payments actually balances.

Complications for floating the pound

There are two main problems when the pound is allowed to float freely.

1. The influence of speculation

The idea behind floating the pound was that the demand for currency for use in trade purposes would be the main determining factor in setting the exchange rate. However, there is considerable speculation in world currencies, with people using them not as a means of financing trade, but as commodities which can be traded in to make profit.

A recent estimate suggests that 95% of all currency transactions in foreign exchange markets are undertaken for speculation rather than for financing foreign trade. If speculators decide that sterling is about to fall in value, they will transfer all their money from sterling to dollars. This will cause a massive growth in demand for dollars and a similar drop in demand (and an increase in supply) of pounds. The result will be that the pound falls in value against the dollar. This is known as speculation.

During 1984 and early 1985 the pound fell to its lowest ever level of £1 to $1.04. This was because foreign speculators were worried that oil prices would fall and that the pound as a so-called 'petro-currency' (because of the importance of oil as a part of the UK economy) would fall.

2. The effect of the exchange rate on domestic inflation

The exchange rate also has a significant effect on the rate of domestic inflation, since the UK is dependent on imported food, raw materials and much else. These have to be bought even if their price goes up. A fall in the value of the pound – which causes import prices to rise – will not result in a significant fall in imports, but merely an increase in their price. If the exchange rate falls 5%, this will cause a 1% increase in domestic inflation.

If a government is trying to minimise inflation, it must keep the value of the pound as high as possible. However, if it does this, it can result in fewer exports (since they will be more expensive abroad) and more imports (because they will be cheaper in the UK), thus worsening the balance of payments. The government must decide what is its more urgent priority: keeping down inflation or eradicating a balance of payments deficit.

Future Prospects for the UK Balance of Payments

The UK has been in balance of payments deficit for most of the last thirty years. However, North Sea oil has meant the UK has become a net exporter of oil, thus adding to the credit side of the balance of payments. It should be noted that this favourable addition to the credit side of the balance is somewhat misleading, since UK exports in products or commodities, other than oil, have actually fallen relative to imports over the same period. Deficits greater than £10 billion are treated now as commonplace. In the first two months of 1992 the current account deficit stood at £1558 million. The trade gap continues to widen: since the 1987 election, which returned a Conservative government to office for the third successive time, only one month has seen the current account in the black.

Means of Controlling the Balance of Payments

If this situation continues what are the possible solutions for the UK government?

Many people believe that the UK should try and protect some of its infant industries. 'Infant industries' are those industries which are only just establishing themselves. For example, the French government places import restrictions on certain electrical products. This is to allow the domestic French economy to develop their production. Traditional industries also may require protection from foreign competition. Imports can be restricted by the use of:

- tariffs

- quotas.

Tariffs are taxes which can be levied on all imports or on specific commodities. The effect of a tariff will depend on the demand for the product. If there is relatively inelastic demand and the domestic industry is unable to produce the product at a price which is less than the import price plus the tariff then the tax will be relatively ineffective. If demand for the import continues then it is in effect a tax on the domestic consumer. It will only be a successful means of curbing imports if the product has an elastic demand or home producers can step in to meet the demand for imports which has been diverted to domestic products because of the import tariff.

Quotas are restrictions placed on the *quantity* of a commodity which is allowed in to the country. Quotas may be statutory (imposed by the government) or voluntary.

There are several problems associated with the introduction of tariffs and quotas.

1.   *The UK is party to a general world agreement which discourages tariffs.*

     This is called GATT (The General Agreement on Tariffs and Trade). This agreement is signed by 170 countries and has led to a general reduction in tariffs and quotas throughout the world. It is based on four principles:

     - that there should be no 'favoured nation status'. In other words, all GATT member nations should receive the same treatment in respect of import controls

     - when import controls are imposed these should be in the form of tariffs and not statutory quotas

     - that there should be consultation between members wherever possible on matters relating to trade restrictions

     GATT members should work to reduce tariffs between members. GATT has proved very successful in reducing the imposition of tariffs and quotas and doing this has led to a significant increase in world trade. GATT has worked hard to reduce the $500 billion that unequal or restricted access to world trade and their financial and labour markets is estimated to cost the poor countries of the world each year.

2. *The UK is a member of the European Economic Community (EC)*. This restricts our freedom to influence trade both within the EC – to and from fellow member countries – as well as outside the EC. The EC has two functions:

   - it is a customs union and as such does not, at least in theory, allow the imposition of any trade restrictions such as tariffs and quotas between its member states; the implications of the Single European Market are considered later

   - it imposes a common external tariff. This means that imports to any country in the EC are subject to the same level of tariff taxation. In this way the EC increases the import price of those goods which are also produced within the EC and so allows Community producers to compete on equal terms with imports which are produced more cheaply abroad. The structure and functions of the EC are more fully discussed later.

3. *There is the possibility that such trade restrictions could actually be disadvantageous if levied on specific countries*. It is suggested that these countries could retaliate in turn and impose similar restrictions on our exports to their countries. However, it has been pointed out that Japan, whose imports are often suggested as a possible target for such *import controls*, does not import on any major scale from the UK and so any retaliation on their part would be relatively ineffective.

Import controls have been suggested as a possible short-term solution to any future balance of payments problem as they would allow a gradual realignment of the UK's industries without the shock of rapid upheaval in our industrial base caused by massive unemployment. Those who hold the opposite view have argued that such measures are merely 'featherbedding' inefficient British industry. In other words, tariffs and quotas would not allow such industries to face the harsh realities of economic life in the world today. If industries are inefficient, then they should be allowed to 'go under', and their resources used in more cost-effective and competitive industries.

Perhaps the reality of the world economic situation is such that if you look at declining industries in most of the Western nations, you will find that they are being subsidised to a much greater extent than those in the UK. Therefore, the UK government could recognise that it must try and combine a realistic economic approach to international trade with the need for an understanding and compassionate approach to those workers faced with long-term unemployment. Such job losses are partly a consequence of the decline in our traditional industries, like coal, steel and shipbuilding, and so the imposition of trade controls should not always been seen as the abandonment of free market ideals but, instead, a recognition that UK governments are prepared to protect the jobs of its workers.

The Government can Stimulate Investment in UK Exporters

A further alternative, which has been suggested and tried in the past, is the encouragement of UK industry to invest and, in so doing, to become more internationally competitive. Such a policy may involve the government in persuading the banks to give loans at cheaper rates to exporters. The government can also give exporters specific tax relief on investment or guarantee that exporters will be paid for their products sold in certain countries.

This can prove difficult in practice, as was found in the early 1970s by the Heath Government. It sought to encourage British industry to re-invest, prior to the UK's entry into the EC. The cheap loans which were given were often not used for investment in exporting industry but instead were used for property speculation and domestic consumption, helping in the process to fuel inflation.

The main policy at the current time is not to directly subsidise exports, but more to encourage businesses to attempt to break into foreign markets. Aid is given in the form of grants to facilitate research into foreign markets and to prepare detailed financial analyses of such export projects. Subsidies for actual products or services are now virtually non-existent.

Deflation of the Economy

Finally, if the balance of payments deficit is sufficiently large, as it was in 1974, 1975 and 1976, the government may be faced with the need to *deflate* the overall economy and in so doing reduce the demand for imports. Unfortunately, this will have the side effect of also making it more difficult for exporters to produce, as interest rates may increase and this can also lead to higher domestic unemployment.

The UK has been extremely lucky to have the cushion of North Sea oil which has cushioned the country from even greater balance of payments problems in recent years. However, when the oil runs out, the UK could well be faced with a disastrous situation. Therefore, policies designed to revitalise export industries – and ensure that the products the UK makes can compete with those of the rest of the world – are even more imperative.

The Single European Market

The Historical Background

The idea of establishing a Single European Market is not a new one. Indeed, the concept dates back to the Treaty of Rome which established the original European Economic Community in 1951. The growth of the EC is shown on the map opposite. The original plans for the establishment of the Single European Market were based on political factors. Europe had just come through a terrible war, and a common desire existed for peace and unity. The EC was perceived as an outstanding opportunity for nations to rebuild after the War and to give to each other mutual support. It was hoped that the possibility of any future conflict in Europe would also be minimised by the 'economic marriage' of various states.

The United Kingdom refused to join the original EC for a number of reasons, some economic some political. However, since 1973 the UK has been a full member of the Community. At present the EC numbers twelve member states.

In 1992 there are four more applications to join the market from Austria, Cyprus, Malta and Turkey. Finland, Norway, Iceland, Sweden and Switzerland are also thinking of applying. Improving relations between East and West, and the establishment of 'market economies' in countries such as Poland, and the old Baltic and Soviet states, makes it likely that there will be a flood of applicants from the old Eastern bloc countries.

In 1985, the EC heads of government committed their states to the formation of a Single European Market by 1992. Their proposals were formalised in the package of Treaty reforms known as the Single European

Act, which came into operation on 1 July 1987. The difference between these new proposals and those of 1951 is that the motive behind them is now primarily economic. Europe as a whole has recognised the need to combine to form a cohesive unit in the face of considerable competition from their major economic rivals. The domestic market within the EC now amounts to some 320 million people, which is almost as large as Japan and the USA combined, but with the potential to become even larger.

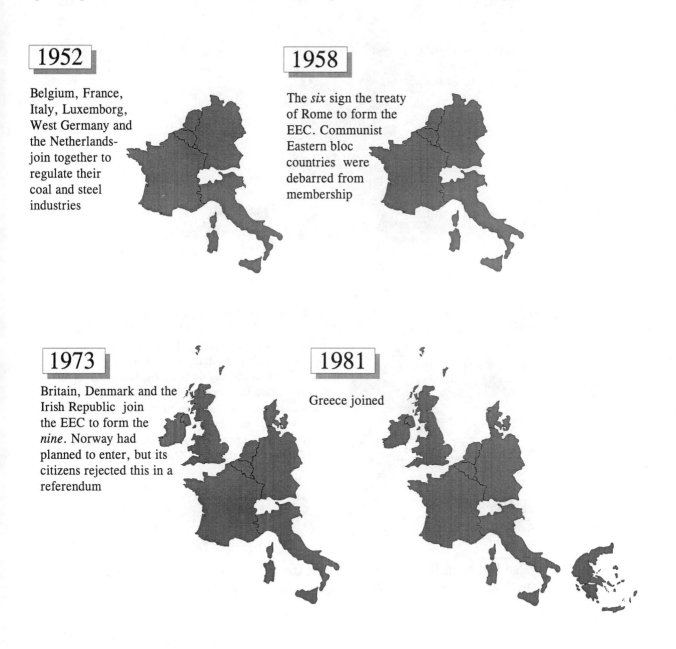

1952

Belgium, France, Italy, Luxemborg, West Germany and the Netherlands-join together to regulate their coal and steel industries

1958

The *six* sign the treaty of Rome to form the EEC. Communist Eastern bloc countries were debarred from membership

1973

Britain, Denmark and the Irish Republic join the EEC to form the *nine*. Norway had planned to enter, but its citizens rejected this in a referendum

1981

Greece joined

1986

Portugal and Spain
joined bringing
the total to 12

1994?

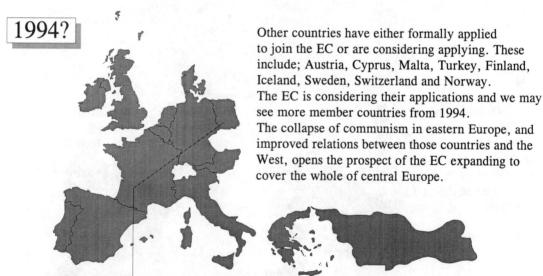

Other countries have either formally applied
to join the EC or are considering applying. These
include; Austria, Cyprus, Malta, Turkey, Finland,
Iceland, Sweden, Switzerland and Norway.
The EC is considering their applications and we may
see more member countries from 1994.
The collapse of communism in eastern Europe, and
improved relations between those countries and the
West, opens the prospect of the EC expanding to
cover the whole of central Europe.

What had been East Germany joined the EC on 3rd
Oct 1990, when it became part of a united Germany

The EC's gradual growth as a trading bloc

In 1991 the EC and EFTA (the European Free Trade Association) agreed to form a single European Economic Area, which would come in to existence on 1 January, 1993, the same day as the Single Market begins to operate. This enlarged nineteen nation Economic Area would hold a market of 380 million consumers, stretching from the Mediterranean Sea to the Arctic Ocean. It will be responsible for almost 50% of world trade. Recent years have seen a considerable rise in the importance of trade between member states: in 1990, 68% of total trade was conducted within the European Economic Area. Almost 50% of UK exports are now destined for EC states, whilst over 50% of our imports come from these same eleven nations.

Economic Pressures Behind the Need for a Single European Market

Various economic factors have played an important part in convincing the member states that the time is right for them to come together. These can be summarised under the following headings:

1. *The evolution of the world economy*

   Japan has emerged now as the strongest economy in the world. The whole area of the Pacific Basin has grown significantly in terms of economic importance, and the growth of high-tech markets has meant that fewer countries can survive on domestic markets alone.

2. *The increased mobility of capital*

   The world financial markets are now so structured as to facilitate easy transfer of funds between countries. However, the problem of this freedom undermining of domestic economic policy has encouraged many EC member states to seek 'safety in numbers'.

3. *The UK government's domestic economic policies*

   Traditional economic thinking in post-war Europe was based on Keynesian demand management policies. As you read earlier, recent years have seen a marked move towards what are known as 'supply side' policies. These involve the creation of the correct circumstances for economic growth and prosperity. One major element of current UK government policy is the encouragement of the application of market principles and the removal of all barriers to trade – exactly the aim of the Single European Market.

The UK Treasury's *Economic Progress Report*, in October 1988, actually describes the move towards the unified Europe as being designed to:

> *'.... improve economic performance by removing unnecessary regulation and exposing economies to market forces. Just as the Government has vigorously pioneered this approach in the UK, so they have vigorously promoted it within the EC.'*

Whether the UK actually continues to promote the new unified market as vigorously is a matter for some speculation.

The Single Market Programme

The underlying theme of the Single European Market is the removal of various barriers to trade from within the EC. In practice this will involve removing some three hundred specific barriers to trade, and thus encouraging the free movement of people, goods, services and capital between member nations. The

European Commission itself has provided a distinction between the various types of barrier which it claims now exist. These can be summarised as follows:

1. *Barriers which increase costs*

    An example of this type of barrier might be unnecessary delays at customs. Whilst this does not technically *prevent* competition, it does increase the cost of the incoming (or, indeed, outgoing) product and, as such, will deter competition.

2. *Barriers which prevent market entry*

    Examples might include the technical requirements laid down by various member states governing the standards required of products; the 'public procurement' policies which are frequently adopted, whereby a government will only buy goods or services from within its own country. A further example would be the lack of universal recognition within the EC of various qualifications, and thus the lack of standardisation. Barriers of this nature will actually prevent competition from taking place.

3. *Barriers which distort the market*

    Specific taxes or subsidies and price controls will distort the level of competition which is possible within a country. This type of policy will invariably favour the 'native nation'.

The task of removing these numerous barriers to trade is not easy. However, in order to facilitate the move towards the Single European Market, a significant change was made to the way in which EC decisions are made. Previously, proposals of this kind would need unanimous support before being accepted as EC policy. Now, the proposals need only to obtain 'qualified majority voting' between ministers, so, in theory, allowing much more flexibility for change.

Potential Gains from the Single European Market

To quote the DTI, the single market means a *process of liberalisation which allows market forces to work ... All new proposals will be assessed for their impact on business.* The aim is therefore to reduce costs to business, in order that these benefits may be passed on to the final consumer in the form of reduced prices and wider choice.

Economists are optimistic in their predictions of the benefits the Single Market will bring. In order to turn the concept into a reality there are many obstacles that must be overcome.

Possible Problems in the Establishment of the Single European Market

Various problems have been identified which could lead to severe problems in the practicalities of the Single European Market. They include:

1. *Taxation*

    A truly united Europe will necessitate some form of *standardisation of indirect taxation*. This will inevitably reduce the power of member countries to set their own tax rates; as such it will remove some of their sovereignty. VAT rates, or its equivalent, vary substantially throughout Europe, both in terms of the level and also the range of goods and services on which it is charged. The thought of VAT on books, food and children's clothes is a notion designed not to win any political friends. Duties on items, such as drink and tobacco, also vary considerably. Should the UK be required to reduce these tax levels on the basis of standardisation, then this might lead to a number of problems; for example, successive British governments have long cited health issues as a major motive for punitive taxes, and will be reticent to alter this policy.

2. *Trade with the rest of the world*

A Single European Market would necessitate a *common policy towards trade* with other nations within the world. Traditional markets would therefore be affected as some countries are made to fall into line with other member states.

3. *Mutual recognition*

Whilst the theory of mutual *recognition of qualifications* is admirable, the practical problems could prove to be insurmountable. Standards of qualifications vary considerably, as do standards of workmanship. The language barrier is also a major hurdle to the establishment of a freely mobile European workforce.

4. *Financial markets*

Again, in theory, banks and other financial institutions will be able to establish themselves freely in all member countries. However, the availability of credit in certain states, such as Germany, could be particularly problematic. Institutions keen to lend money to the German public will find severe opposition from a State government committed to a strict monetary control policy.

5. *Public procurement policies*

The expenditure of public authorities throughout the EC amounts to a significant proportion of total spending. Traditionally, many member states have confined this spending to domestic producers/suppliers. The Single Market will mean freedom of competition in all markets and, as such, public authorities will be expected to open themselves up to competition from other member nations. In practice, this may prove politically difficult to implement. If a government or local authority is concerned solely with cost, then the cheapest product or service may well come from another EC state. However, whether spending outside the domestic market will be *politically* acceptable is more uncertain. Many public authorities have spending criteria other than simple cost; for example, the preservation of local industries and employment. An authority which actively imports, to the detriment of its own domestic workforce might face a potentially disastrous political backlash.

European Monetary Union

In 1991 the present twelve states of the EC signed the Treaty of Maastricht. As well as dealing with the subjects of political union, the Treaty contained a timetable for the establishment of Economic and Monetary Union (EMU). The timetable contained procedures to ensure that, after 1996, each member moves to a single European currency once finance ministers have decided which of the EC currencies comply with the 'convergence' criteria. The five 'convergence' criteria are that each country should:

1. have an inflation rate no higher than 1.5% above the average of the three EC countries with the lowest price rises

2. have interest rates that are within 2% of the average of the three members with the lowest rate

3. have a budget deficit no greater than 3% of its Gross Domestic Product (GDP)

4. have a PSBR no greater than 60% of GDP

5. have a currency that has not been devalued in the previous two years and one that remains within the normal 2.25% fluctuation margin of ERM.

Those countries which fulfil all five of the criteria will adopt the ECU as their single currency by 1999; the UK has reserved the right to opt out.

The Advantage of a Single Currency

It is calculated that, since each EC country has its own currency, a traveller who started a journey with £100, and changed it into the local currency of each member country, would have only £28 remaining at the end of the journey, yet would have spent nothing. This is due to the cost of converting currency as one moves from country to country: a single European currency, such as the ECU, would avoid these charges.

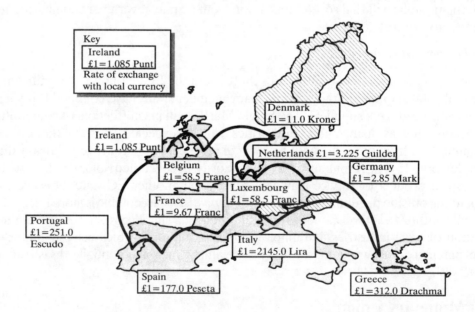

Currency conversion within the EC

Under EMU a single central bank in Europe would set interest rates and regulate exchange rates for all EC member states. If all the member states agreed to implement full monetary union, the pound might become a thing of the past. The present twelve currencies would be merged into a strong, single European currency, the ECU (European Currency Unit). This would allow Europe to compete effectively against the US and Japan – after all, the Americans have the dollar, the Japanese the yen, so why not Europe the ECU? There are two main arguments against EMU:

1. *A single currency can only be created at a punitive cost to some of the poorer members*
   There are significant differences in the economies of the twelve countries; these differences would benefit the richer parts of Europe while causing unemployment in the poorer areas. Poorer countries would be unable to adjust the value of their currency in order to help them to compete with their richer partners. They would have to face up to a period of slow or zero economic growth while they (painfully) lowered their costs.

2. *The loss of control over the currency by national parliaments*
   Since control would pass to a non-elected committee of bankers, they might well take decisions that are against the interests of individual countries.

European Monetary System (EMS)

The European Monetary System is designed to eliminate the problems caused by fluctuating exchange rates. Those countries which are 'full' members of the EMS set agreed ranges of exchange rates for all of their currencies, based on a weighted average of a basket of currencies. When a member state's currency reaches the extremes of its given range, the Central Banks of the other member states buy or sell as appropriate in order to avoid the currency moving outside of its limits.

A three-stage process has been proposed, aimed at achieving full monetary union within the EC. The stages are:

1. All member states to become full participants of the EMS

2. A central decision making body to be established, consisting of the representatives from member states, with the role of centralising financial decision-making. This would lead to a standardisation of all financial variables, such as interest rates, throughout the EC

3. The implementation of a common currency, the (ECU), and thus the total harmonisation of all financial decision-making within the EC.

The 1987-92 Conservative Government was not fully supportive of these moves. Various arguments have been advanced against full monetary union, such as the fact that it is a distortion on the free operation of market forces, but more particularly that it will remove the sovereignty of the government to conduct the UK economy in the manner which they see fit. As such, the UK has so far resisted any temptation to become a full member of the EMS. However, the Prime Minister recently agreed, in principle, to stage one of the process outlined above. This was to be at a time when the UK inflation rate was lower, and therefore more comparable to the rest of the EC. No date was fixed, and stages 2 and 3 still appear to be very distant targets.

The Exchange Rate Mechanism (ERM)

The ERM is the Exchange Rate Mechanism. Until 1992, the UK was a member of the ERM, before the events of 'Black (or 'White') Wednesday' forced the Chancellor to declare that we could no longer belong to it and the pound sterling would be allowed to find its own level. An immediate result of abandoning the ERM was that the value of the £ fell by about 25% against the mark and the dollar. Although the government has declared its intention to rejoin the ERM "when the time is right", many people doubt its commitment to the ERM and would be surprised were the UK to becomae a member again.

As it stands the ERM keeps most European currencies linked to each other within fixed rates or bands. Thus the member currencies move as a block or raft against the yen, dollar and other world currencies. Each member government is obliged to set its currency at a level that will keep it at its ERM rate; thus, if a currency is falling in the money markets, the government must make it more attractive by raising domestic interest rates. When it is rising, the government will cut its interest rates in an attempt to encourage currency traders to divest themselves of their currency.

The ERM is a mechanism for linking the currencies of participating European countries within specified limits; its purpose is to bring about relative currency stability between member countries. If the ERM brings about a stabilisation of currencies, this halts those fluctuations which brings uncertainty to business people who need to be certain of the costs of its imports and its receipts from exports. The ERM keeps currencies within a fixed band, thus giving greater certainty over prices and costs.

The consequences of ERM membership are that if a country's goods are to remain competitively priced, then its prices should not rise quicker or more sharply than those of other countries. This, in turn, means that inflation has to be kept in check since the effects of inflation would be to:

- make that country's goods uncompetitive when sold abroad

- shrink that country's domestic market by 'sucking in' cheaper foreign goods.

Assume an exchange rate of 2 French Francs to the German Mark, and that the rate of inflation in the France in Year 1 is 10% and that it is also 10% in Germany.

	Cost in France	Cost in Germany
Beginning of Year 1		
Renault	120,000 FF	60,000 DM
Volkswagen	120,000 FF	60,000 DM
End of Year 1		
Renault	132,00 FF	66,000 DM
Volkswagen	132,000 FF	66,000 DM

So long as the the inflation rates in France and Germany remain reasonably close, then price parity will remain. Suppose, though, in Year 2 inflation in France remained at 10%, whilst in Germany it was reduced to 5%.

	Cost in France	Cost in Germany
Beginning of Year 2		
Renault	132,000 FF	66,000 DM
Volkswagen	132,000 FF	66,000 DM
End of Year 2		
Renault	145,200 FF	72,600 DM
Volkswagen	138,600 FF	69,300 DM

As under the ERM exchange rates remain relatively fixed, the price of the French-built Renault has became uncompetitive in both France and in Germany when priced against the Volkswagen. In France more car buyers will be attracted to VW by virtue of its price, and likewise in Germany, the potential buyers of Renault many will be put off by its increased price.

In the past, a floating exchange rate would have meant that German consumers would get more francs for their deutschmarks, enabling the real price of a Renault in Germany to remain competitive.

Although control of inflation has always been one of the main objectives of all European governments, it has now assumed an even greater significance if the overall balance of a country's trade within the EC is to be maintained and even improved.

The Social Chapter

Whilst most people are by now aware of the Single Market, few will know of the Social Chapter – other than the Conservative Government's opposition to it. The Chapter is intended to standardise working conditions throughout the Community so that workers in each member state enjoy improved working conditions and worker consultation. The UK government argued that its adoption would make the EC uncompetitive. Member states, except for the UK, gave a commitment to the social chapter and reached a compromise whereby they 'opted in' to the agreement. In July 1993, the House of Commons finally ratified the Maastricht Treaty but only after the Prime Minister had to call for a vote of confidence in order to pull the Tory 'Eurosceptic' rebels into line. However, the ratification does not include agreement to the Social Chapter.

Doubts on the Future of the Single European Market

The predictions of the benefits of the Single European Market were all based on the 'medium term', following what the EC describe as 'adjustments'. The actual nature of these 'adjustments' will necessarily vary from member state to member state. Inevitably, there will be winners and losers. Some domestic markets will find themselves 'overthrown' by fierce foreign competition, with resultant costs in terms of industrial closures and job losses. Other industries will find the opportunity to expand into a much larger market decidedly to their advantage.

Some nations were more prepared than others for 1993. The UK government ran an 'awareness raising' campaign, aimed at consumers, but more specifically at industry. The message is that the Single Market is not the 'end of the process', but the beginning. The UK lagged behind the rest of Europe in its planning for the Single Market, partly because of a lack of awareness of the opportunity which the Single Market will afford to business. The signs are that business is now accepting the need for change and preparation, although this is by no means a universal view.

Many critics claim that the problems of the Single Market are far from being ironed out. The government's commitment to the policy will be tested should its own sovereignty be challenged. Mrs. Thatcher is quoted as saying:

> *'we have not successfully rolled back the frontiers of the state in Britain to see them reimposed* (in Brussels).'

The director-general of Britain's Institute of Directors, Sir John Hoskyns, recently said that 1992:

> *'... will fail to open frontiers, but cripple Europe with regulatory overheads so that a still fragmented Community will have gone down with the old British disease.'*

Such pessimism does not augur well for the future of the Single European Market. Talk of a staggered introduction of the measures may lead to what a leading economic commentator has described as:

> *'... the inner core of countries moving on to economic and monetary union on their own, as the more peripheral countries carry on making noises about sovereignty and imagined freedom of action.'*

Supporters of the Single Market argue that the largest economic benefit of a 'borderless' market will be seen in a reduction in costs to producers and prices to consumers. In addition, economies of scale will eventually reduce costs (and thus prices) even further. In the longer term, the Single Market will bring about a climate where industries of a size that can compete with those of the US and Japan will flourish. The figures below show the relative sizes of these three markets in 1988.

	EC	**US**	**Japan**
Population	324m	246m	123m
Gross Domestic Product	£2.54 bn	£2.63bn	£1.45bn

Whether the programme is a roaring success or an utter disaster remains to be seen.

The Role of Multi-national and Transnational Companies in the International Environment

One of the more significant factors affecting international trade both within the UK and throughout the world is the influence of multi-national companies. A 'multi-national' is a company which owns and controls a business operation outside the country in which it is based. In the UK there are many such multi-nationals. Some have their headquarters in the US, such as Ford, General Motors and IBM; others are based in Europe such as Philips and Nestles. The UK itself is the base for multi-national organisations such as British Petroleum, ICI and Lonrho, all of which have operations in many countries of the world. In most cases, multi-nationals establish domestic subsidiaries to carry out their business in other countries and this will, to some extent, isolate the parent company from the government control of the countries in which they operate. So, in the UK, Vauxhall is owned by General Motors of the US and Nissan (UK) is a wholly-owned subsidiary of its Japanese parent company.

The Growth of the Multi-nationals

One of the most striking characteristics of multi-nationals is their size. The largest multi-national company in 1992 was Royal Dutch Shell, which had a market valuation of $77.82 billion. The top UK multi-national is Glaxo, which is ranked twelfth largest in the world.

One of the largest multi-national companies in the world is Exxon. This may be a name with which you not familiar. In fact, in the UK it trades under the brand name of Esso and you will certainly recognise that particular brand of petrol. Exxon has a turnover throughout the world that matches the Gross National Product of all but the largest manufacturing nations. This is also true of General Motors and Ford who are the second and third largest companies in the world. It is a somewhat daunting fact to realise that the company president of Ford, elected by his shareholders, has control over a greater level of expenditure than the president of most of the nations of Europe. What is more, his corporate objectives are merely to increase the wealth of his shareholders, irrespective of the effect his decisions could have on the people who work for Ford throughout the world or the citizens of the countries in which his organisation has business interests.

Another significant factor to note is that the multi-nationals are growing at a rate which is almost twice that of the developed nations of the world and three times as fast as world trade since 1983. Given the fact that world trade growth fell from 7% to 5% in 1989-90, multi-national investment can be regarded as crucial to promoting economic growth. Indeed, the UN Centre on Transnational Corporations has suggested that corporate investment by these companies has become a dominant force in structuring the world economy. Investments by multi-national companies are a large, if not the largest, factor in determining the patterns of trade, flows of money and transfer of technology between nations. Not all countries are beneficiaries of this, however: whilst the EC, US and Japan account for more than 80% of capital flows in the 1980s, the share of total investment directed to developing countries dropped from 25% to 18% over the decade.

So, in the not too distant future, they could be as economically important as the major industrial nations. It would be impossible in a book of this nature to consider all aspects of the operations of multi-national companies, but here we will make some comment as to their investment and pricing policies.

The Investment Policies of the Multi-national Companies

The multi-national companies are the most significant source of industrial investment for any country in the world. They invest in two ways:

1. through direct investment by building plant or facilities for their subsidiaries in a country

2. by investing in the share capital of domestic companies.

Because of the financial size of this investment and the impact it can have on a particular country, the multi-nationals have considerable power. In the first place, they can decide where and how to invest in a country and, secondly, they can hold over a government the threat to withdraw their investment. So, for example, Ford, a major American multi-national, has been able to influence the domestic economic policy on incomes of the UK government by indicating that it might place a major investment in a new engine works in mainland Europe, rather than in the UK, and a Japanese multi-national, such as Nissan, can persuade the British government to offer it very attractive terms to establish a base in this country, rather than in continental Europe.

Furthermore, it is interesting to note that the strength of the multi-national company has changed to some extent. After 1945, the major multi-nationals were American companies; they tended to place their investments in countries where they felt confident there would continue to be political and economic stability: Europe, Canada and Australia. However, the multi-national companies which have been most prolific in their growth since the 1970s have been Japanese and their investment has often been in the Pacific Basin and close to their home base: Singapore, Taiwan and Hong Kong. The UK has seen a noticeable *disinvestment* or reduction in investment by many of the multi-nationals since the late 1970s, which has resulted in considerable job losses. The reason is that the UK has become less attractive as an industrial base and other countries have become more attractive. As multi-nationals are such large employers, their policy of closing factories can produce major job losses and it is often beyond the power of a national government to prevent such damaging action by them.

The Pricing Policy of the Multi-national Companies

A further important aspect of the operations of the multi-nationals is their pricing policy. Today more than 20% of world trade is between the subsidiaries of multi-nationals. By this is meant the trade within companies, where a subsidiary in one country manufactures a product and sells it to a subsidiary of the same company in another country. This allows the company to take advantage of the taxation differences between countries in order to maximise profit. A simple example may help to illustrate the process.

A multi-national car manufacturer may build cars in Spain for eventual sale in the UK. Spain has a much lower tax on company profits than that in the UK. Therefore the company wishes to make the profit for its Spanish subsidiary, rather than its UK subsidiary, and so consequently pay less tax.

The problem here is that the UK government provides the service which the company may need to operate in Britain and yet gains little tax revenue from the company's activities. It could even be offering substantial incentives to the company to invest in the UK. The investment capital could have come from the profit made from the sale of the car we have just considered.

It is almost impossible for a single government acting on its own to curtail this practice of *transfer pricing*. If the UK government attempted to impose any restrictions on the freedom of the multi-nationals to act in this way, it is likely that there would be considerable disinvestment in this country by them, with consequent job losses. Therefore the power of the multi-nationals to set their own prices is considerable.

Many multi-national companies which have not got a base within the EC are attempting to take over such EC-based businesses. This is partly due to a fear that Europe may close its doors after 1992, and partly an attempt to tap into what has become a huge market.

Challenges to the EC

1. The 'Japanese Miracle'

In the early 1980s a Japanese economist was attending a symposium on the world in the twenty-first century. He predicted that Japan would be the research laboratory of the world and the rest of Asia the factory, while the USA would be the granary. "And what about Europe?" asked one of the Europeans present. "Ah yes," the Japanese speaker said, "Europe will be Japan's boutique."

In the period between 1945, the end of the Second World War, and 1960, the UK failed to seize the opportunity and advantage over the war-damaged economies of Germany and Japan, to re-tool and invest for the future.

In 1945 Japan had been defeated by the US and its allies and had surrendered unconditionally; its people were almost at starvation point and its industries had collapsed. In an over-populated island, with little cultivable land and even fewer resources, the country seemed to face only a bleak future. Yet Japan rebounded from its predicament to become the world's wealthiest nation and a 'superpower' of the 1990s.

1945 saw the American General MacArthur force a democratic constitution and radical reforms upon the occupied nation in an historic clash of cultures. Whilst some of these changes have survived, the Japanese clung to many of their traditions. In the post-war years, an alliance of paternalistic politicians, big business and elite bureaucrats assumed the running of the country: 'Japan Inc.' used military efficiency to create world-beating industries, from cars to computing: so much so that by 1991 it was running a trade surplus of £104 billion and the first six months of 1992 saw the country export $163 billion worth of goods.

A specific instance of this failure by UK manufacturers to exploit their advantage is seen in the way that Japan was allowed to capitalise upon what its researchers found post-austerity consumers wanted: goods like motorbikes, televisions, electronics etc. These were markets which Japan built up aggressively and swiftly, through a determined policy of market penetration.

The emergence of Japan as an 'economic superpower' is a result of several factors:

- the failure of European (especially British) and American businesses to be as aggressive, competitive and innovative: for example, in 1980 the number of UK patent applications was 19,710 and in 1990 it was 19,932; in Japan in the equivalent years the respective numbers of patent applications were 165,730 and 317,353.
- the high levels of investment and re-investment in equipment and machinery
- the drive to secure a larger share of the market rather than being contented with short-term profits
- a workforce which was prepared to be flexible, to accept change, new practices and new technologies and which reacted positively to training in order to secure continuous improvement
- more methodical planning and the patience to implement long-term strategies
- a banking system that had the foresight and patience to wait for returns over the long-term and which made risk-capital available to businesses

- its culture: workers have a lifetime commitment to their company and show more uniformity of purpose – pressure to conform in Japanese society is felt far more keenly by Japanese workers than by their Western counterparts.

The emergence of Japan to a position to where it now occupies second place in the world economic league table with a gross domestic product of $3.4 billion has been hailed as a 'miracle'. However much Japan's emergence as a world economy is due to its willingness to sacrifice short-term objectives in order to gain long-term strategic goals, it has been due also to the West's inability to respond to, and exploit, changing markets. As Japan continues to pose a trading threat to countries, like the West, including the UK, they find themselves seeking protection form partner countries who find themselves similarly threatened: the EC is as much a 'ring fence' against aggressive competition as it is a political and philosophical ideal.

2. The 'Tiger Economies'

A new threat is also beginning to emerge from the Far East. The smaller nations of South East Asia, the 'tiger economies' of Malaysia, Hong Kong, Singapore, Taiwan and South Korea are all blessed with sizable pools of cheap labour; already they are flexing their muscles and giving signs that they are, collectively, the 'new Japan'. Indigenous industries, of car manufacturing, shipbuilding and electronics are growing rapidly and posing a 'second front' on which the UK and EC might well have to fight.

3. Eastern Europe – the New Market?

The years 1989 to 1992 witnessed a startling transformation in the geopolitics of Europe. What was known, until 1991, as the 'Eastern bloc' – those countries of Eastern Europe which were Marxist-Leninist (Socialist) states, many of which belonged to the military alliance, commonly known as the Warsaw Pact – rapidly disintegrated. A timetable of that disintegration reads as follows:

- June 1989   Poland
- October 1989   Hungary
- November 1989   East Germany
- November 1989   Bulgaria
- November 1989   Czechoslovakia
- December 1989   Romania
- July 1990   Yugoslavia
- June 1991   Albania
- August 1991   USSR.

That disintegration was completed when the USSR began the process of 'defederalising' itself into its constituent republics and allowing each state to have the autonomy to decide how to govern itself and run its economy. All of the republics (now known collectively as CIS or the Commonwealth of Independent States) increasingly came to accept the 'Western model' of a free market economy and a more liberal, democratic order.

One of the principal reasons for the disintegration of the Eastern Bloc was not philosophical or a love of freedom, as many right-wing politicians like Bush and Thatcher claimed. Rather, it was a gradual decline in living standards in countries like the USSR. Since the early 1980s, countries like the USSR began to spend more on imports than they earned in exports, principally because the price of raw materials they produced had fallen below the cost of manufactured Western goods. Additionally, they suffered badly from prohibitions that banned the export of technology, especially computer technology, to them. These factors, considered alongside their huge spending on armaments, saw prices of food and consumer goods rising faster than wages, leading to a deterioration in the living standards of the Eastern bloc citizen.

The transformation of Eastern Europe, from socialist satellites of the USSR into a collection of autonomous states who can decide with whom they trade, has opened up countless opportunities for business. Together with the CIS, Eastern Europe is one of the largest underdeveloped markets in the world. Political and economic reforms will create new customers as the distribution and transport infrastructure is improved. As local businesses begin to address the unfulfilled demands of domestic consumers, UK suppliers will need to place themselves in order to take advantage of the new opportunities.

G7

The Group of Seven are the seven advanced leading industrial nations –USA, Japan, Germany, Italy, UK, France and Canada. Between them they account for two-thirds of the world's output of goods and services. The main forum of debate is the World Economic Summit meetings, which have taken place annually since 1975. Since 1986, talks have been going on to create a new framework for global trade; these have been organised by the General Agreement on Tariffs and Trade (GATT), an international body dedicated to free trade.

A major fear of the G7 nations is that the current round of GATT negotiations (the 'Uruguay round) will end in deadlock or disgreement, precipitating the world into a new period of protectionism, such as that which worsened the already deep Great Depression of the 1930s. Such a bleak scenario includes the world dividing itself up into three rival trade blocs: Europe; North America (the US, Canada and Mexico) and the Pacific Rim, dominated by Japan.

The G7 agenda, unlike the GATT agenda, includes 'non economic' as well as economic topics:

- looking for growth in the world economy
- endorsing any GATT agreement that may be reached
- relieving debt to the poorer nations
- global environmental concerns
- co-operation to prevent drug trafficking
- aid for Eastern Europe and the CIS.

Those of a sceptical nature who look at the G7 nations, note that they are all what Third World countries would call 'northern': that is, they are all geographically located above the equator that divides the affluent north from the under-developed and undeveloped south. Sceptics would also note that Third World debt to the 'First World' is now almost US$1.5 trillion, a sum that is equivalent to 44% of the Third World's gross national product. Each year the poor countries pay US$77 billion in interest alone. In 1989 the World Bank lent US$28 billion.

Income disparity between the richest and poorest

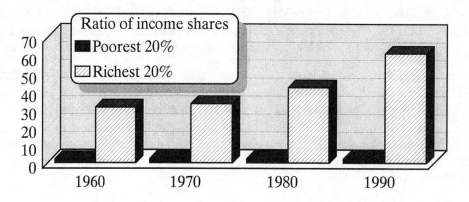

Cost of global markets to developing countries

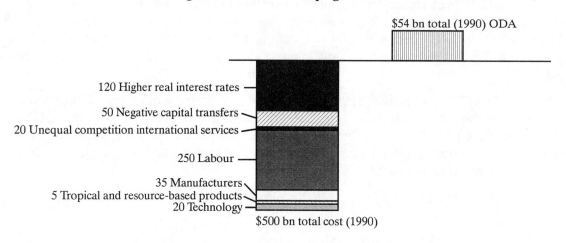

$54 bn total (1990) ODA

120 Higher real interest rates

50 Negative capital transfers

20 Unequal competition international services

250 Labour

35 Manufacturers

5 Tropical and resource-based products

20 Technology

$500 bn total cost (1990)

Money flows into and out of developing countries

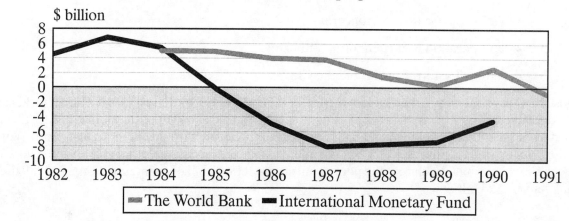

GATT

The General Agreement on Tariffs and Trade is an initiative which was started in 1947 in order to promote free trading between nations. GATT is committed to ending *protectionist* practices:

- whereby one nation safeguards its domestic industries by imposing a limit on the amount of goods that can be imported (the *quota* system)

- whereby imported goods are made to pay a surcharge (or tariff) before they can enter the country, thus making them less competitive.

The bulk of GATT's work is to dismantle tariffs and eliminate quotas, subsidies and other obstacles to free, international trade. It tries to achieve this through 'rounds' of talks. From 1948, early GATT rounds focused on dismantling the barriers to trade in manufactured goods and ignored agricultural products. Currently, GATT is engaged in the so-called 'Uruguay round' of trade talks, involving 108 nations, which began in 1987 and is due to end in 1992.

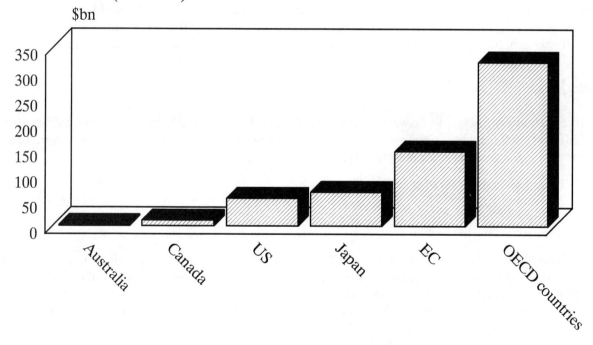

Agricultural support

How much consumers and taxpayers spent supporting agriculture in 1991. US $bn ($1=£1.80)

How farmers are subsidised: the level of agricultural support by: the EC and other countries

The central concern has been the trade in agricultural produce, with the EC bloc of countries resisting American demands to reduce their agricultural subsidies. The amount of support that consumers give to their farmers is graphically illustrated in the Figure below. Some Europeans and Americans want to stem the flood of Japanese imports, especially expensive, technological imports such as cars and consumer goods. The US also believes that the EC is restricting its imports into Europe.

Agreement on agriculture has proved difficult to find. Ranged on one side of the argument is the US and its allies in the Cairns Group of farm exporters (Australia, Argentina, New Zealand etc). They maintain that the Common Agricultural Policy (CAP) disadvantages them in two ways:

1. It stops the entry of cheaper, foreign meat and cereals entering EC countries because of a system of levies and tariffs which make these goods more expensive than the already expensive EC farm products.

2. The CAP awards export subsidies that allow EC farmers to dump their surplus products on the world market at the expense of cheaper and more efficient producers. Although EC produce is expensive within the EC, it can be sold cheaply on the open world market because the EC (that is, the European taxpayer) pays the difference between the price it fetches on that open market and the internal EC price.

The likeliest route out of this impasse seems to be a proposal by EC agriculture commissioner Ray MacSharry who advocates paying farmers a guaranteed income rather than providing financial incentives to produce more. The CAP reforms are, of course, separate from the GATT talks but a European willingness to implement the MacSharry Proposal might well improve the acrimonious relationship that presently exists between the EC and the US over this vexed issue of 'hidden' agricultural subsidies.

The IMF

The International Monetary Fund was set up, like GATT, in 1947 to promote increased international trade. The IMF was established to supervise the operation of a new international monetary order where orderly currency arrangements between member countries could be negotiated.

The IMF has two main areas of responsibility:

- exchange rates
- international liquidity.

The IMF acts as banker to 143 countries, including most western nations as well as China, Hungary, Rumania and Yugoslavia. It accepts annual deposits from each country in a combination of its own currency, foreign currencies and gold. This is referred to as the country's *quota*. The member countries then have the right to draw on these deposits. They are also allowed to borrow in excess of their deposits to help finance a temporary balance of payments deficit. The loan is then repaid in better years. If a country wishes to borrow very substantial sums, the IMF will ask that certain conditions are met by the borrowing country. As the size of the loan increases the stringency of the conditions which the debtor country has to meet also increase. The UK has used these facilities in the past, particularly in 1976 when the restrictions imposed by the IMF at this time were a strong influence on domestic economic freedom forcing the then Labour government to implement very tight monetary control and substantially reduce public spending.

The policies of the IMF are determined by an executive board of governors made up of 22 member nations. These include seven permanent members (the USA, West Germany, France, the UK, Japan, Saudi Arabia and China) and fifteen other members elected on a regular basis from each of the geographical areas in which the other members are located. While the traditional policy of the IMF has been to finance only short-term loans to help solve temporary balance of payments problems, it has in recent years been increasing its longer-term loans to the developing nations to help them develop their economies.

1.   Distinguish between *visible* and *invisible* trade.

2.   What is the *current account* of the balance of payments?

3.   Give an example of *comparitive advantage in trade*.

4.   What do each of the following terms mean:

- reserve currency

- floating exchange rate

- tariff

- quota

- ERM.

5.   Describe the function of the organisations represented by the following initials:

- IMF

- GATT

- EC

- G7.

6.   List the world's main trading blocs.

7.   What are the causes of the disparity between the inputs and the outputs of third world countries?

8.   Give some recent examples of *barriers* to world trade.

9.   Why is the *Social Charter* a political issue in the UK?

10.   What are the advantages to a company of being a *multi-national*?

11.   How do multi-national companies price their product?

12.   Why has Japan been so successful in the post-war era?

13.   Describe the role of *subsidies* in world agriculture.

14.   What is the function of the IMF?

1. In 1989 Jaguar cars blamed their poor profit performance on the fluctuating value of the US dollar. Explain why fluctuations may have had such a impact and analyse what could be done to improve the position in the future.

   AEB P2 1991

2. From 1992 there will be a 'Single European Market'. Discuss the likely implications for UK firms.

   AEB P2 1990

3. *"We will reduce the level of direct taxation and so increase the incentive to work"(Prime Minister: the General Election 1983).*

   Do you think such a policy would achieve its objective?

   UCLES P2 1985

4. You are the Marketing Manager of a firm selling polyunsaturated margarine. In its annual Budget, the Government cuts direct taxation. Soon afterwards, a promotion campaign is launched by the Butter Information Council, and the Government forbids advertising that suggests that margarine is healthier than butter. In the light of these events, what changes would you consider in your marketing strategy?

   UCLES P2 1986

5. The Government is proposing to introduce further credit restrictions.

    (a)   How might this policy be implemented?

    (b)   What effect would you expect these measures to have on:

           (i)   the motor car industry

           (ii)   builders' merchants supplying the Do-it-Yourself trade

           (iii)   the overall level of economic activity?

   UCLES P2 1986

6. *"Most bulk chemical products are priced in US Dollars."*
   (The Financial Times)

   Discuss the problems likely to be encountered by a British company involved in the Chemical markets at home and abroad.

   UCLES P2 1987

7. The Chancellor of the Exchequer, in his Budget, proposes that *tax thresholds* should be lifted, rather than reductions made in *personal tax* rates for *higher income earners*.

(a)   What do the italicised terms mean?

(b)   How might a personnel manager evaluate these changes?

(c)   How would the marketing manager of a package holiday firm expect these changes to affect his business?

UCLES P2 1987

8.   (a)   Briefly explain how you would measure the rate of inflation.

(b)   Discuss the likely consequences for your company, a UK-based washing machine manufacturer, of a significant increase in the rate of inflation.

(c)   What policy measures might you expect a company retailing your products to adopt in reaction to this change?

UCLES P2 1988

9.   (a)   Discuss the possible benefits and difficulties involved in a merger between a UK based manufacture and a similar-sized competitor.

(b)   What additional implications might there be if the competitor firm were based elsewhere in the European Community?

UCLES P2 1991

Other questions

10.   Using as your example one of the following industries,

The high street banks ('The Big Four')

The brewers

PVC manufacturers

Chocolate makers

Car manufacturers

examine the market shares of its principal players and determine whether:

1.   they are oligopolies

2.   their policies act against the public interest.

11.   You are the marketing director of a UK company that imports and distributes a leading brand of German kitchen appliances (ovens, refrigerators and dishwashers).

You recognise that your products have a fairly large price elasticity of demand and also a large positive income elasticity of demand.

(a)   Explain the underlined phrases

(5 marks)

(b)   Write a report for your fellow board members outlining the implications of an increase in the value of the German mark relative to sterling and suggesting adjustments to your marketing strategy.

(20 marks)
UCLES P2 1991

12.   Read the article and answer the questions which follow

(20 marks).

SQUEEZE HITS JOBS AT HOOVER

Britain's biggest manufacturer of washing machines, is expected to announce a large number of redundancies tomorrow because of a 12 per cent fall in spending on "white" goods caused by high interest rates.

The company has 1950 employees at its factory in Merthyr Tydfil, Mid Glamorgan, and 250 in its administrative department. It was hit earlier in the year by the strong pound making imports cheaper, and by a price war. Mr. Anthony Williamson, managing director, said: "We have managed to maintain our position as market leader, but costs have gone up while the price of our goods has not changed."

We are doing what any sharp company must do at the moment and reviewing our operations. He added: "The high interest rates policy of the Chancellor, has contributed significantly to the downturn in business." Hoover is the biggest employer in Merthyr Tydfil and one of the largest in South Wales. Unemployment in the town at present is 12.6 per cent.

(Extracted from the *Daily Telegraph, August 1989*)

(a)   Explain why high interest rates might lead to a fall in consumer spending.

(5 marks)

(b)   Explain why Hoover has been unable to pass on their increased costs to the consumer.

(8 marks)

(c)   Analyse the possible effects in South Wales of the proposed redundancies.

(7 marks)

AEB P1 1991

13.   Read the article and answer the questions which follow.

(25 marks)

Tourism Performance In 1986

The United Kingdom attracts visitors from all over the world. Last year 13.8 million came, 60% from Western Europe, 21% from North America and the rest mainly from the Far East and Australia. Visits from Western Europe increased by 5% over 1985 whilst due to well published but essentially short-term fears those from North America fell by 24%, with the drop largely concentrated during the summer months. But our broad market base meant that overall, visits fell by only 4%, and the picture on spending was even more encouraging. Many of our European competitors fared worse. Recent trends indicate continued long-term growth.

After the sharp fall in numbers overseas visitors early in the year, there was a strong recovery in the last quarter making 1986 the second highest year on record. December visits from North America were 10% above 1985 - which, together with the high level of forward bookings, promises well for 1987.

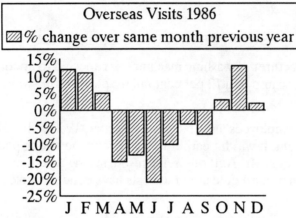

Source: "A Bumper Year for Tourism" *Action for Jobs*, Department of Employment, 1987

(a)   Explain why the data in the diagram on "Overseas Visits 1986" is presented in two different ways.

(2 marks)

(b)   Explain why a "high level of forward bookings" would benefit businesses involved in tourism.

(2 marks)

(c)   Within which category would earnings from foreign tourism appear in the Balance of Payments Current Account?

(2 marks)

(d)   State and explain three positive effects that "continued long-term growth" in overseas visitors is likely to have on United Kingdom industry.

(9 marks)

(e)   Explain how a rise in the value of the pound, via its effects on foreign tourists in the United Kingdom and United Kingdom tourists abroad, would affect the tourist industry in the United Kingdom.

(10 marks)

AEB P1 1989

Case Study

The Trade Deals

Mills and Casson International is an import/export company based in the East End of London. In 1989 the company negotiated two important trading contracts. The first was for the import of cotton shirts from Singapore. The initial contract agreement was made in January and a price of S$6.60 per shirt was agreed. (The currency for Singapore is the Singapore dollar, represented by S$.) The contract was for 20,000 shirts, which were to be delivered in July.

Payment was to be made on delivery and in Singapore dollars. In January the exchange rate was £1 = S$3.30, but by July it had changed to £1 = S$3.20.

The second contract involved the export of £100,000 worth of Harris Tweed cloth to the US. The initial agreement was reached in May and the American buyer promised to pay US$150,000 for the goods on delivery. (The exchange rate in May was £1 = US$1.50). Delivery was not made until late August. The US$150,000 were paid, although by then the exchange rate had changed to £1 = US$1.45

Tasks

You are employed as a trainee in the finance department of Mills and Casson International. Your section head Gerard Dominic, has asked you to examine the financial implications of each of the contracts.

1. Prepare a memorandum to Mr. Dominic in which you explain the cost of the shirts in sterling to the company in the light of the change in the exchange rate.

2. Prepare a second memorandum relating to the American deal. Explain whether Mills and Casson has benefited or not from the change in the exchange rate between the pound and the dollar.

3. Write a report to Mr. Dominic in which you examine the advantages and disadvantages of the company negotiating its import and export deals in sterling or in some other currency.

4. From the financial pages of a quality newspaper obtain the value of sterling against the US dollar, the French franc, the German deutschmark, the Swiss franc and the Italian lira. Plot the changes of the pound against each of these currencies for a month on a chart and produce an explanation of any major fluctuations.

Case Study

The Impact Of Monetary Policy

The Government's monetary policy has had a considerable impact upon the economy in the 1980's and early 1990's. It has affected individuals and organisations in both the public and private sectors. One such organisation is Weller Finance Ltd., a company engaged in providing finance to individuals and businesses. The insurance companies which provide both domestic and commercial mortgages linked to endowment policies. Alan Weller, the managing director of the company, is a competent businessman but readily admits that he is unclear on the rationale for monetary policy and the precise methods the government employs to implement it. He is particularly concerned about changes in the interest rate and its effect on borrowing.

Task

You are employed by Weller Finance Ltd. and Alan Weller has asked you to prepare an outline of the rationale underlying the government's monetary policy, the main methods of monetary control and the economic effects of monetary policy on the economy. Whilst you may have your own views on the appropriateness of such a policy, you should try to make these notes as objective as possible. To help in the preparation of these notes, you should refer to information on unemployment, inflation and growth of the money supply.

Obtain a copy of the Government's Financial Statement and Budget Report for the current year. This is published immediately after the Budget in the spring. From this document identify the main aspects of the its current economy strategy and analyse and evaluate any changes in policy which are included in it.

Case Study

Privatisation

Contract Cleaning Ltd., is a large, private company specialising in office and factory cleaning. It is based in Barnet, Hertfordshire and has mainly dealt with cleaning contracts in the North London area. The managing director of the company is Martin Davies who is keen to see the business expand. He is aware that in certain areas of the country, local authorities and area health authorities have privatised their cleaning operations. Davies wishes to investigate this further, as a possible avenue for expansion, but is aware that there is considerable public opposition to the government's policy for privatisation.

Tasks

You are employed as a management trainee by Contract Cleaning Ltd. Mr. Davies has asked you to prepare a report for him on the issue of privatisation. In the report you should consider the following points:

- (a)   the different ways in which the present government has interpreted the term 'privatisation'

- (b)   the benefits the government claim will result from putting privatisation into practice

- (c)   the economic arguments against the policy of privatisation.

Case Study

The Tall Ships Race

The Tall Ships Race is to be held this year at Newcastle upon Tyne. This spectacular event has attracted entries from throughout the world and up to a quarter of a million spectators are expected to attend.

One of the prime viewing sites is a local cricket ground, sited on the cliff top. It has a view across the whole of the mouth of the River Tyne. The Local Authority has decided that this site can be used as a vantage point from which to view the event. North Tyne Cricket Club, who use the ground, is prepared to rearrange its fixtures for the three weeks surrounding the event in order to allow for preparations to be made and the ground repaired after use. In return, the Council has agreed to pay them a £500 'disturbance fee' as well as a donation of 50p per car; this will go towards North Tyne's 'pavilion fund'.

The Council has estimated that the capacity for the ground would be a thousand cars and, using a sample of its own employees, has produced the following estimates of the demand for a combined parking and entrance fee, at a range of prices:

Price (£)	Demand
0	1000
1	950
2	890
3	820
4	745
5	650
6	545
7	425
8	290
9	150
10	0

The only other cost that the council anticipates is that of stewarding. Local students can be hired to do this task at a rate of £30 for the day. The Safety Committee have suggested that the following numbers of stewards will be necessary.

Number of cars	Number of stewards
1 – 50	1
51 – 100	2
101 – 200	3
201 – 300	4
301 – 400	5
401 – 450	6
451 – 500	7
501 – 550	8
551 – 600	9
601 – 650	10
651 – 700	11
701 – 750	12
751 – 775	13
776 – 800	14
801 – 825	15
826 – 850	16
851 – 875	17
876 – 900	18
901 – 925	20
926 – 950	25
951 – 1000	30

The debate is now centred on what price to charge. At a recent meeting of the full Council, the Conservative Leader of the Council, Nicholas Grabbe, proposed that a price be charged to maximise profit. Kevin Spartley, leader of the Labour Group was outraged and said that the facility should be provided free of charge. An Independent councillor, Timothy Browne, suggested a compromise whereby the Council should merely attempt to break-even if possible. The matter was deferred and a special meeting of the Council was called for two week's time.

Tasks

As a local government employee in the Recreation and Leisure Department, you have been asked to prepare a report on the pricing debate and the result of each proposal, using figures and diagrams where appropriate. In your report, you should refer to the price that will make maximum profit, that price which will result in a break-even position and what costs the council will face if it makes no charge at all, but still has to pay North Tyne Cricket Club and the wages of the stewards.

Your UNISON representative calls you and expresses grave misgivings that non-union labour is to be employed. He asks whether you could supply him with calculations for cost/profit etc, assuming unionised labour is employed, at a minimum rate of £35 per day. You agree to call him back. Prepare notes for this telephone conversation.

Case Study

Hannay Manufacturing

Hannay Manufacturing Plc is a major national company based in Manchester. It has been in existence for more than fifty years and is one of Manchester's largest employers. It has recently been leaked in the national press that the company could be the possible target of a takeover bid by Wilding Engineering Plc. This company is the main competitor in the market in which Hannay Engineering operates and Willding hopes to consolidate its position in this market and become the dominant supplier. The proposed take-over has become a topic of considerable debate in the city.

Task

You are employed as a junior reporter on *The Manchester Evening News* and have been asked by your editor to prepare an article for publication in the paper. In the article you should explain the following points:

   (i)   the problems which could result from a take-over, such as this, in which one company becomes dominant in a particular market

   (ii) the procedures which the government might employ in attempting to decide whether or not the proposed merger is in the public interest

   (iii) the benefits that Wilding Engineering Plc might claim to justify the merger.

Examine the financial pages of one of the 'quality' newspapers for one month. List all the mergers and takeovers which are mentioned as actual or potential. Analyse the action of the government and the Monopolies Commission in each of the cases.

Part Three –
Business Communication and Decision Making

This Part falls into two sections: (a) Communication and Organisation; and (b) Decision-making.

Communication concerns how information flows within a business or other organisation. Information can – and should – flow in two directions: downwards from the directors and managers, through supervisory staff, to employees; upwards from employees until it attains the highest level. Only when information flows freely will a business be effective. These channels, or lines, of communication are called vertical; communications from manager to manager, or employees on the same organisational level, are said to be horizontal. The longer lines of communication become, the greater is the likelihood of communication breaking down.

Information forms the basis of all sound decision-making. Without properly collected and disseminated information, business decisions become haphazard or incorrect. Managers will wish to obtain information, usually in numerical form, in order to analyse it and assess its implications on how they run their business. Information can be obtained at the simplest level by counting the items on shelves, or reading sales ledgers or extracting figures from accounts. How difficult it is to retrieve information depends on the care that is taken when the raw data was first stored; it is much more difficult to retrieve 'intangible' information (data that relates to attitudes and values) than it is to retrieve purely numerical data.

The capability that business has to transmit, store, analyse and use data has been hugely enhanced and accelerated as a result of technological changes, especially advances in computing software and hardware. The whole process of recording, keeping, retrieving and 'crunching' information has been transformed over the last decade. It has been made cheaper, quicker and more comprehensive by the leaps forward that have been made in electronic and silicon technology.

Decision-making

Business is about risk and operating in a changing and uncertain world. The bases of decision-making are assumptions which may or may not, in the fullness of time, be proven valid. Uncertainty begins, as you learned in Part One, with the decision to start up a business. Once made, it triggers an unending sequence of decisions: Do we expand production? Do we develop that new product? Should we break into a new market? Should we go public? Are we under-capitalised? For those who are uninvolved, it is easy to say that a decision should, or should not, have been made; the reality of decision-making is that decisions cannot be deferred indefinitely and the manager's job is to take calculated risks. The key word is the adjective 'calculated'. A manager (and a mathematician) distinguishes between *absolute* uncertainty and *calculated* uncertainty. Calculated uncertainty is what a manager refers to when speaking of 'risk'. One way of assessing (and minimising) risk is by estimating the probability of a particular event, but a manager will have a selection of analytical tools which he can use in order to lessen the risks and avoid the possibility of making a wrong decision.

In Part Three, you will look at how a manager appraises risk and attempts to tip the odds in favour of a 'right' decision. There are two general ways of doing this: by analysing information that is historical (that is, it has already occurred and been documented, but has not been 'worked'); by making information work in an anticipatory or predictive way. Often, using the first method to collect data provides an information 'platform' that can be made use of by the second method.

Thus, as is the case with all tools and models, managers might, for example, use the basic concept of probability. In itself probabilities are of intrinsic interest only to a narrow group of mathematicians, but they are interesting to a manager because, if used properly, they can help to predict the future pattern of sales, possible profit, total sales, losses, seasonal fluctuations and so on. The second half of this Part focuses on the application of numerical techniques in formulating a business strategy.

Business Communication and Organisation

Communication involves transmitting and receiving information in all its many shapes and forms. The most obvious and widespread act of communication is oral communication: word of mouth the next most widespread sort of communication is the written word. Communicating is a basic human activity which enables people to develop relationships. It is vital to the formation and success of any kind of business because businesses need adaptable communication systems.

When communications and business are considered in terms of the relationship between them, it is not difficult to appreciate that a poor communications system might often prevent a business from meeting its objectives and becoming successful.

A business is a *corporate* body which is made up of a highly complex collection of individual components, each of which is designed to work in harmony with all the others. A business, like a human body, has evolved and adapted to make the best use of the environment in which it finds itself. And just as people are not identical so, too, are businesses different: some people have adapted to life at high altitude, or have evolved their skin pigmentation to cope with extreme sunlight, or have heavier layers of fat to withstand the Arctic cold; some businesses have adapted to cope with the specialised environments within which they have to work.

A nuclear power station doesn't just look different from a building society headquarters, it is intrinsically different: the nature of its operations give rise to risks which are unique to it. To counter such risks it has developed specialised physical and administrative mechanisms. Successful businesses are ones which best adapt to their environment – and to do that, they must be able to communicate flexibly.

Communications Systems Involve Control

The human body can walk, run, talk, manipulate, observe, listen and so on. To do any of these things, commands must be given to the various organs and limbs which are capable of carrying out the function. The commands come from the brain; they are passed as minute electric pulses through the nervous system and are picked up by the limb or organ to which they are directed. This is the communications network of the body. The system also works in reverse: instructions received through the senses are passed back by the same route to the brain, where they are interpreted, and acted upon.

The same process is at work in a business. It, too, has a 'brain' made up of those responsible for controlling the activities of the business. The 'brain' is the board of directors or management of a company. Decisions made on that level are communicated to the appropriate parts of the business to carry them out. When the board of directors decides that company spending needs to be reduced, the message is passed to all the 'organs' of the business. A breakdown in any part of the system may have an adverse effect upon a business's performance. The breakdown may originate within the mechanism by which messages are transferred, or with the recipients to whom the messages are directed, or even in the brain itself – those who manage the business. Such possibilities are considered in more detail later.

A Communications Policy

Larger businesses will often adopt a communications policy. Such a policy is likely to describe the purpose of the communications activity and the importance management attaches to it. It is likely to be a statement of the business's philosophy, rather than a practical guide on how to implement and operate a communications network. A policy that both emphasises the overall importance of good communication, and states how this objective is to be realised is beneficial in the following ways:

1.   the existence of such a policy suggests that management is aware of the role of communications and that planning and decision-making should be mindful of the communications issues involved

2.   it lays a foundation upon which to build a more detailed communications network, specifically related to information flows

3.   as a consequence of 1 and 2 the business's internal operations run effectively, because relevant data is available when and where it is needed and staff consultation procedures are improved

4.   attention is paid to developing good public relations, thereby enhancing the image of the business in its relations with the outside world.

A communications policy identifies the following factors that might affect employees personally:

- the importance of good employer/employee relations. In a large business this is achieved by a personnel or welfare officer taking responsibility for the handling of:

    disciplinary measures

    employees' grievances

    the monitoring of career development

    personal problems, such as illness, or the death of a member of the employee's family.

- the need for 'machinery' to enable consultation to take place between management and workforce

- the importance of providing induction for new starters, and of keeping staff generally informed about the business and what is happening within it.

Implementing such a policy helps to ensure good industrial relations.

Many communication systems, however, are simply the outcome of piecemeal developments that have occurred as the business has evolved. As a result, it may contain unseen barriers to communications. In the design of any communication system, it is vital to be aware of the ways in which barriers to communications occur.

Establishing and Maintaining a Communications Network

To build a business around a communications network would be a case of letting the tail wag the dog. However, if the organisational structure neglects its communications, it is unlikely to operate satisfactorily. The communications process involves three distinct components:

1.   the individual or group giving the instructions or information

2.   the individual or group receiving it

3.   the mechanism by which the transfer of information takes place.

Communication breakdown

It is, of course, in the interests of any business to establish and maintain an effective communications system. For a business, failures in its communication system may be both minor and major. For instance, it may be that, as a result of key personnel or equipment being out of action on a temporary basis, the system suffers an information blockage; perhaps accounts are not being prepared, or material cannot be photocopied; or letters remain unanswered. However, when the member of staff returns to work, or the machinery is repaired, the system reverts to its normal operation, and the damage is not significant. But where the damage is major, the effects can be devastating.

Firstly, suppose a large business has a unionised workforce. Management believes that unions in general are against the best interests of the business. The unions for their part regard management as reactionary and unwilling to allow worker participation. Given such different views, there is a serious danger that each side will make it more difficult to operate the business. There might be a breakdown in labour relations; this might rapidly lead to industrial action and a loss of production.

Secondly, suppose a business becomes aware that many of its competitors are diversifying their product ranges. Also, their competitors are using new methods of production that are less labour intensive but which place heavy reliance upon new technology and technological processes. (The newspaper industry in the 1980s provides an example of a major switch from traditional working methods and practices to modern methods of production.)

Despite the business being aware of the threatening changes that are taking place, its own business structure is such that:

- staff lack opportunities to express their views about the need for change

- information received by the business from outside, and which describe the changes taking place within the industry, are not acted upon because they aren't understood or simply don't get passed on to the right person

- there is no monitoring and evaluation procedures within the business or such procedures as there are fail to signal to the business that it is becoming increasingly uncompetitive.

Gradually, through a combination of factors that collectively represent an inadequate internal communications structure, the business will become increasingly ineffective in the market place, its market share will drop, and it will eventually go out of business.

Identifying the Barriers to Communication

Such barriers are the result of poor design and they may be either physical or psychological. They result from a very wide range of causes, some of which can be easily identified and resolved. Other barriers, especially those caused by negative attitudes, require time and delicate handling.

Design faults in communications systems include:

Incompatible organisational structures. For example, a problem could arise in a business where the personnel department deals with disciplinary matters and the heads of section handle the personal problems of staff under them. Because these matters are separately dealt with, this might prevent a connection being made between the two areas: such as abusive behaviour at work and personal problems at home. In other words, the link between cause and effect is not recognised.

Imprecise descriptions of roles and responsibilities. Staff should be clear about the tasks they are required to perform, to whom they are accountable, and the extent of their responsibilities.

Lack of supervision and/or training. Effective supervision can identify difficulties facing members of the workforce which prevent them from performing their jobs effectively. Training programmes can help to overcome these.

Inefficient or inappropriate information systems. For instance, an appraisal of the printing and reprographics work carried out may reveal that existing facilities are too slow or insufficiently cost-effective.

Mechanisms for evaluating the system are inadequate or non-existent. In order to discover whether or not a system is functioning properly, it must be reviewed and its faults diagnosed and remedied. An analysis of the system by a professional outsider, such as a management consultant or a systems analyst, is a valuable tool, especially when the size of the business makes it impossible for its managers to rely on informal structures for control. As growth occurs, there is a tendency towards greater division of labour and this, in turn, requires an increase in the physical size of the workplace. The effect that this has upon a communications system is to formalise it, so that it can cope with the more complex communications patterns that develop. In turn, this may have the effect of masking failures in the system which, in the past when the business was smaller, would have become readily apparent.

Physical Barriers

These include:

Inadequacies in the geographical layout of the workplace. Many people are employed by a business in which a number of physically separated buildings are administered as a single entity. This situation is often the result of superimposing a new organisational structure upon existing sites which were not designed to cope with it. Many schools and colleges are based on split sites as a result of educational re-organisation.

For instance, two schools half a mile away from each other, and previously quite separately administered, are now being operated as a single administrative unit because of an amalgamation. This problem may also be encountered where a business occupying a single site expands its operation as growth takes place. Limitations of space and money can result in an overall building plan that is not conducive to effective communications between departments.

Inadequacies in the provision of equipment may be due to a lack of investment in updating existing equipment, such as typewriters, photocopiers and computers. Perhaps management fails to realise the potential of new systems and the value of the electronic office in improving performance.

Staff problems. The most obvious difficulty is the problem of under-staffing. If the personnel needed to operate the information system is under-strength, the system cannot work satisfactorily.

Attitudinal Barriers

These may occur at any level within the hierarchy of the business. There are usually two clearly discernible elements in the social/psychological climate of the business. There is the official line of command which is found by looking at the administrative arrangements for the business: for instance, how it is structured and what the job descriptions of individual staff contain. This is referred to as the *authority hierarchy* and it can be set out in the form of an organisation chart. At a more subtle level, there is what is referred to as the *status hierarchy*. This is less to do with rank than with the earning of respect. Of course, it is often the most powerful individuals in the business who are also the most respected. However, such respect may be related more to their power to 'hire and fire' than to any belief in their integrity and capability. It does not always follow that you will automatically approach senior staff when you are seeking help or a favour. Instead, you turn to the long-serving employee whom everybody agrees knows the system inside out and can use the contacts developed over years of service to 'get things done'.

Having identified these aspects of authority what attitudinal barriers can exist? They include:

Employee problems

These may be the result of an individual's own personal attitudes. They include phobias, such as the fear of the radiation emitted by VDUs, or basic prejudices against the opposite sex, or people from different racial or cultural backgrounds. Alternatively, the fault may lie with management. An employee's lack of training may affect his or her ability to perform effectively an allotted responsibility. This failing may not be the fault of the employee, but instead be the result of management's inability to recognise the need for training, or to appreciate the skills appropriate to the task. Similarly, an employee who is apathetic and demoralised may be ineffective in his or her work. Such behaviour may stem from the fact that the job is intellectually or physically undemanding. This should be recognised by management and acted upon.

Managerial failures

Certain management styles generate significant barriers to communication. Different types of businesses operate different styles of leadership. An autocratic, or highly paternalistic approach, or even a general indifference to the interests of the workforce, usually will have an adverse effect on the performance of employees. Any communications system in a business relies heavily upon the consultation procedures between management and workforce. It is equally important to delegate. Bottlenecks can occur when an individual in the enterprise is trying to cope with a workload that is too heavy; the consequence is often that information is provided too late or not at all.

Personality conflicts

Closely associated with these communications barriers are the personality conflicts that sometimes plague a business. In the narrowest sense, these conflicts may involve the personal dislike of one member of staff for another. This becomes an issue when both individuals must communicate and transfer information. Such information in the hands of an individual can be used as a means of asserting power over others. This may take the form of retaining the information until a vital meeting and then using it to embarrass or disconcert the other person. It may involve 'forgetting' to pass on a message. At its most extreme, it may involve refusing to deal with the other person other than through an intermediary. Such behaviour can damage the business, especially as 'sides' in the dispute can develop, compounding the problem and creating an emotionally charged atmosphere that is not conducive to the free flow of information.

Information overload

Increased amounts of information within business – and more sophisticated designs of systems to handle that information – can lead to situations where the people operating such systems receive too much information in too short a time and become overloaded. Inevitably, the business will suffer, orders will be lost, services deteriorate and wrong decisions will be made.

As well as the business malfunctioning, there will be an adverse effect on individuals trying to cope with the overload. Such pressures can lead to occupational stress and work-related nervous disorders, both increasingly recognised symptoms of the demands of a working environment.

Aids to Communication

Despite our technical ability to design improved systems, there are always problems that upset business communications systems. Exercising skill in the following areas can help to minimise these problems.

Empathy. This is the act of identifying with the feelings and thoughts of another. It doesn't mean that you agree with the other person, but it does mean that you understand and appreciate why that person has spoken or acted in a particular way.

Listening. A person who is constantly talking is not listening or learning. Listening helps us to discover problems and explore solutions. An average speaking speed is 120 words per minute; you listen at four times that rate.

Reading. There are books and training courses available which raise the speed of reading without a commensurate loss of comprehension.

Observation. Most people miss much by failing to observe important elements in the environment. Using our powers of observation to supplement listening and reading adds measurably to our overall understanding of communications.

Word choice. All businesses create specialist words, but there is a threshold beyond which most people are not able to understand. Presentations need to be direct and simple; jargon confuses.

Body language. This aids oral communication: it conveys thoughts and emotions.

Action. Action is sometimes a more effective form of communication than words.

Information Technology (IT)

As a result of advances in electronics, communications systems have changed rapidly, growing increasingly more automated. Word processors, microcomputers, minicomputers, 'powerbooks' and main-frame computers are commonplace. Indeed, many businesses have become dependent on these machines, especially high street organisations, such as banks, building societies and travel agencies. Developments in storing information on CD and optical disks, telecommunications and video technology have all contributed to change. One factor that has helped bring about this change has been the falling cost of technology.

The Development of Information Technology

Information technology (IT) involves the use of computer-based systems to store, process and transfer information. IT has evolved as a result of developments in two distinct areas:

1. computing
2. telecommunications.

Though there has been a telephone network for several decades and computers have been in existence since the late 1940s, the important advance in recent years has involved the linking of the two. In other words, being able to transfer information quickly and effectively from one computer to another using conventional telephone lines, satellite links and optic fibre cables. The establishment of this link has led to a communications revolution which has wide implications for the way in which businesses communicate both within and between themselves. Consider the uses of information technology as a means of improving a business's internal communications system.

The use of IT within the Organisation

The electronic office

An electronic office involves the performance of many clerical and administrative tasks by a set of computers or other electronic equipment which are linked together into a *network*.

A network

This means that the machines are connected using an internal telephone line or a simple cable. The network allows the machines to:

1. share resources
2. share information.

1. Sharing resources

To operate a computer you need the computer itself (known as the central processing unit or CPU), an input device (such as a keyboard or disk driver), a monitor or visual display unit (VDU) and an output device (printer, monitor, speaker or disk drive). Each of these pieces of equipment is expensive and a 'stand alone' system which is completely self-contained will require all of them. A network system will mean that users can share much of the equipment. So, for example, one central CPU may be linked to a number of terminals, each with its own monitor but without a disk drive or printer. A user will access the machine through the terminal, but will need to go to the central printer for 'hard copy' output. This type of network is known as a 'star' network and is shown below.

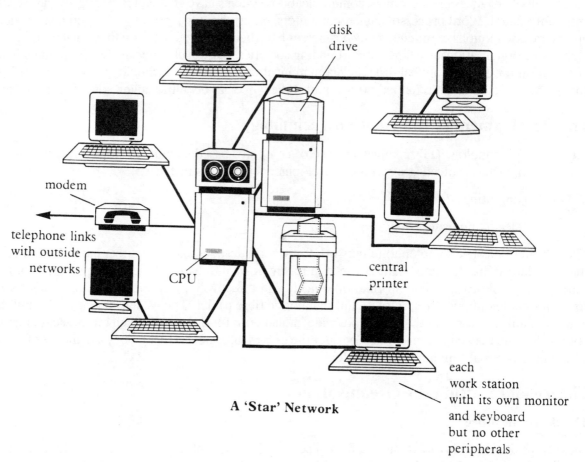

A 'Star' Network

Alternatively, a number of microcomputers each with its own CPU, can be networked together. In this way they can transfer information held on one machine to another almost instantaneously. This allows each to be used either independently or as part of the network. Such a network is known as a 'ring' network and is shown in the figure on the next page.

2. Sharing information

For both the network examples mentioned, a major advantage is that it is possible to access a much greater amount of information than on a single microcomputer. In a network system which has only one large CPU, the memory of the machine will be considerably larger and may be linked to a hard-disk system. These are large-capacity storage units holding magnetic disks (somewhat similar in appearance to a stack of gramophone records) encased in a removable pack. They hold many more times the amount of information than the floppy disks used by microcomputers. However, they are relatively expensive and most businesses would find it uneconomic to have a hard-disk drive for every computer terminal. Networking enables the most efficient use to be made of equipment.

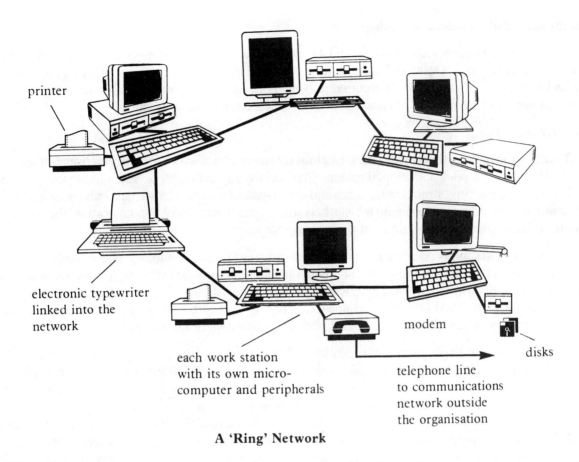

printer

electronic typewriter
linked into the
network

each work station
with its own micro-
computer and peripherals

modem

telephone line
to communications
network outside
the organisation

disks

A 'Ring' Network

The uses of a network

Linking a number of machines can reduce the document flow within the business. There has even been the suggestion of the 'paperless' office. An example may illustrate how this can be achieved.

If goods are delivered into the business, it is the normal procedure for the receiving department to complete a Goods Received Note. Copies of this are sent to the purchasing department, the accounts department and the stores. In other words, a considerable amount of paper work is generated. If instead the goods receipt is entered into a terminal which is networked to the rest of the business, the information that the goods have been received is immediately recorded on the central database. This can be accessed by any other authorised department through its own terminal. Thus the information can be made available to anyone who requires it, in one simple data transfer.

The applications are numerous. Imagine the total amount of paper work generated by every memo which is sent, every notice circulated or report copied in a large business. Clearly, the physical movement of paper is enormous. If, instead, the initiator of the memo simply input the message via a terminal and then directed the machine to transfer it electronically to every named recipient through the IT network, there would be a vast reduction in the amount of paper circulating.

External uses of information technology

Businesses must communicate externally and IT can play a greater role in improving the efficiency of business communications. Data can be transmitted around the world in a matter of seconds, bank deposits made in London, for instance, being credited in New York almost instantly. Trading transactions can be effected in seconds and information passed speedily via electronic mailing systems.

Some current issues

The IT revolution may further divide the world into those countries which are information rich and those which are information poor. Developed nations (particularly Japan and the US) dominate the electronics and IT industries. Vast investment in research and development is necessary to make advances in this field. Such dominance clearly impacts on the job markets since, even in respect of administration, the technology facilitates centralisation in the country of the parent company.

It is said that information is power and that, with the advent of new technology, there has been concern about the abuse of that power; there are threats to individual privacy posed by organisations as diverse as the police and credit rating agencies. The UK has only limited legislative safeguards on this potential abuse, the main one being the 1984 Data Protection Act (which is dealt with in some detail in Part Five), unlike other countries which have much more liberal policies on freedom of information.

Finally there is the challenge which the revolution in IT, and indeed other advanced technologies, present us with. As individuals, the use of personal computers at home and at work presents us with applications to increase our potential in a variety of ways. To businesses, computers enormously enhance efficiency and effectiveness if they and the systems they use are matched to the needs of the enterprise. Indeed, as a society we are seeking to ensure that future generations will be computer literate. For some time all our schools have been equipped with computers. The developments in the new fourth generation 'thinking' computers will provide limitless potential for man's inventiveness in terms of the scope of its applications.

The future shape of businesses?

Change is taken for granted. In a changing world people are growing more aware that the pace of change is accelerating. Whilst change is a feature of people's lives generally, the notion of change can be applied specifically to businesses: in their size; their complexity and sophistication; in their increased use of IT.

At present people generally 'go to work'; they leave home to go to a building which has been designed to use labour in conjunction with capital (equipment, machinery etc). Evidence suggests that, in the future, more jobs will be done from home and the use of IT will transmit them to the business. Most new jobs that will be created will require 'brain power' (not muscle power) and will be essentially concerned with handling and processing information of a great variety. These kinds of jobs, which are sometimes referred to as 'cerebral' jobs, can be done part-time or on short-term contracts, so that the existence of permanent, full-time employment in a business will diminish.

In 1989 Professor Charles Handy suggested that the future shape of organisations would be best described as a 'shamrock model'. This is illustrated in the figure on the following page.

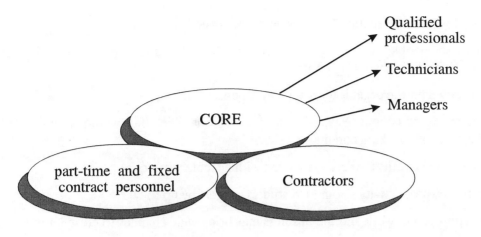

Handy's Shamrock model

Handy argued that people in the core would work long hours and, in addition to being specialists in their own field, would need to know the whole organisation. The organisation would be supplemented by contractors, hired when the need arose and part time, and fixed contract personnel; the emphasis would be on flexibility. Increasingly, personnel may be involved in 'high-tech homeworking' or 'telecommuting'.

Hi-tech homeworking

In the past 'homeworking' has described low-paid work done on a piece rate system, usually by women. Its main advantage to the homeworker was that it offered flexibility in regard to the hours one chose to work,: it negated the need to travel to work and allowed the worker to plan work around the running of home and family. Its main disadvantage was the usually derisory pay which was on offer.

Nowadays 'homeworking' – sometimes known as 'teleworking' or 'telecommuting' – is more likely to describe a form of flexible working which makes use of high technology. It is a trend that is growing most quickly in the independent sector as redundant professionals establish their own home-based businesses. The next fastest growth area is the public sector, such as local government, the Department of Social Security, the Treasury, with the private sector in third place.

Teleworking involves working from home, at some distance from the office, using some form of telecommunication equipment, such as computer, modem, fax and telephone. At present it is estimated that 'teleworkers' now account for 1.5 million (or 1 in 17) of the workforce; this figure is likely to increase to four million by 1995.

Teleworking requires a different style of management in order to monitor it. Managers have to overcome a fear of losing control. Tasks must be devolved and more planning done. Managers have to learn to resist the temptation to check up on employees working away from the office; their focus should be on results.

The advantages to the employer:

- it can tap into a hidden pool of workers at times of full employment

- it cuts down on the rental of expensive office space

- it increases people's efficiency: less travel results in less stress which results in higher productivity during working hours

- it cuts down on the organisation's travel expenses bill

- it retains skilled people (especially mothers) in jobs which they would be unable to do under 'normal' working conditions

- it brings the benefits that are associated with a stable workforce

- it increases productivity – some US studies suggest by up to 60%.

This more flexible approach to work and the business may bring wide changes to lifestyles in this country.

Whether it is welcome or not, change in one form or another is inevitable. It extends not only to the nature of the work being performed, but also to the ways in which it is performed and to the character of the economic and social environment in which business activities are conducted.

A further example of change that will affect businesses lies in the establishment of a single market within Europe. This means that UK business finds itself competing in a single market with a population in excess of 300 million people. In common with other aspects of change, the greater economic and social integration of the UK with the other states of the EC presents both opportunities and threats.

Factors Influencing the Communications System

The composition of an organisation

In nearly all business a distinction is drawn between those who manage (management) and those who carry out their instructions (the workforce). Only in the smallest business is such a division unlikely to exist. In addition, however, there are the owners of the business. The owners may also be the managers – for instance, the owners of the family business which runs as a private limited company will also act as its directors, but in large businesses the owners may be distinct from the managers, whilst retaining the ultimate power to control them. This is the case in a public limited company. The mechanisms that enable the owners to exert control over their managers, and which enable the managers to report to the owners on the performance of the business, are an important feature of the communications system. In the case of public limited companies, it is at company meetings (notably the AGM), that the interaction between owners and managers is most pronounced.

The aims and objectives of business

All forms of business have aims and objectives, even if they are not explicitly stated. Aims and objectives are set by the senior managers of a business. A failure to communicate aims and objectives to the workforce can be detrimental in the following two related ways:

1. Employees are unaware of the broader context within which they are working. Suppose that management, in a business which is threatened with closure, devises a survival package. This aims to hold down wage rises for the next three years with the objective of avoiding redundancies, making the business more cost effective, and anticipating a growth in demand

by that time. If the workforce is denied access to this information, and is merely informed that the company is not prepared to accept an increase in its wage bill, much greater resentment is likely than if management provides a reasoned account for its longer term strategy.

2.   Employees are not encouraged to identify as essential components of the business. This really is an extension of the first point. Companies that convey the importance of the individual to the work of the business as a whole, generally enhance motivation, but inevitably must, in so doing, divulge the aims being pursued by the company. These may be production figures for the next month or year; statements concerning product quality; or perhaps the desire to improve and extend the product range. An indirect way of communicating the last example to the workforce is by means of a system which encourages staff to suggest ways of improving and developing products and systems using suggestion schemes, or discussion groups.

One of the major causes of conflict between management and workforce is the lack of a well-established set of objectives for the working group (i.e. the whole of the business or a section of it) to achieve. A method of attempting to overcome this is *management by objectives*; that is, a systematic approach to management which involves fixing objectives for the business and the individual.

The use of this approach involves managers in producing an action plan which should include:

- establishing the objectives of the business in every significant area of its operation

- assigning these objectives to individuals, providing them with a time scale and quantifiable targets

- agreeing action to be taken. This involves the manager discussing his or her objectives with the staff, and *vice versa*

- carrying out the agreed action

- reviewing the performance of the action.

Management by objectives can significantly improve a business's internal communications system.

The management structure of the business

Management structures vary from business to business, but one of the basic principles of good management is the need to lay down and clearly define lines of authority. This has the effect of identifying the relationship between superiors and inferiors and ensures that individuals are clear to whom it is that they are accountable.

The importance of scale to a communications system

One of the most important factors affecting the suitability of a communication system is the scale of the business. The *scale* of a business can refer to:

- *its annual turnover* or the *level of revenue*. This is a measure of its financial importance.

- *its physical size.* The buildings or the plant that it uses will reflect the nature of the work it carries out and the productive capacity involved. An aluminium smelter demands a substantial plant size to accommodate it. If the existing plant is running at full capacity, but is still not meeting demand, the plant must be physically expanded if demand is to be met. A large business of this type may be compared with a business that has a similar financial turnover but requires a much smaller physical site to do so. An example is provided by the high technology 'sunrise' industries which produce computer software and hardware.

- its *workforce.* Some commercial and industrial activities are highly labour intensive, which means they employ large numbers of staff, whilst others can operate with very low staffing levels. A useful comparison is provided by business in the energy sector. Despite widespread reductions in its labour force in recent years, British Coal still relies heavily upon manpower to operate its mines. There have been substantial improvements in coal extraction methods as the industry becomes more mechanised. However, each tonne of coal produced still needs face workers and supporting staff. The electricity industry, on the other hand, produces electricity at nuclear power stations staffed by small numbers of skilled staff. This is achieved through the use of automated high technology control and monitoring systems which merely require supervision by power station staff.

- the *nature of its markets.* Physically, markets vary tremendously. Some businesses will operate within a very limited geographical location, perhaps the local town and the surrounding area. Others may buy and sell goods and services throughout the UK, or the EC, or perhaps as in the case of multi-nationals, worldwide.

The scale of a business is important because it is an indication, in crude terms, of the amount of communications activity which will take place. It is incorrect to suggest that there is a precise relationship between the type of communications network appropriate to a business and the financial, physical or human scale of its operations. It is, nonetheless, obvious that a business employing 200 staff requires a system of control, such as a personnel department, which would not be needed by a business employing only twenty staff. Similarly, a business with a turnover of £5 million a year is likely to need a larger financial department than one with a turnover of £50,000 a year, even if both use essentially similar financial and accounting systems.

The Organisational Structure of the Business

The organisational structure of a business is concerned with the co-ordination and grouping of related activities to achieve the business's objectives. The responsibilities for each section of the business must be clearly defined and the authority to undertake such responsibilities must be delegated to the appropriate section.

Overall, the business must ensure that there is co-ordination between the various sections of the business and that clear lines of communication have been established. However, the organisational structure must retain sufficient flexibility to allow it to adapt to change.

One important reason for a formal organisational structure is to ensure that each individual is able to identify his or her position within the business. Employees should be aware of their own responsibilities, to whom they are directly accountable and for whom they bear a managerial or supervisory role. A further advantage of a formal structure is that it should allow management to develop areas of specialism and expertise within the business.

Almost certainly, informal structures will also develop within a business as a result of personal relationships, work patterns and practical expediency. Such informal structures are to be encouraged unless they conflict with the efficient operation of the business.

Most businesses fall into one of three organisational structures:

1. Departmental

2. Pyramidal

3. Matrix.

1. Departmental Structure

The departmental structure is simplest to understand and is encountered frequently. The business is comprised of several departments (e.g. Production, Accounting, Personnel, Marketing etc), which may, if the size of the business justifies it, be further divided into sub-departments: Marketing, for example, might be further split into 'Promotions', 'Advertising', 'Product Development', 'Market Research' etc.

The type of division described above occurs along *functional* lines. However, departments can be created according to different sets of criteria, such as:

- geographic departmentalisation: e.g. Levi Strauss, the jeans manufacturer, is divided into one division for North America (US, Canada and Mexico), a second for Europe and a third for the rest of the world..

- process departmentalisation: e.g. a confectionery manufacturer who divides production into chocolate products and non-chocolate products because the manufacturing technique for each is different.

- product departmentalisation: e.g. United Drinks divides itself into the Beverages Division and the Liquor Division.

- customer departmentalisation: e.g. where a business is dependent on a small number of large customers, a single department might be created to totally oversee the requirements of a single customer. A textile company supplying Marks and Spencer might devote a single department to that account; within that department would be found all the usual functions of the business, such as marketing, production, accounts etc. This type of customer departmentalisation is common in the advertising industry.

2. The Pyramid Structure and Communication Flows

Most businesses, which have a pyramidal structure, have a functional departmentalisation and *vice versa*. The pyramid shape is indicative of the hierarchy of the organisation and the status of each rank of employee in each department: authority and responsibility extend downwards in a hierarchical pattern. Senior management makes the executive and policy decisions. It has overall responsibility for the success or failure of such policies and has the authority vested in it to allow it to carry this out. As you move down the pyramid, status, responsibility and authority all decrease. Pyramids can vary from shallow (or flat) to steep (or tall) structures.

However, the lower down the pyramid you go, the larger the number of staff you are likely to find employed. Thus, the pyramid represents both authority and quantity. An organisational pyramid is illustrated below.

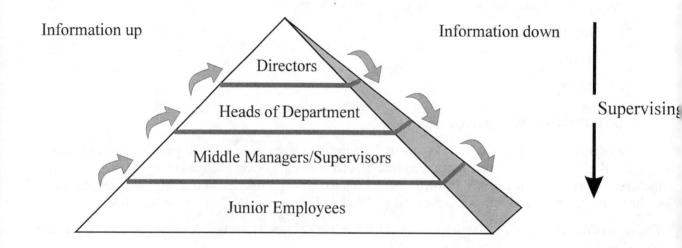

Information up and down

Within the pyramid, information passes both upwards and downwards. Policy decisions, taken at board level by the directors, are implemented by instructing the relevant departmental heads to see that the policy is carried out. Departmental heads will then brief the middle managers, for whom they are responsible, and the final stage in the process is the communication between middle managers and junior staff. This may seem like a tortuous process but, at each stage, the staff involved not only get to know the decision made 'at the top' but are left to use their knowledge and initiative to best determine how to respond to the instructions they have been given.

For instance, it may be that a supervisor needs only to speak to certain of his junior staff and, knowing them personally, will choose the best time and method to inform them of changes to their working practices. A level of fine tuning is introduced, which would probably be lost if the information came from higher up. In a sense, what the pyramid reveals is that, as businesses grow, the need to delegate responsibilities increases. Someone who sets up a business employing only two part-time staff can exercise full control over all aspects of the business. If, in twenty years time, the business has developed and now employs a hundred full time staff, it will no longer be physically possible for the founder to manage the business alone.

The information flow also passes from the bottom upwards. Staff provide feedback to their seniors. This may take many forms: monitoring shortages of materials; absences of staff; production problems; grievances; suggestions for improving work methods in the working environment. Anything which requires the authority or approval of someone further up the business hierarchy, and which has been generated or identified below, will pass back up the system. Only in extreme circumstances is it likely that an issue arising at the bottom of the pyramid will pass right back to the top for consideration and decision.

For the most part, an immediate senior is likely to possess sufficient authority to make a decision, but ultimately it is a question of the extent of the delegated responsibility held by senior employees that determines whether they can deal with the matter personally, or must pass it back to their own superiors. This in turn indicates just how much power the business has vested in them. Clearly, if a middle manager enjoys little autonomy to make decisions, but must, in most cases, refer back to the head of department, the middle manager is in the position of having a title without corresponding authority, making the job virtually impossible; it also means that the chain of communication is unnecessarily extended. This is time-wasting and expensive, for it defeats the purpose of creating a separate managerial tier, and may result in the senior employee carrying too heavy a workload.

As businesses grow bigger, it is inevitable that communication flows, the messages passing within the business, have further to travel. This is not ideal, since it is likely to take longer to transmit communications and there is a greater divide between giver and receiver, which can lead to a 'them and us' view of the business by junior staff. However, it is clear that as the business grows, so its communication system must become increasingly refined, for the bigger the business, the greater are its communication demands.

Information passing across the business

Within each of the levels identified in the pyramid, communications also take place horizontally, between staff of broadly the same status within the bands. Since most businesses consist of a number of component parts, usually referred to as departments (which are often further broken down into sections), these horizontal communications will invariably involve messages being transferred between departments, for most of the workforce will be attached to a particular department. Thus heads of department are likely to meet regularly. Junior staff may need to work together to deal with invoices, and in a business engaged in production processes, production line workers, each with his or her own particular responsibility, will need to co-operate with fellow workers to ensure the smooth running of the line.

When horizontal communication is impaired, serious damage can be caused to the entire enterprise, for each department, inevitably, is heavily dependent upon other departments if it is to function effectively. The interrelationship of departments, and the significance of it for the communication system, is examined in more detail below.

Information passing diagonally

This occurs when staff at different levels within the business and who work in different departments, are involved in communicating with each other. For instance, a Marketing Manager may request financial information from an assistant in the accounts department, or a junior employee in the production department may need personal details about a newly-appointed employee to the department that are held by the Personnel Manager. Both in the case of diagonal communications, and those across the business, care and tact are called for, since staff in one department are not accountable to staff in another department. Thus it would be 'out of order' for a senior member of department A to issue an instruction to an employee in department B, or seek to discipline someone in department C.

The diagram below illustrates communication flows within a business, and indicates the types of communication that are likely to be involved.

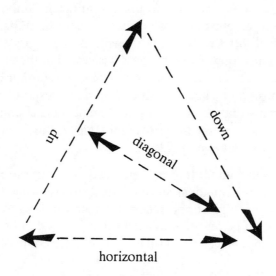

The direction of communications in a business

Using the diagram above, you can see the likely content of the communications involved.

Downwards communications will predominantly involve the issuing of:

- *directives* i.e. general orders, such as a rule that no one below a certain level shall make long-distance telephone calls before 1 p.m.

- specific *orders*, such as an instruction to prepare a report or clean a machine

- *requests*.

Additionally, downwards communications will often involve the granting of authority to a subordinate, or confirmation of the action taken by a subordinate.

Upwards communications involve seeking information and advice and obtaining authority to act, and include suggestions and criticisms presented by subordinates to superiors.

Horizontal communications are essentially concerned with information exchange, for example, the giving and receiving of data between departments, and working on joint or group projects.

Diagonal communications are concerned with requests for information and advice, between staff of differing status, located in different departments.

3. Matrix Structure

The matrix structure is found less often in business than the pyramid structure, but it can be used effectively where greater flexibility is required and where innovative and creative thinking are required, for example in one-off decision-making situations. It is sometimes combined with the pyramid structure. The matrix structure can be used to guide through individual projects, where a manager or director needs to be appointed for the duration of the project. The project director can withdraw (or second) staff from normal duties to work under his or her direction, thus enabling a team that combines all of the appropriate skills to be assembled. The major disadvantage of the matrix structure is that there is an ever-present danger of contradictory or conflicting instructions being given, on the one hand, by the line manager and, on the other hand, by the project manager. Its other major disadvantage is that it can engender a lack of discipline and make accountability difficult to enforce.

Organisation Charts

The traditional organisation chart looks like the following:

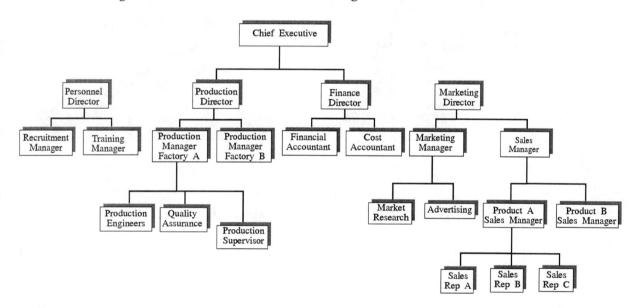

Notice that if you were to draw in all the posts in each department you would produce a very complicated chart. However, if such a chart were then produced, you would need to be aware of three features of the organisation represented by it:

1. line relationships
2. staff relationships
3. functional relationships.

1. Line relationships

Organisation charts show, through the use of connecting lines, who has responsibilities and authority. In general, authority flows down from the top and accountability flows upwards: there is an organisational hierarchy. The obvious advantage is that people know who is responsible for particular functions and to whom they are accountable. In very large organisations the hierarchy may involve many levels and the communications process can become very slow, particularly upward communication.

Using such a chart can show at a glance a manager's 'span of control', that is, the number of subordinates that a manager can effectively control and direct. The number of subordinates will vary according to a given situation.

Shapes of organisation

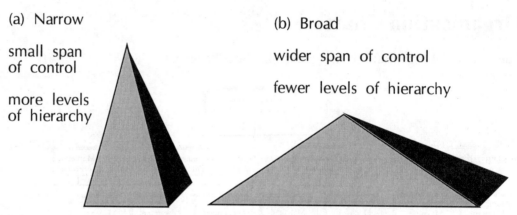

(a) Narrow

small span of control

more levels of hierarchy

(b) Broad

wider span of control

fewer levels of hierarchy

Organisation structure and span of control

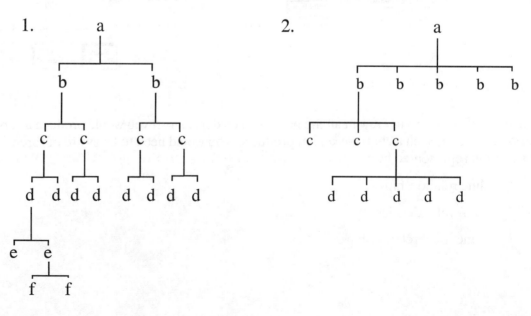

2. *Staff relationships*

A staff function is one which serves some part of the organisation. Thus a personnel department has a staff function, though the department also has a line relationship in that there is a hierarchy of responsibility and accountability. The clearer staff relationship is where there is no line relationship: for example, a personal assistant to the chief executive or a head of department. The authority of such a position is derived from the person to whom he or she is personal assistant. Another way to explain a staff relationship is to emphasise the importance of advice compared to authority.

3. *Functional relationships*

A functional department is one which serves an organisation-wide 'function' and which has authority and responsibility for that function which affects the line departments. Thus quality inspectors (or any other kind of inspectorate) are in a functional relationship to other departments.

Organisation charts are an attempt to record the formal structure of the business, showing some of the relationships, the downward flow of authority and responsibility and the main lines of communication. They have the advantage of forcing senior management to clearly define organisational relationships. For outsiders, particularly new employees, they are a useful introduction to the organisation and they can form a starting point from which management can initiate change or evaluate the strengths and weaknesses of the operation. However, they can quickly become out-of-date as personnel and operational relationships change and they often introduce a degree of rigidity into the organisation as people feel that they are constrained by the defined limits of their position in the organisation chart.

In terms of both line and functional authority, the simplicity or complexity of the organisation chart will be a reflection of the scale of the organisation. The organisation charts we show on this page and the next

An organisation chart for a professional partnership

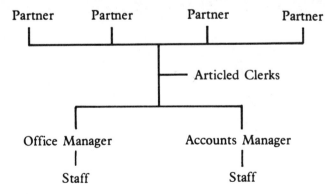

provide a comparison between two private sector organisations, one of a professional partnership, the other of a large private limited company.

An organisation chart for a large private limited company

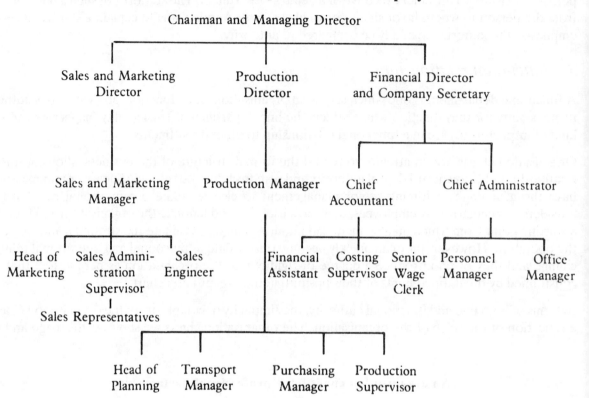

Thus organisation charts, by identifying lines of authority and responsibility, can be of great assistance in the improvement of the communications system by managers. They may, for example, reveal that an existing structure is such that it inhibits change and development in the organisation: for example, where it becomes apparent that research and development work is spread too widely and is not co-ordinated. The structure should be carefully monitored to ensure that it does not become outdated and begin to introduce rigidity into the roles and responsibilities of the workforce.

The value of an organisation chart

The value of an organisation chart is that:

1.   the task of preparing it enables the individual components of the business to be brought under review

2.   an assessment can be made of the relationship of each component part of the business to the others

3.   management must consider the authority required by individuals within the structure to carry out their responsibilities adequately

4.   it assists staff in locating their role and status within the business.

1. Explain the function of a *communication system*.

2. List the features of a *communications policy*.

3. What are the *three* components of a communication process?

4. Explain the dangers of communications breakdown.

5. Identify *five* possible design faults in a communication system.

6. Distinguish between *physical* and *attitudinal* barriers to communication.

7. What is an *electronic office*?

8. Explain the two main advantages of a *network*.

9. In what ways does information technology improve communication?

10. Explain Handy's 'Shamrock' model.

11. List the main advantages and disadvantages of *homeworking*.

12. Describe the main factors influencing a communications system.

13. Describe the main features of the following organisational structures:

    - departmental
    - pyramidal
    - matrix.

14. State the main purpose of an *organisation chart*.

15. Distinguish between:

    - line relationships
    - staff relationships
    - functional relationships.

16. What is meant by *span of control*?

Decision-making in Business

Effective decision-making is an important part of business success. If a business is to function smoothly and minimise the risk that results from any decision-making process, then decision-making must be approached in a logical and methodical manner.

Whether it is an individual acting in a personal capacity, or as a representative or employee of a business, some general observations can be made about the decision-making process. Decisions are likely to take longer to make (the time-span of decisions) when:

- costs associated with the decision are high
- risk is great
- many people are involved in the process
- the information required is substantial
- the problem to be solved is not urgent or immediate
- many people will be affected
- options are many
- opponents are many and/or influential and/or vociferous.

Business finds some approaches to decision-making more valuable than others for some projects. How might a business, for example, evaluate a decision which is to be made concerning whether it should, or should not, invest in a particular project?

Take, for example, a company which currently meets its energy requirements by taking electricity from the National Grid and paying its bills quarterly. Because of rising energy costs, a team is set up, consisting mainly of engineers and accountants, to assess the possibility of reducing these costs. A simple process the team might follow is:

1. Identify the problem
2. Brainstorm possible solutions
3. Refine ideas
4. Collect financial and statistical information on options
5. Assess the non-numerical factors
6. Analyse the information using decision-making tools
7. Make the decision

8.   Implement the decision

9.   Review the decision.

1. Identify the problem

Identifying the problem is often not as easy as it appears. The problem may seem evident: energy costs are rising. To solve the problem, it is important to discover the root cause of the problem. For example, the increased costs may have arisen because:

a.   the electricity suppliers have increased their prices

b.   more electricity is being consumed than is necessary.

The latter cause may require entirely different measures to be taken than former. For example, with the first option the team might look at the feasibility of the business building and operating its own electricity generator, using gas to power the generator. The team's decision might specify that the business sticks with its existing system or buys a generator for its own use. This is, probably, an entirely inappropriate solution if the problem is excessive use of electricity – in which case individual energy-saving devices, fitted to machines and equipment, would be a much more appropriate solution.

Solving the 'wrong problem' is a very costly exercise and must be avoided. One way of ensuring this is by allocating sufficient time for this stage of the investigation to be properly carried out.

2. Brainstorm solutions

Often, people are selected for a problem-solving team on the basis of their creativity. Particularly in a marketing environment, lateral and creative thinkers are capable of producing numerous ideas. Even when the problem seems mundane or very technical, one spark of imaginative thinking may be all that is required for the solution to emerge. One of the techniques used for this sort of ideas generation is known as brainstorming. *Brainstorming* involves a group of people shouting out ideas in a random and spontaneous manner. The ideas are then sorted and sifted afterwards and evaluated for their feasibility.

3. Refine ideas

This stage involves refining the ideas generated by the brainstorming process. Brainstorming produces random ideas: they are raw and unsifted. Many of the ideas would prove to be unfeasible if an attempt was made to implement them. The ideas must be checked against three basic areas if they are to progress to the next stage of the process:

- *business objectives*: any possible solution must match with existing business objectives, otherwise conflict is likely to occur

- *internal constraints*, such as shortage of available finance or a lack of certain skills in the workforce, may invalidate a particular idea

- *external factors*, such as interest rates, level of competition, exchange rates will influence a decision. Other external factors will include changes in technology, or in the law, which must be anticipated if an informed decision is to be made.

4. Collect financial and statistical information on options

Once the root of the problem has been identified and ideas have been sorted, sifted and measured against the objectives and constraints that might affect the business, then the information connected with each option can be collected. If the problem is one associated with money, output, consumption of materials etc. – and most business problems tend to be of this type – then the collection of numerical information can proceed. Numerical information is often referred to as *quantitative* (that is, it can be expressed in numbers or quantities).

5. Assess the non-numerical factors

All business decisions will involve some non-numerical factors. These factors may include such things as:

- the effect of the decisions on employee motivation and attitudes
- the social or environmental costs and benefits of the decision
- the effect on competitors.

This is known as *qualitative* information. However much effort is put into the collection of quantitative information, it is frequently the qualitative factors which ultimately determine the success or failure of the decision.

6. Analyse the information using decision-making tools

There exist numerous tools which help business managers analyse the effect of alternative decisions; some of these are examined later in this Part. All of the tools involve setting up a model of some type so that the likely outcomes of particular decisions can be projected. Computers are now used extensively for this type of modelling: spreadsheets are an example of a computer-based modelling tool with which you may be familiar. Spreadsheets take numerical information and manipulate it within parameters set by the business manager or decision maker. 'What if?' situations can be easily shown and the best quantitative decision can be identified. As already mentioned, non-numerical considerations will weigh heavily in the analysis stage.

7. Make the decision

At this stage, where the actual decision is made, there is always a choice. At the most basic level it is: to do something or to do nothing. Sometimes, a range of options have been investigated and the problem lies in making a choice between them. The final decision will rest on four main criteria:

(i)   *financial costs*: the money costs and benefits of a decision

(ii)   *opportunity costs*: this is the value of the best alternative opportunity which has to be forgone as a result of making a particular choice

(iii) *social costs*: the costs to society, such as the loss of trade in a town if a by-pass is constructed around it. (See Part Five.)

(iv)   *human costs*: the effects of the decision on the workforce.

8. Implement the decision

Implementation is putting a decision into practice. Implementation may involve buying and installing equipment and setting up systems to monitor and control a process. Control is a vital part of any decision-making process as it must:

- guide the project towards achieving its goal
- set a standard for measurement of achievement
- measure planned activity against what actually happens.

Controlling the implementation stage allows managers the chance to correct their actions; this increases the likelihood of success.

9. Review the decision

The review of a decision is, sometimes, neglected, yet it is an important step in collecting feedback on the success of the decision. The review will provide valuable information which can be used to increase the chance of success for future projects.

Levels of decision-making

The types of decision to be made should determine the structure of the decision-making process. Day-to-day decisions, such as choosing a new supplier of paper clips, are qualitatively different from major decisions, such as deciding where to locate a new factory. To use the same structure of decision-making to solve both problems will be wasteful of resources and result in unwanted outcomes. A routine decision, such as choosing a paper clip supplier, will require little time being spent on it and should involve very few people. The larger, more complex decision needs careful, detailed analysis and will need careful scrutiny, since to arrive at the wrong decision will prove, at best, costly and, at worst, irreversible.

Let's consider the two levels of decision-making that are furthest away from each other on the spectrum. Decisions which have to be made periodically and are 'operational' can be made by junior and middle managers who are involved in routine administrative matters rather than by senior management. The motto of the day should be: routine decisions are dealt with by routine procedures.

On the other hand, senior management will concern itself only with those decisions which are non-routine, non-recurrent, strategic and whose outcomes are uncertain. That is, those which require a greater input of judgment and creativity of thought. When senior management does become involved in straightforward and mundane decision-making, then the motivation of more junior management will suffer and the time that would be better spent on long-term, strategic objectives (that is, *development*) is squandered on short-term *control*.

Summarised by management experts, the moral is clear:

> '... *insofar as it is possible to generalise, the primary concern of senior management should be with strategic decisions, whilst short-term operational decisions should be left in the hands of operating management. Middle management then acts as the meeting point between the two, taking as its focus the periodic control decisions.*'
> Gilligan, Neale and Murray: *Business Decision Making* (Philip Allan 1983)

Working in business involves making a constant stream of decisions, some of which are more urgent, complex and important than others. However, in the long-run, whatever the nature of the decision, the more systematic and planned management's approach to decision-making is, then the more successful the business will be in achieving its objectives.

Numerical Tools for Decision-making

Many textbooks on business include a section on methods of presenting numerical data. Usually, the content of that section will focus on methods of graphical presentation and will explain:

bar charts
pie charts
histograms
pictograms.

With the introduction of the National Curriculum in mathematics and its focus, in Attainment Target 5, on statistical knowledge and skills, most students approaching the age of 17 are now expected to possess a number of such skills to a satisfactory level. This book assumes that this is the case and continues from that state of knowledge: it looks specifically at numerical aids to decision-making, rather than just the presentational skills.

This section will examine techniques for:

Building decision trees
Investment Appraisal
Constructing indices
Forecasting
Network analysis
Blending: allocating resources
Using normal distribution.

Decision Trees

In business, almost all decisions that are taken involve some degree of risk and uncertainty. A new product launch may be a failure. A share which has been recommended to investment clients may fall in value. Construction of a new factory may be far more expensive than expected, and so on. In order to ensure that only *acceptable* risks are taken, you need to be able to evaluate each alternative so that you know how likely each of a number of possible outcomes might be.

You will already know that there are several means of estimating the likelihood of occurrence and this array of techniques is called 'probability', and you need to know, too, that comparing relative probabilities is a useful, basic aid in a manager's decision-making.

A basic understanding of probability is a vital starting point for the learning about decision trees. Probability is a topic studied by all mathematics students who follow the National Curriculum, but 'probability' is something that affects us all – even those who have never heard of it. In October 1987 a large swathe of the South and West of England was devastated by a violent storm that caused widespread destruction and loss of life; it resulted in insurance companies facing a liability that ran into billions of pounds. The 'duty weatherman' at the Met. Office that evening was Mr. Michael Fish, who received severe public criticism for his failure to warn the country of the storm threat. In 1991 a set of climactic conditions occurred, similar to those of October 1987, and the Met. Office duly issued a warning. In the event, the weather system tracked to the south and east and left Britain undisturbed and undamaged. On both occasions, the Met. Office forecast the likelihood of an event happening and, on both occasions, it was wrong; for the majority of the time when it forecasts correctly, its success is ignored.

If you should feel confident that you can apply your understanding of the word 'probability' to the situation just described, then you will have no difficulty in understanding its application to the following business situations:

> *"I think there's an 80% chance that our advertising campaign will result in increased sales."*

This statement implies that there is a 20% chance of the campaign being unsuccessful in achieving increased sales.

> *"The chances of the share issue being a success are no better than 50%."*

> *"That machine is unreliable – on the basis of our records, there is a 30% chance it will break down and lose us production this week."*

In each of these situations the people concerned are making a speculative statement about the likely occurrence of an event. (The happening might be what is called a 'random event'.) The statements may be based on information that managers have collected from the past or it may be pure speculation about the future: it is more likely to be a combination of the two. Implicit, though, is their understanding that the combined chance of something happening, or not happening, is 1.

Trying to assess the possible outcomes from various decision options is something which lends itself particularly well to being represented as a diagram. Decision trees are often used for this purpose and to use them involves understanding some basic terms:

Decisions: these are within the control of the decision-maker: the decision-maker has a choice between various courses of action. Decision points are represented in a decision tree by means of a square.

Outcomes: as a result of one decision, two or more outcomes are possible. Each outcome has a probability associated with it. Outcomes are represented in decision trees by means of circles.

Expected values: these are the result of multiplying

(1)   the probability of a particular outcome occurring

by

(2)   the return in money terms that would be expected if that occurrence actually happened.

Example

A football club is in trouble – its team is locked in a relegation battle at the bottom of the league. Should the team be relegated, it will have major repercussions on the club's financial situation. At an emergency meeting of the Board of Directors, held to discuss the crisis, a sub-committee presents the following options:

Option 1

- the existing manager be replaced. It will cost £0.3 million to terminate his contract before its natural expiry. Should the Board decide to replace the manager, it has a further decision to make: it can replace him with a high-profile manager, who will cost £0.5 million, or a low-profile manager at a cost of £0.3 million.

Option 2

- the existing manager is retained.

The club's Financial Director estimates the revenues for the following year:

	Relegated	**Avoid Relegation**
Existing manager	£1.2 m	£3.2 m
High-profile manager	£1.3 m	£3.6 m
Low-profile manager	£1.3 m	£3.0 m

Based on the past records of clubs which have experienced similar situations, the Board assesses that a high-profile manager, and the enthusiasm he would bring, will mean the club has a 70% chance of avoiding the drop to a lower division, while a lower profile manager's chances would be 60%. Meanwhile the existing manager's chance of avoiding relegation, largely because of the low morale of his players, is only 40%.

Because of the complexity of the situation, a decision tree is used to represent and evaluate the decisions involved.

Drawing the decision tree

Step 1

Decisions are represented by squares and the first decision is whether or not to replace the manager.

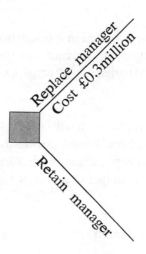

Step 2

As a result of retaining the manager, there are only two possible outcomes: the team will either be relegated (0.6 chance) or avoid relegation (0.4 chance). Outcomes are shown by circles and each outcome has a financial return.

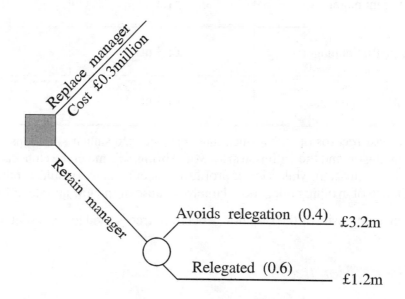

Step 3

If it is decided to replace the manager, a further decision must be made: whether to employ a high- or low-profile manager, taking into account the estimated chances of avoiding relegation.

All the possible decisions and alternative outcomes are now shown by the tree.

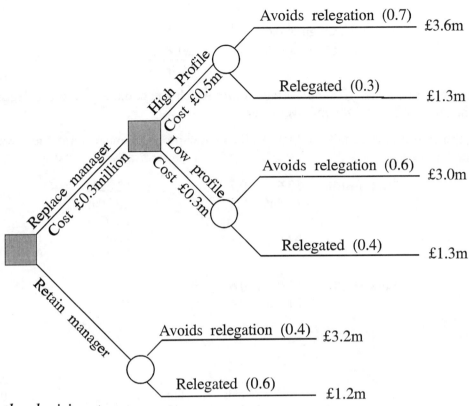

Evaluating the decision tree

Evaluating a decision tree involves calculating the expected values of each mutually exclusive event. To do this, it is necessary to work back from right to left through the tree.

If the existing manager is retained, there is a 40% chance of earning £3.2 million next year and a 60% chance of earning £1.2 million. The expected value of the 'existing manager' option is calculated by multiplying the return from an outcome by its probability. The result is shown in the following figure:

£3.2m x 0.4 = £1.28m

£1.2m x 0.6 = £0.72m
_____

£2.0m

$$£3.2m \times 0.4 \quad = \quad £1.28m$$
$$£1.2m \times 0.6 \quad = \quad \underline{£0.72m}$$
$$\underline{£2.00m}$$

This expected value of 2.0 m gives the average return which you could expect if the decision to keep the existing manager were taken over and over again.

Calculating the expected values, if the high-profile or low-profile managers are employed, produces the following results:

High-profile

$$£3.6m \times 0.7 \quad = \quad £2.52m$$
$$£1.3m \times 0.3 \quad = \quad \underline{£0.39m}$$
$$\underline{£2.91m}$$
$$\text{less cost} \qquad \underline{£0.50m}$$
$$\underline{£2.41m}$$

Low-profile

$$£3.0m \times 0.6 \quad = \quad £1.80m$$
$$£1.3m \times 0.4 \quad = \quad \underline{£0.52m}$$
$$\underline{£2.32m}$$
$$\text{less cost} \qquad \underline{£0.30m}$$
$$\underline{£2.02 \text{ m}}$$

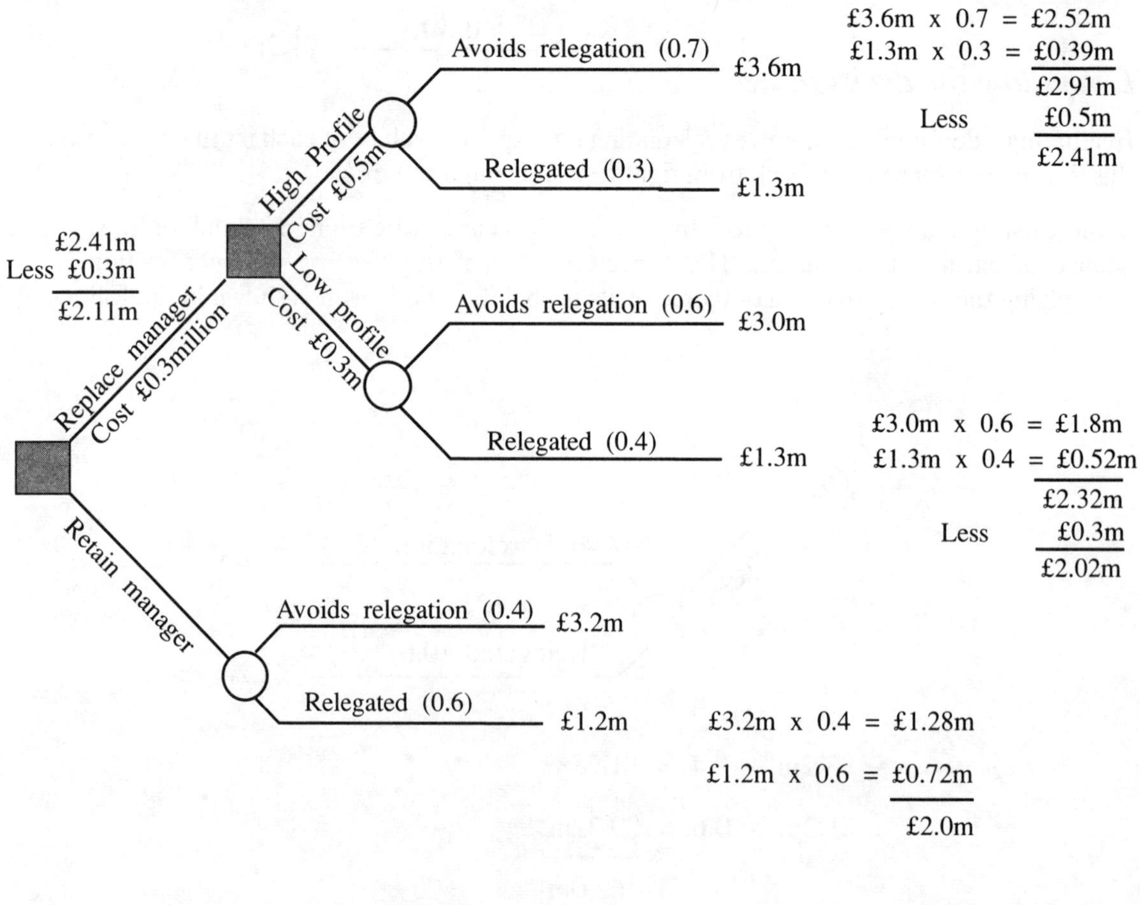

If the manager is to be replaced then, on average, replacing him with a high-profile manager will yield the highest expected return (£2.41m against £2.02 m). The choice between these options now having been made, it remains to deduct the cost of terminating the existing manager's contract (£0.3m) from the expected value of the decision made (£2.41m). The resulting figure of £2.11m compares favourably with the option of retaining the existing manager (£2.0m), so the decision should be to dismiss the existing manager and hire a new high-profile replacement.

Clearly, few decisions of the type you've just looked at are likely to be taken on purely financial grounds.

As with any financial technique, decision trees have their limitations.

Limitations of decision trees

- decision trees can be time-consuming to research – it may take months to produce useful figures. The expense of this must be weighed against the importance of the decision.

- the information needed may not be available or may be incomplete. The decision may not have been taken before so any figures used will contain an element of subjectivity.

- the time-span of the decision may be considerable and, therefore, figures cannot be taken as exact. Caution must be exercised in the evaluation process; this sometimes leads to the production of two versions of the tree: one will show an optimistic view of possible outcomes, whilst a second will demonstrate the outcome if pessimistic circumstances prevail.

- non-financial factors may weigh as heavily in the decision as purely financial factors. In the football club example, the opinion and attitudes of the press and supporters will have a major influence; loyalty to the existing manager may be a factor and the availability of possible replacement managers is also a point to bear in mind.

Advantages of decision trees

- they show clearly and logically the decision options which are open: this can produce new ideas and provoke discussion

- they encourage quantification, thereby allowing managers to consider the financial implications of their decisions

- they can be combined with other tools of decision-making, such as network analysis, to enable the thorough planning of projects.

Investment Appraisal

'Investment appraisal' is a process whereby a manager, or management team, weighs up the advantages and disadvantages of spending money (capital) on a particular project. Every effort will be made to ensure that the costs and benefits of the project are measured and quantified so that it can be compared favourably or unfavourably with other projects that might be under consideration.

In a business, there are a number of different situations when managers may have to consider capital investment. These situations will include occasions when:

    a.   the business requires new plant or machinery

    b.   obsolete plant or machinery needs replacing

    c.   budget cuts and alternative means of cost savings need to be assessed

    d.   there is a possibility of expansion where new products are needed.

Investments such as these are the focus of major decisions for any business, especially since such projects usually:

- have a large, initial cost
- are expected to continue for a number of years
- are expected to improve profits, either through increasing the revenues of the business or cutting its costs.

New assets, such as plant, machinery or buildings, may be bought with profit accumulated and retained from previous years, but it is more often the case that a business is forced to borrow funds to pay for its capital investments. Such funds are available from several sources, but each has a cost attached to it.

A manager who decides to invest must be confident that the immediate cost of the project will be eventually outweighed by the benefits that it will bring to the business. Here, such 'benefits' are not always purely financial in their nature; they can be social benefits, or health and safety benefits, or in terms of recruitment. Rather than examining these more intangible benefits, it is on the purely financial appraisal of an investment that you will now concentrate. There are four main methods used to appraise projects:

    1.   Average Accounting Rate of Return

    2.   Payback

    3.   Net Present Value (NPV)

    4.   Internal Rate of Return (IRR).

Methods 3 and 4 are collectively referred to as Discounted Cash Flow (DCF) methods; these are examined later.

For the purpose of illustrating the usefulness and suitability of each method, consider two alternative project proposals: Project A and Project B. The proposals have been thoroughly researched as preparation for the decision-making process. From that research, the following information has been made available:

Project A	Cash outflow	Cash inflow
Year 0	£15,000	
Year 1		£7,000
Year 2		£8,000
Year 3		£9,000

For Project A, the initial investment is £15,000. This is considered to be Year 0, as the investment is made now. The life of the project is three years and, in each of these three years, a cash inflow is received.

Project B	Cash outflow	Cash inflow
Year 0	£25,000	
Year 1		£5,000
Year 2		£10,000
Year 3		£10,000
Year 4		£5,000
Year 5		£10,000

Project B involves an initial spending of £25,000. The project has a five year life.

Method 1 Average accounting rate of return

Method of calculation

Stage 1

$$\frac{\text{Cash inflows} - \text{Cash outflows}}{\text{Number of years of investment}} = \text{average return per year (£)}$$

Stage 2

This stage converts the result of Stage 1 into a percentage figure, the percentage being the average annual rate of return on the initial investment.

$$\frac{\text{Average return per year(£)}}{\text{Initial investment}} \times 100 = \text{Average annual rate of return (\%)}$$

Performing the calculations for Project A produces the following result:

Stage 1 $\frac{£24,000 - £15,000}{3} = £3,000 \text{ per annum (Year)}$

Stage 2 $\frac{£3,000}{£15,000} \times 100 = 20\%$

Thus the average annual rate of return for Project A is 20%. You might like to practice this method on the figures for Project B: you should arrive at a return of 12%.

Clearly, 20% is a better return on an investment than is 12%. If a choice has to be made between the projects using this method – and on *purely financial* grounds – Project A will be chosen.

The business would also need to consider whether 20% constitutes an acceptable return, bearing in mind the *cost of capital*. The benefits of the average accounting rate of return method is that it:

- is simple to calculate
- provides a quick (but rough) rule-of-thumb approach to appraising the financial attractiveness of a project
- is readily understood by managers who are not financial specialists or accountants.

However, it suffers from these drawbacks:

- it fails to take account of the 'time value of money'. Receiving £8,000 in two years' time is *not* the same as having that money available now. £8,000 now could, through investment, be converted into a larger sum in Year 2

- it fails to indicate the *risk* of a project. The sooner you recoup your initial investment, the less risk you run of losing it.

Method 2 Payback

The payback method is a useful indicator for telling a business how quickly it will recover its initial investment.

Project A involves an initial investment of £15,000. Cash inflows of £7,000 and £8,000 in Years 1 and 2 means that the initial investment has been recovered. Hence, the payback period for Project A is two years. Look at the data for Project B and confirm that the payback period is three years.

Both projects have nice round 'numbers of years' as the payback period, but it is usual for a payback period to be specified in years and months. For example, suppose the project has £5,000 left to recover at the beginning of Year 4 of its life, and the projected cash inflow for that year is £20,000. It is assumed that the investment will be recovered three months into Year 4 and that the payback period can be stated, therefore, as 3 years 3 months.

The benefits of the payback method are:

- its calculations are simple and quick

- the result can be easily understood by non-accountants

- it assesses the risk of a project.

Its limitations are:

- it fails to measure the profitability or the rate of return of the project

- it fails to consider the 'time value of money'.

The method is especially suitable when capital for investment is in very short supply and the element of risk is management's prime consideration. It is a method frequently used in combination with another method which measures rate of return.

Discounted Cash Flow (DCF) Methods

Method 3, Net Present Value and Method 4, Internal Rate of Return, are jointly known as DCF methods. The critical difference between DCF methods and the two methods you have looked at so far is that DCF methods consider the 'time value of money'.

Method 3 Net Present Value (NPV)

The time value of money

Most people, if asked the question, "Would you prefer £100 now or in five years' time?" would not hesitate to choose to have that £100 now. Their probable reasons are that:

- either they need the money now so they can spend it immediately

- or the £100 can be invested immediately and, if left untouched, will have grown to be more than £100 by the end of Year 5.

It is the second of these two reasons which you need to know if you wish to understand DCF methods. Investing money is an idea with which most of us are familiar. If you place a sum of money in a National Savings Certificate or in a building society, for example, it will have interest added to it at a specified rate, known as the *rate of interest*. Assuming an interest rate of 10%, then a £100 investment would grow in the following way:

Year					
1	£100.00	×	1.10	=	£110.00
2	£110.00	×	1.10	=	£121.00
3	£121.00	×	1.10	=	£133.10
4	£133.10	×	1.10	=	£146.41
5	£146.41	×	1.10	=	£161.05

So £100, invested at a rate of 10% interest for five years, will grow to be worth £161.05 in five years' time. Looking at the 'flip-side' of this, £161.05, to be received in five years' time, is worth £100 now. Developing this idea further, any cash flows from a project, which are to be received in the future, are worth less than that amount in today's money terms.

Looking at Project A, the figure below shows what needs to be calculated if the time value of money is to be considered.

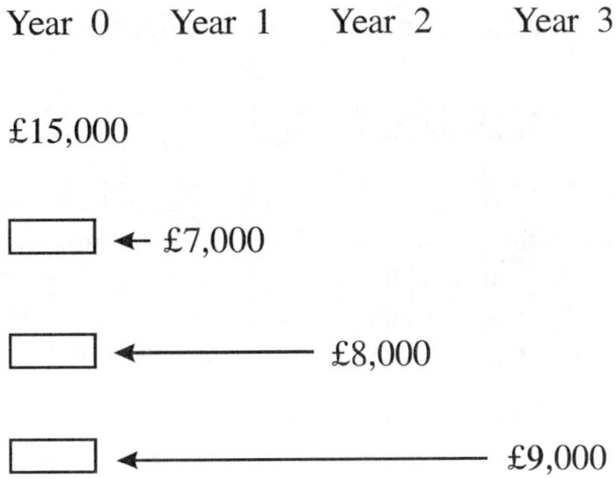

Year 0   Year 1   Year 2   Year 3

£15,000

☐ ← £7,000

☐ ← £8,000

☐ ← £9,000

The time value of money

The three cash inflows need to be converted back into Year 0 terms, so that their true worth can be compared with the initial investment of £15,000. Fortunately, at your current level of study, you can use a set of tables to assist with this process. You need not know how the tables were produced – simply how to use them. The table below is an extract from a set of discount tables and includes most of the values you are likely to need. You might like to find a full set of tables and identify where the extract is from.

Years Hence	1%	2%	4%	6%	8%	10%	12%	14%	15%	16%	18%	20%	22%	24%	25%	26%	28%	30%
1...	0.990	0.980	0.962	0.943	0.926	0.909	0.893	0.877	0.870	0.862	0.847	0.833	0.820	0.806	0.800	0.794	0.781	0.769
2...	0.980	0.961	0.925	0.890	0.857	0.826	0.797	0.769	0.756	0.743	0.718	0.694	0.672	0.650	0.640	0.630	0.610	0.592
3...	0.971	0.942	0.889	0.840	0.794	0.751	0.712	0.675	0.658	0.641	0.609	0.579	0.551	0.524	0.512	0.500	0.477	0.455
4...	0.961	0.924	0.855	0.792	0.735	0.683	0.636	0.592	0.572	0.552	0.516	0.482	0.451	0.423	0.410	0.397	0.373	0.350
5...	0.951	0.906	0.822	0.747	0.681	0.621	0.567	0.519	0.497	0.476	0.437	0.402	0.370	0.341	0.328	0.315	0.291	0.269
6...	0.942	0.888	0.790	0.705	0.630	0.564	0.507	0.456	0.432	0.410	0.370	0.335	0.303	0.275	0.262	0.250	0.227	0.207
7...	0.933	0.971	0.760	0.665	0.583	0.513	0.452	0.400	0.376	0.354	0.314	0.279	0.249	0.222	0.210	0.198	0.178	0.159
8...	0.923	0.853	0.731	0.627	0.540	0.467	0.404	0.351	0.327	0.305	0.266	0.233	0.204	0.179	0.168	0.157	0.139	0.123
9...	0.914	0.837	0.703	0.592	0.500	0.424	0.361	0.308	0.284	0.263	0.225	0.194	0.167	0.144	0.134	0.125	0.108	0.094
10...	0.905	0.820	0.676	0.558	0.463	0.386	0.322	0.270	0.247	0.227	0.191	0.162	0.137	0.116	0.107	0.099	0.085	0.073

The Present value of £1

Assuming a discount rate of 10%, and applying the appropriate values in the table to the cash flows in Project A, produces the following result.

Project A   – discount rate 10%

	Year 0	**Year 1**	**Year 2**	**Year 3**
	–£15,000			
	£6,363	←(.909 × £7,000)		
	£6,608	←	(.826 × £8,000),	
	£6,759	←		(.751 × £9,000)
	£4,730	NPV		

The three discount values used in calculating the net present values of the cash flows are circled in the DCF tables shown below.

Years Hence	1%	2%	4%	6%	8%	10%	12%	14%	15%	16%	18%	20%	22%	24%	25%	26%	28%	30%
1...	0.990	0.980	0.962	0.943	0.926	(0.909)	0.893	0.877	0.870	0.862	0.847	0.833	0.820	0.806	0.800	0.794	0.781	0.769
2...	0.980	0.961	0.925	0.890	0.857	(0.826)	0.797	0.769	0.756	0.743	0.718	0.694	0.672	0.650	0.640	0.630	0.610	0.592
3...	0.971	0.942	0.889	0.840	0.794	(0.751)	0.712	0.675	0.658	0.641	0.609	0.579	0.551	0.524	0.512	0.500	0.477	0.455
4...	0.961	0.924	0.855	0.792	0.735	0.683	0.636	0.592	0.572	0.552	0.516	0.482	0.451	0.423	0.410	0.397	0.373	0.350
5...	0.951	0.906	0.822	0.747	0.681	0.621	0.567	0.519	0.497	0.476	0.437	0.402	0.370	0.341	0.328	0.315	0.291	0.269
6...	0.942	0.888	0.790	0.705	0.630	0.564	0.507	0.456	0.432	0.410	0.370	0.335	0.303	0.275	0.262	0.250	0.227	0.207
7...	0.933	0.971	0.760	0.665	0.583	0.513	0.452	0.400	0.376	0.354	0.314	0.279	0.249	0.222	0.210	0.198	0.178	0.159
8...	0.923	0.853	0.731	0.627	0.540	0.467	0.404	0.351	0.327	0.305	0.266	0.233	0.204	0.179	0.168	0.157	0.139	0.123
9...	0.914	0.837	0.703	0.592	0.500	0.424	0.361	0.308	0.284	0.263	0.225	0.194	0.167	0.144	0.134	0.125	0.108	0.094
10...	0.905	0.820	0.676	0.558	0.463	0.386	0.322	0.270	0.247	0.227	0.191	0.162	0.137	0.116	0.107	0.099	0.085	0.073

e.g. £7,000 received in Year 1, when a discount value of 10% is used, results in the calculation:

£7,000 × .909 =£6,363

The NPV of £7,000 received in Year 1 is £6,363. Once the NPVs have been found for Year 2 and 3 cash flows, the overall NPV of the project can be calculated. Take the negative cash flows from the positive cash flows to leave a surplus NPV of £4,730. This means that £15,000 invested now in Project A, with an interest rate of 10%, will yield a surplus of £4,730. Clearly, on financial grounds alone, the investment is a worthwhile one.

Once again, you might like to practice the method on Project B. Use a 10% discount rate. You should end up with an NPV of £4,940; clearly, Project B is also an attractive investment.

In a situation where only one project will be given the 'go ahead', then, on financial grounds, Project B gives the slightly better NPV. However, in such a marginal decision, the degree of risk will figure largely in the decision-making process, as well as other, non-financial considerations.

The results of the NPV calculations have proved that with, interest rates at 10%, both projects are attractive propositions. But NPV doesn't tell you what the return on the projects actually is. You know that the return is greater than 10%, but you don't know by how much. Method 4, Internal Rate of Return, can provide you with that information.

Method 4 Internal Rate of Return (IRR)

The IRR is found when the percentage discount factor applied to the cash flows produces a Net Present Value of 0.

To establish the IRR of Project A you can use one of two techniques:

- trial and error
- interpolation.

Trial and error involves trying different discount rates until an NPV of zero – or nearly zero – is produced. For Project A, try 20% – the discount factors for this can be found from the previous table.

Project A	– discount rate 20%		
Year 0	Year 1	Year 2	Year 3
– £15,000			
£5,831	←(.833 × £7,000)		
£5,552	←——————— (.694 × £8,000)		
£5,211	←————————————— (.579 × £9,000)		
£1,584	NPV		

A positive NPV of £1,584 indicates that the return of Project A exceeds 20%. Trial and error means trying again with a higher rate: remember the objective is to reach an NPV of 0.

Project A – discount rate 28%

	Year 0	Year 1	Year 2	Year 3

Year 0   − £15,000
£5,467 ←—(.781 × £7,000)
£4,880 ←——————— (.610 × £8,000)
£4,293 ←————————————— (.477 × £9,000)

−£340   NPV

An NPV of –£340 indicates that the rate of return is *less* than 28%: it must, then, be between 20% and 28%. Using trial and error would involve choosing another discount rate, say 26%, and applying that to the cash flow in the hope that it would be close to 0 NPV. A quicker, and sufficiently accurate, alternative technique is to use *interpolation*.

So far it has been established that the IRR lies somewhere between 20% and 28%.

20% ——————————|——————— 28%

If you represent the NPVs on a similar scale, the idea of interpolation should become clear.

£1,584 ——————————— £0 —— –£340

If you mark £0 on this scale, it will be nearer to –£340 than +£1,584. The line estimates its position.

The range between £1,584 and –£340 is £1,924.

$$\frac{£1,584}{£1,924} \times 100 = 82\%$$

NPV of £0 lies 82% of the distance along the line from £1,584. Transferring this finding to the discount rates will establish the IRR of Project A. 8% is the difference in rates. Find 82% of 8 and add it to the 20% discount rate.

$$\frac{82}{100} \times 8 = 6.60$$ The IRR of Project A is 26.66%.

Practise the technique of interpolation on Project B. You should discover the IRR to be about 17.5%

On the basis of IRR, Project A, in percentage terms, has a much higher return. Project B runs over five years and the further into the future that the cash flows are, the less will be the NPV of the cash.

Project A or Project B?

In making a final decision between the project proposals, the following points must be considered:

In favour of Project A

- using the crude average accounting rate of return method, Project A yields 20% against the 12% for Project B
- Project A has a shorter pay back period: 2 years, rather than the 3 years of Project B

- Project A involves the initial investment of a smaller capital sum; £15,000 as opposed to the £25,000 of Project B

- the estimated cash flows from Project A are over a shorter time period (3 years) than from Project B (5 years) and, therefore, will tend to be more reliable and less prone to economic fluctuations.

In favour of Project B

Although everything seems to militate against Project B, it is worth considering two factors before a final decision is made:

- the IRR of Project A is 26.6%: 26.6% of £15,000 = £3,990

- the IRR of Project B is 17.5%: 17.5% of £25,000 = £4,375

Although the cash sum invested in Project B is larger, so is the net present value of the actual cash returns.

Non-financial factors must be discussed. What are the implications of not going ahead with Project B; will health/safety be threatened; will ground be lost to competitors etc?

Measuring the risk factor

The largest single factor a potential investor has to consider is *risk*. This, like its opposite – returns, may be great or small, low or high. Imagine if you were in a gaming club and you were feeding a succession of £1 coins into a one-armed bandit. Each pound coin that you push in to the slot represents a nexus of three factors that are at work:

- the forecasted payback time is extremely short (seconds, in fact)
- the returns are proportionally huge (perhaps 100 for a £1 'investment')
- the risk of totally losing your investment is high (perhaps 1000 to 1 in the machine's favour).

You may still consider 'staking' your pound, however, because it is a small amount of money and because the high forecasted returns make taking the risk a worthwhile one for you. Whether trying the pools, or buying a lottery ticket, or backing a horse the 'long odds' are the same – the attraction is that for an insignificant outlay (investment) you might have an almost instant and disproportionately high return on your stake. In short, you consider it worth the risk of losing your money.

Let's look at the three parts of the investment/ risk /return equation from a different perspective. You walk into a High Street bank and instead of standing in front of a one-armed bandit you are now standing in front of a two-armed cashier. You pay the cashier some money to pay into a 10 year National Savings Certificate. This cash nexus shows the same three factors at work but the balance between the three is different:

- the forecasted pay back period is long (10 years at least)
- the returns on investment are modest
- the risk to your money is almost non-existent.

This is an investment that you would probably decide is still worthwhile, since the amount you are investing is relatively small and, despite the fact that any return is going to be modest, you are running no appreciable risk of losing out.

These two examples of high and low investment risk may also illustrate how important knowledge is in the investment equation – even though it's not always apparent. An investment that is made without any knowledge of the three other investment factors is not really an investment at all but is merely gambling. Investors must 'do their homework' and analyse as accurately, as possible, the risks that any investment carries. An investor's 'homework' needs to include:

- forecasting returns
- calculating Net Present Values
- assessing one investment against an alternative
- deciding whether potential returns outweigh any risk of loss.

In the business world, thorough research is more valuable and more widely used than guesswork; business people want to make the correct investment decision in order to secure the best return that they can on their money. However, once the investment manager has applied formulae, consulted DCF tables, programmed computers and compared the forecasts with the projected returns, a human choice remains to be made: which investment will be preferred to others that may be only marginally less attractive.

So, while NPVs remain a useful tool in a manager's investment decisions, they remain just that – useful. NPVs are simply an aid that helps the manager to distinguish between what is an 'acceptable' and an 'unacceptable' investment proposal. But, at the end of the decision-making process, it will still be a human being who makes the ultimate choice (sometimes subjectively); it is the manager who will have to put up with the praise when the decision works to the company's advantage or with the criticism when the decision is declared 'wrong'.

What, apart from direct loss, does an investment manager need to consider? There are many considerations. For example, an investment proposition that appears to offer excellent returns for the company may be rejected, simply because it appears to work against the corporate image. Drug running may offer excellent returns, but investment in it would hardly sit well with Coca Cola's benevolent corporate image – apart from the illegality of such a venture! Another example might be that of a company that is tempted to invest heavily in new technology knowing that the returns on that investment will be high but which rejects the investment proposal since implementing the decision will bring unacceptable disruption to its workforce.

There are two other things to consider in our investment equation.

1.   The first, like 'knowledge' is an invisible part of our equation – it's called 'luck', and it comes in two varieties, good and bad. 'Luck' of both kinds is what upsets an otherwise true statement: high risks usually bring high returns.
      If you examine this statement you see it's not true; for example, you might have invented and developed a product that the world is crying out for, or you might be the sole source of supply of a particular commodity or service. Whatever the case, your returns are likely to be extremely high, but you will not have put your investment to any significant risk.

2.   Time is our second invisible factor and it is often linked with luck since the longer one has to wait for one's returns the greater is the likelihood of things going wrong with one's

investment or the unpredictable happening. Investments are likely to have a greater guarantee of return in the short-term rather than the long-term since risk is consequently minimised and predictions and forecasts are likelier to be accurate.

Even with the most copper-bottomed, cast-iron, gilt-edged proposition things can go wrong – in business there are no 'racing certainties'. So it is true to say that money which comes back sooner is better than money which is predicted to come back later. Ploughing your investment capital into a project which has the potential for high returns but only in the distant future, opens up the possibilities of unforeseen events occurring that would lead to things going wrong (for example, wars, development of alternative products, changes of government or consumer taste are all dependent on what is jokingly referred to as 'the fickle finger of fate'). Such a realisation of the unpredictable havoc that time can bring can lead to 'short termism' amongst managers.

As part of this gloomy picture let's consider one other phrase: downside risk. This phrase (a cousin of another Americanism – worst case scenario) means what you would lose if everything went wrong – in other words, your downside risk is the greatest loss you would sustain in any particular set of circumstances. So, for example, our one-armed bandit gambler has a downside risk of 1 every time he inserts a coin; our national saver has a downside risk equal to the total amount of money he has handed over to the cashier up to and including his present visit. Living with downside risk and worst case scenarios are the wallpaper of management – you may not like the wallpaper but you've just gotta live with it. Making investment decisions, awaiting returns and living with the consequences of your decisions requires strong nerves, an unflappable temperament and a willingness to accept responsibility – as an American president once said, "The buck stops here". Investment decisions are wise, sound, inspired or just plain lucky – and it is this last adjective that is often used most widely by the managers themselves.

Network Analysis

Sometimes referred to as *critical path analysis*, this technique is used extensively in the construction industry. When you consider the word 'construction', think as widely as you can; it really refers to any object or structure which is:

- built or made over a considerable time span
- requires substantial co-ordination of resources
- needs to be thoroughly planned well in advance.

Such projects may be as massive as the Channel Tunnel or the new bridge over the Thames at Dartford; or it might be the building of a tanker or aircraft; it could even be a new school or hospital.

Whatever the project, it will have features which make it suitable for analysis and planning by means of a network; specific activities which can be identified and for which a time or duration can be estimated.

The objectives of network analysis are:

- to calculate the overall duration or time-scale of a project – how long will it take from start to finish?

- to identify those activities which are critical; that is, which activities, if delayed, will cause the whole project to be delayed?

- to identify those activities on which slack exists; that is, if an activity takes longer than expected, then its delay may not jeopardise the time-scale of the whole project.

This sort of information is invaluable to the project manager. In a complex project, where time available for management control and supervision is at a premium, it allows 'management by exception'. This means that managers will observe most closely those activities which are critical to the punctual completion of the project; those activities on which slack exists will merit less attention.

Network analysis can allow reallocation of resources - if slack exists on an activity which uses labour, can that labour be moved and utilised elsewhere? When the critical activities have been identified and the duration of the project has been worked out, it can help also in a situation when a client applies pressure to accelerate work on a project and complete it more quickly. The project manager can establish that, by working overtime or obtaining materials more quickly, the project can be completed in a shorter time and, when it can, what the cost and benefits of this might be.

Consider a building project, such as an extension to a factory. An example of this is the construction of an extension to a car plant at Sunderland so that Nissan is able to manufacture a replacement for its Micra. The cost of the project has been worked out and the expenditure approved by the management of the company. What will planning the project involve? Before building can even begin, management needs to know how long the work will take. Clearly, the earlier the work is completed, the sooner Nissan can begin to use its new extension, thereby generating earlier and additional revenue and profit. Thus, once a completion date has been estimated, any delays will be costly to the business. Network analysis will identify particular activities which are likely to be important or critical to the project's punctual completion.

Constructing the network

In practice, most projects involve large and complex network diagrams; often the data is processed by computers. You can quickly understand the nature of network analysis through considering a much simpler example.

In any building project some operations or activities need to be completed before others can begin. To state an obvious example, building the walls cannot begin until the foundations are in place. On the other hand, there are numerous activities which can be taking place simultaneously, in parallel. For example, plumbing can probably be done at the same time as electrical work; tiles can be affixed whilst windows are being glazed. The more jobs that can be done simultaneously, the shorter the duration of the project, but it must be borne in mind that some jobs have a practical and logical dependency on others.

Example

Suppose that a project has been broken down into twelve key activities and that, for simplicity, each activity is given a letter for ease of reference. For example, laying the concrete floor is Activity J. This Activity is estimated to take six days and this is noted as its duration. The full list of activities, estimated durations, and sequencing are as follows:

Activity	Estimated Duration	Must be preceded by
A	4	–
B	3	A
C	8	B
D	6	B
E	5	C
F	1	D
G	11	E,F
H	6	F
I	7	G,H
J	6	I
K	4	J
L	8	I

Adding up the durations will give a total project length of 69 days, but this is not hugely significant because some activities can take place simultaneously, as you are about to find out.

To draw up a network diagram you use circles and lines.

Circles

These are known as nodes and signify the end of one activity and the beginning of another. Nodes are numbered for ease of reference. In order that the network can be analysed, each circle is sectioned in the following way:

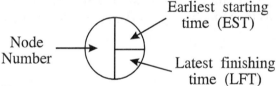

In the 'earliest starting time' section is written the earliest day on which the activity can begin. The 'latest finishing time' section will contain the latest day on which the previous activity can finish without extending the duration of the whole project.

Lines

Lines represent the activities themselves; they have a node at each end. They are annotated with a letter (which identifies the activity) and a number (which gives the expected duration of the activity).

Network analysis involves working through the information in the example in three stages;

Stage 1   Construct a diagram showing the sequence and logical dependency of each activity in the project. Number the nodes for ease of reference and work out the earliest time each activity can begin.

Stage 2   Calculate the duration of the project and identify those activities which are critical if the project is to be completed on time.

Stage 3   Analyse the network diagram to identify those activities on which slack exists and which could be managed in a more efficient and beneficial way.

Stage 1

Activity A is the start of the project and is, therefore, not preceded by any other activities. The first activity in a network diagram always starts on Day 0. Activity A lasts for four days. Note how the node at the end of the activity is not added: this is not done until you know which activity is next.

Activity B follows on from Activity A and has a duration of three days. A node is added and labelled as Node 2. As the preceding activity took four days, the earliest time Activity B can begin is Day 4, so this is noted in the appropriate section of the node. The latest starting time cannot be determined until the whole diagram is complete, so we will return to this later.

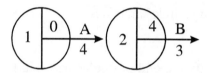

Activities C and D follow B, with durations of eight and six days respectively. The earliest time these activities can begin is Day 7, as they follow Activity A (4 days) and Activity B (3 days), so this is noted in Node 3.

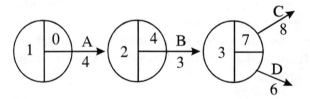

Activity E (duration 5 days) follows Activity C.

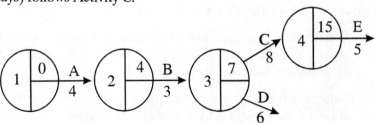

Activity F follows Activity D.

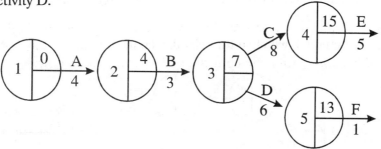

Activity G follows Activity E and F. This means both E and F must be complete before G can begin. The earliest time (EST) Activity G can start is Day 20.

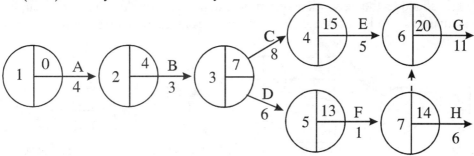

Activity H must also be preceded by Activity F. But if you look back to the previous diagram, this will clearly give rise to a problem. One thought might be to have H also emerging from Node 6. If you look closely, though, this would indicate that Activity H is dependent, not just on Activity F, also on Activity E; this is not so. The solution to this dilemma is to introduce a *dummy activity*. A dummy activity has a duration of 0 days and is used purely to show logical dependencies. A dotted line is used for a dummy.

The use of the arrow on the dotted line is vital in signifying the dependency of activities. Activity G is dependent on both E and F; Activity H is dependent only on F.

Activity I must be preceded by G and H, and the earliest time Activity I can start is on Day 31. (Check this now if you like!)

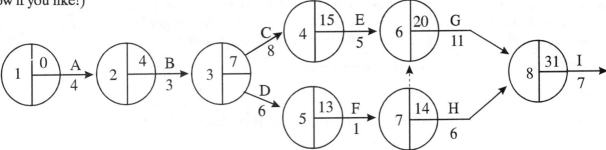

Before this point, Activities A, B, C, E, D and F must have been completed. You can see that Activities D and F have considerable slack. Activities D and F can start on Day 7, as they take only seven days in total; they don't need to be finished until Day 20; the other path (C-E) determines that fact.

Activities D and F can, and will, be performed in parallel with Activities C and E. It is just that they take less time.

Activity I is followed by Activity J, which in turn is followed by Activity K.

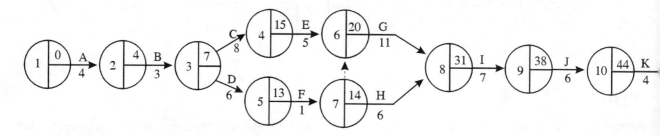

Finally, Activity L is added to the network diagram. It is dependent on Activity I, so it can be performed in parallel with Activities J and K. It takes eight days and ends at the final node with Activity K.

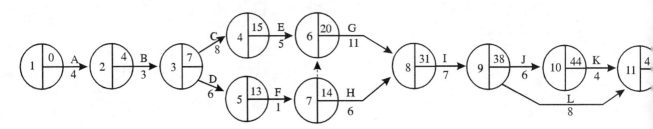

The 48 days in Node 11 represents the duration of the project if all goes to plan. From the start of Activity A, to the completion of Activity K, will take 48 days. This compares very favourably with the 69 days which it would take if activities were done one at a time in sequence.

Already network analysis has provided useful information: you can already inform the customer or client of the time from the start to the end of the project. You may have competitors for the project and they may be quoting a different delivery or completion date to you. Whatever you quote, you must feel confident that you can abide by the time-scale since the reputation of your business may depend on this factor. You must control the process so that it does not overrun. Network analysis can assist in your need to establish which activities are critical to the project's punctual completion. More specifically, it can tell you which activities, if held up, will delay or extend the completion of the project.

Stage 2 of the analysis will provide that information.

Stage 2

In constructing the network, you work from left to right. In completing the latest finishing times (LFTs), you work from right to left.

Clearly, the latest time Activities K and L must finish is on Day 48, as this is the last day of the project. So 48 is entered in Node 11.

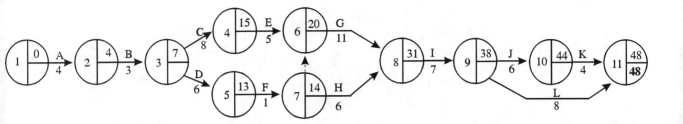

The LFT for Activity J must be day 44 because, unless it finishes by this day, the project will overrun (since Activity K needs four days).

In the same way, Activity I must be completed by Day 38 if the project is to remain on schedule.

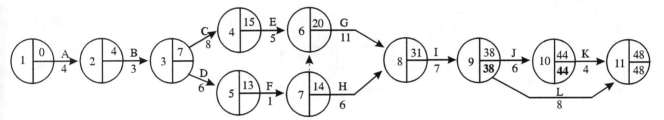

Activities G and H both feed into Node 8 – and the LFT for either of them is Day 31. If it is any later than Day 31, then the total of 17 days for Activities I, J, and K will cause the project to be delayed.

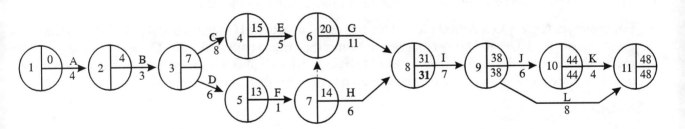

Turning our attention to Node 7 gives rise to an interesting and important dilemma. It would be tempting to say that the LFT for Activity F should be Day 25 - after all, Activity H can be completed in six days, meaning the deadline of Day 31 at Node 8 can be met. This solution to the dilemma would, however tempting, be wrong, because Activity G also relies on the completion of Activity F before it can begin. Thus, Activity F must finish by Day 20 at the latest, in order that the project stays on time. If it were to finish any later than this, then Activity G (11 days), Activity I (7 days), Activity J (6 Days) and Activity K (6 days), would mean an overall finish date later than the 44th day.

Following this line of reasoning, the LFT of Activity E (at Node 6) must be Day 20.

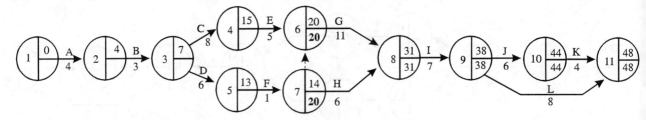

Following this process back through to Node 1, produces the completed network diagram you see below.

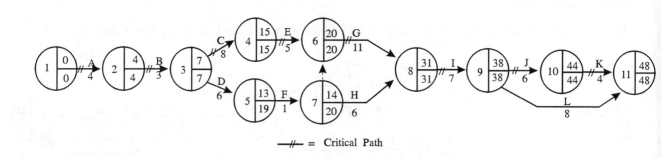

—//— = Critical Path

The Critical Path

The critical path can be identified as consisting of those activities whose EST + Duration = LFT.

For example, Activity G is critical (20 + 11 = 31) whereas activity H in non-critical (14 + 16 = 31). Check these out on the diagram. The last diagram indicates the critical path as A – B – C – E – G – I –J – K. This means that a delay of even one day on any of these activities will cause the project to be delayed by one day. In a network diagram, there may be sometimes be more than one critical path.

Stage 3

This stage involves working out the *floats* or slack time on each of the non-critical activities. This allows resources to be deployed elsewhere, or managed more efficiently. To achieve this objective, there are two main floats which need to be calculated: *total* float and *free* float.

Total Float

The best way to illustrate the calculation of floats is to use an activity from the example which has been used so far. Let's take Activity F.

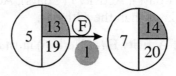

The total float for Activity F is found by deducting EST and duration from the LFT of the activity. The shaded sections show the numbers used.

LFT of Activity F – Duration of activity F – EST of activity F = Total float for Activity F

20 – 1 – 13 = 6

Caution must be used when interpreting total float. It refers not to the slack on Activity F alone, but in all activities up to and including Activity F (ABDF). As Activities A and B are on the critical path, this does tell us that between Activities D and F there is some slack time, a float of six days.

Free Float

This is used to calculate the float on one activity alone. It is found by deducting the EST at the beginning of the activity and the duration of the activity from the EST of the next activity. Let's take Activity F as an example.

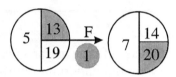

EST of next Activity – Duration – EST of Activity F = Free float for activity F

14 – 1 – 13 = 0

So, F on its own has no free float. Why is this?

If the previous activity (Activity D) had overrun by six days, this would effectively remove any slack from the path. Examining the previous activity should shed some light on it.

Check the total float of Activity D and you'll find it to be six days.

LFT – Duration – EST

19 – 6 – 7 = 6 days

Obviously, it's only ever worth working out floats on non-critical activities. Critical activities don't have floats! You might like to try working out the floats on the non-critical activities before checking your answers in the table overleaf.

Activity	Total Float	Free Float
A	0	0
B	0	0
C	0	0
D	6	0
E	0	0
F	6	0
G	0	0
H	11	11
I	0	0
J	0	0
K	0	0
L	2	2

Networks as a control tool

Earlier you became familiar with some of the uses of network analysis. With your knowledge of how to produce a network diagram, it's worth reviewing the important points. A network is merely a model: a model of a real-life situation. That model can be manipulated to simulate different circumstances. The effect which various occurrences would have on the duration and cost of the project can be demonstrated in advance by means of the model. Network analysis is an under-used tool in industry. Although only a model, it can:

- minimise working capital requirement by ordering and receiving delivery of materials 'just in time'

- help utilise labour to its fullest potential, indicating where float exists or where pressure points are likely to occur

- clarify the thinking process: even the very act of constructing the network does this

- provide a visual aid which can help to explain the importance of the roles of those involved in the project in helping the project to meet its targets

- assist in management 'by exception' – management time and expertise are concentrated on the real problems, not on time-consuming trivia

- identify, prepare and plan for critical activities and events in advance in order to make sure that the whole project runs smoothly.

Networks are highly suited to computer analysis. The time-hungry job of completing the diagram and calculating floats etc. can all be done for you. However, this gives rise to one cautionary note. As with all processes in network analysis, the quality of the output depends on the accuracy and the quality of the input. If inaccurate estimates of the durations of activities is input into the computer, or into the human calculation, then the product - the analysis - will be of little use. As in other walks of life, the golden equation applies: *GARBAGE IN = GARBAGE OUT.*

Blending

Blending is a management tool designed to allocate the resources of a business in the most cost-effective and profitable way.

One of the main applications of blending is in manufacturing industry, where allocating time on different machines to different products is of great importance. The method which you are about to learn is a much simpler version of that which would be used in industry, but it is a good way of grasping the principle of blending and is certainly sufficient for your current level of study. The more mathematically complex method is known as 'simplex' and nowadays tends to be the preserve of the computer.

Blending is used to solve problems where the allocation of resources is juggled between two products; when more than two products is involved, then 'simplex' is required.

Example

A business makes fishing rods of two main types: fly rods (FR) and spinning rods (SR). The manufacture of the rods involves many processes, but three of the processes are considered critical. These three processes are:

Blanking (B)
Forming (F)
Whipping (W).

Each process is performed by an expensive machine with only limited hours available.

The business knows that it makes a contribution of £12 per fly rod and £8 per spinning rod. It also knows that each type of rod requires the following amount of time, expressed in minutes, on each process:

	Fly rod (FR)	Spinning Rod (SR)	Weekly time available
Blanking (B)	120	40	2,400
Forming (F)	60	40	1,800
Whipping (W)	40	50	2,000

The purpose of the blending technique is to show what combination of fly rods and spinning rods should be made, bearing in mind the constraints of time per machine, in order to achieve the maximum contribution.

This is best illustrated by means of a graph but, first, some calculations need to be done.

Blanking constraint

The constraint is that in one week no more than 2,400 minutes of time is available on the blanking machine.

If only fly rods are made, then a simple piece of arithmetic tells you that twenty can be made:

$$\frac{2,400}{120} \quad = \quad 20 \text{ fly rods}$$

And if only spinning rods are made:

$$\frac{2,400}{40} \quad = \quad 60 \text{ spinning rods}$$

So, at the extreme, either twenty fly rods or sixty spinning rods can be made. But, as you probably realise, there are numerous combinations in between. These possible combinations can be quickly spotted if a line that represents the equation is drawn and labelled on a graph.

The line can be simply drawn between the two extremes of 20 fly rods and 60 spinning rods but, if you're feeling mathematical, it can be drawn to represent the equation:

20 FR + 60 SR ≤ 2,400

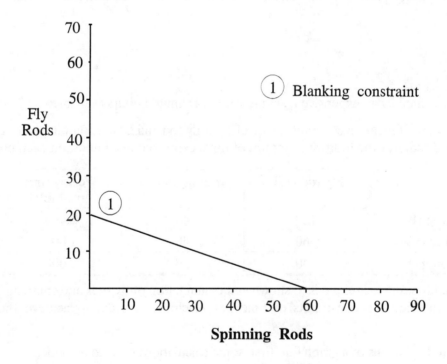

The line itself, and every point below the line, represents a combination of fly and spinning rods which it is possible to produce, given the blanking constraint. This is known as the *feasible area*.

For example, according to our graph, ten fly rods and twenty spinning rods can be blanked. Just to be sure, check the sums:

10 FR + 20 SR ≤ 2,400

10 x 120 + 20 x 40 = 2,000

If contribution is to be maximised, then the best or optimum solution will always be somewhere on the line, rather than somewhere below it.

Forming constraint

The available forming time is 1,800 minutes per week. This produces the equation;

60 FR + 40 SR ≤ 1,800

Again, at either extreme, 30 fly rods or 45 spinning rods could be made. This is now plotted on the graph as line 2 .

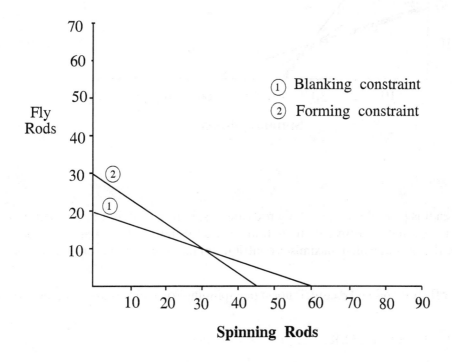

Whipping constraint

The equation for whipping is:

40 FR + 50 SR ≤ 2,000

which produces line 3 on the graph.

The feasible area on the graph contains all combinations of fly and spinning rods which it is possible to make, taking into account the constraints. The feasible area is, therefore, that area that lies below the perimeter of lines 1, 2 and 3 shown by the shaded line.

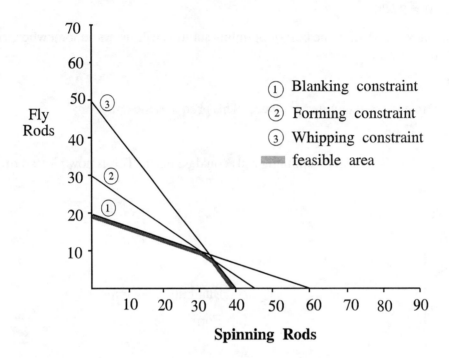

Within the feasible area it is possible to make 0 fly rods and 0 spinning rods, but in a business situation – where each rod sold is making a positive contribution to the business – that would not be a sensible approach. The level of the output which maximises contribution has to be a point on the perimeter of the line.

A £12 contribution per fly rod and an £8 contribution per spinning rod can be expressed by the following equation:

Contribution (C) = £12 FR + £8 SR

Because the relationship between the contributions of fly rods and spinning rods is linear, it is possible to plot this line on the graph.

The line is found by taking an assumed contribution; say £96. If no fly rods are made, 12 spinning rods need to be made to achieve a £96 contribution:

£96 = (£12 × 0) + (£8 × 12).

Or, reversing the situation:

£96 = (£12 × 8) + (£8 × 0)

Plotting this on the graph gives the contribution line (4).

Moving the contribution line parallel with the original line, until it intersects the uppermost part of the perimeter of the feasible area, will identify the optimum (best) solution.

As the line is parallel with constraint 2, the intersection comes at the points marked on the diagram.

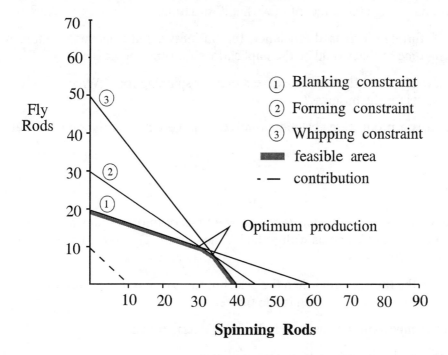

The intersection is at 10 fly rods and 30 spinning rods. Substituting these values in the contribution equation gives:

C = £12 FR + £8 SR

C = (£12 × 10) + (£8 × 30)

C = £360

The best contribution which can be achieved is £360. Any level of production between the two points marked will produce the same contribution, as the contribution line intersects it at every point between the two points marked.

Other uses of the model

As well as vital information about the production needed to ensure maximum contribution, following the model also provides information about the utilisation of resources. For example, if more minutes could be squeezed from the forming machinery, it would have the effect of moving line 2 upwards, parallel to its current position. All three lines would intersect at one point, indicating an efficient use of resources. All processes are being used to their full potential. No new line is needed from blanking or whipping machinery – extra minutes on forming will ensure a higher level of contribution.

The model can be used to gauge the effect of the 'what if' situation:

- What if, through increased efficiency, the business could achieve 200 more minutes blanking time? What would be the implications for other processes?

- What if demand for fly rods far exceeds that for spinning rods? What are the resource implications for the business?

The blending method is a production technique and, to a large extent, it ignores market demand for products.

Forecasting

The soundest business decisions are usually taken on the basis of information which has been collected and provided by people and departments within the business itself. The more accurate the information, the better the decision is likely to be.

Decisions take effect in the future, rather than the past, but the past is a very useful source of information and indicator of what possibly might happen in the future.

Some examples of how important the past is in influencing decision-making:

- every month the inflation rate, the unemployment rate and the balance of trade figures are announced. The government, business, and 'the City' await the news with interest, expectation and sometimes even trepidation. When announced, the figures are immediately compared with past figures in order to identify a trend.

- a factory that produces cars is concerned about its level of absenteeism. Figures fluctuate from month to month, but it is the overall trend which interests management. If the trend is rising, will it continue to rise? What can be done to halt the rise? If the trend is one of a declining rate of absenteeism, how can it be maintained and even accelerated?

- a tourist board is looking at the occupancy rates for hotel rooms in its area. Figures vary widely according to season; this is to be expected. But what is the overall trend? Are occupancy rates, in general, increasing or decreasing? This information is vital if decisions are to be made and action is to be taken.

Part 4 looks at the role of the marketing function in providing information about consumers and their likely buying patterns in the future. To assist with putting together this picture of the future, it is also possible to collect data from the past (historic data), process it, and analyse it to see if any pattern emerges.

Time Series Data

Most business data will come in the form of a *time-series*. This is simply a set of numbers arranged in chronological (time) order.

The following raw (or unprocessed) data represents the sales from fourteen consecutive quarters of a company's operation.

Year/Quarter	Sales (£000s)	Quarters	Sales (£000s)
1/1	48	2/4	61
1/2	51	3/1	65
1/3	53	3/2	68
1/4	60	3/3	75
2/1	55	3/4	70
2/2	58	4/1	73
2/3	61	4/2	69

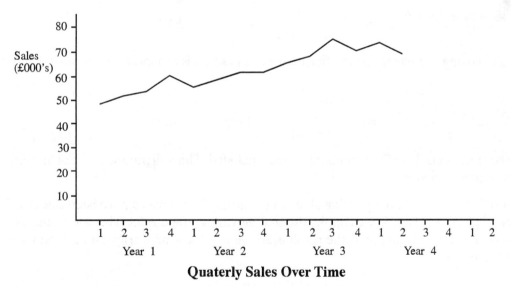

Quaterly Sales Over Time

By presenting the raw data in graphical form, it is possible to establish that:

- the overall pattern of sales seems to be rising
- there are very noticeable peaks and troughs in sales: e.g. Quarter 4 is always well above Quarter 1.

Although even this raw data can assist with planning, the more accurately sales can be predicted for the future, the more reliable decision-making becomes. To assist with this, the data can be broken into components.

The components of a time series

The three components of a time series are

1. Trend

2. Seasonal or Cyclical Variation

3. Random Variation.

1. Trend

The conclusions which can be drawn from the raw data are not very precise. To predict future demand accurately requires a line that reveals the underlying trend. That line could then be extended so that forecasts of future demand could be made.

How can we smooth the line on the graph to help us to do this? The answer lies in the technique of moving *averages.*

In our example the data can be split nicely into groups of four (i.e. periods 1, 2, 3, 4). An average of the sales of the first four periods can be found.

$$\frac{48 + 51 + 53 + 60}{4} \quad = \quad \frac{212}{4} \quad = \quad 53$$

The idea of the moving average is that the first quarter's sales (48) is dropped, and the next in the sequence is used (55).

$$\frac{51 + 53 + 60 + 55}{4} \quad = \quad \frac{219}{4} \quad = \quad 54.75$$

This process continues until the final number has been included. This will produce a set of 'moving average' figures ready to plot on a graph.

However, there is a problem in the plotting of moving average figures which have been calculated from an even number of pieces of data. For example, the first moving average is 53. This was found by using the data for periods 1/1, 1/2, 1/3 and 1/4. If the result is an average then, on a graph, it must be plotted at the mid-point of the periods.

| 1/1 | 1/2 | ↑ | 1/3 | 1/4 |

This mid-point is half way between periods 2 and 3. On a graph, this is not accurate and may lead to difficulties when making predictions. All subsequent moving averages in the series would then need to be plotted between actual time periods. The problem will always occur when even numbers of pieces of data are used in a moving average. To overcome this problem, an additional technique called *centring* is used.

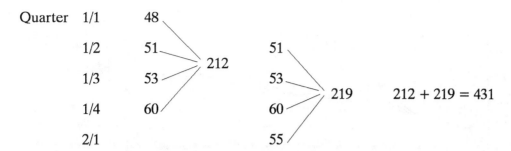

In this technique, two four-period moving totals are added together to give an eight- period moving total.

Quarters 1/1 and 2/1 have been used once
Quarters 1/2 and 1/4 have been used twice

and that means Quarter 1/3 is the mid-point.

If the eight-period moving total is then divided by 8, it will give a moving average which can be accurately plotted against Quarter 1/3. Using the technique of centring and eight-period moving averages, produces the table shown below.

Year/Quarter (a)	Sales (£000s) (b)	4period moving total (c)	8period moving total (d)	Trend (e) (d) ÷ 8
1/1	48			
1/2	51			
		212		
1/3	53		431	53.875
		219		
1/4	60		445	56.625
		226		
2/1	55		460	57.5
		234		
2/2	58		477	59.625
		243		
2/3	61		492	61.5
		249		
2/4	69		505	63.125
		256		
3/1	61		519	64.875
		263		
3/2	65		532	66.5
		269		
3/3	68		547	68.375
		278		
3/4	75		564	70.5
		286		
4/1	70			
4/2	73			

An 8Period Moving Average

Plotting these trend figures on the original graph will result in the following graph.

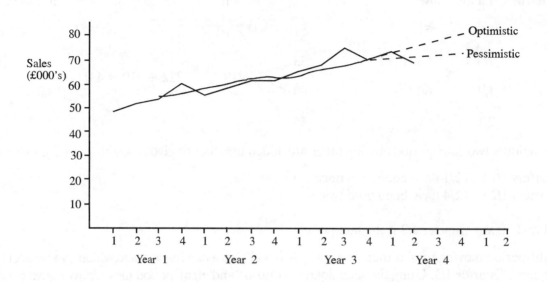

Trend using 8-Period Moving Average

Notice how it now becomes possible to extend the trend line, using a dotted line to show what future demand might be.

Sometimes it may be necessary to make optimistic, or pessimistic, predictions, depending on prevailing market or economic conditions. For example, it may be known that a competitor is having difficulty supplying its customers. This could lead to a higher demand for the product and, therefore, you would be more optimistic when you draw in the trend line and predict sales.

2a. Seasonal Variation

Assume that it is necessary to forecast the likely demand in Quarter 4/4. In the previous figure, the trend line indicates sales of approximately £78,500. Clearly, this is not going to be an accurate forecast, as smoothing the line has ironed out the seasonal variation. Therefore, the seasonal factor must be found and added back to the forecast in order to make it realistic.

Seasonal variation = Actual sales – Trend.

The following table showing the seasonal variations calculated by subtracting column (e) from column (b).

Year/Quarter (a)	Sales (£000s) (b)	4-Period moving total (c)	8-period moving total (d)	Trend (e) (d) ÷ 8	Seasonal Variation (b) – (e)
1/1	48				
1/2	51				
		212			
1/3	53		431	53.875	–0.875
		219			
1/4	60		445	56.625	3.375
		226			
2/1	55		460	57.5	–2.5
		234			
2/2	58		477	59.625	–1.625
		243			
2/3	61		492	61.5	–0.5
		249			
2/4	69		505	63.125	5.875
		256			
3/1	61		519	64.875	–3.875
		263			
3/2	65		532	66.5	–1.5
		269			
3/3	68		547	68.375	–0.375
		278			
3/4	75		564	70.5	4.5
		286			
4/1	70				
4/2	73				

Table Showing Seasonal Variations

The seasonal variations for every fourth quarter are 3.375, 5.875, and 4.5. An average of the three variations is found and that average is, in this instance, added back to the trend figure predicted from the graph.

$$\text{Average seasonal variation for Quarter 4} = \frac{3.375 + 5.875 + 4.5}{3} = 4.58 \text{ or } £4,580$$

Therefore, the forecast sales for Year 4 Quarter 4 = £78,500 + £4,580 = £83,080

In contrast:

$$\text{Average seasonal variation for Quarter 1} = \frac{-2.5 + -3.875}{2} = -3.187 \text{ or } -£3,187$$

The average seasonal variation for Quarter 1 uses only two numbers: these are all that are available from the table. Notice the negative sign, which indicates the average seasonal variation, must be subtracted from any trend figure for Quarter 1 taken from the graph.

2b. Cyclical Variation

Sometimes the pattern of data is cyclical rather than seasonal. This means it does not peak and trough in line with the seasons, but more with trade cycles that occur over several years. One of the most widely quoted examples is the cycle of economic activity which provides booms and recessions within a national economy. The same process as for seasonal variation is applied, although the time-scale is different.

3. Random Variation

A random variation is something which occurs as a result of an unexpected event. It has no regular pattern and is, to a large extent, unpredictable. Examples of such occurrences are strikes in suppliers' factories and freak weather conditions. These might cause peaks and troughs on the graphs which are totally out of character with the pattern of the rest of the data. Fortunately, the moving average process minimises the effect of these random variations and allows, by smoothing, a clear trend to be discerned.

Conclusion

Although it is advisable to use forecasting techniques when attempting to predict future demand, it is not the full story. Computers can produce graphs and forecasts to lend objectivity to decision-making but, with their own sensitivity and foresight, business managers provide the human factor which is so important throughout the decision-making process.

Index Numbers

When examining a set of numbers that is large, or which is taken in isolation, it is often difficult, or even impossible, to make comparisons. This difficulty can be made worse when sets of numbers are measured in different units. In many cases, it is not the numbers themselves that are of interest or even importance, but more the relationships that they reveal and the relative increases or decreases which they expose. Increases from one year to the next are difficult to interpret from raw data, but expressing the data in index form can make comparison much easier.

Simple binary index numbers

The provision of school meals has recently been opened up to competitive tendering. In the past, this service was provided exclusively by the School Meals Service of the respective local authorities. Now private catering companies are able to bid (or 'tender') for contracts, in competition with the local authority.

In the example you are about to examine, the local authority has recently secured the contract for a five year period. The authority re-named its schools' catering department 'Commercial Catering Services' (CCS) and, as part of its business plan, has looked at the numbers of school meals sold in its schools over the previous nine years.

	1982	1983	1984	1985	1986	1987	1988	1989	1990	1991
(000s)	3,800	3,900	3,950	4,050	4,100	4,250	4,200	4,180	4,150	4,070

Looking at these raw figures you can see a clear and gradual rise in the numbers of children taking school meals up until 1987, when the trend is reversed and the number starts to decline. Even though this trend can be discerned, it would be much more evident and useful if those figures were presented in index form.

To convert them to index numbers requires the selection of a base year. The base year is the starting point for the index and it is always assigned a value of 100; in this example, the base year is 1982.

To calculate the index number for 1983:

$$\frac{\text{Number of school meals in 1983}}{\text{Number of school meals in 1982}} \times 100 = \text{Index for 1983}$$

$$\frac{3900}{3800} \times 100 = 102.6$$

The index for 1984 is:

$$\frac{\text{Number of school meals in 1984 (3950)}}{\text{Number of school meals in 1982 (3800)}} \times 100 = 103.9$$

Continuing this process gives the full index:

1982	1983	1984	1985	1986	1987	1988	1989	1990	1991
100	102.6	103.9	106.6	107.9	111.8	110.5	110	109.2	107.1

By looking at this set of figures you can immediately see that in 1985 there were 6.6% more meals sold than there were in 1982 and yet, by 1991, the number of school meals sold was only 7.1% higher than it was in 1982.

The important point to bear in mind here is that all the index numbers are related to the base year. A common mistake students make is to misuse the method when they are comparing two years other than the *base* year. If asked to find out the increase between the two years, 1984 and 1985, which, you remember, are not base years:

Wrong	$106.6 - 103.9 =$	2.7%
Correct	$\dfrac{106.6 - 103.9}{103.9} =$	2.6%

The correct answer is that the number of school meals sold has increased by 2.6% between 1984 and 1985.

Comparing quantities

An index, such as the one you've just looked at, is useful on its own, but becomes even more useful when it is used in comparison with another index. For example, a sensible question is to ask, 'Have school meals really become more popular over the last nine years?' Clearly, from one set of figures they look as though they have: 7.1% more meals were sold in 1991 than were sold in 1982.

But you may well ask, 'Are there more students in the school than there were in 1982?' Look at the following index of the school populations over the same nine years.

1982	1983	1984	1985	1986	1987	1988	1989	1990	1991
100	100.4	100.9	102.1	104.4	107	110.3	111.8	112.1	112.3

Index of school populations

The school population in 1991 was 12.3% higher than it was in 1982 and, yet, the number of children taking school meals had only increased by 7.1%. So, what looked like an encouraging increase, in fact, turns out to be, proportionately, a 'real' decrease.

Plotting the two indexes on a graph will show this clearly.

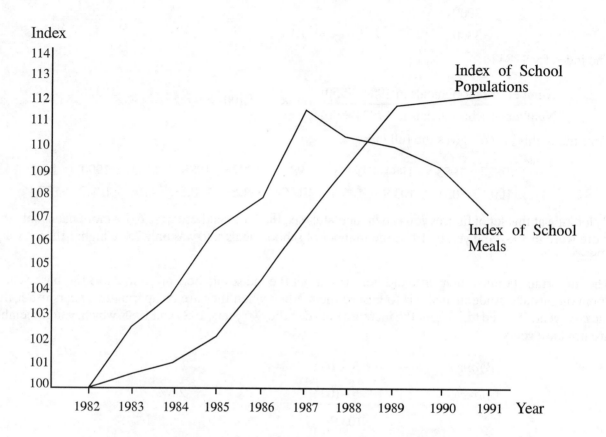

**Graph showing index for numbers of school
meals plotted against index of school populations**

One of the great uses of index numbers is in comparing numbers which are measured in different units.

For example, you can plot on the same graph, in index form, such data as:

- the average price of school meals over the last ten years
- the retail price index showing the rate of inflation.

These two sets of data will show whether school meals have become relatively more expensive and, if so, whether this might have influenced the number of meals sold.

Sometimes, indexes which need to be compared have different base years when, to make a true and reliable comparison, both ought to have the same base year. Fortunately, the conversion process is relatively straight-forward. We illustrate the problem below.

Year	1985	1986	1987	1988	1989	1990	1991
Index 1	100	116	121	125	126	128	131
Index 2	93	98	100	104	106	109	111

To convert Index 1, with a base year of 100 (to match Index 2), each value in Index 1 must be multiplied by a factor of 100/121. This produces the following result:

Year	1985	1986	1987	1988	1989	1990	1991
Index 1	82.6	95.9	100	103.3	104.1	105.8	108.3
Index 2	93	98	100	104	106	109	111

Adjusting the base year makes the indices look much closer to each other than they did at first sight.

Weighted index numbers

In a business which has two direct costs, labour and materials, the indices for the past five years are as follows:

Year	1987	1988	1989	1990	1991
Material	100	104	109	114	117
Labour	100	106	113	117	125

It is evident from the indices that materials costs are 17% higher in 1991 than they were in 1987 and that labour costs are 25% higher in 1991 than they were in 1987. Assuming that 50% of the direct costs are labour costs and 50% are materials costs, then the average increase will be:

$$\frac{117 + 125}{2} = 121 \quad \text{or} \quad 21\%$$

But, on looking at the make up of the company's products, you find that only 20% of the direct cost of the product is labour, as against the 80% that is materials cost. This means that to be accurate, any average must be weighted according to each item's importance in the overall cost of the product.

Weighted index for 1991 = 117 × 80% = 93.6

125 × 20% = 25.0 / 118.6

So the increase, taking into account the weights of the items, is actually 18.6%.
Overall, the direct costs have increased by 18.6%, rather than the 21% which was originally calculated.

The full weighted index is calculated as follows:

YEAR	1987	1988	1989	1990	1991
Materials	100	$(104 \times .8) = 83.2$	$(109 \times .8) = 87.2$	$(114 \times .8) = 91.2$	$(117 \times .8) = 93.6$
Labour	100	$(106 \times .2) = 21.2$	$(113 \times .2) = 22.6$	$(117 \times .2)= 23.4$	$(125 \times .2) = 25.0$
Weighted Index	100	104.4	109.8	114.6	118.6

Different approaches to weighting

In the previous example you saw how the weightings attached to particular components of an index can influence the overall picture: the apparent average increase in costs of 21% was, in fact, 18.6% when the respective weightings were considered. However, a dilemma exists when selecting the weightings to be used in such an index. In your example, it is unlikely that the balance of direct costs between labour and materials has remained unaltered over the five years from 1987 to 1991. It may well be that in 1987 the 80 :20 ratio of material to labour costs was accurate, but by 1991 this ratio may have changed to 90 :10, due to further automation of a production process which came to require proportionately less labour. The dilemma which exists is whether the weighting of 80 :20 that prevailed in the the base year of 1987 should be used in calculating the full index or whether the current year's weighting of 90 : 10 should be used; i.e. the 1991 weighting.

The base year (Laspeyre) method

Named after its originator, this method involves using base year weightings throughout the index. It is the method used to calculate the direct costs in the index above. Its main advantage is that weightings do not have to be re-calculated each year.

The current year (Paasche) method

This involves re-calculating the index each year based on the most recent year (current year) weights. The affect of applying this approach to the direct costs in the example would be:

YEAR	1987	1988	1989	1990	1991
Materials	100	$(104 \times .9) = 93.6$	$(109 \times .9) = 98.1$	$(114 \times .9) =102.6$	$(117 \times .9)=105.3$
Labour	100	$(106 \times .1) = 10.6$	$(113 \times .1) = 11.3$	$(117 \times .1)= 11.7$	$(125 \times .1) = 12.5$
Weighted Index	100	104.2	109.4	114.3	117.8

Even a relatively small change in weightings has affected the index. The Paasche index is particularly applicable when the relative weightings of elements in the index change frequently. It provides a more relevant set of data in this circumstance. The increased relevance must be offset against the possible expense of collecting information from which to update the weightings.

As well as indices which a business will compile from its own data, there are numerous indices updated and published annually, monthly and sometimes even daily. Perhaps the best known of these is the RPI (the Retail Price Index).This is published monthly and is primarily used as a measure of inflation. It consists of a 'basket' of goods and services, each with its own weighting. The price of the basket is updated each month and from that is calculated the RPI. The RPI is illustrated in more detail in Part Two.

Normal Distribution

Normal distribution is a statistical model which has many applications in business situations. It is particularly useful in quality-control decision-making as well as in other fields of business, such as the interpretation of the data from market surveys. It is the quality-control aspect which you will explore later, but for now let us concentrate on establishing a basic understanding of normal distribution.

Consider a girl, two years old, visiting her doctor's surgery for a routine check on her growth. The doctor will have a very clear idea what height he expects the infant to be: the doctor will know this from previous experience of thousands of children of the same age and from records collected nationally and at regular intervals about the normal height of children at various ages.

From your existing knowledge of mathematics, you will appreciate that there will be an average (or mean) height for girls of two years: this average will have been found by adding together the heights of thousands of children of this age and dividing the total by the number of children used in the calculation. Let us suppose that the average height of a two year old girl is 85 cms. Logic tells us that many girls of two years who are measured will be around this height; in fact, some will be exactly 85 cms. Once again, logic tells us that the further away from the mean we move, the fewer children there are who will measure that height. This *distribution* can be shown by means of a diagram.

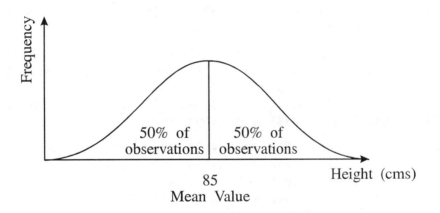

The Normal Distribution Curve

Notice the bell shape of the curve indicating that a height of 85 cms is the mean height and that most girls of two years measure close to this height. It also indicates that 50% of all girls of this age will be taller than 85 cms and 50% will be shorter.

When doctors check the height of a two year old girl, they will have a knowledge of this distribution: they will be aware of what range of height is usual and what range of height gives cause for concern, perhaps needing further investigation. This awareness will be governed by how far a particular measurement *deviates* from the mean.

z	.00	.01	.02	.03	.04	.05	.06	.07	.08	.09
0.0	.0000	.0040	.0080	.0120	.0160	.0199	.0239	.0279	.0319	.0359
0.1	.0398	.0438	.0478	.0517	.0557	.0596	.0636	.0675	.0714	.0753
0.2	.0793	.0832	.0871	.0910	.0948	.0987	.1026	.1064	.1103	.1141
0.3	.1179	.1217	.1255	.1293	.1331	.1368	.1406	.1443	.1480	.1517
0.4	.1554	.1591	.1628	.1664	.1700	.1736	.1772	.1808	.1844	.1879
0.5	.1915	.1950	.1985	.2019	.2054	.2088	.2123	.2157	.2190	.2224
0.6	.2257	.2291	.2324	.2357	.2389	.2422	.2454	.2486	.2517	.2549
0.7	.2580	.2611	.2642	.2673	.2704	.2734	.2764	.2794	.2823	.2852
0.8	.2881	.2910	.2939	.2967	.2995	.3023	.3051	.3078	.3106	.3133
0.9	.3159	.3186	.3212	.3238	.3264	.3289	.3315	.3340	.3365	.3389
1.0	.3413	.3438	.3461	.3485	.3508	.3531	.3554	.3577	.3599	.3621
1.1	.3643	.3665	.3686	.3708	.3729	.3749	.3770	.3790	.3810	.3830
1.2	.3849	.3869	.3888	.3907	.3925	.3944	.3962	.3980	.3997	.4015
1.3	.4032	.4049	.4066	.4082	.4099	.4115	.4131	.4147	.4162	.4177
1.4	.4192	.4207	.4222	.4236	.4251	.4265	.4279	.4292	.4306	.4319
1.5	.4332	.4345	.4357	.4370	.4382	.4394	.4406	.4418	.4429	.4441
1.6	.4452	.4463	.4474	.4484	.4495	.4505	.4515	.4525	.4535	.4545
1.7	.4554	.4564	.4573	.4582	.4591	.4599	.4608	.4616	.4625	4633
1.8	.4641	.4649	.4656	.4664	.4671	.4678	.4686	.4693	.4699	.4706
1.9	.4713	.4719	.4726	.4732	.4738	.4744	.4750	.4756	.4761	.4767
2.0	.4772	.4778	.4783	.4788	.4793	.4798	.4803	.4808	.4812	.4817
2.1	.4821	.4826	.4830	.4834	.4838	.4842	.4846	.4850	.4854	.4857
2.2	.4861	.4864	.4868	.4871	.4875	.4878	.4881	.4884	.4887	.4890
2.3	.4893	.4896	.4898	.4901	.4904	.4906	.4909	.4911	.4913	.4916
2.4	.4918	.4920	.4922	.4925	.4927	.4929	.4931	.4932	.4934	.4936
2.5	.4938	.4940	.4941	.4943	.4945	.4946	.4948	.4949	.4951	.4952
2.6	.4953	.4955	.4956	.4957	.4959	.4960	.4961	.4962	.4963	.4964
2.7	.4965	.4966	.4967	.4968	.4969	.4970	.4971	.4972	.4973	.4974
2.8	.4974	.4975	.4976	.4977	.4977	.4978	.4979	.4979	.4980	.4981
2.9	.4981	.4982	.4982	.4983	.4984	.4984	.4985	.4985	.4986	.4986
3.0	.4987	.4987	.4987	.4988	.4988	.4989	.4989	.4989	.4990	.4990

Table of Standard Normal Curve Areas

There are thousands of examples of measurements which are normally distributed. Some further examples can be seen in the next figure.

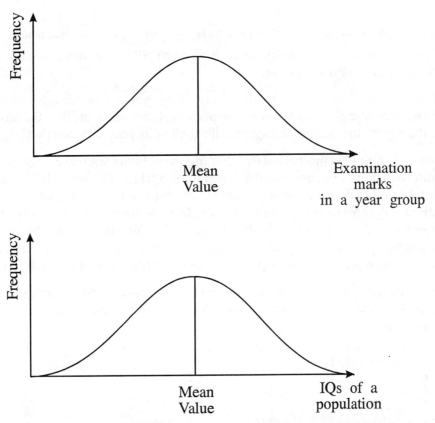

Examples of measurements which are Normally Distributed

The normal distribution curve shows all the possible outcomes and the frequency with which they will take place. Some normal distributions are very steep-sided, whilst others are shallow: all are bell-shaped, however, and as such are normal. The factor which determines the shallowness or steepness is the *spread* or *standard deviation*. If observations are very closely packed together, then the spread (or standard deviation) will be small; if the observations are thinly spread the standard deviation is relatively large. The common feature of any normal distribution, however the observations are spread, is that 50% of observations will lie on either side of the mean.

The standard deviation is a challenging concept for many students of business studies. Specialist statistics textbooks will show you its origins and explain the method for its calculation, but for business studies at this level you need only understand its potential uses.

To recap: standard deviation is a measure of spread. The more widespread the observations, the larger the standard deviation. A more compact, normal curve indicates a relatively smaller standard deviation.

Applying the normal distribution

Consider the filling of yogurt pots, an example where the normal distribution can be applied to an industrial situation:

Fruit Farms Yogurts Ltd. produce speciality yogurts in 150 gram pots. They have a machine which automatically fills the pots and seals them with a foil lid. Each pot is sold with a label that clearly states that the contents of each pot weighs 150 grams.

The filling machine is not precise – few machines are. If the pots are underfilled, then the business may run into trouble with the Weights and Measures inspectors; if they are overfilled, the business will be losing profit. Clearly, the nearer the business can get to filling all of its pots with exactly 150 grams, the better.

The manufacturer of the filling machine states that the mean filling volume is, indeed, 150 grams, with a standard deviation of 5 grams. For any industrial operation, a table, 'The normal distribution', can be used. This normal distribution table states what proportion of observations will fall within a certain number of standard deviations (or *range*) from the mean; for example, 68% of all yogurt pots will be filled with between 145 and 155 grams and 95% with between 140 and 160 grams. Whether or not this is an acceptable level of precision for the filling machine is a decision that management must make; if it is not the manufacturers may need to service the machine or, perhaps, a new, more accurate machine needs to be bought.

It is important to understand that the manufacturer may also have a filling machine which fills 170 gram pots: if the standard deviation of this machine is also 5 grams, it is represented by a curve of identical shape that is just shifted along the horizontal line.

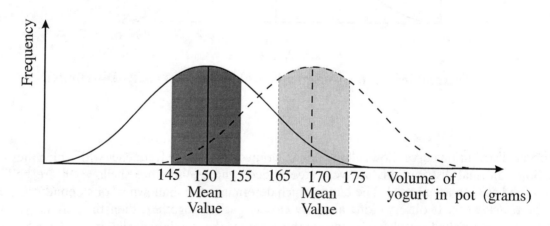

The Normal curves for the 150 and 170 gram machines with same Standard Deviation

On the other hand, as well as the mean being changed, the 170 gram machine may have a wider tolerance – its standard deviation may be 7.5 grams. In this case, as well as shifting, the curve will change shape as the spread of observations will be wider.

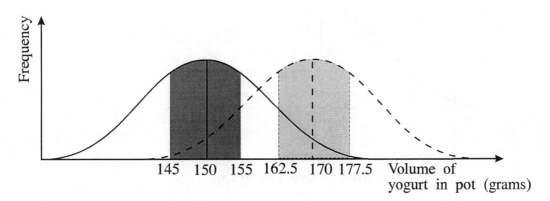

**The Normal curves for the 150 and 170 gram
machines with Different Standard Deviations**

Looking at the table will provide you with some useful information about the original yogurt filling machine, and about other normal distributions. Knowing that the machine has a mean of 150 grams, and a standard deviation of 5 grams, will allow us, through the tables, to discover what proportion of the filled pots you would expect to contain:

- over 155 grams of yogurt*

- over 160 grams of yogurt and;

- between 146 and 148 grams of yogurt

- etc.

*over 155 grams (greater than 1 standard deviation (sd) higher than the mean. The number of standard deviations from the mean is known as the *Z value*)

1. Look down the left-hand column of the tables until you find 1.0 (representing 1.0 sd)

2. Multiply the 0.3413 by 100. This tells you that the percentage of pots which are filled with between 150 and 155 grams of yogurt (34.13%).

3. You are aware from an earlier statement that, as the normal curve is symmetrical, 50% of all observations will be greater than the mean. As this is so, and 34.13% are between 150 and 155 grams, it follows that you would expect 15.87% of the pots to be filled with more than 155 grams of yogurt.

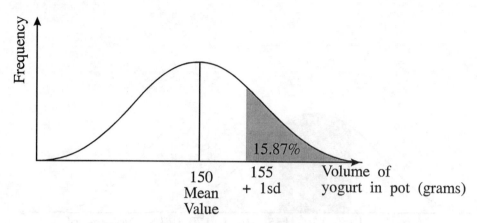

Frequencies above 155 grams

What proportion of the pots would you expect to contain over 160 grams (+2.0 sds from the mean)?

1. Find the Z value for 2.0 sds from the mean (.4772). This indicates that the probability of a yogurt pot being filled with between 150 and 160 grams is .4772 or 47.72%.

2. As the distribution is symmetrical, the likelihood of a pot containing more than 160 grams is 2.28%. Put another way, on average, about two pots in every hundred are likely to contain more than 160 grams.

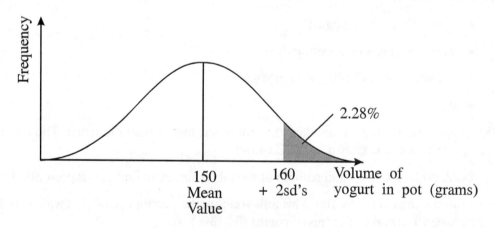

Frequencies above 160 grams

What proportion of the pots would you expect to contain between 146 and 148 grams?

1. On this occasion, it is necessary to find out how many sds 146 grams is from the mean (the Z value).

Method:

$$\text{Z value} \quad = \quad \frac{\text{Mean} - \text{value}}{\text{standard deviation}}$$

or using mathematical symbols

$$Z \quad = \quad \frac{x - m}{s}$$

$$\frac{150 - 146}{5} \quad = 0.8$$

2. Finding the Z value of 0.8 in the table gives 0.2881, indicating 28.81% of all pots contain between 146 and 150 grams of yogurt.

3. Find the Z value for 148 grams.

$$\frac{150 - 148}{5} \quad = 0.4$$

4. Using the Z value of 0.4 gives 0.1554, indicating that 15.54% of all pots filled contain between 148 and 150 grams of yogurt.

5. Subtract 15.54 from 28.81 to discover that you would expect 13.27% of all yogurts will be filled with between 146 and 148 grams of yogurt.

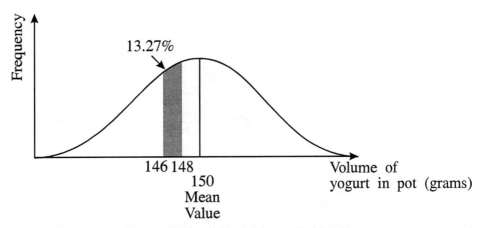

Frequency of yogurt pots filled with between 146 and 148 grams

As you are probably becoming aware, this is a very useful quality-control technique. Regular sampling of yogurts pots after they have been filled may indicate that the standard deviation has changed, indicating that the range or spread of the distribution has changed. In other words, although the mean remains 150 grams, more pots are being filled with amounts of yogurt which are further away from the mean. Such a change could have major repercussions for the business: the filling machine has become less precise.

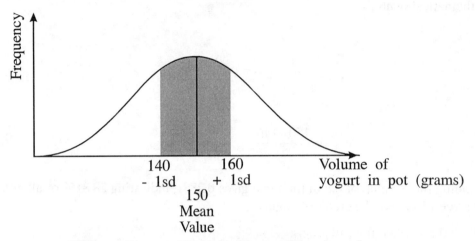

Filling of yogurt pots with a wider spead

Alternatively, the mean itself may have moved, thereby shifting the whole distribution. For example, the machine might be set up incorrectly and be filling pots with a mean of 160 grams: the standard deviation may still be 5 grams, but many more pots are being filled with incorrect amounts and the business is losing lots of money.

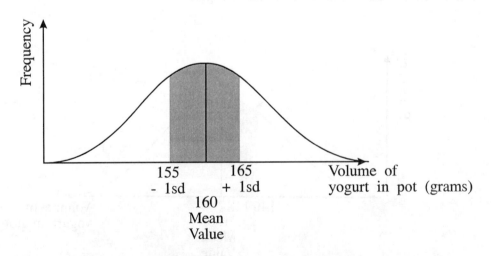

Filling of yogurt pots with a shifted mean

You have only scratched the surface of the potential applications of the normal distribution in business situations, but you may be able to appreciate how it is possible for a producer to:

- specify the 'tolerance' of components which are delivered by suppliers: if seats are being delivered to a car factory, then the holes for fixing the seats into the car must be in the correct position, otherwise the bolts will not fit. It is unrealistic to expect the boltholes to be in exactly the same position in each seat, as the position of holes is normally distributed. What it *is* possible to do, is to specify tolerance limits for the position of the bolthole, thereby controlling quality of supplies. The supplier will then decide whether they are able to meet these limits with their existing equipment. If they are not, then they must turn down the order, improve their existing equipment, or buy new equipment which can produce to the specification. Clearly, it is unwise for any producer to place impossible demands on a supplier by specifying tolerances which are unnecessarily tight, since this not only reduces the number of potential suppliers, but also is likely to push up the price of seats as the supplier buys unnecessarily sophisticated equipment in an attempt to meet the specification.

- specify the performance of equipment when they are buying. A machine for automatically bagging sand in a builders' merchants will have a specification in the same way as a scanner in a hospital. Measurement of their performances will each produce normal distributions and, yet, the deviation is bound to be much more significant in the case of the scanner.

A cautionary note

When taking samples to check quality, it is important not to read too much into an individual reading. If it is a long way from the original mean it may be a one-off from a correctly set and functioning machine. On the other hand, if on further sampling the occurrence of such measurements is frequent, this is more convincing evidence that the machine is malfunctioning.

Also, to ensure that the sample is more likely to represent what is really happening, a larger random sample should be taken: smaller samples are more likely to be unreliable.

1.   Identify and explain the main stages in the decision-making process.
2.   What is meant by *levels* of decision-making?
3.   Explain the purpose of *decision trees*.
4.   List the main advantages and disadvantages of decision trees.
5.   In decision trees, what are:
     - outcomes
     - expected values?
6.   List the four investment appraisal techniques.
7.   Explain what is meant by the *time value of money*.
8.   Explain the process of *discounting*.
9.   What is meant by Net Present Value?
10. Distinguish between NPV and IRR.
11. What is the purpose of a *base period* in calculating an index?
12. Show, by means of an example, how an *index number* is calculated.
13. How can indices with different base years be compared?
14. Explain a *weighted* index.
15. Explain, with examples, the different approaches to weighting.
16. What is the RPI and how is it calculated?
17. What is a *time-series*?
18. Explain, with examples:
     - trend
     - seasonal variation
     - random variation.
19. Why is the process of *centring* sometimes needed in the calculation of moving averages?
20. What are the objectives of network analysis?
21. Explain the process of *management by exception*.
22. Explain your understanding of *earliest starting time* (EST) and *latest finishing time* (LFT).
23. Why are dummy activities important in network analysis?
24. What is meant by the *critical path*?
25. Distinguish between *total float* and *free float*.
26. List the advantages to management of network analysis.
27. How can the technique of *blending* assist decision-making?
28. Sketch the normal distribution curve.
29. Give some examples of how normal distribution might be applied in industry.
30. Show, with an example, how the normal distribution table is used.

1.   (a)   What is the role of the Average Rate of Return when evaluating investment projects?

       (b)   When might the Pay Back Period be a better technique?

       (c)   What advantages and disadvantages would the Discounted Cash Flow technique have over other methods when evaluating investment decisions?

UCLES P2 1986

2.   (a)   Distinguish between autocratic and democratic styles of management.

       (b)   Why is 'span of control' relevant in any discussion of management style?

       (c)   Compare and contrast the advantages and disadvantages of the following methods of communication, and say to which management style they might be appropriate:

           (i)   letters;

           (ii)   notice boards;

           (iii)   telephones;

           (iv)   meetings.   *UCLES P2 1987*

3.   (a)   Compare and contrast what is meant by 'line' and 'staff' relationships within an organisation.

       (b)   Distinguish between cost centres and profit centres. How do these help organisations in planning and controlling their operations?   *UCLES P2 1988*

4.   "All businesses maximise profits." Discuss this statement.   *UCLES P2 1990*

5.   (a)   Differentiate between one-way and two-way communication and comment on their significance for different styles of management.

       (b)   Discuss the likely implications of the introduction of new technology to a company's communications framework.   *UCLES P2 1990*

6.   (a)   Why is change often so difficult to implement in organisations?

       (b)   How may these difficulties be minimised?   *AS UCLES 1991*

7.   (a)   What do you understand by the phrase 'hierarchy of objectives' as it relates to a business organisation?

       (b)   Discuss the relationship between objectives and the organisational structure.

UCLES P2 1989

8.   A company is reviewing its policy for disposal of industrial waste. Currently, waste is used to fill old quarry sites, but an alternative scheme for large machinery to crush and burn the waste has been suggested.

   (a)   Identify and explain the types of cost involved in such a decision.

   (b)   Discuss and evaluate various methods of investment appraisal that might be appropriate in aiding the decision-making process in this case.   *UCLES P2 1991*

9.   One of the advantages which small firms often possess over large ones is good communications. Why does larger size tend to cause communications to deteriorate and what steps can be taken to ease the situation?   *AEB P2 1990*

10.   CKL is a manufacturer of capital equipment who set up in business 15 years ago (Year 1 in the table below). Its yearly sales, and the five and eight period moving averages, are shown below in index form.

Year	1	2	3	4	5	6	7	8
Sales Index	100	132	160	173	181	174	158	140
5 period moving averages			149.2	164	169.2	165.2	160.2	156.8
8 period moving averages					155.25	159.75	163.75	167.25
Year	9	10	11	12	13	14	15	16
Sales Index	148	164	184	205	209	198	178	164
5 period moving averages	156.8	168.2	182.0	192.0	196.8	190.8		
8 period moving averages	171	174.25	177	179.75				

   (a)   Time series data, such as that in the table above, can be analysed into three major components. Identify these three components.   *(3 marks)*

   (b)   (i)   What factors should you bear in mind when choosing the number of observations you will use in a moving average?   *(2 marks)*

         (ii)   Show how the five and eight period moving averages for year 10 have been calculated.   *(6 marks)*

         (iii)   Plot a graph of the sales index and trend lines and comment on your result.   *(9 marks)*

   (c)   (i)   Stating clearly any assumptions you make, predict a trend value for year 18.   *(2 marks)*

         (ii)   How would you attempt to make a useful forecast of the actual sales for year 18?   *(3 marks)*
         UCLES P1 1987

11.   (a)   Discuss the main advantages and disadvantages of using decision trees in decision making.   *(4 marks)*

      (b)   What is the purpose of using the concept of expected value in decision trees?   *(4 marks)*

(c)   An investor is deciding whether to buy £10,000 worth of unit trusts or an investment bond. Unit trusts have been quite volatile in price lately, investment bonds less so. Whatever he buys he contemplates selling either six months ahead or a year ahead. His objective is to maximise the expected cash value of the deal on the basis of capital gain alone.

His subjective evaluations of the likely price movements are as follows:

Unit Trusts

After six months: 50% probability of £1200 and 50% probability of £1000.

After one year:

(i)   if price after 6 months was £1200, 50% probability of £1500 and 50% probability of £1000;

(ii)   if price after 6 months was £1000, 50% probability of £1200 and 50% probability of £900.

Investment Bond

After six months: 50% probability of £1500 and 50% probability of £700.

After one year:

(i)   if the price after 6 months was £1500, 50% probability of £2500 and 50% probability of £1200;

(ii)   if the price after 6 months was £700, 50% probability of £800 and 50% probability of £500.

Draw a decision tree to show the features of this problem.   *(8 marks)*

(d) Calculate the expected values and on the basis of these decide which is the better investment.   *(6 marks)*

(e)   What practical difficulties would you be likely to encounter in applying this concept and how might they affect your decision?   *(3 marks)*
        UCLES P1 1985

12. The Pirongs Company has hitherto produced just one product which seems to be at the end of its life cycle. The company has two projects to develop new products that are encouraging but, since capital is short, it feels that it could undertake no more than one of these projects. No immediate capital expenditure is required in either project. The financial details are given on the following page:

	Year (End of year figures)				
	1	**2**	**3**	**4**	**5**
Project I					
Net Cash Inflow/Outflow	−10000	−5000	10000	15000	20000
Less Depreciation	0	0	5000	5000	5000
Net Profit	−10000	−5000	5000	10000	15000
Project II					
Net Cash Inflow/Outflow	0	0	10000	10000	10000
Less Depreciation	0	0	2000	2000	2000
Net Profit	0	0	8000	8000	8000

(a)　Examine what is meant by the phrase "product life cycle" and recommend to Pirongs how this may be extended in their company.　*(4 marks)*

(b)　Define what is meant by the term "depreciation" and comment on the depreciation policy of the Pirongs company.　*(4 marks)*

(c)　Calculate the net present value of the two projects on the assumption that the cost of capital is 10%. On the basis of this decide which, if either, of the projects should be undertaken.　*(8 marks)*

(d)　What other methods of capital investment appraisal could have been used? Compare the advantages of these to the net present value method.　*(4 marks)*

(e)　What other considerations would you take into account in choosing whether to prolong the present product life cycle or to undertake one of the new projects?

Present values of 1 in future are given below at various rates:

	10%	**12%**	**14%**	**16%**
One year hence	0.91	0.89	0.88	0.86
Two years hence	0.83	0.80	0.77	0.74
Three years hence	0.75	0.71	0.68	0.64
Four years hence	0.68	0.64	0.59	0.55
Five years hence	0.62	0.57	0.52	0.48

(5 marks)
UCLES P1 1985

13. Below is the index of labour costs facing Bloggs Seaside Hotel Ltd. The value of quarter 1 of 1986 is set at 100.

Year	Quarter	Index
1985	3	118
1985	4	101
1986	1	100
1986	2	99
1986	3	122
1986	4	105
1987	1	112
1987	2	103
1987	3	142
1987	4	101
1988	1	132
1988	2	107

(a) (i) Explain why you would use a 4-quarter moving average to establish the trend in these data. *(2 marks)*

   (ii) What is meant by centring a moving average and why is it done? *(2 marks)*

(b) Calculate the following information.

   (i) The trend for as many quarters as possible. *(2 marks)*

   (ii) The seasonal variation for each quarter. *(2 marks)*

   (iii) The average seasonal variation for each quarter. *(1 mark)*

(c) Draw a suitable graph on the graph paper provided to show the trend only. Predict labour costs in quarter 3 of 1988. *(4 marks)*

(d) What are the shortcomings of the forecasting technique used above? *(3 marks)*

(e) What factors other than the data shown above might Bloggs wish to take into account in attempting a forecast of labour costs? *(5 marks)*

(f) As a seaside hotel, Bloggs employs much casual labour.

   (i) Explain two reasons why Bloggs adopts this manpower strategy. *(2 marks)*

   (ii) Explain two reasons why this strategy may not suit another business of your choice. *(2 marks)*

   UCLES P1 1989

14. Manor Road playschool operates for 12+ hours per week during 40 weeks each year. Two members of staff are employed, who are paid only during term time, whereas the rent is paid throughout the 52 week year. The table below represents the costs incurred by the playschool over the past three years.

	1983	1984	1985
Salaries (£ per hour)	2.00	2.10	2.30
Rent (£ per week)	10	11	12
Rates (£ per year)	180	180	198
Electricity (p per unit)	6	6.9	7.5
Repairs (index 1983 = 100)	100	107	117
Equipment (index 1980 = 100)	120	144	150

In 1983, repairs and equipment each accounted for one eighth of total costs, and an average of 1,250 units of electricity were used per quarter.

(a)   Construct a base weighted index for playschool costs for 1984 and 1985 (1983 = 100), using annual expenditure as the basis for relative weights. Comment on the answers you obtain.   *(12 marks)*

(b)   What are the advantages and disadvantages of base year weighting compared with current year weighting? Compare these advantages and disadvantages with those of other methods of weighting.   *(5 marks)*

(c)   An index for the playschool fees is as follows:

1981	**1982**	**1983**	**1984**	**1985**
100	104.5	110	121	132

Adjust the base period of this index so that a direct comparison can be made between costs and fees. Comment on your result.   *(5 marks)*

(d)   In 1985, total playschool expenditure exceeded fees taken by £320. Given that in 1983 income from fees was £4,120, can you reconcile this information with your results from part (c)? Explain your answer.   *(3 marks)*

UCLES P1 1986

15. (a)   What are the advantages and limitations of presenting data in index number form?   *(4 marks)*

(b)   Smithers Toy Factory collect cost data in the following categories:

Table 1

	1979	1989
wages per worker per week (£)	75	120
rent/rates (per quarter)	6250	8250
materials used (£000s per annum)	250	400
administration (index, 1984 = 100)	80	120
promotion/distribution/sales (£000s p.a.)	200	242
production overheads (£ per toy)	0.5	0.64

There were 100 workers employed in each 50 week year. In 1979 administration overheads were £50,000 and 200,000 toys were made.

    (i)   Calculate the 1989 index number for each category (1979 = 100).   *(3 marks)*

    (ii)   Calculate the ANNUAL cost of each category in 1979 only.   *(2 marks)*

    (iii)   Construct a base-weighted TOTAL cost index for 1989 (1979 = 100). Use annual expenditures as the weights.   *(5 marks)*

(c)   Smithers' workforce is about to make a pay claim for the year starting August 1990.

    (i)   What is meant by a real increase in pay?   *(2 marks)*

    (ii)   How could Smithers' management use the data in Tables 1 and 2 in the pay negotiations?   *(5 marks)*

    (iii)   How could the data be effectively presented in visual form to support the management's case?   *(4 marks)*

Table 2

	National Retail Price Index	Smithers' sales revenue (£mns)
1979	100	1.20
1984	105	1.17
1989	121	1.42

16. (a)   Outline briefly the operational research approach to problems.

     (b)   Johnston Ltd is a small firm of jobbing builders. They have received an order for the construction of a small prefabricated building and are using network analysis to plan the project. Draw the network for the project, given the following information.

Activity	Must be preceded by:
A	-
B	A
C	A
D	C
E	B
F	B
G	D
H	D,E
I	H,G

(c) The company is involved in a second project. The network is shown below:

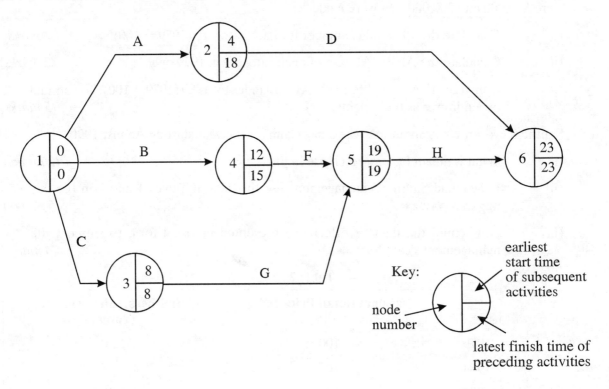

Activity:	A	B	C	D	E	F	G	H
Estimated Duration (days)	4	7	8	5	4	4	11	4

(i)   Show that the total floats on activities A and D are both 14 days. What would the total float on activity D be if activity A over-ran by 3 days? Explain your answer.   *(5 marks)*

(ii) Calculate the total float for all other activities and, using your answer, confirm that the critical path is via nodes 1, 3, 5 and 6.   *(4 marks)*

(iii) The number of men needed for each activity is shown below:

Activity:	A	B	C	D	E	F	G	H
No of men:	2	2	4	6	2	4	4	2

Each activity uses employees of the same skill level and no activity can be started with fewer than the number of employees required to carry out the activity. There are only six employees available for the project.

Explain how you would use float to ensure the optimum allocation of employees and show that the project cannot be completed in 23 days.

(7 marks)
UCLES P1 1988

17.   (a)   Explain the differences between the following types of sample:

      (i)   random,

      (ii)   stratified,

      (iii)   quota.   *(6 marks)*

    (b)   A firm wishes to fix a piece work rate for its employees and to do this it needs to know the average number of operations per person per day. Rather than make this calculation for all its staff, the firm decides to take a sample.

      (i)   Describe how the firm might decide on the kind and size of sample it would need.
    (4 marks)

      (ii)   Discuss which of the measures of central tendency would be the most appropriate to use and explain why you think this is the case.   *(4 marks)*

  (c)   Suppose that workmen had previously been paid a flat rate of £25 per day, on the basis of an arithmetic average of 100 operations per day. Suggest why, and at what levels of operations, you might introduce bonus payments, if the results of the sample showed that the arithmetic mean was 100 operations, with a standard deviation of 30. (You may use the table below if you think this is appropriate.)   *(5 marks)*

Proportionate parts of the area under the normal curve				
Distances from Mean in terms of standard deviation in one direction	0-1	1-2	2-3	over 3
Proportion of area in above range	34%	14%	2%	Negligible

  (d)   Suppose a workman performed the following set of operations over a 10 day period:

$$180,\ 180,\ 150,\ 130,\ 190,\ 200,\ 150,\ 160,\ 170,\ 180$$

What would you conclude about the workman and/or the sample results? Explain your reasons (You may assume that the standard deviation remains at 30).   *(6 marks)*
UCLES P1 1985

18.   Newlin's Ltd has to decide whether to continue producing its traditional range of goods next year or whether to produce an entirely new line. To help in making this decision, it is considering spending £5,000 on a market research survey to assess the level of interest in this new line, which may be high, medium, or low. Whichever range Newlin's finally produces, it believes that the sales will be either "successful" or "unsuccessful". The decision tree overleaf illustrates the situation.

Key

Trad – Traditional Range
New – New Range
Suc – Sales are successful
Un – Sales are unsuccessful

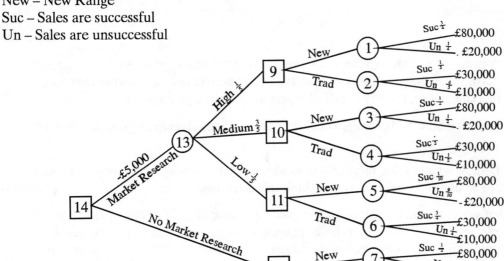

The numbers in the circles
and squares are for identifying
each node in part (b).

(a)   In the diagram, explain the significance of:

   (i)   the squares;

   (ii)   the circles;

   (iii)   the fractions on the lines;

   (iv)   the numbers at the end of the lines.   *(4 marks)*

(b)   (i)   What do you understand by the term 'expected value' in the decision tree analysis?   *(2 marks)*

   (ii)   Calculate the expected values at each node in the decision tree.   *(7 marks)*

(c)   What action would you recommend Newlin's to take? Give reasons for your recommendation. What reservations might you have about your recommendation?   *(3 marks)*

(d)   Newlin's has just been offered the lease of additional machinery. This would enable it to produce both traditional and new ranges of goods, or a larger number of each range. Also, if it began by concentrating on a single range and this proved unsuccessful, it could change to producing a mixed range halfway through the season. (It cannot completely stop production of any range at this point because contracts with its purchasers guarantee supply of the initial range throughout the season). An immediate decision must be made as to whether or not to lease the additional machinery, so Newlin's cannot undertake any market research before deciding.

Draw and label the additional branch of the decision tree. (You do not need to put in any numerical data on the diagram you draw.) *(5 marks)*

(e) State the assumptions that have been made to enable the decision tree to be drawn. How do these assumptions affect the conclusions that you draw from the tree? *(4 marks)*

UCLES P1 1987

19. (a) Briefly explain the advantages and limitations of Critical Path Analysis as a control tool for management.

(b) Use the critical path diagram below to calculate the earliest and latest start times of each activity, the critical path and the minimum possible duration of the whole project. Show your workings. *(7 marks)*

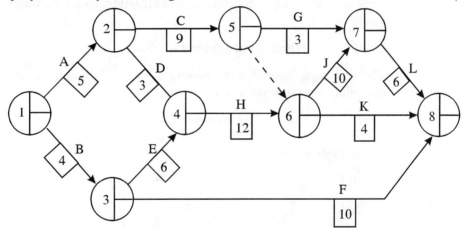

(c) Six days must now be cut from the minimum project duration. No single activity can be reduced by more than 2 days. Using the information given, find the cheapest way of achieving this. What is the new critical path?

Further information

activity	cost of reducing by one day (£)
A	4
B	4
C	1
D	4
E	3
F	1
G	2
H	4
J	2
K	4
L	1

(d)   Assume that the cuts in question (c) are NOT introduced. Activities C, D, E and F require labour of skill X as below:

activity	units of skill X needed per day
C	10
D	12
E	10
F	8

   (i)   Assuming each activity starts at its earliest time, and using the graph paper provided, draw a histogram to show the total utilisation of X.   *(3 marks)*

   (ii)   What are the implications if only 17 units of X are available?

20.   (a)   Why is 'weighting' necessary in constructing index numbers? Give a brief example.

   (b)   Identify the limitations of a typical retail price index.

   (c)   The following figures were provided by the Utopian Statistical Service for compiling a retail price index:

Item	Price Relative (June 1988 Jan 1980 = 100)	Weights (1987 average)	
			(3 marks)
			ULCES P1 1990
Food	110.3	25	
Fuel	122.1	20	
Housing	141.3	25	
Services	126.9	15	
Miscellaneous	118.2	10	
		$\overline{100}$	

   (i)   Explain why the weights refer to a period other than the base period (January 1980).   *(3 marks)*

   (ii)   What is meant by the term 'price relative'?   *(1 mark)*

   (iii)   Calculate a weighted aggregate price index for June 1988.   *(6 marks)*

(d)   A company calculates details of wage rates, material costs and factory overheads in index form, and in June 1988 these stood at 150, 60 and 130 respectively (January 1980 = 100). A particular product had the following cost structure in January 1980:

	£/unit
Labour	0.80
Materials	0.80
Factory overheads	0.40
	$\overline{2.00}$

(i) Estimate the mean percentage increase in the costs of producing the product between January 1980 and June 1988. *(4 marks)*

(ii) State any assumptions you have made. *(2 marks)*

UCLES P1 1988

Other questions

21. Make a list of three products and three services which have a seasonal demand.

22. Try to think of three recent world or national events which might have caused a random variation in demand for a product.

23. In what circumstances is it necessary to use the centring process in establishing a trend?

24. Mr. Dixon is the owner of a small business and is about to retire. He is considering selling his business. The agent who is to handle the sale needs information about the sales performance in order to set a realistic price for the business. Prospective buyers will want to know its history in order that they can begin to predict the potential of the business. Mr. Dixon's accountant has prepared the following figures;

Quarters

	1	2	3	4
Year 1	33	51	48	27
Year 2	26	42	43	24
Year 3	21	33	30	18
Year 4	24	33	36	24
Year 5	25	36		

All figures are × £1,000.

(a) By using moving averages calculate the trend and seasonal variations.

(b) Plot the original data and the trend figures you have calculated.

(c) Predict sales turnover for quarters 3 and 4 of Year 5.

(d) What conclusions can you draw about the position of the business and its prospects?

(e) Other than turnover, what factors might buyers consider when assessing the potential of the business?

14.   How do you decide on how many observations should be included in a moving average?

15.   Explain how the owner of a small, but expanding, business might use forecasting techniques in order to improve decision-making.

Case Study

Owen Print Ltd.

Owen Print Ltd. is a private limited company employing over 90 staff spread across six departments: Sales and Administration; Finance; General Office; Production; Technical and Dispatch.

The company is an established family business that has rapidly expanded its production over the past five years. It is operated from two sites in the market town of Hereford. The main site houses the production, technical and dispatch departments. A new building, first used four years ago when expansion forced the company to increase its accommodation, houses the other three departments.

As a family business, the company is run on rather old-fashioned lines. It is autocratic. Of the four directors, three are members of the family. The Chairman and Managing Director is Cecil Owen; his son Colin, and daughter Madeleine, are also directors, and Larry Grant, who is not a member of the family, is the remaining director. Cecil Owen still sees the company as it used to be many years ago: a small business in which everyone knew each other and he knew exactly what was going on everywhere within the company. He is still referred to by older members as the 'gaffer' and, if they have problems, Cecil Owen is always willing to hear them. But he is not a man who likes labels for people so most employees have no formal job descriptions. Nor does the company have any formally stated aims and objectives, other than those contained in its Memorandum of Association.

Larry Grant, as well as being director, is also Company Secretary and in overall charge of the Sales and Administration Department, Finance and the General Office.

Recently, Mr. Grant has become increasingly anxious about the inadequacies of the communication/information system operating within the company. He has identified that:

  (i)   new and existing staff are often unclear about their role within the company

  (ii)   no single individual has responsibility for personnel matters

  (iii) the physical and organisational structure of the company is not helpful to effective communication.

Task

You are an employee of the company and you are directly responsible to Larry Grant. You have been asked to produce an informal report for Mr. Grant to present to the next meeting of the Board of Directors. In the report you should take each of the concerns (i), (ii), and (iii) that are raised by Mr. Grant. You should indicate:

  (a)   the reasons why the problems exist

  (b)   how the communication system might be improved

  (c)   how the situation might best be overcome.

Part Four – Business Functions

Once a business grows beyond a certain size, it begins to employ specialists. These specialists are grouped together within the business and together perform a function. The number of specialist functions grows as the business continues to expand: these often become know as departments.

At your current level of study, it is impractical to gain a knowledge of some of the more intricate functional departments of a business: the Public Relations Department is likely to be a feature of most medium and large -sized businesses and, although you will touch on the importance of a business image and information in the study of marketing, a detailed account of the work of such a department is outsisde the scope of this book and, indeed, outside most courses of study other than for professional qualifications.

Instead, you will concentrate on the four major functional areas of business with which you will be expected to have a detailed working knowledge. They are:

Accounting	• whose function it is to be responsible for the stewardship of the financial affairs of a business
Marketing	• whose function it is to be responsible for identifying a market and developing a strategy to attack it
Production	• whose function it is to be responsible for manufacturing the products that customers need, to the required quality
Personnel	• whose function it is to be responsible for recruiting and retaining employees of the right calibre to maintain the position of the business

Amongst its many entries, a dictionary might give you the following definitions of an account:

1. To reckon up the credit and debit of a person or business

2. A record of goods and services expended, with balance

3. A statement of money held in trust.

Accounting is defined as 'the art of keeping and verifying accounts' and an accountant as a 'professional keeper and inspector of accounts'. These definitions are a useful starting point to a subject that, though it has grown increasingly complex, is, in essence, a simple and straightforward process that is carried out according to well-established practices and conventions.

What is an Accountant's Responsibility?

An accountant's job is to provide financial statements that will allow interested parties – such as an owner or client – to monitor and control the activities of the business. This is done by devising a system of *internal record keeping*. The accountant will ensure that an accurate *record* is kept of payments, receipts, stock movements, sales, purchase of supplies, use of assets, consumable stocks; accountants will control misappropriation and theft by employees.

This is done for two reasons:

1. For purposes of *comparison*. To give management an overall view of how its cost centres, departments, plant are performing in relation to each other in order to maximise the efficiency of the business; also to compare how the business is performing at one time as compared to another.

2. So that any *external comparison* with another business can be carried out fairly ('like is compared to like'), accountants draw up financial records that conform with accepted standards of business practice. These records will be scrutinised by external agencies, such as the Inland Revenue and shareholders.

Financial Statements

There are three classifications of business in the private sector:

-   *Sole Trader* (one person operating the business)
-   *Partnership* (two or more persons operating the business jointly)
-   *Limited Liability Company* (at least two persons owning shares in a business, which has the advantage of Limited Liability for the shareholders).

A Limited Liability Company may fall into one of two categories:

- a *Private Limited Company* (Ltd.) or
- a *Public Limited Company* (plc.).

It is the Plc which we will use as our model for explaining in detail the items which are contained in financial statements.

Financial Statements of Limited Companies

Financial statements of limited liability companies must be:

- prepared annually
- conform to certain standards of presentation (these are set out in the *Companies Act* 1985).

For each financial year, limited companies produce sets of accounts which are published and are available for public inspection. These sets of accounts consist of:

a.   *The Profit and Loss Account* (including appropriate explanatory notes and additional information required by the Companies Act)

b.   *The Balance Sheet* (also including appropriate explanatory notes and additional information required by the Companies Act)

c.   *The Funds Flow Statement*

d.   *The Director's Report*

e.   *The Auditor's Report.*

In addition to the Companies Act 1985, laying down the required format for accounts, there are also Statements of Standard Accounting Practice (SSAPs) which have been drawn up by the professional accountancy bodies and which cover particular aspects of accounts and their presentation (such as stock valuation, depreciation, taxation etc). The Funds Flow Statement, for example, is drawn up and presented in accordance with the requirements of SSAP 10: *'Statements of source and application of funds'*.

Who Uses the Financial Statements?

The users of financial statements are of two broad types:

- those not connected with running the company (external users)
- those involved in the management of the company (internal users).

External users of accounting information

These include:

- shareholders
- lenders

- suppliers
- government
- the Inland Revenue
- employees
- the local community.

Shareholders

The shareholders' interest in the financial statements of a business may, on the face of it, seem an obvious one: their interest is in knowing what return they will receive from their investment. But that 'obvious' perception depends upon your view of who the shareholders are and, at this point, it is worth pausing to take a more detailed look at the nature of their involvement and interest.

In a private limited company, the transfer of shares is subject to restrictions. Shares are often held by a small number of investors, some of whom will be directors, many of whom will be employees; some will have a family interest in the business.

These types of shareholder are relatively loyal to the business and poor financial results are unlikely to influence them into selling their shares, and, in so doing, withdrawing their interest and stake in the business. Clearly, from their point of view, the greater the return is on their investment, the happier they are likely to be, but the size of the return on investment alone is not so critical a factor in the decision to buy or sell a shareholding as it would be in a public limited company. As you are aware by now, the shares in a plc are available for purchase on the open market. Most investors buy shares with the help of a broker. The broker will advise on the various investment opportunities which are available, make the purchase on behalf of the client and complete administration matters.

This may give you an image, of thousands or even millions, of members of the public queuing up to buy shares in all sorts of companies, but is this the case in practice?

Since 1979, the order of the day has been for successive Conservative governments to pursue a policy of 'privatising' nationalised industries. (Part Two of this book looked at this process in some detail.) One of the main features of each privatisation has been the encouragement for the small investor to buy shares. Mr. and Mrs. Joe Public have been given considerable financial incentives to become shareholders, either for the first time or to extend their range of investments.

One recent example of this preferential policy of giving priority to the individual shareholder could be seen in 1991 when the Government initiated the sale of its remaining 49% stake in British Telecom. Small investors (that is, members of the public and BT customers) were offered BT shares at a price of £1.10 each. Small investors had to make a commitment to buy at least one hundred shares. In contrast, the large institutional investors faced a price of £1.25 and a commitment to purchase many more shares. This approach continued when the third tranche of BT shares was sold in 1993 ("BT 3").

In theory, this sort of preferential policy should broaden the base of share ownership in the UK. In practice, many small shareholders sell a short time after buying the shares, in some instances making a lucrative short-term profit. Almost inevitably these shares are then bought up by the large institutional investors.

Given the pattern of share ownership which has been described, let's return to the investor's interest in the financial statements.

An investor is likely to assess the investment in two main ways and will seek answers to these questions:

- what is the dividend which is being paid? How does it relate to my investment and any alternative investments I might have made?
- what proportion of the earnings on my investment has been ploughed back into the business for future growth?

Both of these factors can be measured by means of financial calculations and ratios which you'll study later in this section, but it's worth exploring the idea behind these factors a little more right now.

If an institutional investor originally bought 10,000 shares in a public company at £6.00 per share, that represents an investment by the institution of £60,000. Suppose, at the accounting year end, the company declares a dividend of 60p per share, then this represents a 'short-term' return of 10%. The money will be received in the form of a cheque and gives an immediate return on investment.

However, shareholders often have as much concern in the re-investment of their earnings as they do in immediate dividends. All profits, which are really the property of the shareholders, can be paid out in the form of dividends if the directors of the company so recommend, but a more usual policy is to retain profit for re-investment in the business. In the example you've just been given, suppose that the dividends represented only 50% of the profits. Then, clearly, each shareholder is effectively re-investing a further 60p per share in the business. Although an investor may initially have been disappointed with the 10% return (a building society account may have yielded as good a return), when the 10% reinvested return is added, the picture is much improved.

In summary: the shareholders' use of the accounting information is very much determined by their viewpoint. Are they short-termists, interested only in dividends and a quick return on their money investment? Or are they more concerned about long-term growth and security?

Whatever their perspective, the financial statement will yield them some useful information.

Lenders

Almost every business needs to borrow money. Some business borrowing will be short-term, perhaps in the form of a bank overdraft; other borrowing will be medium-term (over a period of three to ten years); some will be long-term (repayable over ten or more years).

The criteria for the sort of borrowing which a business decides and the choice of lender is a decision-making topic in itself; it has been explored in some detail in Part One.

Once the finance has been arranged, one thing is common to all types of borrowing: the lender must repay the sum borrowed (the *capital sum*) plus the interest accruing at a rate agreed earlier between business and lender.

Both in advance of the loan, and after the loan has been granted, the lender will watch the financial affairs of the borrower with great interest. The lender will want assurance that the loan is 'secure' and that repayments and interest will continue to be paid on time.

In recent years, several of the larger banks in the UK have been badly affected by businesses 'defaulting' on their loan repayments.

Large losses incurred by some lenders, combined with recession squeezing the profit margins of businesses, has led to increased attention being paid to the financial performance of borrowers, as reported through their published financial statements.

As in the case of shareholders, lenders have particular methods of evaluating the risk of their decision to lend. These methods are explored later in this Part of the book.

Suppliers

All businesses need suppliers. A manufacturing business will be sold a wide range of goods and services by its many suppliers. Such supplies may include raw materials and components. Even the smallest business will buy supplies. A one-person consultancy business, although not producing anything tangible, will still need office stationery, telephones and toilet paper. So, every business needs suppliers and, in the business world, goods and services can only be purchased in two ways:

- by cash
- by credit.

Smaller businesses frequently have to pay for goods from suppliers *before* they receive them. The reason for this is that suppliers want to safeguard themselves against possible bad debts. Such a method of pre-payment for goods cuts out any financial risk they might otherwise expose themselves to: they receive their money for the goods even before they are despatched. Many suppliers, in order to do business, need to offer a credit facility. That is, they are prepared to deliver goods to a customer before receiving payment. This is a form of loan – the supplier is simply supplying goods or service rather than money.

Suppliers of goods or credit will want to be assured that they will receive payment and analysis of the accounting statements of a customer will provide some evidence of how 'safe' a particular customer is. As well as unquantifiable feedback, such as market news and hearsay, suppliers will also use ratios to quantify the risk they are taking when extending credit.

Government

The Government will be more interested in the general well-being of the economy rather than the prosperity or otherwise of individual companies. However, in an industrially based economy, such as the UK, there are companies whose results will reflect the economic climate. If the retail trade is going through a bad spell then a cross-section of the accounts of such companies as Marks & Spencer, Sainsbury and W.H. Smith would reflect this.

Importantly though, any government has at its disposal a series of measures which it can take to stimulate or subdue business activity. Such measures include:

1. *Changing the rate of Corporation Tax*

    This is the tax that companies pay on their annual profits. A reduction in the rate of this tax means a lower proportion of profit is payable to the Inland Revenue; therefore more profit is available to distribute to shareholders or retain within the company for further investment.

2.   *Changing the rate of Income Tax*

This is a measure which has the effect of increasing or decreasing the income of individuals. All people who work, and receive payment over a certain sum, pay Income Tax on their earnings. If income tax is increased, then more is deducted from an individual's earnings, leaving the taxpayer less to spend. If income tax is reduced, then the individual will have more left to spend (that is, more *disposable income*) once tax has been paid.

Theoretically, a reduction in income tax should increase demand from consumers with more money to spend and this should be reflected in the sales revenue and profits of companies in the retail sector of the economy. A reduction in the rate of income tax should also, in theory, leave more disposable income to be saved. Saving represents an investment, since a consumer depositing money in a building society or bank results in the institution investing more money in business and commerce in order to earn even greater returns.

It must be stressed how *theoretical* these economic measures are. If life, and managing the economy, were as simple as the last two points have perhaps made them seem, then the UK and other national governments would have a much easier job. Every decision has its *downside* (or *risk*) and, in the instance of reducing income tax, a very real risk is the possibility that increasing the amount of money consumers have, leads to a higher demand for more goods. Higher demand leads to higher prices; consumers then demand higher wages in order to pay for the goods; higher wages then lead to increased costs and business passes these on to the consumer in the form of higher prices, thus setting in motion an inflationary spiral.

These are complex matters, more appropriate to a textbook of economics than a business studies book, but they are explored in more detail and from a different angle in Part Two. You may well ask, after that diversion, what has all this got to do with accounts? Well, the annual accounts show the performance and well-being of a business. The government can look at the performance of the top two or three hundred companies in order to get an overview of the success or failure of their measures.

The Inland Revenue

The interest of the Inland Revenue in the accounts of a business is a purely pragmatic/practical one. Are the accounting records correct (i.e. have they been checked and certified accurate by an auditor)? If they have, how much Corporation Tax does the business owe?

Employees

In the past, many employees of business seemed satisfied just to have a job and a weekly pay packet. Recently, things have changed. Many employees are now shareholders in the company for which they work and so have an interest in the company's results as reported in the annual accounts.

Even if they are not shareholders, employees – and certainly their union representatives – are acutely aware that a prosperous company usually means increased job security, better promotion possibilities and career progression and higher financial rewards. Many employers are aware, perhaps more than ever, that a prosperous employee depends on a prosperous business and, whilst the annual accounts don't tell the full story, they are a useful short-term reflection of the prosperity of the business.

Local Community

Many local communities around the UK depend upon certain major employers. The major employer not only employs a lot of local people but also generates and sustains numerous jobs in local suppliers. The performance and prosperity of a whole community may well depend upon the performance and prosperity of a single large employer. Historical examples in the UK will include: the influence of ICI in Cheshire and Teesside; British Coal in the valleys of South Wales; IBM in Greeenock, Scotland; Harland and Wolfe in Belfast.

The dependency of local communities on such industries has evolved and developed over time. Local communities know to their cost that poor company results in one year may mean redundancies the next.

Internal Users of Accounting Information

The internal users of accounting information are, broadly speaking, management. In a 'good' business which has systems set up for gathering and reporting accountancy information during the course of the financial year, the annual accounts will merely be a confirmation of what was already known.

The annual financial statements summarise the performance and position of the business, but managers need earlier and more detailed information in order that they can properly control and review the operation of the business and make decisions. Such information is provided primarily by management and cost accountants and is looked at in a later section.

Accounting Systems

Accounting systems are complex and a detailed study of them is outside the scope of this book. Accounting systems comprise a topic in themselves; they are really the preserve of the accounting student. You must know that such systems exist, but you do not need to know the details of how the system is operated.

The foundation of any system of book-keeping is a book which is called a *ledger*. It consists of a number of pages, each page being called an *account*. Each account is given a name or a title and a distinctive number for reference purposes. Each supplier to the business will have an account and this account will record the amount owed to that supplier. In the same way the amount owed to the business by each customer will be recorded in an account. Every transaction with a customer or supplier will be entered in the relevant account. This means that, at any time, it is possible to determine how much is owed to suppliers or due from customers. The accounts of suppliers and customers are called *Personal Accounts*.

A second category of accounts is known as *Impersonal* or *Nominal Accounts*. These are records of transactions to do with impersonal things, such as wages, heat and light, property and so on.

Daily transactions are recorded by means of a process called *book-keeping*. This is based on a principle of *double-entry* which we will examine shortly.

The Balance Sheet

The double entry principle which is central to the accounting process is, for your purpose, best examined through the study of a balance sheet of a business. Remember: *unless you are doing an accountancy course you need only grasp the principle and not the practice.*

Any balance sheet, whether it be that of the smallest sole trader or the largest public limited company, is merely a summary of two things:

- where the funds of the business have come from (*source of funds*)

- where the funds have been deployed (*use of funds*).

In broad terms there are only two places funds can come from:

- capital from the owners (shareholders/partners/sole proprietors). This is known as *equity capital* or just plain *equity*

- capital from lenders. This is known as *debt capital* or *debt.*

There are two broad ways in which funds of money can be used:

- to purchase *fixed assets* such as land, buildings and machinery

- to provide *working capital* to keep the business running on a day-to-day basis.

This seems too simple to be true. A lot of business students freeze when they see a balance sheet: you needn't be one of them! Simply remember the basic principle that a balance sheet shows:

1. Where funds have come from and

2. Where funds have been used.

Let's take a first look at a balance sheet to show the truth of that statement. Advent Cards plc is a company which manufactures and sells all sorts of cards for different occasions: gift; birthday; anniversary etc. Advent Cards plc has several factories and sells to the wholesale and retail trades. Its financial position last year was summarised as follows:

Advent Cards plc
Balance Sheet as at 31 August 1993

	1992 £000	1992 £000	1993 £000	1993 £000
USE OF FUNDS				
Fixed Assets:				
Tangible Fixed Assets (Note 1)		2190		2632
Intangible Fixed Assets (Note 2)		210		168
Financial Fixed Assets (at cost)		100		200
		2500		**3000**
Current Assets:				
Stock (Note 3)	3620		4180	
Debtors	3630		4680	
Cash	235		170	
	7485		**9030**	
Current Liabilities				
Creditors	3335		4000	
Corporation Tax	165		390	
Dividend Proposed	280		230	
	3780		**4620**	
Current Assets Less Current Liabilities (Working Capital)		**3705**		**4410**
NET ASSETS		6205		7410
SOURCE OF FUNDS				
Shareholders' Funds				
Ordinary Share Capital (Note 4)		2500		3000
Share Premium		-		250
Revaluation Reserve		150		150
Retained Profits		2275		2730
		4925		**6130**
Long-Term Liabilities				
Debentures		**1280**		**1280**
CAPITAL EMPLOYED		6205		7410

Notes to the Balance Sheet

1. Tangible fixed assets are as follows:

	31 August 1993			31 August 1992		
	Cost or Valuation	Dep'n	NBV	Cost or Valuation	Dep'n	NBV
	£000	£000	£000	£000	£000	£000
Land and buildings	1750	-	1750	1200	-	1200
Plant and equipment	650	354	296	560	280	280
Motor vehicles	990	540	450	940	390	550
Office equipment	230	94	136	230	70	160
	3620	**988**	**2632**	**2930**	**740**	**2190**

No fixed assets were disposed of during the year ended 31 August 1993.

Land and buildings (freehold) have been revalued from £1.2 million to £1.75 million.

2. Intangible fixed assets consist of Goodwill and Research and Development Expenditure of which £42,000 was written off during the year ended 31 August 1993.

3. Stock is valued at cost or net realisable value, whichever is the lower.

4. The authorised capital is £4,000,000 consisting of 8,000,000 ordinary shares of 50 pence each.

The issued share capital is as follows:

	31 August 1993 £ 000	31 August 1992 £ 000
Ordinary shares of 50p each fully paid	3,000	2,500

There had been an issue of ordinary shares during the year ended 31 August 1993.

Let us examine each item on the balance sheet in turn.

Fixed Assets

These are items which have been bought for the business to use over a number of years. Some, such as land and buildings, rarely lose value and their value stays static at 'cost'. It may sometimes need to be revalued to represent a value nearer its realistic worth. However, many fixed assets do lose value, especially things such as tools, machinery, equipment and vehicles. These are used up by the business over a period of years and their value is reduced by 'depreciating' them. The subject of depreciation is dealt with in detail in a following section.

There are three broad categories of fixed asset:

Tangible Fixed Assets

These are items which can be seen and touched; examples might include plant and equipment. As well as the items discussed earlier, such as land and buildings, this sort of asset will include fork lift trucks, storage equipment, desks, computers etc. You will often find that these are grouped together on the balance sheet for convenience under the heading of 'plant and equipment'.

Intangible Fixed Assets

These are items which have a financial value to the business (and which can be assessed) but which cannot be seen or touched. Examples of this might include patents which have been paid for and are held by the business or the mineral rights to a quarry. In each of these instances – as the patent gets nearer to running out and as the quarry is stripped of its resources – so the value of the intangible asset falls. The value of such assets is reduced by a process called *amortisation* (this is similar to 'depreciation' of tangible assets). Goodwill can be shown as an intangible asset of a business. It is usually only shown in company accounts when a takeover has recently taken place and the value of goodwill can be accurately valued.

Financial Fixed Assets

These are usually investments in other companies. The investments should always be valued in the balance sheet at cost – never at market value. However, if the market value is significantly different from cost, then this should be recorded in a note attached to the accounts. Attaching such a note ensures that the users of accounts are made aware of possible gains or losses made in respect of investments.

Working Capital

Working capital = Current assets – Current liabilities.

All businesses, from the smallest sole trader to the largest multi-national, need working capital. Working capital keeps the business running on a day-to-day basis. It provides funds for wages, heat, light and the payment of creditors.

In a later section we will examine the importance of working capital and its control, but for now it is sufficient to look at the components of working capital as seen in a balance sheet.

Current Assets

These are things of financial value, which the business owns, and which are in the form of cash, or which will be converted into cash over the course of the following twelve months. The main current assets which you are likely to see in business accounts are:

Stock

This is the closing stock of goods, which the company has purchased and/or manufactured, but which it has not yet sold.

Stock should always be valued at cost or net realisable value (the value the stock could be sold for), whichever is the lower. Stock should never be valued at selling price (unless selling price has somehow fallen below cost price) since there is no guarantee that the goods will be sold for that amount. To represent stock in the balance sheet at selling price would be anticipating profit before it had been earned; this would violate the *prudence concept* of accounting which we will refer to later.

In a corner shop, stock consists of those goods which the owner has bought at cost but which have not yet been sold.

In a manufacturing company, stock can be of three types:

1. *Raw materials* and components are goods which have been bought from a supplier ready for use in the manufacturing process.

2. *Work in Process* comprises goods in the factory which are in various stages of completion: they are part-processed.

3. *Finished goods* are goods which have been manufactured and are awaiting dispatch to the customer.

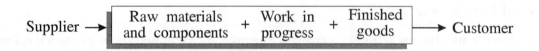

Types of stock in a manufacturing business

Debtors

Debtors are customers of the business who have bought goods on credit. They have received goods but have not yet paid for them. The money sum in the balance sheet states the total amount which is owed by customers on a given date.

Cash

Some cash in a business will be in the form which we are familiar; notes and coins on the premises of the business. However, in business terms, money which has been banked is always referred to as 'cash'.

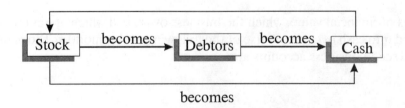

The current assets of a business

Cash is known as a *liquid resource* of a business; that is, it can be spent immediately. *Debtors* are less liquid since the money needs first to be collected before it can be spent. *Stock* is the least liquid of the current assets since in most businesses it needs to be turned first into debtors and following that, into cash. Accounting convention dictates that *the least liquid current asset is listed first in the balance sheet and the most liquid asset is listed last.*

Current Liabilities

Current liabilities are amounts owed (debts) to organisations outside the business. Frequently, in the balance sheet, you will see this category of current liabilities referred to as 'amounts falling due within one year', or creditors.

Creditors

Creditors are organisations which have supplied goods or services to the business, but have not yet been paid for them. They will, however, be paid within the next twelve months.

Bank overdraft

This is money borrowed from a bank in the short-term. It is often used to finance the day-to-day running of the business. For example, suppose a business is expecting, within the next week, a payment from a customer of £5,000. At the same time the business must pay its employees their wages of £1,500, but it does not have the cash to do so. The business can issue cheques or draw cash from their bank account to a certain 'overdraft limit', even though it has no funds in its account. The bank will 'clear' the cheques or issue cash in order that the employees can be paid. When the £5,000 is received from the customer, it is paid into the bank account, thereby 'clearing' the overdraft. Thus an overdraft is a very short-term loan used to finance peaks and troughs in cash flows through a business.

Corporation Tax payable

When a business makes a profit it pays Corporation Tax. This tax is assessed on the basis of the end of the accounting statements but the tax will not be payable until the following year. Funds need to be put aside for this payment and these are therefore included as a current liability – an amount which is to paid out within the next twelve months.

Dividends proposed

When a company makes a profit, then it usually declares a *dividend* to its shareholders. A dividend is a cash sum which is paid on the basis of so many pence per share. The proposed dividend in any year must be approved by the Annual General Meeting of the shareholders before the dividend is paid. Therefore, in the balance sheet, the amount set aside to be paid out in dividends is classified as a current liability.

As you will see when you look, in a later section, at the Profit and Loss Account for Advent Cards plc, the total dividends for the year are £505,000. That indicates £275,000 has already been paid out as an interim dividend: the remainder (£230,000) remains as a current liability and will not be paid out until the dividend is approved by the shareholders at the AGM.

As a group, current liabilities represent money which is owed to organisations outside the business. In reality, these organisations are providing funds or a form of short-term loan which assists the financial operation of the business. Why should a business use its own funds when it can use those of other organisations, cost-free?

Shareholders' Funds

The classification 'shareholders' funds' includes all money invested by the shareholders in the business. This investment can be of two types:

a.   their initial investment – the amount they paid for their shares when they were first bought

b.   their re-investment – earnings which have not been paid out in dividend but have been put back into the company to buy further equipment, fund expansion etc. Such re-investment is often shown under the general heading of 'reserves'.

a. Initial investment

1. Authorised share capital

In Part One it was explained how, when a company is incorporated, it must state, in its Articles of Association, what is to be the maximum number of shares it is allowed to issue. This becomes its 'authorised share capital' and must be entered in the 'Notes to the Accounts'. It does not mean that a company will want or need to issue all those shares, but simply what is available to issue if required.

2. Ordinary share capital

The purchase of ordinary shares entitles the shareholder to:

- appoint directors
- appoint and fix the amount to be paid to the auditor
- to vote in general meetings on all matters relating to the general conduct of the company
- a share of an unspecified amount of the company's assets remaining after any dividends to preference shareholders have been paid
- if the company is 'wound up' or ceases trading, a proportionate share of the company's assets remaining after prior claims have been settled. Prior claim on the company's assets is held, firstly, by those who have loaned money to, or are creditors of the business, and, secondly, by preference shareholders.

Suppose in a company, the ordinary shareholders hold 2,000 shares of £1 each, 75p called and paid. This means they have paid £15,000 for these shares (20,000 × 75p) but, should the business be wound up and it has insufficient funds to pay its debts, then ordinary shareholders are liable to contribute the remaining £5,000 (20,000 × 25p) for the purpose of settling such debt.

3. Preference share capital

This category of shares gives holders preferential rights in respect of dividends. Preference shares are issued at a set percentage rate; for example 8%. This entitles the shareholders to a dividend of 8% on their shareholding every year before any payments are made to ordinary shareholders. Unless otherwise stated in the Articles of Association, preference shares are presumed to be 'cumulative'. With cumulative preference shares, fixed dividends not paid in one year are carried forward to future years and any accumulated arrears have priority over dividend payments to ordinary shareholders. Sometimes preference shares are redeemable; that is, they can be bought back by the company after a stated period of time.

b. Reinvestment

The broad heading for this on the balance sheet is 'reserves'. Reserves are amounts retained by a business in order to help it make future profits. Reserves can be of three types:

1. Revenue reserves

These are profits retained by the business. They can be used to fund the purchase of assets, or can be used to pay dividends.

2. Capital reserves

These result mainly from the revaluation of assets, such as land. For example, if a business has valued its land at £250,000 and a revaluation places a value of £500,000 on that same land then the business is worth more. As a result, the shareholders' stake is increased. Capital reserves cannot be used for dividend purposes.

3. Share premium

Shares issued always have a 'nominal value'; that is, the stated price of a share when it was first issued. If further shares are issued at a price greater than its nominal value, then the excess revenue is recorded as a share premium. By law the premium must be kept in a separate account and cannot be used for dividend purposes.

Long-Term Liabilities

This section of the balance sheet includes all long-term funds derived from sources outside the business. 'Long-term' in this context means the amounts are repayable to the lender over a period of more than one year. Long-term liabilities are sometimes referred to as *loan* or *debt* capital. The most common sources of such funds are:

- debentures or loan stock
- bank loans.

These and other sources of debt capital are explained in detail in Part One. Having looked at individual categories in the balance sheet, it is a good idea to take a step back and try to gain an overview once more.

$$\text{Assets} = \text{Shareholders' Funds} + \text{Liabilities}$$
$$\text{or}$$
$$\text{Use of Funds} = \text{Source of Funds}$$

The traditional accounting equation (Assets = Shareholders' Funds + Liabilities) is simply a way of saying that everything of value which the company possesses (its assets) has a claim upon it from either the shareholders (shareholders' funds) or those organisations who have loaned it money or goods and services (long-term and current liabilities).

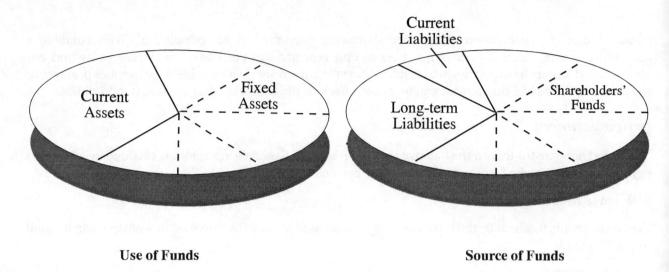

Use of Funds   **Source of Funds**

In a balance sheet, you will sometimes see 'assets employed' and 'financed by' as two sub-headings. 'Assets employed' will be followed by a list of assets which the business owns, their valuation and a total sum: 'Financed by' will be a breakdown of shareholders' funds and other organisations who have financed the assets of the business.

Now that you have some background knowledge of the balance sheet, the concept of double entry will make some sense to you.

Double Entry

The concept originates from the fact that any business transaction will have two effects. Let us take a look at a series of transactions and note their effect on the balance sheet of a small business

Fern Potteries Ltd. is a small, privately owned business whose balance sheet at the end of the year looked as follows:

Fern Potteries Limited
Balance Sheet as at 31 March 1993

Assets employed	£	£	£
Fixed Assets			
Land		35000	
Buildings		20000	
Plant & equipment	12000		
less depreciation	2000	10000	65000
Current Assets			
Stock	6000		
Debtors	9000		
Cash	2000	17000	
Less Current Liabilities			
Creditors	4000		
Dividends Proposed	2000	6000	11000
NET ASSETS			**76000**
Financed by			
Shareholders' funds			
Ordinary Share Capital			
(30000 shares at £1 per share)		30000	
Retained Profit		28000	58000
Long-Term Liabilities			
Mortgage		12000	
Loans		6000	18000
CAPITAL EMPLOYED			76000

Take the following set of transactions which occur in sequence in the new financial year.

Transaction 1

> £500 cash is received from a debtor
> The double entry is:
> > Cash increases to £2,500
> > Debtors decrease to £8,500
> The 'balance' of the balance sheet is unaltered by this transaction. One use of funds (debtors) has been transferred to a different use of funds (cash).
> The balance sheet equation holds true
> > Assets = Shareholders' Funds + Liabilities
> > £82,000 = £58,000 + £24,000

Transaction 2

> £1,000 is paid to a creditor
> The double entry is:
> > Cash decreased by £1,000 to £1,500
> > Creditors decrease by £1,000 to £3,000
> Once again the 'balance' of the balance sheet is unaltered by this transaction although the total does change.
> > Assets = Shareholders' Funds + Liabilities
> > £81,000 = £58,000 + £23,000

Transaction 3

> An additional loan for £5,000 is taken out to finance an extension to a building.
> The double entry is:
> > Buildings increases by £5,000
> > Loans increase by £5,000
> > Assets = Shareholders' Funds + Liabilities
> > £86,000 = £58,000 + £28,000

Again, the balance sheet balances. There are now more assets in the business; it has grown as a result of lenders providing funds. The shareholders' stake remains unaltered.

Transaction 4

> The proposed dividends of £2,000 are actually paid but, rather than using cash, a separate short-term loan is arranged.
> The double entry reads:
> > Dividends proposed is reduced by £2,000
> > Short-term loan is increased by £2,000
> In this instance, one liability is replaced by another liability, leaving the balance sheet in balance:
> > Assets = Shareholders' Funds + Liabilities
> > £86,000 = £58,000 + £28,000

To summarise:

Transaction 1   Assets +
Assets –

Transaction 2

Assets –
Liabilities –

Transaction 3   Assets +
Liabilities +

Transaction 4   Liabilities +
Liabilities –

Through these four transactions you have looked at the four ways in which assets and liabilities can change, always leaving the balance sheet in balance (source of funds always equals use of funds).

You might like to put this to the test further by thinking of some transactions and trying them out for yourself; try categorising them into one of the four types above.

So far, the transactions looked at have not affected shareholders' funds, yet we know shareholders' funds increase when profits are made and decrease when losses are made. If more shares are issued, then we would also expect to see a change. Let us consider two transactions which illustrate this point.

Transaction 5

The company issues a further 5,000 shares for £1 each.
The double entry is:
Cash increases by £5,000
Ordinary share capital increases by £5,000
Assets = Shareholders Funds + Liabilities
£91,000 = £63,000 + £28,000

Transaction 6

The company sells stock, which it bought for £1,000 to a customer, on credit, for £2,000. On the face of it, this transaction looks the trickiest you have looked at so far, but apply a bit of common sense and all will become clear.

- The business has sold stock – so stock (asset) decreases by £1,000.

- Creditors owe £2,000 for the goods, so creditors (liabilities) increases by £2,000.

- The business has made a profit of £1,000 on the transaction, a profit which is made on behalf of its shareholders. Therefore, retained profits are increased by £1,000.

To summarise, the double entry will be:

Stock decreased by £1,000
Debtors increased by £2,000
Shareholders' Funds increased by £1,000.

The 'balance' now reads:
Assets = Shareholders' Funds + Liabilities
£92,000 = £64,000 + £28,000

So after six transactions the balance sheet would look like this:

Assets employed	£	£	£
Fixed Assets			
Land		35000	
Buildings		25000	
Plant & equipment	12000		
less depreciation	2000	10000	70000
Current Assets			
Stock	5000		
Debtors	10500		
Cash	6500	22000	
Less Current Liabilities			
Creditors	3000		
Short-term Loan	2000	5000	17000
NET ASSETS			**87000**
Financed by			
Shareholders' funds			
Ordinary Share Capital			
(35,000 shares at £1 per share)		35000	
Retained Profit		29000	64000
Long-Term Liabilities			
Mortgage		12000	
Loans		11000	23000
CAPITAL EMPLOYED			**87000**

This balance sheet has been drawn up after six transactions; it might have been drawn up after each transaction. If you are uncertain about how the figures have been reached, try running through each transaction.

Practically no business is required to, or would want to, go through this process, but it is a useful way to learn about the principal of double entry accounting.

As stated earlier, transactions are recorded in individual ledger accounts and at the end of the accounting year balances on these accounts are incorporated into the balance sheet.

Factors Influencing Valuations in the Balance Sheet

Depreciation

Fixed assets are bought for use in a business over a number of years. The value of some fixed assets does not reduce as they age; land and buildings are the usual example of this. Other categories of fixed assets, such as machinery, equipment, vehicles and so on, lose value over a period of years. This lost value is known as *depreciation*. Accountants must always show assets in the balance sheet at *true value*: they must therefore reduce their value on an annual basis. The procedure for accomplishing this is to deduct the annual amount of depreciation from the sales revenue, thus reducing the profit in that year.

Think hard about this and how it affects the 'balance' of the balance sheet in the following way:

- the value of the assets is reduced
- shareholders' funds are reduced, since the profit which is retained is reduced.

Both the value of the assets, and therefore the shareholders' stake in the business, is reduced.

Think about the effect if an asset was *not* depreciated gradually in annual steps over its lifetime. Suppose the cost of a machine, bought for £20,000 with a life expectancy of five years, was simply deducted as an expense in the Profit & Loss account from the profit in a single year. That year's profit would be reduced, before tax, by £20,000, thereby reducing the profits transferred to shareholders' funds by £20,000. Remember that the asset would then be shown in the balance sheet as being worth nothing: thus, in effect, the shareholders would own nothing of value. This is clearly an untruth: the asset *is* worth something. In fact, a fair estimate is that it is worth £16,000 (£20,000 – £4,000). It has lost only £4,000 of its value.

Even intangible assets are depreciated, such depreciation being referred to as *amortisation*. This would apply, for example in the case of the purchase of the right to quarry a piece of land. The right may cost £100,000 but twenty years later it may be virtually worthless since the mineral resources are nearly exhausted. The intangible asset has lost value and, therefore, should have been depreciated over the years of the quarry's useful economic life.

How is depreciation calculated?

There are two methods of calculating depreciation:

- the straight line method.
- the reducing balance method.

Before a depreciation calculation can be performed, the following four pieces of information must be known;

- the original cost of the asset
- the estimated useful life of the asset (how long it is likely to be of productive value to the business)
- the scrap or residual value of the asset (that is, the value at the end of its estimated life)
- the method of depreciation which is to be used: straight line or reducing balance.

Take the same information in order to show the calculations for each method. Suppose a business buys an asset for £10,000. It has an estimated life of five years and a residual value of £1,000.

Using the straight line method

The annual amount for depreciation is found by;

$$\frac{\text{Original cost} - \text{Residual value}}{\text{Estimated life of asset}}$$

In this instance

$$\frac{£10,000 - £1,000}{5} = £1,800 \text{ per annum}$$

Using the reducing balance method

This involves a set percentage being deducted from the value of the asset at the end of each year. The method for deciding the percentage to be applied in the calculation is, at this stage, beyond the scope of your studies. However, the percentage applied will reduce the value to approximately the residual value after the appropriate number of years.

Comparing the two methods

Both methods spread the cost of an asset over its expected life. The difference is in the pattern of the depreciation charge. Straight line depreciation involves spreading the expense of the asset equally over its expected useful life. In contrast, declining balance applies a set percentage to the net book value of assets at each year end. This method produces a higher amount of depreciation in the early part of an asset's life than it does towards the end.

	Straight Line Method		**Reducing Balance Method**
Rate to be applied	£1,800 per annum		40% per annum
	Cumulative depreciation £		Cumulative depreciation £
Cost of Asset Year 1	10,000		10,000
Depreciation Year 1	1,800	(40%)	4,000
Net Book Value	8,200		6,000
Depreciation Year 2	1,800	(40%)	2,400
Net Book Value	6,400		3,800
Depreciation Year 3	1,800	(40%)	1,520
Net Book Value	4,600		2,280
Depreciation Year 4	1,800	(40%)	912
Net Book Value	2,800		1,368
Depreciation Year 5	1,800	(40%)	547
Net Book Value	1,000		821

The reducing balance method more realistically represents the way the value of those goods changes in real life, i.e. most assets lose value at a greater rate soon after they are bought and less as they get older – ask any car owner about this! Also, as an asset grows older, so the cost of repairing and maintaining the asset is likely to increase. By using the reducing balance method, the total expenses (depreciation plus maintenance) are evened out over the life of the asset.

For these reasons, declining balance is often considered a better, more realistic method of depreciation. However, largely as a result of tradition and custom, the majority of businesses in the UK favour using the straight line method.

Revaluing Fixed Assets

Depreciation is *the loss of value of an asset*. The accountant must present a 'true and fair view' of the financial affairs of a business so this loss of value is shown in the balance sheet as 'accumulative depreciation'. But what of those assets that *appreciate*, or increase in value or worth? Surely, the accountant has an obligation to present this fact also? Well, the prudence concept of accounting means that the accountant is wary of showing the increased value of an asset in the balance sheet; that is, unless it could be 'realised' with reasonable certainty. The value of land and buildings in recent years has gone up, at times dramatically so. There have been falls from time to time, but the overall trend has been of increasing land and buildings value. This presents a dilemma to all accountants. Do they revalue the assets nearer their market value, or maintain them at historic cost (the cost when originally purchased)?

Revaluing assets nearer their market value:

- may go against the accounting concept of prudence (discussed later)
- risks the worth of the company being unrealistic if the value of the land and/or buildings subsequently falls.
- increases the worth of the shareholders' stake in the business. Shareholders and lenders effectively 'own', or have claim to, the assets of the business. If the value of those assets increases, then so does the value of shareholders' claims on them and, thereby, their stake in the business.
- may have the effect of dissuading other businesses from mounting a takeover bid. The potential bidders may be interested in business whose assets are undervalued. They may wish to acquire them through a takeover, only to sell them shortly afterwards for their true market value. This process is often referred to as 'asset stripping'.

    Revaluation of fixed assets is shown through their increased value in the balance sheet. This increased value is also added to a 'revaluation reserve' in the shareholders' funds section of the balance sheet. Revaluation of fixed assets is *not* regarded as profit. This is logical since any 'profit' to the shareholders would only be realised if the business were wound up.

Consider an example of this. The example is much oversimplified, but it clearly illustrates the difference the revaluation transaction can make to a balance sheet.

ABC Builders Ltd. have drawn up their balance sheet for the current year. ABC then decides that the revaluation of their premises is long overdue. Land and buildings were bought for £20,000 when the company was formed ten years ago. Since then the demand for land in the area has greatly increased and a conservative estimate puts its present value at £65,000. The balance sheets before and after this transaction can be simplified and seen on the next page.

The revaluation 'reserve' which has been created is not profit, nor is it cash. It simply represents the real worth of the shareholders' stake in the business.

Valuing Stock

As stated and explained earlier in this chapter, in accounts any stock is always valued at *cost or net realisable value.*

In the case of a business which simply buys and sells its goods without 'adding value' to those goods, the stock will be valued at the amount it cost to buy.

In a manufacturing company, value is added to original goods as they travel through the manufacturing process. Thus, by the end of the process, the goods have labour and overheads added as part of their cost. Such costs must be reflected in the value of those goods in the balance sheet.

Net Realisable Value

Sometimes the worth of the stock is less than it cost to buy. In this case, the goods must be shown in the balance sheet at their realisable value.

ABC Builders Ltd
Balance Sheet as at 30 April 1993

	Before Revaluation		After Revaluation	
	£	£		£
Assets employed				
Fixed Assets				
Land and buildings	20000		65000	
Plant and equipment	10000	30000	10000	75000
Current Assets	7000		7000	
less				
Current Liabilities	4000	3000	4000	3000
NET ASSETS		33000		78000
Financed by				
Shareholders' Funds				
Ordinary Share Capital	10000		10000	
Retained profit	18000	28000	18000	
Revaluation reserve			45000	73000
Long-Term Liabilities		5000		5000
CAPITAL EMPLOYED		33000		78000

The reasons for stock being valued at less than cost might be:

- Tastes change – goods are bought into stock with a particular group of consumers in mind. The tastes and preferences of those consumers change, leaving the stock unsaleable even at cost price.
- Physical damage – stock may have been shop-soiled or damaged by the weather. The stock may be saleable (everything has its price), but perhaps at considerably less than the stock cost to buy, or produce.

Stock which has been affected by these factors must be valued in the balance sheet at their *realistic realisable value.*

Identifying Stock

Identifying stock in accounting terms does not refer to physically locating a particular item, or groups of items, in the warehouse or storeroom. It refers to being able to put an accurate value on stock, depending on when the stock was purchased. In times of constant prices, such identification is unnecessary. In times of rising and falling prices, identification becomes important because as you will see shortly, profits are affected by the closing value of goods in stock. There are three main methods of stock identification with which you should be familiar:

1.   First in First Out (FIFO) – this assumes that the first items bought into stock are the first to be sold. The opening stock is used first followed by the earliest purchases, leaving the most recent purchases in stock at the end of the year. This is the usual way of identifying stocks in the UK.

2.   Last in First Out (LIFO) not normally used in the UK. This method assumes that the first items bought into stock are the last to be sold. It is an accounting technique which constantly undervalues the closing stock but ensures that stock sold or issued is at its most recent cost.

3.   Average Cost – a simple method which assumes the value of the closing stock is an average of the cost of the stock received over the accounting period under consideration.

These methods are best looked at through an example.

Consider a garden centre which buys 25kg bags of compost from the manufacturer and sells on to the public. The cost of compost from the manufacturer is £2.50 per bag, but in the month we are to examine the cost of compost rises significantly due to the shortage of supply combined with greatly increased demand. The stock records at the garden centre for the first two weeks in April (a busy time in the gardener's calendar) show the following transactions:

Opening stock: 50 bags at a cost of £2.50 each

Receipts	Number of Bags	Cost per Bag
2 April	100	£2.50
6 April	100	£2.80
9 April	100	£3.00
Total	**300**	
Sales		
Week ending 7 April	150	
Week ending 14 April	150	
Total	**300**	

Total receipts were 300 bags; total sales 300 bags; this left 50 bags in stock at the end of two weeks' trading. Physically the stock may have been rotated; in other words the opening stock of compost would have been sold first and the closing stock would be 50 bags from the last delivery on 9 April. With items such as fresh food in a supermarket's stock rotation is vital if customers are to be guaranteed fresh food and waste is to be minimised. In the case of compost, which has a very long 'shelf life', the physical rotation of stock is much less important. In our example it may well be that the 50 bags in stock at the end of the fortnight are the same bags as those in stock on 1 April.

The valuation of stock is completely independent of the way the stock has been physically rotated and depends entirely on the accounting method used; FIFO, LIFO or average cost.

FIFO Method

Date	Receipt/Sale	Value	Stock	Value
1 April	opening stock		50 @ £2.50	£125
2 April	receipt 100 @ £2.50	£250	50 @ £2.50	
			100 @ £2.50	£375
6 April	receipt 100 @ £2.80	£280	50 @ £2.50	
			100 @ £2.50	
			100 @ £2.80	£655
7 April	sales 150 @ £2.50	£375	100 @ £2.80	£280
9 April	receipt 100 @ £3.00	£300	100 @ £2.80	
			100 @ £3.00	£580
14 April	sales 100 @ £2.80	£280		
	50 @ £3.00	£150	50 @ £3.00	£150

So the closing stock on 14 April is valued at cost: £150. Reading carefully through the transactions above shows that the FIFO method assumes the first items in stock are the first to be issued or sold. The significance of this is that the opening stock is the first to be sold and the closing stock is the most recently received.

LIFO Method

Date	Receipt/Sale		Value	Stock	Value
1 April	opening stock			50 @ £2.50	£125
2 April	receipt 100 @ £2.50		£250	50 @ £2.50	
				100 @ £2.50	£375
6 April	receipt 100 @ £2.80		£280	50 @ £2.50	
				100 @ £2.50	
				100 @ £2.80	£655
7 April	sales	100 @ £2.80			
		50 @ £2.50	£405	100 @ £2.50	£250
9 April	receipt 100 @ £3.00		£300	100 @ £2.50	
				100 @ £3.00	£550
14 April	sales	100 @ £3.00			
		50 @ £2.50	£425	50 @ £2.50	£125

With the LIFO method the closing stock of 50 bags has the same value as the opening stock: £125. This form of accounting assumes that the most recently received stock is the stock which is issued first. The value of the closing stock is out of date, but the value of the stock which has been issued very closely reflects current costs.

Average Cost Method

Date	Receipt/Sale		Value	Stock	Value
1 April	opening stock			50 @ £2.50	£125
2 April	receipt 100 @ £2.50		£250	50 @ £2.50	
				100 @ £2.50	£375
				(average £2.50)	
6 April	receipt 100 @ £2.80		£280	50 @ £2.50	
				100 @ £2.50	
				100 @ £2.80	£655
				(average £2.62)	
7 April	sales	150 @ £2.62	£393	100 @ £2.62	£262
9 April	receipt 100 @ £3.00		£300	100 @ £2.62	
				100 @ £3.00	£562
				(average £2.81)	
14 April	sales	150 @ £2.81	£421.50	50 @ £2.81	£140.50

Average cost is a compromise between LIFO and FIFO. The final value of the stock in this example is £140.50. The process of averaging the value of the stock, and also issues/sales, means the stock valuation is a closer reflection of current costs than that produced by the LIFO method.

The effect on profit

Despite the increasing cost of the compost the garden centre has fixed its price to the customer for the full fortnight at £4.00 per bag. Let's now look at the effect which the method of stock valuation has on profit in such circumstances.

	FIFO		LIFO		Average Cost	
Sales		1200		1200		1200
Opening Stock	125		125		125	
+ Purchases	830		830		830	
	955		955		955	
– Closing Stock	150		125		140	
Cost of Stock Sold		805		830		815
Trading Profit		395		370		385

So, as you can see from the figures, in periods of rising costs, the LIFO method will understate profits. This is because the cost of stock sold is at the most recent cost.

The Profit and Loss Account

To understand fully all of the financial aspects of a business, requires three lots of information. Each lot of information can be found in an accounting document whose purpose is to provide the answers to the questions different categories of people are likely to ask.

The *balance sheet* provides answers to questions about the present; it provides any interested person who can read it with a financial snapshot of the present state of health of the business at a particular instant of time. If read with care, the balance sheet will reveal answers to the following questions: How much money does the business have at the moment? Where is the money at this moment? How safe is it at the moment? How much of it can the business use at this moment?

Having answers to those questions is essential, but that information alone does not provide a full picture of where the business has been and where it is going in the future. Questions about its past and future performances are equally important to ask: What level of revenue has been earned in the past year? What costs and expenses have been incurred? After costs and expenses have been deducted from revenue, has the business made a profit or loss? All of these questions can be answered by gaining an appreciation and understanding of *the profit and loss account.* The *funds flow statement* will also provide useful information in this connection and that document will be examined later in this Part.

Let's look at the profit and loss acount for Advent Cards plc and see how the business has done in the past year.

Advent Cards plc
Profit and Loss Account for the year ended 31 August 1993

1992 £000		£000	£000
33100	Turnover		36400
	Cost of Sales:		
3130	Stock as at 1 September	3620	
25815	Purchases	27860	
28945		31480	
3620	Less: Stock as at 31 August 1992	4180	
25325			27300
7775	Gross Profit		9100
	Less: Expenses		
6110	Wages and Salaries	6612	
75	Heating and Lighting	80	
227	Rates	315	
175	Advertising	155	
100	Motor running expenses	110	
28	Telephone	33	
40	Insurance	47	
320	Depreciation	290	
7075			7642
700	Operating Profit		1458
10	Add: Investment Income		22
710	Profit before Interest and Tax		1480
130	Less: Debenture Interest		130
580	Profit before Tax		1350
165	Less: Provision for Corporation Tax		390
415	Profit after Tax		960
335	Less: Ordinary Share Dividend		505
80	Retained Profit for the year		455

The Profit and Loss Account is headed, and is always stated as being for a specific period of time (for example, *Year ended 31 August 1993*). This means that the Account is a summary of the trading activities of the company for the period commencing on 1 September 1991 and finishing on 31 August 1992. You will notice that the account also shows figures relating to the previous year: this is to enable comparisons to be made between the current year and the previous year.

The top part of the Profit and Loss Account, from turnover to gross profit, is often called the 'Trading' part of the Account. Once this part has been calculated the rest of the Account is relatively straightforward.

Turnover

This is the amount of income derived from selling the product or products in which the company deals. It does not necessarily mean the amount of cash collected, because sales are often made on credit. Income is deemed to arise from sales at the time when the sale is made and not when the cash is received.

Cost of Sales

This figure represents the net cost of buying the products which have been sold during the same period of time, and consists of three basic items:

Opening stock

This is the value of the stock which had not been sold by the end of the previous year, and is therefore part of the cost of goods sold in the current year.

Purchases

This is the cost of buying goods for resale during the current year. Purchases do not include the purchase of any items which are not for resale (such as stationery etc). In some businesses which are involved in manufacturing, purchases will refer to the purchase of materials and components for use in the production process: all other purchases are either an expense or a fixed asset. In businesses which simply buy in and then resell, purchases simply means the expenditure incurred on goods bought for resale.

Closing stock

This is the value of goods bought for resale which have not been sold, and they are thus still held in stock. The value of these goods at cost price is deducted from the purchase figure so that the cost of goods sold equates with the income derived from the sale of those goods. This closing stock will, of course be the opening stock of the following year. As you have seen, it also appears on the balance sheet as an asset.

To summarise, you can see that: opening stock *plus* purchases *minus* closing stock *equals* cost of sales.

Gross Profit

This figure represents the difference between sales revenue (turnover) and cost of goods sold; it is the profit earned on trading, before deduction of other expenses (overheads) essential to the running of the business. It effectively reflects the difference between the selling price and the cost price of the goods being traded.

Expenses

These are the overhead expenses of running the business incurred during the accounting year.

Operating Profit

This is the profit from the usual activities of the business. For example, it does not include income from and expenditure on investments, as these are not part of the normal trading activities of the business.

Investment Income

This is additional income, derived from the investments which the business has made in subsidiaries and such like.

Profit before Interest and Tax

This is the profit which is directly controllable by the management of the business. Rates of interest and levels of taxation are influenced and governed by factors external to the business.

Debenture Interest

This is the annual amount payable to those individuals and organisations which have loaned money to the business through buying debentures.

Provision for Corporation Tax

Corporation Tax is payable on company profits. It is set by the government: the rate may be altered by the Chancellor of the Exchequer, usually in the annual budget statement. The amount is 'provided for' as the actual amount will not become payable until the following year.

Ordinary Share Dividend

Dividends are paid to shareholders from profits. The dividend is usually declared as a percentage or in pence per share.

Retained Profit for the Year

This is profit kept back from the shareholders for reinvestment in the company. It will be used to purchase fixed assets or to increase working capital. The amount will be added to the retained profits for previous years and the updated figure will appear in the balance sheet.

The Funds Flow Statement

The Balance Sheet and the Profit and Loss accounts of a business show, between them, the position with regard to its assets and liabilities at the beginning and at the end of the financial year, and the amount of profit or loss made between those two points. However, the profit and loss account deals with *revenue items only*, taking into consideration sales made on credit for which the cash is still owing, and purchases and other expenses incurred for which the money has not yet been paid. The Balance Sheet *shows the position at two dates only*, and it may not be evident where money has come from, nor in which way it has been spent. In recent years the practice has been to provide an additional statement with the Balance Sheet and Profit and Loss account which summarises the movement of cash in and out of the business. This statement is called the *Source and Application of Funds Statement*, usually simply referred to as the 'Funds Flow Statement'. It is not a substitute for the Balance Sheet and the Profit and Loss account, but is supplementary to them.

The purpose of the funds flow statement is to show where the business has obtained money from during the year and in which areas it has been spent. Normally the statement illustrates this in two parts. The first part shows *the change in working capital between the two balance sheet dates*; the reason for this is that although cash is part of working capital, any increase or decrease in working capital is not necessarily the same as the increase or decrease in cash, because of the changes in debtors, stock, creditors, etc. The second part shows *the changes in the individual components of working capital* and highlights specifically the change in the current liquidity position.

Sources of funds are:

> share capital contributed by the owners
> borrowed capital (debentures, etc)
> net profit before tax
> depreciation
> proceeds of the sale of fixed assets.

Applications of funds are:

> purchase of fixed assets
> repayment of capital or loans (not dividends or interest)
> net losses before tax
> payment of taxes
> payment of dividends.

Most of the above items are easily understood, but the inclusion of depreciation as a source of funds needs further clarification. Depreciation is *not* a cash transaction: the cash was paid out when the equipment was originally bought: to consider the depreciation expense each year as being cash would be to double count. Depreciation has been deducted from Net Profit as a source of funds and to be accurate it must be shown as a source of funds in itself.

One of the major uses of the funds statement is that it links the balance sheet position at the beginning of a trading period, the profit and loss account, and the balance sheet position at the end of the period. To enable this to be easily interpreted the statement should itemise major changes in the position of the company.

To illustrate the funds flow statement we will use the information contained in the account of Advent Cards plc as our model.

Advent Cards plc
Statement of Sources and Application of Funds for the Year Ended 31 August 1993

	£000	£000
Source of Funds		
Net profit before taxation		1350
Depreciation		290
Issue of share capital		750
		2390
Application of Funds		
Purchase of fixed assets	690	
Purchase of investments	100	
Corporation tax paid	165	
Dividends paid	555	1510
Increase (Decrease) in Working Capital		
Increase in stock	560	
Increase in debtors	1050	
Decrease in cash	(65)	
Increase in creditors	(665)	
		880
		2390

Source of Funds for Advent Cards plc

As you can see the profit before taxation was £1,350,000. To that figure you add back depreciation of £290,000. This gives you the flow of funds from profit. After that you show other sources of funds, which in this case is an issue of 1,000,000 ordinary shares of 50p each at a price of 75p each. This makes the total source of funds £2,390,000.

Application of funds for Advent Cards plc

The company has acquired fixed assets costing £690,000 , and has also spent £100,000 on investments (see the balance sheet for the change in figures between 31 August 1992 and 31 August 1993.
Taxation actually paid during the year was £165,000 (the provision for year ended 31 August 1992).

Dividends paid during the year are £555,000 (the £280,000 proposed from the previous year plus the £275,000 already paid as an interim dividend this year). The total of applications is £1,510,000 and deducted from the total sources it shows an increase in working capital of £880,000.

Movement of working capital of Advent Cards plc

The overall movement of working capital is +£880,000.
This is made up of an increase in working capital in:

1. stock of £560,000 (£4,180,000 – £3,620,000)
2. debtors of £1,050,000 (£4,680,000 – £3,630,000)

This is counteracted by a decrease of working capital in:

1. creditors of £665,000 (£4,000,000 – £3,335,000)
2. cash £65,000 (£235,000 – £170,000)

The working capital needs of Advent Cards plc have increased by £880,000 over the year. This has the effect of balancing the sources and applications of funds.

The Notes to the Financial Statements

Certain items will always be found in the notes. These are:

(i)   details of the accounting policies used in the preparation of the Financial Statements. These are the specific methods chosen by the organisation to apply the fundamental accounting concepts, which we discuss later in this Part;
(ii) details of the Balance Sheet items, such as the types of fixed assets owned by the organisation;
(iii) details of the Profit and Loss Account items. For example, it will show Corporation Tax and the notes will show how this charge has been estimated, when it is payable and any corrections due as a result of adjustments to the previous year's provision for Corporation Tax.

The Director's Report

The Director's Report is a statement issued by the Directors of a company to their shareholders. It normally contains:

(i)   a summary of the company's performance for the financial year just ended, and its expected performance in the coming year
(ii) details of the directors of the company and their shareholdings in it
(iii) a statement of the principal activities of the company
(iv) details of the proposed dividend.

The Auditor's Report

Often the shareholders of a company are not the people who run the company. This task falls to the directors and it is their responsibility to prepare the financial statements and present them to the members. The shareholders need to know if the financial statements are a reasonably accurate reflection of the profit the company has made and of its financial position at the balance sheet date. In order to know this, the shareholders appoint an independent qualified person to examine the financial statements and to pass an opinion on them. That independent person is the *auditor*.

The Auditor's Report is an expression of opinion as to the 'truth and fairness' of the financial statements and of the profit of the company. This opinion is based upon an examination of the financial statements and upon various financial tests which have been carried out. Auditor's reports can be 'unqualified', where the auditor states the financial statements show a true and fair view, or they may be 'qualified'. Where the auditor's report is qualified, the auditor will explain those aspects with which he or she is not satisfied and the effect that this has upon the financial statements.

Managing Cash and Working Capital

It is a fact that more British businesses fail because they run out of cash and working capital rather than through lack of profitability.

Most business people are astute enough to know the costs of their business and what they must charge for their product or service in order to cover those costs and also make a profit. The problem arises when money doesn't come in to the business when expected: money needs to be paid out and there is no cash available.

It follows that good cash and working capital management are vital for the survival of any business and a necessity if stable growth in the business is to be achieved. Because of this importance, a student of business must be aware of the distinction between *cost* and *profit* and the implications for a business of this distinction.

Let us look at these from the perspective of a newly-formed and promising business: Anne's Ices.

Anne Robinson formed her business in 1992 after taking voluntary redundancy from her job as a catering lecturer. She had always wanted to run her own business and saw a market opportunity in the sale of special ice cream to traders in nearby seaside holiday resorts. The business was naturally seasonal but Anne had worked hard to develop a good, all year round trade with local restaurants.

She started off the business as a sole trader with £20,000 of her own capital and £15,000 provided by a local bank on the basis of her business plan. The start-up capital was used to secure a lease on a small factory unit, to buy a delivery vehicle, and equip the factory and office with necessary equipment.

The first year went reasonably well and Anne's Ices made a small profit. She felt this was satisfactory and she expected that in the next twelve months the business will expand.

The balance sheet and summarised profit and loss account for the year was as follows:

Anne's Ices
Balance sheet as at 30 June 1993

	£	£
Fixed Assets		
Premises	19000	
Vehicle	7500	
Equipment	4000	
		30500
Current Assets		
Stock	1500	
Debtors	3000	4500
Current Liabilities		
Creditors	300	
Bank Overdraft	200	500
		4000
NET ASSETS		**34500**
Owner's Capital	20000	
+ Retained Profit	500	20500
Loan		14000
CAPITAL EMPLOYED		**34500**

The equipment originally purchased for £5,000 is depreciated over 5 years on a straight line basis.

A vehicle originally purchased for £10,000 is depreciated over 4 years on a straight line basis.

The 20 year lease on the factory, purchased for £20,000, is to be depreciated by £1,000 each year.

Anne's Ices
Profit and Loss Account for year ended 30 June 1993

		£
Sales		**30000**
Opening stock	0	
+ purchases	18000	
– closing stock	1500	16500
Gross Profit		**13500**
Wages	4500	
Business rates	1000	
Depreciation	4500	
Other expenses	600	
Interest on loan	1400	
Loan repayment	1000	13000
Net Profit		**500**

Anne's forecasts for the next 12 months are:

> Monthly Sales will increase
> to £2,500 per month for October – March
> to £3,500 per month from April – September

All sales are made on credit and Anne has agreed to give her customers two months to pay, instead of the one month credit period she operated in her first year. She considers this one of the necessary pains of business growth: it provides an added incentive for buyers to use Anne's Ices.

Purchases will make up 50% of goods sold. Anne has recently negotiated one month's credit from her suppliers, as having been in business for one year they now consider her a better risk. Stock will always be equivalent to one month's sales at cost. Anne intends to increase her wages and take a monthly wage of £750 out of the business.

Monthly expenses will amount to £50. Interest on her loans £100, will be paid monthly and she decides to pay off the loan at the rate of £100 per month.

Business rates are payable quarterly in July, October, January, April: they are £250 per quarter. Anne has agreed with the bank manager a maximum overdraft limit of £500.

Just to check that her budget for the forthcoming year is realistic, she draws up a draft Profit and Loss Account (P&L A/C).

Anne's Ices
Profit and Loss Account for year ended 30 June 1994

			£
Sales			**36000**
Opening stock	1500		
Purchases	18000		
	19500		
– Closing stock	1750		17750
Gross Profit			**18250**
Wages		9000	
Business rates		1000	
Depreciation		4500	
Other expenses		600	
Interest on loan		1200	
Loan repayment		1200	17500
Net Profit			**750**

Even after increasing her own salary for working in the business, Anne feels satisfied as her net profit is increasing by 50%.

However, if a cash flow projection is drawn up, it becomes clear that potentially serious problems lie just around the corner for Anne's Ices.

Anne's Ices Cash Flow Projection July 1993 – January 1994

		July	Aug	Sept	Oct	Nov	Dec	Jan
IN		**1500**	**1500**	**3500**	**3500**	**3500**	**2500**	**2500**
OUT	Purchases	300	1750	1750	1750	1250	1250	1250
	Salary	750	750	750	750	750	750	750
	Interest	100	100	100	100	100	100	100
	Loan Repayment	100	100	100	100	100	100	100
	Expenses	50	50	50	50	50	50	50
	Rates	250			250			250
	Total Out	**1550**	**2750**	**2750**	**3000**	**2250**	**2250**	**2500**
Cash Balance	**–200**	**–250**	**–1500**	**–750**	**–250**	**+1000**	**+1250**	**+1250**

Problem 1

Since Anne's business is expanding, she needs to purchase more stock well in advance of receiving money for the sales. Take August as an example:

Cash In

She will receive cash in from the sales she made in June of the previous accounting year – remember Anne is allowing her debtors two months to pay.

Cash Out

In July she sold goods worth £3,500 (although she will not receive this money until September). Purchases make up 50% of the goods sold, so in July she needed to buy £1,750 of goods. This £1,750 is payable in August, one month after purchase. This time gap between paying suppliers and receiving money from customers is critical to the success or failure of Anne's business.

Other cash out in August totals £1,000.

The net effect of these receipts and payments is that Anne's overdraft leaps to £1,500 – £1,000 more than her authorised limit. Looking at the following months, it takes Anne's Ices until October to get back within her authorised overdraft limit.

So, although profit is acceptable to Anne, the cash flow situation will almost certainly be unacceptable to her bank manager. This highlights the need for businesses to forecast cash flow well ahead, so that if a potential problem arises it can quickly be identified and action taken to remedy it.

Possible actions in Anne's case include:

- showing the cash flow forecast to her bank manager and requesting an increased overdraft limit until the cash flow situation eases in October/November.

- giving incentives to her debtors for early settlement by offering say a 2½% discount for invoices paid within 10 days. This will, however, erode her already slender profit figure.

- sell the debts of the business to a factoring business. In return for a commission the factoring company will pay Anne's invoices immediately on behalf of the debtors, then collect the money at the due date themselves. Once again the commission paid to the factors will erode Anne's profit margins.

- reduce her own wages in the critical months, increasing them later when the cash flow position improves. She may have her own personal commitments, such as a mortgage to pay, which make this course of action impossible.

In many instances, if a cash flow problem is spotted well in advance, it can be managed and the business will survive. However, if it is not seen until it happens, lenders will interpret this as poor financial management and it may well result in a lack of confidence in the business and its subsequent closure.

Problem 2

Anne is making a living from her business and is retaining a small profit for re-investment. Most of the re-investment is taken up by increasing her working capital as the business expands.

However, Anne has overlooked the effects of depreciation on her business. In four years time the book value of her delivery vehicle will be zero – and it will certainly need replacing. Where will the money come from to buy the replacement? Certainly not from profits if they remain at their current level. A bank loan is a possibility, but this would add to the existing loan. As this will not be repaid for several years, interest payments will put further pressure on profit levels.

So, any profits earned must be sufficient to allow for replacement of worn out fixed assets, the purchase of new assets to expand capacity, as well as to meet the increased working capital needs of the business.

Ratio Analysis

Earlier in Part Four you will have read of the individuals and groups who are interested in the financial statements of a business. Although management has access to detailed financial and cost information outsiders have access only to the published reports and accounts. These are based on historical data; what has happened in the past two years is shown in the financial statements and often trends are shown by means of graphs and charts.

Courtaulds plc – *Financial Highlights*

	1990	1991	change
Operating profit	£53.0m	£53.2m	+0.4%
Profit before tax			
Pre exceptional charge	£41.6m	£46.9m	+12.7%
Post exceptional charge	£40.3m	£42.2m	+4.7%
Earnings per share	30.9p	31.1p	+0.6%
Earnings per share pre exceptional charge	32.2p	35.8p	+11.2%
Net dividend per share	12.3p	13.0p	+5.7%
Year - end borrowing	£74.6m	£35.6m	DOWN £39.0m
Gearing	29.6%	14.1%	
Return on capital employed	16.1%	18.3%	

Operating Profit by Business Area

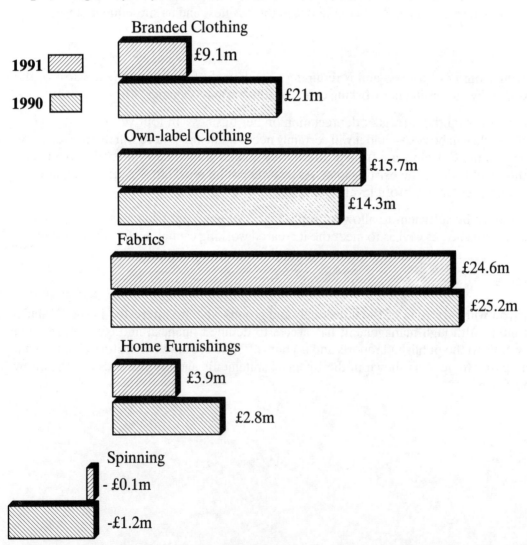

1991

1990

Branded Clothing
£9.1m
£21m

Own-label Clothing
£15.7m
£14.3m

Fabrics
£24.6m
£25.2m

Home Furnishings
£3.9m
£2.8m

Spinning
- £0.1m
-£1.2m

Though company accounts are not overprinted in the same way as cigarette packets, with a public health warning about their contents, there is a case for doing so: you consume them at your own risk. In recent years the accuracy and veracity of accounting systems and statements has come under increased scrutiny. The financial statements of companies are often the only basis upon which investors and lenders make their investment decisions. However, the recent experience of investors in businesses such as Polly Peck, the Bank of Credit and Commerce International (BCCI) and the Maxwell Communication Corporation (MCC) has led to a call for the re-appraisal of what constitutes sound accounting practices.

At the time of writing, the Accounting Standards Board (ASB) has been drawing up proposals that are intended to tighten corporate reporting procedures and lead to a 'new look' balance sheet and profit and loss account. Amongst the ASB's provisional recommendations which are likely to be adopted are:

- the *quality* of a company's earnings must be reported as well as the *quantity* – extraordinary items will no longer be permitted to appear in the profit and loss account without a qualifying note
- the abuse of capital instruments, for example the disguising of company debt as 'share capital', will be prohibited
- the earnings per share ratio must be shown *after* all extraordinary costs are charged and not before they are charged.

The proposal for a qualitative breakdown of the profit and loss account is intended to make accounts more accessible by focussing on a business's organic growth and growth through acquisitions. The minimum requirement is for a split of turnover, operating profit (profit before interest) and exceptional items into categories for continuing operations, acquisitions and discontinued operations.

The way in which capital instruments (various forms of shares, debentures and loans) are accounted for is also expected to change, considerably altering the look of the balance sheet:

- capital instruments, other than shares and warrants, will be treated as liabilities
- convertible debt will be separately disclosed as a liability until such time as it is converted
- shares which have a restricted dividend entitlement, or are redeemable, will not be treated as equity.

Though the ASB proposals, if adopted, will no doubt strengthen reporting procedures, would-be investors should still be aware of the shortcomings of the system. Consider its weaknesses and deficiencies, what it leaves unreported as well as what it reports:

- the nature of information contained in accounts can be unreliable (and selective).
- a potential investor is well advised to corroborate evidence before drawing any conclusions from reported information.
- the reported information doesn't necessarily show the potential that a business has or necessarily highlight any of its intrinsic problem.
- it needs to be compared objectively with the previous year's accounts – and not necessarily in the same way that the business itself would carry out that comparison.
- it doesn't give a comparison with other companies in the same industry.
- accounts don't indicate market share or the attitudes and loyalty of customers.

- accounts don't include the experience, expertise and ability of the workforce (including management); the most important resource of the business doesn't occur in the balance sheet.

- financial information concerns the past and present: it doesn't look to the future economic climate.

What is a ratio?

A ratio is a measure of the relative size of two numbers expressed as a proportion. You will understand what is meant if a teacher says to you, "The ratio of boys to girls in my class is 2 to 1 (2 : 1)". The ratio states the *proportion* of girls to boys in the class.

The same principle is used in business. Ratio analysis is useful as a technique that allows comparison between figures in accounts or between the same figure in different sets of accounts; it is a tool that helps you to judge the financial performance of a business. Since a ratio is *a comparison of one piece of financial data with anothe*r, it can be expressed appropriately as a percentage, a proportion or as a ratio. The following example may illustrate this.

You will know that if you deposit £100 in a building society you may receive £8 interest at the end of the year. This can be expressed as a performance indicator on your savings in the following way:

$$\frac{\text{Interest paid}}{\text{Money invested}} \qquad \frac{£8}{£100} \qquad \times \quad 100 = 8\%$$

Therefore, you find that you are getting an 8% return on your savings. Is this a good return? The answer to such a question depends on the rate of return you might get if you invested your money elsewhere, as well as on a number of other important considerations. With your money in the building society you know that it is safe, so you may be willing to accept a lower rate of return than you might receive on a more risky investment. A further consideration might be that you were able to get 10% from the same building society last year before interest rates fell, so you are less satisfied with your 8% now. These, and other factors, will influence your feelings as to whether or not you are getting a good return, but in each case you are using a *performance ratio indicator* to make a judgment. Businesses use similar ratios to measure their performance and in the next section we will examine some of them.

Consider the financial statements of Advent Cards plc to illustrate the points we are making. You should refer to the Balance Sheet and the Profit and Loss Account of Advent Cards plc to examine and calculate the ratios as they are explained.

Accounting and financial ratios are often grouped in the following way:

- Performance measures
- Liquidity measures
- Investment measures.

Performance Measures

Return on capital employed or return on net assets

You have already noted how the capital invested in a business can come from a number of sources. For sole traders and partnerships, the money usually comes from the owners themselves. This will be either from their own savings or from borrowing, normally from a bank. In a limited company, the capital consists of share capital provided by the shareholders plus reserves. In the case of a small private company there may be only a few shareholders, whilst in a large public company there may be hundreds or thousands of investors.

Wherever the initial investment comes from, all persons or institutions providing it have similar objectives – they wish to see a return on the money which they have invested in the business. The prime means of assessing this is by *the return on capital employed*.

If you understand the 'balance' of the balance sheet, discussed earlier in this Part, you will know that capital employed in the business (*source* of funds) can only be used to provide fixed assets and working capital (*use* of funds). Fixed assets and working capital are collectively referred to as *net assets*.

Capital employed always equals net assets so, whatever you call this ratio, the calculation remains the same.

$$\frac{\text{Operating profit}}{\text{Capital employed}} \times 100 \qquad\qquad \frac{\text{Operating profit}}{\text{Net assets}} \times 100$$

Operating profit is *the profit which a company has made before charging interest and tax.*

Capital employed is *shareholders' funds plus long term liabilities.*

Net assets is *fixed assets plus working capital* (current assets - current liabilities).

There are other ways of doing this calculation, but it is usually sufficient to understand one thoroughly. Once this one has been mastered and understood, further reading will introduce you to others.

Return on capital employed for Advent Cards plc

1992	1993
$\dfrac{£700,000}{£6,205,000} \times 100 = 11.3\%$	$\dfrac{£1,458,000}{£7,410,000} \times 100 = 19.7\%$

The return on capital employed or net assets for Advent Cards plc for 1993 is 19.7%. Expressed a different way, this means for every £1 which has been invested in the business, through equity and debt capital, 19.7 pence has been earned before interest and tax. This figure is not what is paid out in cash; it is the return on the total sum of money in the business; some of the 'return' will be retained for reinvestment in the business.

Whether or not this is a good return can only be determined by comparing it with returns for other companies, or with its own returns for earlier years.

Profit margin

Profit margin is calculated by expressing *operating profit as a percentage of sales turnover;* it is used to compare:

- the results of one time period against another
- the results of one business against another
- the results of one particular business against the standard for that type of business.

The calculation is:

$$\frac{\text{Operating profit}}{\text{Sales turnover}} \quad \times \quad 100$$

This can then be used as a basis of comparison with the margin earned in earlier accounting periods. If there are any major deviations from earlier years, then these should be investigated. The major causes of decreases in profit margin are:

- increases in costs or expenses without a corresponding increase in selling price.

The best way to illustrate this is by looking at an individual item; for example, an apple. Suppose apples cost a greengrocer 40p per kilo to buy and they were sold for £1 per kilo. The profit margin is 60%. If the cost was to rise to 50p per kilo, but the greengrocer was unable to increase selling price, then the profit margin would fall to 50%.

- decreased selling prices without a corresponding decrease in costs.

Increases in profit margins are brought about by the reverse of the above events happening.

Profit margin can be used to compare one business with another – providing both carry out the same type of business. It would be pointless for a bakery business to compare its returns with those of a car dealer or a petrol company since they will have vastly different profit margins. Generally speaking, the more rapid is the turnover, then the lower is the profit margin. Hence the petrol company may only get a profit margin of, say, 5% against the car dealer's 60%. The former gets its profit from the rapid turnover of petrol, whereas the latter will have to hold large volumes of stock of very slow turnover goods, so that when a sale is made a larger margin is needed to compensate for the slowness of that turnover.

Profit margin for Advent Cards plc

1992	1993
$\dfrac{£700,000}{£33,100,000} \quad \times \quad 100 = 2.1\%$	$\dfrac{£1,458,000}{£36,400,000} \quad \times \quad 100 = 4.0\%$

The Advent Cards plc Profit and Loss Account for the year ended 31 August 1993 shows that the company had an operating profit of £1,458,000 and that this profit was earned on a sales revenue of £36,400,000. In other words, for every £1 of goods sold, an operating profit of 4p was made.

It is worth noting at this point that it is possible to express any expense item in the Profit and Loss Account as a percentage of sales revenue. For example, if you wished to find the percentage of sales revenue spent on advertising, you know that sales are £1,458,000 and the advertising expenditure is £155,000; the percentage will be 0.4% (1991 – 0.5%). Thus, in the current trading year, every 4p spent on advertising generated £10 in sales. You can use similar calculations to show wages/sales ratio, or any other ratio you need to calculate, in order to assess whether any element of cost is excessive and requires monitoring.

Asset turnover

This ratio measures the use that has been made of the business's assets in producing the levels of the sales. In other words, has the capital employed – which has financed the business assets – been fully utilised in the period? It is normally expressed, not as a percentage, but as a turnover of capital. A very low turnover of capital would indicate that the business has not produced a great level of sales in comparison to the amount of capital it holds. It is calculated simply by *comparing the sales revenue with the capital employed.* So, if an engineering company has the capital of £300,000, which is represented by plant and machinery and earns sales figures of £900,000, you can say that it has a turnover of capital of 'three times'. Note that this is *not* given as a percentage but as a *multiple of the capital employed.*

Asset turnover for Advent Cards plc

1992

$$\frac{£33,100}{£6,205} = 5.3 \text{ times}$$

1993

$$\frac{£36,400}{£7,410} = 4.9 \text{ times}$$

The Relationship between the Three Performance Measures

You have just examined three important ratios

- the return on capital employed
- profit margin;
- asset turnover.

All three ratios are concerned with the profitability of the business and the rate of return on capital invested. In fact, all three are interlinked. The return on capital is determined by the relationship between the net profit to sales and the turnover of capital. Using the following example, this relationship can be illustrated.

Assume that a business has a profit of £100,000, sales of £1,600,000 and capital employed of £800,000.

From the previous example you can see the *interdependency* of the ratios. Clearly, an increase or decrease of profit, capital employed or sales, will influence the others.

However, it also means that you find similar returns on capital employed in industries operating on very different profit margins. So, for example, food retailing, which has a rapid turnover and very competitive prices, may have a profit margin of only 3% or 4%. However, it has a high asset turnover because of the high volume of trade, so the low profit margin of 3%– 4% may be compensated for by an asset turnover of 5 times which would give a return on capital employed of 15% –20%.

Alternatively, a manufacturing industry might expect a profit margin of about 8%–10% but, because of the relatively long time required to produce each individual product, may have a comparatively low asset turnover of 1.5 giving a return on capital employed of between 12% and 15%. As you can see, a potential investor would be well advised to scrutinise carefully all of these ratios before determining where to place his investments.

Liquidity Measures

You have seen that a business must attempt to maintain its profitability if it is to provide a satisfactory return to those who have provided it with capital. However, in order to survive it must also remain solvent and to ensure that this is done, it becomes necessary to keep a close watch on its short-term liquidity position. This means asking whether the business has the ability to pay its immediate debts; that is, whether or not it is 'liquid'.

A business can easily become insolvent and, as a consequence, find itself being wound up. Its employees will expect to be paid and certain creditors, such as landlords or suppliers of materials, may be unwilling to give the business any degree of extended credit. If the business cannot get credit from its suppliers, or from the bank, then it may be unable to produce and may be forced to close. Thus it is important that a business has some means of assessing its liquidity position and to do this it can use two ratios:

- current ratio
- liquidity (acid test) ratio.

Current Ratio

The current ratio expresses the relationship between the *current assets* and the *current liabilities* of a business. Current liabilities are those liabilities which have to paid within a short period of time. The funds available to meet them are contained within the current assets: first, as cash in hand and at the bank (the most liquid of current assets); next as debtors (the next most liquid of current assets) on the grounds that debtors are the next in line to produce the cash; finally, as stock (generally the least liquid of current assets). The latter will take longer to turn into cash because it has to be sold first; then the money represented by the sale has to be collected from the debtors. One possible exception to this is if the business is the type which has a large proportion of its sales made on a cash basis. If it is, then cash will obviously be collected at the time the stock is sold.

Current ratios are always expressed in ratio format; that is, as 'something' to 1 (for example, 5 : 1). The current ratio is expressed as:

Current Assets : Current Liabilities

The current liabilities should always be represented by the '1'. The ratio is calculated by dividing both sides of the equation by the current liabilities. For example, a business with current assets of £7500 and current liabilities of £5,000 would have a current ratio of £7,500 : 5000 or 1.5 : 1.

It is difficult to generalise about what is an acceptable current ratio but any business would be very wary of having a ratio which was less than 1 : 1, since such a ratio would mean that current liabilities exceeded current assets and the business may not be able to pay its immediate debts. However, it is almost as bad to have a current ratio which is too high, since this might mean that too much cash was tied up in stocks, or that the debtors were taking too long to pay. Most business would, therefore, be satisfied with a current ratio of between 1.3 : 1 and 2.5 : 1.

Current ratio for Advent Cards plc

At 31 August 1993 Advent Cards plc has current assets of £9,030,000 and current liabilities of £4,620,000 and so its current ratio is

1.95 : 1

At 31 August 1992 the ratio was

1.98 : 1

There has been little change in the ratio over the two years, and the company looks to be reasonably solvent in that the current liabilities are covered by current assets about two times.

Liquidity ratio

The liquidity ratio is expressed as *liquid current assets* (current assets excluding stock) to *current liabilities*, and as with current ratio, is expressed as 'something' to 1, with the current liabilities being expressed as the '1'. This ratio is often described as the quick assets ratio, or 'acid' test. It has earned this name because it is a much more stringent test of a business's solvency, since it leaves stock out of the equation, the reason being that stock takes longer than any other current asset to convert into cash. In other words, it is better at revealing how much ready money will be available when the creditors are queuing at the door. 'Ready money' here includes all available cash, short-term investments, such as government stock or shares which can be quickly cashed in, and debtors who can be pressed for payment. It is expressed as follows

Current Assets (less stock) : Current liabilities
or
Debtors and Cash balances : Current liabilities

Some businesses can operate with a liquidity ratio of less than 1; in other words, with current liabilities exceeding available liquid assets. This can happen if a business has a bank overdraft facility which is not at its limit and can be drawn on at short notice. It may also be possible to relieve a short-term liquidity crisis by re-scheduling the debt and paying off short-term loans with longer-term credit. In the case of Advent Cards plc, the current assets excluding stock are £4.85 million (31/8/91 £3.865m), current liabilities are as used before in calculating the current ratio; that is 4.62m (31/8/91 £3.78m). The liquidity ratios are, therefore,

At 31 August 1993 1.05 : 1
At 31 August 1992 1.02 : 1

In both cases the ratios indicate that the company is, and has been, reasonably solvent in that its immediate liabilities are covered just about equally by quick assets. When looking at liquidity ratios it is well to note that you are measuring the liquidity at a particular point in time (the date of the balance sheet from which the ratio is taken), but this gives us no idea of the time element involved in:

a.   converting stock and debtors into cash; and

b.   payments being made to the creditors of the company.

You can, therefore, use a further series of ratios which will give an indication of the time-span involved in the cashflow. These are

- Stock turnover (cash in)
- Debtors turnover (cash in)
- Creditors turnover (cash out).

Stock turnover

This can be expressed in two inter-related ways:

a.   the number of times the average stock is turned over (or 'moved') in a trading period (usually 1 year)

b.   the length of time it takes (in days) to turn over the average stock.

To determine the stock turnover ratio, you need to know *the average stock figure*, which can usually be determined by adding the opening stock to the closing stock and dividing the result by two; and also the *cost of sales figure*, which can be obtained from the Profit and Loss Account.

For example if a business had sales of £6,000,000, an opening stock of £40,000, purchases of £460,000 and a closing stock of £50,000, then the cost of sales would be £40,000 + £460,000 – £50,000 = £450,000. The stock turnover is therefore:

$$\frac{£450,000}{£45,000} \quad = \quad 10 \text{ times}$$

This means that the average stock is turned over (sold) 10 times in one year. This can then be expressed in days by dividing 365 by 10 to give 36.5 days. This means that, in 36 or 37 days, the money tied up in stocks will be released by the sale of that stock. It does *not* mean that there will be no stock left after 36 or 37 days, as any stock sold will be replaced by new purchases, which then become part of the next cycle. Neither does it mean that the actual cash represented by the stock will be available for the payment of creditors, because if the sales are made on credit terms, there will be a further delay before the cash is finally collected.

Stock turnover for Advent Cards plc

1992		1993	
$\dfrac{£25,325,000}{£3375}$	= 7.5 times	$\dfrac{£27,300,000}{£3,900}$	= 7 times

It should be made clear that the higher the stock turnover rate, the sooner profit is earned on the stock sold. Therefore, a business with a high stock turnover is able to operate on lower profit margins. In essence, the profit is determined by the speed of turnover. Businesses with a quick turnover, such as petrol filling stations and fruit and vegetable shops, can still make acceptable profits with low profit margins. On the other hand, a slower stock turnover rate means that higher margins must be earned when stock is finally sold, to compensate for the slower turnover. For example, a car dealer, who must carry high stocks to attract customers, may have a low stock turnover rate, but relies on higher profit margins.

You should also note that it is *the cost price* of stock which is used in the calculation of the stock turnover rate and *not* the price at which it is sold. This is because the selling price would include the profit margin and any other costs incurred in the sale, whilst this ratio is concerned about how often the stock is replaced at cost price.

Debtors Turnover

This is very similar to the stock turnover in the method of its calculation, in so far as it expresses the relationship between sales on credit and the debtors arising from those sales. As with the stock turnover figure, you may express it either as the number of times the average debtors are turned over in a year, or as the number of days it will take to collect the average debt. Since the *age* of debts is important, it is preferable to express the debtors turnover ratio in terms of days. The equation is therefore as follows:

$$\frac{\text{Average Debtors}}{\text{Credit Sales}} \quad \times \quad 365 \quad = \quad \text{Number of days}$$

Carrying on the example which we used as the stock turnover figures, if the debtors at the start of the year had been £90,000 and at the end of the year £110,000, the average for the year would be £100,000. If the whole of the sales of £600,000 had been on credit, the debtors turnover ratio would be:

$$\frac{£100,000}{£600,000} \quad \times \quad 365 \quad = \quad 61 \text{ days}$$

This means that, from the figures given, it will take on average 61 days to collect the average debts once. However: this does *not* mean that nothing will be collected for 61 days and then all outstanding debtors from 61 days ago suddenly pay up. What it *does* mean is that, even though money comes in from debtors daily, it will normally be 61 days before all the debtors represented by a debtors figure will have finally cleared their debts. In the meanwhile, new debtors will continue to be created by the act of making further sales to them on credit terms.

The debtors turnover for Advent Cards plc is as follows:

1992		1993	
$\frac{£3.63m}{£33.1m} \quad \times \quad 365 = 40 \text{ days}$		$\frac{£4.68m}{£36.4m} \quad \times \quad 365 = 47 \text{ days}$	

Now we can see that if we add the debtors collection period of 47 days to the stock turnover period of 52 days, we can say that it will be 99 days before the average cash tied up in stock (at 31/8/92 £4.18m) will be recovered and that it will be 47 days before the current level of debtors will be converted back into liquid funds (cash). In other words, we have established a speed of cash flow into the business, which we can compare with earlier years, and also with the speed of cash outflow.

In retail outlets, such as supermarkets and department stores, which mainly deal on a cash over the counter basis, the turnover rate will be more important than the debtors turnover rate, because credit sales will tend to be a very small proportion of the total sales. However, even retail outlets can have substantial debtors, particularly if they accept credit cards, such as Access or Barclaycard from their customers, or as is the tendency nowadays, if they issue their own credit cards.

Creditors Turnover

In the examples above we have considered the length of time it takes a business to receive money from its debtors. However, it is important to recognise that there are two sides to the picture and it is more than likely that the business itself is taking time to pay its creditors. The length of time taken to pay creditors can be calculated in the same way as the debtors turnover. The figures used in the calculation will be *creditors* and *credit purchases* made during the year:

$$\frac{\text{Creditors}}{\text{Purchases}} \qquad \times \qquad 365 \qquad = \qquad \text{Number of days}$$

Creditors turnover for Advent Cards plc

1992	1993
$\dfrac{£3.335m}{£25.815m} \times 365 = 47 \text{ days}$	$\dfrac{£4.0m}{£27.86m} \times 365 = 52 \text{ days}$

At this point it is worth making a comparison between the stock and debtors turnover figures and the creditors turnover figure for Advent Cards plc. As we saw earlier, the stock turnover for the business was 52 days. In other words, the average item of stock stays on Advent Cards' shelves for 52 days. Yet, as we have seen, the creditors turnover for 1993 is also 52 days. This means that the creditors are, in effect, being paid at the same time the stock is sold to customers. This may place a strain on the company's cashflow as the outflow to creditors is quicker than the inflow from customers, as the debtors turnover rate is a further 47 days. Effectively, what is happening is creditors are being paid almost twice as quickly as cash is being received from sales and this could lead to liquidity problems arising in future. However, it should be recognised that each sale should earn a profit for the company above the cost of the purchase, which means that when cash is finally collected, it will be more than was expended. This, coupled with the fact that cash is continually being collected from earlier sales, will keep the company buoyant for some time. Nevertheless, steps should be taken to narrow the gap between the two turnover rates, perhaps by decreasing the stock levels or by chasing up debtors to get them to pay more promptly. What should be avoided is the necessity to increase the delay in settling creditors, as this could only result in the company gaining a reputation as a poor credit risk.

Investment Measures

Having looked at the main accounting ratios used to measure the performance and the liquidity position of a business, it will now be of benefit to look at some ratios which are used by those investors who have no interest in running the business, but who spread their money around and look for the best returns they can get. This type of investor is looking for a good return in terms of income from, and also capital appreciation of, the investment.

Some of the ratios which may help investors to make the correct decisions about how and where to place their money are:

- earnings per share
- earnings yield
- price/earnings ratio
- dividend per share and dividend yield
- dividend cover.

Earnings per share

When the profit of a limited company is finally determined in respect of a particular financial year, there are certain claims (*appropriations*) made on that profit. The first claim is by the Inland Revenue in respect of Corporation Tax. After tax is provided for, the remainder of the profit is available for the ordinary or 'equity' shareholders.
This amount is divided by the number of ordinary shares issued to give the earnings per share ratio.

$$\frac{\text{Profit after tax}}{\text{Number of ordinary shares}} = \text{Earnings per share (EPS)}$$

This figure shows a shareholder exactly how much the company has earned for him or her after all other claims have been met.

Care must be taken when calculating this ratio, since it is the number of shares which have been issued which is used. A company with an issued capital of £50,000 may have 50,000 shares of £1 each, 100,000 shares of 50p each or 500,000 shares of 10p each.

Note that the key phrase is 'earned for', which means that during the year the company has accumulated a sum of money for its shareholders from its trading activities. It does not mean that this amount is actually paid to shareholders, because the company may wish to retain some profit for expansion or for some other purpose. The amount actually paid to shareholders is described as the 'dividend', which is usually expressed as a percentage of the issued share capital; so a dividend of £8,000 on an issued share capital of £80,000 would be expressed as a dividend of 10%, or 10p per £1 share or 5p per 50p share.

The EPS for Advent Cards plc for 1991 and 1992 would therefore be as follows:

1992		1993
$\dfrac{£415,000}{5,000,000}$ = 8.3p		$\dfrac{£960,000}{6,000,000}$ = 16p

Earnings Yield

Rarely will the nominal value of a share be the same as its *market value*. The latter is the price at which the share will change hands on the market, and is determined by a number of factors, such as the value of a company's net assets as represented by ordinary share capital plus reserves, its performance in terms of profitability, and other market forces. For instance, if a company has an issued ordinary share capital of £50,000 and reserves of £50,000, its net worth can be expressed as £100,000. If the nominal value of its ordinary shares is £1, each share could be worth £2 on the market, determined by the balance sheet value of the company.

A more accurate picture of the relationship between earnings and investment is obtained by expressing the earnings per share as a percentage of the market value of the share. This is calculated by using the following formula:

$$\frac{\text{Earnings per share}}{\text{Market value of share}} \times 100 = \text{Percentage yield}$$

For example, if a company has an issued share capital of £100,000 in ordinary shares of 50p, and reserves of £50,000, it has a balance sheet value of £150,000 which (using the above criteria) gives a market value of 75p per share. If it earned an after tax profit of £30,000, the earnings per share would be:

$$\frac{£30,000}{200,000} = \text{15p per share}$$

The earnings yield would be:

$$\frac{15p}{75p} \times 100 = 20\%$$

This means that, if you were thinking of investing in that particular company, you would receive a return in terms of earnings (not dividends) of 20% on the cost of your investment (the amount you would have had to pay for it on the market). To determine whether this is a good or a bad investment, you would have to compare it with the earnings yield figures from other companies or the yields from this company in earlier years.

For Advent Cards plc, in order to work out the earnings yield, we have to assume a market price for the ordinary shares. Based on the level of reserves, this could be £1.10 per share, so this is the market price which we will work on. The earnings yield now becomes:

$$\frac{16p}{110p} \quad \overset{1993}{\times} \quad 100 \ = 14.5\%$$

Price/Earnings Ratio

This is the relationship between *the market price of the share and its earnings,* and is in fact the earnings yield ratio inverted, the formula being:

$$\frac{\text{Market value of share}}{\text{Earnings per share}} \quad = \quad \text{Price/Earnings Ratio}$$

In the example used above, the P/E ratio will be calculated as follows:

$$\frac{75p}{15p} \quad = \quad 5 \text{ times}$$

This means that, on current figures, it will take 5 years to recover in earnings the price that would have to be paid for the share. Obviously there is a relationship between the P/E ratio and the earnings yield. In effect, the higher the P/E ratio, the lower the yield and therefore the less favourable are the prospects for an investor.

Generally speaking, the lower the P/E ratio the better it is to invest in that particular share. It may mean, however, that the share is undervalued by the market and since other factors, not necessarily highlighted by the above ratios, may influence the share's valuation, further enquiries should be made before making a decision to invest. Other examples of the relationship between the P/E ratio and the earnings yield are:

P/E Ratio 10:   Earnings Yield 10%
P/E Ratio 8:   Earnings Yield 12.5%
P/E Ratio 20:   Earnings Yield 5%

You will notice that, as a check, the P/E ratio multiplied by the earnings yield always equals 100.

The P/E ratio for Advent Cards plc is:

$$\frac{110p}{16p} \quad \overset{1993}{=} \quad 6.875 \text{ times}$$

Dividend Per Share and Dividend Yield

For most investors the dividend per share, and subsequently the dividend yield, are probably more important ratios than the earnings ones already discussed. This is because these particular ratios measure exactly what the shareholder receives in the pocket from the investment. Dividend per share is calculated by dividing the *total ordinary share dividend (paid and proposed for the year) by the number of ordinary shares issued,* and expressing the result as *X*p per share. Alternatively, the dividend may be expressed as a percentage of the issued ordinary share capital by using the formula:

$$\frac{\text{Dividends paid and proposed}}{\text{Ordinary share capital}} \quad \times \quad 100$$

Leading on from this, as with the earnings ratios above, it is easy to calculate the dividend yield, which represents the actual return that an investor would receive in the pocket if he purchased the shares at the current market price. As with the earnings ratios, the calculation of dividend yield is: dividend per share divided by the market price of the share, multiplied by 100, and expressed as a percentage.

For Advent Cards plc the dividend per share is:

1993

$$\frac{£505,000}{5,000,000} \quad = \quad \text{8.4p per share}$$

This represents a dividend rate of 16.8%, since the ordinary shares have a value of 50p each.

Using the same assumed market share value of 110p

The dividend yield for Advent Cards plc is:

$$\frac{8.4p}{110p} \quad \times \quad 100 \quad = 7.6\%$$

The above figures mean that for every share held by an investor in Advent Cards plc a shareholder will receive 8.4p (or 16.8% of the nominal value of the share) in dividend, which represents a yield of 7.6% on the current market price of the share.

Dividend Cover

Another important aspect of investment is *capital growth*, and anyone who is looking to invest in a company will wish to see how much of the company's profits, after tax and preference dividend has been provided for, is retained by the company for expansion and growth. This can be done by calculating the dividend cover, which is effectively the number of times the dividend is covered by the profit available out of which the dividend is to be paid. For example if a company with an issued ordinary share capital of £500,000, earns a profit after tax of £100,000, out of which a dividend of 10% (£50,000) is paid, the dividend cover is 2 (£100,000 divided by £50,000). In other words, the company is keeping half of the available profit for expansion and distributing half of it to its shareholders as dividend. If the dividend had been, say, 5% (£25,000), the cover would have been 4 (£100,000 divided by £25,000).

Dividend cover shows the relationship between *earnings per share and dividend per share*, which is perhaps best illustrated by referring to Advent Cards plc. In that company the profit after tax was £960,000: this was the amount available for ordinary shareholders. Since they received a dividend of £505,000 the cover can be calculated as:

1993

$$\frac{£960,000}{£505,000} \quad = 1.9 \text{ times}$$

Generally speaking, the higher the dividend cover the better the retention (growth) policy, but, unless profits are very high, it will probably mean a smaller dividend per share, with a correspondingly smaller yield. An investor looking for growth would probably be quite happy with that situation, but one looking for good short-term returns would not be.

Capital Gearing

No section on interpretation of accounts would be complete without discussing capital gearing. We have already seen that capital can be raised from different sources. These are loans, preference shares, and ordinary shares plus reserves (equity). The first two carry fixed rates of interest and dividend, whilst the latter receive what is left, so if profits are not very high they will receive very little but, if profits are high, they stand to gain quite substantially. For this reason, the ordinary share capital is classed as the *risk taking capital*.

Gearing shows the relationship *between equity capital and fixed interest/dividend bearing capital* and can be expressed as:

$$\frac{\text{Loan capital} + \text{preference share capital}}{\text{Ordinary share capital} + \text{reserves}}$$

expressed in ratio format similar to the liquidity ratios discussed earlier,

or:

$$\frac{\text{Loan capital} + \text{preference share capital}}{\text{Total capital (Loan} + \text{preference} + \text{equity})} \times 100$$

expressed as a percentage that the fixed interest/dividend bearing capital bears to the total capital.

A company is said to be highly geared when the fixed interest/dividend bearing capital is high in relation to its equity capital. If the ratio is high, it indicates a higher geared company than one with a lower ratio (2 : 1 is high geared; 1 : 3 is low geared).

Suppose we have the following capital structures for three separate, but similar, companies:

	Company A	Company B	Company C
	£000	£000	£000
15% Debentures	1,000	500	200
10% Preference Shares	1,000	500	200
Ordinary Shares	500	1,000	1,500
Reserves	500	1,000	1,100
Total Capital	3,000	3,000	3,000
Gearing (%)	66.67	33.33	13.33
	High		Low

Suppose each of the three companies makes a net profit of £300,000 after tax, but before interest and dividends are paid. The distribution (share out) of that profit would be as follows:

Debentures interest	150	75	30
Preference dividend	100	50	20
Balance remaining for ordinary shareholders	50	175	250
Return on equity to shareholders as a percentage of capital invested	5%	8.75%	9.6%

Note that the return to shareholders is fairly small in all three companies, but that the lower the gearing, the better returns are made on investment in risk capital.

Now see what happened using exactly the same capital structures as above. With a net profit of £400,000 after tax, and before interest and dividends are paid, the amount available for ordinary shareholders is:

In £000s	150	275	350
% Return on equity	15%	13.75%	13.46%

If the profits were £500,000 the respective figures would now be as follows:

Profit available £000s	250	375	450
% Return on equity	25%	18.75%	17.3%

From the above, you can see that, as profits get higher, in a highly geared company, the returns to ordinary shareholders get progressively better than they do in a lower geared company. This means that a highly geared company offers more risk to its ordinary shareholders than does a low geared one, because there is a higher prior claim on profits, which must be met before any consideration is given to its ordinary shareholders. Put another way, 'the greater the fluctuation in profits is from one year to another, the greater will be the fluctuation in returns to ordinary shareholders in a highly geared company. In lower geared companies the returns to ordinary shareholders are steadier, even in times of fluctuating profits. To sum up: the rewards for ordinary shareholders can be very good in a highly geared company, but they must be prepared to take small returns when profits are low.

The gearing ratio for Advent Cards plc at 31 August 1992

$$\frac{£1,280,000 \text{ (debentures)}}{£7,410,000 \text{ (total capital)}} \times 100 = 17.3\%$$

This is quite low.

Finally, it must be said that the use of accounting ratios must be tempered with common sense. It is all too easy to come to incorrect conclusions, using accounting information, without balancing it against other business information which may be available. Accounting ratios are very useful tools for the measurement and comparison of profitability, solvency and the investment potential of a business, but care must be taken not to jump to the wrong conclusions without looking at other sources of information.

The use of non-financial ratios

Management teams use ratios when making decisions. Financial ratios do not always make a lot of sense on the shopfloor where managers and supervisors are often more practical.

The Japanese approach is to use ratios which mean more at this level of management. Non-financial ratios are becoming more widely used in the UK, too. They include ratios which evaluate such things as:

- quality
- number of customer complaints and warranty claims
- delivery to time
- non-productive hours etc.

All of the above have costing implications and any improvement in these indices will result in profitability gains through a better ability to meet target costs.

Does Accounting Work?

The UK has more accountants *per capita* than any other country; they have been called 'the invigilators of capitalism', though in recent years various spectacular business failures (Coloroll, BCCI, MGN, Barlow Clowes, Polly Peck, British & Commonwealth etc) have drawn attention to the failings of the system and its practitioners. Such large collapses have highlighted weaknesses in accounting and auditing, compounded by accounts users' inability to understand the limitations of accounting. The consequences of negligent accountancy and auditing are serious: if accountants and auditors are not responsible for maintaining standards and ethics, then they have no responsibility to shareholders, employees and the general public. The result would be that chief executives are not restrained in what they do: Robert Maxwell's activities are a prime example of this.

As result of malpractice in the 1980s and early 1990s, the Accounting Standards Board (ASB) was instructed to tighten its procedures and improve standards, so that corporate reporting was reformed. Company accounts were no longer trusted to give a clear, unbiased representation of a business's performance since issues, such as foreign currency translation, the valuation of assets (such as property or brands), the offering of convertible bonds and 'put' options caused problems.

However effective such procedural reforms are, they must be accompanied by a different attitude on the part of users of accounts as well as preparers and auditors. Bank analysts can be tempted by simplifications – focusing on a handful of key ratios rather than taking a more comprehensive view of how a company is doing. This has led to businesses presenting their accounts in order to produce the most favourable ratios. One example of this will be enough to give the general flavour.

In recent years, most businesses have been tempted to boost their reported profits; to do this they have maximised their 'earnings per share' figure, a practice that has already been criticised by the ASB.

The usual profit figure is 'earnings after interest and tax'. This figure includes 'exceptional items' but not 'extraordinary items', which are deducted after the reported profit figure. But any distinction between what is 'extraordinary' and what is 'exceptional' is likely to be subjective; many businesses have exploited this 'grey area' by placing all unusual expenditure under the 'extraordinary expenditure' heading, and in so doing appearing to boost their profits. The ASB has now attempted to block this loophole by directing accountants to define extraordinary items so that they rarely appear in accounts. (50% of UK firms were following this practice, as opposed to only 5% of American businesses.)

FRED 1: Statement of Recognised Gains and Losses

The ASB has shown its concern at the inconsistent ways in which accountants were presenting the balance sheet. In its first Financial Reporting Exposure Draft (or FRED, for short), the ASB proposed a new primary financial statement, a Statement of Recognised Gains and Losses which is designed to show clearly any changes in the net assets of the business. We show an example at the top of the next page.

Presentation of Final Accounts

The purpose of presenting final accounts is to make them understandable to those who need to read them.

There are a number of ways of laying out balance sheets, profit and loss accounts and funds statements but in the previous examples we have given the most commonly used method. The layout is similar for all types of businesses, the main difference being in the way in which any profit (or loss) made in the trading period is shown. For example, a sole trader receives all the trading profit made and is liable for personal tax on the entire amount after any capital and personal allowances are made. In the same way a partnership divides the profit according to the respective partnership shares and each partner is taxed accordingly through personal income tax. In the Advent Cards plc examples given above, as the business is a limited company the trading profit is taxed through Corporation Tax. The profit which remains after Corporation Tax has been paid may then be retained by the company and included in its reserves or it could be shared out among its shareholders as a dividend. Any dividend which the directors decide to declare is obviously distributed among the shareholders in proportion to the percentage of the company's shares that they hold.

Statement of Recognised Gains and Losses

	1993 (£m)	1992 (£m)
Profit attributable to members of the company	6	27
Unrealised surplus on revaluation of properties	4	4
Unrealised loss/gain on trade investment	(3)	7
Total gains and losses for the year before currency adjustments	7	40
Currency translation differences	(2)	5
Total recognised gains and losses for the year	5	45
Dividends	(5)	(7)
Total recognised gains and losses after dividends	0	38
Prior year adjustment	(10)	0
Net deduction from/addition to net assets	(10)	38

Source: Accounting Standards Board (Fred 1)

Accounting Concepts

Financial statements are structured and presented in a conventional way; there are certain *principles* in the way they are drawn up, often referred to as accounting concepts. It is the use and limitations of such concepts which this section considers.

As you may appreciate, financial information can be presented and interpreted in a number of ways. In order that accounts can be understood, it became necessary to establish some general rules and regulations which people working with financial information would understand, accept and use. They are the basic concepts of accountancy that allow you to interpret financial information consistently. When reading textbooks on accounting, you will see the terms *concepts*, *conventions*, *principles* and *rules* used almost interchangeably.

Four broad assumptions underlie the periodic accounts of business enterprises. These are:

1.   the 'going concern' concept

2.   the 'accruals' concept

3.   the 'consistency' concept

4.   the 'prudence' concept.

The concepts are so widely used that accountants do not bother to explain that they are using them when they publish accounts: they assume that you know what the concepts are, and they presume you know they are observing them – unless they state something to the contrary.

The 'Going Concern' Concept

When a balance sheet is prepared it is assumed that the business will continue to operate in the future, in other words that it is a 'going concern'. For this reason the assets of the business are valued *at their worth to the business* and not at the price they would fetch if they were sold on the open market. So, for instance, an engineering company may have a factory which has been converted for its use and has had special overhead cranes installed. The initial cost of the factory, its conversion and machinery was £100,000. Yet, if the business closes and the factory and its equipment are put up for sale, there may be little demand in that locality for a fully-equipped engineering factory. But an accountant will value the assets at *cost less depreciation* if the business continues to operate. That represents their assessed worth to the engineering company rather than the value they might fetch if they were sold.

The same principle can be applied to stock or to debtors. They would be valued on the assumption that the business was a going concern, although they may clearly be worth less should the business cease.

The 'Accruals' Concept

You already know that the profit and loss account should reflect the costs incurred in the trading period so that they compare accurately against the income earned in the same period. However, many of the expenses incurred by the business are not likely to be charged over the same accounting period as that adopted for its financial year.

For example, the business's financial year may run from 1 May in one year to 30 April in the following year, yet it may pay the rent for its premises on a calendar year basis, from 1 January to 31 December of the same year. If it pays the rent in advance, then it would be wrong to allot the full calendar year's rent to the financial year which ended part way through the calendar year. A simple example may illustrate the point.

An organisation is charged a rent of £1,200 for the calendar year 1992. However, for the calendar year 1993, the landlord increases the rent to £1,500 with the agreement of the business as the tenant. The business's financial year runs from the beginning of May 1992 until the end of April 1993. Thus the amount of rent which should be included in that financial year's Profit and Loss Account will be calculated as follows:

> 8 months (May to December 1992) of the 1992 calendar
> year's rent which is 8/12 of £1200 equal to £800
>
> plus
>
> 4 months (January to April 1993) of the 1993 calendar
> year's rent which is 4/12 of £1,500 equal to £500.
>
> The total rent to be included in the Profit and Loss Account
> for 1 May 1992 until 30 April 1993 is £1,300.

Obviously, some bills will be less easy to divide (such as fuel or telephone bills) and as accurate an estimate as it is possible to arrive at is included in the accounts. The principle of accrual will apply equally if the bill has been paid or has yet to be paid. In the example on the previous page it is assumed that the bill was paid in advance. Perhaps it may be paid in arrears. In either case the total rent owed by the business in its 1992-93 trading period is £1,300 and this is the amount which should appear in the Profit and Loss Account.

The 'Consistency' Concept

You already know that one of the main reasons for preparing financial statements is that they will allow a comparison of the performance of the business over a period of time. It would be misleading to regularly change the basis on which business accounts are prepared – accounts should be consistently prepared in the same way.

If the initial cost concept is applied in one year's accounts, it should be used continually. For instance,if a business valued its stock on an average value in one accounting period, it would cause difficulties in financial interpretation if in the next set of accounts it adopted a first in first out (FIFO) valuation approach. Accepting the convention of consistency does not mean that the business can never change the basis on which it prepares its accounts: it simply means that any significant change in its methods must be made clear.

The Concept of 'Prudence'

In finance, it is wiser to err on the side of prudence rather than over-expectation. Accountants accept the *highest* level of projected *expenditure* and the *lowest* level of projected *income*. Following this prudent approach means the projected profit of a business will be the least that is probably expected. This may appear to be an over-cautious approach; however, better to be pleasantly surprised if profit turns out higher than anticipated than to be disappointed when profit turns out disappointingly low.

'Prudence' has drawbacks: riskier projects may not be pursued because the projected level of profit seems insufficient to make it worthwhile; nevertheless, adopting this approach will save the over-optimistic businessman from bankruptcy.

Other accounting concepts or conventions

The four concepts discussed above are the major concepts defined by the Statement of Standard Accounting Practice. There are several others which you should know about. These are:

5. money measurement

6. separate business entity

7. stability – the cost concept

8. the realisation concept

9. materiality.

Let's consider each in turn.

Money measurement

In finance, *transactions are measured in money*. For example, if one used-car dealer stated that he has sold 200 cars, while another said he had sold 300 cars, you might assume that the second dealer had the larger turnover. However, if the average price of the first dealer's sales was £5,000 per car and that for the second was £3,000 per car, then you can see that the first has a turnover of £100,0000 (200 cars at £5,000 each) while the second has only a turnover of £900,000 (300 cars at £3,000 each). Thus, to allow accurate comparison of turnover, performance must be measured in money terms and not in terms of the quantity of actual goods and services bought and sold.

Other factors may be vital to the success of the business. A well-established shop may have built up much goodwill. Customers are used to trading with that business. Goodwill is a valuable asset since an established customer base is clearly an asset and an advantage over a business which has just started. It is not an easy task to value that goodwill when preparing a balance sheet: if it cannot easily be measured in monetary terms it is omitted. Of course, when an established business is sold it is normally the case that the seller and the buyer agree upon a value for the business goodwill, and this is included in the selling price, though this will really depend on the buyer's assessment of its worth.

Similarly, an efficient workforce not only increases profits in the current trading year but is also a valuable asset for the future. Should 'efficient workforce' be included as an item in the balance sheet? As you cannot put a money value on it, you should not include it, although it may well influence the price if the business is sold.

Stating business information in monetary terms provides a way of *objectively* comparing business performance, over the same trading period or between different organisations. However, a note of caution:. the value of money changes over time as a result of inflation. A business with a net profit in 1992 of £20,000 and a net profit of £30,000 in 1997 has not necessarily become more profitable. If over that period inflation rises by 230%, the value of money falls proportionately and then the business needs a profit of £67,000 in 1997 to keep its profitability, in real terms, at the same level. The causes of and possible solutions to inflation as an economic problem are examined in Part Two of this book.

Separate business entity

Always regard a set of accounts from the viewpoint of the business. In other words, the business, whether it is a sole trader, partnership or limited company, should be seen as a separate business entity. If the business is either a sole trader or a partnership, then the owner's personal accounts should be separated from those of the business. So, for instance, if the owner introduces money into the business, this should be recorded as capital introduced (or as a loan) under the liabilities of the business, while it would be regarded as an asset in the owner's personal accounts.

Of course, there is the possibility of confusion for the business is not a separate legal entity and its assets and liabilities are regarded *under the law* as being those of the owner. However, within this concept it is important to see owner and business as separate *accounting* entities, even though they are not separate legal entities. The situation is clearer in the case of a limited company, for limited companies are both separate *legal* entities and separate *business* entities distinct from their owners – the shareholders.

Stability – the cost concept

When preparing a balance sheet it is usual to show the business's *assets at their cost price*. This means that the value of the assets shown does not represent their true current market value. However, it is impossible to accurately assess the market value of every asset each time a balance sheet is prepared so, in the interests of consistency and objectivity, you assume the current value of the asset by taking its initial cost and depreciating its worth as it is used. In this way you can allocate a part of the assets value to each trading period in which it is used. It is often the owner's choice as to how quickly assets are 'written down'. Assets, such as buildings and freehold land which do not depreciate in the same as machinery or other assets, are not normally written down in this way. Instead, they are re-valued from time to time so that the balance sheet will more truly reflect their worth to the business. Such re-valuations usually bear in mind the convention of *prudence*. At times of high inflation it is usual for financial statements to carry a note to the accounts which points out the possible effects of inflation on particular assets or transactions.

The realisation concept

This concept is similar in nature to the 'accruals' concept. When looking at the Profit and Loss Account it is important to record all transactions in the trading period in which they occur, and *not* in the period in which money is received or paid. It is normal practice for a business to send an invoice to a customer at the time the goods are despatched or the service is completed. Business customers often expect a period of trade credit or are simply slow payers. Because of this probable delay, which could obviously stretch from weeks to months, you record a sale in the accounts at the time the invoice is sent. If money is still owing at the end of the trading period for work done or goods delivered, then this amount will be shown as trade debtors in the balance sheet and will not affect the Profit and Loss Account.

Materiality

Not every transaction, every asset acquired and every liability incurred will be recorded. Whether a transaction is recorded will be determined by assessing the material needs of the business. So, for example, most businesses would not bother to list every item of office equipment as a fixed asset – despite the fact that its working life may extend into a number of trading periods. It would be a time-consuming exercise to record a stapler (at a cost of £3.50) in the assets column of the balance sheet and then to depreciate it over the next four years. Such minor items are included as a current expense in the Profit and Loss Account and are, in effect, 'written off' immediately.

The level of 'materiality' depends on the size of the business. An office photocopier might be regarded as a major item of expenditure for a sole trader but would not be a fixed asset in the accounts of a multi-national corporation.

It is important to bear these concepts and conventions in mind when you attempt to understand and interpret the Balance Sheet and Profit and Loss Accounts. It is always worth your while turning to the end of the accounts to see if the concepts or conventions under which they have been prepared have been specified and to check whether the accountants who verified them have qualified them in any way.

Costs and Costing Methods

Despite any deficiencies that financial statements may have, they are widely used by business analysts, commentators and investors. However, they are of limited use to the *internal* managers of the business. Management is not interested so much in the past but in what is happening now and what the future might hold. This is where management accounting comes into its own.

Management accounting involves the systematic analysis of the costs and revenues of a business. Once analysed by management accountants, the information is presented to the other managers in the business in order to help them in their decision-making roles.

The Different Sorts of 'Costs'

The nature of costs and their behaviour is important to a business. The nature and behaviour of costs can change with time. For convenience of understanding, time can be split into:

a.   the short-run

b.   the long-run

a.   The short-run, or short-term as it is sometimes called, refers to the period of time into the future over which fixed costs *cannot* be altered. It is assumed that rent, insurance, factory overheads cannot be changed in the short-run. Even labour costs are sometimes considered to be fixed in the short-run. Take, for example, semi-skilled workers on a car assembly line. One would think that the fewer cars which are produced, the fewer the workers that would be needed. In theory this is so: in practice, though, most workers have to be served a period of notice before they can be made redundant and the effect of this is to make the cost of their labour fixed in the short-run.

b.   The long run (or long-term) is the time period over which even fixed costs can be changed. For example, a retail business may have sixteen shops. In the short-run the fixed costs of those shops are made up of rent, rates, insurance, depreciation etc. It is assumed that in the short-run these costs of the whole business are fixed. However, should the business plan to open more branches then, clearly, in the long-run even those fixed costs begin to vary.

Costs are often classified into two main types :

Fixed costs are generally regarded as those costs of the business which in the short-run do not increase as output, production or sales increase. Frequently quoted examples of such costs are: insurance; lighting; heating; rent; rates and depreciation.

Variable costs. These are sometimes referred to as *direct* costs. They increase in direct proportion to the level of output, production or sales. The best example of this is the cost of materials. In a factory making shirts, the cost of materials that go in to producing one shirt is £3; the cost of materials to produce two shirts will be £6. For each additional shirt the cost of materials will be £3, whether it be the third shirt or the three millionth.

Some businesses will have an additional cost types: that of *semi-variable* or *semi-fixed* costs. An example of a semi-variable cost is that of maintenance staff. Clearly the higher the production of shirts that is achieved, the greater will the need be for maintaining the production equipment. The cost of maintenance in this instance is not fixed: it is increasing. Nor is it variable, because it is unlikely to be increasing in direct proportion to output.

An analogy of the costs of running a car might clear up any difficulties in distinguishing the different types of costs. Take three costs of running a car, which fall clearly into each of the fixed, variable and semi-variable categories

1. *Fixed cost.* A car owner currently pays £110 a year in road tax. Meeting such a legal requirement is clearly a fixed cost in having a car. Whether you do ten miles a year or a hundred thousand miles a year, the cost remains fixed. Obviously, if you wished to spread the cost of the road tax over the number of miles you do the more miles you drive in a year means that the average cost of road tax becomes less and less with each mile that you travel.

   Example

Motorist A does 5,000 miles a year

$$\frac{£110}{5,000} \quad = \quad \text{2.2p per mile}$$

Motorist B does 15,000 miles per year

$$\frac{£110}{15,000} \quad = \quad \text{0.7p per mile}$$

The way the fixed costs are spread in this way is an important idea to understand and one to which we will return later.

2. *Variable cost*: petrol. Clearly, the more miles you travel, the more petrol you consume. The quantity of petrol consumed will increase in direct proportion to the number of miles travelled: petrol is a variable cost of running a car.

3. *Semi-variable cost*: maintenance. The more miles you cover in a year, the more maintenance your vehicle is likely to need. Maintenance isn't a fixed cost since it increases as the number of miles driven increases. Neither is it a variable cost, since it does not increase in direct proportion to the number of miles travelled. It's a sort of halfway house: a *semi*-variable cost.

You might like to continue this classification exercise with other items of expenditure involved in running a car (insurance, depreciation, tyres etc.) If you don't already drive a car, you probably will do so soon: this exercise will heighten your awareness of the financial costs of motoring.

Determining the Level of Output/Sales

Break-even Analysis

Break-even analysis is a technique used to estimate, on purely financial costs and revenue basis, the number of units which must be produced or sold for a project to break even. With this simple technique, a manager can calculate the effect of different marketing strategies on the business.

The break-even point is where *total costs* equal *total revenue*: in other words, no profit is being made and no loss is being incurred. The break-even point gives a business an initial target at which to aim.

It can also be used to estimate the number of units which must be produced/sold in order to make a stated or target profit.

There are two basic ways to determine the break-even point (or target level) of production/sales:

- by graphical means
- by means of calculations.

A shirt manufacturer can be used to illustrate each method.

CSC Shirts Ltd manufactures men's shirts. It has a factory which has a maximum output of 100,000 shirts a year. It is currently producing 70,000 shirts a year. The management accountant has provided the following information so that the break-even level of output can be pinpointed:

Selling price per shirt £15
Variable cost per shirt £7

Total fixed cost per year £440,000

By graphical means

Step 1

Draw the fixed cost line on the graph.

This line will be horizontal and straight as fixed costs are set at £440,000 irrespective of the level of output.

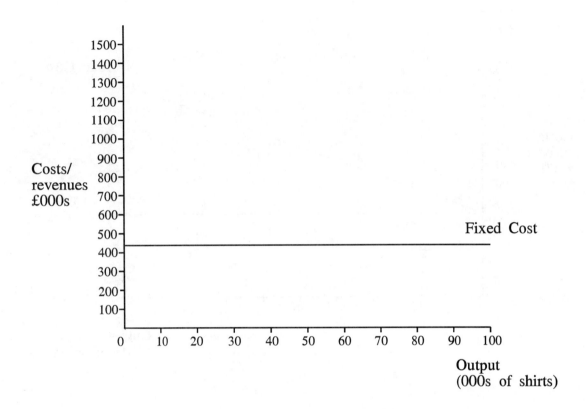

Step 2

Add the total cost line to the graph.

Total costs are fixed costs plus variable costs. An output of 0 shirts has an actual cost of £440,000 (£440,000 fixed costs + £0 variable cost). One shirt produced will have a total cost of £440,007 (£440,000 fixed cost + £7 variable costs of producing one shirt). An output of 100,000 shirts (the maximum capacity) will cost £1,140,000 (£440,000 fixed cost + £7 variable cost on 100,000 shirts).

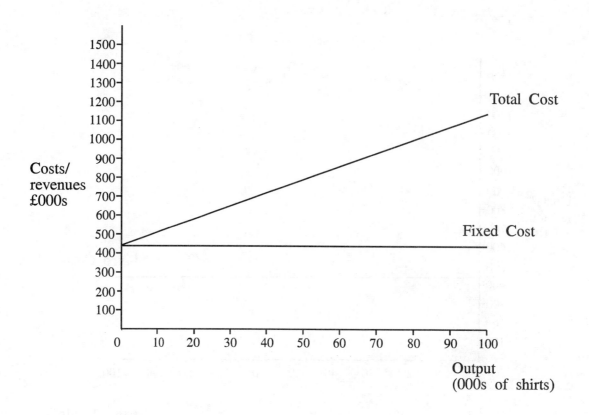

Step 3

Add the total revenue curve to the graph.

The total revenue for one shirt is £15, two shirts £30 and for 100,000 shirts it is £1,500,000 (100,000 shirts x £15 selling price per shirt).

Step 4

Identify the break-even point (BEP) on the graph.

The BEP is the level of output/sales when total revenue equals total cost. Remember: it is the point of output when neither a profit nor loss is made. It tells the business how many shirts it must make before it will begin to earn itself a profit. In CSC's case the BEP is 55,000 shirts.

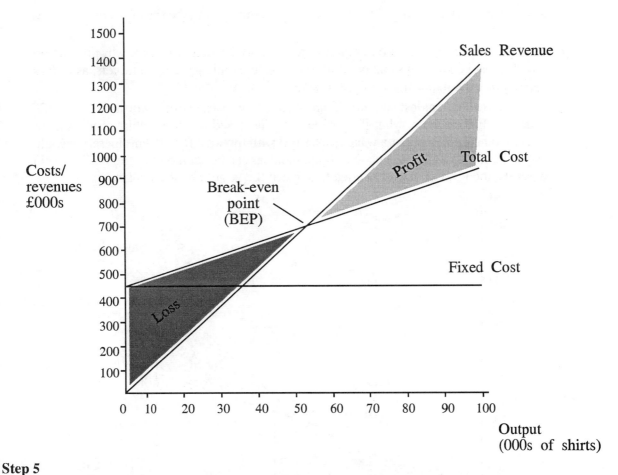

Step 5

Identify the margin of safety on the graph.

Margin of safety = Current level of output – BEP level of sales

The margin of safety is the gap between the number of shirts being produced and the number needed to break even. CSC's margin of safety is 15,000 shirts.

Step 6

Identify level of output needed to achieve target profit.

CSC has set an objective of making a £200,000 profit next year. By locating that level of profit on the graph, it is possible to read off the level of output/sales which must be achieved in order to meet that objective. The business must produce and sell 80,000 shirts in the following year if it wishes to make a profit of £200,000.

Summary

The graphical method has several benefits:

- it shows output decisions clearly and simply

- it assists in 'profit planning'. Managers can plot estimates and see the effect of variations of cost, revenue or volume.
- it can be used as a tool to show situations to the workforce: they can see why production targets must be met. This can be used to motivate people to achieve targets, as well as highlighting the implications of falling short of targets.
- it can be used to demonstrate the effects of changing costs, in other words the *'What if?'* situation. For example, what if variable costs increased to £8 per shirt as a result of increased material costs or a wage rise agreed with the workforce? This increase would cause the total cost line to become steeper and, as can be seen below, the BEP, margin of safety and level of output needed to achieve the target profit are all changed.

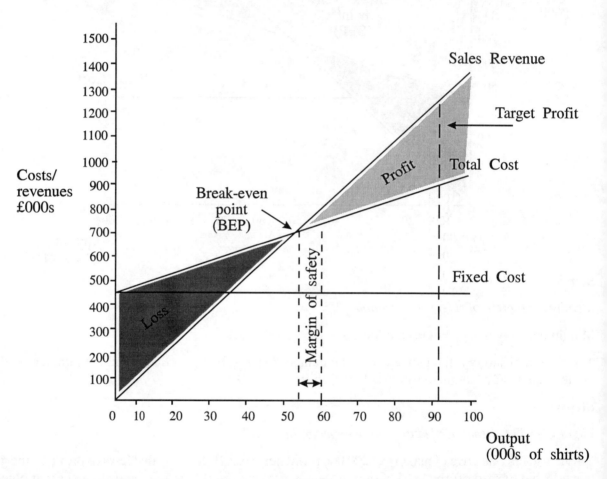

Using pieces of string on a pin board – or better still a graphics package on a computer – can quickly show the effects of even small changes. This is known as manipulating the break-even model.

However, the break-even model does have some major drawbacks and limitations to its usefulness:

- it can only show simple production decision-making. For example, suppose CSC Shirts made more than one type of shirt, with each type having its own cost structure and a different selling price. Would a break-even graph be drawn for each type of shirt and, if so, how would the fixed costs be treated? (This is the subject of a later section of this book.)

- in practice, cost and revenue lines are rarely straight. For example, it is possible that if CSC wishes to produce and sell 90,000 shirts, rather than the 70,000 they currently produce, then the selling price may need to be reduced on the increased volume. CSC may sell the additional 20,000 shirts as 'own label' shirts to a chain of department stores at £14, whilst retaining a £15 price level for their its own CSC-labelled shirts. What would the revenue line look like in these circumstances? It certainly won't be straight and yet it is a perfectly realistic situation for a business to find itself in.

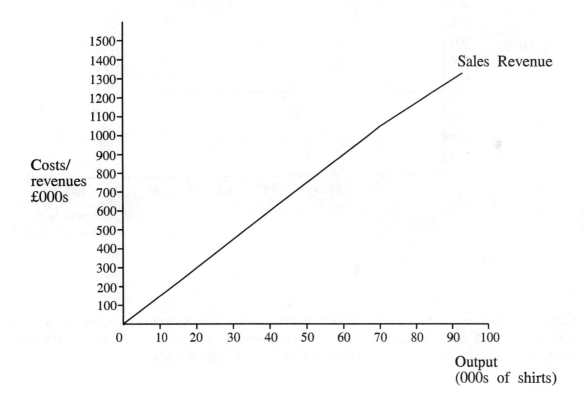

At the same time as production increases, it is perfectly reasonable to expect economies of scale to occur. In increasing production by 20,000 shirts, perhaps the buyers of materials for making the shirts can gain a cost reduction because they are now buying in increased volume – they might be asking for a discount for 'buying in bulk'. Such a cost reduction will decrease variable cost per unit and this will affect the total cost line.

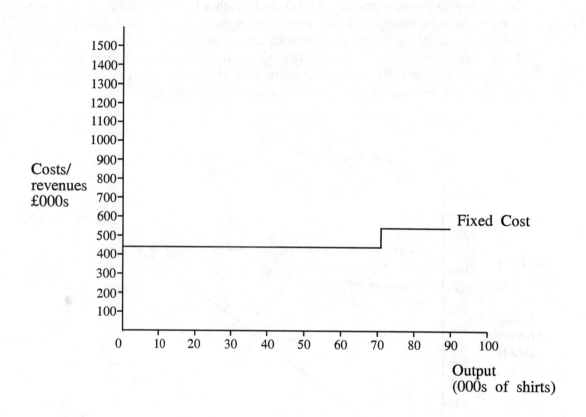

Often, even fixed cost lines are not straight but 'stepped'. Such stepping happens when extra storage facilities need to be hired in order to cope with the increase in volume from 70,000 for 90,000 shirts. Extra storage in turn means increased rent, rates, insurance etc – all *fixed* costs.

By means of calculations

This method cannot show the *'What if?'* situation which is so clear in the graphical method, nor is it quite so pretty to look at! Its main advantage is that it is a much quicker and more accurate way of analysing a break-even situation.

Calculating break-even point

Break-even point occurs when fixed costs are covered by the proceeds from units made or sold. But this depends on how much is made on each unit made or sold.

	Selling price per shirt	£15
less	Variable cost per shirt	£7
=	Contribution	£8

'Contribution' is the difference between selling price and variable cost. Each shirt produced/sold contributes £8 towards paying the fixed costs of the business. Once fixed costs are covered, then the business has reached break-even point.

Therefore:

$$\frac{\text{Total Fixed costs}}{\text{Contribution per unit}} \quad = \quad \text{Break even point}$$

$$\frac{£440,000}{£8} \quad = \quad 55,000 \text{ shirts}$$

Calculating margin of safety

Margin of safety = current level of production - breakeven level of production

$$70,000 - 55,000 \quad = \quad 15,000 \text{ shirts.}$$

CSC can afford to reduce production by 15,000 shirts before a loss making situation is reached.

Calculating level of output needed to achieve target profit

When setting a target profit to achieve, it is not really different from setting a target level of fixed costs which need to be covered. CSC have a target level of £440,000 of fixed costs to cover and a target level of £200,000 profit to achieve.

Every shirt made/sold contributes £8 to pay fixed costs. Once fixed costs are covered, this £8 per shirt becomes profit.

Therefore, level of output needed to achieve target profit is simply a modified version of the calculation which established break-even point.

$$\frac{\text{Total fixed cost + Target profit}}{\text{Contribution per unit}} \quad = \quad \text{level of output to achieve target profit}$$

$$\frac{£440,000 + £200,000}{£8} = 80,000 \text{ shirts}$$

To cover fixed costs and make a profit of £200,000, CSC must make and sell 80,000 shirts.

Costing Decisions

The way costs are internally organised by management accountants can have a major bearing on production and selling decisions.

The starting point to illustrate this is by examining the method of 'contribution' or 'marginal' costing.

Contribution or marginal costing.

Layatease Ltd manufacture beds. Operating solely in the 'budget' segment of the bed market they have a range of only three beds. The beds are sold to retailers for the following prices:

Single bed	Double	Ortho-double
£80	£120	£140

The beds are all made in the same factory. The variable cost of manufacture per bed is as follows:

£50	£80	£90

In some companies variable cost is referred to as 'marginal cost' Marginal cost is *the increase in total cost as a result of increasing output by one more unit.* The marginal cost of producing one more single bed is £50.

For our purpose the terms *variable* and *marginal* cost are interchangeable.

Fixed costs for the business as a whole are £300,000.

Any manufacturer of a range of products will be interested to know which product provides the most profit for the business. However, it should be 'contribution', not 'profit', which is the yardstick. The reasons for this is that profit is found after deducting the fixed costs of the business. As they are a total £300,000 they cannot be deducted until total contribution has been established.

Consider the following information:

	Single	**Double**	**Ortho-double**
Selling Price	£80	£120	£140
Variable Cost	£50	£80	£90
Contribution per Bed	£30	£40	£50
Sold in Year	4,500	4,500	1,500
Total Contribution by Bed Type	£135,000	£180,000	£75,000
Total Contribution		£390,000	
Less Fixed Costs		£300,000	
Profit		£90,000	

From the information you should be able to verify the following facts:

- each single bed contributes £30 towards the fixed costs and profit of the business
- double beds contribute a total of £180,000 towards the fixed costs and profit of the business.
- ortho-doubles make the largest contribution per bed (£50 as against £40 for double and £30 for singles)
- doubles make the largest total contribution (£180,000)
- Layatease Ltd are making a profit of £90,000 after deducting fixed costs of £300,000 from a total contribution of £390,000.

But one question still remaining is:

'Which bed type is contributing the most to the business?' The question has a number of 'right' answers. The contribution can be measured as:

Contribution per unit

On this basis ortho-doubles are the best contributors. They contribute £50 per bed against the £40 and £30 of doubles and singles respectively.

Contribution by cost centre

A 'cost centre' is an area (or department or division) of a business for which costs can be clearly identified. In our example the cost centres are single beds, double beds and ortho-double.

The best contribution by a cost centre is that of 'doubles' which contributes £180,000.

Contribution as a % of selling price

It is very useful for a business to know the contribution, which a product makes, as a percentage of its selling price. Percentages always uncover some hidden truths behind raw figures.

Take two chocolate bars as an example. Both bars are popular with consumers, but a shopkeeper is wondering which bar makes her more.

    Bar A costs 10p and sells for 15p
    Bar B costs 13p and sells for 19p.

Clearly, the shopkeeper makes 6p on Bar B as against only 5p on Bar A, so Bar B is better for the shopkeeper. However, if the shopkeeper does her sums she'll find:

	Bar A	Bar B
Selling Price	15p	19p
Cost	10p	13p
Contribution	5p	6p

$$\frac{\text{Contribution per bar}}{\text{selling price}} \qquad 100 \quad = \text{33.3\% for Bar A and 31.6\% for Bar B}$$

So, as a percentage of selling price, Bar A contributes more.

Performing a similar calculation for Layatease Ltd produces the figures:

Single	Double	Ortho-double
37.7%	33.3%	35.7%

As a percentage of selling price, single beds contribute the most.

Contribution as a % of marginal (variable) cost

When money is in short supply, firms often look to products which yield maximum return for minimum spending. Layatease need only spend, in variable cost, £50 to produce a single bed as against the £80 and £90 needed to produce the other types. So if a good return can be achieved on marginal cost, then it makes single beds a better proposition.

	Single	Double	Ortho-double
$\dfrac{\text{Contribution per bed}}{\text{Marginal cost per bed}} \times 100$	60%	50%	55.5%

On the basis of contribution as a percentage of marginal cost, single beds do the best.

To summarise Ranking of products by:	Single	Double	Ortho-double
Contribution per unit	3	2	1
Contribution per cost centre	2	1	3
Contribution as a % of selling price	1	3	2
Contribution as a % of marginal cost	1	3	2

As you can see there is no 'right' answer to the question of which product contributes most. It depends very much on

- what you are trying to find out

- what purpose you are wanting the answer for

- what method of measurement you use.

It is another illustration of how figures can be made to mean different things to different people.

Allocating Fixed Costs to Cost Centres

The main strength of contribution costing lies in its ability to encourage those responsible for controlling variable costs to see the importance of their task. They are responsible for only the costs over which they can exert control and this leads to motivation to improve efficiency and compete with other cost centres.

One criticism of the system is, however, that individual cost centres are distanced from the fixed costs and overheads of the business. Control of those costs is seen as someone else's responsibility. They lack awareness of the level and nature of the fixed costs.

One method used to overcome this lack of ownership of fixed costs is to attempt to allocate them to individual costs centres. Each cost centre is made to take its 'fair share' of the fixed costs. In accounting terms, this is known as *absorption*.

Absorption Costing

Suppose Layatease Ltd decides to share out the fixed costs between its three production departments. A simple way to do this is to divide the fixed costs of £300,000 equally between them. Each department would have to absorb £100,000 of fixed costs.

The result of this would be:

	Single	Double	Ortho-double
Contribution	£135,000	£180,000	£75,000
Share of Fixed Costs	£100,000	£100,000	£100,000
Profit/Loss per Department	£35,000	£80,000	–£25,000

Notice how the total profit still adds up to £90,000.

Clearly the ortho-double department would be most unhappy about the basis of the fixed cost allocation. The allocation has been made regardless of the size of the department.

A much fairer way to allocate would be on the basis of sales volume, which would produce the following result.

	Single	Double	Ortho-double
Calculation	$\frac{4,500}{10,500} \times £300,000$	$\frac{4,500}{10,500} \times £300,000$	$\frac{1,500}{10,500} \times £300,000$
Share of Fixed Costs	£128,571	£128,571	£42,858
Profit per Department	£6,429	£51,429	£32,142

Once again the profit still adds up to £90,000.

Other methods of allocating fixed costs and overheads can be by:

- number of employees in department
- floor space occupied
- sales target.

The benefits of raising awareness of fixed costs in cost centres must be weighed against the attitudes of managers to the arbitrary method of a fixed cost allocation and absorption.

Traditional costing is changing. Technology means that in many manufacturing companies, direct labour is as low as 10 per cent of all costs, or even lower. The practice of spreading 'the overheads' over the various units passing through each cost centre – which you know as absorption costing – would not make sense – they couldn't cope with these very large amounts and it would be impossible to base any sensible business decisions on the results.

The traditional division between fixed and variable costs is becoming less relevant today. Perhaps the only really significant variable costs left are materials and sub-contract labour.

Budgeting

Budgeting is the process of setting and monitoring the short-term objectives of different aspects of the organisation's operation. It involves the day-to-day financial management of each department of the business and so should be based on the individual objectives, targets and goals which each department must have. This precise management of the organisation's resources is an essential part of the achievement of the overall plan.

Any budget essentially has three distinct aims:

1. to allow the business to meet its objectives through the co-ordination of a range of activities

2. to allow the allocation of the appropriate level of finance to allow the achievement of these objectives

3. to permit the efficient management of the organisation's financial resources and ensure that it is aware of the extent of, and timing of, requirements for finance.

Without sticking closely to individual budgets the business's wider objectives may be hindered. As an integral part of the overall plan the process of budgeting should progress through three main stages:

1. construction (including Consultation)

2. co-ordination

3. control.

Constructing Budgets

It is a normal practice in most businesses for senior management to negotiate a budget for their own departments. This will take place in the previous financial year and will obviously be constrained by the overall budget of the business.

The Board of Directors will meet to share out the organisation's spending according to their cost requirements. However, budgeting should not be seen solely as the preserve of senior management. There should be a great deal of *consultation* with the workers of the business who are going to have to live with the budget once it is allocated. It is often the management style employed in the business which determines the extent of employee participation in decision-making. Yet it is in this area of financial budgeting that many of the problems of worker dissatisfaction can emerge. Therefore, a sensible management will avoid imposing a stringent budget on its workforce without previous participation or consultation.

Budgeting for operational and capital expenditure

It is important to distinguish between budgets for operational and capital expenditure. With the former, a sufficient budget must be allocated which allows for the efficient working of a department at its anticipated level of operation for the coming year. There is a tendency, when proposing a departmental budget, to take the amount that was spent in the present year and to increase it in line with inflation. This is a negative approach since it does not evaluate the changing needs or level of output of the department for the coming year. This is why *departmental* objectives are so important. The departmental managers should carefully cost out their spending requirements to meet the targets they have been set by the overall corporate plan. This requires foresight to avoid an over-estimation of the costs involved, which might mean that other departments are left with insufficient finance to operate efficiently. Conversely, an under-estimation can result in the departmental staff feeling that they have not been given enough finance to carry out their jobs properly.

The operational budget

The production department should be able to identify the amount it will need to spend on materials and labour to meet a specified level of output. This may well involve the department in producing separate purchasing and manpower budgets.

Thus the operational budget will include:

- all costs incurred in the operation of the department for the time period of the budget, irrespective of when payment is actually made.

The operational budget will exclude:

- the purchase of capital equipment, even if when purchased during that budgetary period
- the depreciation on capital assets used during the budgetary period.

The cash budget

The business will also prepare a cash flow forecast for the coming year, also referred to as the *cash budget*. This will allow the financial management of the business to plan its borrowing needs by scheduling expenditure in each department against anticipated income. All sources of income would be included in the cash budget but care should be taken not to include cash as being received as soon as a sale is made. Most commercial customers require a period of trade credit and this must be taken into consideration.

The capital budget

The capital budget of the business is determined by its level of profitability, projected growth and the need to replace capital assets which are becoming inefficient or obsolete. Because of the long lifespan of most capital assets, such as machinery, there is a need for considerable forward planning. Thus the capital expenditure budget must be interlinked with the corporate strategy to allow sufficient finance to be made available in the accounting year when the asset is to be purchased. This may entail each department planning its own capital expenditure over a period of years and submitting this to form part of the organisation's overall capital budget.

Co-ordinating Budgets

The budget must show a high degree of co-ordination so that one department is not under financed to the detriment of the rest. For instance, the marketing department must be given sufficient expenditure to advertise and sell the business's products. It would be highly inefficient to have a production department manufacturing a high output which was not being sold.

Controlling Budgets

It is normal practice to break the financial year into budgetary periods. These may be monthly, quarterly or half yearly, depending on the nature and size of the business. This subdivision allows the department manager to monitor and control the progress of budget expenditure in his own area more effectively and to adjust spending, should it become necessary.

It is usual to compare the budgeted figure with the actual expenditure and assess whether there is any variance. A deviation from the budget in one month may not be of concern if the variance is in the other direction in other months. The normal practice is to prepare a cumulative budget report to show the current month's position as well as the cumulative picture for the year. An example of a budget report is given beneath.

Production Department Monthly Budgetary Report						
Cost Heading	Month			Cumulative (1st 10 months)		
	Budget	Actual	Variance	Budget	Actual	Variance
Raw Materials	145	149	+4	1,580	1,650	+70
Labour	289	272	−17	2,970	2,900	−75

Budget variances

To illustrate the effect of budget variances consider the following case:

A company has budgeted to make and sell 1,500 desks over a six month period. The selling price is budgeted at £120. Costs per desk are planned on the basis of;

Materials	£35
Labour	£25
Overheads	£15

At the end of the six month period the following information about actual spending is presented.

Sales only 1,300 desks at £115 per desk due to market conditions

Materials   £44,800
Labour   £32,700
Overheads   £21,000

Sales variance

	Budget	**Actual**	**Variance**
Sales Revenue	£180,000 (1500 x £120)	£149,500 (1300 x £115)	–£30,500
Materials	£52,500	£44,800	+£7,700
Labour	£37,500	£32,700	+£4,800
Overheads	£22,500	£21,000	+£1,500
Profit	£67,500	£51,000	–£16,500

Any variance which has a negative effect on profit is considered a negative variance: any variance which has the effect of increasing profit is considered a positive variance. So, actual sales revenue less than budget sales revenue is a negative variance and actual material cost less than budget material cost is a positive variance.

It is possible to do further variance analysis. Clearly, some of the negative sales revenue variance is due to a lower volume of units being sold, and some is down to the lower than anticipated price. This can be analysed as follows:

Total sales revenue variance   –£30,500
Accounted for by sales price variance: £156,000 (1500 × £120) – £149,500 (1500 × £115) = – £7,500
and a sales volume variance: £172,500 (1500 × £115) – £149,500 (1300 × £115) = – £23,000

So the larger part of the variance was accounted for by selling fewer units than it had budgeted to sell, rather than selling at a lower price.

Similar analysis can be done on costs. For example, if a business knows the hours of labour per unit and the price of labour per hour, it is possible to analyse any variance between both factors.

A problem exists, though, with the analysis done earlier. If a lower volume of goods has been produced and sold then, naturally, labour and material costs as a total should be lower. It was not suprising to find that when 1,300 units were made and sold, rather than 1,500, costs decreased. The real question is – what level should they have reduced to?

On the basis of 1,300 units, costs are:

	Budget	**Actual**	**Variance**
Materials	1,300 × £35 = £45,500	£44,800	+ £700
Labour	1,300 × £25 = £32,500	£32,700	–£200
Overheads	1,300 × £15 = £19,500	£21,000	–£1,500

So, what initially seemed positive variances on labour and overheads, in fact, are negative variances. Spending was greater on these costs than it should have been for an output of 1,300 units.

Budget and actual figures are fed to accountants who incorporate them into a 'rolling' budget for the business as a whole. This provides a regular check on both over- and under-spending and permits them to more effectively control the organisation's borrowing requirements. They will normally prepare a set of 'management accounts' at regular intervals; these are, in effect, an up-to-date profit and loss account. Large businesses will prepare these at monthly intervals, while smaller businesses may find that half yearly management accounts provide a satisfactory check.

Budgetary adjustments

Budgets are estimates of expenditure needs and so can be inaccurate. The business must, therefore, have some mechanism which allows it to adjust budgets as the year progresses. The factors which will make such changes necessary are either over- or under-achievement of departmental targets or external changes, such as an unexpected growth or decline in demand. This approach is called 'flexible budgeting' and is particularly important in businesses which experience constant fluctuations in costs and output. If flexible budgeting is implemented, then departmental budgets need to be monitored closely. It would be inefficient for a business to find itself in a position where it cannot expand output to cope with a surge in demand because the production budget is exhausted – only to discover that there is a considerable underspend in the transport budget.

Such a process can be summarised by saying that each department must:

- *Review*
- *React*

    and

- *Revise.*

Review involves the frequent monitoring of actual costs incurred against those planned in the budget. The department will either be operating under-budget, over-budget or exactly to budget.

React involves adjusting spending to take account of variances from the planned budget.

Revise involves adjusting the budget to incorporate the changes made.

If there is continuous need for major budgetary adjustments every year, this suggests that the business is not undertaking its budgetary process as thoroughly as it should do in the first place. It may require an examination of the manner in which budget allocation is made.

However, budgets have the major objective of requiring managers to control their expenditure. As such, they need to be reasonably fixed. There is little incentive to a manager to insist on cost control if he or she knows that as soon as his or her budget is used up s/he can simply ask the board for an extra budgetary allocation. If the budget is prepared properly in the first place, and no major changes have occurred which have been recognised by senior management, then the budget should be adhered to wherever possible.

1. Explain the role of an accountant.

2. What documents must be included in the accounts of a public limited company?

3. List the *external* users of accounting information.

4. What is the purpose of the balance sheet?

5. Explain, with examples:

    - tangible fixed assets
    - intangible fixed assets
    - financial fixed assets.

6. Define *working capital*.

7. List and explain the main types of *current assets*.

8. List and explain the main types of *current liability*.

9. What is meant by *unpaid share capital?*

10. Distinguish between:

    - revenue reserves
    - capital reserves
    - share premium.

11. What is a *debenture*?

12. Explain, by means of examples, the concept of *double entry*.

13. What are the two methods of *depreciation*?

14. What is meant by the term *residual value*?

15. Compare and contrast the two methods of depreciation.

16. Explain why assets may need to be revalued.

17. What is meant by *net realisable value*?

18. List and explain the three main methods of *stock valuation*.

19. Explain the function of the profit and loss account.

20. Show how *cost of goods sold* is calculated.

21. Explain how profits can be distributed.

22.   List some *sources* and *applications of funds*.

23.   Explain, with an example, the difference between *cash* and *profit*.

24.   State the formulas for the three ratios which measure business performance.

25.   Explain the difference between the *current* and *liquidity* ratio.

26.   What information do *debtors' turnover* and *creditors' turnover* provide for a business?

27.   List, with formulas, the main measures of investment performance.

28.   Explain what is meant by *capital gearing*.

29.   List and explain the main accounting concepts.

30.   Give examples of some misleading accounting reporting and practices.

31.   Distinguish between *short-run* and *long-run*.

32.   Explain with examples:

- fixed costs
- variable costs
- semi-variable costs.

33.   Sketch and label a break-even graph.

34.   Explain what is meant by:

- target profit
- margin of safety
- break-even point.

35.   What is *contribution*?

36.   Distinguish between *contribution* and *profit*.

37.   Explain how contribution, or marginal, costing can be used to assess the viability of a product or department.

38.   Explain how absorption costing might work in a business.

39.   What are the aims of the budgeting process?

40.   Explain, by means of an example, what is meant by a *budget variance*.

It's not just a fizzy brown drink in a funny-shaped bottle. It's a way of life – A director of Coca Cola.

Introduction

Effective marketing is almost always based on a thorough and accurate analysis of the selling situation faced by a business.

Margaret Crimp clearly describes the purpose of the marketing process as one which locates *'a target group of consumers or users who have an unsatisfied need which could be met by a branded product.'*

Margaret Crimp: *The Marketing Research Process*

To find a group of consumers with 'an unsatisfied need' requires the ability to explore, identify and interpret customers' behaviour, attitudes and preferences. The success of marketing relies on a deep understanding of who those customers are and the society in which they live. As Crimp says, an accurate analysis will *'define a target group in the market and specify the characteristics of a product to suit this group'*.

This first section further examines: how markets and consumers are analysed; how customers are divided into groups; the kind of research techniques that marketers use to carry out their exploration of the markets. It then goes on to consider the marketing mix.

A Definition of Marketing

So what about a definition of marketing? Most people reply with the word 'advertising'. This is an understandable response since we see so much of it. Marketing, however, is *not* advertising. Nor is it promotion, nor is it selling. Some people say 'market research', but that still does not cover it. Others say 'service', which is getting much warmer but still is not quite right.

Marketing is about organising the business to meet the needs of customers, not just today and tomorrow but also in five or even ten years time. It is about supplying customers with well-designed, good quality, reliable products, at a price which those customers consider to be fair. It is about providing the level of service that customers have a right to expect before, during and after the placing of an order.

Marketing, therefore, is all about making the company outward-looking or *customer oriented*. To do this you have to be able to put yourself in the customers' shoes, (or, even better, inside their minds) in order to really understand what they want and what they feel about things. Only in this way can a business organise itself successfully to meet the needs of its present and potential customers.

Marketing is a Philosophy

Marketing should be seen as a philosophy. It is a way of thinking, from the customer's perspective, about how a business can meet the needs of its customers.

Although the marketing department is responsible for planning marketing strategies and activities, everybody in the business has some role in helping to implement them. Staff at all levels have some impact on the business's ability to keep its customers satisfied. It is a key responsibility of marketers to ensure that this marketing philosophy, about serving customers, is the spirit which motivates the behaviour of everyone in the business, however little contact they have with customers.

This is perfectly illustrated by an extract from *Iacocca* , the autobiography of Lee Iacocca who ran the Ford Motor Company in the 1970s and rescued the Chrysler Motor Company in the 1980s, very much as a result of implementing marketing principles. Iacocca illustrates his understanding of the marketing philosophy by relating an incident which occurred in a restaurant when he was young. The food was good, the surroundings were clean and comfortable, but the family's meal had been somewhat spoilt by the surly, offhand attitude of the waitress. At the end of the meal, when it came to bill settling and tipping time, Iacocca's father called the waitress over and said:

> *'Now I'm going to give you a real tip. Why are you so unhappy in this job? We're out for a nice time and you're wrecking it. If you want to be a waitress you should work on being the best damn waitress in the world. Otherwise, find yourself another line of work.'*

A little harsh maybe, but if businesses are going to be successful in the long run everyone in the business must strive to be the, best damn, waitress, fitter, cleaner, receptionist, designer (or any other position), since the most successful businesses will usually be those whose staff take the most trouble to serve their customers.

Inward-looking or Outward-looking?

Many businesses are not at all outward-looking. They are inward looking or *product oriented*. They think in terms of their own products, their own activities and their own priorities rather than in terms of their customers' needs and preferences. They think that the key to success in business lies inside their organisation. Some believe that the key is to be an efficient producer, enabling the company to cut its costs and therefore sell at a lower price. A well-known exponent of this 'production concept' was Henry Ford, who pioneered mass production, in itself a very good thing, but who was then obsessed by making greater and greater economies of scale. Everything in his company was built around the need for production efficiency. Ford was famous in the 1920s for its slogan, 'You can have any colour as long as it's black'. It was more efficient to produce only black cars and as a result Ford sold the cheapest car on the market.

However, General Motors wondered whether customers would welcome more choice. They offered red car, blue cars as well as several other colours, and many additional and (apparently) unnecessary luxury items inside the car. All this added to the cost; General Motors could not compete on price with Ford, but, despite this, their sales kept on growing. By the 1930s GM had overtaken Ford. GM has never since lost its position as the world's leading manufacturer of cars, a position based simply on giving customers what they want.

The marketing concept sees the business as a *customer-satisfying* process.

You can contrast the inward-looking product and sales oriented approach with the outward-looking market oriented approach in the following way. Imagine that someone is starting a new business. The thought processes of the inward-looking entrepreneur might go something like this:

> This new electric hammer would be a good idea!
> Let's make some.
> Let's make 1,000.
> Let's charge £1 each.
> Now let's try and sell them.

The outward-looking entrepreneur would tackle the exercise in a very different way. The entrepreneur's thoughts might develop like this:

> Let's find out what people want.
> Let's find out how many they want.
> Let's find out how much they will pay.
> Let's decide if it's profitable.
> Now let's make them.

The writer on management, Peter Drucker, has said that *'the aim of marketing is to make selling superfluous'*.

Put simply, marketing is about ensuring that the business provides products that people want to buy. Selling is concerned with persuading people to buy the products that the business offers.

In effect, marketing is a kind of matching process. It seeks to learn what people want and then tries to match the resources of the company to supplying those wants. Of course, this does not mean that companies can supply whatever people want. A private school cannot suddenly turn itself into a private hospital if it finds that there is more demand for medical care than there is for education. Businesses have to be realistic about their abilities.

You can, therefore, define marketing as a creative process which seeks to *identify and satisfy customer needs profitably by matching company strengths to market opportunities*.

The Marketing Process – A Short Story

In the early years of this century a man made an appointment with the chief of a well-known New York advertising agency. He walked in and asked if the agency was capable of making for him the world's best ever advertisement for shampoo. Not inclined to modesty, the advertising man replied that of course his agency could do that – it was the world's best advertising agency. 'Good,' said the client, getting up to leave, 'get on with it and let me know when you've finished.'

'Hold on a minute,' said the agent. 'Where's the product? What's it like? What does it do? What colour is it? What's the packaging like?'

'We'll have to wait and see,' said the client. 'I'll know the answers when you've come up with the advert'. And he took his leave.

The agent was gobsmacked. This was not at all the normal way of going about things. Where should he start? Not knowing anything about shampoo, he decided that the first job was to educate himself. His staff went and asked people which shampoo was best, how they used it, what problems they had with it, what kind of packaging they found most convenient and attractive. They used the answers to design an advertisement for a fictional product – the ideal shampoo.

They contacted the client, who came back in and was delighted with what he saw. He went away and had the shampoo made and packaged according to the ideal formula. The agency then promoted it. The client's name was Alberto Culver and his company has been extremely successful in the American shampoo market ever since. That story has almost passed into marketing folklore. Alberto Culver followed to the letter the marketing process, starting with 'Let's find out what people want'. He was outward-looking, concerned only with 'doing the right things'.

Doing the Right Things Out of Town

In the early 1970s, British milk and dairy products were not as buoyant as they had been. There were a number of reasons, including competition from the EC milk lake, cuts in free school milk and growing health fears regarding cholesterol. Dairies faced two choices. They could look inwards, tighten their belts, and become more efficient in the hope of weathering the storm. Many chose this alternative. Many dairies' profits did decline over the ensuing years – and many dairies disappeared altogether.

A second, more risky, option was to look for newer, growing areas of need into which the profits from the dairy market could be invested while the going was still good. One company which chose this option was a medium sized regional dairy based in Yorkshire called Associated Dairies Ltd. They pioneered the hypermarket concept in the UK. Being the first to move food shopping out of the town centre was a very bold move, but it paid off. Asda is now one of the largest food retailers in the country and others have followed them into out-of-town superstores.

A more recent arrival to British out of town shopping is IKEA, a Swedish furniture retailer which has almost a hundred stores in twenty countries. IKEA opened its first UK store in Warrington in October 1987, and its second in Neasden, west London, in September 1988.

IKEA was founded in 1943 by Ingvar Kamprad as a small mail-order furniture operation and opened its first out of town furniture store in 1953. It was soon spreading overseas, firstly to Switzerland and then across western Europe, with West Germany now its biggest single market. It now has stores in such far-flung places as Iceland, Kuwait, Saudi Arabia, Hong Kong and Australia.

The success of IKEA is based firmly on doing the right things. Like Asda it has been prepared to take the risk of breaking new ground with its huge out of town furniture superstores. IKEA's smallest stores cover 1,600,000 square feet, three times the size of the biggest stores operated by its two main British rivals, MFI and Harris Queensway. More importantly, the company is effective in terms of exploiting market opportunities at the right time. According to Birger Lund, the managing director of IKEA (UK), as well as identifying the growing preference of the British shopper to visit out of town superstores, the company has also spotted a gap in the British furniture market. According to Lund, the best, high-quality furniture is extremely expensive in the UK, but the low-cost alternative is of very poor quality. IKEA aims to fill that gap in the middle with good quality, reasonably priced furniture.

As well as getting its planning right, IKEA does the right things from day-to-day to keep its customers satisfied. Correctly identifying the view that the public is increasingly taking – that shopping (especially for clothing, durables and luxuries) is a *leisure* activity rather than a chore, IKEA ensures that a visit to one of its stores will be as pleasant and interesting an experience as possible. The stores have a restaurant, selling both English and Swedish food (including reindeer steaks), a video room, a supervised children's playroom and huge car parks. Only seven months after the opening of its Warrington store, IKEA's millionth customer walked through the door – the company knew it must be doing something right.

Marketing Planning

Situation Overview

People cannot plan effectively unless they know exactly where they are starting from. The most common way of analysing the current situation of a business is to perform a SWOT analysis (see figure below) which examines its internal strengths and weaknesses and the external opportunities and threats which it faces in the immediate and more distant future. The directors of the business must steer it towards opportunities and away from threats. The business must locate a group of customers with an unsatisfied need, which can be met by that business. It is the accuracy with which a company matches its internal strengths with any external opportunities which is primarily responsible for success in the marketplace.

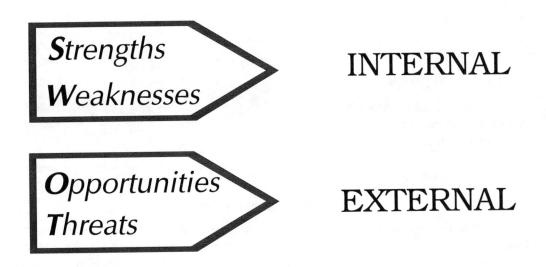

SWOT analysis

Setting Marketing Objectives

The matching process should lead logically to a statement of company objectives. The objectives should be stated as precisely and in as much detail as possible, otherwise it will prove impossible for the business to monitor its progress towards achieving them.

For example, a publisher of diaries might decide to enter the growing personal organiser market. The objective might be to secure a firm foothold in that market, but it would be impossible to know when the objective had been achieved if it was stated in such a vague way. A better way of stating the objective would be to quantify it: for the business to say that it intends to gain a 20% share of the personal organiser market within two years.

Objectives can be quantified in monetary or volume terms. Interim targets might be set, against which progress can be monitored and, if necessary, remedial action taken. The larger the business, the more important it is to have detailed and unambiguous targets so that the whole workforce strives to achieve that common goal.

Formulating a Marketing Strategy

Having decided where it wants to go, and defined it accurately, the business has to decide how it is going to get there. Of course, a marketing strategy must be realistic and consistent with the strengths and weaknesses of the business. As the figure below shows, its strategy should cover the medium-to long-term. It will concentrate on developments, such as the planned dates for the introduction of new products or the opening of new outlets.

1.   STRATEGIC ASPECTS

    ....up to 10 years
    –Broad Objectives
    –New Products
    –New Markets
    –New Initiatives

2.   TACTICAL ASPECTS

    ....less than 1 Year
    – Short-term Activities
    – Doing it better than the Competition
    – Adding Value
    – Effective Promotion

Marketing strategy and tactics

As the figure illustrates, tactical plans are to do with competing in the marketplace, or 'doing it better than the competition'. Tactics are often focused on getting the customer to perceive the 'added value' of their particular product and are often ways of effectively promoting the company's products in the marketplace.

What makes companies successful?

Peters and Waterman in their book, *In Search of Excellence,* summarise this as 'being close to the customer'.

Understanding the marketing environment

Businesses must understand all outside forces which could have an effect upon their operations. These outside forces can be placed in four categories, neatly summarised by the acronym 'PEST'. They are:

1. Political factors

2. Economic factors

3. Social factors

4. Technological factors.

Understanding the Political Environment

There are three aspects of the political environment which can affect a company's ability to carry out its business:

- the attitude of the government towards business activity
- legal controls on business activity
- the influence of pressure groups.

Government's Attitude Towards Business Activity

Some countries are accused of 'economic nationalism', of over-protecting their own industries against foreign competition. In such countries the government's objective often appears to outsiders to be one of making life as difficult as possible for foreign business. This can lead to the kind of administrative harassment which makes it very difficult for a business to trade in that country.

An example is the Japanese insistence that Trebor Sherbert Lemons must be made in a more subdued yellow, not because the colouring poses a health hazard to consumers, but because the colouring has a 'potentially harmful effect on the eyesight'. Trebor's sales to Japan run at only £250,000 per year and, given such problems, Trebor questions whether it is worth the effort – which is, perhaps, the effect the Japanese wish to achieve.

Legal Controls on Business Activity

Legislation can affect business life. In the UK, the Sunday trading laws have made it difficult for many retailers who would like to open for business on Sundays to do so. Cigarette manufacturers have found their freedom to advertise progressively curtailed. Brewers and pubs have had to adjust to the effects of 'drink drive' legislation.

Opportunities can arise from legislation. When the income tax regulations on company cars were changed, Ford saw the opportunity to introduce a new 1.4 litre engine to offer motorists the largest permissible engine size in the bottom tax band and a 1.8 litre engine to do the same in the middle tax band. New health and safety regulations present opportunities to makers of safety equipment which many businesses are obliged to use under the new laws.

Legal constraints do not have to be formal regulations. They may be unwritten 'gentlemen's agreements', such as the informal arrangement between the UK and Japan that imports of Japanese cars into the UK will be kept to 10% of new vehicle registrations. The opening of the Nissan factory in Sunderland, and the arrangement which enables Rover to manufacture Honda cars in the UK, are two examples of Japanese companies reacting to their political environment and finding new ways to sell more cars in this country.

The Influence of Pressure Groups

The influence of pressure groups can often lead to the introduction of the kind of legal constraints mentioned in the previous section. ASH and other anti-smoking pressure groups were instrumental in bringing about the tightening of restrictions on TV advertising of cigarettes.

Many pressure groups are currently seeking to persuade governments to impose further legal constraints on business activities of various kinds. Ecological pressure groups, such as Greenpeace and Friends of the Earth, are trying to curb business activities that have adverse effects on our natural environment. Such groups favour the introduction of a 'carbon tax' on the use of all fuels that come from non-renewable sources.

Ecological pressure groups favour further regulations to reduce the lead content in petrol; the Government has already responded by introducing tax advantages on lead free petrol, but the pressure groups see this as only a start since most petrol sold still contains lead. They would like to see the complete banning of CFCs and similar gases that are harmful to the ozone layer.Some companies, such as Johnsons, have already responded by investing in more expensive aerosol manufacturing plant to produce propellant gases that do not have this harmful effect. Pressure groups are examined in more detail in Part Five.

The Economic Environment

The economic environment within a country will often be directly influenced by the political attitude of its government. However, national economies are becoming increasingly dependent upon world economic trends and marketers need to be alert to all economic factors which might influence their business.

In analysing investment potential in any particular country, the marketer will need to be aware of the following economic factors.

Income levels

The most accurate measure of a country's wealth is its 'per capita income': that is, its national income divided by its population. This ratio gives a rough indication of that country's standard of living. A typical Gulf State might have a per capita income of around $20,000 pa, whereas some African countries would struggle to exceed $100 pa. Most western economies have per capita incomes of around $10,000 per annum, with the US in the lead and the UK lagging some way behind wealthier European countries, such as Switzerland, Germany, Sweden and Austria.

Inflation

Inflation erodes the purchasing power of the consumer. It causes severe problems for marketers who have to set prices accurately and estimate demand. At times of high inflation, people feel worse off. They may spend less or they may 'trade down'. For example, it is possible that high UK inflation in the 1970s contributed to the move away from branded groceries towards cheaper 'own label' products.

Purchasing Power

There are two kinds of purchasing power in which marketers are interested:

1.   'Disposable income': this is the amount of money that people have left after deductions, such as tax and National Insurance contributions, have been made. This is a more useful measure than per capita income, but may still not describe the amount of money people actually have to spend.

2.   'Discretionary income' is a better indicator of spending power. It describes the amount of money people have left over to spend as they choose once they have made their essential expenditure on housing, food, basic clothing etc.

Distribution of Income

Marketers want to know how a country's wealth is distributed. For example, Sweden has a higher per capita income that the UK. Income is much more evenly distributed. There are few very poor or very rich people and there is a very large, comfortable middle-income bracket. The UK's (lower) national income is distributed much less evenly, with a much larger population of poor people, a smaller middle class and a much larger percentage of rich people. Although there are several countries with a higher per capita income than the UK, the British market is, after the US and Germany, the third best market for BMW cars. Some very poor countries can be surprisingly good markets for luxury products because. although the large majority of the population is very poor, the ruling elite is extremely wealthy. Some African countries, for example, are very good markets for Mercedes cars and malt whisky.

The Social Environment

The Social Environment – Demographic Aspects

Demography is the study of populations. a subject of great interest to the marketer since people are the end result of most of his activities. Ultimately, the marketer is interested in people buying his product or service in sufficient volumes to make business profitable. The demographic make-up of the populations will help him to work out whether he is likely to achieve this objective.

There are five main demographic factors of interest to the marketer.

Population size

The sheer size of the population may be more relevant to some products than to others. For luxury goods consumed only by a wealthy elite, total population size will be of little relevance, but will be much more important for basic goods which may be bought by a high percentage of the population.

Population growth

For basic products, strong population growth means an increasing potential market.

Geographical distribution

The marketer needs to know where the people are and whether the market is densely or sparsely populated. A densely populated market, such as Singapore, is easier and less costly to penetrate than a more sparsely populated market, such as exists in neighbouring Malaysia.

Age distribution

Since different age groups often buy various goods and services, the age distribution of the population is highly relevant to marketing planning. In the UK, a number of demographic trends are currently apparent. Since the birth rate fell from the mid-1960s, the youth market is declining. This will have adverse repercussions for companies which rely heavily on that market e.g. pop records, teenage magazines and fashion shops. The next generation, the 25-45 year olds, often known as the baby boomers, since they were born in the years of high birth rate after the Second World War, will be a large market. The other demographic group showing strong growth is retired people. In particular a new, younger, more affluent retired group is emerging, keen to spend money, especially on leisure. Activities, from gardening to foreign holidays, represent significant market opportunities here.

Demographic changes also have an significant impact on the labour market and this is examined later on.

Changing family patterns

The typical family is no more. Mr. and Mrs. Average, both in their first marriage with two kids, the husband at work and the wife at home, now represents less than 4% of all families. Divorces are increasingly common, as are single-parent families. Such trends mean that the number of households is increasing at a faster rate than the population. Thus, items such as fridges – which are purchased by households rather than individuals – have more potential sales growth than is apparent from the bare population statistics. The huge growth in the working women population has revolutionised many markets – the growth in convenience food and labour-saving appliances being two of the more obvious examples.

The Social Environment – Behavioural Aspects

Marketing is a *behavioural* discipline. It is about people and the way people behave when purchasing goods and services.

Social trends

Any community will have a large variety of secondary cultural or social values. These may be attitudes, beliefs or trends which are less firmly adhered to than the core cultural values; indeed, they may be accepted only by certain sections of the community. Current examples in the UK would be physical fitness and healthy eating, both clear national trends, both followed more determinedly by some sections of society than by others, but both affording considerable marketing opportunities.

Aesthetic values

A marketer needs to know what a society rates as attractive and unattractive in terms of design, styling, fashion and colour. Early Japanese cars, for example, suffered in European markets because their styling was geared to American tastes. This resulted in a brash, chromy image from which they struggled to recover.

The Technological Environment

Technology is changing continuously and at an ever increasing rate. Think of just a few of the major inventions which have occurred in the twentieth century: electric lighting; radio; television; photocopying; X-rays; life support machines; synthetic fibres; plastics; electronic circuits; the computer. A business that does not keep up with technological advances will fail, sooner or later. As far as the technological environment is concerned, the marketer should be concerned with three main factors in his planning:

- new processes
- new materials
- generic replacements.

New processes

New ways of doing things are being constantly fuelled by technological innovation. One has only to think of cash dispensers outside banks, EPOS tills in supermarkets (the tills which record the price of each item simply by reading its bar code), flexible manufacturing systems which enable many of the operations involved in building a car to be performed automatically by robots. The firm has to keep up with these changes. If it does not, and its competitors adopt them, it will soon become uncompetitive.

New materials

Carbon fibres, graphite, and kevlar are just three of the new high performance materials which have come to prominence in recent years. They are now widely used in the manufacture of sporting equipment from squash rackets to racing cars, from fishing rods to catamarans. Any manufacturer of high performance sporting goods who had not adapted to these new materials would find sales falling dramatically.

Generic replacements

A generic product is a product class. Coffee is a generic product, Nescafe is not: it is a particular brand of coffee. From time to time, a technological innovation will make a generic product (and obviously all the specific products within that class) obsolete. Cassette recorders took over from reel-to-reel tape recorders. Calculators made slide-rules obsolete. Drawing office equipment is gradually being replaced by computer aided design (CAD).

The American marketing professor, Theodore Levitt, has explained why this happens. Nobody, says Levitt, buys drills. Customers buy holes. It is not the drill itself which they value, but its hole making capabilities because it is the holes for which they have a need. If a new, more cost-effective method of making holes was developed (lasers, perhaps), customers would soon abandon traditional steel twist drills and turn to the new hole making method. If drill manufacturers could not supply the new hole makers, they would soon find themselves without a business. As Levitt says, customers do not buy products, they buy the service which that product performs for them.

Market Structure and Performance

According to Kotler, a market is: *A collection of individuals and organisations who are actual or potential buyers of a product or service.*

There are a number of important factors concerning the market itself which must be analysed. These are:

- buyers
- purchasers
- market size
- market potential
- market growth
- barriers to entry.

Buyers

The historical view of a market was that of a physical space in which buyers and sellers could meet to buy and sell goods and services. Economists have kept the same basic definition of markets, but see this market place activity in its abstract form. They see markets as involving all the potential buyers and sellers of a particular good or service and regard the economic exchange process as the essential activity within that arena.

Marketing, in contrast, limits its definition to the buying side of these transactions. The market for instant custard refers to all those consumers who buy instant custard. The businesses which sell instant custard will be referred to as 'the industry' or 'the competition'.

As far as markets are concerned, there are two basic types of market:

- consumer markets
- organisational markets.

Consumer markets are made up of individuals who buy items for personal domestic consumption. Typically they buy from middlemen, such as retailers, and transactions are of a low value. A £5,000 purchase (e.g. a car) is a highly important, and very infrequent, transaction for most buyers in consumer markets.

Organisational markets can be further split into *industrial markets*, where buyers purchase goods and services to use in the production of other goods or services; re-seller markets, where organisations, such as shops, buy goods for re-sale, and *government markets*, where public sector organisations buy goods and services which they consume in the provision of state services. For most organisational buyers £5,000 will represent a relatively small transaction. Orders worth millions of pounds frequently occur in organisational markets.

In your study of marketing you will concentrate on *consumer markets*.

Purchases

Buyers, by definition, must be buying something. This 'something' is a purchase. Markets can be classified according to the type of purchase being made. There are two different methods of classifying markets according to the nature of the purchases made:

1. on the tangibility of the purchases, it can be divided into three sections: durables; non-durables; services.

2. on the way in which buyers make such purchases; it can be divided into three categories: *convenience* goods; *shopping* goods; *speciality* goods.

Durables

These are tangible goods, which are expected to last for a long time in use, at least for over a year; e.g. furniture; tools.

Non-durables

These are tangible goods which are normally used up quickly, after one or a few uses; e.g. food; batteries.

Services

These are intangible items, such as activities, manual or intellectual forms of assistance or even ideas. They cannot be touched or stored, but they do offer benefits to buyers. Hairdressing, decorating, education and advertising are all services.

The second method is based on the way in which buyers make such purchases and can also be divided into three categories:

Convenience goods

Usually purchased on a regular basis, often of relatively low value, purchases of convenience goods are made with very little thought or pre-planning. They are usually habitual purchases, but may also be made on impulse. Basic foodstuffs, sweets, beer and newspapers would all come into this category.

Shopping goods

These purchases require more consideration. Buyers will often 'shop around', comparing competing brands, with the objective of obtaining the best value for their money. Shopping goods also include high visibility items (often called 'conspicuous purchases'), which may affect the way they are viewed by other people, and whose purchase, therefore, involves particular care. Examples of shopping goods are clothes, furniture, holidays and some special food purchases, such as wine.

Speciality goods

These purchases have the same attributes as shopping goods, but are also special interest purchases, typical of the behaviour of the 'connoisseur consumer'. For these purchases, consumers will be prepared to go out of their way to buy exactly what they want. They will be more knowledgeable about these goods and the relative attributes of competing brands and they will often want to buy the best they can afford, rather than going for value for money. Speciality goods include cameras, hi-fi and sporting equipment.

Market analysis, however, will often concentrate on the more dynamic aspects of markets, such as those outlined below.

Market Size

For common consumer goods and services in western markets, market size figures, expressed in *value* or *volume terms*, are usually quite easy to find in published form. Market size statistics are difficult to obtain for obscure goods and many industrial goods. In less developed countries, statistics are almost impossible to obtain for any good.

Market Potential

Market size refers to the existing total of purchases of that product type but, as our original definition indicated, marketers regard markets as including *all potential future buyers as well as existing buyers*. The potential UK market for domestic dishwashers includes every household, but the existing market size is still only a low proportion of its potential.

Market Growth

If potential is greater than existing market size, the marketer would like to know how quickly the market is likely to grow towards that potential. Marketers always seek high growth markets because they are often more profitable. In low growth, static or declining markets, competition tends to be very fierce, with sellers often resorting to extreme tactics such as large price cuts. This is often felt necessary as the only way in which companies can increase their sales is to take business from competitors. In high growth markets it is much easier for suppliers to meet their growth targets. A company, seeking an annual growth in sales of

10% operating in a market with a growth rate of 10%, needs to perform only at the industry average to achieve its objectives. It does not need to take business from competitors but can rely on the fact that the market is getting bigger. In the early days of personal computers, when the market was showing rapid growth, many UK manufacturers performed extremely well. But as market size began to approach market potential, growth slowed and competition intensified. Many smaller manufacturers went out of business (e.g. Sinclair) and even the more famous, such as Acorn, experienced extreme difficulties.

Barriers to Entry

Some markets are made artificially less attractive because governments erect barriers to entry against foreign suppliers. Usually in the form of tariff barriers, they can also take the form of administrative or safety procedures to which it is difficult and expensive to conform. Barriers to entry can also be commercial. In the washing powder market, for example, the two dominating suppliers, Lever Bros. and Proctor and Gamble, try to make it very difficult for new competitors to enter the market. Each company produces a wide range of similar brands, filling the supermarket shelves and making it very difficult for a new entrant to find an opening. By maintaining extremely high advertising expenditures, they make the promotion of any new competing product extremely expensive.

Understanding Customers

Markets fall into the two broad categories: consumer and organisational. The customers in these two kinds of market can be very different, as can their buying behaviour. Let us examine each in turn.

Understanding Buyers in Consumer Markets

According to Kotler, a consumer market is: *a collection of all the individuals and households who buy or acquire goods or services for personal consumption.*

In order to fully understand customers, the marketer needs to be able to answer four straightforward questions:

1. Who buys?
2. What do they buy?
3. How do they buy?
4. How do they make their buying decisions?

Who Buys?

A detailed knowledge of the type or types of consumer who buy the product is essential to marketers who will want to know all about their age, gender, family position, occupation, income, interests and activities. Marketers also need to acquire information about their home and the neighbourhood in which it is found, the kind of newspaper and magazines they read, the car they drive: in fact, all about their lifestyle in general. Through the possession of such detailed knowledge, marketers can match the benefits offered by their product or service to the right group of consumers. Many people believe that this process – matching the product or service very accurately to segments of the market – lies at the heart of marketing success.

What do they Buy?

Marketers must know exactly what products are currently bought by those consumers. This is one of the reasons why consumer marketers find market share figures so important. Market share figures provide the basis for answering this question. It is important to know whether buyers prefer an Escort, Nova, Cavalier, Golf or Tipo. For most common consumer products, businesses will study share statistics on a monthly basis. They will look for the effects of minor modifications in the marketing mix, such as a new sales promotion, as well as major developments, such as the introduction of a new model. The marketers' ultimate objective is not to build the world's best car, but to produce a model which most closely matches 'what consumers want to buy'.

How do they Buy?

This question concerns the way that people behave when they are buying the product or service. There are four main questions that the marketer will want answered.

- Where do they buy?
- When do they buy?
- How often do they buy?
- How loyally do they buy?

Where do they buy?

Some goods, such as most groceries, are bought at huge superstores. Some, like bread, meat and fresh vegetables at local shops. Some, such as fashion clothing or cameras, are bought in specialist stores. Some, like soft drinks, are bought almost anywhere that is convenient, from the newsagent's to the railway station, from the fish and chip shop to the petrol station.

There are certain products people like to choose at home. Leisure purchases often come into this category. Some people like to spend hours studying the seed catalogue before buying next year's seeds for their garden. For products like this, people enjoy the actual process of buying. The way they are sold must, therefore, cater to this need, so seed companies usually provide interesting, detailed catalogues, whilst sailboard manufacturers will produce exciting brochures full of dramatic photographs.

When do they buy?

There are two aspects to this question. Firstly, there is the time of day or week when products are bought. Milk and newspapers, for example, are required early in the morning. Supermarkets have discovered that more and more people like to do their grocery shopping in the early evening after work, so most are now open until eight o'clock. Petrol stations have discovered that there is a range of basic essential items that households can run out of at any time and need to buy urgently. Many have, therefore, opened small convenience stores since their site is already open for business for petrol for long hours.

How often do they buy?

Frequency of purchase is very important to the marketer. The less frequently a product is purchased, the more likely it is to be a significant act for the buyer, who therefore gives the whole buying process more thought. Very often, marketers will divide buyers into heavy, medium and light users. Light users of the same product may buy in a different way from heavy users. A heavy magazine buyer, for example, will probably have a regular weekly order for a particular magazine, or several magazines, and will tend to stick to the same titles. An occasional magazine buyer, who buys a magazine to read on a long train journey perhaps, is likely to take much more care over the purchase of that magazine, flicking through several titles and inspecting the contents before making a decision. This leads into the fourth question.

How loyally do people buy?

Some products command a very high degree of brand loyalty. National newspapers are a good example. The higher the buyer's level of loyalty the more difficult it is to break into a market. Eddie Shah discovered this with his *Today* newspaper, which did not reach the level of sales he predicted. Even now, long after Shah's departure, the circulation of *Today* is well below its main rivals, such as the *Express* and *Mail*. In general, magazines have a less loyal following, with many chosen at the newsagent's or kiosk by buyers who are sometimes in a rush and who often choose a different title each time. This different buyer behaviour is reflected in the much greater numbers of launches of new magazines.

How do they make their buying decisions?

Understanding the way in which consumers make their decision to purchase a product or service is a vital part of the marketing manager's job.

Customers do differ from one another in many ways, a fact which forms the basis of the concept of *market segmentation*. To give one example, a poor 65 year old married lady is a different person to a very wealthy unmarried 22 year old man. Each will buy different products and services; each will have different priorities and each will follow a different lifestyle. Quite simply, they have different needs and it would not be possible for marketers of most products to treat them in the same way. Market segments are *groups of customers who have something in common*.

Customers within segments will be similar to each other; customers in different segments will be dissimilar to each other. However, the method by which the marketer divides the market into segments is extremely important. One method might be to divide the population into groups according to hair colour. You might end up with people with black hair, people with fair hair, people with red hair and people with no hair. This would be a perfectly valid method of classifying people into groups whose members were similar to each other and dissimilar from members of other groups. But what use would it be to the marketer of frozen peas, designer jeans, gloss paint or domestic electrical services? Very little. The most important aspect of market segmentation is *the choice of criteria used to divide customers into groups*. Choosing the right criteria is a critical task for marketers who are often faced with several alternative ways of grouping customers. This section will examine the more common criteria used to segment markets.

The basic steps in this decision making process are shown in the figure below.

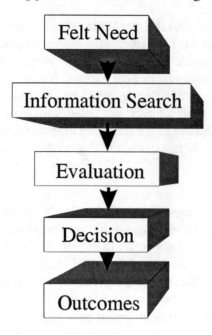

The purchase decision-making process

Demographic Segmentation

There are a number of demographic criteria which may be of relevance to different markets.

Age

Segmenting customers to age bands is very common. Children are clearly different from retired people, but quite narrow age bands can help to describe variations in purchasing behaviour for some products. Take the following female fashion chains: Chelsea Girl; Miss Selfridge; Top Girl; Etam; and Dorothy Perkins.

Each is aimed at a slightly older age band than the previous one, starting with teenage girls and ending with women in their thirties and forties. The age bands overlap, but the steps in the age segments catered for are not large.

Sex

Sex is a relevant segmentation criterion for many markets. Some products, like the fashions in Top Girl, are aimed exclusively at one sex. Many other products, like beer, are aimed primarily at one sex. It is not likely that sex will be used as a criterion on its own. It is more usual for it to be used, in conjunction with other criteria, to describe the members of a segment. The practice of using more than one variable to segment markets is very common. Etam, for example, might be aiming at a segment of 30-45 year old women; two variables – age and gender – are used to define the segment. In fact, Etam is much more likely to use at least three variables: age; gender; customer spending power.

Demographic Trends

By the year 2030, deaths will exceed births and the UK population will begin to shrink; there will be 3.4 million aged over 80 – 60% more than in 1992 – and 360% greater than in 1961. The reason for this decline lies in what demographers call the Period Total Fertility Rate (PTFR), which in the UK has settled down at 1.8 children per family. This falls beneath the figure of 2.1 children that is needed for long-term population replacement.

The lack of young people means more than just a lack of young employees: it also means a lack of consumers, consumers with large disposable income. Businesses selling to 'the youth market' need to be cautious: the number of 15 to 19-year olds has declined from 1987's total of 3.8 million to a present total of 3.2 million. This decline is projected to continue throughout the 1990s but will reach its low point in 1996 when the number falls to 3.1 million. Between now and 2000, the sectors of the UK population predicted to grow quickest are the over-75s and the middle-aged (those between 45 and 54 wield 'Grey Power' and collectively are known as the 'grey market').

By 1995 there will be more consumers over the age of 45 than under 30.

Another demographic trend is that of the disintegrating family. The number marrying is falling, the divorce rate is rising and the proportion of illegitimate births has exceeded 30%. The editor of *Social Trends* (Central Statistical Office) has said, 'If it goes on at this rate, there will be no births within marriage in 20 years.' Professor David Coleman in his book, *The British Population* (1992) points out that in the 1980s 73% of illegitimate births were jointly registered by parents who gave the same address and could be inferred to be co-habiting in what are known as 'optional families'. 25% of households in 1990 were single-person, with the total expected to rise by over a million by 2000, mainly because of divorce and widowhood.

Consider what are the implications of these trends are for the following:

- manufacturers of Reebok trainers
- the brewing industry
- advertisers
- Saga Holidays
- insurance companies.

Income

For many products, income levels can be a sure discriminator. Products. like dish washers, video cameras and holidays to the Caribbean, are not likely to be bought by consumers with very low levels of income. Even within a product class, top of the range and bargain basement versions will often be designed to appeal to buyers with differing income levels. An Escort XR3i is aimed at a more affluent buyer than an Escort Popular. This can also be the case with everyday products. Nescafe Gold Blend coffee is targeted at a more affluent consumer than a basic own-label instant coffee, which will usually be half its price.

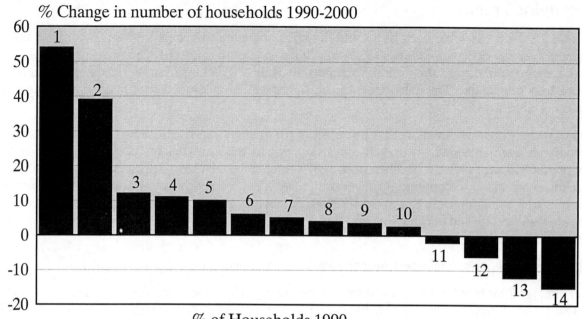

1. 35-44 yearold single person	8. family, youngest child over 5
2. 45-54 year old single person	9. family, youngest child under 5
3. one parent family	10. couple with non-dependent children
4. 60+ year old single person	11. 18-34 year old couple wthout children
5. 45-54 year old couple without children	12. 60+ year old couple without children
6. one parent with non-dependent children	13. other
7. 35-44 year old couple without children	14. 18-34 year old couple without children

The Changing Household Structure

Level of education

Sometimes, the age at which people left full-time education is used as a segmentation variable. This criterion has obvious value with products requiring a certain level of intellectual application, such as books, but has also been found to influence other products as well. For example, research has shown that people with a university degree are more likely to make an objective analysis of value for money when buying groceries, and will often buy own-label products rather than more expensive, branded equivalents. People with lower levels of education often opt for the 'safety' of the well-known brand, even though their income may be lower.

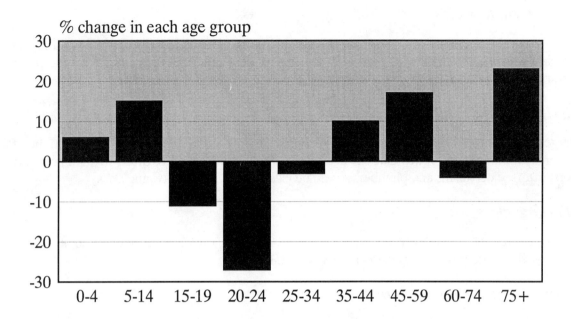

% Change in each Age Group 1989 to 2000

As you can see, segmentation is a complex issue. Will the well-educated, affluent coffee consumer buy own-label or Gold Blend? To answer this question, the marketer will need to understand consumers very well and to segment the market according to several variables.

Social Class

Segmentation by social class is used very frequently by consumer marketers in the UK. There are a number of methods of dividing the British population into social classes, most of which are broadly similar. The method most commonly used by marketers is that devised by the National Readership Survey (NRS). NRS breaks down the population into six social classes:

A: Upper middle class

Forming 3% of the population, social class A covers higher managerial, administrative and professional occupations. The head of the household will be a successful business or professional person, or may have considerable inherited wealth. They would normally live in expensive detached houses in provincial areas or, if in London, in expensive flats or town houses in the better parts of town. Social class A occupations include barristers, bishops, brain surgeons and top business people.

B: Middle class

Defined as intermediate managerial, administrative or professional occupations, social class B people are quite senior, but not yet at the top of their profession. Social class B can include younger people, destined for social class A but who have not yet climbed so far up their career ladder. They are well off, but their lifestyle is respectable rather than rich or luxurious. 10% of Britons are in this class.

C1: Lower middle class

Covering supervisory, clerical and junior managerial positions, often called white collar workers, the lower middle class will often be significantly less affluent than classes A and B. It includes 24% of the population. Most nurses, and many civil servants, are in social class C1.

C2: Skilled working class

The largest class, with 30% of the population, it consists mainly of skilled workers. Tending to be of lower educational attainment and status than social class C1, they can nevertheless often be higher earners. Print workers, fitters, electricians and plumbers would be classified as skilled working class.

D: Working class

Consisting entirely of manual workers, semi-skilled or unskilled, this class includes assembly line workers and farm workers and unskilled workers in service industries.

E: Those at the lowest levels of subsistence

Social class E is made up largely of the unemployed and the poorest pensioners. Together, social classes D and E comprise one third of the population.

Geographic Segmentation

Even in a small country like the UK, the same can be true. If one were to analyse consumption patterns of whisky, beer and wine, significant regional variations would be found between Scotland, the North of England and the South East of England. Increasingly, marketers are making distinctions between affluent and poor areas. This is not necessarily regional but can be applied to much smaller geographic areas.

Benefit segmentation

Many markets can be segmented in terms of benefits sought by customers. Car buyers may be looking primarily for reliability, high mileage to the gallon, speed, interior comfort or exterior appearance. There are said to be five main segments in the toothpaste market. Some buy for cosmetic reasons: they want white shining teeth. Second, there are those who buy strong toothpaste to avoid bad breath. A third segment buys mainly for medical reasons, to prevent tooth decay. Fourth, there are those buying for children who want 'flavour'. Finally, there is the price conscious segment. Shampoo is often sold on a *benefits* basis: good for greasy or dry hair; good for daily washing; good for fighting dandruff.

Geo-demographic Segmentation

The criticism of the social class-based NRS method of segmentation has prompted a search for more accurate methods of segmentation which will give more reliable predictors of buying behaviour.

Amongst the most successful of the new methods are those which seek to combine geographic and demographic principles of segmentation. The most well-known of these new methods is ACORN which stands for 'A Classification of Residential Neighbourhoods'. Developed by Richard Webber in the late

1970s, and based on detailed information from the 1971 census (later updated from the 1981 data), ACORN classifies households according to the neighbourhood in which they are found. The underlying philosophy of ACORN (and other geo-demographic methods of segmentation) is that certain types of neighbourhood will not only display similar housing but also will have residents with similar demographic and social characteristics who will share common lifestyles and will tend to display similar purchasing behaviour.

The eleven ACORN types now in common use, and the percentage of popultion they comprise, are:

A: Agricultural areas 3.3% of households

B: Modern family housing, higher incomes 14.8%

C: Older housing of intermediate status 18.7%

D: Poor quality older terraced housing 4.6%

E: Better off council estates 12.2%

F: Less well-off council estates 10.4%

G: Poorest council estates 6.8%

H: Multi-racial areas 3.5%

I: High status non-family areas 4.9%

J: Affluent suburban housing 18.9%

K: Better off retirement areas 4.8%

Life-style Segmentation

The *lifestyle* concept was developed originally by the Leo Burnett advertising agency, in conjunction with the University of Chicago.

It covers people's day-to-day habits, work patterns, leisure interests, attitudes and values. Lifestyle segments would be based on distinctive ways of living and social values portrayed by certain types of people. In fact, the lifestyle concept is sometimes, more accurately, referred to as values and lifestyles.

The findings from a survey of the lifestyles of people in fifteen countries in Europe found that for every one person interested in morality and maintaining social values, there are two people who are more interested in material wealth and consumerism. This is of critical concern to those interested in 'the market'.

The survey, known by the title 'Lifestyles', is a departure from the usual market research method of classifying/ categorising groups into the rich, the not-so-rich and the poor. This new method analyses consumers by their personalities and the way they choose to live, rather than by their demographics.

Businesses large and small have seized upon the results of the survey, which was carried out by a number of market research companies using a 150 page questionnaire, with the purpose of tailoring their market strategies for both the multi-national and regional markets as the deadline approaches for the lowering of EC trade barriers in 1992.

The Lifestyles survey concludes that 63% of the 24,000 respondents were interested in materialism while 37% felt that moral and social issues played a central part in their lives.

British consumers, like their EC counterparts, fall into six main categories or 'mentalities'. They can be categorised as: the ambitious; the dreamers; the withdrawn; the contesters; the militants; the notables. The first three groups are broadly described as 'the materialists'; the latter groups are 'the moralists'.

Businesses regard the new classification of consumer as an essential marketing tool for the 1990s and beyond. They believe that it is no longer enough to know *who* is buying your product; the competitive edge is gained by knowing *why* they buy them. Market research companies maintain that the traditional demographic breakdown using age, income, family size and cultural level is inadequate, since it does not help forecast how people behave and fails to reveal people's motivation in buying.

The findings are not likely to change for a considerable time. Those people who answered questions such as, 'What is the ideal car you see yourself driving in 2001?' or 'What do you like to do most during your free time?' are giving information about their attitudes and about their motivation. That information is like gold as far as anticipating consumers' decisions is concerned.

The Lifestyles survey showed that 28% of UK respondents are 'ambitious'. These are generally young, urban people who have benefited from a good education and who wish to succeed and, in order to be seen to have succeeded, spend: they are big spenders who seek variety and choice. 'Business', a sub-group of the ambitious category, is made up of single people who are not very religious. They are elitist, competitive and ambitious and are looking forward to the Single Market and 1992 with eagerness. They tend to work in commerce and services.

This group is of particular interest to manufacturers of high-tech equipment and producers of pre-cooked meals and convenience foods. This category is well equipped in quality products; they want the latest and best television and demand a VCR that matches the TV. They own microwaves because they regard cooking as a waste of their valuable time – time they might be using to make money. Their philosophy is Gordon Gecko's philosophy: 'Lunch is for wimps'. They like choice and the atmosphere and ambience of a shop is important to them. Easy access for shopping is also important, since they don't want to queue. Price is of little concern to them, but they are susceptible to special offers. If one saw a pair of Reebok trainers at £65.99 instead of £70, one would certainly buy them and would not worry that a pair of good trainers without the brand name could be obtained across the street for £19.99.

The 'withdrawn' category (23%) earns less than the EC average and is made up of people who tend to be conservative. A sub-group is characterised by the label 'prudent'. They are concerned about money, probably because they don't have very much of it. Many will never have been outside their own locality or region. They are often rural, retired and would probably regard people who haven't lived in the locality for at least twenty years as 'incomers' or 'blow ins'.

The 'withdrawn' are worried about the influence of foreigners. They tend to produce as much of their own food as they can, shop locally and bargain hunt. Spending on clothes is a tiny part of their expenditure. Probably they don't have a bank account. They economise wherever they can and they are considered by marketers to be 'under equipped'.

Like the ambitious and the withdrawn, the 'dreamers' are also interested in money and what it can buy. But they are far more concerned with building a comfortable lifestyle for their family. They tend to have a romantic view of life and want to have a nice home and live comfortably, but they don't want to have to work sixteen hours a day to achieve it.

The next category is the 'notables': well-heeled, ultra-conservative, middle aged. One of its sub-groups is the 'gentry', who are uninterested in money since they've always had it and probably always will. They play golf, drive nice cars, consume luxury goods and are well-equipped in sophisticated products for domestic comfort.

'Militants' and 'contesters' are groups which are roughly equal in size. They are concerned about the environment and show a sense of community spirit. The militants are mostly middle-aged and tend to be 'joiners'; often they will be involved in Neighbourhood Watch and various community associations. They are regular voters in local and national elections and they are opposed to racial and religious extremism.

Contesters tend to be people who challenge. They were probably in the students' union at university or college and they have protested at everything from contraception to abortion. They are between 30 and 40 years of age and don't see consumerism as a way of life. They tend to be buyers of second-hand clothes and second-hand items.

The Lifestyles system is being promoted as a database which is unique and which offers a wide variety of applications and 'customised services'. To access it, a business or marketeer must be ready to pay up an initial £2,000, with an additional £1,500 for a specialised report on a particular report or product. Already Lifestyles has helped some businesses to identify or anticipate problems in the run up to the Single Market. Conservativism and tight budget controls are forcing many companies to go after niche markets and specialised marketing efforts so that there is no wastage. But two consumers with similar incomes and of similar age may have very, very different buying habits and lifestyles.

Targeting

The marketer will try to match the strengths of the company and its products with the market segment or segments exhibiting the most suitable needs and priorities. This is the process of targeting, which is the next logical step after segmentation.

Targeting Strategies

When selecting the most appropriate segments to target, the marketer has three broad strategies to choose from.

1. Mass Marketing
One product for the whole market

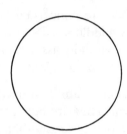

2. Selective Marketing
Several segments targeted with a different marketing mix offered to each segment

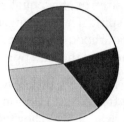

3. Niche Marketing
Concentration of the firm's resources on one small part of the market

Three broad targeting strategies

Mass marketing

Sometimes called *undifferentiated marketing,* this involves selling one product to the entire market, or at least to a very large proportion of it. Well-known examples in the past have been the Model T Ford and Coca Cola. Mass marketing has to focus on what is similar in the needs of customers, rather than on what is different, and must develop a product and marketing programme that aims to appeal to most buyers.

Mass marketing has some major advantages for the supplier. The economies of scale afforded by mass production, distribution in bulk and global advertising help to make the business more efficient, enabling it to reduce its costs and become more price competitive.

Selective marketing

A selective marketing strategy is the sort adopted by most medium- and large-sized companies. It involves covering several, or even all, of the segments of the market but, in contrast to mass marketing, will offer a different mix that is carefully designed to meet the needs of each segment served. Most of the large car manufacturers sell a range of models designed to cover most market segments.

Niche marketing

Often most suited to the strengths of small companies, niche marketing means that a business concentrates its resources on just one small segment or, at most, a small number of tiny segments or *niches.* Such a strategy makes a lot of sense for small companies for two reasons:

- it allows them to concentrate their limited resources on being one of the best suppliers in a precise market

- many niches are ignored by large companies because they are not considered sufficiently worthwhile opportunities. The small business may find that it faces less competition from large companies in carefully chosen niche markets.

Morgan Cars has been extremely successful with its niche marketing strategy. Morgan faces no direct competition from large companies because that market segment is much too small for a large company, such as Ford or Nissan to contemplate.

In the free-spending 1980s, businesses such as Sock Shop, Knickerbox and Tie Rack successfully exploited their respective niche markets; in the recession of the early 1990s all suffered badly, not because they misjudged their market, but because they took on debt in order to expand and then failed to service those debts as interest rates rose.

Marketing Research

Information is essential to marketers and the marketing success of a business may well depend on how efficient it is at gathering and analysing relevant information. The gathering and analysing of such information is known as *market research*.

There are three sources of the information which the marketing researcher may have to gather:

1.   The researcher can look at information which already exists within the business. These are *internal* sources of information.

2.   The next step, which usually involves more work and more cost, is to look outside the company, to *external* sources of information which already exist, perhaps in the form of published market reports or government statistics. These are *secondary* sources of information.

3.   The most expensive step of all is to look for information which does not already exist in any retrievable form. This information has to be gathered from consumers and usually involves asking questions to find out the desired facts or opinions. These are *primary* sources of information. Look, in turn, at each of these ways of gathering information.

1. Internal Sources of Information

Internal marketing information might include:

a.   Summaries of past sales figures, broken down by company size or market segment.

b.   Competitor information, including brochures and product information.

c.   The sales force is the company's eyes and ears in the market place. Sales people should report back any interesting information they have gleaned about customers or activity in the market place.

2. Secondary Sources of Information

There is a wealth of information from secondary sources available to the marketer. Some of the more commonly used examples are:

Information about markets

Information is big business and many companies make very handsome profits by gathering information about markets, compiling it into reports and selling them to anyone who wants to buy them. The government produces statistics and information on markets which can also be consulted. Listed below are some of the more common sources of market information.

Mintel reports

Mintel produce a monthly journal containing about six reports on markets of interest, almost always consumer markets. Monthly Mintel reports are about ten to twenty pages long and give the kind of basic information that marketers need for a preliminary scan of the market, such as: market size, projected growth; main competitors; market share of main products; advertising spend of main brands; significant trends.

Key Note reports

Key Note reports differ in that they produce reports for business to business markets. They do not have a regular monthly edition but cover a range of business markets and update the reports on a regular basis. Around 75 pages long, they provide a fairly detailed introduction to marketers.

Government statistics

There is an almost equally large and bewildering range of government statistics available to the marketer. The best place to start is the free guide from the CSO (Central Statistical Office) entitled, *Government Statistics: A Brief Guide to Sources*.

Audits

Retail audits record sales to consumers through a sample of retail outlets, usually at two monthly intervals. Though retail audits have existed for many years, the spread of EPOS (electronic point of sale) tills has greatly facilitated the task of data collection. Two companies, A. C. Nielsen and Retail Audits, are the most well-known in this field. They collect data of retail sales, typically goods sold through supermarkets or major retail chains, and sell the figures to anyone who wants to buy them. Both retailers and manufacturers find such detailed, up-to-date tracking of sales useful, since it enables them to work out matters such as market shares, the performance of new products, the effect of a price change, a sales promotion or a new advertising campaign. It offers continuous monitoring of their performance in the market place.

Panels

Panels are groups of consumers who record their purchases, their media habits and/or their attitudes in a regularly kept diary. The diary will be very easy to keep; usually it is simply a matter of ticking boxes.

Primary Sources of Information

To meet their specific research needs, marketers often need to generate primary information. There are four main methods of primary marketing research: observation; experimentation; survey; discussion groups.

Observation

An observer (or hidden camera) watches consumers, usually in the act of buying or choosing. It is most commonly used to observe consumer behaviour in stores, recording details like how consumers move through the store, whether they notice and stop at special in-store displays and, probably most commonly, how they scan the shelves, since the shelf space and shelf location given to competing brands in supermarkets can often be significant factors in their sales.

Survey

The survey is the most used method of data collection in marketing research.

Simple random sampling

Sometimes called *probability sampling*, the researcher starts with a complete list (the population or sample frame) of the market or group to be surveyed. He or she then determines the size of sample required and chooses that sample from the complete list on a random basis, which means that each individual in the sample frame has the same likelihood of ending up in the same sample.

Stratified random sampling

Random sampling can sometimes distort results in markets where some customers are more important than others. In this case, *stratified* random sampling would be used. This involves the weighting of the sample on the basis of the importance of the various segments making up the market. Imagine that a company has 10,000 customers segmented as follows: 5000 light users accounting for £5m turnover; 3,000 medium users accounting for £20m turnover; 2,000 heavy users, accounting for £25m. turnover.

A randomly chosen sample of 200 would not be fully representative of the company's business. Since heavy users account for half the turnover, they should also make up half the sample; the medium users representing 40% of turnover should be 40% of the sample. The light users, although half the population, make up only 10% of sales and should, therefore, form no more than 10% of the sample.

Thus the 'strata' of the stratified sample would be:

> 100 heavy users randomly chosen from the heavy user population of 2,000
> 80 medium users randomly chosen from the medium user population of 3,000
> 20 light users randomly chosen from the light user population of 5,000.

Cluster sampling

There is also a third, less costly and very commonly used, way of producing a random sample. Cluster sampling reduces the cost of the marketing research by concentrating the sampling in one or several representative areas.

Random samples are therefore often drawn from small numbers of tightly defined locations (clusters) which are typical of the target market. This method is considered to be statistically accurate enough for most commercial market research.

Quota samples

Quota controlled samples are frequently used by commercial marketing research agencies to minimise the cost of fieldwork. The research agency initially uses secondary sources to divide the population into groups. In the case of the consumer research these groups will often be social and/or age. The research agency then decides, on the basis of published statistics, on controlled quotas (or groups) of respondents for each interviewer, in the field. For example, the interviewer might be told to question 20 housewives aged 20 - 35, 15 housewives aged 36 - 50 and 25 housewives aged 51 and over. Using this method the agency can be certain that the quotas are an accurate reflection of the total population.

However, there is no guarantee that the individuals within those age bands will represent an accurate sample of all housewives within that age band. The interviewer will simply question the first twenty housewives who agree to be interviewed in the 20 - 35 year old age band. This method is very commonly employed in commercial research, simply because it is often considered to be the most cost-effective way of producing data of sufficient accuracy.

Administering the survey

Personal interviews

Personal interviews may be highly structured, with the interviewer reading through a list of questions, often with a limited choice of set answers. This would lead to the collection of 'quantitative data'. These are data to which statistical techniques can be applied and from which specific conclusions can be drawn. For example, 20% of the target market finds new 'Washing Powder X' makes their whites whiter, or 47% of working women between the ages of 20 and 35 and from social classes A, B and C1 do not believe that any brand of washing powder has significantly superior whitening capabilities than any other.

On the other hand, personal interviews can be far less structured, with the interviewer working through the list of topics but allowing the respondents to develop their views as they wish. This kind of interviewing produces 'qualitative' information. The emphasis is on insight, attitudes, explanation and depth of understanding. Although of great value in helping the marketer to get closer to his customers, conclusions cannot be justified statistically and projections cannot be made.

There are a number of advantages of using personal interviews: much information can be obtained in great depth; the interviewer can explain exactly what is required; products, photographs or other stimuli can be used; the interviewer can also record observations; the interviewer can persuade people to agree to be questioned and relatively high response rates can usually be achieved.

There are some disadvantages: they are usually expensive to administer; there is a danger of interviewer bias; some types of respondent may distort answers to please the interviewer or to avoid appearing foolish; some types of respondent, e.g. busy executives, are reluctant to agree to lengthy personal interviews.

Telephone interviews

Often used in business to business research and increasingly in consumer research, telephone interviews are quick and often very cost-effective. They are particularly useful if cluster sampling is not acceptable. Telephone interviews must be short and to the point or the respondent may become irritated and discontinue the interview.

The main advantages of telephone interviews are:

- two-way communication, enabling explanations to be made where necessary
- they are quick and cost-effective
- national and international samples are possible
- easy identification of respondents facilitates later recall if necessary
- lack of eye contact reduces respondent embarrassment
- the interviewer can key responses directly into a computer
- response rates are quite high.

The main disadvantages of telephone surveys are:

- questions must be simple and total interview time short
- they are restricted to respondents with telephones
- they are suitable only for target markets where the vast majority of buyers are telephone subscribers
- some people regard telephone surveys as an invasion of their privacy and refuse to participate.

Postal surveys

This involves mailing, or distributing door-to-door, a written questionnaire to a sample of buyers for their completion at home or at work. Questionnaires must then be collected or the respondent left to post it back. Two methods are being increasingly used in an effort to boost responses. Firstly, an incentive may be offered to all respondents who complete and return the questionnaire. This may be a small incentive for which all respondents qualify, e.g. a book token. This kind of incentive is popular in business to business research and is almost to be seen as recompense for the considerable amount of time that may be involved in the completion of some written questionnaires. Alternatively, an attractive prize (e.g. colour TV and video recorder) may be offered to the first completed questionnaire drawn out. This is popular for surveys requiring a large number of responses, usually in consumer markets.

The advantages of postal questionnaires are:

- they cost little
- they lack any interviewer bias
- total anonymity for respondents

- long; thought-provoking or complex questions can be asked to suitable target audiences
- respondents, who are reluctant to agree to personal or telephone interviews, may be prepared to co-operate
- diverse audiences can be reached.

The disadvantages of postal surveys are:

- questionnaires must be short unless sufficient incentive is offered
- for many types of respondent the questions must be simple
- without incentives, response rates are low
- questions may be misinterpreted or missed
- the meaning of questions cannot be explained
- those who respond may not be typical of the whole sample.

Questionnaire design

Having made the decisions about sampling and type of questionnaire, the researcher must design a questionnaire. All methods of collecting data will require some kind of data collection form. Its design should reflect both the survey method and the target group to whom the questionnaire will be distributed.

There are a number of types of question which may be asked.

Closed questions

Closed questions give respondents a fixed selection of answers to choose from. They are very popular with market researchers because they are the quickest and easiest to administer and analyse, offer the least scope for interviewer or respondent error and produce quantitative data. The interviewer (or respondent in a self-completion questionnaire) need only tick the relevant box.

Closed questions are frequently 'dichotomous', meaning that only two optional answers are given. The following are dichotomous questions:

> *Did you buy any soup yesterday?*   YES/NO
> *Do you agree that soup is nutritious?*   YES/NO

Sometimes more than two possible answers are given, as in the example below. Such questions are usually called multiple choice questions.

> *Which of these flavours of soup to you prefer?*
>
> TOMATO   OXTAIL   VEGETABLE   FISH

Open questions

Sometimes the researcher does not want to 'lead' the respondent in any way whatsoever, so open questions are used: *When do you serve soup?*

Such a question may be useful if marketers suspect that consumption patterns are changing. Perhaps, instead of the traditional starter to a three-course lunch, it is suspected that people are making soup as an evening or mid-morning snack. (It was this kind of shifting behaviour that led to the introduction of 'cuppa soup'.)

Rating scales

Sometimes researchers need to quantify the strength of an answer. It may not be adequate to know which, from a list of four soups, was most liked by the respondents in the sample. It will be more useful to know the degree of liking for each kind of soup. The two most commonly used rating scales are 'Likert scales' and 'semantic differential scales'.

Likert scales are used to qualify the respondent's reaction to the question on a scale which goes through a range of degrees from one extreme to the other. For example:

How much do you like tomato soup?

VERY MUCH　　QUITE A LOT　　NOT MUCH　　NOT AT ALL

A score can be given to each response, the final average score representing an overall preference rating for tomato flavoured soup. This rating can be compared with the scores given for the other three types of soup. Comparisons can also be made between ratings given by different groups of consumers, such as different social classes, which can help in the segmentation of markets.

Conclusion

You have seen how the researcher usually has a wealth of information at his or her disposal, both inside the business and outside it, in both secondary and primary form. Primary research techniques are diverse: from the very basic, commonsense approach to weird and wonderful psychological exercises. It is marketing research that enables businesses to describe and segment markets, to understand buyers in those segments and to predict their likely responses to its marketing activities.

The Marketing Mix

So far you've concentrated on the 'analysing' activities which the marketer must perform if the right kind of strategy is to be developed. The marketer's objective is to identify a group of potential buyers with an unsatisfied need which will be met by that business. The marketer identifies such needs through marketing research, initially looking broadly at different aspects of his company's operating environment and progressively narrowing the field of analysis until the needs of individual consumers are being studied. By this time the marketer will have segmented the market, dividing customers into groups which display similar needs. The marketer will hope to have identified an unsatisfied (or poorly met) need in a particular market segment which the business can exploit.

Once the marketer turns to meet such a need, he or she is moving away from analysis and planning and into the realm of 'doing' or implementation. To compete successfully in the market segment, a business must meet customers' needs more closely than they are being met by any other suppliers. Meeting customers' needs involves more than just selling them a suitable product. It involves 'giving them what they want', in the broadest sense of the phrase. Sir John Egan, past Chairman of Jaguar, expressed it in this way:

> *'Business is about making money from satisfied customers. Without satisfied customers there can be no future for any commercial organisation.'*

Customers usually want to satisfy a number of needs when they purchase a product. Very often these needs are fairly clear and relate almost entirely to the product itself. For example, when people buy table salt, they want it to be dry, fine, white, free-flowing and salty. But is that *all* they want? Surely, they want also to buy it in a suitable container which will keep it dry and free-flowing, with a hole of the right size in the top etc? In other words, customers are also interested in the packaging. Is that it? Not really, because as with most buyers of most products, they certainly do not want to pay more than a reasonable price for it. Anything else? Yes because, ideally, they do not want to be put to too much inconvenience when they have to buy salt. Having to travel to a specialist salt shop on the edge of town, or to send away to the Salt Mail Order Co. Ltd., would be rather inconvenient. Most people would much prefer to be able to buy salt at no extra inconvenience at the same time and in the same place as they buy their other groceries. In other words, customers are interested in the *availability and accessibility of the product*.

And there can be more. The factors already outlined cover very practical aspects of purchase, which you would expect to concern most buyers of most products, but there may also be less practical, more emotional criteria which can also affect the purchase decision. For example, what if one of the salt companies were sponsoring the British athletics team for the Olympic games, with a donation made for every carton top sent in? That might affect the consumer's purchase decision. More basic promotional offers, such as an extra product free or money off incentives, will also be very attractive to buyers of salt. Customers are also interested, therefore, in a host of factors which come under the heading of *promotion*.

In fact, any buyer of salt is interested in the four Ps:

Product   Price   Place   Promotion

If this mix of benefits is sought – even by people making such a routine purchase as salt – how much more varied must be consumers' purchase criteria for many other products? It is safe to say that, for virtually all purchases, customers seek a mix of benefits, which is called the marketing mix, or the four Ps. Let's examine each element of the marketing mix.

What is a Product?

A firm's product is whatever it sells. As far as marketers are concerned, products do not have to be physical goods. A window cleaning service is a product, just as much as a bucket, a ladder or a wash leather are products. Remember that people buy holes, not drills. They buy the service that products perform for them, so really, it helps to see all products as services rather than as physical goods.

Philip Kotler has developed an all-embracing definition of a product. According to him a product is:

> *'Anything that can be offered to a market for attention, acquisition or consumption that might satisfy a want or a need. It includes physical objects, services, persons, places, organisations and ideas.'*

Of course, there must be much more to a product than the glib statement 'whatever we sell'. According to Theodore Levitt, the product should be viewed at four levels:

The total product concept

The Generic Product

The word 'generic' means type, so the generic product is, simply, the basic product type. At one time, virtually all groceries were bought as generic products. Flour, tea, butter, would be weighed out by the grocer and placed in a plain wrapping. Although packaged, branded goods have taken over in the twentieth century, generic grocery products have made a certain comeback in recent years, with some supermarkets having bins containing generic products which can be scooped out, weighed and placed in a plain polythene bag by customers. Many health stores also sell generic products.

Kotler refers to this first product level as the core product or *core benefit*. What is the basic thing that people are buying? If it's a drill, they are buying the ability to make holes; if it's a portable radio/cassette, they are buying the ability to receive radio transmissions and listen to music.

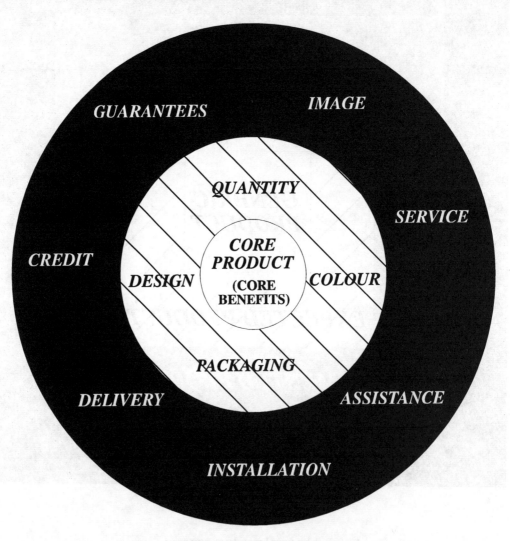

The concept of the augmented product

The Expected Product

However, when people buy a radio/cassette, they don't just want any old box which will pick up broadcasts and produce a sound vaguely reminiscent of music. They expect additional things from a radio/cassette player. They expect a certain quality of sound; they expect stereo; they expect an FM wave band; they expect the controls to look sophisticated; they expect the choice of battery or mains operation and they seem to expect it to be very, very loud! These additional requirements for the expected product become the industry norm. Features that were once extras become standard, and radio/cassettes simply have to have them if they are to stand a chance of competing in that market. Any business which falls behind on these expected features will certainly lose sales. Austin Rover, for example, were very slow with the introduction of diesel engines, which then cost them sales at the heavy user, business end of the market. As time goes on, markets become more competitive, technology improves and consumers' expectations become ever higher. More and more standard features are added to the radio/cassette, the family car and virtually any other consumer durable.

The Augmented Product

In order to gain an advantage over their competitors, suppliers always try to offer something over and above the expected product, since it may be that something extra which clinches the sale over a rival product. The product can be augmented in major ways, by adding a second cassette to facilitate tape copying, for example. More usually, however, the product is not augmented in such a tangible way.

Additional benefits become less tangible as one moves out from the core product. Any of the benefits can be offered to augment the expected product. Design features and colour have recently been used to differentiate radio/cassettes. Instant credit is often available to would-be purchasers, likewise guarantees. Some electrical goods are offered with five year guarantees to offer an extra benefit over the competition. As far as suppliers are concerned, the augmented product has one problem. Today's augmented product becomes tomorrow's expected product. The dual cassette deck, initially a much sought after extra, has become a standard feature on most models within a few years. To overcome this problem, and to keep ahead of the competition, the marketer has to move to the potential product.

The Potential Product

According to Levitt, the potential product includes 'everything that might be done to attract and hold customers'. Even for the most basic and mature of products, alert marketers can discover new ways of making their product more attractive to buyers. A good example is steel, a very mature product which one would expect to be very difficult to distinguish from its competitors. Not at all. In the 1980s, suppliers of steel used the concept of the potential product to offer new and valuable benefits to buyers. For example, Swedish steel maker Avesta AB developed an 'improved machinability steel', which is actually easier to drill than normal stainless steel, so causing less wear and tear to very expensive tools – a significant benefit to buyers. BSC Stainless in Sheffield now offers stainless steel sheet with a range of patterned finishes, which is opening up new uses for the material, such as exterior cladding for buildings. They have added real value to their product in the eyes of suppliers. It is the role of marketing management to identify the best ways to add value, and, according to Levitt, the most successful companies in many markets are the ones whose marketing departments are most thorough in their identification of the potential product. If you sell soap, beer, banking services, fast food or any competitive product, you have constantly to look forward towards the potential product.

A Range of Products

Products are continuously evolving to meet ever-changing market needs. The potential product becomes the augmented product, which in turn becomes the expected product. Companies dependent on one product, or a very restricted range of products, are always in a vulnerable position in today's rapidly changing environment.

Product Life Cycles

Each product has a beginning, followed by a rapid or steady growth in sales; sales eventually peak. The product may maintain this level of sales for some time, but sooner or later its sales will be adversely affected by changes in the environment, the market or technology and they will begin to decline, to be replaced by products more suited to the times.

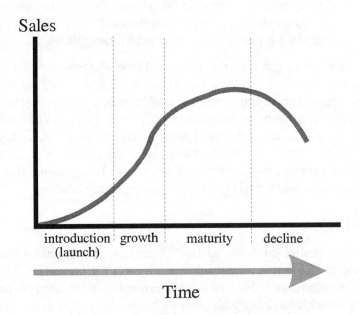

The product life cycle curve

Although it is widely accepted that all products do follow a life cycle, the exact pattern and duration of the life cycle will differ for each product. The generic product, bread, is at the mature stage of an extremely long life cycle, but if you look at specific bread products you will see that the branded white sliced loaf, which underwent rapid growth after the Second World War and was at its mature stage in the 1960s and most of the 1970s, has now been in decline for several years. It has suffered from the move away from highly processed food towards more healthy, traditional, high-fibre diets. Many of these high-fibre, unsliced, bread products are currently at the growth stage of their life cycle.

Thus the time horizon, represented by the horizontal axis on the graph is of indeterminate length, as are the sales figures represented by the vertical axis. The shape of the curve will also vary. Some products may have a longer, flatter curve if their peak in sales follows very gradual growth over a long period of time. Other products typically exhibit much more rapid growth, and some an equally rapid decline. Examples of such product life cycle curves are shown in the folowing two graphs. The first graph shows a typical 'fashion' product life cycle. Most items of clothing now come into this category with two buying seasons per annum. Sales rise quickly each autumn for the winter fashions, followed by a short mature stage and an equally quick decline. By the end of the January sales very little additional business is done with the winter fashions which is why summer clothes can appear in the shops whilst there is still snow on the ground. Although their life lasts longer (about five years on average), most individual car models show a similar life cycle pattern, with a strong rise in sales for their first year, a two to three year mature period and declining sales for their last year to eighteen months as buyers become rather tired of the model.

A 'Fashion' Product Life Cycle

Fashion products may give their manufacturers the problem of having to produce a continuous stream of new designs, but the problem is predictable: it is in the nature of their business, so they have to plan accordingly. Life cycles of some products, however, are much less predicable: they are known as 'fads'. Their sales can escalate dramatically, there can be shortages of the product as everyone clamours to buy but, for some reason, the trend can subside as quickly as it grew, often leaving manufacturers and retailers with excessively high stocks. Skateboards are the most well-known example of the 1980s. An even better example from thirty years ago was the 'hoola-hoop', a fad which, unlike skateboards, gripped everyone. Every household had to have its hoola hoop but the sales explosion lasted for only one summer. The figure overleaf shows a typical 'fad' life cycle with its steeply rising growth curve, the short or non-existent mature phase followed by an equally sudden decline.

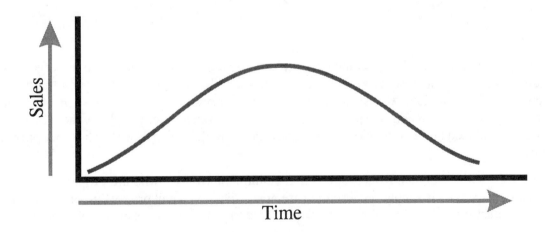

A 'fashion' product life cycle

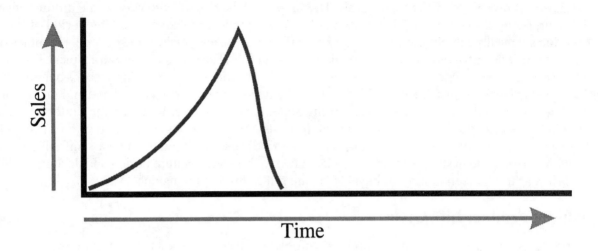

A 'fad' product life cycle

Managing the Product Life Cycle

The marketer will have two objectives in the management of the product life cycle and will want both axes to extend as far as possible. To be more specific, at the growth stage the marketer will want sales to continue growing to their highest possible level, and at the mature stage will want to continue at this plateau level for as long as possible before decline sets in. Let's examine the marketer's tactics at each stage of the life cycle.

Introduction

This stage begins when the product is launched onto the market. It may already have undergone a long development stage, including 'test marketing', but the product life cycle begins only when the product is fully launched on to the market. At first, sales growth can be very slow, mainly because most people are hesitant about trying new ideas and new products. They prefer to watch other people try them first. In 1962 Everett Rogers produced his famous 'adoption of innovations' model which describes how people react to innovations.

As can be seen from the diagram, Rogers states that genuine innovators, who are prepared to take risks and like having new products simply because they are new, are a very small proportion of the population, only 2.5%. Manufacturers, therefore, have to work very hard to push the sales of most new products beyond this group during the introductory stage of the product life cycle.

Moreover, the manufacturer will almost certainly be losing money at this stage. Development costs may have been considerable, and the marketing costs at this introductory stage will also be high. Advertising, direct mail, exhibitions and sales promotions are all communications techniques which may need to be used at this stage in order to generate awareness of the new product and to give consumers an incentive to try it. Distributors may have to be offered financial incentives to stock the product or to give it favourable shelf space and special display material may have to be produced for them. With low production volumes, costs will also be high, so it is most unlikely that the product will manage to reach breakeven point. Some genuine innovative new products can be profitable at this stage because marketers are able to charge a very high price for them. They can afford to go for the top end of the market where the small group of 'innovators' will be prepared to pay handsomely for the status value of such a conspicuous purchase. The first CD players and the discs themselves would be good examples.

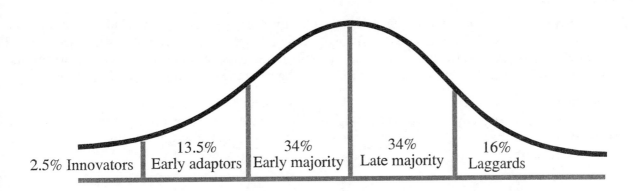

Everett Rogers' Innovation Adoption Model

Growth

The growth stage is the 'take-off' phase when the 'early adopters' begin to purchase the product. They are typically fashionable, successful and keen to be associated with new ideas and products once it is clear that they are socially acceptable. They will be joined later in the growth stage by the 'early majority' who do want to be fashionable but are followers rather than leaders.

Sales will now be climbing rapidly. This will attract attention in the business world and new competitors will be attracted to the market. Their products may even have new features or be offered at a lower price. The Japanese company, Brother, is the world leader in portable electronic typewriters. When they launched the first electronic typewriter they had an eighteen month opportunity to exploit the market and build their position before they faced highly aggressive competition. As the market has matured this period has shortened. Now, when they introduce a new model, they expect to have a 'window of opportunity' of only four weeks before a competitor comes out with a product which does the same things at a lower price, or offers more benefits at the same price.

At the growth stage, whether it is four weeks or four years, prices are likely to remain quite high although, as competition begins to intensify, the first pressures on prices will be seen. Thus price competition affects growth products, such as fax machines, car' phones and, to a lesser extent so far, compact discs. Manufacturers will continue to push hard with promotional activities at this stage, especially advertising designed to increase interest and build brand loyalty. Although marketing costs are still high, they are now a much smaller proportion of the growing sales which help to move the product into profitability.

Maturity

Sales growth for all products slows down sooner or later as market penetration approaches its maximum. Products such as video recorders or microwave ovens have now reached their mature stage.

During the mature stage most remaining potential consumers will become customers. The 'late majority' tend to be sceptical and old-fashioned but will change when the evidence is overwhelming. Such people would now buy an automatic washing machine, but are most unlikely to have been converted to the concept of dish washers at the present time.

The maturity stage should last much longer than the introduction and growth stages, but competition will now be intense and this will be reflected in falling prices or frequent sales promotions that seek to add value in customers' eyes. Advertising, and perhaps public relations activities, such as sponsorship, will continue but will be more defensive, concentrating on image and the encouragement of loyal customers.

By now, however, marketers may have to consider more tangible ways of supporting the stagnating sales of their brand. Their objective will be to prolong the mature stage and stave off the decline stage for as long as possible. Product modifications may have be made in the hope of giving the brand a new lease of life, as shown below.

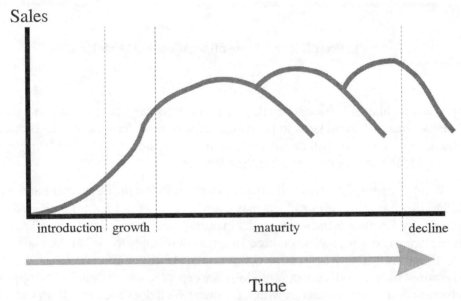

Extending the product life cycle

Extending the product life cycle

This is a tactic particularly favoured by car manufacturers. During the early part of the mature stage, product modifications can be purely cosmetic. Often called 'concept cars', a special model will be introduced with a number of extra features, such as superior upholstery, sun roof, and perhaps an improved stereo as standard. Often they will have a special exterior appearance to increase their distinctiveness. As the mature stage proceeds, such modifications may need to become more fundamental, a completely updated model may need to be introduced, probably retaining most of the mechanical parts of its predecessor, but with a new external appearance. Fords have been masters of extending the product life cycle in this way, giving models a timely facelift before their sales began to decline. Extending the product life cycle in this way can be much cheaper and less risky than launching a completely new product. Ford discovered this to its cost when it replaced the very successful Cortina with the Sierra. The Sierra was initially unpopular, largely because of its different exterior appearance. Loyal Cortina buyers deserted in droves, mainly to the Cavalier, a more conventional looking car which offered the option of a boot, and it was five years before the Sierra regained market leadership of a segment which the Cortina had previously dominated for a decade.

Decline

All products eventually enter a stage of declining sales, perhaps because they have become obsolete or because the competition has a rival product which offers much better value. Declining sales result in over-capacity and a consequent temptation to cut prices, simply to keep production lines going and employees in jobs. The remaining Ford Capris in the car showrooms in 1987 could be bought for very low prices. Small black and white televisions cost no more now than they did fifteen years ago, which means that in real terms they cost considerably less.

Fierce price competition hits profits, with the result that manufacturers' first reaction is to make marketing economies elsewhere. Product modifications and development come to an end, advertising is cut or curtailed. Despite such economies, the declining products may still be unprofitable as sales and prices continue to fall. As a result, many suppliers will withdraw from the market. Some products simply disappear: slide rules, for example, have been replaced by calculators.

A Basket of Products

Perhaps the most valuable message of the product life cycle is to remind management that products, however successful they are today, do not go on for ever. The company must replace products which are reaching their decline stage with new products which can take their place. The risk of having 'all your eggs in one basket' is a generally accepted principle in all walks of life. People and businesses avoid this risk by giving themselves more than one option; businesses usually have a range of products, with the more successful ones making up for any losses incurred through the poorer performing products.

Peter Drucker has suggested that a business needs a range of products, each at a different stage of its life cycle, so that a succession of profitable products will always be on stream. Shown in the figure on the following page, Drucker labels this stream of products as 'today's breadwinners', 'tomorrow's breadwinners' and 'yesterday's breadwinners'. The profits from today's breadwinners must be used to finance the development of tomorrow's breadwinners, which will be able to replace yesterday's breadwinners.

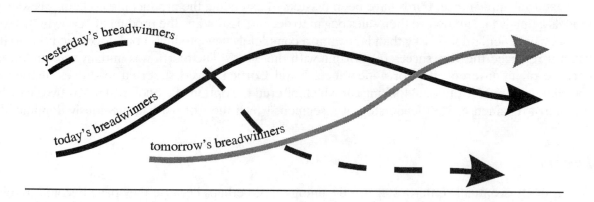

Peter Drucker's Breadwinners

Product Portfolio Analysis

The main problem with the product life cycle concept, and Drucker's breadwinners, is that it is, in practice, very difficult to know when your product has reached a certain stage. With the objective of helping marketers to tackle this problem, the Boston Consulting Group in the US developed an approach known as product portfolio analysis.

The BCG theory uses the analogy of stocks and shares. Serious investors on the stock market will try to cover their risk by investing in a portfolio of shares, so that they are cushioned from the full effects of unexpected sharp falls in an individual share price. Extending the same approach to products, a company is recommended to have a portfolio of products, the more successful ones financing the weaker ones

BCG portfolio analysis does not link in strongly with the product life cycle. Proceeding round the diagram in an anti-clockwise direction, equivalent to the introduction stage, are 'problem children', aptly named since many new product launches fail to get beyond this stage. Products which successfully reach the growth stage are 'stars', and become 'cash cows' at the mature stage. Products in decline are known as 'dogs'.

So far no different, but the advance comes in the way the marketer places his products into these categories, by using the two variables of market growth and market share. Products in the top half of the box are in the early stages of the product life cycle. They are in growth markets, like the coffee market up to 1975. Other things being equal, this means they are products with a future, tomorrow's breadwinners, and should be invested in. However, although all these products consume the company's cash, they are not all equal. Those on the left-hand side of the box enjoy a high market share. If not market leaders, they will not be far behind the market leaders. Nescafe was a star, as was Blend 37 in the 1960s and Gold Blend in the 1970s. Such products, though they may be unprofitable in the short-term due to high development and promotional costs, should receive continued financial support as the breadwinners of the future.

Not so problem children. Their sales have never really taken off and they have a very poor market share. Sometimes called 'question marks', the business must really scrutinise their performance and ask if they are ever likely to be a real commercial success. If not, it may be better to withdraw them straightaway, rather than waste funds on the marketing of losers, since those funds could be more profitably allocated to supporting stars or the development of new products.

Products in the lower half of the box are in the later stages of their life cycle. They are in mature markets whose growth has slowed or even stopped. This is not necessarily a bad thing, because a cash cow, a mature product with a high share of its market segment, is usually a very profitable product. Nescafe is an excellent example. Although it advertises heavily, expenditure of £10 million per annum is relatively small when compared with annual sales of £280 million. Its development costs have long since been recovered, and high production volume leads to economies of scale which keep down costs. Allied to the fact that Nescafe is not a cheap product (it costs twice as much as the average own-label coffee and more than its main branded competitors), it can be seen that it must be a very profitable one. It is said that cash cows should be 'milked' to provide the funds to support stars, problem children which do appear to have good future prospects and the development of new products.

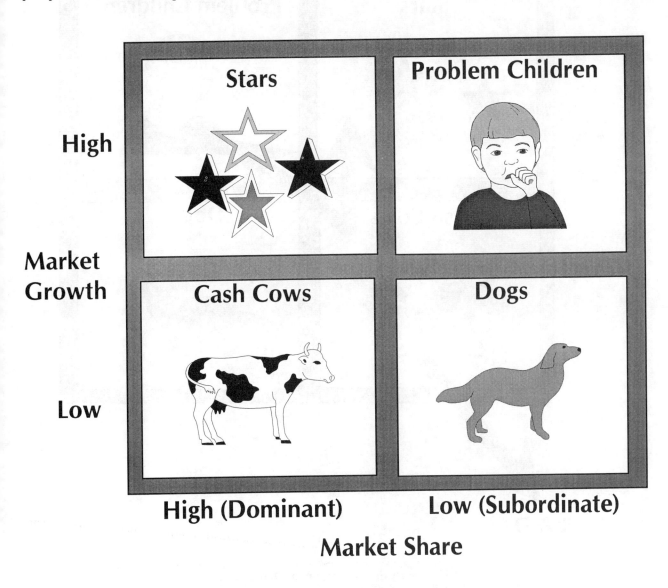

BCG Portfolio Approach

Dogs have the twin characteristics of low share and low growth. They tend to have low profits – or incur losses – and poor future prospects. If the dog is relatively close to the market leader and can maintain a positive cash flow in a stable market, then it may be a 'cash dog'. By minimising marketing costs, such as promotion and product development, cash dogs can sometimes be milked like a cash cow. If, on the other hand, the product is a genuine dog, with no prospects for an extension of its life cycle or for its introduction to another segment (e.g. an export market), then liquidation, either immediate or gradual, will be the only strategy.

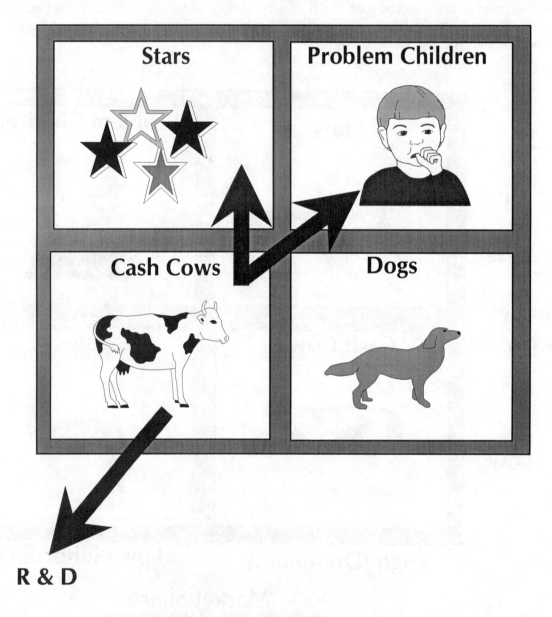

BCG Analysis – the internal flow of funds

The Product Mix

It is a good idea for most businesses to offer a range of products, each at different stages of its life cycle, if future profitability is to be ensured. The total set of products a business sells is called its 'product mix', which may include a number of 'product lines' and a large number of products.

The Product Line

A product line consists of a group of products that are closely related because they are intended for the same end use (e.g. running shoes), are sold to the same customer group (e.g. Next Accessories, aimed at the 25-45 year old woman), or fall within a certain price range (e.g. budget records and cassettes).

Breadth of the Product Mix

Breadth refers to the number of different product lines in the product mix. The product mix of large firms is tending to become broader, largely as a result of amalgamations. When Cadbury merged with Schweppes, the confectionery and hot drinks product lines of the former were added to the soft drinks product lines of the latter, thus increasing the breadth of the product mix.

Depth of the Product Mix

Depth refers to the number of items within each product line. Some large businesses try to crowd smaller businesses out of the market by increasing the depth of their product lines. The two detergent giants, Unilever and Proctor and Gamble, both have very deep washing powder lines, to the extent that they are prepared to risk some of their brands competing with each other. However, the strategy seems to be effective because even the supermarkets' own-label products find the market difficult to penetrate.

Branding

According to Margaret Crimp: *A brand is a product or service which has been given an identity; it has a brand name and the added value of a brand image.*

Other distinctive aspects of a branded product:

- it is likely to have recognisable packaging, like the Nescafe jar
- it might have a logo or a trademark.

Its brand image will enable people to recall identifiable aspects or benefits of the product. These may be directly related to the product, such as the quality of the coffee, the strength of the toilet paper, or they may be less tangible, such as the Dulux dog or the Andrex puppy.

Many people go further than Crimp and say that a brand is *a product with a personality*, which consumers can see almost as a friend rather than just a purchase. You can see this idea coming through in the advertising of many consumer products, such as 'mild green Fairy Liquid – kind to your hands'.

However, there is more to the concept of branding than giving a personality to a product. In fact, there are four main advantages of branding from the marketer's point of view.

1. Differentiation

Differentiation means making things different, and it will always be one of the main objectives of marketers to differentiate their product from their competitors' product. Occasionally, a new product is so innovative that it differentiates itself from other similar products. The first Polaroid camera did not need a creative genius to distinguish it from conventional cameras. With some products, differentiation is not quite so obvious, but it is not too difficult for marketers to achieve. Cars, for example, look distinctive and have their own unique performance characteristics which can be stressed by the marketer although, as time goes on, cars are becoming similar.

Some products, however, are known as 'undifferentiated products'. The definition of an undifferentiated product is: a standard product produced to a commonly accepted specification, usually the subject of a routine purchase decision, ordered in response to basic and essential needs.

Examples are soft margarine, sugar, petrol, floppy disks, paper clips, screws, steel and polythene bags and many, many more basic products in consumer and industrial markets. Such products are essentially indistinguishable from other products in their class. Branding will be one of the key weapons which gives an identity to an undifferentiated product.

There are a number of ways in which this might be done.

2. Brand Name

There can be a lot in a brand name. Beanz Meanz Heinz to a lot of people. The main reason why a lot of products are perceived as undifferentiated, especially in industrial markets, is that their manufacturers don't even try to differentiate them. They do not even take the first step of giving them a name. There can be a lot of promotional mileage in a name, especially if it is distinctive. The Guinness – 'pure genius' advertising is one good example. Look at this list of the top ten selling sugar confectionery counter lines in the UK.

1.   Rowntree's Fruit Pastilles
2.   Opal Fruits
3.   Polo
4.   Trebor Extra Strong Mints
5.   Tunes
6.   Chewits
7.   Wrigley's Spearmint
8.   Bassett's Liquorice Allsorts
9.   Locketts
10   Cadbury's Chocolate Eclairs

Sweet eaters or not, all of those names are recognisable. Ideally, a name should be short and it should mean something. Both of those things help it to be recognised and remembered.

3. Trademarks

A trademark can be any word, symbol, picture or device which is associated with a particular product or service brand. Although the brand name is what most people would ask for in a shop, the trademark will probably help them to recognise the product they are looking for.

4. Colour

Colour can be used to differentiate almost any product.

Other Recognisable Features

It is often better if a name can be linked with some other feature to produce a stronger identity. So, for the paraffin, Pink became the name and the colour. The hole in the Polo, the Andrex puppy and the Dulux dog are all universally recognisable and are all used by creative marketers to give their brands a likable personality rather than a simple identity.

USP

A USP is an advantage much sought after by all marketers. Short for 'unique selling proposition', it is the ultimate differentiating factor. It makes a product unique. Even the most uninteresting of products in consumer and industrial markets can develop a USP. Of course, the more technical the product the easier it is to establish a USP which is inherent to the product, such as the first Polaroid camera, but any product can develop an intangible USP, such as a mint with a hole, pink coloured paraffin or toilet paper which is associated with a soft cuddly puppy.

Added value

There are two main ways in which marketers seek to add value through branding

- to associate the brand with high quality
- to associate the brand with excellent customer service.

The benefits of quality and service do, of course, lie at the heart of the marketing philosophy.

Quality

It is generally recognised that quality is an important factor in success in the market place. Research carried out for books like *In Search of Excellence* and *The Winning Streak* showed that successful companies, like Marks and Spencer, Sainsbury, Clark's Shoes, MacDonald's and IBM all place great emphasis on maintaining quality standards throughout the business.

Quality should be seen as 'fitness for purpose'. MacDonald's do not serve the most *cordon bleu* dishes in town, but that is not the point. For what the consumer expects from a fast-food hamburger restaurant, MacDonald's can rarely be faulted. Sainsbury's are so keen on quality that they have an objective that all their own-label products should be of higher quality than their branded equivalents – even though they usually sell for a lower price.

Customer service

Branding can also add value in customers' eyes by establishing an association with high levels of customer service. IBM have always maintained that not only is their product quality the highest, but so is the service they offer to customers. Theodore Levitt has pointed out that the more technologically sophisticated the product, the more customers are dependent upon the service back-up offered by the supplier. The buyer of a new computer system may need installation, may need help in the choice of software, may need training for staff in how to use the computer and may also require maintenance support in the future.

Services can also use branding to great effect in this respect. The American care hire company Avis, second in the market behind Hertz, ran a very successful advertising campaign with the slogan, 'Because we're second we try harder'. There is no doubt that some companies do build a reputation for offering unusually high levels of customer service. The best example is Marks and Spencer, where the customer knows he or she is always right.

Self-service

Attaining high levels of customer service is not relevant to some products because they are sold in circumstances where the consumer serves himself. Branding however is also very important in this self-service situation. There are two main factors here: packaging and merchandising.

Packaging

In the supermarket, products have to speak for themselves, and sometimes customers certainly select the brand which shouts the loudest, i.e. the one that is most visible on the shelf. Companies devote considerable resources to designing and testing packs which will stand out in the self-service situation.

There are two factors which are rigorously tested:

- the visual impact made by the pack, compared to a selection of similar packs
- the 'find time'. The manufacturer may have no control over the shelf space or position allocated to its brand by the supermarkets, so will want to ensure that loyal customers who do recognise the pack are able to identify it quickly even when placed in an obscure position.

The pack also has to reinforce the brand's image. In other words, it has to project those qualities which make the brand different from and better than its competitors. There is evidence that when a consumer comes across a new product in the supermarket the decision whether to try it is influenced by ideas conveyed by the pack about the product.

The packaging also needs to incorporate the brand name, trademark, any slogans used by the brand and, perhaps, some additional promotional material which is to be carried on the pack.

Merchandising

If products have to speak for themselves in the supermarket, then anything which can help them to shout louder must be considered. Money off, flash packs offering some extra product, premium offers and competitions are all promoted on packaging in the hope of giving consumers that extra little incentive to buy.

As far as branding is concerned however, merchandising which reinforces the brand image is ideal. POS (point of sale) display material which can convey more of the product benefits is of great value, but many supermarkets refuse to accept such items, preferring to be in full control of their own in-store displays. Sampling sessions can also be useful as can anything which reinforces the brand image, such as permanent storage jars (e.g. Mr. Homepride flour).

The importance of services

In the UK more people are employed in the service sector than in all other sectors of the economy put together; the same is true in the US and most western economies. In the UK, income from services contributes more than any other sector to the Gross National Product, and income from selling services overseas, called 'invisible earnings', plays an increasingly important role in our balance of trade.

Examples of services

With over half the workforce employed in the service sector, you would be right to expect the range of service activities to be vast. This section describes the breadth of the sector by highlighting a few examples.

1. The financial services industry is probably the most buoyant area of the service sector. It includes high street banks, building societies, merchant banks and stockbrokers. Insurance, (incorporating property insurance, motor insurance, life insurance and pensions) is another growth market.

2. Professional services include accountants, solicitors, consultants of many kinds, architects and surveyors.

3. Marketing services are growing as are advertising agencies. There are market research companies, PR companies, hospitality companies and sales agents.

4. Catering is also buoyant, including hotels, restaurants, fast food takeaways.

5. Leisure and recreation cover sports centres and clubs, theme parks, zoos, amusement arcades, libraries, cinemas, sports events and music.

6. There are cleaning services such as contract office cleaning, domestic cleaning and window cleaning. Decorating covers internal and external painting, sand blasting and interior design.

7. Transport services employ thousands of people, as do health services (both in the public and private sectors), education and training, social services, travel agents, telecommunications, the delivery of letters and hair dressing.

Reasons for the growth of services

As manufacturing industry creates wealth with ever fewer people and ever increasing use of technology, western governments have had to place more emphasis on the development of the service sector. Reduction of employment in manufacturing industry, since productivity has continued to increase, has not meant less wealth. On the contrary, western countries continue to grow richer and, as they do so, there is an ever-increasing demand for all the kinds of service mentioned above.

In the years after the Second World War, the introduction of the Welfare State led to a huge growth in public sector services. Since 1979 privatisation has begun to reduce the activities of the public sector, although the core services, health, education and social services are still provided mainly by the state. Increasing competition from the private sector, however, is being seen throughout these services.

The buoyancy of the service sector has resulted in increased competition and greater investment in marketing by service companies. One clear sign of this is the growth of service sector advertising. For over twenty years TV advertising was dominated by well-known branded goods. In the 1980s the big grocery brands have seen increasing competition for the audience's attention from the banks, building societies, insurance companies, airlines, telecommunications companies and the government advertising its own services.

Service companies therefore are facing exciting growth opportunities and are keen to recruit marketing expertise to help them to exploit their markets.

Developing New Products

Ideas

Ideas are the basis of all new products. Some products are more innovative than others. Some, such as penicillin, nylon, kevlar or the jet engine represent a totally new breakthrough, often the result of many years of slow and expensive research and development. Other new products are 'adaptive', which means that they are improved versions of an existing product. The degree of innovation in an adaptive product can vary enormously, but they are not classified as inventions, just modifications. Some new products do not appear to offer any kind of improvements or modification compared to existing products in the market place. Such products are often referred to as 'me too' products.

The first task of a business intent on an effective new product development programme is to create an atmosphere in which the communication of new ideas flourishes. In addition to sustaining the kind of corporate culture in which ideas can flourish, a number of specific techniques may be used to stimulate the generation of ideas.

Brainstorming

Brainstorming might involve a number of people, (usually around eight to twelve), placed in fairly comfortable, relaxed surroundings with a leader to guide the session. The leader will have already prepared certain key words or concepts thought to be appropriate for stimulating the thoughts of the participants. The leader introduces one of these words and the other participants shout out the first word or idea that comes into their head. It does not matter how ridiculous the idea appears, the participant should shout it out because the whole session relies for its effectiveness on group dynamics. One person's banal suggestion might spark off another idea from a second participant, which in turn prompts a really good idea from a third member of the group. Most ideas will be voiced spontaneously, so it is often chaotic and might at times degenerate into farce. A record is kept of all points (ideally, on tape) and if two or three good ideas emerge from a session it is time well spent.

The suggestion box

Internal idea generation can be maximised by involving the entire workforce of the business in the process. Many businesses have suggestion boxes, with financial incentives to contribute. Employees, whose suggestions are taken up, are paid for their suggestion according to how much money it makes or saves the company. Suggestions may not be exclusively concerned with new product developments. They can include ideas for cost saving in the workplace or for a new way of promoting a product, but new product ideas will often be a significant proportion of all suggestions. Many of these are successfully implemented. Smith's, for example successfully introduced square crisps on to the market, an idea originally suggested by a shopfloor employee.

Research and development

Larger companies, like ICI, employ very large numbers of staff in their research and development (R&D) departments. Being at the forefront of new technological development is important for many businesses, but in some industries, such as pharmaceuticals or computers, it is essential.

The sales force

It is often said that the sales force is the company's eyes and ears in the market place. This information-gathering role should always be fully exploited by companies, because the close relationships which sales people often have with customers can be a very fruitful source of new product ideas.

Marketing research

For many companies, especially those in consumer markets, marketing research will be the most fruitful source of ideas for new product development.

Competitors

It is fairly common for firms to use competitors as sources of new product ideas. Most companies gather and file all their competitors' literature, and some take the process a stage further by buying, using and dismantling their competitors' new products. Although it is essential to maintain extensive and up-to-date knowledge of competitors' activities, to make sure your own company is not slipping behind, using competitors' products as sources of new ideas is of much more dubious value. At best, the copying of a competitor's product results in a 'me too' product. At worst, the firm may find itself copying a product for which there is no demand, particularly if the competitor has not based the product on a thorough analysis of customers' needs

Screening

The purpose of idea generation is to develop as many new ideas as possible. From the start of the screening stage, the new product development process concentrates on reducing the number of ideas down to the tiny number which are worthy of launching on to the market.

Compatibility with company strengths

Many ideas can be eliminated quickly and easily on the grounds that they are not really appropriate to the company's strengths and resources. If the firm believes that other businesses would be better at developing a particular idea, they should abandon it (or possibly sell it to another business). At the screening stage most ideas can be eliminated if the company makes a ruthless assessment of its own ability to exploit them.

Compatibility with existing products

The company must also ask itself how well a prospective new product would fit in with its existing range of products. If the new product is complementary to its existing products, it will impose less strain on the company's resources because it will build upon existing customer relationships, sales visits, and distribution channels.

Values engineering

Once it is decided that the new idea is compatible with the company's strengths, financial resources and existing product range, it may still need to satisfy itself that the manufacture of the product is feasible.

Market demand

The final screening step would involve a quick assessment of the likely demand for the new product. The aim at this stage would be to identify those ideas for which the likely demand would be too small to generate sufficient sales to enable the company to recover the anticipated development costs of the new product.

The whole point of the screening stage is that it should be performed quickly and inexpensively in order to identify early those products which are unlikely to make it through the remainder of the process – before too much money has been invested in their development.

Marketing Analysis

Most of the original ideas have been eliminated by this stage, but the cost incurred in the development of those which remain begins to escalate, especially from the product development stage. The objective is still to eliminate potential losers at the earliest possible stage in order to minimise the potential loss. It is now that a comprehensive marketing analysis and forecast is made, before the very costly product development stage is entered, since the business wishes to satisfy itself that the new product is a potential winner.

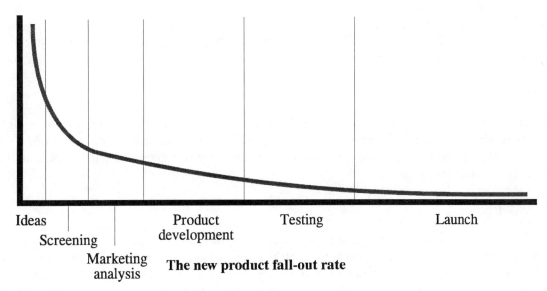

The new product fall-out rate

Pricing

Price is a very important element of the marketing mix. It is not just an accountancy task, but a central part of the marketing package that the company is to offer to is customers.

There are four reasons why price is such an important element of the marketing mix:

1. quality

2. image

3. a fair price

4. price bands.

Price

Quality

Everything about a product and the company communicates messages to the customer. This is certainly true of price. Above all, the price communicates messages about a product's quality. Customers often have a very incomplete knowledge of the real attributes of competing products. They may have seen a few adverts, heard opinions from friends and tried some – but not all – of the product choices. In the absence of complete knowledge, customers tend to assume that more expensive products are of a higher quality than cheaper competing products.

Image

Some products have 'pose value'. They are the car, the jeans, the pub or the wellies to be seen in. In some pubs, the tables are covered by empty lager bottles. They are shapely bottles with attractive labels and gold foil around the neck. The lager inside costs around twice as much as the humble draught variety, although it costs no more to make and its taste may be virtually indistinguishable. The consumers are buying the image of the bottles more than the lager inside, which is why they go to the trouble of bringing the bottle as well as the glass back to the table. Those bottles are like badges. They make a statement about the buyers. They have pose value. A relatively high price is essential if a product is to have this prestige value.

A fair price

There is evidence of a 'plateau effect' in price. People resist a very expensive price which seems to be a 'rip off' but are also suspicious of a very cheap price, which tends to be associated with poor quality. Most people are price conscious, seeking good value for money, but this does not usually result in their buying the cheapest available product.

Price bands

Although the price plateau principle almost certainly applies, it may exist at different levels for different groups of buyers. When buying groceries an affluent middle-class family will have a different notion of 'good value for money' than an 'unemployed' family. Therefore, marketers will often try to offer a range of products priced within certain bands, roughly in line with what the customers expect to pay, e.g. £9.99, £14.99 and £19.99. This price banding is particularly popular in the clothing market.

If a company is introducing a new product, or reviewing the price structure for its existing products, it must take seven main underlying factors into account.

Costs

Cost plus

In arriving at a price, most companies will start by calculating their own costs because they will not want to sell at a price which is insufficient to cover those costs. In its simplest form this results in 'mark-up' or 'cost plus' pricing. This involves the addition of a predetermined percentage to the firm's costs, and is particularly popular with some retailers. For example, a clothing retailer might work on a 50% mark-up. This would involve adding 50% to the purchase price of all products. A pullover bought from the manufacturer for £16 would be sold in the shop for £24. This 50% margin would cover overheads and profits. It would probably be an 'industry norm'. In other words, years of experience would have taught the industry that a 50% mark-up would be a sufficient margin to yield a satisfactory profit. This may work well as long as traditional conditions prevail but, in a changing market environment, it can be very dangerous to rely on cost plus methods of pricing.

Target pricing

A more scientific approach would be target pricing based on breakeven analysis. Breakeven analysis is examined in the accounting section.

The big drawback with all cost-based approaches to pricing is that they are inward looking. They take into account only factors internal to the firm. In reality, factors outside the firm are much more likely to influence the price that the company will be able to charge.

However, breakeven analysis is very useful for establishing a base line for pricing, a price below which the firm cannot trade without making a loss.

Company objectives

It cannot be taken for granted, however, that a business will not, under any circumstances, be prepared to trade at a loss. Company objectives will, therefore, be a second relevant factor to consider when setting prices. The company's goals may influence pricing in a number of ways.

Marginal costing

If a firm has spare capacity, due to a shortage of work, the directors of the business may have the objective – at least in the short term – of seeking work at virtually any price in order to keep the factory busy and avoid making employees redundant. They may therefore have a 'marginal costing' policy which seeks to cover the variable cost and makes only a contribution to overheads. The remainder of the fixed costs which are not covered would represent a loss to the company.

The concept of marginal costing is particularly appropriate to service industries. If a commercial aircraft takes off with empty seats, the opportunity to sell those seats on that flight has been lost for ever. If the airline had managed to sell tickets for some of those empty seats, even at a greatly reduced price, it would have been better, financially, than leaving them empty. The small additional revenue brought in by the cut price tickets would have helped to offset a small proportion of the very high fixed costs. This is why airlines offer cheap stand-by tickets for passengers who are prepared to travel at very short notice on a flight with spare capacity. The same marginal costing policy leads to tour operators offering bargain holidays, again for buyers who are prepared to book at very short notice.

Buying market share

Pricing at below breakeven level can result from a very different objective. A strong company, seeking to expand, may choose to sell at less than a breakeven price in order to drive competitors from the market place. If it believes it can sustain the losses for longer than the competition, such a pricing strategy, known as 'penetration pricing' may be feasible. When it has secured a dominant position in the market, prices can gradually be increased. The Japanese penetration of the British motorcycle market was achieved in this way.

High profit margins

Far from selling at a loss, some companies want to achieve very high profit margins. This may be feasible with a new type of product, such as the first Polaroid camera, video recorder or compact disc. With such an innovative product in a new market, there may be an opportunity to make unusually high profits, with prices set well above costs. This is known as 'price skimming', the high price skimming the cream from the new market. This is often feasible because some customers are willing to pay for exclusivity and the latest developments. As time passes, the firm can lower prices to draw in more price-sensitive groups of customers. Price skimming enables a firm to recover its development costs quickly. This can be necessary in markets with unusually high R & D costs (e.g. pharmaceuticals) and essential in fast-changing markets (e.g. fashion).

Demand

A firm cannot decide on the price for a product without looking outside the business at conditions in the market place. One of the most important factors will be the level of demand. During the early stages of the product life cycle, when demand is strong and growing, it is usually possible to charge higher prices than in the later stages, when demand is weakening. Products at the decline stage of their life cycle will often have to be priced at a low level. End of season fashion sales is an example of products reaching the decline stage of a very short life cycle.

Sometimes demand fluctuates as a result of trade cycles beyond the control of the manufacturer. When industry was depressed in the early 1980s, demand for steel fell considerably. Steel producers were forced to lower their prices as a result. By the end of the decade, renewed world economic growth, coupled with reductions in capacity made by most steel producing countries in the early 1980s, had substantially altered the balance of demand and supply and prices had risen considerably.

Demand can also fluctuate on a more regular and predictable basis. Companies can often respond in a planned way to these changes in demand by charging different prices for the same product under different conditions of market demand. This is known as 'price discrimination'.

There are many examples of price discrimination. Seasonal products such as holidays are much cheaper in the low season. The buyer of fourteen days on the Costa del Sol in May receives exactly the same product offering for a much lower price than the sun seeker who departs in August. Telephone calls are cheaper when demand is lower in the evening and at weekends, as are rail fares. In this way the seller can try to sell spare capacity at times of low demand by offering attractive prices.

Perceived quality

Consumers tend to associate a high price with high quality. This quality may be perceived in the mind of the customer, rather than being inherent in the product, but if it is there sellers can charge for it. Leading brands of perfume can command a much higher price than less established brands. It is debatable whether the core product is significantly superior, but the augmented product, enhanced by stylish packaging and years of successful advertising, has attained a very high value market position, and is priced accordingly. This is known as 'perceived value pricing'.

A variation of this pricing strategy can be adopted for the luxury versions of standard products. Known as 'product line pricing', it involves charging significantly higher prices for 'top of the range' products due to their higher perceived value. Cars are a good example. The top of the range Cosworth Sierra costs almost three times as much to buy as the cheapest two door 1.3 litre version. It does not cost three times as much to produce. The profit margin is much higher, but the pricing is in accordance with the relative values pereived by customers.

The competition

Some companies base their prices largely on those charged by the competition. This 'competition oriented pricing' is very common in extremely price sensitive markets and is more likely to be practised by the weaker companies. Petrol companies often respond to competitors' price changes within hours. Supermarkets and retailers of electrical goods in the same town will keep a eye on prices charged by their competitors. It is now common for retailers to offer to refund customers the difference if they can find the same product sold cheaper elsewhere.

Competition oriented pricing can be very dangerous, leading to rash price cutting and a downward spiral in prices which only leaves the industry as a whole much less profitable. Many of the most successful companies are those which have refused to cut prices, relying instead on their higher quality, better service or some other benefit which offers value for money. Kelloggs does not try to be as cheap as its own-label competitors. Rover refused to respond to competitors' heavy discounting when it introduced its new 800 model because of the adverse effect such price cutting could have on perceived quality.

In today's highly competitive markets, however, virtually all companies must take some account of the prices charged by competitors. However good the rest of their marketing mix, few companies can afford to be too far out of line with the rest of the industry.

Distributors

In some industries distributors exert a powerful influence over the pricing strategies of manufacturers. Today, the large retail chains in the UK often dominate their smaller suppliers and can, should they choose, more or less dictate prices to them. Even where the manufacturer is stronger and is in full control of his pricing strategy, if he sells through distributors he must take account of their needs.

Legal constraints

In some countries there will be extensive legal constraints on pricing. There are no longer statutory controls on pricing in the UK, but there are certain rules designed to ensure that consumers are not misled by pricing. Under the *Consumer Protection Act* 1987, for example, the once common practice of buying in special cheap goods for sales and advertising them at apparently massively reduced prices is no longer permitted. Only genuine price reductions can be marked up or advertised. Goods displaying a price reduction (e.g. 'Now only £19.95 – was £35') must have been previously stocked and offered for sale at that higher price.

Tactical pricing

A company's pricing strategy will probably result not in a single fixed price but a price range, a minimum and a maximum price at which the company will sell. Tactical pricing refers to the task of setting specific prices within that range and altering them if necessary as conditions change or to secure a short term tactical advantage over the competition. There are many examples of pricing tactics, some of which are described below.

Promotional discounts

They are a very popular form of price cutting. To be effective, they must offer the customer sufficient incentive to buy extra, or to change brands, and they must have a time limit in order to induce action now. It is also believed that price discounts, which are clearly of a short-term nature, do not have a detrimental effect on the product's perceived quality, because consumers see them as a promotion and not as the 'real price'.

Loss leaders

Loss leaders would be a small number of products at an incredibly cheap price (a loss-making price). They are designed to attract customers into the store in the hope that, once there, they will also buy many normally priced items. Very popular with retailers, especially supermarkets at one time, this price tactic has become less common in recent years.

Psychological pricing

How many prices in the shops end in 99p? Probably, the overwhelming majority. There are sound psychological reasons for charging £9.99 rather than £10. Research has shown that although many customers will mentally round up the price, many will round it down, particularly if, subconsciously, they want to give themselves a reason for buying.

Customary pricing

Sometimes customers become accustomed to seeing a certain price for a product or product type. It becomes difficult to raise the price without having a major adverse effect on demand (e.g. chocolate bars). Rather than increase the price, a supplier might be tempted to reduce the amount of product, aided perhaps by a creative re-design of the packaging. These tactics led to the phenomenon of shrinking bars of chocolate in the inflationary 1970s, which in turn created the conditions for the success of Yorkie, as Rowntree recognised the demand for a decent-sized, chunky, chocolate bar.

Distribution

Having developed a product or a service and determined a price, the company needs to decide how to distribute it to customers. This is the third 'P' in the marketing mix and is all about place. In fact, distribution is about places – places where the product will be made, stored, bought and used. Two words accurately describe the concept of distribution, 'availability' and 'accessibility'. A company needs to ensure that its products are available, that it is in fact possible for customers to buy them. This sounds obvious, but in the 1960s lack of availability was one of the big failings of British industry. As competition increases, however, being widely available may still not be enough to ensure success in the market place. Consumers can be notoriously fickle and very lazy. They will often opt for the product which is easiest to buy, rather than the ideal product. It will always be an important objective of any marketer to make his product or service more accessible (easier to buy) than those of his competitors (although the exclusivity associated with some 'difficult to buy' products can be highly valued by some customers).

Basic definitions

Place – As an element of the marketing mix, place or distribution involves those management tasks concerned with making the product available and accessible to buyers and potential buyers.

Availability – Availability describes the fact that a product or service is capable of being acquired and used by buyers and potential buyers.

Accessibility – A product is accessible if buyers and potential buyers find it easy and convenient to acquire and use.

Physical distribution – The management tasks concerned with efficient movement of goods and services both into the company and outwards to the customer.

Channels of distribution – The system of organisations through which goods or services are transferred from the original producer to end users.

Middlemen - Middlemen, or distributors, are those businesses which handle goods or services in the channel of distribution between the producer and the end users.

The Economics of Middlemen

There is a a cost attached to using middlemen. They have to be given their cut of the profits. So why do manufacturers use middlemen, and not keep all the profits for themselves? There are two main reasons why manufacturers feel it is beneficial to use middlemen. They are: lower costs and higher sales.

Lower costs

Fewer lines of contact

The basic economic reason for the use of middlemen is that they reduce the lines of contact between producers and end users, as shown in the diagram below.

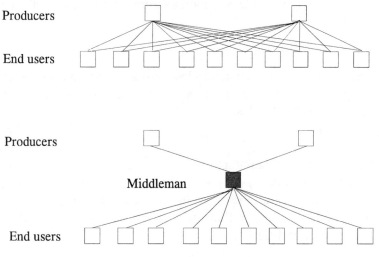

The economics of middlemen

Without the middleman there are 24 lines of contact. With the middleman, there are fourteen lines of contact. The cost of delivering goods to one middleman, rather than twelve end users, will be much lower. Clearly, it is more efficient to use middlemen. Imagine how much more efficient it becomes when there are millions of customers rather than twelve.

Lower stockholding costs

Using middlemen saves the producer money because the producer now needs to hold lower stocks. The middlemen assume the responsibility of holding sufficient stocks to meet end user demand.

Lower sales administration costs

If the manufacturer is dealing with thousands of customers, sales administration costs will be enormous. The manufacturer will need to employ a small army in tele-sales for incoming orders and the associated paperwork with confirmation of order slips, delivery notes, invoices and statements, will be very costly. Dealing with a relatively small number of distributors relieves the manufacturer of a large proportion of these costs.

Lower sales force costs

With distributors a much smaller sales force can be employed. The distributors' sales people perform that task in their local area, leaving the manufacturer's sales force to sell to the distributors themselves and possibly to a small number of very important customers.

Higher sales

The second broad reason for using distributors is that it should enable a manufacturer to increase sales. There are three main reasons for this:

1. *Accessibility*

    Being placed in the area, normally in a good location, distributors make it much easier for customers to buy.

2. *Knowledge of the local market*

    The locally based distributor is also much closer to customers in other ways, understanding their needs and priorities much better than a remote manufacturer. This would be especially true when referring to export sales.

3. *Specialisation*

    Manufacturers specialise in manufacturing. That's what they are good at. Retailers specialise in displaying large numbers of goods and making it easy for customers to buy them. That's what they are good at. Research into successful companies has shown that an important factor in their success is that they concentrate on what they're good at, but do not try to be good at everything.

The functions of middlemen

The basic role of middlemen, therefore, is to make the product more available and accessible to customers and potential customers in a more cost-effective way than might be achieved by the manufacturer alone. They do this by performing some or all of the following functions:

Breaking bulk

They take goods in the large quantities which the manufacturers want to sell but are prepared to sell them in the much smaller quantities that end users usually wish to buy.

Storage

This relieves manufacturers' storage problems and costs and increases availability to customers.

Stockholding

The buffer stocks held by distributors reduce delivery times to end users and reduce the risk of stock-outs.

Delivery

Whereas manufacturers typically deliver to distributors with 38 tonne articulated lorries, the distributor probably delivers to many small customers with a small van, thus increasing accessibility.

After sales service

Dealers often provide a valuable local point for after sales service, as in the case of cars or electrical goods.

Price setting

Distributors may have the authority to decide their own pricing or may be required to sell at prices laid down by the manufacturer.

Promotion

Local distributors often perform a valuable role promoting manufacturers' products on a local basis. Sometimes manufacturers will recognise this and reach co-operative advertising agreements with their middlemen, with both parties sharing the cost.

Personal selling

This can take two forms. A local retail outlet provides an obvious sales advantage to a manufacturer. For industrial products, a similar cash and carry type sales desk may exist but the distributor may also have its own sales force calling on local companies. This is a valuable extension to a manufacturer's selling capabilities.

Channels of distribution

The marketer has a number of decisions to make as far as channels of distribution are concerned. The marketer must decide how many middlemen (if any) are required between the manufacturer and the consumer, what kind of distribution network would be most suitable for the product, how to select individual distributors and how to manage the system once it is in place.

Channel levels

The number and type of middlemen in a channel of distribution can vary as shown in the Figure overleaf.

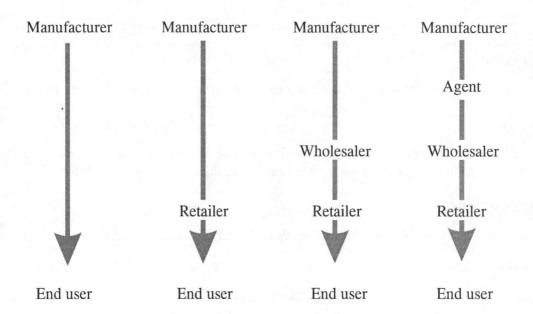

Channels of distribution

The number of levels or tiers between a manufacturer and end user can be as few as none (a zero level channel) or as many as three (a three level channel). It can be more, but that is unusual. One level or two level channels are by far the most common.

A zero level channel is more correctly termed *direct marketing* and is growing in popularity. Mill shops attached to large textile factories are becoming more common and many small companies concentrate on selling their products direct to the end user.

In consumer markets, the one level channel is becoming the most common because of the growth of the large retail chains who buy directly from the manufacturer, rather than from wholesalers. In business to business markets, many transactions are made without middlemen but, where channels are used, the most normal arrangement will be one agent or wholesaler between manufacturer and end user.

Two level channels are still common in consumer markets, since many small retailers do not have the buying power to purchase directly from the manufacturer and therefore have to buy their stock through whole-salers. Sometimes small retailers band together into a buying syndicate (e.g. Spar or Mace) to increase their buying power. An organisation, like Spar, in reality acts as a wholesaler, but since it is owned by its customers (the retailers) its margins are lower than those of an independent wholesaler.

Agents differ from distributors in that they do not normally hold stock or own it. They concentrate on promoting and selling manufacturers' products and receive a commission on all sales from the manufac-turer, who delivers the product straight to the customer. Such practices are common with items such as machinery, which is often purpose-built or would be very expensive to hold in stock for long periods of time.

Most manufacturers will not choose between these different channel levels. They will adopt some combinations of all four. A computer manufacturer, for example, will deal directly with its largest customers who are spending very large sums of money. Medium-sized computer systems, typically bought by smaller businesses, will be sold through professional local dealers, fully-qualified and competent to provide advice, training, installation, servicing etc. Their cheapest products, perhaps a small home computer, may be available from many high street shops and small computer dealers. If the manufacturer has a minimum order size, the small dealers will have to buy through wholesalers. The manufacturer may also use agents, especially abroad, where the company may not be well known, which makes distributors reluctant to carry stocks.

Channel networks

Not all one level or two level channels are the same. Distribution networks can vary and a manufacturer needs to decide on the type of network which best suits his product. There are three broad choices:

1. *Intensive distribution*

   The aim of intensive distribution strategy is to secure as many outlets as possible in order to maximise availability and accessibility to potential buyers. This type of distribution is most suited to products where convenience of purchase and impulse buying are important factors influencing sales. Examples of products requiring intensive distribution would be petrol, cigarettes, ice cream and crisps. The manufacturer of such products wants his brands on sale in every conceivable outlet. A regional manufacturer of soft drinks for example will want his products on sale in supermarkets, small grocery shops, fish and chip shops, newsagents, confectioners, pubs, cafes, fast food outlets, vending machines, and any other outlet which will stock the product.

2. *Exclusive distribution*

   At the other end of the spectrum, availability and accessibility are deliberately restricted. Prestige products which need to protect their image of up-market exclusivity will grant sole dealerships to distributors in each area. The dealers will be chosen very carefully because their image and competence must match up to the high standards demanded by the manufacturer. You would not expect to find Porsche cars sold by a back street garage. A dealer of IBM business computers has to meet a number of very stringent requirements.

3. *Selective distribution*

   Selective distribution involves the use of more than one, but less than all, of the distributors who are willing to stock the product in a particular area. The manufacturer may want the distribution of the product to be as intensive as possible but may also want to protect the image of the company and its brands by exercising some control over the type of retailers selling it. An example is that of white goods (e.g. washing machines), brown goods (e.g. televisions) and other domestic appliances.

Competition is fierce and a manufacturer will want his brand on show in as many retail outlets as possible, but there will still be some criteria that retailers are required to meet, such as minimum stockholding levels and standard premises.

Vertical integration

In addition to the three broad classes of channel network, other variations are possible. *Vertical integration* describes a co-ordinated channel of distribution, where all the members work together for the common good with the aim of achieving greater efficiency and, thereby, a competitive advantage. Vertically integrated channels may or may not be under common ownership.

In the past Burton's was the ideal of a vertically integrated channel. Burton's motto used to be 'From sheep to shop' and Burton's did, indeed, control all activities involved in transforming the wool from the sheep's back into a made-to-measure suit bought at its store. Nowadays, Burton's is a retailer, sourcing much of its merchandise from other manufacturers.

Thornton's is a good example of *forward integration*. The Derbyshire manufacturer of quality confectionery has gradually developed a network of its own high street shops.

C & J Clark the shoe manufacturers, practise both forward and backward integration, acquiring retail outlets at one end of the chain of demand and building up a substantial shoe machinery business at the other.

Channel members in vertically integrated channels do not have to be under common ownership. Many large retail chains practise backward integration by exercising very tight control over their suppliers.

Franchising is a very popular method of forward integration. Benetton shops for example are all franchises. A Benetton shop is an independent business which was started by its owner under a franchise arrangement with Benetton. Under a franchising agreement the franchiser (Benetton) agrees to supply the shop with merchandise, and to provide management and promotional help. In return the franchisee (the individual store) agrees to buy exclusively from Benetton and to pay the franchiser a royalty on all sales. Franchising is an increasingly popular form of business ownership.

Selecting channel members

For all but the most intensive of distribution networks the manufacturer will need to exercise some control over the recruitment of channel members. A number of criteria may be used.

1. *Image of the product*

    The more exclusive and expensive the product, the more up-market the image of the distributor will have to be.

2. *The standing of the company*

    Distributors buy a large volume of goods on credit from manufacturers. The manufacturer will want to be satisfied that all distributors are of sound financial standing and able to meet their debts

3. *Complexity of the product*

    Technical products such as business computers demand a high level of knowledge on the part of dealers. The ability to train buyer's staff and to service products may also be required.

4. *Perishability of the product*

    Products requiring special equipment, such as freezers, obviously can be sold only through outlets with the correct equipment. Manufacturers requiring intensive distribution (e.g. ice cream companies) will often supply the middleman with suitable equipment.

5. *Location of customers*

    Manufacturers will obviously want more middlemen in areas where they have the greatest concentration of customers.

The Marketing Tools – Main Strengths

Personal Selling

1. Achieving conviction and purchase – 'closing the sale' to use selling jargon

2. Negotiating terms, such as price, delivery times, credit terms

3. Explaining complex issues, which is usually an important task with highly technical products

4. Maintaining good relationships with regular customers

5. Enhancing the credibility of the 'product' – particularly important for service industries.

Tele-sales

1. Order taking

2. Qualifying leads and arranging sales calls

3. Reminding regular customers to place their order

4. Closing very straightforward sales, or sales which have been virtually concluded by previous personal visits.

Exhibitions

1. Demonstrating the benefits of products, especially if they are expensive, complex or technical

2. Reaching large numbers of potential customers in a face-to-face situation

3. Enhancing the company's image through a good display

4. Selling (N.B. at some exhibitions no selling can take place, only display and demonstration).

Direct Mail

1. Targeting precise segments of the market

2. Sending long or complicated messages

3.   Making impact, by doing something special with the mailer contents

4.   Improving awareness and knowledge on a wide scale

5.   Achieving action, e.g. attending a shop opening or applying to test drive a car

6.   Selling simple items, e.g. typical catalogue items.

Public Relations

1.   Increasing understanding

2.   Sending complex or highly technical messages, e.g. through an article in a specialist magazine or through a conference

3.   Generating awareness or building image, e.g. through sponsorship or open days.

Literature

1.   Informing briefly or in great detail

2.   Explaining product benefits

3.   Stimulating interest

4.   Building image.

Sales Promotion

1.   Stimulating trial or impulse purchase

2.   Provoking attention in stores

3.   Encouraging repeat purchase.

Advertising

1.   Reaching mass audiences

2.   Sending simple messages

3.   Generating awareness

4.   Stimulating interest and excitement

5.   Building image.

Advertising

Introduction

Advertising is big business. In 1990, £7.9 billion was spent on advertising in the UK. Over £7.9 billion seems like a lot of money to spend on advertising but it's little more than one tenth of American advertising expenditure. In fact, the UK is only the fourth largest advertiser in the world, with Japan coming second and Germany third. However, before you look at how and why all this money is spent, some basic concepts need to be defined.

Advertising can be defined as:

> *'all forms of non-personal communication conducted through paid media under clear sponsorship.'*

This includes adverts on the television, radio and cinema, as well as print adverts in newspapers, magazines and directories. It also includes roadside posters, usually referred to as 'outdoor advertising'. It does not include any promotional material on a product's packaging, any sponsorship, any articles in the press or news features on TV or radio. Nor does it include special events, company brochures, competitions or merchandising. At one time, direct mail was commonly seen as just another form of advertising but, as it becomes increasingly prevalent, many people are coming to see it as a discipline in itself.

Advertising Agencies

Advertising agencies are big business, and many of the most successful ones are British. The largest advertising agencies in the UK are:

Saatchi and Saatchi	£N/A
J.Walter Thompson	£340 m
BSB Dorland	£340 m
D'Arcy, Masius Benton & Bowles	£242 m
Lowe Howard Spink	£235 m
Ogilvy and Mather	£211 m
McCann Erickson	£146 m

The figures represent the agency's billings, i.e.the value of the advertising they place on behalf of their clients. (*Source*: BRAD January 1992)

Most large advertisers will employ an agency to handle their advertising. However, it must be borne in mind that the use of an advertising agency is not compulsory. Many companies, usually smaller companies, create and run advertising campaigns without the help of an agency. It is likely that most of the advertising you see in your local newspaper has been developed without the use of an advertising agency. Even TV and radio adverts are often produced without an agency, since the TV or radio company will often help the small advertiser with basic creative work and copywriting.

Media

However good the creative concept behind the advert, its effectiveness will still depend very much upon intelligent media selection. There is a vast choice of media through which the message can be communicated to the target market. There are a dozen national daily newspapers and hundreds of regional and local ones. There are over five hundred consumer magazines and even more trade journals. Television offers the advertiser fourteen ITV regions, Channel 4, BSkyB and the growth in cable and satellite stations. There are around one hundred ILR (Independent Local Radio) stations, a thousand cinemas and a vast number of outdoor advertising opportunities. Let's look at the decisions that need to be taken by the media planner.

Media planning

The chief objective of the media is to ensure that an acceptable proportion of the target audience (= COVERAGE) sees the advert a sufficient number of times (= FREQUENCY). The media planner must decide what coverage and frequency should be aimed for, how much can be afforded, and how these can be achieved. The media planner will need to take account of the following factors.

Budget constraints

A small advertising budget will automatically cut out the more expensive media such as television. The media planner will, therefore, need to be conscious from the outset of his budgetary constraints and choose only between those media which can be afforded.

The target audience

The media planner needs a very accurate profile of the members of the target audience, their sex, age, social class, income, level of education, geographical location and lifestyle.

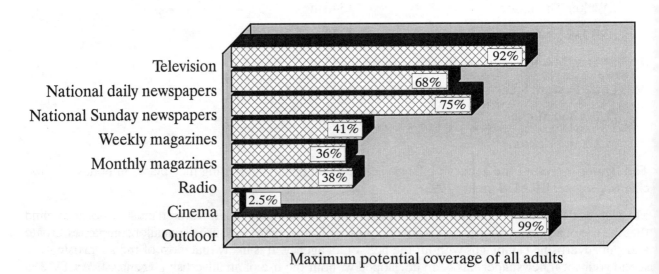

Maximum potential coverage of all adults

Average weekly coverage of all adults

Coverage

All media publish detailed profiles of their typical readers (viewers, listeners etc.) You can find out the difference between a typical *Guardian* reader and a typical *Sun* reader. You can find out the profile of ITV viewers at 9 pm on a Wednesday evening. Unbiased breakdowns can be found in directories, such as Benn's Media Directory or BRAD (British Rate and Data). The media planner must, therefore, match the target audience profile to the closest profile of users of different media. It will almost certainly be necessary to send the message via several different media so as to maximise coverage of the target audience.

Cost effectiveness

If there is a choice of media through which the target audience can be reached, the planner will not simply want to use the most effective media but will want to use the most cost effective media. £1,000 spent on advertising will not reach exactly the same number of people, whatever the medium that is used. When you include costs in the calculations, the most effective media may not turn out to be the most cost effective media because of their very high price

Frequency

It may not be enough simply to cover the target audience, however cost-effective that coverage, if the members of that audience do not see the message a sufficient number of times. Simon Broadbent developed the 'threshold concept', which suggests that unless people are exposed to a message a certain number of times, they will remember little if any of it. To be effective, advertising must cross that threshold level.

Media selection

The success of the media in achieving objectives will depend very much on the ability to select the right media, each of which has its own distinguishing characteristics.

In 1990, the £7.9 billion spent on advertising in the UK was distributed across the media in the following way:

> Press 64%
> Television 30%
> Posters 4.0%
> Radio and Cinema 2.0%

The characteristics of each of these different media are:

Newspapers

There is a wide range of national newspapers and magazines. New national newspapers have appeared in recent years (e.g. The *Independent* and *Today*) and many new, free local newspapers have been launched.

Newspapers vary widely in their circulation, as shown by the following table for national newspapers:

Daily Newspapers	
The Sun	3,521,855
Daily Mirror	2,695,266
Daily Mail	1,758,994
Daily Express	1,441,077
Daily Telegraph	1,035,573
The Star	782,378
The Guardian	421,175
The Times	375,144
Today	532,509
The Independent	358,102
The Financial Times	291,535

Sunday Newspapers	
News of the World	4,664,092
Sunday Mirror	2,451,778
The People	2,038,908
Sunday Express	1,719,627
Mail on Sunday	2,050,228
The Sunday Times	1,216,179
Observer	533,670
Sunday Telegraph	580,899
The Independent on Sunday	402,584
Sunday Sport	275,140

National newspaper circulation Oct - March 1993. Figures show average sales for that period

Source: BRAD Newspaper Circulation Bulletin.

It is interesting to note that British people feel they have more time for newspaper reading on Sundays than on weekdays, with three million extra copies being sold – 14.8 million. There is evidence that Sunday newspapers are read more carefully and in a more leisurely fashion than daily newspapers.

Advantages of newspaper advertising

1. *High national coverage*. Over 85% of the population can be reached through national and local newspapers, although in practice, advertisements would have to be placed in a very large number of newspapers to achieve this level of coverage.

2. *Audience segmentation.* National newspapers attract different types of readers which allows advertisers to target specific audiences. The regional and local press allow very accurate geographical segmentation.

3. *Credibility.* It is often felt that people believe the printed word more than certain other forms of advertising, though, of course, some national newspapers will enhance the credibility of the message more than others.

4. *Messages.* Long or complex ones can be sent if a large space is booked and long copy is written.

5. *Frequency of publication.* Some advertising messages have great urgency. The ability to send a message at very short notice can be important. Daily newspapers offer this possibility.

6. *Split runs.* A big advantage offered to the advertiser by most national newspapers is the facility of split runs, where half the print run can carry one form of copy and the other half can carry different copy. This enables the advertiser to test two different adverts.

7. *Economical.* For many advertisers newspapers will prove to be the cheapest way of reaching large numbers of people with an advertising message.

8. *Specialisation.* Certain days become known for special features. A good example would be job advertisements which appear in the quality nationals on certain days for certain careers. This improves targeting as people in the relevant target audience are likely to make a point of buying on that day.

9. *Colour supplements.* An increasing number of colour supplements are now being included with newspapers. Originally offered with certain Sunday newspapers, they have now spread to some other newspapers. Supplements help to overcome some of the disadvantages of newspaper advertising. They are appropriate for products which require high quality, colour advertising and they are often read by several people and kept for several days, or even weeks, thus helping to overcome the first two disadvantages of newspaper advertising given below.

Disadvantages of newspaper advertising

1. *Poor impact.* This is due to the volume of competing advertising messages and the fact that newspapers result in rather 'flat', uninteresting adverts, though the use of colour in newspapers is reducing this to a certain extent.

2. *Short life.* Daily newspapers have a short life and are often only partially read.

3. *Quantity.* There is a proliferation of local newspapers, making it difficult for national advertisers to make accurate judgments on their value, particularly since there is often a dearth of readership information too. This problem has been exacerbated by the growing number of free newspapers. Usually local or regional, there is often a higher proportion of advertising matter to editorial matter than in a typical paid for newspaper. Often delivered on a door-to-door basis, the 'opportunity to see', in the area of distribution, is very high in theory, but in practice there is a great deal of uncertainty over the actual level of readership

of free newspapers. The net effect of the spread of free newspapers, as far as most advertisers are concerned, is to increase the fragmentation of media and make the media selection process more difficult.

Costs

Costs can vary dramatically between the national and local press. In 1991 the published rates for the *Daily Mail* for a black and white full page display was £27,500. The Holme Valley Express, a paid for weekly covering the Holmfirth area of West Yorkshire, would charge somewhat less: £504 for a full page.

In conclusion, many newspapers enjoy reader loyalty which may enhance the credibility of the advertiser's message, which makes them very useful for prestige and reminder advertising. They can also be useful for product launches, such as new cars, because of editorial support and the newsy, urgent nature of the medium. However, as they are read hurriedly, adverts will often go unnoticed and lengthy copy may be wasted, although the Sunday papers are read in a much more leisurely fashion.

Television

Television viewing is nearly equally divided between BBC and the IBA (Independent Broadcasting Authority). ITV is split into fourteen regions, each of which is run by an independent company under a franchise arrangement. The following list shows the companies running each region and the share of the national audience which each reaches.

The Advantages of Television

1. Mass communication of simple messages. Since it reaches virtually all homes almost everyone has an opportunity to see TV advertising.

2. Impact is very good, helped by colour, sound and often a very high standard of creativity.

3. The message is received in a relaxed atmosphere at home.

4. Regional segmentation is good, provided the regional boundaries are appropriate.

5. Extensive viewing data helps to target specific audiences.

6. Attractive discounts and other assistance will often be available to new advertisers.

Region	Company	Share of Audience
London	London Weekend & Thames (weekdays)	22%
Midlands	Central	16%
North West	Granada	13%
Yorkshire, N. Midlands	Yorkshire	11%
Wales and West	Harlech	7%
South	TV South	7%
North East	Tyne Tees	6%
Central Scotland	Scottish	5%
East	Anglia	5%
South West	TV South West	3%
N. Ireland	Ulster	2%
N. Scotland	Grampian	2%
S. Scotland, N. England	Border	1%
Channel Islands	Channel	tiny

Disadvantages of Television

1. Airtime is very expensive at peak viewing times.

2. Production costs for highly creative advertising are very high.

3. Coverage is poor with higher income/education groups tending to be light TV viewers and difficult to reach through this medium.

4. Viewers' attention often wanders during the commercial breaks.

5. Remote control has aggravated this problem, with viewers often 'channel flicking' during commercial breaks.

6. The growing use of videos also causes problems – most viewers fast forward the adverts when watching recorded programmes.

Buying Time

Each TV company sells airtime in commercial breaks between and during programmes. There are three or four breaks per hour with a maximum limit of seven minutes per hour for advertising allowed. Different advertising rates are charged at different times of day, roughly corresponding with audience size, with the highest rate occurring during the peak early evening time. Prices also vary considerably between the large ITV companies and the smaller ones. The prices shown below are taken from the November 1991 issue of BRAD and refer to the cost of 30 second slots.

Peak time ITV:
Thames: £52,000
Anglia: £14,000
Border: £1,200

Off peak:
Thames: £500
Anglia: £250
Border: £45

Magazines

Magazines vary from quarterlies to weeklies and from very general magazines with a wide readership such as *The Radio Times* to highly specialist journals with much smaller circulations. There are well over a thousand magazines of one kind or another published in the UK, though the numbers are constantly changing. The main difference between newspapers and magazines is that magazines pre-select their audience by their content and are, therefore, much better for targeting purposes.

Magazines can be divided into seven broad categories:

Special interest

Interests of all kinds are covered by specialist magazines. from photography to skateboarding, from dog breeding to chess.

General interest

Women's magazines form the bulk of this category but there are also children's magazines, broadcasting magazines and current affairs magazines.

Trade journals

Aimed typically at the distribution trade, they cover items of topical interest and are a major vehicle for supplier information to the trade, either in the form of editorial (written largely from manufacturers' press releases), or advertising. A typical example would be *The Grocer*.

Technical journals

Aimed at companies in manufacturing or service industries, these journals often contain long, technical articles as well as shorter, more topical items. Again, a large volume of advertising will be found. Typical examples would be *Plastics and Rubber Weekly* and *Woodworking Industry*.

Professional journals

These are aimed across industry divisions at members of specific professions such as accountants, personnel managers, solicitors or engineers. Many professional bodies have their own magazine. Job advertising features prominently in these journals.

Regional magazines

Traditionally these were rather up-market social publications such as *Northumberland Life* but, with the ever decreasing costs of publishing, a large number of locally based, free magazines are appearing which are aimed both at households and local businesses.

Advantages of Magazine Advertising

1. They have a longer life than newspapers and one copy may be read by several people – even by hundreds if it ends up in a doctor's waiting room!

2. Segmentation and targeting can be very precise.

3. Special interest magazines will often be read avidly by enthusiasts who will be prepared to devote considerable time and attention to all of its contents, including advertisements and editorial content. In addition to improving the chances of an advert being noticed, it enables advertisers to use long and complicated copy if necessary.

4. High-quality paper and print is suitable for up-market advertising, e.g. fashion, perfume, quality furniture.

5. Some magazines are kept by subscribers as sources of reference.

6. Some respected journals may add credibility to advertising messages.

Disadvantages of Magazine Advertising

1. High-quality production means high cost since very high-quality originals are necessary to take full advantage of the glossy medium.

2. Infrequent publication causes long lead and cancellation times and makes really topical advertising impossible.

3. Advertisers face considerable competition for their message from editorial and other adverts.

4. The long life of some magazines makes monitoring and evaluation difficult.

5. Readership details are much less comprehensive for most magazines than they are for newspapers. Smaller journals may not even have independently audited circulation figures.

6. Cost per thousand is typically high but is, arguably, offset by the greater intrinsic value of the advert to the reader, particularly in the specialist magazines.

Cost of advertising space

Costs vary widely according to the circulation and prestige of the magazine. It is best to illustrate this point with some examples. All are taken from BRAD, which is by far the most comprehensive source of advertising media and their costs in the UK.

Colour page

Woman's Own	£26,500
Cosmopolitan	£9,900
Just Seventeen	£7,930

Black & white page

Woman's Own	£15,500
Radio Times	£12,700
TV Times	£9,600
Prima	£9,135
Smash Hits	£7,780

Outdoor

As well as poster sites, outdoor advertising includes transport advertising opportunities (such as buses, taxis, underground trains and stations, railway stations and airports), sports stadia perimeter boards and even milk bottles, parking meters and balloons. Outdoor posters are usually sited on the sides of buildings, by the roadside, around car parks, in shopping centres and precincts and even on litter bins.

Advantages of Outdoor Advertising

1. By far the lowest CPT of all media.

2. High coverage and OTS – theoretically 94% of the population has the opportunity to see a poster advertisement in a week and almost everyone over a long period.

3. Large poster sites can be very dramatic.

4. Adverts are in full colour.

5. There is a very wide choice of locations and sites.

6. Little direct competition from advertising matter.

7. Some poster sites may achieve 'sole attraction' status, where people have little else to do but read the advert when standing on the underground platform, riding up the escalator or waiting for the bus.

8. Many poster sites are booked for 13 weeks and it is said that poster advertising may come close to achieving the 'subliminal effect' (where people sub-consciously absorb a message without realising it) as people pass the poster site maybe twice a day during that period.

Disadvantages of Outdoor Advertising

1. *Wallpaper effect.* Since they are always there and have very little opportunity to make impact, the main criticism of the outdoor media is that messages go totally unnoticed by many people. A notable exception to this rule was the outdoor advertising which accompanied the introduction of Araldite, when a real Ford Cortina, (albeit minus the heavy bits

such as engine and transmission) was stuck to a billboard. Needless to say, as well as being noticed on the spot, this creative coup also generated much additional publicity in the media, and was arguably one of the most brilliant pieces of advertising of all time.

2.   Printing costs for the large sheets, ordered in relatively small quantities, are expensive.

3.   Booking and cancellation lead times are long.

4.   Audience research is very scanty.

5.   Graffiti is a problem on some sites.

6.   Most sites suffer from plenty of extraneous matter to distract the attention of passers-by, especially drivers.

7.   Suitable only for very simple messages due to the often short exposure time (maybe less than five seconds) to the audience.

Cost of outdoor advertising

A single, small poster site can be booked for a few pounds, but this virtually never happens. Sites are bought in packages. Mills and Allen sells 14 day packages on their poster sites in Greater London at £190,000. Production costs are also steep, tending to add around 30% to the cost of a typical package.

Radio

There are over 150 commercial independent local radio stations at present. Programming is generally middle of the road, in contrast to BBC's five highly segmented national services. Although ILR is currently receivable by around 85% of the population, only about 45% listen in a typical week. This figure rises to over 60% for the 15-24 year olds but gradually declines to below 30% for over-60s. The visual transfer concept can be adapted on an audio level with songs or jingles associated with well-known TV adverts helping to increase the impact of radio advertising. A recent ILR development has been networking, starting with the Network Chart show on Sundays, which offers advertisers the possibility of genuinely national advertising on ILR.

Advantages of Radio Advertising

1.   Precise local coverage.

2.   Commercials are transmitted serially, so they do not have to compete at that point in time for listeners' attention with other adverts or with programme matter. (Unlike newspapers, for example, where a large amount of competing material faces the reader.)

3.   Radio is an excellent medium for conveying urgency, e.g. 'Hurry to Joe's store on Main Road NOW, while stocks last.'

4.   Campaigns can be booked or cancelled at short notice; this facilitates topical and urgent advertising.

5.   Sound quality is much better than TV which does offer the possibility of making impact through the use of creative sound effects.

6.   Production costs can be very low due to very simple production technology. Radio stations will help advertisers with production of their ads.

7.   Discounts will be available for first-time advertisers.

Disadvantages of Radio Advertising

1.   Planning is difficult because, apart from the excellent local targeting, radio research is still not sufficiently comprehensive to enable media planners to plan national campaigns in the way they would like.

2.   Radio is generally assumed to be very poor on impact. It is seen as 'aural wallpaper', always there in the background, but rarely paid full attention.

3.   Booked nationally, ILR is an expensive medium.

Cost of radio advertising

Costs vary widely. Discounts will be widely available, especially for quantity bookings. The most expensive thirty second spot on a local station would be Capital 95.8 FM's price of £1,800 for a commercial on Sunday morning between 9 am and noon.

Cinema

The number of cinemas has been declining for over thirty years, although it has slowed down considerably over the last ten years. Hit initially by the spread of the television, the medium has also had to contend with the threat of video rental in more recent years. As a result it has become increasingly dependent upon the latest 'Big Films' with star names and much publicity. There are now around 1,580 screens in the UK in total. The cinema is a very young medium, with 30% of 15 to 24 year olds claiming to attend once a week and 76% attending at least once a month. The attendance figures drop rapidly amongst older age groups, although the audience at cinemas in the West End of London shows an older profile. The cinema is, therefore, used mainly as a way of targeting this young audience, with products like jeans, cosmetics, motorcycles, new bank accounts and local entertainment likely to feature prominently amongst adverts.

Advantages of Cinema Advertising

1.   Reproduction quality of both sound and picture is superb.

2.   Local advertising is feasible.

3.   Excellent targeting of young adults.

4.   Ideal conditions for holding the attention of the audience, with the impact of the big screen and the absence of distractions.

5.   Research shows that people recall cinema commercials better than TV commercials.

Disadvantages of Cinema Advertising

1. Low audiences.

2. Very slow build up of coverage and frequency, since commercials are shown only once during a programme and most individuals, even in the young adult group, will not attend the cinema more than once a month.

3. Production costs are extremely high. Initial filming is no more expensive than for television, but then the costs start to escalate. The cinema contractors demand two very high quality 70mm colour prints per screen, which is a lot of films if a national cinema is contemplated, especially since they cost several hundred pounds each. Thus, many advertisers use alternate weeks in advertising at each cinema (or screen) to halve the print costs.

4. Many cinema adverts, especially the local ones, are of poor quality, and this image may rub off on the whole commercial break.

Cost of cinema advertising

Spots can be booked with individual cinemas at a cost of around £30 for a thirty-second spot for one week. Of course, with the production costs taken into account, it would make sense only to book a number of weeks (or several different cinemas). To book a thirty-second slot nationally, on all 1,580 screens, for one week would cost £83,483.

Direct Mail

The popular impression of direct mail is a vision of millions of consumers and businesses being submerged each day beneath a mountain of direct mail. This is a misconception. Although the irritation factor caused by individual mailshots which are inappropriately targeted may be very high, the volume of direct mail received – even by business – is not particularly large. In fact, UK households and businesses receive, on average, only a small proportion of the mail that would be received by a typical American consumer or business buyer. An even greater misconception is that all mailshots take the most direct route to the wastebin and must, therefore, be a waste of money. In fact, many transactions are completed as a result of mailshots. Even a seemingly tiny response rate, below 1% for example, can make many mailshots a highly cost effective form of promotion.

Reasons for the growth of direct mail

In reality, direct mail is currently the most rapidly increasing form of promotion. In 1986 banks alone sent out no less than 109 million items by direct mail. Many businesses are beginning to use direct mail because of the considerable advantages it can offer, including:

Selectivity

Targeting can be very precise, and there are many readily available methods, e.g. ACORN or MOSAIC, to help users of direct mail to aim their message at the correct audience.

Cost effectiveness

The ability to target precise segments makes it possible to eliminate a large proportion of unlikely buyers. This eliminates the waste factor which is such a problem when advertising through the main media such as TV and national newspapers.

Impact

Mailshots to make impact. A 1986 survey (by Survey Research Associates) showed that 80% of recipients read some of the leaflets included with regular bills, while 40% read most of them. Companies which are prepared to spend money on making an impact (e.g. offering a free draw with a valuable prize) get a very high rate of attention from the audience.

Complex messages

Unlike most forms of media advertising, direct mail can cope with detailed copy, allowing long and complicated messages to be sent. If impact has been made, and the receivers are interested in the general message, they will be prepared to read quite lengthy copy. This is ideal for complex offerings such as financial services.

Measurability

Direct mail is the measurable form of promotion. The marketer knows exactly how many mailshots have been sent and exactly how much the whole campaign has cost. By recording the responses the effectiveness of the campaign can be measured and, since it is usually a simple task to trace the proportion of responses which resulted in sales, it is possible to work out whether the campaign paid for itself.

Testability

More than any other medium, direct mail is testable. A small number of mailshots can be sent out and the response monitored. Individual features of the mailshot can be changed and different versions compared for response rate. Different copy, photographs, mailing lists, envelopes, incentives – almost variable – can be tested. For a valid test, however, it is important to change only one variable at a time otherwise it would be impossible to isolate the effects of each change.

Sales Promotion

Sales promotions include 'money off' coupons, scratch cards, competitions, small plastic soldiers inside boxes of breakfast cereals, free samples, 'buy one and get one free', and they come in many more varieties besides. But what exactly are sales promotions? The definition of sales promotions is simple. It is 'short term incentives to buy'. The objectives of advertising are usually more long term, such as generating awareness and building brand image. The objectives of sales promotions are almost always short-term and induce people to act immediately. James Adams summed up the difference between advertising and sales promotion. Advertising is 'to increase preference for the brand in the mind of the potential customer through paid for media space or time'. A sales promotion is 'any device for triggering purchase of the brand where it would not otherwise have been chosen.' Adams adds that a sales promotion will usually seek to achieve this objective by 'increasing perceived value for money'.

Promotions out of the pipeline

Moving products off the shelves is big business. The manufacturers are still responsible for the bulk of 'out of the pipeline' promotional expenditure but the retailers are becoming increasingly involved. Typical promotions include the following:

Free samples

The most effective method of getting people to try a new product, and also the most expensive. It can be done on a door-to-door basis or, as is more popular nowadays, as part of a joint promotion of non-competing products, such as the bounty packs of baby products given to mothers who have recently given birth.

Coupon offers

Usually in the form of 'money off', they can be distributed door-to-door, be part of a press advertisement, or be on-pack and offering money off the next purchase. Sometimes coupon offers are distributed as part of an 'FSI' (a free standing insert). An FSI would typically be found in a magazine such as *Prima* or *Woman's Own*, and would contain nothing but adverts and coupons for non-competing products. Coupons do, of course, involve the buyer in some effort and therefore have a redemption rate of only around 20%.

Reduced price

Usually in the form of 'money off', these promotions are very popular with consumers, but are the most expensive of all the manufacturer or retailer concerned. It is far cheaper to give away free products or other merchandise which can be purchased in bulk quite cheaply. Also some of the money given away in reduced price offers will be wasted since regular purchasers of the product would have bought anyway.

Banded offers

This type of promotion takes two forms: 'two for the price of one' (very common with soap and shampoo) or a well-known brand carrying a sample of another non-competing product.

Premium offer

There are three main types of premium offer:

The free gift

This may be contained in the pack (plastic animals in breakfast cereals or cards in tea). It may be the pack itself (instant coffee in storage jars), or it may be given at the checkout (for example a free mug with every gallon can of oil purchased). A common objective with such promotions is to build brand loyalty through encouraging a collecting habit.

Free sendaway gift

This type of promotion offers a free gift in exchange for the proof of purchase of a certain product, usually demonstrated by a collection of tokens or packet tops. The consumer has to claim the free gift by sending away the tops. An example would be a free guide to the Tour of Britain cycling race in exchange for eight Kellogg's Bran Flakes tokens. This can be a cost-effective form of promotion for the manufacturer, since many of the people who buy the product and start collecting the tokens never send off for the free item.

Self-liquidating premiums

Here the consumer has to send both money and proof of purchase to obtain the premium offer. Through buying in bulk and maybe striking an agreement with the manufacturer of the offered item (who gains valuable publicity) the self-liquidating offer can appear to be very good value to the consumer but actually pays for itself.

Competitions

Interest in competitions can be considerable, particularly if there is an attraction of a very large prize, coupled with a sufficient number of small consolation prizes, to encourage people to try their luck. It is popular with petrol companies: the Shell 'make money' promotion (packets containing half a bank note which had to be matched with its corresponding half) was both very original and very popular with motorists.

Bonus packs

Sometimes called 'flashpacks', usually they come in the form of a brightly coloured extra portion, such as '20% extra free'. These promotions can be very popular with consumers since the extra value is obvious, and they are popular with manufacturers because giving away a free product is less costly than knocking money off, while the packs have considerable impact in the store and the promotion can sometimes be part of a campaign to trade customers up to larger sizes. The disadvantages are the considerable extra packaging costs incurred and the logistical problems of fitting the larger packs onto supermarket shelves, pallets and lorries.

Charity promotions

Customers collect box tops or wrappers and send into the manufacturer who makes a donation to charity for each wrapper sent in. The Ski yogurt Stoke Mandeville appeal is typical. Sporting appeals, e.g. donations to help athletes train for the Olympic Games, are also popular. Probably the best example is the Andrex appeal for guide dogs for the blind.

Personal Selling

Introduction

The standard definition of personal selling is:

'Oral presentation in a conversation with one or more prospective purchasers for the purpose of making sales.' (Philip Kotler).

This is a good definition of the traditional view of personal selling which is seen to involve a sales presentation, the objective of which is to persuade someone to buy something. Increasingly, however, the role of personal selling is being seen as something much wider than the very narrow view of the hard sell door-to-door salesperson. In most cases the final act of the marketing process involves personal contact between buyer and seller. The act of personal selling is usually the culmination of the marketing mix. A product which meets customers' needs has been developed and produced, has been priced, has been made available and accessible to buyers; promotion has raised customer awareness and stimulated their interest and, finally, a deal is struck between buyer and seller.

The importance of personal selling

In arriving at an acceptable deal, the importance of personal selling will vary between different types of business, but in general it is important in three ways:

Making sales

Whenever a sale is made the role of the sales person can be critical. Even for the most mundane of items well-trained sales people will always sell more than untrained sales people.

Relationships

Sometimes sales are the result of a much longer dialogue between suppliers and customers. In this situation personal interaction between buyers and sellers is very important because the final sale may be the culmination of long negotiations.

Service

Making the sale, and fostering the relationship which precedes it, are very important, but together they still do not fully encompass the personal role in successful marketing, because, if the marketing process is all about the delivery of satisfaction to customers, there is a much more central role for people to play. People are fundamental to the winning and keeping of satisfied customers, so much so that it is now suggested that the marketing mix should have a fifth 'P' – People.

In fact, 'personal communications' would be a more accurate term to fully describe the role and importance of personal selling in the marketing process.

Telephone selling

Because of the high total cost of maintaining a salesforce (estimated at over £30,000, including overheads, to keep one sales person on the road for a year) and the relatively small proportion of sales force time spent selling, companies are always looking for ways to increase the efficiency of their sales effort. In recent years, this has led to a rapid growth in tele-sales, a method of selling now employed by many companies.

It is not usual for telephone selling to replace all the tasks of the sales person described. It can be feasible for the sales of fairly simple, low value products bought on a repetitive basis. A good example would be supplies of tea, coffee, milk, sugar etc. to replenish drinks machines. Lots of companies have these machines and need to re-order supplies weekly or monthly. To employ a sales person to drive round to take orders in person would be very expensive, but a tele-sales operation can be used to ring customers on a regular basis to take their orders.

Conclusion

This section has explored the function of marketing in a business. There is no doubt that in recent years marketing has taken on much greater significance than in times gone by. No business must lose sight of the fact that, once demand has been created by the marketing process, that demand must be capable of being fulfilled. In a manufacturing business that satisfaction of demand involves producing goods which will meet consumers needs: the production function is examined in the next section. With some people, marketing is a contentious subject: some of the social implications of marketing are examined in the section 'Consumerism' in Part Five.

1. Explain the difference between a *market* and a *market segment*.
2. What is the principal purpose of marketing?
3. Name three sources of data a marketer might use.
4. Why might a business benefit from more effective marketing?
5. What do you understand as the difference between *product orientated* and *market driven*?
6. What is meant by the phrases *SWOT analysis* and *PEST*?
7. In what demographic factors are marketers most interested?
8. What is described by the term *buying decision*?
9. Summarise the effectiveness of anti-union legislation in the 1980s.
10. What strategies might marketers use to target a market?
11. Describe the differences between *niche*, *mass* and *selective* marketing.
12. List the *primary sources of information* a business might use in its marketing.
13. Name the '4Ps'.
14. Define a *product* and a *brand*.
15. Sketch a typical product life cycle.
16. Describe the *stages* of a product life cycle.
17. Explain a possible strategy to extend the life cycle of a product.
18. State the advantages of *branding* a product.
19. Describe some methods of developing new products.
20. Why is *price* an important element of the marketing mix?
21. List the factors that a business must consider when deciding a price structure for its product.
22. What is meant by *tactical pricing*?
23. Sketch a diagram to show the main channels of distribution.
24. List the main functions of *middlemen*.
25. State what is meant by *vertical integration* within a channel network.
26. List the main forms of advertising.
27. Construct a table that compares and contrasts the main methods of advertising.
28. List the advantages and disadvantages of advertising through the different media.
29. Distinguish between *advertising* and *sales promotion*.
30. Explain what you understand by *personal selling*.

Introduction

Essentially, a business is a structured system which uses its resources to provide goods or services to customers or clients. The managers of that business may often find themselves heavily involved with such matters as financial control, methods of work, materials purchasing, marketing and all the administrative and managerial tasks that are necessary to the running of a modern business. However, the most important resource in a business is the people that it employs; adequate management time must be devoted to meeting their needs.

It is possible to examine the importance of a business's personnel from several viewpoints. These are:

1. the financial approach
2. the altruistic approach
3. the potential approach
4. the productivity approach
5. the development approach.

1. The Financial Approach

Few people who watch or read the news will be unaware of the call for all businesses to implement financial cutbacks, limit budgets, lower costs and set competitive prices. The people who ask for business to take such measures point to the need for careful control of the business's spending. If they are right, then attention must be given to the resource which normally makes up the largest share of a business's costs: the human resource or, as they are better known, people.

Many businesses, especially those in the service sector, are 'people (or 'labour') intensive': up to 65-75% of their total budget may be taken up by staff costs, such as wages, pensions, facilities etc. Staff costs are by far the largest element in their budget and become the focus of any cost-cutting exercise.

Take the case of the National Health Service which has an annual budget of more than £18 billion. More than two-thirds of this total is spent on personnel costs, so it is essential for the NHS management to seek value for money from each of its employees.

2. The Altruistic Approach

A very high proportion of employed people's active time is spent at work. Therefore, there is an argument that it is only morally right that their work should be interesting and rewarding. However, the question is: What should a job ideally provide? Everyone has their own ideas about their 'perfect' job.

For most people, this would include: a reasonable wage or salary; interesting and challenging tasks; meeting and working with other people; some chance to display initiative and demonstrate worth; and an opportunity to 'get on'. Some people's jobs do contain all of these elements and their work becomes a central life interest. Work often overlaps with their leisure time and some activities can blur the distinction between work and leisure. There are many examples of this, such as friends discussing work and social activities connected with the place of work. However, the opposite is also true for many other jobs.

Some jobs are designed for 'efficient working', with easily learnt, repetitive tasks being carried out as part of the production process. Here people work in a strictly ordered manner and so have little opportunity to display initiative. Such jobs tend to treat people like machines; it would be pleasing to think that this type of work has been eliminated by managers keen to look after their staff. Unfortunately, this has not happened – despite the fact that machine-like jobs are best carried out by machines.

There have never been greater opportunities to automate repetitive processes by introducing new methods and machines, or replacing human movements entirely by machines for tasks such as spot welding or simple assembly. It is important to design jobs in which people can use new technology, such as word processors and computer-aided design, to remove some of the repetitiveness of certain processes and allow people to carry out those tasks which need the flexible approach of the human being.

3. The Potential Approach

Engineers, by improving design, have managed to extract more power from engines of a similar basic design. For example, a two litre car engine in the early part of this century could produce only 40 brake horse power (bhp) while today a two litre family saloon can produce around 115 bhp – and a two litre racing car engine up to 400 bhp. In other words, the engine had the potential to produce more power and skillful engineering managed to bring out the greater capability. The same may be said of the way people are managed: is their 'potential' being fully tapped? A business with a thousand employees has a thousand brains at its disposal. The business should use the potential of the workforce to develop new ideas about work methods, what it produces and the services it provides. Businesses invariably waste this potential, simply through a failure to recognise it.

Some businesses have tried to capitalise on this potential by allowing employees a greater opportunity to participate in the decision-making process, especially when it affects their work. A variety of methods are used, ranging from suggestion schemes in which individuals can propose improvements or amendments to their work, to discussion meetings which aim at group problem-solving. Such approaches enable a greater breadth of experience to be brought to bear upon a business's problems. This may constructively change the way in which management and the workforce co-operate and may improve human relations once the benefits of such improvements are felt by employees. This, in turn, might lead to a more co-operative attitude between management and unions, thus benefiting industrial relations.

4. The Productivity Approach

If the cost of manpower is high, it needs to be paid for by high output. At the beginning of the century, FW Taylor suggested that only high productivity could solve the problem of providing high wages while maintaining low average labour costs per article produced. For example, if the output per worker could be increased, prices could be reduced and so the customer would benefit. If this resulted in higher sales of the product, then more profit would be generated for the business; this, in turn, would lead to higher dividends for its shareholders.

The problem is the need to motivate the workforce so that higher levels of output can be achieved by the same number of workers. FW Taylor believed that money was the major incentive to increase production and his 'scientific management' approach attempted to find the best method of working and rewarding the workforce if they produced more. The workforce was expected to follow rigidly the prescribed method of working: if the specified levels of output were achieved, then bonus payments were made. One problem with this approach is that specified levels of output may be set unfairly high. This can be the cause of poor industrial relations, leading in some cases to industrial action in the form of go-slows and strikes.

Modern workstudy methods seek a fairer approach to setting targets of work. However, if the work which employees are required to perform is simple and repetitive, this will not provide sufficient job satisfaction and financial incentives themselves may be insufficient to motivate the workforce.

5. The Development Approach

Any enterprise needs to keep an up-to-date account of the value of its business in the form of a balance sheet, where the value of its assets and liabilities are expressed in financial terms. The business will wish to see improvements in its balance sheet provision from year to year. One asset which is *not* recorded in the balance sheet is the workforce. Yet, as already noted, the workforce is often the business's most valuable resource. An efficient manager will wish to evaluate the worth of the workorce, on a regular basis, by undertaking an audit of the skills and experience of the business's employees. That manager may then attempt to ensure that the 'value' of those employees increases each year by enhancing their skills and abilities through training and staff development.

Personnel Management

The manner in which employees are treated is of critical importance to the successful management of any business. Those involved in the management of staff must be guided in the way in which they carry out this function. To help achieve this objective, many businesses now have separate personnel departments whose responsibility is to give advice and guidance to managers on all aspects of personnel work, such as health and safety, welfare, recruitment, termination of employment, job specification and matters related to industrial relations and collective bargaining. An important, though difficult, area within personnel is manpower planning and it is to this that we look next.

1. Manpower Planning

It is a function of the business's senior management to decide overall policy and objectives. An important aspect of this function is the establishment of a personnel policy and personnel objectives for the business as a whole. This is often referred to as 'the manpower plan'. A long-term strategy is needed for the business and the manpower plan is an integral part of this overall corporate strategy. Manpower planning may be defined as *the means by which a business may plan its future employee requirements*.

Manpower planning will involve determining the number and quality of employees that will be required in the future. Obviously, the business's requirement for manpower will be determined by the anticipated future demand for its product or service and, as such, is part of the long-term development of the business. Clearly, it is important to establish whether or not this future demand can be met by the present work force; if it cannot, then there is the need to establish plans to ensure that the present staff can be trained or developed, or that new employees can be recruited to fill the gap.

2. The Aims of Manpower Planning

In order to survive, every business must meet its own needs and demands for employees. This may be expressed under the following headings:

a. *Recruitment*

The business must ensure that the right kind of employee is attracted. Thus its recruitment policy is determined by its specific manning needs.

b. *Experience*

Well-trained and experienced employees must be encouraged to stay with the business. This is achieved by creating an appropriate working environment, career structure and building in adequate rewards.

c. *Task performance*

All employees must carry out their duties and responsibilities in an efficient and effective way and the employer must be able to monitor this and rectify any deficiencies in an employee's performance.

d. *Motivation*

Employees must be motivated so that they will do more than just carry out instructions. For the business to survive and grow, it must have employees who are willing to seek improvements in their work tasks and use their ingenuity to achieve this.

3. The Use of Manpower Planning in Guiding Management

Manpower plans can guide management decision-making in a number of respects. These include: recruitment; staff development, including management development; training; anticipating the need for redundancies; productivity bargaining; improving industrial relations; estimating labour costs; health, safety and welfare; accommodation requirements; disciplinary procedures.

4. The Need to Update the Business's Manpower Plan

The manpower plan will need updating, at intervals, as a result of changes in:

a. *New technology*

To maintain a competitive position, the business must adapt to changes in technology. This may mean updating the skills of existing employees or hiring new employees with new skills. New technology may require changes in the method of work, as well as in the equipment which is used. This may also involve a corresponding change in the attitude of the workforce to new technology.

b.   *Government intervention*

The government from time to time introduces legislation which requires a modification of a business's manpower plans. An example is the change in the compulsory retirement age of women that is contained in the Sex Discrimination Act 1986.

c.   *New organisational goals*

Changes in market conditions often force a business to re-think its business strategy. This can mean a major revision of its manpower requirements.

d.   *The changing needs of society*

The public's ideas, tastes and needs tend to change. Such changes may cause a business to grow or decline. For example, tobacco firms have been forced to diversify into the manufacture of other products as smoking has become more socially unacceptable. This has obviously meant a reduction in the number of workers in the tobacco industry.

5. The Time Scale of Manpower Planning

Planning, by its very nature, involves the anticipation of future events. The further ahead the prediction, the less certain will be the plan. Manpower planning, therefore, falls into different time-scales.

Short-term manpower planning

Planning up to one to two years ahead provides for the personnel needs of the business in its present form. Examples are: the replacement of people who retire or training and induction programmes for new starters. The business should have job descriptions of all existing staff and personnel records will indicate the age of individuals so that it can accurately anticipate retirements. Usually, a computer system is used to hold a database for personnel information. This enables information, such as identification of workers within a given range, to be retrieved very quickly.

Long-term manpower planning

If a business looks further ahead, say to the next five years, obviously, there will be a greater degree of uncertainty. However, the training of certain employees, such as accountants or engineers, may require a considerable amount of such forward planning. Also, if the nature of the business means it is involved in long-term projects, then manpower needs will have to be anticipated well in advance so that sufficient time is allowed for the recruitment and training of staff.

Long-term manpower planning attempts to provide for the personnel needs of the business as they may develop in the future. This provision has to take into account any new objectives the business may wish to pursue. There are three factors which are usually associated with new advances:

1.   an increase in productivity

2.   the opportunity to gain an increase in quality

3.   a change in skills required by personnel who will be closely involved with it.

Predictions based on current developments in new technology suggest that staff in the future may have to change their work skills, on average, three times in their working career. Technological advances, which demonstrate the three factors previously listed, can be found in almost every manufacturing and service industry.

6. Personnel Selection

When an economy grows, more jobs are generated and more movement between jobs becomes likely. Businesses must, therefore, seek to be efficient and effective in recruitment and selection of the personnel needed for the future of the business.

Recruitment can be seen as the first step in filling a vacancy. It involves: examining the job to be done; identifying where the best candidates are likely to be found; how best to make contact and attract them.

Selection is the next part of the process and a variety of means are employed to choose the most suitable candidate. These means can be expensive involving, as they often do, advertising, expenses incurred by candidates and, above all, the administrative time expended. Subsequent expense will emerge in the form of employee induction and other training costs.

7. Industrial Relations and Manpower Planning

By industrial relations is meant *the relationships which exist between the business and its workforce*. Every business should attempt to develop good industrial relations, as the effects of industrial action can be severely damaging in terms of morale, motivation and finances. As businesses increase in size, individual bargaining between a manager and an individual worker becomes impractical. In such circumstances the trade unions will undertake this role on behalf of their individual members. This process is referred to as 'collective bargaining'. A climate where good communications and morale are present is usually conducive to good industrial relations. The effect of poor industrial relations may damage industrial output and confidence in UK industry, both domestically and internationally and so government agencies have been established to assist in the promotion of industrial relations. The most important of these is ACAS (the Advisory, Conciliation and Arbitration Service). Codes of Practice designed by ACAS are intended to assist the promotion of good industrial relations.

A Manpower Plan for the 1990s

A phrase that was originated in the 1980s, is likely to become even more widely used as the year 2000 approaches; that phrase is 'the demographic time bomb'. It sums up the dramatic changes that are occurring in the shape and structure of the UK population over the 1990s, the potentially explosive effects those changes are having on the national workforce and the consequences for business in particular and the economy in general.

The elements of the demographic time bomb are:

- the population of the UK will be aging
- fewer young people will be joining the workforce
- there will be a shortage of workers of the right quality
- people will become increasingly valuable as a 'human resource' and will be critical to a business retaining its competitive edge.

The implications of this are clear:

- employers will wish to retain their employees
- employers will wish to be seen as attractive to potential recruits
- employers will need to offer the right incentives in order to recruit, retain and motivate their employees.

The 1990s will see business focusing on its employees, since there will be a heightened realisation that, unless they are offered the opportunity to exercise their qualities, skills, training and ideas, then they are likely to look for job satisfaction elsewhere. Training is a highly motivating factor to an employee: employees offered quality training see it as part of their own career planning and development and are likely to remain loyal to its provider. A business which offers quality training as part of a broad 'people' strategy gains greater involvement and commitment from its personnel and is unlikely to see them 'poached' away.

Some of the strategies businesses will have to develop in order to become successful in this is through the re-skilling and re-training of current, committed employees. Businesses which regard training as a clear priority and divert resources to it will have such investment richly rewarded, since personnel repay the training through increased performance and reduced operating costs. All employees, including senior management, need to communicate, secure understanding and treat the 'human resource' with respect. There must be clear communication and a free flow of ideas and, as an accelerated pace of change exacerbates feelings of insecurity and uncertainty among employees, these need to be met and resolved. Overall, the business that firmly places a premium on the individual and develops a management style that formulates the new relationship is likely to be competitively well placed to meet the demographic challenges of this decade and the next.

The Functions of a Personnel Department

There are many functions involved in a comprehensive personnel department. These have been defined by the Institute of Personnel Management (IPM) as follows:

Personnel management is concerned with the development and application of policies governing:

1. manpower planning, recruitment, selection, placement and termination
2. education and training; career development
3. terms of employment; methods and standards of remuneration
4. working conditions and employee services

5.   negotiation and application of agreements on wages and working conditions; procedures for the accordance and settlement of disputes

6.   the human and social implications of change in internal business and methods of working, and of social and economic changes in the community.

These aspects are examined in the following section.

Recruitment, Selection and Training

The efficiency and effectiveness of a business depends upon it having the right people in the right jobs, with the right skills and training. Hence the process of recruitment, selection and training is a very important feature of business. In small businesses, recruitment will be the responsibility of the departmental manager. In larger businesses, the personnel department will fulfil this function, probably in consultation with the department involved. For some key posts, the services of employment or recruitment consultants will be sought and the consultants will work with the personnel department and any other department which needs to be involved.

A systematic approach to the recruitment process will involve the following:

1.   job analysis, involving job description, job specification, person specification

2 .   job evaluation

3.   attracting a field of candidates

4.   interviewing

5.   selection

6.   employment involving induction and training and development.

1. Job analysis

There are three parts to job analysis:

a.   A *job description*. This is a statement of the tasks, duties, objectives and standards attached to the job.

b.   A *job specification*. This is the production of a specification of the skills, knowledge and qualities needed to perform the job.

c.   A *person specification*. This is a re-wording of the job specification in terms of the kind of person needed to perform the job.

These three components represent an 'ideal' and you will often find that the term 'job description' is used loosely to describe all three components.

2. Job evaluation

This is concerned with comparing one job with others before finding a suitable grade or salary for it.

Elaborate systems involving the allocation of points are widely used. Another method is the design of a grading system into which all jobs can be slotted. The Institute of Administrative Management (IAM) suggests the following grading scheme for office jobs:

- Grade I – routine, unskilled work requiring little or no training and carried out under close supervision

- Grade II – supervised work requiring basic mechanical skills or clerical work requiring some aptitude

- Grade III – skilled work requiring a longer period of training/experience and some degree of responsibility/initiative

- Grade IV – responsibility for a group or work requiring semi-professional training

- Grade V – responsibility for a department or complex work; requiring specialist or professional training

- Grade VI – control of a wide range of people and activities; requiring experience and specialist training/qualifications.

Care must be taken with these 'scientific' approaches to grading and payment. They provide a useful framework, but there are still 'grey' areas that involve people making a subjective judgment. Take, for example, Grade V. How do you define 'complex' work? Similarly, such schemes do not decide the salary, or structure in terms of actual salaries, or the differences between grades. This is further complicated by the state of the labour market: supply and demand factors can force employers to pay salaries which contradict the general job evaluation scheme.

3. Attracting a field of candidates

There are various practices and methods used to attract candidates.

a. *Internal advertising*

Many businesses advertise internally, depending on the job on offer and the policy of the business. Balancing the need to reward internally (by promotion) with the need to transfuse new ideas and new approaches from outside into the business, is an area of management that requires considerable judgement. The commonest ways of internal advertising are staff bulletins, notice boards, and circulating copies of advertisements to each section or department.

b. *External advertising*

Ways of advertising externally are:

(i) the local and national press

Advertising in national papers is expensive, but for senior jobs where the widest possible field is required the cost is justified by alerting a very wide market to the available post.

(ii) specialist journals – trade and professional

These are two platforms that are frequently used because the press and journals have expert staff who assist advertisers with layout and with knowledge of circulation and re-ordering of their publications.

    (iii)   recruitment agencies and consultants

This method has become more widespread in recent years, demonstrating the willingness of businesses to use the specialist services available from these agencies. When a business is looking for a particularly important post to be filled, and actively pursues candidates without first having been approached by them, the process is known as 'headhunting'.

    (iv)   schools, colleges and universities

This source of candidates can be tapped either by printed material or by visits to give talks and create a favourable image, or by specific recruitment visits. Increasingly, educational institutions tend to organise career conventions as a means by which potential candidates and employers can meet (sometimes referred to as 'the milk round'). Many employers have professionally designed and highly portable displays which can be taken to any organised convention. Such displays are also used within the company for various image-enhancing purposes, such as visits to the workplace by organised groups.

c.   *Local shops and personal contact*

Many small businesses will rely upon advertisements in local shops or simple word of mouth to fill vacancies. Many part-time jobs are also filled this way.

d.   *Department of Employment agencies*

The Department of Employment assists employers to find suitable candidates through various schemes. A common method is the Job Shop, where advertisements are displayed on postcards and help is available from officials. Publicising vacancies using the media necessitates sending out information to applicants – usually an application form and 'further particulars' relating to the job and business.

4. Interviewing

The number of applications received can dictate the pattern of the selection process. If there are a hundred applicants chasing a single job, then a process of matching them to the job will reduce the candidates to a manageable shortlist.

A typical shortlist includes five or six applicants. If matching applicants to jobs fails to reduce the number of applicants to a manageable number, then some other filtering and elimination process is required. All candidates might be invited to a pre-selection interview or test in order to whittle down the candidates. They will then be further interviewed to determine who will be offered the job.

A shortage of applicants will require a different approach. Suppose, for a very senior post in your business, which has been nationally advertised, there is only one applicant. You would want to know why the response proved so poor; whether it is worth re- advertising the vacancy. Consider how many people may not see an advertisement which appears only once. Inevitably, questions about the job, level of salary, location, benefits, the business, and the supply of certain skills will need to be considered when responses to advertisements are very low.

Assuming there are enough candidates of sufficient calibre to draw up a shortlist, interviews can be held. The process involves three phases :

a. Arranging the interview

The arrangements will include:

- agreeing the composition and size of the interviewing panel

- agreeing a date for the selection interviews

- seeking responses from referees

- inviting shortlisted candidates to the interview and specifying date, time, place and any other details; asking if it is their intention to be present; arranging a room and other facilities for the interview e.g. refreshments.

b. The interview

Interviews are seen differently by interviewers and interviewees.
Interviewers should:

- be familiar with job descriptions/specification

- study application forms and surnames, together with references

- decide a strategy for the interview. For example, is it to be highly structured and formal, with a list of specific questions? Or more informal? How will a decision be made: by discussion in order to arrive at a consensus, or by a vote?

- if specific questions are to be asked, these will need to be typed, and may be given to the candidates a few minutes before the interview

- candidates should be welcomed and the interview procedure explained

- the panel should be introduced, an indication of who they are given and a brief explanation of their role

- questions should be clearly asked and candidates allowed to answer without interruptions

- responses should be listened to carefully and any questions arising, or any points to be later considered, should be noted as unobtrusively as possible until the interview is finished; then any detailed notes and observations may help in the decision to appoint

- questions should aim to discover facts, experience, qualifications and so on. Questions can also discover attitudes, values, opinions on specific issues related to the job, the business or the industry. Equally, they can be directed towards values and views related to life, the economy, social change or whatever

- candidates should be invited to ask any questions about the job and the business

- the interviewer should finish appropriately by thanking the candidate and explaining subsequent procedure. For example, it might be explained that a decision will be made that same day and candidates should wait, or that a decision will be made in a few days and notification will be made by telephone or letter.

Techniques for interviewees/applicants

- Find out as much as you can about the business, its products or services, its size, its budget and so on. This helps to put the job in context and assists with broad questions that might be asked.

- Ensure you know how to get to the interview, who to ask for; take the invitation to your interview with you.

- Consider any important questions you might be able to ask about the job, the business, future prospects, training policies and so on.

- Present yourself appropriately attired. Use your interpersonal skills and communication skills: be attentive; construct answers carefully; avoid speaking too quickly.

- Ask questions when and if invited. Do not ask questions for the sake of asking them.

- At the end of the interview, express your thanks appropriately.

c. After the interview

- Communicate the decision to the successful and unsuccessful candidates, either face to face if they have waited, or in writing and/or by telephone otherwise.

- If face to face, the successful candidate is normally invited back into the interview room to receive the offer and to arrange any further details, including starting date.

- Arrange any necessary medical clearance or other clearance necessary for the job (for example, verification of certain qualifications).

- Prepare a contract of employment and initiate a personnel file in order to bring the new employee onto the payroll and onto other records.

5. Selection

How is the selection of the successful candidate made? Apart from liking the candidate, or being guided by intuition, there are some more scientific approaches available, which reflect the job description and personal specification referred to earlier.

The factors usually included in a plan to assess candidates are :

- physical attributes (appearance, speech etc.)

- educational attainment

- special aptitudes

- disposition (e.g. sociable, extrovert and communicative)
- background and motivation.

Jobs vary so much that it is impossible to suggest that these factors are always used. What is important is that a systematic approach is better than an intuitive, haphazard approach to the selection of staff.

6. Employment

Arrangements to begin work are the final phase in the recruitment process. Yet, in many ways, it is the beginning of a new relationship: hence the importance of an induction process. How a person is received, briefed, introduced to organisational facilities and to other staff is important to a new job holder. Finding one's way around helps the new employee to settle in to what is, inevitably, a strange environment.

Induction is the beginning or continuation of a career and good employers continue the training and development of staff by in-house and off the job training and education.

By signing a 'Contract of Employment' the employer and employee acknowledge certain duties and obligations to each other.

Employees' duties

These can be summarised as:

a. *The duty of good faith* – this duty is the most fundamental obligation of an employee and involves serving his employer faithfully. Faithful service involves working competently, respecting the employer's property and not taking industrial action, such as strikes and go-slows, which would disrupt the employer's business.

b. *To account for money received* – an employee must not accept any bribes, commissions or fees for his work other than from his employer.

c. *To respect trade secrets* – an employee would be in breach of this duty by working for a competitor in his or her spare time.

Employer's duties

a. *To pay wages*

In most cases, when the contract of employment is signed, a rate of pay is agreed. Every employee is entitled to receive a written, itemised statement of pay, including deductions.

b. *To provide work, indemnify and provide a reference*

Generally, there is no duty on an employer to provide work for employees as long as their contracted remuneration is paid. If, however, an employee's pay depends upon the performance of work (piece work), then the employer is under an obligation to provide sufficient work to enable a reasonable wage to be earned.

An employee is entitled to be indemnified for expense incurred in the course of employment.

There is no legal duty to provide a reference, but if one is provided it must not include any false statements which are likely to damage the employee's character.

c.   *To provide a safe system of work*

Statutory duties are imposed under various Acts, for example the Factories Act 1961 and the Office Shops and Railway Premises Act 1963 (the contents of which are incorporated into the Health and Safety at Work Act 1974).

An employer has a duty to provide safe fellow workers. If an employer is aware of an employee who may create a dangerous situation at work, by incompetence or practical jokes, the employer should discipline the employee and, if the practice continues, dismiss him. Such a dismissal would be regarded, in the circumstances, as justifiable.

The law also places an obligation on an employer to provide safe plant, safe appliances, safe working methods and safe working premises. To determine whether an employer is providing safe working methods, it is necessary to consider a number of factors, including the layout of the workplace, training and supervision, warnings, and whether protective equipment is provided. The duty is on an employer to take reasonable care, and if an employer gives proper instructions which the employee fails to observe, the employer will not be liable if the employee is then injured.

Health and Safety at Work

In 1974, Parliament passed the Health and Safety at Work Act, which is designed to provide a comprehensive system of law to govern health and safety at work. The Act lays down general duties on employers, employees, suppliers of plant and equipment etc. The principal duty is that an employer must ensure, so far as is reasonably practicable, the health and safety of his workers. This duty includes:

- providing and maintaining safe plant and a safe work system

- making arrangements for the use, handling, storage and transport of articles and substances

- providing any necessary information, instruction, training and supervision

- maintaining a safe place of work and a safe entry to and exit from it

- maintaining a safe working environment.

Equal Opportunities Legislation

The three major pieces of UK legislation have been amended to comply with Article 119 of the Treaty of Rome. Article 119 demands that each member country should ensure that 'men and women receive equal pay for equal work.'

The three statutes that deal with 'equal opportunities' are:

1. *The Equal Pay Act* 1970 (amended by the Equal Pay Amendment Regulations 1983). This outlaws discrimination involving terms and conditions of employment between men and women. Most of the cases so far have been brought by women who feel that they are entitled to be paid the same because they are 'on *like* work or work *which is rated as equivalent* with that of a man in the same employment'.

    Four factors which help to decide whether or not work is 'like' are:

    *   the duties involved

    *   the hours

    *   the responsibilities involved

    *   the location of the work.

2. *The Sex Discrimination Act* 1975 (amended by *The Sex Discrimination Act* 1976) makes it illegal to discriminate against someone on the grounds of his or her sex or because a person is married. The Act holds that discrimination takes three forms:

    *   direct or intentional

    *   indirect or inferred

    *   victimisation.

    The Act holds that there are five occasions when discrimination arises in employment:

    *   in the arrangements made for employing people (e.g. adverts and job interviews)

    *   in the terms of employment

    *   in refusal to employ because of gender

    *   in promotion and training opportunities

    *   in dismissal because of gender.

3. *The Race Relations Act* 1976 makes it unlawful to discriminate against anyone on the grounds of race, colour, nationality or ethic origin. (It does *not* apply to discrimination on religious grounds, though this creates legal complications since race and religion are often inseparable.)

    As in The Sex Discrimination Act, discrimination is adjudged to be direct, indirect or victimisation. In the field of employment it is unlawful to discriminate in the 'arrangements for employment', which are:

    *   in the interview or advertisement

    *   in the terms of employment

    *   by refusing employment because of colour, race, nationality or ethnic origin

- in promotion and training
- by dismissing a person because of colour, race, nationality or ethnic origin.

Redundancy: the 1980s' Growth Area

Redundancy, as defined by the *Employment Protection (Consolidation) Act* 1978, occurs for one of three reasons:

1. The employer has ceased, or intends to cease, a business for the purpose for which the employee is employed.

2. The employer ceases business *in the place* where the employee is employed.

3. The requirements of the business have ceased or have now diminished; e.g. so that a reduced workforce only is needed.

If an employee is dismissed because redundancy occurs, then that dismissal is unfair. The employer is not entitled to make an employee redundant unless proper warning is given and there has been proper consultation with the relevant trade union. One of the trade union's less pleasant jobs will be to monitor that those chosen for redundancy are not being selected on a discriminatory basis. Usually, unions and employers will try to reach agreement on an equitable system, such as 'last in, first out'.

Unfair Dismissal

Most legislation on this issue is contained within the various Employment Protection Acts. These were designed to afford employees some protection against employees who were intent on dismissing them unfairly or who refused to proffer a reason for dismissal.

The relationship between an employer and an employee is in the form of a contract of employment. Since 1971 an employer has been given the statutory obligation to give employees a reason or reasons why they are being dismissed. A business is still entitled to dismiss an employee for any number of good reasons. Such reasons for 'fair dismissal' may include:

1. the employee is deemed incapable of doing the work

2. the employee is unqualified to do the work

3. the employee is found guity of misconduct in the workplace

4. the job has ceased to exist (see 'redundancy')

5. to continue to employ the person would be illegal

6. any other substantial reason e.g. an employee marrying someone from a competitor business may lead to the divulgence of trade secrets.

A business must operate within a set disciplinary code which is known to all employees. By law, the employee must be offered the opportunity to explain his or her alleged misconduct or transgression. The employer must decide whether the alleged misconduct is 'minor', 'major' or 'gross':

Flow Chart: Unfair Dismissal

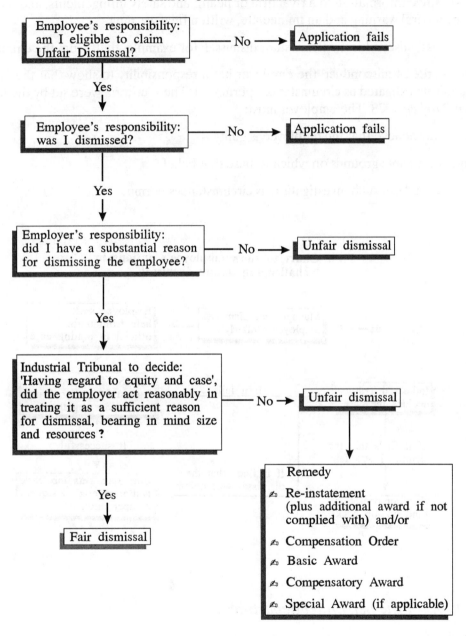

- 'Minor' misconduct: includes trivial offences, such as unpunctuality and dismissal is judged to be too severe a penalty unless the misconduct is persistent

- 'Major' misconduct covers more serious acts, such as fighting, disclosing commercially sensitive information to a rival firm or health and safety infingements, and is dealt with by an oral warning and an immediate, written final warning

- 'Gross' misconduct invites instant dismissal; for example, theft from the employer.

Whatever the degree of misconduct, the employer has a responsibility to show that the employee's case was as thoroughly investigated as circumstances permitted. These criteria were set by the test case *British Home Stores v Burchell* 1978. The employer must:

1.   genuinely believe that the employee is guilty

2.   have reasonable grounds on which to base that belief

3.   have carried out such investigation as circumstances permit.

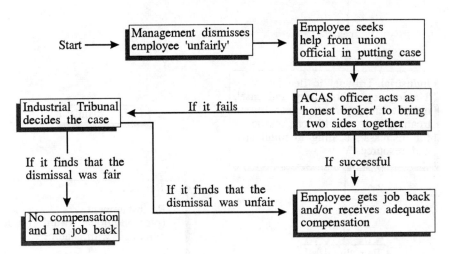

Flow Chart to show employee's options in challenging unfair dismissal

Other functions of the personnel department

The responsibility for

1.   bargaining and

2.   social and welfare organisation usually falls within the scope of the personnel department.

Bargaining

The department will have the responsibility for putting the business's viewpoint in all situations which have direct relevance to its employees. This might include situations related to:

- wages and salaries
- working conditions
- working practices
- payment systems and methods
- disciplinary matters
- redundancy and dismissal.

Negotiations about such matters are conducted with the elected representatives of the employees. Sometimes the employee representatives will be from within the organisation, but often they are regional representatives from the relevant employee trade union. Trades unions and their changing roles are discussed in more detail in Part Five.

Social and welfare organisation

Large employers often provide a range of sports, recreation and social facilities for their employees. The personnel department will discuss with employee representatives the nature and appropriateness of such a provision.

1. What is the role of a personnel department?
2. List and explain the different approaches to personnel management.
3. What is a *manpower plan*?
4. What are the aims of manpower planning?
5. Explain the factors that may change a manpower plan.
6. Describe the challenges of producing a manpower plan for the 1990s.
7. List the stages in the recruitment process.
8. Explain the process of *job analysis*.
9. How might *job evaluation* be approached?
10. List the main ways to attract a field of candidates to a job vacancy.
11. Describe the process of interview and selection.
12. List and explain the responsibilities and duties of:
    - employees
    - employers.
13. List and explain the main equal opportunities legislation.
14. What constitutes *unfair dismissal*?

An economist might well define the word 'production' as the act of combining factor inputs (labour, capital etc) by firms to produce outputs of goods and services. A non-economist might conjure up any one of several images in lieu of a definition. 'Production' might evoke a picture of a skyline dominated by tall chimney stacks belching smoke, with steam issuing from pipes and valves and the clang and clamour of hammers and pistons filling the air. Everywhere is black with soot and grime. Workers – men, women and children – emerge like some great, defeated army from mill and pit, foundry and factory.

'Production' might evoke a second picture: a factory turning out masses of goods, its workforce attending constantly to an assembly line which moves continuously at a pre-determined pace; component parts are stacked high awaiting assembly and mountains of materials await processing; finished goods await dispatch.

No doubt such scenes, though increasingly rare, can still be found in Britain, but they do not accurately reflect what is happening in today's factories. Such images of the 'production function' are narrow and out-of-date; production is a vital aspect of the UK economy, but it embraces much more than the production activities of heavy industry or of the 'traditional' assembly line.

What Does 'Production' Include?

To widen your thinking about what production is, consider which of the following activities might be described as production:

- open-cast coal mining
- the provision of airline meals for in-flight consumption
- the writing of computer software
- the sale of goods through an electric retailer
- a builder constructing a house
- a broker selling insurance.

Your first thoughts might be guided by the knowledge you already have of the way in which commercial activity is categorised into primary, secondary and tertiary levels. (This was explained more fully in Part One.) Secondary activity, which is made up of the manufacturing sector of the economy, is considered as consisting of businesses which processes and produces goods. But, when you look at the above list, would you consider open-cast coal mining to be a 'production' activity? Your probable answer is yes – and yet open-cast coal mining is a *primary l*evel activity.

So what are the criteria by which you might judge whether an activity is truly 'production'? There are two of them: *added value* and *change in physical appearance*.

Added Value

If raw materials, components or goods are bought by a business and value is added to them before they are sold, then that business is a producer. The important question to ask in order to distinguish between a business that is a producer and one that is a non-producer is: *Does the business 'add value' to the goods or does it simply increase the price by 'marking up' the goods?*

Take as an example an electrical retailer who sells a personal compact disc player. The CD player will have been purchased from the manufacturer and will be re-sold to the consumer in the same form as it was bought. The retailer has not 'added value' to the CD player but has merely 'marked-up' the price in order to make a profit. Although the retailer is providing a valuable service to both manufacturer and consumer, such activity has not 'produced' anything.

In contrast, the writing of computer software can be said to be 'production'. Before the software is written the product does not exist; it had no value. Once written, it has a value. The software 'manufacturer' has written software which has added value; the manufacturer has thereby produced a good.

You might like to try using the concept of added value in order to classify the remaining activities in the list into production or non-production activities.

Change in Physical Appearance

A cruder, but equally effective, method of identifying a production activity is to look for any physical change in the appearance of the goods.

For example, the supplier of airline meals for in-flight consumption is buying raw vegetables or basic ingredients, preparing and cooking them, then packaging them in an appropriate way. Clearly, by the end of this process the food will look considerably different from when first purchased; using the criterion of changed physical appearance tells us that production is taking place.

A broker selling insurance, however, does not change the appearance of the goods. The insurance policy already exists and the broker is merely promoting and retailing an existing product to the consumer.

Methods of Production

Methods of producing goods can be broadly categorized:

- job production
- batch production
- flow production.

Job Production

Job production is a method of production found mainly in the civil engineering and construction industries. A 'job' is a one-off product; if it is repeated there will be a considerable interval between similar jobs.

Consider the following activities, which are all examples of job production:

- building the Channel Tunnel

- building an extension to a house

- repairing a road

- landscaping gardens.

The main features of a business involved in job production are:

- it usually offers some individual design and planning facility for its clients

- it may co-ordinate the work of sub-contractors who are needed to complete the project

- it will employ people who have high levels of creative ability

- it employs people with specialities, but who are also adaptable and can cope with non-standard job specifications and situations.

Buying a product which is 'job produced' or 'custom-built/made' usually means paying more than you would when buying a product from a standard range. For example, buying an individual architect-designed house will be considerably more expensive than buying a house among houses of the same type and design on an estate.

One of the main reasons for the higher price of the 'one-off' job relative to the 'off-the-shelf' house is that the average cost per house decreases as the number of houses with the same design are built. As more houses are built the initial cost of design and development is spread over a larger number of units, thus reducing the production cost of each individual unit

In addition, other economies of scale can be enjoyed, such as the purchase of materials in bulk at discounted prices and the most effective utilisation of specialist labour.

The time that elapses between the initial order for a job and it being finished (or having it delivered) is referred to as the 'lead time'. In job production the lead time can be considerable: the Channel Tunnel took years to design, plan, and build. (At the opposite end of the spectrum is the non-existent lead time which is often a characteristic of flow or mass production which you will look at shortly.)

Batch Production

Batch production involves a group of products of the same design passing through the production process together. Examples of batch production are:

- a builder constructing a small estate of twenty houses, all of the same design and construction

- a wine producer who produces a batch of cases of wine all from the same type and crop of grapes. Further batches may use different crops or types of grapes and therefore form a separate batch

- a wallpaper manufacturer making a batch of rolls of a particular design in a given production run. The inks and prints are unique to that batch. When the batch is complete the manufacturer may change to a different design or even just a different set of colours.

- a clothes manufacturer.

Once a producer moves from job to batch production. several potential gains emerge:

- more specialised labour can be employed, thus enabling labour costs per unit to be reduced

- materials can be ordered in greater volumes, thus making it easier to negotiate discounts and reduce the material costs per unit

- production can become more organised and systematic

- design costs are offset over a greater volume of output

- 'set up' time for machinery and equipment is reduced as a proportion of total manufacturing time.

You may wonder why, if the potential gains are so significant, most manufacturers have not moved to batch production methods. The answer lies with the preferences, tastes and requirements of the consumer and client.

There will always exist a need for 'one-off' projects, particularly in the civil engineering and construction industries. Sometimes, as in the case of the Channel Tunnel, the project is by necessity a one and only product.

However, some consumers prefer, and are able to afford, individually designed clothes, designed and tailored to their own unique specifications. (Look up the word 'bespoke' in a dictionary, you'll find it useful.)

So any business engaged mainly on job methods of production must be conscious that a move away from this method, however small, may undermine and threaten its customer base and service which is the initial reason for its success.

Flow Production

Flow production is an image of production with which people are most familiar. The image includes:

- large volume (bulk) deliveries of materials for use in production

- highly automated equipment

- highly specialised workforce, mainly semi-skilled

- high volume product

- product of standard design and construction

- systematic and well-organised machinery and equipment

- a hierarchical, one-way system of workforce organisation:
  e.g. worker   supervisor   foreman   production manager

- stockpiles of finished goods awaiting dispatch to customers.

Whilst this image of flow production may be true of the way some businesses do things, it is far from typical of the most modern production units. New technology, new methods of organising production and changing management styles have radically altered the traditional image of 'the factory'. Whilst such changes are not restricted solely to flow production, it is through businesses which use its methods that most of the progress has been achieved.

A modern, efficient and productive unit for flow production will have some of the following characteristics:

- a critical emphasis on organised stock control to reduce working capital, perhaps using a just-in-time (JIT or 'stockless production') system

- the minimising of production costs through the constant review and improvement of production techniques

- a 'team' approach to working and work methods

- a two-way communication system between 'shop floor' and management

- a commitment to quality and the satisfaction of consumer need.

Comparisons of Methods of Production

One business may operate more than one method of production. The method of production which is chosen by a business is dependent on:

- the market in which the business is involved

- the type of product

- the size of the business and the resources at its disposal.

Taking the baking industry as an example, one large business could be organised to produce a range of products, including:

- standard white, sliced loaves produced continuously by the *flow production* method. Demand is large, continuous, and for a standard product. The price of the product is relatively low, meaning subsequent costs must also be low in order to achieve profit objectives. A high level of mechanisation requires high investment and therefore the business would need to have substantial capital at its disposal.

- batches of products such as wholemeal, bran-based and high-fibre bread for a more specialised market. The demand for each of these products might not justify an exclusive flow production line, so a system of *batch production* would operate. A particular type and volume of loaf would be produced before the same machinery is cleaned and reset for a different product batch. This batch method is more expensive and results in a higher unit cost. However, consumers will be prepared to pay more for these product so profit margins can be maintained or even improved.

In contrast, the small family baker may use a combination of batch and job production methods. As a business, it is likely to have limited capital and, as a result, only limited equipment. The same equipment will be used to produce all the standard lines. White sliced loaves might be the first batch through, followed by brown sliced, high-bran and so on.

As well as the batch method, the small family baker may undertake to make personalised wedding anniversary and birthday cakes. Such cakes are 'one-off'; this activity is an example of *job production*.

As has already been mentioned, hybrid or mixed methods are fairly common. For example, the mass producer of white loaves may set the slicing machine to 'thick sliced' for a batch, 'medium sliced' for a batch before finishing off with a batch of 'thin sliced'. The standard product – 'the white loaf' – is flow produced, but the slicing is done by batches according to consumer demand.

The figure below gives a summary of how the main features of production vary according to production method – use it only as a rough guide. Each business is unique and may confound even what you think is a mostly safe assumption.

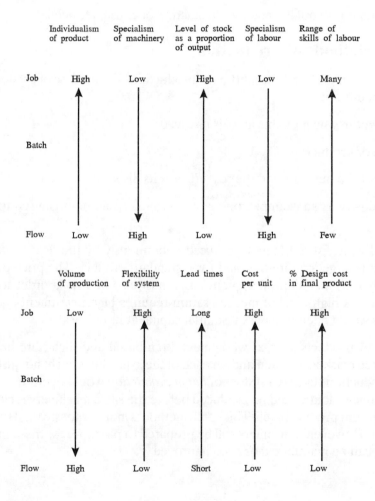

The main features of production methods

The Location Decision

The principal factors influencing the location of a business are:

- the nature of the market for its goods or service
- the size of the business
- the objectives of the owners and managers.

All businesses may need to make location decisions, whether they be a local chemist, a large DIY chain or a multi-national car manufacturer. However, because of the variable influence of the factors mentioned above, the nature of that decision is fundamentally different.

The Chemist's Shop

A chemist, who owns one shop, is seeking to expand by opening a second branch. As the chemist is unlikely to want to move far away from the area of her first shop, she is likely to locate in a nearby town. The location decision then becomes a matter of choosing an appropriate site for the shop within that town. Her main considerations will be:

1. the sites of an existing chemist's

2. the position in the town of doctors' surgeries and hospitals, since prescriptions will form a significant part of the anticipated revenue

3. the main pedestrian thoroughfares

4. the availability of appropriate premises

5. the rent and rates of suitable premises in the town

6. other considerations, such as security.

A large DIY chain

Chains, such as Do-It-All, B & Q and Texas, have expanded rapidly over the last ten years. As the DIY market has grown, so chain stores have extended their network of shops to cover large parts of the UK. In considering locating a new branch, their management is likely to base its decision on:

1. *The size of the market in the target area*. This will be analysed by marketing experts who will study the size and nature of the population of the area. Target groups will be identified and their current buying habits established. As the new store will be seeking primarily to attract 'local' customers, this sort of research is vital if the new store is to be a success.

2. *The existing competition in the area*. Although this will be a consideration, it does not seem to have a great influence on the siting of the store. Frequently, such DIY stores occupy 'out of town' sites; these are often part of a retail park. Location in such developments usually means competing directly with at least one other DIY chain store in the same location.

3.   *The availability of a suitable site.* Many of the DIY chains prefer purpose-built, new accommodation for their stores. The site is invariably 'out of town'; it is usually on an industrial estate or in a retail park. Such a location is chosen because:

- premises can be purpose designed

- rents are significantly lower than in town centre sites

- space is often unavailable in a town centre or a site is not suitable

- the target market segment consists of consumers who are prepared to travel by car to sites that have what they want 'all under one roof'

- because of the space available an in-store ambience can be created; this has added appeal to the shopper

4.   *The location of their nearest existing store.* The business will have considerable information about how far customers already travel to their existing stores in order to shop. It will not want to open a store in such close proximity to an existing store, since this would unduly damage the customer base it already has.

5.   *The objectives of the company.* It may be that a prime site is available in a particular part of the country, but is outside the area which management has designated as its target market area. For example, a site may be available in Norwich, yet the strategy of the company is to concentrate its resources on building up its base in Scotland and the North of England. To divert from that strategy would mean an isolated branch, far from existing distribution channels and networks.

A multi-national car manufacturer

In the 1980s two major Japanese car makers, Nissan and Toyota, decided to locate manufacturing plants in the UK. Compared with the chemist and the DIY business, these two international companies had a far greater number of complex issues to consider. Large manufacturers tend to operate in world-wide markets: as the town is to the sole trader, so the continent is to the multi-national company.

When a manufacturer decides to locate, or relocate, in an area, this is referred to as 'inward investment', a phrase that reflects the fact that a particular business is committing its money and its future to that area. The factors which most large manufacturer will consider longest when making their location decision are:

1. The Nature of the Market

Nissan and Toyota both want to penetrate the large and lucrative market which is the EC. To penetrate from outside the EC meant they would be subject to tariff barriers and, possibly, import quotas. Locating manufacturing plants in an EC country meant that they became, effectively, European manufacturers and, as such, able to compete on equal terms with the long-established European manufacturers, such as Ford, General Motors, Austin Rover, Fiat, BMW etc. Once, on the basis of the market, the decision to locate in an EC country was made, it then became a question of which country. Other factors are then considered.

2. The Availability of Labour

A company will need to find out whether:

- there is a pool of labour sufficiently large to meet its requirements
- if the labour in the area has the skills needed for the type of work to be done
- if worker attitudes in the area are positive towards inward investment
- if worker attitudes are positive towards training.

In assessing the quality and quantity of labour, businesses must analyse what is happening demographically and identify any possible future implications.

3. The Cost of Transport

The cost of transport involves looking at two main elements:

- the cost and time involved in transporting, from suppliers to the factory, the raw materials and components that will be used in manufacture
- the cost of delivering to the customers the finished product from the factory.

Both of these transport costs are important, as they will affect the price of the final product; ultimately, costs and price may determine how competitive the firm becomes.

Businesses that locate *nearer their market than their sources of supply* (raw materials), are usually operating in a *bulk-increasing* industry: as the goods are manufactured, their bulk – and therefore the cost of transport – increases, thereby making it more practical and economic to locate nearer to the market than to the sources of supply.

Businesses that locate *nearer their sources of supply than their market* are usually *bulk-decreasing* in their manufacturing process: that is, they convert bulky materials, which are expensive to transport, into less bulky, finished products.

The North East of England has good examples of each of these types of firms.

Press Offshore constructs gas and oil exploration rigs for the North Sea production fields. When the rigs are completed, they are very huge, unwieldy and difficult to transport. When locating their business, Press Offshore chose Wallsend on the banks of the River Tyne to base their construction site. Press gave as their over-riding reason for location the fact that completed rigs could be towed by other sea-going vessels to their nearby destination.

British Alcan produce aluminium at their smelter in Lynemouth on the Northumberland coast. Aluminium production requires large quantities of alumina (bauxite in its ore form) and substantial amounts of power in the form of electricity. From a transport perspective, Alcan chose Lynemouth as the location for its plant because of its close proximity to Blyth, a port which was able and willing to provide off-loading facilities for the alumina which is imported from Jamaica and South America. In addition, because of the vast amounts of electricity which a smelter consumes, Alcan decided to build its own coal-fired power station, selling any excess power it produced back to the National Grid. Within a couple of miles of the site for its power station lay Ellington Colliery, one of the largest deep mines in the UK. So, despite the fact that very few customers for its aluminium were located in the North East of England, the site was chosen for its advantageous effects on the costs of inputs to the manufacturing process.

4. The Availability of Utilities

Utilities are supplies of gas, electricity and water, as well as the treatment of sewage and industrial effluents. Many industries use huge volumes of water in their manufacturing processes. In recent years, the shortage of water in the South of England has caused drought conditions and has been a major factor in discouraging large water users from locating there. Although there has not been an interruption in supply to industrial users as a result of the water shortage, one might speculate that, if low levels of rainfall become the norm, supplies of water will be rationed in the future. A national water grid, such as that which exists for electricity, may be the answer to this particular problem, but the costs of such a project appear at present to be prohibitive.

5. The Availability and Price of Land

The availability and price of land will vary from area to area. Clearly, the larger the area any production facility occupies, the more significant will this factor become in its decision over where to locate. Many areas of the UK, which are seeking to rejuvenate their local economies, have set aside generous parcels of land to encourage inward investment.

6. Regional Policies

As you read in Part Two, certain areas of the UK have seen their traditional industries decline and sometimes diappear altogether. The reasons for this are sometimes complex, but tend to be the result of exhausted supplies of raw materials (e.g. coal, iron ore), or the shift in the balance of world trade (e.g. the expansion of the textiles industry in the Far East). The government now offers fewer incentives for businesses to expand or relocate in these areas than has hitherto been the case; indeed, the EC is a larger provider of aid under its Regional Development Fund than is the UK government. Such schemes, however welcome they may be to the local communities, do have drawbacks:

- many of the firms which locate in the regions do so when the economy is expanding: they will open another factory to respond to increased demand for their products and locate it in a region where grants are available. When a recession begins to bite and demand falls, the first areas to be affected are those where the new factories located – it is those units which will be closed first

- in the past, it was common practice for certain companies to locate in an area so that they could take advantage of grants for the purchase of capital equipment. Once the qualifying period had elapsed, the firm closed the factory and moved the equipment, purchased at a very attractive price, to another location where grants were not on offer.

7. Communications

The proximity of major road networks, railway links and an airport will influence particular types of business. For example, the Channel Tunnel is likely to draw a lot of firms who specialise in export and import to Kent and the South East of England. Areas which are part of the rail network which feeds the Tunnel, are also likely to benefit from businesses wishing to take advantage of the improved communication and transport links with continental Europe.

The location of a factory is a most important business decision. The commitment will result in large amounts of investment taking place and any decision taken is difficult, if not impossible, to reverse. A business approaching the decision will assess the sorts of factors already discussed and weigh them according to their own requirements and specialisms. Because of the complexity of this process, and the crucial importance of its outcome, the time-span of a location decision is likely to be long.

The Importance of Business Size

Generally, a business increases in size by increasing the volume of goods it produces or sells. Any goods which can be mass produced (and/or mass-marketed) are likely to cost less as economies of scale come into play. Economies of scale can be defined as *reductions in unit costs arising from an increased scale of operation.*

As a business becomes larger, it tends to be able to organise itself more efficiently. This results in economies in the following areas:

- *technical economies.* Large firms are able to employ production equipment which is financially and technically out of reach of smaller producers. Small producers are unable to specialise as they have insufficient volume to make it worthwhile. Even in the building trade, technical economies are present. The small, jobbing builder may have bought a cement mixer to mix mortar for laying bricks etc. The mortar is mixed in small quantities, lasts only a short time before hardening and is relatively expensive. A large construction company will buy in special mortar, mixed in large amounts and delivered to the site by the supplier. As well as being cheaper than conventionally mixed mortar, the product is technically more efficient by virtue of the fact that it remains workable for about forty eight hours.

- *labour economies.* In large businesses, highly specialised workers can be trained and used to increase efficiency and lower the cost of production. In the small building firm one employee may need to turn their hand to bricklaying, concreting as well as mixing their own materials. The switching between jobs is time-consuming and reduces the speed of each particular task. The large construction company will employ tens, or even hundreds, of specialised bricklayers, trained specifically for the task of bricklaying: they will be highly proficient at laying bricks. The cost per brick laid by these workers is likely to be significantly less than the cost per brick laid by the non-specialised worker.

In addition, larger firms will be able to employ specialised managers to control and organise the operation of the business.

- *commercial economies*. Large firms are able to wield more power in the commercial world. A large construction company will have commercial advantages over the jobbing builder. These advantages may include:

  – buying materials in bulk, thereby securing discounts
  – arranging beneficial credit terms with suppliers
  – setting up a specialised marketing department
  – spending considerable sums on promoting the company image
  – accessing prime building land through reputation and contacts
  – setting money aside for training its workforce.

- *financial economies*. As businesses expand, so usually does their reputation and standing in the world of business finance. Smaller firms are likely to suffer four main disadvantages:

1. they will pay higher rates of interest than their larger counterparts

2. they will need to provide much more detailed information in order to justify a loan application. Preparation of this information can be expensive for the small business.

3. they will have less access to extended periods of credit from their suppliers.

4. they will have larger customers as creditors and these may be reluctant to settle their bills in a reasonable time.

In the 1980s and early 1990s, this final disadvantage became a particularly acute problem for the small business. The resultant effect on cash flow contributed to the downfall of thousands of small businesses. The impact of this was so drastic that, in the Spring Budget of 1992, the Chancellor announced some measures to help alleviate the problem. All contracts awarded by public sector purchasers were required to include a clause which guaranteed payment within thirty days of contract completion: this, it is hoped will 'set an example' for other larger firms and institutions to follow.

Production Layout

A manufacturing business will always seek to minimise the time it takes to produce its goods. A shorter time span in the production process means a faster response to consumer demand is possible, as well as minimising the cost of work in progress stocks. A business will always seek to make its manufacturing process more cost-effective and, in mass production, this is mainly accomplished through automation. However, the layout of equipment has a vital role to play in reducing costs: if people have to travel further than necessary to complete an operation, then this is time lost. And lost time means that an unnecessary cost is added to the product. Similarly, if a part-finished product needs to travel to the next process, then the time this takes must be optimised if costs are to be minimised.

Stock Control

The principal objective of stock control can be stated simply: it is *to ensure that the volume of stock and the costs of holding it are reduced to the minimum without any interruption or stoppage to production.*

Stock is a vital requirement of any business that is engaged in production. At different points in time, stock might exist in three distinct forms:

- materials or components
- work-in-progress
- finished goods

Materials and components are the 'ingredients' from which a product is made. They are purchased from suppliers.

Work-in-progress consists of part-processed materials and components. Their 'cost' will also include the labour which has been used up to that point in their production.

Finished goods are goods whose production is complete and that are awaiting dispatch to customers.

Stock is a part of the working capital of a business. From your knowledge of accounting and finance, you will understand that the more working capital a business needs, the greater is the cost of acquiring that capital. Materials and components need to be paid for, as does the labour and overheads in work-in-progress and finished goods.

The money used to pay for these could be used for an alternative purpose, such as the purchase of fixed assets or investments in other companies. If a business holds total stocks of £500,000, then that represents money tied up which otherwise might be used for other purposes. Of course, most businesses need stock, but even if this stock holding could be reduced to £400,000 it would mean £100,000 is released for use elsewhere in the business.

It is worth bearing in mind two additional points:

- the business may have had to borrow the £500,000 to finance the stock, so that borrowing will be incurring interest charges
- stock needs space, handling and it needs also to be insured. As well as freeing money for use elsewhere in the business, reducing stock reduces these other expenses, ultimately helping to make the business more cost-effective.

So, clearly, the lower the volume of stock held, the more effectively the funds of the business are being managed. The obverse of this is the enormous costs which can be incurred should an interruption in production occur as a result of stock having been run down too severely. Machinery and labour then become idle and production is lost. Delivery times to customers may also be affected and the reputation of the business for reliability is jeopardized.

The extreme model in stock control is exemplified by SOMO or 'Sell One, Make One'. In this model, exemplified by Nissan Motors at its Sunderland plant, no production is undertaken without a definite sale already having been made: this minimizes stock in the form of components but, more especially, it also avoids stockpiling finished goods that have no firm buyer.

Methods of Stock Control

A most exciting innovation in manufacturing business since the late 1960s has been the Just In Time (JIT) or 'stockless production' method of stock control. The JIT approach was developed in Japanese manufacturing but it has spread internationally to revolutionise business thinking about production and stock control in industry. To fully appreciate its impact, it is worth reminding ourselves of the situation that persisted before its inception.

Pre-JIT: traditional method

Although JIT has revolutionised thinking about stock control, it is not appropriate for all forms of business or types of industry. Traditional methods still survive and flourish but they have been streamlined as a result of the influence of JIT.

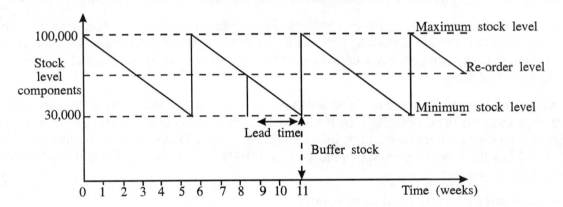

The graph shows that:

- 10,000 components are used per week

- the maximum stock level is 100,000 components (10 weeks' usage)

- the number of components in stock should never be fewer than 30,000 (3 weeks' usage)

- stock should be re-ordered when the level reaches 70,000 components (7 weeks' usage)

- it will take four weeks between the date on which the order is placed with the supplier and the date the components are received into stock. This is referred to as 'lead time'.

- the buffer is 30,000 components. This protects against delays in receiving the next delivery.

It must be emphasised that this is just a model. Indeed, it is a model which can be managed easily by computers. Supplied with information about maximum stock, minimum stock and re-ordering levels, demand per week and lead time, a computer will produce, indicate and remind the purchasing department when decisions need to be made.

Humans prepare and input data on the basis of information they have available and this information needs to be constantly updated. The model you have just looked at is based on a demand for 10,000 components per week. If production is to be cut back because of falling customer demand for the final product, then the inputs must be adjusted accordingly.

As well as taking action on changing demand, the model will be affected by a changing business environment. These might include:

- bulk discounts or 'special savings' which can be made by increasing re-order quantity. This potential saving must be offset against the increased costs of holding the stock (space, insurance etc.)

- difficulties with sources of supply. It may be that a supplier is likely to experience problems with their workforce (a go-slow or strike) which will result in delays or extended lead times. Alternative suppliers must be found or the model needs to be adjusted to take account of any delays

- if materials are imported ,then problems with any of the transport links, such as the ports will be important.

Just In Time (JIT) method

JIT began in a Japanese shipbuilding industry that was suffering from over-capacity, with too many shipyards chasing after too few orders. The result of this fierce competition was that the suppliers of steel to the shipyards were eager for business and prepared to supply steel to the yards at very short notice, usually within three working days.

Traditionally, the shipyards had held more than a month's stock; since steel is a high cost item this had resulted in high levels of working capital. The shipyards began to demand their steel 'Just in Time'; they wanted only that steel that would be put to almost immediate use. As a result, they cut their working capital needs drastically. This novel practice brought them to the attention of other Japanese industries, notably car manufacturing.

Since the early 1980s the approach has spread to European manufacturing and the method been recognised as one of the ways by which profit, quality and customer satisfaction can be improved.

(It has been said, with as much seriousness as humour, that 'Japanese industry works Just in Time but Western industry works Just in Case'. However, Western business is now more acutely aware of the benefits of such practices.)

Central to the Japanese Just in Time philosophy are the objectives of reducing

MURI – excess
MUDA – waste
MURA – unevenness of quality.

Ideally, the aim is to 'produce instantaneously with perfect quality and minimum waste'. Realistically, it is recognised that this is an ideal which business might aspire to but which it will never achieve.

JIT sees stock as wasted investment – what could be cash is tied up in raw materials, work in progress and finished goods awaiting dispatch or buyers. If a business can cut back on this stock, more capital is thereby released to re-invest elsewhere in the business.

As you saw in the earlier section on traditional stock control, a *buffer* is usually retained to protect against irregularities and fluctuations in demand. The buffer is the 'safety net' for the production manager. In addition, the economic order quantity (EOQ) is assumed to be a quantity where discounts from supplier and transport costs are at their optimum level.

But to lower stock levels and cut 'excess', economic order quantities must be reduced as far as possible. JIT working virtually eliminates buffer or safety stocks. One practice adopted to achieve this is summed up in the Japanese word 'Kanban'.

Kanban seeks to ease the flow of materials through the production line; it is a way of working that 'pulls' components on to the line when they are needed. The word itself means 'visible record' and the visible records that show whether the flow of materials is smooth enough, are the containers or bins that are part of each workstation on the line and which contain the components ready to be added to the car, television or computer.

Kanban relies on a 'downstream' workstation telling an 'upstream' workstation of a demand for components. In the Nissan car factory this is done with a microchip; in other businesses it may be signalled by card or by a container of standard size showing empty.

Minimizing the level of stock carried exposes any production problems caused by irregularities of demand and the workforce can set about solving them. Removing the safety net concentrates the mind and focuses efforts on improving the efficiency and effectiveness of production systems.

Traditional stock control starts from the point where it is assumed that a producer must hold stock, often in quite large volumes. JIT assumes that suppliers exist to supply customers with:

- goods of the quality they demand
- goods at the time the customer requires them
- goods at what the customer considers to be a fair price.

It puts the customer in the position of a consumer in a consumer-oriented society. To sell to a business, a supplier must meet certain stringent conditions, one of the most important of which is minimising the stock holding costs of its customer. The customer knows that stock holding and stock handling costs money: if the burden of these costs can be partly shifted onto suppliers, then the customer's business becomes more streamlined, cost effective and competitive.

Therefore, if JIT is to function successfully, a close relationship with suppliers must be established. The supplier also needs to recognise the benefits of JIT. To the supplier these are:

- a long-term, guaranteed contract
- a steady demand which does not fluctuate from week to week
- a reduced amount of administration.

These benefits to the supplier will, in turn, allow them to plan more effectively and encourage their own adoption of the JIT idea. Ideally, suppliers should be:

- local or easily accessible
- able to produce to an agreed quality
- able to demonstrate a good record in industrial relations.

Risk will be minimised if selection of suppliers is based on these criteria.

The implementation of JIT

Any alteration in working practices or systems are usually viewed suspiciously by a workforce, certainly in the initial stages of change. Yet, for JIT to work effectively requires total commitment from all the employees of that business. For this to be achieved, employees must be convinced of its benefits, not just for the company but also for themselves as individuals.

The benefits to the workforce can be summarised as:

- increased opportunities for team work
- active involvement in decision-making and problem-solving as part of MURA (the elimination of unevenness)
- higher quality of workmanship and lower levels of rejects resulting in greater job satisfaction
- less time spent on rectifying faulty products, reducing the demoralising effects of the task
- productivity is improved, ultimately leading to increased rewards
- training becomes a central focus, with resulting improvements in skills and attitudes. In turn this increases the bargaining power of employees.
- improvement in 'worker/management' communications which in turn helps to minimise the likelihood of production stoppages due to disputes.

Quality

'Quality' is now a familiar word to consumers. It has a straightforward definition: *The level of product or service which it takes to satisfy the customer.*

When a consumer considers buying a product, three main questions will be borne in mind:

- Is the product suitable for the purpose I have in mind?
- Is the price right?
- Is it available for purchase?

It is most likely that the consumer will have products from several manufacturers to consider, and that each manufacturer will attempt to persuade the consumer to buy their product by the use of various promotional and marketing techniques; these were explained in some detail in the section on Marketing.

Increasingly, though, consumers will discriminate between products according to their *actual* or *perceived* quality. Actual quality is that which can be clearly and definitely established; for example, the quality of upholstery inside a new car. Perceived quality is what the consumer believes to be the quality, either by the image which the product portrays or the reputation which it has built. For example, no-one questions the quality of the Jaguar motor-car; it is 'perceived' to be a quality product.

To illustrate the concept of quality, consider a couple contemplating the purchase of a new lawn mower. They visit their local garden centre, where they know there is a wide selection from which to choose. On arrival they find there are three different manufacturers who have products which meet their need, which is to mow a small lawn in a family garden. The price differential between all three models of lawnmower is only £5 and the product specifications of all three machines are similar.

On what basis might the couple make a decision? Promotional techniques, such as a free first service or discount coupons for other garden products, might influence the decision, but an increasingly important factor for the discerning consumer is the issue of quality. The couple might try to establish:

- the quality of the 'finish' on the lawn mower
- whether the paint work, cabling and cutting blade on one mower is significantly better than on its competitors
- the length of product guarantee: is a longer guarantee a statement of confidence in the product quality?
- the efficiency and convenience of after sales service: are service depots close at hand?
- the availability of spares
- the clarity of instructions in the instruction booklet.

How Does a Producer Achieve Quality?

Once it recognises the importance of quality to its customers, a business must have a strategy for achieving the necessary quality from its production facility.

The ability of a business to produce 'quality' goods is dependent on two main factors:

its suppliers: They must deliver material and components of the right quality, otherwise the product will never be right. The implementation of Just in Time, in full or some of its main principles, can help with this process.

its workforce: The importance of the quality concept must be recognised by them. Traditionally, managers have kept the issues of special training and knowledge of quality and customer satisfaction to themselves. Many managers fail to educate their workforce's to understand quality and its impact on competitiveness. They have also failed to empower their workers to make suggestions and act to improve quality. Improving quality is a gradual process; constant improvement is needed. Workers must understand and own the objective of improved quality and be motivated to make it a reality.

Investment in training, consultative processes, new machines and techniques is vital for the maintenance of a highly skilled and motivated workforce which can generate the crucial, constant improvements in products that win customers.

Quality is about people and their attitudes rather than simply methods and systems of production. The responsibility for management of quality lies with all employees – managers and shop floor together.

Quality Circles

One technique for achieving improved quality, which has spread in recent years, is that of the quality circle. There are several variations on the technique but the basic model is the one explored here.

A quality circle is a small group of people doing similar work who meet regularly to identify, analyse and solve problems related to their workplace. They usually meet weekly, in or near their workplace. Circle members are trained in basic methods of statistics and communication under the guidance of their leader.

Quality circles explore many types of work related problems. Among them are problems related to quality, maintenance, safety, motivation, waste reduction and communications. There are no limits to the areas in which a quality circle can be effective.

The main reasons why quality circles can be so effective are:

- the importance of people in the production process is emphasised
- they are voluntary
- team work is central to its success
- projects and investigations are group efforts
- the usual hierarchical structures are abandoned
- creativity is encouraged
- training is integral to the process
- real problems are solved for self– and mutual benefit
- the use of fact rather than opinion is encouraged.

Total Quality Management

Traditionally, the UK approach to quality control in industry has been based on the practice of post-production inspection. At the end of the manufacturing process the product was examined and measured to see whether it measured up (conformed) to a set specification.

The disadvantages of this approach are:

- it depends on outcome only
- it is expensive

- it wastes valuable material (talent and time)
- it wastes production time and effort in making scrapped or failed products.

Since the late 1970s the emphasis has begun to shift from systems of end-inspection to one where systematic and scrupulous inspection is integral to the process itself so that sub-standard products are eliminated. This approach depends on

- a specification of the process
- close monitoring of the process
- continuous inspection of the product at all stages.
- every participant in the process being 'quality conscious' and accountable for quality at each stage of the process.

This approach is often referred to as 'total quality management' and ensures that products meet stringent international standards. It is the approach favoured particularly by Japanese industries which seek quality assurance. Its advantages are:

- it is efficient
- it makes the best use of resources
- it provides reliable and early feedback loops to ensure consistent products
- it leads eventually to increased customer satisfaction.

1. Give some examples of production.

2. What is meant by *added value*?

3. Compare and contrast *job, batch* and *flow* production.

4. List and explain the principal factors influencing location of business.

5. Identify the main factors which influence the location of a manufacturing plant.

6. Define *economies of scale.*

7. List and explain some examples of how economies of scale might be achieved.

8. Why must stock be controlled?

9. Sketch a model of traditional stock control.

10. Explain the process of JIT.

11. What are the advantages of JIT?

12. Define *quality.*

13. Explain how a producer might achieve quality.

14. What are the advantages of quality circles?

15. Explain the concept of *total quality management.*

Essay questions
Accounting

1. Explain the differences between a profit and loss account, a balance sheet and a funds flow statement.

    Why are they all needed in order to give a clearer picture of a company's performance?

    AEB P2 1991

2. Distinguish between fixed assets and current assets. Discuss the factors that influence how a company might decide to deploy its capital between a variety of assets.

    AEB P2 1990

3. (a) What does an accountant understand by the term 'liquidity'?

    (b) Outline a method by which a firm might predict future liquidity problems and explain how these may be averted.

    (c) Does the method of depreciation of fixed assets have any bearing on a firm's cash position, and if so, why?

    UCLES P2 1988

4. (a) Show how the following accountancy ratios are calculated:

    (i) dividend cover

    (ii) current ratio

    (iii) return on net assets

    (iv) gearing.

    (b) Explain their usefulness. Are there circumstances in which any of the above might provide misleading information?

    UCLES P2 1990

5. "More small businesses fail through lack of liquidity than through lack of profitability." Explain why this statement is likely to be true and suggest ways in which firms might attempt to avoid such failure.

    UCLES P2 1991

6. "Ratios extracted from one company's accounts are virtually useless without additional information."

    What other information would you need in order to make them valuable?

    AEB P2 1989

7. "The simple break-even model provides an easily understood, and effective, aid to decision making." Discuss limitations to its usefulness, and evaluate possible modifications that might be made to overcome them.

UCLES P2 1989

8. A local menswear shop has asked you to help establish a dress suit hire section in response to many requests from existing customers to hire formal wear for weddings and other social events.

    (a)   Explain the nature and types of costs that this might involve.

    (b)   Outline techniques with which the shop owner might assess the viability of such an enterprise.

    (c)   What other considerations or constraints might affect the decision?

UCLES P2 1990

9. Explain the concept of break-even analysis.

To what extent is the concept useful in the making of business decisions?

AEB P2 1991

10.   (a)   Differentiate between fixed and variable costs.

    (b)   How would you anticipate Sunday Trading affecting a large retailer's cost structure and its overall profitability?

UCLES P2 1988

11.   (a)   Distinguish between "contribution" and profit.

    (b)   Under what circumstances would "contribution" be used as an indicator of the values of a cost centre to a firm?

    (c)   Is profit important to a business? Explain your answer.

UCLES P2 1989

12. Barton & Sons make sets of cooking utensils. They are currently making and selling 16,000 sets a year, 4,000 units below the maximum capacity of the plant. Mr Barton is preparing for a meeting of the marketing and production managers to discuss proposals for the next year. He has decided to use a straight line break-even approach to analyse the company's position. The company earned a 5% return on its net assets which are currently £320,000. Unit total costs at this level of output are £39.00 of which variable costs are £24.00.

    (a)   What are the limitations and advantages of the break-even model in this case?

(4 marks)

    (b)   (i)   What is the present profit?

(2 marks)

(ii)   Calculate the present selling price per unit

(2 marks)

(iii)   Calculate the present contribution per unit

(1mark)

(iv)   What is the company's revenue at break-even?

(4 marks)

(c)   As a means of raising the company's return on assets to 10%, Mr Barton is keen
to increase sales by reducing prices by 10%. The plant's capacity can be increased
from 20,000 units to 30,000 units per year but this will involve additional fixed
overheads of £52,000 per year. Net assets will not rise because Mr Barton is
considering leasing the new equipment. The lease agreement would last for ten
years.

(i)   How many additional sets would the company have to sell?

(5 marks)

(ii)   Consider the marketing and production implications of the new,
higher output. Would you advise Mr Barton to go ahead with this
plan?

(7 marks)
UCLES P1 1988

13.   (a)   The following information is available about Wizard telephones.

Average calls sold per day (minutes)	20 million
(of which 15 million between 7 am and 1 pm)	
Variable cost per call per minute	2p
Fixed cost per call per minute (on average)	2p
of which the first 10 million at 1p and the second 10 million at 3p	
Price charged per minute	5p
Rental of line to customers	NIL

Wizard has a poor reputation for quality and reliability as its equipment keeps breaking
down in the mornings. Customers unable to get through are transferring to the competitor
Quicksilver.

(i)   Calculate Wizard's break-even daily sales (in minutes)

(ii)   Calculate Wizard's daily profit at the present sales quantity

(iii)   Account for the different levels of fixed cost

(10 marks)

(b)   Wizard is thinking of introducing price discrimination so that charges for calls will be 15p per minute between 7 am and 1 pm and 3p per minute at other times. Wizard's economist believes that after the price changes there will be 10 million minutes of calls per day between 7 am and 1 pm with the other 10 million spread evenly throughout the rest of the day.

(i)   How might this pricing policy affect Wizard's reputation?

(3 marks)

(ii)   What do you think are the economist's assumptions?

(4 marks)

(iii)   Calculate the effect on Wizard's profitability and explain it.

(4 marks)

(iv)   Firms often attempt to segment the markets they serve. Explain and give an example.

(4 marks)

UCLES P1 1990

14.   (a)   Why do firms use budgets?

(6 marks)

(b)   Hooson's actual and budgeted sales for 1990 were:

	Budgeted	Actual
Sale Price	£4.40	£4.50
Number sold	220,000	206,000
Total Revenue	£968,000	£927,000
Direct costs per unit	260p	278p
Total direct costs	£572,000	£572,680
Contribution	£396,000	£354,320
Total Fixed Costs	£350,345	£342,127
Pre-tax profit	£45,655	£12,193

(i)   Define and give examples of:

- direct costs

- fixed costs

(4 marks)

(ii)   Produce a statement, using variances, analysing the shortfall in profit. Explain how it may have occurred.

(10 marks)

(c)   Conditions often change between the setting of a budget and its implementation. Explain how firms may take this into account.

(5 marks)
UCLES P1 1991

15.   Warwick Ltd wish to replace 10 vans in their distribution fleet. The vans cost £1,000 new, have a useful life of 5 years and have a residual value of £1,000.

(a)   Define "useful life" and "residual value". How might these be estimated?

(4 marks)

(b)   Alternative ways of replacing the vans are:

  - outright purchase, payment terms being cash one year after delivery;

  - leasing, rental £30,000 per annum, 30% tax relief one year in arrears;

  - hire purchase, total price to be paid calculated as 130% of the outright purchase cost: 20% of this total price to be paid at once and the balance in 5 equal annual instalments.

(i)   Construct the CASH FLOWS for each alternative for each year.

(4 marks)

(ii)   Use an appropriate investment appraisal technique to calculate the cheapest way of replacing the vans. Explain and evaluate the technique you use.

(6 marks)

NB All cash flows occur at the end of the year.

Discount factors at 10% are:

End of year	0	1	2	3	4	5	6
Factor	1.000	0.909	0.826	0.751	0.683	0.621	0.564

(c)   (i)   Which fixed assets do firms depreciate and why?

         (ii)   Warwick could depreciate these new vans on a "straight line" basis or "declining balance" basis at 38%.

If the vans were purchased outright, how would the choice of depreciation method affect Warwick's profit in the first two years after the acquisition of the vans?

(6 marks)
UCLES P1 1990

16.   (21 marks)
Coley Ltd is an engineering firm. It is the largest supplier of a particular tool in a market where, at a standard price of £500, there is very little competition. The home market is reaching saturation point, but Coley Ltd is not yet working at full capacity. Present output is 1500 units, while full capacity is 2500 units.

An order for 500 units has been received from an Italian firm on condition that the tools can be delivered to their factory all expenses paid at a price of £400 each.

Coley Ltd's present cost structures are:

Materials per unit	£120
Direct labour per unit	£100
Variable overheads per unit	£60
Fixed overheads	£300,000

However to these must be added the costs associated with exporting to Italy. A sum of £20,000 is thought to be ample to cover this order.

The company's first reaction was to reject the order on the basis that it meant a loss of £70 per unit, while at present, sales produced £20 profit per unit. However, further consideration of the financial and commercial aspects of the deal swung the decision in favour of accepting the order.

(a)   Use appropriate financial calculations to demonstrate whether the decision to accept the order was justified. Show all your workings.

(9 marks)

(b)   Discuss three other reasons for accepting the order.

(6 marks)

(c)   Explain two problems that might be encountered if the order is accepted.

(6 marks)
AEB P1 1990

17. A machine costs £20,000 to purchase. It has a useful life of 5 years and a residual value at the end of this period of £3,000.

Depreciation figures, using the Reducing Balance Method are as follows:

Year	Depreciation Provision (£)	Net Book Value (£)
1	6315	13685
2	4321	9364
3	2957	6407
4	2023	4384
5	1384	3000

(a)   Explain the term "depreciation"

(3 marks)

(b)   Suggest three factors that influence the useful life of an asset

(3 marks)

(c)   Calculate the annual depreciation provision using the Straight Line Method

(3 marks)

(d)   Compare the Reducing Balance Method with the Straight Line Method of depreciation.

(6 marks)

(e)   On a graph, show the annual Net Book Value for each of the following methods of calculating depreciation:

(i) the Straight Line Method and

(ii) the Reducing Balance Method

(7 marks)

(f)   Why is depreciation a provision rather than an expense?

(3 marks)

AEB P1 1989

Other questions

Aspen plc is a large public company which was originally founded as a brewery, but which is now engaged in a wide range of activities. At a recent board meeting it was decided to further diversify into food retailing. In the board's view the safest and most prudent way to do this would be to acquire an existing business already operating in this field. Two relatively small companies have been identified, Foodline Ltd. and Handy Stores Ltd. as possibilities for takeover. Both are suitable for acquisition by Aspen and the final decision as to which of the companies to takeover rests on the issue of their relative financial positions. The final accounts of Foodline and Handy Stores are given on the following two pages:

Balance Sheets as at 31 July 1992

	Foodline Ltd.		Handy Stores Ltd	
Fixed Assets	£'000	£'000	£'000	£'000
		345		270
Current Assets				
Stock	160		135	
Debtors	260		219	
Balance at Bank	45		—	
	465		354	
Creditors: Amounts due within One Year	180		306	
Current Assets less Current Liabilities		285		48
Total Assets less Current Liabilities		630		318
Creditors: Amounts due after more than one year (10% Debentures)		—		90
		630		228
Share Capital and Reserves				
Issued Share Capital*		300		150
Reserves		330		78
		630		228
Market Value of an Ordinary Share at the Balance Sheet Date		£1.80		40p

* The Shares issued by Foodline Ltd are £1 shares and those issued by Handy Stores Ltd are 25p shares.

Profit and Loss Accounts for the Year Ending 31 July 1992

	Foodline Ltd		Handy Stores Ltd	
	£'000	£'000	£'000	£'000
Sales		1,080		1,290
Less: Cost of Sales				
Opening Stock	111		123	
Purchases	742		942	
	853		1065	
Less: Closing Stock	159		135	
	694		930	
Other Costs of Sales	116	810	102	1,032
Gross Profit		270		258
Selling and Distribution Costs	105		86	
Administration Expenses	90		103	
Interest on Debentures	—	195	9	198
Net Profit for the Year before Tax		75		60
Less Corporation Tax Provided		30		22
Net Profit for the Year after Tax		45		38
Less Dividend Proposed		15		18
Retained Profit for the Year		30		20

You are employed as an assistant to the financial manager of Aspen. You are required to advise on the possible takeover of Foodline Ltd or Handy Stores Ltd. For this purpose produce a report in which you:

(a) use suitable accounting ratios to draw a comparison between the two companies in relation to their profitablity, liquidity and investment potential;

(b) make recommendations on the basis of your findings;

(c) state further information about each of the companies which would be useful to have before arriving at a final decision.

Case Study

Hairy Hadrian and his Roman Walls

This year the town of Morpeth celebrates its 900th anniversary. As part of its festivities, the Borough Council resolves that it should hold a series of concerts reflecting the town's musical heritage. The Director of Leisure Services, Mr Chris Booth, is given the task of promoting these concerts and, although the Borough Council has allocated a substantial budget for these events, it is clear that some will make considerable losses while others will prove profitable.

The concerts will include early church music, medieval music, chamber music and rock and roll. One of the events that it is hoped will prove profitable is a 'gig' to be given by 'Hairy' Hadrian and the Roman Walls. 'Hairy' Hadrian – real name Dave Spigot – is an aging thrash rock star, a 'local boy made good' and should prove to be a crowdpuller. However, the Director is wary in case crowd trouble should break out and blemish the festival, so he insists that there must be a more than adequate number of bouncers to control fans. The event is to be held in the Chantry, one of the Borough Council's public halls in the town centre. The hall is very old and not particularly safe, and so stringent conditions have to be laid down.

Under these conditions, there must be: at least thirty bouncers if 3,000 or fewer tickets are sold; one extra bouncer for each 20 tickets sold, between 3,000 and 4,000; and one extra bouncer for each 10 extra tickets sold over 4,000. Each bouncer is to be paid £40 per night. The capacity of the hall is 5,000. The price of tickets is set at £6 each. The cost of heating, lighting and administrative staff for the event is £2,500 and this must be paid, regardless of the number of tickets sold. 'Hairy' Hadrian's specially discounted fee for his performance is £2,000, and £850 must be spent on hiring a PA system for the evening.

It is clear that, in order to sell tickets for the concert, it must be advertised, and this can be done in three ways: on posters at a cost of £40 each; in the local papers at £80 per advert; and on the local radio at £200 per spot. The Director estimates that to attract 3,000 customers it is necessary to spend £400 on posters and £800 on newspaper ads. If local radio is used, however, more tickets can be sold, as follows:

> 1st radio ad sells 1,000 more tickets;
> 2nd radio ad sells an extra 500 tickets;
> 3rd radio ad sells an extra 250 tickets;
> 4th radio ad sells an extra 50 tickets.

Task

As an officer in the Leisure Services Department of the Borough Council, advise the Director on the following points:

(a) what the fixed costs of the concert are and what its variable costs are;

(b) how many tickets will have to be sold in order to reach break-even;

(c) how many tickets should be sold to make the maximum profit;

(d) how much advertising should be carried out.

Explain your advice in words and in the form of a break-even chart.

Case Study

Howard's Dilemma

'Why have we never got enough money to pay the bills?' thought Howard Ratcliffe, as he arranged yet another meeting with his bank manager to extend the overdraft facility of his business. 'We seem to be increasing our sales all the time and yet the bills seem to go up every month.'

Howard is the founder and Managing Director of Ratcliffe Potteries, a small limited company based in Kidsgrove near Stoke on Trent. The company makes a wide variety of pottery and earthenware and has been established for six years. Howard's background has been mainly in sales and marketing and he has concentrated his efforts on the promotion and distribution of his company's products. He has generally left the internal management of the company's operations to the Works Manager, Sam Hazley and, while output has continually increased and quality standards have been improved, the general financial control of the manufacturing aspect of the business has been rather slipshod and badly managed.

Howard is sufficiently concerned about the financial state of the business that he decides to introduce a strict budgetary control. He calls Sam to a meeting in his office. In that meeting he outlines his proposed financial controls. Sam is clearly suspicious of the changes, as he feels that they are a means of monitoring how he, and other sections heads, are performing. He asks for time to consider the proposals and Howard arranges a meeting of the management team to discuss the matter further in two weeks' time.

Tasks

1. You are employed by Ratcliffe Potteries as a personal assistant to Howard. He believes that he must have a sound and reasoned case for introducing the budgetary control measures into the company. Prepare briefing notes for Mr Ratcliffe; in them you are to outline the advantages the company will gain from introducing budgetary control.

2. A second agenda item of the management meeting is a consideration of the purchase of a new kiln for the production of porcelain. The cost of the new kiln is £50,000, which must be paid immediately. Howard anticipates that the kiln will generate £12,000 per year in extra revenue for the business in each of the next five years. He is concerned that this is an insufficient return to justify the purchase of the kiln. Using a discount rate of 12%, prepare a discounted cash flow statement which will determine the financial viability of the new kiln. Prepare a memo to Mr Ratcliffe in which you inform him of your conclusion. (Discounted cash flow is covered in Part Three of this book).

Case Study

Closing The Restaurant

Doggards Ltd. is a private company which runs a department store in the small market town of Northallerton. The store sells the usual range of goods which are normally found in a department store: ladies' wear; menswear; hardware; electrical goods; perfumes; groceries and sports equipment. It also has a restaurant which serves morning coffee, lunch, afternoon teas and high tea. The restaurant occupies approximately half the area of the second floor of Doggard's building. The store has five floors altogether, including the basement, but the top floor is given over entirely to staff accommodation, store rooms and offices. All the floors are of equal size.

The managing director of the company believes that the restaurant is not contributing to the profitability of the store. Indeed, he suspects that it is actually running at a loss. He has asked the company's accountant for a complete analysis of the store's activities, department by department, and finds that, while all departments involved in selling are making profits, the restaurant is making a loss. In response, he is considering closing down the restaurant and using the space that would release to expand the toy department, which is one of the most profitable departments. Another director of the company is unconvinced that this proposal is in the best interests of the business and wishes the restaurant to remain open.

Tasks

1. As a management trainee with the store, you have been asked to investigate the situation and produce a report which will eventually be used as a basis for deciding whether the restaurant should be closed or remain open. Draw up a checklist, prior to producing the report, in which you carefully identify, for your own benefit, the various factors which you consider relevant in arriving at a decision about closing the restaurant.

2. Write the report on the proposed closure to the Board of Directors.

3. Produce a simple questionnaire, that could be completed by customers to the store and which would provide you with data on their attitudes to a possible closure of the restaurant.

Case Study

Charming Children's Chairs

You are employed as an Administrative Assistant by Charming Children's Chairs, a company which specialises in the manufacture of children's chairs for sale to indulgent parents. Having been in business for some six months, the company is finding that they are overstretched in terms of sales staff and have decided to expand. It is time to employ some sales representatives. These 'reps' will visit retailers and also attend various meetings, playgroups and so on that are held throughout the region in an attempt to secure orders. Drawing on past experiences and knowledge of the market, the company estimates that the following numbers of representatives would sell the following quantities of chairs:

Number of Representatives	Total Number of Sales per Week
1	6
2	15
3	25
4	36
5	48
6	60
7	69
8	75
9	80
10	75

The unit costs of the chairs have been calculated as £60 per chair, and this figure includes all materials, administration costs etc, but not the wages of the reps. It has been decided to advertise for sales people at the rate of £120 per week.

The chairs are currently sold as a unit price of £75.

Where possible, the following tasks should be produced using a spreadsheet on the computer.

Tasks

You have been asked to calculate how many sales representatives should be employed in order to earn maximum profit per week. Prepare a brief report for the Managing Director, Mr. Gordon Bartram, to explain your answer in words, figures and diagrams.

Having been somewhat disappointed with recent sales, the company has decided to advertise its product in the local Mothers' Institute Magazine. This advertising campaign, undertaken at a negligible cost, has resulted in a boost to sales and the potential sales figures have been recalculated by adding a further four chairs to the sales of each rep. Recalculate the number of representatives which the company should now employ, using the higher projected sales figures, and forward them to Mr. Bartram in the form of a memorandum.

Having achieved these higher sales figures, the sales reps are keen to see an increase in their pay. In order to asses the possibility of a pay rise, you have been asked to recalculate your figures, using a wage rate of £150 per week. Draft a memo which will illustrate to management how this will affect profit levels and the number of reps that the company should employ.

Essay questions   *Marketing*

1. Examine the different ways a firm manufacturing chocolates might determine the nature and size of its potential market.

    AEB P2 1990

2. "If a product is good enough, it shouldn't need marketing. All marketing does is to mask poor quality products." Assess the arguments for and against these statements, and say why you agree or disagree.

    AEB P2 1991

3. Filocopy Ltd. believes it has identified a market opportunity in a field dominated by one firm – the originator of a novel product. Filocopy have asked you as marketing consultant, to advise them of actions they should take.

    AEB P2 1989

4. Explain and illustrate what is meant by "the product life cycle". Using appropriate examples explore the implications for management of this concept.

    AEB P2 1990

5.   Distinguish between cost-based pricing methods. Discuss the relative merits of each group of methods and suggest where they would be most appropriately used.

UCLES P2 1988

6.   You have been asked, by an Egg Marketing Board, to advise them about various forms of packaging.
Write a report, in reply, explaining the main functions of packaging and how these relate to other aspects of the marketing mix.

UCLES P2 1988

7.   (a)   Why do suppliers of key products such as British Gas, an Electricity Board or British Telecom operate a pricing policy which includes a fixed charge?

     (b)   Why do such organisations often charge different prices to various types of customer?

UCLES P2 1989

8.   (a)   How might the marketing mix, adopted by a large carpet retailer with many outlets, differ during its annual January sale from that used for the rest of the year?

     (b)   What are the benefits to companies of holding such sales?

UCLES P2 1989

9.   (a)   A UK. based manufacturer of paper tissue has launched a new range of paper towels. What factors might influence the company's choice of distribution channel?

     (b)   Discuss the likely implications for such a firm of a fall in the effective exchange rate of the sterling.

UCLES P2 1990

10.   (a)   Differentiate between 'brand substitution' and 'product substitution'.

      (b)   Using appropriate examples, explain how marketing strategies aimed at achieving each of the above might differ.

UCLES P2 1990

11.   (a)   Explain what is meant by product life cycle.

      (b)   Why is it important for a firm to maintain a range of products?

      (c)   Suggest ways in which ideas for product development could be encouraged and harnessed.

UCLES P2 1991

12.   A brewery is preparing to add an alcohol-free lager to its existing product range although this is already a highly competitive market.

(a)   What factors should be considered when branding the product?

(b)   How might the firm make use of a test market for the product?

(c)   Discuss alternative pricing strategies for the new lager.

UCLES P2 1991

13.   (a)   Suggest how the marketing mix for a consumer durable may change as it moves through its product life cycle.

(b)   Why is it necessary for many firms to become increasingly market orientated in the UK?

AS UCLES 1991

14.   (a)   What is meant by Full Cost Pricing?

(b)   In what circumstances would you advise the use of Marginal Cost Pricing, and why?

(c)   Why is the profit earned on a product important?

UCLES P2 1985

15.   (a)   What pricing strategies are available to a firm launching a new variety of non-stick frying pan on the market?

(b)   What might be the differences in pricing policy for the longer term, and what information and analysis is likely to be necessary?

UCLES P2 1986

16.   "The role of advertising is to awaken customers to wants that they never had." Discuss.

UCLES P2 1986

17.   How might the manufacturer of a new chocolate bar decide to market the product?

UCLES P2 1987

18. (a)   Vincent Ltd. make trousers. Production capacity is 250,000 units *per annum*. Sales volume is currently 100,000 units per annum. Vincent's cost structure is as below:

Unit costs at different production levels

	nil-120,000	120,001-200,000	200,001-250,000
Materials	240p	280p	300p
Labour	300p	360p	420p
Maintenance	60p	60p	80p

Per unit costs at maximum capacity

Depreciation	80p
Rent	40p
Loan interest	9p
Advertising	21p
Administration	50p

The trousers are sold by Vincent to retailers at £14 each.

(i)   Calculate Vincent's total fixed cost.

(ii)   Calculate Vincent's break-even output.

(iii) Define "margin of safety" and explain its usefulness.

(iv)   Describe the behaviour of Vincent's costs as output rises and suggest reasons for this behaviour.

(13 marks)

(b)   About 60 million pairs of trousers are sold in the domestic market per annum. About 1 million pairs are sold by prestigious department stores and "quality" tailors who buy supplies almost entirely from domestic makers at prices between £13 and £18 per unit. About 13 million pairs are sold by multiple tailors and independents who buy supplies at between £7 and £12 per unit: imports account for 25% of these sales. About 46 million pairs are sold by supermarkets and chain stores who buy supplies at between £3 and £6 per unit: imports account for 75% of these sales.

(i)   Define "market segment" and "marketing mix"

(2 marks)

(ii)   Give possible reasons for the above segmentation

(5 marks)

(iii) Explain possible changes to Vincent's marketing mix if it were to reduce its price to retailers.

(5 marks)
UCLES P1 1991

19. (20 marks)
Read the extract and answer the questions which follow.

MINERAL WATERS IN THE UK

During the 1970's, Perrier (UK) built the market almost single handed, aided by the "Eau so successful" advertising campaign. By the early 80's, there were five major competitors each contributing to spending on advertising and stimulating market growth. In 1983, there was a major marketing windfall - a national water strike - which caused the market to leap by almost 50% in one year. At the same time, the market began to segment on a price basis, as the premium brands gained national distribution through outlets and own labels were introduced.

The UK Mineral Water Market
(Million litres)

1980	25
1982	34
1984	65
1986	105
1987	150
1990 (Est)	210

Source: Perrier UK *estimates*

Today, the ownership of the mineral water brands can be divided between those companies which have a diversified product range, e.g. Nestle, Cadbury Schweppes, and those who are purely mineral water producers (e.g. Perrier, Highland Spring).

Whilst product life-cycle theory suggests that volume growth will inevitably slow down, the Chief Executive Officer of Perrier (UK) estimates that the average Briton will be drinking ten litres of bottled water a year within two decades (Financial Times 1986). A British Market Research Bureau (1986) survey showed that 34% UK adults claimed to drink bottled mineral water. 25% of these claimed to drink it once a month or more.

The UK consumer and derived brand benefits

Forty one per cent of UK mineral water is consumed by Londoners, perhaps due to the fact that the original 'eau' campaign was targeted upon "image-conscious trendies" who saw mineral water as a status symbol.

As the distribution base broadens (56% of national sales are now distributed through major multiples - Mintel Market Intelligence, 1988) and the market structure changes, it seems likely that with increasing consumer demand, a mass market will develop from the niche position previously occupied.

There is considerable evidence to suggest that other environmental and social factors are also encouraging these structural changes.

(Source: *The Quarterly Review of Marketing - Summer 1989*)

(a)   What factors might affect a grocery outlet's decision to introduce 'own label' products?

(5 marks)

(b)   Assume that total advertising expenditure in the UK Mineral Water Industry was £2m in 1986 and £2.5m in 1987. If other factors remain the same, calculate the advertising elasticity of demand for the UK Mineral Water Market between 1986 and 1987, and comment on the significance of the result.

(5 marks)

(c)   How might those "who saw mineral water as a status symbol" have been targeted by the marketing department?

(4 marks)

(d)   How might marketing strategies change as a distribution broadens and the market structure changes to a mass market from a "niche position" in the market?

(3 marks)

(e)   What factors other than marketing might have led to the increase in sales of mineral water?

(3 marks)
AEB P1 1991

Essay Questions   *Personnel*

1.   In what ways might the functions of a firm's personnel department be affected by falling levels of unemployment?

AEB P2 1989

2.   In the 1990s population trends will reduce the number of young people entering the workforce.
How might a firm respond to this situation?

AEB P2 1991

3.   (a)   Discuss the role of the Personnel Department in a large organisation.

        (b)   How might the performance of such a department be evaluated and controlled?

UCLES P2 1991

4.   Discuss how systems of wage payments may sometimes conflict with quality standards.

UCLES P2 1987

5.   (25 marks)
     Read the information and answer the questions which follow.

A job description

Job Title: Office Services Supervisor

Department: Administration

Main purpose of Job: To ensure the provision of efficient typing, reprographic and switchboard services to company personnel

Scope of job: Responsible to: administration manager
Responsible for: five staff; equipment to value of £300,000

Main duties:

1. To allocate suitable personnel to switchboard, telex, offset printer and photocopiers, as required.

2. To ensure the provision and maintenance of an accurate and efficient typing and reprographic service.

3. To ensure the maintenance and upkeep of equipment.

4. To collate control information on departmental costs, etc.

5. To order stationery, reprographic chemicals and other materials, recording use and maintaining suitable stock levels.

6. To train and assist in selection of new staff.

(Adapted from Recruitment and Selection, ACAS)

A job specification

Seven-Point Plan

Essential	Desirable
Physical make-up Good health record. Acceptable bearing and speech.	Pleasant appearance, bearing and speech.
Attainments GCSE English Language. Ability to type, and to operate office machines. Experience of general office work.	GCSE maths or equivalent. RSA II typing. Experience of using simple statistical information and experience of staff supervision.
General Intelligence Above average.	
Special aptitudes Reasonable manual dexterity. Facility with figures.	
Interests	Social activities.
Disposition Persuasive and influential. Self-reliant.	Good degree of acceptability, dependability and self-reliance. Steady under pressure.
Circumstances No special circumstances	

(a)   Using examples given in the data, distinguish between a Job Description and a Job Specification

(2 marks)

(b)   How might a firm recruit for this post?

(4 marks)

(c) What factors might be important in the conduct of an interview?

(5 marks)

(d) The firm has appointed someone to fill the post without interview, what information might they have used in making their selection?

(6 marks)

(e) Outline four pieces of legislation that might be taken into account during the recruitment and selection process

(8 marks)
AEB P1 1991

6. The Head of a School/College will be interviewing a short-list of three candidates for the post of A-level Business Studies teacher. Candidate A is professionally well-qualified, has worked in industry but has no teaching experience. Candidate B is moderately-qualified and has two years' successful teaching experience. Candidate C has just qualified as a teacher of Business Studies. Suggest factors which would influence the Head's choice and consider:

(a) how the Head might brief himself for the interviews;

(b) the questions he might ask each candidate;

(c) the information he might seek before making his decision.

UCLES P2 1986

Essay questions   *Production*

1. (a) Do entrepreneurs always aim to minimise average costs when deciding on a location for a new factory?

(b) Identify other factors which might influence the decision and explain difficulties which are likely to arise in reaching such a decision.

UCLES P2 1988

2. (a) Differentiate between job and batch production systems.

(b) How might a biscuit manufacturer benefit from changing production processes from batch to flow?

(c) Discuss the potential problems that might arise from such a change.

UCLES P2 1989

3. (a) Discuss methods of production that would be appropriate for an aeroplane manufacturer. Justify your answer.

    (b) Why do capital good manufacturers have particular problems in relating production output to demand? How might they deal with this problem?

UCLES P2 1991

4. (a) Explain how a washing machine manufacturer might develop a stock control model for bought-in components like electrical motors.

    (b) What would be the implications for the firm of the introduction of 'just-in-time' production principles?

UCLES P2 1991

5. (a) What are the objectives of stock management?

    (b) How might each of these objectives be achieved?

UCLES P2 1985

6. (a) What are the principal types of production system?

    (b) How would the management of a catering establishment choose between them?

    (c) What problems might arise in moving from one system of production to another?

UCLES P2 1985

7. (a) What factors should determine the level of stock held by a company?

    (b) How might you use ratios or other methods to achieve satisfactory control of stocks?

UCLES P2 1987

8. (a) Why are changes in the structure of the population of interest to producers?

    (b) In what ways will these changes be viewed by:

    (i) builders of old people's residences;

    (ii) manufacturers of school uniforms?

    (c) Distinguish between the production systems which might be used in producing

    (i) white shirts; and

    (ii) school ties.

UCLES P2 1987

9.   (25 marks)
   Read the article and answer the questions which follow.

JCB

JCB has many of the qualities of UK engineering in its heyday; pragmatic, determined and more than a little pushy.

Such qualities have helped to make it extremely successful. Still a family-owned firm, it has hacked out a growing place in the ferociously competitive global construction equipment market. JCB funds all its 20 million-a-year capital investment from internal cash flow. And it doesn't believe in debt.

The reason for this atypical performance is, unfortunately, also atypical: unlike 90% of firms, JCB has a manufacturing strategy. It knows what it wants manufacturing to deliver, and manufacturing has a pretty good idea how to do it. Getting closer to the customer is a fetish at JCB. In this aim, manufacturing is viewed as a support to sales and marketing. 'My job,' says manufacturing director John Sussens, 'is to give the sales force total flexibility. We want to drive the whole factory on what the customers want.' In turn, this dictates manufacturing policy and organisations. Rocester, which builds JCB's four different types of product, is a world-class factory, but it is not a technological marvel. Rather, its excellence derives from its principles, supported at key points by appropriate technology.

The principles are responsiveness and quality. Traditionally, quality meant final build. It still means final build - but also fitness for purpose, timely delivery, cost competitiveness and after-sales service as well. The pursuit of this demands a whole new toolkit of techniques. Rocester uses the classic ones of just-in-time manufacturing and quality. The beauty of the

system is its dynamic, the effectiveness of which is perhaps best encapsulated in JCB's prices. Between 1980 and 1987, the list price for a back-hoe leader went up just 4%, compared with RPI's 52.7%.

A constant industry leader
Activity: Production of construction equipment
Production workforce: 800
Turnover: £300 million
Manufacturing features: Just in time, total quality, continuous improvement
Record: Highest per employee figures in industry for turnover, profits and investment; expanding product line, three times greater turnover from same factory with reduced workforce; since 1979 direct labour productivity up 125% +, stock turn up from 3.2 to 15.3, supplier base reduced from 730 to under 400 (eventual aim 100), quality improved, total order to delivery time eight weeks

JCB spends substantially on modern capital equipment. It has islands of automation, is introducing CAD-CAM (Computer Aided Design-Computer Assisted Manufacture) to cut product development lead times, uses robots and plenty of CNC (Computerised Numerically Controlled) machine tools. Yet it has a healthy distrust of technology for its own sake.

(Adapted from Best Factories, Management Today 1988)

(a)   (i)   Suggest advantages and/or disadvantages to JCB of funding 'capital investment from internal cash flow'.

(3 marks)

(ii)   List two alternative methods of funding capital investment.

(2 marks)

(b)   Explain the view of 'manufacturing ... as a support to sales and marketing'

(3 marks)

(c)   Explain the term 'just-in-time' manufacturing and state two advantages and two disadvantages of the system

(7 marks)

(d)   JCB has made significant gains since 1979, comment on the likely effects of these on the organisation

(10 marks)

Part Five – Business and Society

The final section in this book deals with several issues which appear at first glance to be unrelated to each other. It deals, too, with various organisations which appear to have little in common with each other: they appear different, if not disparate. You might, then, be tempted to see this Part as a 'ragbag' that contains many bits of 'business' that cannot be found a home anywhere else in the book. You would be mistaken in doing this. All of the issues and organisations that are discussed here can be found at the interfaces between the world of business and society at large.

Society and business are not two neighbours who occupy separate houses and have gardens that butt on to one another, but have nothing to say to or do with each other. They are neighbours who do not always see eye to eye and who, over the years have quarrelled with each other, copied each other, made up with each other, squabbled again. They share the same neighbourhood streets and facilities and are constrained by the same disadvantages. They cannot (or perhaps will not) leave the neighbourhood and each is anxious to know what the other is doing. The windows of their respective houses reflect back each other's values in an intimate and infinite process. What happens in society invariably influences what happens in business and *vice versa* and this is discussed when you look at the relationship between the way business operates and the mostly unwritten 'codes' of ethics by which it is expected to abide.

Society and business try to mould each other in their own images. Society, or at least segments of it, tries to influence business through various interest groups, such as organisations that are concerned with consumers' rights or health issues. Government acts on business by insisting it follows the legal constraints imposed upon by legislation. Business tries to influence society by exerting pressure on the government to amend or initiate or abandon legislation. At any point, the balance between the 'rights' of the public and the 'rights' of business will be tilted in the favour of one party rather than the other, on issues such as data protection, pollution and environmental control and consumers' rights. One major function of pressure groups is to redress such imbalance.

The final section in this Part deals with some of the more complex issues and conflicts of interest that result when an 'individual member of the public' takes on the role of 'business person'. This section examines the argument, and counter-argument, that there is no essential distinction between the two.

Society and Conflict

Despite 1980s' protestations to the contrary, there is such a thing as society – and a complex organism it is, too. 'Society' is people living in the same place, a majority of whom follow the same customs, who are part of the same organisation and share a similar or common objective. Society is made up of number of systems, each of which has its own objective; within society each individual will also have a number of personal objectives which he or she strives to attain. It is when those personal objectives and social objectives fail to coincide within the system that conflict is engendered.

'Conflict' is the noun used to label overtly aggressive behaviour by individuals; (this is, in its most extreme manifestation, murder). Conflict also describes aggressive behaviour by society (this is, in its most extreme form, warfare). Since it is a part of society, the business world is one of several areas where there exists a high potential for conflict at many different levels. For example, within the business itself there will be people whose business and personal objectives clash with those of other people within the business: you've seen already that the objectives of the owners of a business may be very different from those of its managers, which again may be different from those of its shareholders – and even more different from those of its employees. When you consider the six categories of interest within a business, it is little wonder that there is scope for conflict:

- those who finance it
- those employed by it
- those who lend and extend credit to it
- those who buy from it
- those who live around it
- the 'country' within which it locates itself and which benefits from its output.

The relationship between employers and employees, or managers and workers, or one manager and another manager, can be a recipe for conflict. Where employees belong to a trade union, or where 'macho' management responds belligerently to a troublesome situation by making threats of plant closures and job losses through 'rationalisation', there is likely to be more overt conflict than might otherwise be the case.

The consequences of conflict resulting from unshared objectives are likely to be: low morale; bad or non-existent industrial relations; the need for management to intervene in trivial decisions which have become too sensitive to be left to their subordinates. Conflict in a business is likely to stem from a failure, on the part of those responsible, to stimulate, maintain and motivate those whom they employ within their business.

In the UK, throughout the 1980s – and even in to the 1990s – there was a strong tendency on the part of those in power to view all individuals and organisations as being in constant competition with each other. Perhaps naively, there was an underlying assumption that as long as individuals and organisations successfully pursued their own objectives then, somehow and magically, they would contribute to the general good. That such an outcome has not yet happened is evidence of the disparate power that individuals and organisations hold and wield; competition that begins on an unequal footing is destined to end in the same way: conflict leads not to growth and harmony, but to more conflict.

At times in the 1980s, supporters of the free market economy made pronouncements that might well have been uttered by Adam Smith over two hundred years before. Smith believed that unfettered competition, with no government interference, would always work to society's advantage. He argued that if producers were left alone to pursue profit through the provision of goods and services, then the 'invisible hand' of market forces would ensure that the right goods and the right services were produced. If markets were left free of any kind of government interference, then *'laissez faire'* competition would result in production being directed in ways that could only improve social well-being.

Smith insisted that this would only happen if government avoided the temptation to interfere with the market mechanism and shunned attempts to regulate economic activity. A second condition that needed to be met if the economy were to benefit the common good was that producers had to openly compete with each other. Smith harboured a deep mistrust of, and animosity towards, any form of monopoly or oligopoly, seeing such as conspiracies directed against the consumer.

'Business' is not a disinterested party that passively and patiently waits for government (and others) to impose their will upon it. Instead, it attempts to shape or mould government policy and national and international law to its greatest advantage. One of the principal determinants of the success of a business will be the health and well-being of the economy, which traditionally has been the government's responsibility. On the other hand, it is absurd to claim that business and enterprise have no power to affect the economy. However, the role of government changed markedly in the 1980s when a course of non-intervention was followed and government avoided taking on any increases of its regulatory roles and powers.

Pressure Groups

Pressure groups (or lobbyists) have been neatly defined as *"organisations with objectives that lie within the sphere of politics but without the political power to achieve them directly"*. A pressure group, as the name implies, will exert pressure on local or central government in order that its viewpoint is taken into account and considered in the decision-making process. The group may try to exert pressure directly or indirectly; it may simply exert pressure in order to get its views noted, or it may combine pressure with more practical measures in order to achieve its objective.

There are thousands of pressure groups in the UK, ranging from *single cause pressure groups*, such as Help the Aged, to *spectrum pressure groups* which will embrace a wide range of concerns that radiate from a single concern e.g. Greenpeace; Friends of the Earth. Some pressure groups are transient; they appear to further a cause, disappearing again when that cause is attained or irremediably lost; for example, some environmental groups opposed to the dumping or incineration of toxic waste in a particular locality.

Historically, one of the most powerful lobbies in UK politics has been the trade unions. In the generally hostile environment of the 1980s, there was a diminution in their power and their ability to influence events. However, they have successfully adapted, evolved and broadened their functions to take into account the changing European scene so that they continue to put pressure on politicians in London, Brussels and Strasbourg to further the interests and protect their members.

A pressure group, whether it is 'political' or not, will usually operate by collecting data and information that can be used to further its particular stance or viewpoint. It will normally seek to give its cause as wide and as much publicity as is possible, so that it can influence public opinion in its favour and thereby put indirect pressure on politicians through their electorate.

Take as an example the smoking and non-smoking lobbies in the UK. Pressure groups which oppose smoking, and the sale and advertising of tobacco products, include the British Medical Association (BMA) and Action on Smoking & Health (ASH), whilst the opposite side of the issue might be promoted by FOREST and pressure groups which are funded by tobacco interests and cigarette manufacturers. Each set of pressure groups will be determined to influence public and political opinion as much in its favour as possible. As the Chancellor prepares for the Budget, each side will be pleading its case, one for increasing the revenues from tobacco products, the other urging that duties on tobacco are lowered.

Pressure groups vary in size, power and the sophistication of their organisation. These three factors do not always determine the degree of success of the pressure group or its impact upon business or government The first successful environmental protest in the UK was carried out by a group of dissatisfied housewives in Swansea who successfully blocked the access road leading to the Carbon Black factory after they had sustained a vigorous campaign to have emissions from the plant stopped.

Pressure groups vary in their resources. The most powerful pressure groups will cross international frontiers, have almost unlimited access to finance, will be well staffed, employ full-time researchers and will be capable of almost instant response; their promotional activities will be lavish and they will spend large sums of money in protecting and enhancing their image. Contacts with politicians and parliamentarians are likely to be strong.

On the other hand, some pressure groups are simply *ad hoc* gatherings of souls who take up a common cause; the degree of organisation may be rudimentary and they will be doing it because they believe in it, not because they are paid for it. The come together over a single issue and promptly disband themselves once the issue is resolved.

How might pressure groups adversely affect businesses?

1. By directing unwelcome publicity on a particular firm and its products: for example, by opposing the re-location of a plant in their neighbourhood because the group claims its emissions are dangerous.

2. By affecting public opinion, so that the public's sympathies move away from a particular business, or business sector, and its products.

3. By involving a business in increased costs; at worst, this may mean the business incurring huge costs if it has to re-locate plant or production facilities; at best, a business may have to expend larger sums on promotional work in order to maintain or enhance its image.

4. By deterring potential job seekers applying to a company whose image they perceive as 'negative'.

5. By causing a fall in sales (e.g. through a customer boycott) and thereby increasing costs.

Trade Unions

The Need for Trade Unions

In a market, businesses sell and buy capital, land, materials, goods, services and labour. In a completely unrestricted market, employers would be free to buy the services of employees at the lowest possible cost to them, whilst employees would compete with each other to secure from an employer the highest possible price for their labour. In the middle ages, and even in to the nineteenth century, agricultural workers and farmers met on certain quarter days at just such labour markets, which were known as 'hirings', to do just that.

Just as employers might band together to form a cartel that will secure the highest price for their products so, too, can employees band together in an attempt to secure for themselves the best possible price for their labour. Trade unions are the result of workers realising that, if they grouped together, then the price they could secure for their services would be higher than if they bargained individually, a process that has become known as *collective bargaining*. The principal weapon which workers wielded against employers in order to get what they wanted, was the strike.

The objectives of unions

Securing the highest possible reward for services is the principal – but not the only – objective of trade unions. They try also to:

- improve the working conditions of their members, especially when those conditions threaten the health and safety of workers e.g. cases in the early 1990s where bank employees (Midland Bank), journalists (*Financial Times*), data processors (British Telecom), suffered repetitive strain injuries (RSI) as a result of the work they did; unions like the BIFU, NUJ, National Communication Union, GMBU, IRSF and CPSA all successfully fought for compensation for their members

- improve the conditions of employment of members e.g. by reducing the number of hours worked or the patterns of work that are followed

- give protection against unjust or illegal actions e.g. unfair dismissal; help enforce equal opportunities

- safeguard jobs

- promote training and 'upskilling'

- provide the advantages of collectivity: 'Strength in numbers'; 'United we stand; divided, we fall'.

Unions might also be expected to negotiate in situations relating to:

- wages and salaries

- working conditions

- working practices

- payment systems and methods
- disciplinary matters
- redundancy and dismissal.

The elected representatives of the employees (usually elected and paid officers) conduct negotiations about such matters with the employers or their representatives. Sometimes the employee representatives will be from within the business, but more usually they are regional representatives from the relevant trade union.

In an ideal world, employers and employees would resolve any problems – whether over pay, conditions or training – swiftly and harmoniously, through a process of discussion and negotiation and without any conflict arising. This has, historically, failed to happen: conflict has occurred whenever employers tried to exploit workers and unions responded through the threat, or reality, of various types of industrial action. The main types of action are:

- working to rule
- picketing
- striking.

Attitudes to Trade Unions in the 1960s and 1970s

The attitude to unions in these decades was remarkably consensual, with both the Conservative and Labour governments treating the unions as the 'fifth estate', behind Parliament and the press. Union leaders were regarded as being an integral part of the constitutional process and they were well represented on parliamentary and quasi-parliamentary committees; no one doubted that they should be represented on the National Economic Development Council (more familiarly known as NEDDY and abolished by Chancellor Norman Lamont in 1992) or that they should regularly meet with industrialists and ministers as equals.

By 1979, things were different. Prime Minister Thatcher refused to have anything to do with the unions and she, her ministers and political colleagues did everything in their power, by passing legislation as well as more unorthodox means, to strip them of any influence and power. (The effectiveness of their endeavours can be gauged from a study of the statistics on strikes and union membership that appear below.)

The Conservative government reinforced the spectre that many people already carried with them: that of union members fighting with police at the Orgreave Cokeworks during the prolonged miners' strike of 1984-5; of print workers and police clashing violently at the new headquarters of Rupert Murdoch's News International in Wapping in 1986. The gloom engendered by 'The Winter of Discontent' of 1979 has been periodically re-invoked by the Conservatives in the election campaigns of 1983, 1987 and 1992 to remind the British people of the dire consequences that can result when the balance of political power tilts towards the unions.

By 1992, union membership had declined for the thirteenth consecutive year, from 12.3 million in 1979 to under 8.2 million in 1992, a loss over that period of one member in every four. In order to compensate for their rapidly dwindling membership, some unions which, traditionally, competed fiercely for members, have opted to merge into 'super unions': the AEU with the EEPTU; the old railway workers and seamen's unions into the RMT and a current proposal whereby NUPE, NALGO and COHSE merge together to form a single union which will account for half of the total membership of the TUC.

The unions have presented a far more positive and varied image than of old. In an effort to shed their obsolete, strike-bound image they have concentrated upon pressurising employers into improving conditions in the workplace. It is a role they are well suited to as people begin to realise that the 'second industrial revolution', with its pervasive use of computers and robots, spawns its own sets of new physical and psychological afflictions and re-invigorates older ones.

The increasing isolation of the unions from the mainstream of British political and economic decision-making has also forced its leadership to look outside the UK for support and hope, especially towards the EC. As a result, the TUC is now more pro-European than the government. The turning point occurred in 1988 when Jacques Delors addressed the annual TUC conference. As Norman Willis, TUC general secretary puts it, "We realised that we must not just put up with the European Community, but make the best of it. And we got a response from the Community which was totally lacking from the government. We found a home in a Social Europe, not just on the rebound, but in a positive sense. Now I believe that we have a responsibility to show that European democracies can deliver the goods economically".

UK unions and their counterparts from continental Europe have joined together to form their own trans-European federation, the European Trade Union Confederation.. Its role mirrors in Europe that of the TUC in the UK: to bring all unions together under one collective umbrella. Trade unions have voiced their support for the EC's Social Charter, a series of new laws designed to standardise working conditions, health and safety protection, child care provisions and training. The Conservative government has opposed the Charter so far and Mrs. Thatcher, when in office, went so far as to say that it was 'inspired by the values of Karl Marx and the class struggle'.

The European Social Chapter

UK trade unions are amongst the strongest supporters of the Social Chapter, the purpose of which is to raise and standardise working conditions throughout the EC. One of the purposes behind the Chapter is to try and ensure that the (more affluent) EC countries that provide superior working conditions do not become economically disadvantaged because of the money that they allocate to improved workplace conditions – money that raises their costs. Without a Social Chapter the free movement of workers between member states will also be discouraged.

Areas where signing up to the Chapter will have the greatest effect are:

- Health and safety at work
- Limits on the length and patterns of working hours
- The rights and conditions of part-time and temporary workers.

The policy which is incorporated in the Chapter has been strongly opposed by successive Conservative governments, though Labour look upon it favourably and are committed to its adoption and implementation when they return to power. In 1991, at the Maastricht Treaty, the UK reserved its right not to become a signatory to the Chapter. In July 1993 the House of Commons tied 317 to 317 in an amendment to the bill that would have ratified the Maastricht Treaty. The Speaker of the House cast her vote in favour of the government and the amendment was defeated. Thus, the UK was the only EC country to ratify the Treaty but not its Social Chapter.

The loss of union power has caused a significant gap in representation both in the workplace as well as in other areas of life where people are either too unorganised or too low-paid to influence events and government. (The unions find it difficult to recruit amongst part-time workers and financial services employees, especially when they are women.) The TUC has traditionally represented not only its membership but also the social underclass which now lacks a watchdog which will bark on its behalf.

Unions, employers and government may meet on any of three levels:

1. Local level: minor disputes, workplace grievances, unfair dismissal and complaints and concerns expressed by individual union members are generally dealt with on this level.

2. National level: this is the area where the most widely seen conflict between unions and employers occurs. Basic rates of pay, conditions of service and contracts are dealt with on this level by full-time, paid union officials and the representatives of the employers.

3. National advisory level: despite the attempts of successive governments to reduce the influence of the unions and remove their opportunities for expression, some still remain. The National Advisory Council (NAC) includes representatives of the TUC, the Confederation of British Industry (CBI) and the government. Its role is to establish guidelines within which collective bargaining can take place.

Recent Legislation to Curb Union Power

Legislation, mainly passed in the 1980s, and the introduction of different approaches to work, have led to a diminution in the effectiveness of the three union 'weapons'. 'Working to rule' becomes redundant in an industrial situation where managers and workers regard themselves as equals in a problem-solving team which relies upon flexibility, multi-skilling and a common, positive approach.

Picketing, if it involved any form of secondary industrial action, was made illegal. As the law stands at present, it is unlawful to picket anywhere other than outside the business which is directly a party in the dispute; equally it is illegal to 'black' the customers or suppliers of that business,

Several major pieces of industrial legislation in the 1980s radically curbed the 'right to strike'. 'Wildcat' strikes are now illegal and no strike may be called without all union members being balloted and a majority being declared in favour of strike action. The introduction of the secret ballot in *The Employment Act,* 1984, has proved extremely effective in restraining the more impetuous union leadership.

The 1980s saw the introduction of several pieces of legislation that fitted in to the Conservative strategic plan to erode the significance of union power:

- 1980: *The Employment Act* outlawed secondary picketing, ended 'closed shop'
- 1982: *The Employment Act* meant that unions could be sued
- 1984: *The Trade Union Act* initiated secret ballots on trade disputes
- 1988: *The Employment Act* gave union members the right not to strike
- 1990: *The Employment Act* made unions liable for action taken against customers or suppliers.

The effectiveness of such anti-union legislation occurred at the same time as union power was being weakened in other ways, too.

- Membership was in decline because of rising unemployment

- The number of strikes declined as a result of legislation

- Public sympathy was diverted by the media portrayal of unions as being politically subversive, with their leaders either out of touch with the membership or as megalomaniacal e.g. Mr. Arthur Scargill of the NUM

- New approaches, such as 'human resource management', placed the emphasis on persuading an individual that it was in everyone's interest to co-operate and give corporate commitment

- Regional and local pay bargaining partly replaced national, collective negotiations

- Single-union and 'no strike' agreements became features of union/employer agreements which were designed to avoid conflict e.g. Nissan's deal with the Amalgamated Engineering Union; such deals where unions competed with each other to become sole representative were disparaged as 'beauty contests' by some.

The Effectiveness of Anti-union Legislation

If you accept that statistics, such as those below, reflect the effectiveness of the legislation passed to curb union power, then it is remarkable how consistently effective that tranche of legislation has been. Its effectiveness has been enhanced since it has been enacted against a background of two economic recessions, two cycles of deep unemployment occurring against broad structural unemployment, and the widespread replacement of full-time jobs in the manufacturing sector by part-time jobs in the service sector. In the 1970s 12.9 million working days were lost, on average, in each year; in the 1980s, an average of 7.2 million days were lost; in 1991 fewer working days were lost to strikes than in any year since records were first kept and the first time the total fell below the one million mark since 1940. To put strikes into their proper perspective, it is worth noting that four million days were lost in 1989, but 120 million days were lost as a result of absenteeism, sickness and injury.

1982	5.3
1983	3.8
1984	27.1
1985	6.4
1986	1.9
1987	3.5
1988	3.7
1989	4.1
1990	1.0
1991	0.8

Number of Working Days Lost through Strikes (in millions)

Union	representing	1989	1988
TGWU	(transport and manufacturing workers)	1.27	1.32
GMB	(unskilled workers in most industries)	.82	.86
NALGO	(public service workers)	.75	.75
AEU	(engineering workers)	.74	.79
MSF	(car production, universities, NHS, banks)	.65	.65
NUPE	(local government, water workers)	.63	.64
USDAW	(shopworkers; distributive trades)	.38	.40
UCATT	(construction workers)	.25	.26
COHSE	(NHS)	.21	.22
UCW	(Post Office; British Telecom)	.20	.20

The decline in membership of the UK's ten biggest unions (Figures in millions)

Competition Policy and Consumer Protection

While suppliers of goods and services wish to pursue their own interests, this may be to the detriment of competitors or consumers. Certain markets for goods and services develop in a way which conflicts with the broad public interest: that is, they are economically or socially undesirable. This section describes the three strategies that have been adopted in order to regulate and control the operation of the market.

The three ways are:

- regulating the market structure through monopolies and mergers legislation
- controlling anti-competitive practices through restrictive practices legislation
- consumer protection.

Regulating the Market Structure through Monopolies and Mergers Legislation

One of the surest ways of bringing a high level of competition to a market is for there to be many buyers and many sellers, none of whom has such a significantly large market share that a single buyer or seller can influence the price. All must accept the market price: that is, they are *price takers*.

However, the UK market since 1945 has developed a more concentrated structure. The most prevalent market form is *oligopoly*. Producers are described as *price searchers*. The government has attempted to lessen this trend towards concentration by passing legislation designed to control the growth of dominant suppliers.

The Increase in Merger Activity

A merger occurs when one business throws in its lot with another business or when one major organisation takes over another. 'Giant' mergers have become a common feature of the commercial scene and many people make a comfortable living 'merely' by advising on takeovers and mergers.

The advent of the Single European Market has led to an increase in the frequency of mergers and takeovers. There are two reasons for this:

1. businesses already within the market attempt to grow to a size which will allow them to benefit fully from the potentially increased market: having 'branches' in as many member countries as possible makes sound commercial sense

2. businesses which are based outside the EC are also aware of the size of this new market. Fearing some form of customs blockade against the rest of the world, they are rushing to buy up European companies in order to take advantage of 1992.

Businesses which have re-located or set up on UK greenfield sites to take advantage of the UK as a 'launch pad' into the EC are Toyota in Derbyshire and Nissan in Sunderland. Despite the large amounts of publicity that attend such foreign 'inward investment', it's worth knowing that foreign buy-outs of UK companies are not as common as UK buy-outs of foreign companies. Since the 1980s a rising tide of UK purchasers have eagerly snapped up European and US businesses, though there have been few if any attempts by British firms to buy into Japanese companies.

It is an interesting exercise to browse through the reference book *Who Owns Whom*. From it you can find the owners of many household names; few people realise that the control of so many companies actually lies in so few hands. Choice is not what it seems!

Legal Control of Monopolies and Mergers

The first major piece of legislation was *The Monopolies and Trade Practices Act* 1948. This created the body called the Monopolies and Mergers Commission (MMC). Legal powers were strengthened by *The Monopolies and Mergers Act* 1965. The Commission's main responsibility is to act as a watchdog; it enquires into possible monopoly or oligopoly situations and reports its findings to the government for possible further action.

The Fair Trading Act of 1973 established the Office of the Director General of Fair Trading. The Director General was authorised to refer to the Commission areas where market concentration might possibly prove detrimental to the public interest. The DG was also given authority to assist the Commission in its investigation into such situations.

The 1973 Act:

- defines both a monopoly situation and a merger situation
- grants investigatory powers to the MMC

- grants powers to the Secretary of State for Trade and Industry to issue orders to deal with monopolies and mergers.

A monopoly/ merger situation

The 1973 Act defines a monopoly/oligopoly/merger situation as existing if the following circumstances arise:

- either a single enterprise has (or through a merger is likely to have) control of 25% of an individual market (a monopoly share); or
- if the total assets of the merged organisations will exceed £5 million.

Monopolies and Mergers Commission

This body is technically independent of the government. It has the duty to investigate and report on any question 'with respect to the existence of a monopoly situation ... or with respect to the creation of a merger situation'. Both the Secretary of State and the Director General of Fair Trading can report matters to the Commission for investigation.

In its report the Commission will decide if either of the above circumstances exists and, if so, whether or not there are any factors which might justify the government in allowing them to continue.

There are many instances of activities in which there is one company with more than 25% of the market. For instance, in the biscuit market, United Biscuits has a 40% market share, and in baked beans, Heinz has a 64% market share. The fact that these have not been referred to the Commission reflects the belief of successive governments that competition in those areas of activity is adequate.

If a referral is made, the Commission will consider whether or not the merger or the level of concentration operates in the public interest. To decide this, the Commission must bear in mind factors such as the need:

- to promote effective competition within the UK
- to protect consumer's interests regarding the price and variety of goods
- minimise the costs of production
- to develop new techniques and products
- to ensure unrestricted entry for new competitors into existing markets
- to ensure a balanced distribution of industry and employment nationally.

These factors may be somewhat contradictory. The first and third, for example, seek to improve economic efficiency within organisations or within the economy as a whole, while others, such as the fifth, aim to restrict the free movement of business and so impose certain constraints on it, thus making it less efficient. For instance, a manufacturing business may be most efficient if it is situated in the south east of England, close to its major markets, yet the Commission would encourage a more balanced distribution of industry throughout the UK and so would encourage it to locate regionally.

One example of a highly publicised takeover which was allowed to proceed, was that of the chocolate company Rowntree Mackintosh by the Swiss manufacturer Nestle. Despite severe opposition from the work force, management, and many of the British public, the takeover took place with little hindrance from the MMC.

When the Commission's report indicates areas of concern, the Secretary of State for Trade and Industry has the following options:

- to require the transfer of property from one organisation to another
- to require the adjustment of contracts
- to require the re-allocation of shares in an organisation
- to prohibit a merger taking place.

These are enforceable by court action through an injunction – that is, a court order prohibiting or requiring specified action.

A recent example of the MMC 'in action' was the case of the takeover bid from Elders Walker for Scottish and Newcastle Breweries. It was a 'hostile' bid (i.e. it was not welcomed by the workers or management of the target company). The MMC ruled that the bid should not go ahead, as Elders Walker already owned Courage Brewers, and ownership of S & N would give them a 40% share of the UK beer industry. The MMC recommended, and the government subsequently ordered, that Elders reduce its share holding in S&N to 9.9%, from the 23% it had acquired in the run up to its full takeover bid.

The MMC's unanimous decision to prevent the takeover was made on the grounds that such a merger would operate against the public interest. The Elders bid was stopped on five counts, all of which relate to competition.

1. A reduction of consumer choice between brands and a corresponding increase in the control of one brewer.

2. A reduction in competition in the supply of beer to the free trade.

3. A reduction in competition in the supply of beer to off-licences.

4. A reduction in competition in Scotland.

5. The creation of a second major beer group who, with Bass, would control more than 40% of the supply of beer.

The final count seems to suggest that it would be unlikely that a merger of any of the top six brewers (who control 75% of the market) would, for the present, be likely to succeed and, consequently, the market leadership of Bass will remain unchallenged for many years. The argument that the creation of a beer group, equivalent in size to Bass, would favour competition, was rejected by the MMC. On the contrary, it considered that the creation of a second large group would result in reduced competition and increased difficulty in supply and distribution for other brewers.

Whilst on the subject of the brewing industry, the MMC also published a report of an investigation into the industry as a whole and what it perceived as its lack of real competition. The report focused on the practice of 'tied houses' – pubs which can sell only the owner-brewer's products. The MMC recommended that the industry, which is dominated by six large breweries, should sell off some 21,000 of its 33,000 tied houses. The report also criticised prices and lack of choice for the consumer.

The Minister's job is to consider the report, and make recommendations.

There followed an intense campaign, by the brewing lobby, designed to discredit the report of the MMC. The success of its campaign can be measured by the actual recommendations that the Minister, Lord Young, made on the future of the brewing industry. The report's recommendation was that they sell off (or 'divest') any public houses in excess of the 2,000 owned by any single brewery; this was rejected by Lord Young. He decided that only one half of that excess of public houses should be divested, but not by outright sale. The method favoured by Lord Young to improve competition within the industry, was to require breweries to lease this number of pubs as 'free houses'. Even existing tied houses will now have the opportunity to sell other breweries' products, and as part of his package of proposals, Lord Young indicated that the licensing laws were to be liberalised.

The Control of Anti-competitive Practices through Restrictive Practices Legislation

One of the major factors which ensures a competitive market is an absence of barriers that may prevent the establishment of new businesses within that market. It is in consumers' interests that, where high profits are being made in a particular market by existing suppliers, there should be no restrictions on new businesses entering that market, thus bringing about healthier competition.

In real life, many markets are *oligopolistic,* and the producers who control them can effectively prevent new competitors from entering their market by *price control*. In addition, free market entry may be restricted by businesses using restrictive trade practices.

Restrictive trade practices include:

- *suppliers who form agreements or associations with other suppliers in the same industry* in order to:

        limit the supply of goods or services
        fix a standard price
        standardise contractual terms of sale
        purchase raw materials through a 'common pool' at an agreed price.

- *agreements between suppliers and distributors or retailers*

        Suppliers who are dominant in a market may enter into agreements with distributors or retailers under which a minimum price is set for the re-sale of the supplier's products. These agreements may also restrict a distributor who may be required to stock the supplier's products exclusively. In return, the retailer may be granted sole dealership over the product in a particular area and substantial discounts on the supplier's standard price.

- *Full-line forcing* involves a supplier requiring a distributor or retailer, who wishes to stock the supplier's major product, to carry the full range of his products. For example, a shopkeeper wishing to sell a major brand of baked beans may be required to carry the full range of the supplier's canned products.

- *Tie-in sales* is a less extreme form of the same arrangement, whereby the sale of one product is tied to the sale of others. Thus, a distributor of a certain type of photocopier may have to enter into a service agreement with the supplier to purchase all photocopying paper from him also.

- *Reciprocal trading* involves businesses agreeing to purchase only each other's products, thereby excluding other competitors' products which cannot be purchased where such an agreement is in force.

Long-term contracts: Here a distributor agrees to carry the supplier's products exclusively for a long period, thus effectively restricting competitors from entering the market.

The above practices are examples of the ways in which dominant suppliers exert pressure on distributors or retailers. The ultimate sanction, which may be used against distributors or retailers who fail to agree to such practices, is a *withdrawal of supplies.*

The Legal Control of Anti-competitive Practices

Legislation specifically designed to prohibit anti-competitive practices is contained in both EC and UK law. The lines of demarcation between EC and UK law can be seen by studying the background to the takeover bid for Midland Bank by its 'suitor', the Hong Kong and Shanghai Bank and its rival, Lloyds Bank, in 1992.

EC Competition Law

The main provisions of the law prohibit trade agreements that endanger freedom of trade between member states by preventing, restricting or distorting competition within the European Community.

Some examples of anti-competitive practices are:

- fixing prices or trading conditions
- limiting production, markets, technical developments or investment
- sharing markets or sources of supply
- applying dissimilar conditions to equivalent transactions with other trading parties.

Fines can be imposed, by the EC Commission, on each or all of the parties to such agreement.

UK Competition Law

The Competition Act 1980 is, obviously, restricted to UK markets.

All alleged anti-competitive practices are subject to a preliminary investigation by the Director General of Fair Trading. If the practice is proven to be anti-competitive, action can be taken by the Minister for Trade and Industry.

Particular practices by individual organisations may be investigated and, if necessary, prevented – without the need to investigate the industry as a whole. However, only *large* organisations are brought under scrutiny; that is, companies with a turnover of more than £5m or more than a 25% share of their particular market.

In determining what is, or what is not, against the public interest, the Commission takes into account all matters which appear to be relevant in the particular circumstances. For example, a manufacturer may offer his product to supermarkets at much bigger discounts than he offers it to corner shops. The practice of offering such discounts may be referred to the Commission as being 'anti-competitive' since the number of corner shops is likely to be reduced as a result of this practice. The Commission, in deciding the question of 'public interest', would have to balance the advantage to the consumer in obtaining a lower-priced product against the added convenience that the consumer gains by shopping locally.

Having reached a conclusion on a reference, the Commission must then report to the Minister for Trade who has the power, by order, to declare an anti-competitive practice unlawful if the offender refuses to refrain from that type of conduct.

The Act also grants the Minister for Trade and Industry the power to refer to the Commission any matters concerning the cost and efficiency of public corporations if they act as monopolies (e.g. the Post Office, British Rail). This is an example of the government using an independent body to keep its own house in order although, of course, the government has discretion whether it will make a reference to the Commission.

The Restrictive Trade Practices Act 1976

Under this Act, duties are imposed on the Director General (DG) of Fair Trading. The DG is required to:

- compile and maintain a register of restrictive agreements
- to bring such agreements before the Restrictive Practices Court, which has the function of deciding whether they are contrary to the public interest.

There are six types of agreement registrable under the Act. They are those made by *suppliers of goods* which lead to restrictions in:

1. the *price* charged for goods
2. the *terms and conditions* of supply of goods
3. the *quantities or descriptions* of goods to be supplied
4. the *process of manufacture* to be applied to any goods
5. those who may obtain the goods
6. the *area* in which the goods may be obtained.

Consumer Protection

Consumption is a fundamental characteristic of economic activity. The legal issues associated with the process of consumption is complex. Here two issues are the focus of attention:

1.   the rights that consumers have in relation to the goods they use and the services they receive

2.   the steps consumers can take if their rights are not respected by producers and suppliers.

The *Caveat Emptor* Approach

The traditional attitude to consumers' rights was summed up in the expression *caveat emptor:* "Let the buyer beware". Today, it is more realistic to describe consumers' rights as *caveat venditor*, "Let the seller beware". There are many factors which account for this shift; legislation aimed at strengthening the consumer's position being the main one.

The fact that legislation has been necessary, to effect changes in the market methods employed by sellers, demonstrates the unwillingness (or inability) of business to meet, through mechanisms of self regulation, the changing social demands placed upon it. (Another aspect of the difficult question of whether to regulate or not is examined later in this Part.)

Specific Consumer Protection Legislation

The Food Act 1984

The principal objectives of the *Food Act* 1984 (previously the *Food and Drugs Act* 1955) are to prohibit the sale of food which is adulterated or which contains harmful additives, foreign bodies or mould. The Act also prohibits misleading advertising or labelling of food, and lays down standards of quality for certain foods.

The Weights and Measures Act 1951

The Act provides for the inspection and testing of weighing and measuring equipment in use for trade. Under the Act it is an offence to use for trade, or to have in one's possession for use in trade, any weighing or measuring equipment which is false or unjust. It is also an offence to give short weight or short measure.

The Act restricts the units of measurement which can lawfully be used by a trader. It lays down detailed requirements as to the packing, marking and making up of certain types of goods, and provides that, in relation to pre-packed or containerised goods, a written statement must be marked on the container giving information about the net quantity of its contents.

Consumer Credit Act 1974

To a large extent, this Act contains the law in relation to consumer credit transactions such as hire purchase, personal loans, overdrafts, credit cards, credit sales and budget accounts. Schedule 1 of the Consumer Credit Act 1974 contains a list of over 35 criminal offences associated with contravention of the Act. These include, for example, trading without a licence; failure to supply copies of consumer credit agreements;

refusal of a trader to give the name of a credit reference agency which he has consulted; failure by a credit reference agency to correct information on its files; and obstruction of enforcement authority officers. The Act further provides that credit agreements must be in a prescribed form and that the consumer is supplied with all necessary information; e.g. rights of rebate on early settlement; right of cancellation; termination of the agreement.

The Unsolicited Goods and Services Act 1971

This Act was passed to impose criminal and civil liability on traders carrying on the practice of inertia selling. This involves sending goods or providing services which have not been ordered and demanding payment or threatening legal action if payment is not made. The Act provides that unsolicited goods or services need not be paid for, and unordered goods may be retained by the recipient if they are not collected by the sender within six months of delivery. It is an offence for the sender to demand payment for unsolicited goods or services.

The Trade Descriptions Act 1968

Two principal offences under this Act relate to false description of goods, and making misleading statements about services.

Two different types of conduct will amount to offences under this section:

1. Where the trader himself applies the false trade description; e.g. by turning back the mileometer of a car to make it appear that the car has not travelled as many miles as it actually has.

2. Instances which involve supplying, or offering to supply, goods to which a false trade description has been applied by another person; e.g. where a retailer sells a garment to which the label 'pure new wool' has been attached by the manufacturer, where the garment is partly composed of man-made fibres.

A false trade description may be applied verbally or in writing, for example in a label on a product or in an advertisement. The term 'trade description' covers *statements relating to quantity, size, composition, method of manufacture, fitness for purpose, place or date of manufacture and approval by any person of other history including previous ownership* of goods.

The Consumer Protection Act 1987

1. Prices

The 1987 Act deals with the pricing of goods and services. It provides that:

> *'A person shall be guilty of an offence if, in the course of any business of his, he gives (by any means whatever) to any consumer an indication which is misleading as to the price at which any goods, services, accommodation or facilities are available.'*

Types of statements which are caught by the Act include:

- false comparisons with recommended prices, for example a false claim that goods are £20 less than the recommended price; or

- indications that the price is less than the real price, for example where hidden extras are added to an advertised price; or

- false comparisons with a previous price, for example a false statement that goods were £50 and are now £30; or

- where the stated method of determining the price is different to the method actually used.

2. Product safety

Part II of the *Consumer Protection Act* 1987 is connected with product safety. In deciding whether goods are reasonably safe, the court must examine all the circumstances, including:

- the way in which the goods are marketed

- the use of any mark, for example indicating compliance with safety standards

- instructions or warnings as to the use of the goods

- whether the goods comply with relevant published safety standards

- whether there is a way in which the goods could reasonably have been made safer.

An offence can be committed only in relation to *consumer goods*. Consumer goods are those which are *ordinarily intended for private use or consumption,* with the exception of food, water, gas, motor vehicles, medical products and tobacco.

Under the 1987 Act, any person who suffers injury or loss as a result of a breach of the safety regulations has the right to sue the trader for damages.

Computers and personal privacy

Since the 1960s, there has been growing public concern about the threat that computers pose to personal privacy. Most countries, including the UK, have introduced legislation to safeguard the privacy of the individual. The Data Protection Act of 1984 was passed after a number of government commissioned reports on the subject. The Younger Report of 1972 identified ten principles which were intended as guidelines to computer users in the private sector. A government White Paper was published in 1975 in response to the Younger Report, but no legislation followed. The Lindop Report of 1978 was followed by a White Paper in 1982 and this resulted in the Data Protection Act of 1984. The principles detailed in the Younger Report formed the foundation for future reports and the Data Protection Act. They are listed below.

1. Information should be regarded as being held for a specific purpose and should not be used, without appropriate authorisation, for other purposes.

2. Access to information should be confined to those authorised to have it for the purpose for which it was supplied.

3. The amount of information collected and held should be the minimum necessary for the achievement of a specified purpose.

4. In computerised systems handling information for statistical purposes, adequate provision should be made in their design and programs for separating identities from the rest of the data.

5. There should be arrangements whereby a subject could be told about the information held concerning him or her.

6. The level of security to be achieved by a system should be specified in advance by the user and should include precautions against the deliberate abuse or misuse of information.

7. A monitoring system should be provided to facilitate the detection of any violation of the security system.

8. In the design of information systems, a period should be specified beyond which information should not be retained.

9. Data held should be accurate. There should be machinery for the correction of inaccuracy and updating of information.

10. Care should be taken in coding value judgements.

The White Paper which followed the Younger Report identified certain features of computerised information systems which could be a threat to personal privacy:

1. The facility for storing vast quantities of data

2. The speed and power of computers make it possible for data to be retrieved quickly and easily from many access points

3. Data can be rapidly transferred between interconnected systems

4. Computers make it possible for data to be combined in ways which might otherwise not be practicable

5. Data is often transferred in a form not directly intelligible.

The 1984 Data Protection Act sets boundaries for the gathering and use of personal data. It requires all holders of computerised personal files to register with a Registrar appointed by the Home Secretary. The holder of personal data is required to keep to both the general terms of the Act, and to the specific purposes declared in the application for registration.

From the individual's point of view, the Act can be said to have a number of weaknesses

1. The penalties for infringing its rules are thought to be weak and ineffective

2. There are a number of exemptions from the Act. Some holders do not need to register and there are exceptions to the right of access to one's own file. There are also limits to confidentiality

3. The Registrar is appointed by the Home Secretary and cannot therefore, be wholly independent.

Consumerism

'Consumerism' is a term that is used to describe individuals and groups who believe that consumers need protection in their relationships with more powerful businesses. It has become a movement that tries to defend and extend the rights and power of consumers in relation to sellers.

The consumerist 'movement' has grown for three main reasons:

1. people have become: increasingly concerned in obtaining better value for money for their purchases

2. people feel that powerful businesses are exploiting and manipulating vulnerable consumers

3. people feel that human values are being eroded by material values.

Buying and selling – what an economist calls 'the exchange relationship' – is based on both parties having certain rights. Both buyer and seller should have an *equality*. The seller has the right to:

-   sell any product, as long as it is not dangerous (though even hazardous products can be sold as long as they have warnings)

-   set any price

-   promote the product in whatever way is thought desirable, as long as the law is complied with

-   encourage people to buy by offering an incentive.

The buyer has the right to:

-   buy or refuse to buy

-   expect a product to be safe

-   expect a product to be what the seller claims it to be.

Consumerism feels that the equality that should be the basis of the relationship between the two parties has been tilted too far in favour of the seller. People have turned to organised movements and to governments for protection. They ask for their rights to be extended so that:

-   they are fully informed about all important aspects of the product (e.g. ingredients, quantities of ingredients etc.)

-   they are protected against questionable products or marketing practices

-   they can influence products and marketing practices in socially desirable directions (e.g. into making manufacturers give up the use of CFCs in aerosols or bleach and dioxins in papermaking).

Research shows that consumerism is more prominent after a period of rapidly rising prices has caused a fall in consumers' purchasing power, strengthening the belief that the buyer/seller relationship has veered strongly in favour of the seller. However, the recent upsurge in consumerism is more credibly explained by:

1.   consumers' increasing awareness, through television, of fraudulent or unethical commercial practices

2.   consumers are more conscious of health and safety issues

3.   awareness of the link between crime and alcohol consumption in certain age groups.

1. Consumers have becoming more aware of shoddy and underhand practices through such programmes as Esther Rantzen's *'That's Life'* and Roger Cook's *'Checkpoint'*. Such programmes are beneficial since they heighten consumer awareness; from a retailer's point of view, however, they cast a cloud of suspicion over all businesses, even those who view the interests of consumers as paramount. The American consumer movement owes much to Ralph Nader, who campaigned tirelessly for improved safety standards in cars manufactured in the US.

2. Increasing consciousness of health and safety has shown itself in such anti-smoking campaigns as those of the British Medical Association and ASH or the pressure placed on manufacturers to properly label additives in foodstuffs, following the publication of Maurice Hanssen's book, *E for Additives*.

3. The link between alcohol and crime amongst the 18-24 year old age group has been firmly established. The UK suffers disproportionately from drink-related problems amongst this age group. Research has suggested that the dramatic growth in alcohol consumption amongst young people can be ascribed to the marketing campaigns of the brewers. Derek Rutherford of the Institute of Alcohol Studies points out that forty years ago this age group had the lowest alcohol consumption of any age range over 18. He suggests that the brewers, afraid of missing out on the youth market, began deliberately to target their advertising at this segment, with the result that there has been massive growth amongst young people – so much so that the peak age for alcohol consumption is now twenty.

A major complaint of the consumerist movement is misrepresentation by marketers. This includes misleading advertising, labelling and promotion, as well as the failure of products to live up to their advance billing. Much of their concern has focused on advertising. Vance Packard's *The Hidden Persuaders*, published in the early 1960s, has helped to fuel fears that advertising is often deceptive, leading consumers with an impression or belief that is different from the one they would form if they had perfect knowledge.

An ethical consideration that has become increasingly prominent from the 1980s has been a belief that the putting the pursuit of wealth before the preservation of the planet is indefensible and wrong. This has led to the formation of some powerful pressure groups, such as Greenpeace and Friends of the Earth.

Social Costs (or Externalities)

Social costs never appear in the balance sheet: they are costs that are external to the business, hence their alternative name, 'externalities'. Since they are not direct financial costs to businesses themselves, some have tended to underestimate their importance or even to ignore them altogether. Social costs are borne by 'society', very often by the community, rather than by the business that incurs them. Since a business usually makes its decisions on the basis of costs within the business, and 'society' (that is, people like you and me) decides whether a decision will have effects which are beneficial or detrimental to it, clearly, there is much scope for conflict.

What exactly is a social cost?

Social costs are the costs that society bears as a result of the implementation of business decisions:

- a social cost is usually undesirable (a social benefit, on the other hand, is generally welcome). For example, refining petrol has several social costs: it increases pollution from car exhausts; it creates pollution around the refinery itself; its lead content can cause physical harm to young children; it leads to environmental damage through oil spillages at sea

- social costs are often unquantifiable

- the repercussions to the business itself can be severe: for example, bad publicity can dent or damage a company's image or affect the sales of its products.

Business Cost versus Social Cost

Many students buy their first car when they are teenagers. Often the car will be second-, third- or tenth-hand and the only direct *cost* to the student will be a small financial outlay for the vehicle itself and, perhaps, some minor repairs. Thereafter, the direct costs to the student-driver are for oil and petrol, spare parts, car parking, fines for parking offences, servicing and MOT tests. The *benefits* that accrue to the student are: increased mobility; increased leisure or work time (since travelling on public transport and on foot are minimised); no expenditure on public transport; an enhanced social life.

But what about costs and benefits to other people – to society as a whole? Does society gain or lose anything as a result of our student's 'investment decision'?

Society can gain in some ways:

- the purchase and maintenance of the car might lead to a marginal increase in employment, servicing, parts manufacture etc.)

- there will be a marginal rise in consumption (petrol, parts etc.)

But society loses in other ways by:

- increased pollution

- lower revenue for public transport

- increased road traffic.

If we move from our small example of the student motorist and look at a slightly larger-scale example that is currently enjoying a high news profile, how might we balance the costs and benefits of the Twyford Down 'overpass'?

The *social benefits* of the bypass scheme to the residents of Winchester will be:

- fewer accidents

- less congestion

- less damage to the fabric of buildings because of the atmospheric pollution created by exhaust gases

- less noise pollution

- better parking facilities

- 'more desirable' residential area (which means higher house prices)

- some new but temporary construction jobs for local people.

The *social costs* which they must meet are:

- less revenue for community since fewer people stop to shop

- the land lost in the process of road construction

- the loss of a recreational amenity

- environmental damage to the flora and fauna of the area

At present the debate is continuing as to which route British Rail will choose its line to follow from London to the Channel Tunnel. The possible routes, and the impact they would have on people in London and Kent, were the focus of numerous newspaper articles in the 'quality' newspapers in 1991.

Using a quick-retrieval facility, such as a CD-ROM player and discs of *The Guardian, the Times* and *The Sunday Times, The Independent* etc., assess the respective costs and benefits to any one community which might be affected by the proposal. Draw up your conclusions in the form of a table, using whatever headings you feel are appropriate.

Cost benefit analysis

Conflict arises when business persists in making decisions purely in terms of its own financial criteria rather than in terms of broader political or social criteria. One way of attempting to defuse the potential for conflict that results from the divergence of interests between business and society is to carry out a cost benefit analysis of a particular situation. Cost benefit analysis comprises *a range of techniques which attempts objectively to measure the utility of a proposal made by a business and measure it against a range of community values which are quantified on a common monetary scale.*

Cost benefit analyses are usually carried out by large public agencies when they evaluate large-scale public investment projects in order to assess what the social benefits might be that accrue from them. Such analyses will be carried out before work begins on major projects, such as the Channel Tunnel or the construction of the M25; they tend to take into account longer-term and broader views than would a private business whose primary objective is profitability.

Business and Ethics

What is 'ethics'?

The conduct of individuals, groups and society is governed by a set of values and moral principles that are known collectively as 'ethics'. Most people, without consciously thinking about them, conduct their lives by a set of rules which they rarely, if ever, question and which they have absorbed and assimilated as they have grown to adulthood: this is a process that is known as *socialisation*.

Ethical behaviour is, by and large, governed by ideas of taking responsibility for one's actions, with individuals seeing themselves acting as part of a wider community and owing something to society at large. Most people have clear ideas about what is right and what is wrong; what is fair and what is unfair; what confers status and what reduces status. Thus, for example, in the UK having a job is generally seen as preferable to not working; working is seen as lending purpose, structure and meaning to a person's life, whilst unemployment is widely regarded as demeaning and undesirable.

Such considerations feed through in to other spheres of life and activity, so that an individual's perception of work as 'a good thing' becomes reflected in the tenacity shown by the individual's trade union when the prospect of redundancies looms. The desire by the individual to protect what he or she regards as valuable, can lead also to some stronger forms of jealous protectiveness: the industrial demarcation dispute or organised opposition to the introduction of new technology are but two examples.

Surveys have shown that a larger majority of people in the 'lower' socio-economic groups subscribe to the ethical belief that workers are responsible for their actions and accountable for their conduct and its consequences, than do people from the 'higher' socio-economic groups. But does 'business', generally, share their views?

'Business ethics'

Blue Arrow, Robert Maxwell, Ivan Boesky, 'obscene' salary increases for chief executives, the Lockheed Bribes Scandal, insider dealing, Barlow Clowes, Ernest Saunders, Guinness, Gordon Gecko, junk bonds, pyramid selling, BCCI ... such names are not exactly synonymous with honesty and straight dealing, are they? Scandal in the business world is not new, but it is, increasingly, the subject of debate. 'Business ethics' now can be found as a component of many business studies courses where future managers are reminded of the potential conflict which they will encounter when their obligations to their board of directors and market meet their sense of social responsibility head on.

Are business people any different from the rest of us?

Some business gurus maintain that there is, rightly, no such thing as 'business ethics'; others suggest that ethics is inseparable from the way we govern the rest of our lives by moral rules and considerations. Being truthful, fair and not breaking promises, govern (or should govern) everyone's life, so why should business people be exempt from them? Because business people pursue self-interest, corporate goals or the profit motive, why should they be spared what the rest of us have to put up with: the discipline of abiding by a set of ethical rules? Or are business people different from ordinary citizens because they have an additional set of social responsibilities?

Traditionally, civilised people have placed the 'common good' before their own self-interest; civilised people (reasonably) expect business people to show a concern for the environment in which they live and work and make a profit. They expect business not to trade with, or invest in, countries with whose politics the majority of people have little or no sympathy (e.g. South African apartheid regimes before 1992). They expect business, as employers, to be vigilant with the lives of employees and consumers alike. Such approaches may result in smaller profits and diminished dividends, higher prices for products and lower wages for workers: most would think this is a price worth paying.

In the popular mind, 'business interests' is a term that covers those shady activities which, though strictly falling within the law, are still considered to be reprehensible. An example of this sort of conduct might be the use of privileged or confidential information, or information gathered illegally, in order to gain a commercial or negotiating advantage – the phrase 'insider dealing', and the prosecutions that have resulted from it, exemplify this kind of conduct.

A recent study showed that, in 1991, eight out of the top ten takeovers were prefaced by an upward surge in share price (on average 4%) of the target company *before* an announcement of an offer was made public. Although such surges are not conclusive evidence that there is insider dealing, several recent takeovers have resulted in substantial speculative gains: for example, BTR's offer for Hawker Siddeley.

Many business people object to the widespread public belief that they are expected, morally, to follow practices which Joe Public is not expected to follow: business has to be seen as socially responsible, even if it means denting potential profits.

The Friedmanite view of ethics

In the 1980s, in the US and UK especially, a body of thought voiced its opinion that sentiments, such as those above, were dangerously collectivist or interventionist. Following Milton Friedman's belief that business has no social responsibility other than to obey the law in the same way as any other citizen, they considered it absurd that responsibility could be attributed to a 'collective' entity, such as business or 'the State', when it is only individuals who can choose, think, act, decide and repent. Friedman's views were echoed by prominent politicians, such as Margaret Thatcher and Ronald Reagan; Friedman's thoughts were reflected in their use of phrases, such as 'the Nanny State' and pronouncements that 'There is no such thing as Society'.

Friedman argued that politics and business are separate compartments of experience and it is wrong to confuse the two. The business executive should not cut the price of his or her product in an attempt to battle against inflation, nor introduce anti-pollution devices which the law does not require fitted, nor hire the long-term unemployed as part of a moral duty to ameliorate unemployment. Why not? The reason, says Friedman, is: were the executive to do this, s/he would be acting as an *agent of government*, not as an agent of his/her shareholders. Better to leave alone the private enterprise free market economy, which will, if left to itself, make life better for all of us.

Many examples of business ethics involve straightforward breaches of the law: selling unsafe products; taking bribes; harming our environment are the obvious ones. Problems raise their heads only when the law itself is vague or ambiguous. Peter Drucker cites the example of the US company Lockheed which 'gave in' to demands and was found to be 'paying off' a Japanese airline so as to secure lucrative orders for its jets. Drucker concludes that there is little difference between the corporation paying off the Japanese in this fashion and the victim of a mugging in Central Park who 'voluntarily' hands over his wallet. No one would consider the victim to have acted 'unethically', yet Lockheed was widely condemned for its action. (As events transpired, Lockheed would have been better off financially had it abandoned the contract: it persevered with it because 'business ethics' demanded that it do so – there was a US government subvention involved which was designed to secure the jobs of 25,000 workers.)

A major argument against the notion of 'business ethics' asserts that the idea of 'corporate responsibility' is meaningless; a corporation cannot have a 'conscience' or a 'corporate morality' (but it is interesting to see how businesses like Benetton and Body Shop put this to the test). Traditionally, moral actions are ascribed to individuals; responsibility (or its downside, blame) are attached to people, not to corporate entities.

How does the law cope with this? The short answer, perhaps, is 'badly'. Though it is possible under the criminal law to prosecute a company for crimes, such actions are consistently unsuccessful or are aborted; you have only to look at recent cases, or at least putative cases, to see this: the Piper Alpha oil rig disaster or *The Herald of Free Enterprise* sinking at Zeebrugge.

The public perception of business ethics

Though many in business might plausibly argue that, individually and corporately, they act ethically and legally, the public at large, reading of those actions, may well disagree with them. It is difficult to convince the average, honest citizen that Lloyd's syndicates are beyond reproach when its practices in the re-insurance market securely insulate its own members from risk, but expose 'names' to devastating personal losses. And it is even harder to convince Mr. and Mrs. Joe Public that they are living under, and obeying, the same set of ethical and legal rules when a government, committed to the untrammelled workings of the free market, bales out Lloyd's names and syndicates when running the market risk proves the reverse of profitable for them.

Mr. Public, having put his money on a sure-fire winner of a greyhound, would not expect the bookie at Walthamstow dog track to return his stake money when his selection fails to romp home! Nor would Mrs. Public, having taken out a 25 year building society mortgage, expect sympathetic treatment when she fails to meet her mortgage repayments and finds that her home proves to be worth less than the debt she owes to the building society that is repossessing it.

Business and Ethics in the 1990s: time for a change?

The 1980s are now widely regarded as a 'me too' decade whose overriding philosophy centred on self interest and a scramble for money. The harsh (or rigorous, depending on which side of the fence you are) doctrines of monetarism and Friedmanite free marketism left little or no room for the niceties of ethical decision-making. There were some honourable exceptions, notably in the shape of unit and investment trusts whose policies promised there would be no acquisition of shares in companies whose behaviour they considered to be politically unacceptable or environmentally damaging or socially divisive.

EIRIS, an ethical investment research body found, in 1992, that only fourteen of the stock market's top fifty businesses were completely uninvolved in doing business with the ninety countries which might be accurately described as 'oppressive'.

In the 1990s there seems to be a reaction to such an unrestrained free enterprise culture. Significantly, consumers and customers are becoming increasingly sensitive about how business and commerce impact upon society and there are louder calls for businesses to prove that they are 'principled'.

In 1992 the Co-operative Bank canvassed the views of its customers and found that 84.2% thought it was a good idea for their bank to have a clear ethical policy; only 5% of those surveyed felt that ethical issues had nothing to do with banking. They placed the issues in the following order of priority:

- human rights   90%
- arms exports   87%
- animal experimentation   80%
- fur trade   66%
- tobacco manufacturing   60%.

Lesser issues included pollution, recycling and energy conservation. The Bank's MD said, 'As a bank we are constitutionally neither partisan nor political but we aim to be responsible members of society and this must affect the choice of person or organisation with whom we will do business.' The Bank believes that the 'ethos of responsible banking' will have a strong appeal for many of its potential customers, 'particularly the younger, better educated, more aware and concerned members of society'.

The Co-operative Bank's Ethical Policy

The bank's position is that it:

1. will not invest in or supply financial services to any regime or organisation which oppresses the human spirit, takes away the rights of individuals or manufactures any instrument of torture.

2. will not finance or in any way facilitate the manufacture or sale of weapons to any country which has an oppressive regime.

3. will not invest in any businesses involved in animal experimentation for cosmetic purposes.

4. will not support any person or company using exploitative factory farm methods.

5. will not engage in business with any farm or other organisation engaged in the production of animal fur.

6. will not support any organisation involved in blood sports.

7. will not provide financial services to tobacco manufacturers.

8. will try to ensure its financial services are not exploited for the purposes of money laundering, drug trafficking or tax evasion by the continued application and development of its successful internal monitoring and control procedures.

9. will encourage business customers to take a pro-active stance on the environmental impact of their own activities.

10. will actively seek out individuals, commercial enterprises and non-commercial organisations which have a complementary ethical stance.

11. will continue to extend and strengthen its Customer Charter, which has already established new standards of banking practice through adopting innovative procedures on status enquiries and customer confidentiality, ahead of any other British bank.

12. will regularly re-appraise customers' views on these and other issues and develop its ethical stance accordingly.

Can business be trusted to police itself? To regulate or not to regulate ... that is the question

Given the nature and frequency of the more scandalous financial events and spectacular corporate fraud of the late 1980s and early '90s, it was small wonder that the Cadbury Committee was set up in 1991. The Committee's remit was to make proposals that would lead to companies reforming the way that they run themselves and the ways in which they answer to their shareholders.

The Committee seeks to clean up corporate practice through self-regulation by the Stock Exchange, non-executive directors and institutional shareholders. Non-executive directors would be given a stronger role so that they could monitor the ethics of executives and liaise with external auditors. The changed role of auditors would mean that they would have a duty to explain clearly to shareholders their 'duty of care' and that their reporting of accounts would not attempt to bolster the expectations of prospective buyers of shares.

Auditors have, generally, welcomed these proposals, but are quick to point out that they would do little to prevent a future Robert Maxwell taking advantage of a company in order to fraudulently bolster its value.

Sir Adrian Cadbury (former chairman of the confectionery company) proposes a voluntary code of practice for all listed companies but reserves the right to regulate by statute. The code includes recommendations that:

- no individual within a business should have complete power over decision-making and the roles of chairman and chief executive should be separated
- the number and status of non-executive directors should be such that their views carry significant weight
- a majority of non-executives should have no financial interest in the company
- executives' pay should be decided by a committee to be made up of non-executive directors
- directors should establish audit committees and explain to their shareholders what their assumptions were at the time the accounts were prepared; these should be accompanied by the auditors' explanation of their responsibilities
- directors should report on the effectiveness of internal financial controls and should state in their report that the business is a going concern, together with any supporting assumptions.

Whether Cadbury is proved right in believing that there is not yet a need for statutory regulation is an optimistic view that experience has shown in the past is not necessarily an accurate one.

1. Describe two examples of *social* or *organisational* conflict.

2. What is the principal purpose of a *pressure group*?

3. What means might a pressure group use to achieve its ends?

4. Why might a business be sensitive to the work of a particular pressure group?

5. How, if at all, do trade unions fit into the 'market mechanism'?

6. List the functions of trade unions.

7. What reasons can be found to explain the decline in union membership in the 1980s?

8. How are unions attempting to keep their national relevance in the 1990s?

9. Summarise the effectiveness of anti-union legislation in the 1980s.

10. What strategies have governments followed in order to control 'the market'?

11. Describe briefly the role of the Monopolies & Mergers Commission.

12. How does EC anti-competition law differ from the work of the M&MC?

13. What is meant by the phrase 'the rights of consumers'?

14. Who does the Data Protection Act of 1984 seek to protect? Why?

15. Define the word *consumerism*.

16. What are *externalities*? Why are they becoming increasingly important?

17. Describe, using an example, what you understand by the term *cost benefit analysis*.

18. What is the case for treating 'business ethics' differently from 'normal' ethics?

19. Give examples where ethical considerations form part of the overall strategy of a business or organisation.

20. "Conflict is always the result of unshared objectives": give examples to support or contradict this assertion.

1. A number of trade unions have reached 'no strike' agreements with some employers. How do these unions justify such agreements and why do some other unions dislike these agreements?

AEB P2 1990

2. "The main obstacle to change in manufacturing industry in the UK is still multi-unionism, whereby each group of workers is represented by different Trades Unions." Discuss.

UCLES P2 1989

3. As leader of a Union negotiating team, which has just had an initial pay claim for an 8% increase in wages (3% more than the current inflation rate) rejected by the Board of Directors of a Cross Channel Ferry Line, prepare a discussion document for other members of your team outlining alternative dispute procedures and their likely effectiveness.

UCLES P2 1986

4. "Legislation such as that concerned with employee and consumer protection and the regulation of potential monopolies cause the loss of international competitiveness. This is too high a price to pay." To what extent to you agree?

AEB P2 1989

5. Argue the case for the reform of British Trade Unions.

UCLES P2 1985

6. Some major manufacturing companies have attempted to replace annual wage negotiations with longer-term agreements. Discuss the relative merits of this as might be perceived by each of the following:

    (a)   the Company

    (b)   Trade Unions and Employees

    (c)   the Government.

UCLES P2 1991

Index

A

Accounting, 319-402
Accounting Concepts, 379-383
Accruals, 380
ACORN, 426-427
Active Selling Skills , 486-489
Added Value , 512
Advertising, 472-488, 499-500
    agencies, 473
    agencies register
    rates, 481-485
Age, 414, 422
Alberto Culver, 407
Annual General Meeting, 31
Application of funds, 350-353
Articles of Association, 28-32, 71
Assets, 328-331, 341-347
Attitudes
    lifestyle, 427
Attitudinal barriers, 227-228
Auditor's report, 354
Audits, 320-324, 432
Augmented product,441
Authorised Capital, 29, 72
Autonomous group working, 80-82
Average Accounting Rate of Return, 258-260

B

Balance of Payments, 150, 181-190
Balance sheet, 326-347
Bank lending, 65-69
Bankruptcy, 42-43
Barriers
    to communication, 55, 225-228

Benefit segmentation, 426
Blending, 277-282
Bonus schemes, 105-106
Bookkeeping, 334
Brainstorming, 248, 456
Brand , 451-453
Branding, 135-136, 451-458
Break even analysis, 386-394
British Petroleum (BP), 40-41
British Telecom (BT), 165-168
Budget, 58, 62, 158, 398-402
    control, 400-402
Business
    failure, 41-46
    finance, 65-76
    performance, 57-63
    plan, 26, 65-67
    strategy, 5, 14, 49-64
    structure, 5-7, 19-46
Campaign planning, 474 .
Capital, 29, 60, 72, 326
    employed, 23
    gearing, 375-377
    investment
Cash, 354-359
    control, 354-359
    flow, 66-67
Caveat emptor, 572
Caveat venditor, 572
Channel
    of distribution, 467-470
Charles Handy, 232-233
Cinema, 484-485
Circulation of working capital, 329
Collective bargaining, 560-564
Commercial breaks, 478-480
Communication, 223-246
    network, 225
    policy, 224
    system, 223-236

F

Factoring, 68
Fayol, H, 93-94
Final accounts, 319-320
Financial information, 319-354
Financial Statements, 319-351
Fiscal policy, 157-160
Fixed
  charge, 70
  exchange rates, 187-190
Floating
  charge, 70
  exchange rates, 187-190
Forecasting, 282-288
Franchising, 33-34
Funds Flow Statement, 350-353

G

G7, 207-209
GATT, 190, 207-210
Generic product, 440
Going concern concept, 380
Goodwill, 329
Government economic policy, 139-170
Gross profit, 349
Group, 84-90
  characteristics, 85
  effectiveness, 87-89
  types of, 85-88
Growth rate, 150

H

Hawthorne studies, 87
Health and safety, 504

I

Imperfectly competitive markets, 134-137
Imports, 181-190
Income, 125
  elasticity of demand, 125
  tax, 157-160
Index numbers, 288-292
Industrial relations, 496, 560-565
Inelastic demand, see Elasticity of demand
Inflation, 140-150
Information technology, 229-234
Inland Revenue, 324
Insolvency, 41-46
  practitioner, 43-46
International Trade, 181-192
Internal Rate of Return, 258, 263-265
International Monetary Fund, 210-211
Interpersonal skills, 96-105
Interview, 500-502
Investment Appraisal, 257-265
Investment ratios, 371-377
Investments, 371-377
Invisible trade, 182-183

J

Japan, 202, 205-206
Job
  analysis, 498
  design, 79-83
  enlargement, 80-81
  enrichment, 80-83
  evaluation, 98-99, 498-499
  production, 512-513
  rotation, 81-82
Journals, 480-481
Just in Time, 524-527

K

Key note reports, 432

Selective marketing, 430
Selling, 488-489
Sex, 422
Share capital, 29-32, 43-44, 55-56
Shareholders, 29-32, 43-44, 55-56, 321
Shares, 29-32, 71-75, 332-333
    ordinary, 29-32, 332-333
preference, 29-32, 332-333
Shopping goods, 418
Single European Market, 192-197
Social
    Chapter, the, 200-202, 562-563
    class, 425-426
    costs, 577-579
Sole trader, 24, 71, 319
Speciality goods, 418
Star network, 231-232
Stock, 342-347, 368-369
    control, 368-369, 522-527
    exchange, 22, 28-32, 38, 72-74
Straight line method, 340-341
Strategy, see Business strategy
Suggestion box, 457
Suppliers, 133-137, 323
Supply, 117, 125-133
    curve, 127-133
Supply side economics, 156-157
Survey, 433-437
SWOT analysis, 409-411

T

Target pricing, 463
Targeting, 429-431
Taylor, F.W., 93, 104
Technology, 11, 415-416
Telephone selling, 471
Television, 478-479
Termination
    of a partnership, 42
    of business, 41-46
    of corporate bodies, 42-46
Tiger Economies, 206
Time series, 283-288
Trade

deficit, 181-184
    Descriptions Act, 573
unions, 102-103, 560-565
Trademarks, 453
Trading and profit and loss account, 347-350
Training, 498-503
Turnover, 22, 60

U

Ultra vires, 71
Unemployment, 141-143
    cyclical, 142-143
    frictional, 142-143
    seasonal, 142-143
    structural, 142-143
Unfair dismissal, 506-508
Unsolicited Goods and Services, 573
USP, 453

V

Value Added Tax, 43, 158
Vertical integration, 36
Virgin Group plc, 4, 8, 12-15, 28, 38-39, 51
Visible trade, 181-182

W

Winding up, 42-46
Work,
    measurement, 99-100
    study, 99-100
Worker
    control, 101-102
    participation, 101
Working capital, 329, 354-359